Lecture Notes in Computer Science 1750

Donald E. Knuth

MMIXware

A RISC Computer for the Third Millennium

Author

Donald E. Knuth
Computer Science Department
Stanford University
Stanford, CA 94305-9045, USA

ISSN 0302-9743 e-ISSN 1611-3349
ISBN 978-3-540-66938-8 e-ISBN 978-3-540-46611-6
DOI 10.1007/3-540-46611-8
Springer Heidelberg New York Dordrecht London

LNCS Sublibrary: SL 2 – Programming and Software Engineering

Printed on acid-free paper

Springer is part of Springer Science+Business Media (www.springer.com)

README

`MMIX` is a computer intended to illustrate machine-level aspects of programming. In my books *The Art of Computer Programming*, it replaces `MIX`, the 1960s-style machine that formerly played such a role. `MMIX`'s so-called RISC ("Reduced Instruction Set Computer") architecture is much better able to represent the computers being built at the turn of the millennium.

I strove to design `MMIX` so that its machine language would be simple, elegant, and easy to learn. At the same time I was careful to include all of the complexities needed to achieve high performance in practice, so that `MMIX` could in principle be built and even perhaps be competitive with some of the fastest general-purpose computers in the marketplace. I hope that `MMIX` will therefore prove to be a useful vehicle for people who are studying how to improve compilers and operating systems, and that other authors will like `MMIX` well enough to make use of it in their own textbooks. My goal in this work is to provide a clean, complete, and well-documented "machine-independent machine" that people all over the world will be able to use as a testbed for long-term research projects of lasting value, even as real computers continue to change rapidly.

This book is a collection of programs that make `MMIX` a virtual reality. One of the programs is an assembler, MMIXAL, which converts `MMIX` symbolic files to `MMIX` object files. There also are two simulators, which execute the programs in given object files. The first simulator, called MMIX-SIM or simply MMIX, executes a program one instruction at a time and allows convenient debugging. The second simulator, MMMIX, simulates a high-performance pipeline in which many aspects of the computation are overlapped in time. MMMIX is in fact a highly configurable "meta-simulator," capable of simulating an enormous variety of different kinds of pipelines with any number of functional units and with many possible strategies for caching, virtual address translation, branch prediction, super-scalar instruction issue, etc., etc.

The programs in this book are somewhat primitive, because they all are based on a simple terminal interface: Users type commands and the computer types out a reply. Still, these programs are adequate to provide a basis for future developments. I'm hoping that at least one reader of this book will discover how much fun `MMIX` programming can be and will be motivated to create a nice graphical interface, so that other people will more easily be able to join in the fun. I don't have the time or talent to construct a good GUI myself, but I've tried to write the programs in such a way that modifications and enhancements will be easy to make.

The latest versions of all these programs can be downloaded from `MMIX`'s home page

`http://mmix.cs.hm.edu/`

in a file named `mmix-YYYYMMDD.tar.gz`. The programs are copyrighted, but anyone can use them without charge. Furthermore I explicitly allow anybody to copy and modify the programs in any way they like, provided only that the computer files are given different names whenever they have been changed. Only my designated successors in Munich are allowed to make a correction or addition to the copyrighted file `mmixal.w`, for example, unless the corrected file is identified by some other name (possibly '`turbo-mmixal.w`' or '`mmixal++.w`', etc.).

The programs are all written in `CWEB`, a language that combines C with TEX in such a way that standard preprocessors can easily convert `mmixal.w` into a compilable file `mmixal.c` or a documentation file `mmixal.tex`. `CWEB` also includes a "change file" mechanism by which people can easily customize a master source file like `mmixal.w` without changing the master file in any way. (See

`http://www-cs-faculty.stanford.edu/~knuth/cweb.html`

for complete information about `CWEB`, including installation instructions for the related software.) Readers of the present book who are unfamiliar with `CWEB` might want to refer to the notes on "How to read `CWEB` programs" that appear on pages 70–73 of my book *The Stanford GraphBase* (New York: ACM Press, 1993), but the general ideas are almost self-explanatory so I decided not to reprint those notes here.

During the next several years, as I write Volume 4 of *The Art of Computer Programming*, I plan to prepare updates to Volumes 1–3 whenever Volume 4 needs to refer to new material that belongs more properly in earlier volumes. These updates, called "fascicles," will be available on the Internet via

`http://www-cs-faculty.stanford.edu/~knuth/taocp.html`

and they will also be published in hardcopy form. The first such fascicle is already finished and available for downloading; it is a tutorial introduction to `MMIX` and the `MMIX` assembly language. Everybody who is seriously interested in `MMIX` should read that First Fascicle, preferably before reading the programs in the present book.

I've tried to make the `MMIX`ware programs interesting to read as well as useful. Indeed, the MMIX-PIPE program, which is the chief component of the MMMIX metasimulator, is one of the most instructive programs I've ever had the pleasure of writing. But I don't expect a great number of people to study every part of this book closely, or even to study every part of MMIX-PIPE. The main purpose of this book is to provide a complete documentation of the `MMIX` computer and its assembly language. Many details about `MMIX` were too "picky" or too system-oriented to be appropriate for the First Fascicle, but every detail about `MMIX` can be found in the present book.

After the `MMIX`ware programs have been installed on a UNIX-like system, they are typically used as follows. First a user program is written in assembly language and put into a file, say `foo.mms`. (The suffix `.mms` stands for "`MMIX` symbolic.") Then the command

```
mmixal foo.mms
```

will translate it into an object file, `foo.mmo`. Alternatively, a command such as

```
mmixal -l foo.lst foo.mms
```

could be used; this would produce a listing file, `foo.lst`, in addition to `foo.mmo`. The listing file, when printed, would show the contents of `foo.mms` together with the assembled machine language instructions.

Once an object file like foo.mmo exists, it can be run on the simple simulator by issuing a command such as

```
mmix foo
```

(or mmix foo.mmo). Many options are also possible; for example,

```
mmix -s foo
```

will print running time statistics when the program ends;

```
mmix -P foo
```

will print a profile that shows exactly how often each instruction was executed;

```
mmix -v foo
```

will give "verbose" details about everything the simulator did;

```
mmix -t2 foo
```

will trace each instruction the first two times it is performed; and so on. Also

```
mmix -i foo
```

will run the simulator in interactive mode, obeying various online commands by which the user can watch exactly what is happening when key parts of the program are reached. The command

```
mmix foo bar
```

will run the simulator as if MMIX itself were running the command 'foo bar' with a rudimentary operating system; any number of command-line arguments can follow the name of the program being simulated.

The MMMIX meta-simulator can also be applied to the same program, although a bit more preparation is necessary. First the command

```
mmix -Dfoo.mmb foo bar
```

will dump out a binary file foo.mmb containing the information needed to load 'foo bar' into MMIX's memory. Then a command like

```
mmmix plain.mmconfig foo.mmb
```

will invoke the meta-simulator with a "plain" pipeline configuration. The meta-simulator always runs interactively, using the prompt 'mmmix>' when it wants instructions about what to do next. Users can type '?' in response to this prompt if they want to be reminded about what the simulator can do. Typical responses are 'vff' (run verbosely); 'v0' (run quietly); 'p' (show the pipeline); 'g255' (show global register 255); 'D' (show the D-cache); 'b200' (pause when location #200 is fetched); '1000' (run 1000 cycles); etc. Some familiarity with MMIX-PIPE is necessary to understand the meta-simulator's reports of its activity, but users of mmmix are assumed to be able to extract high-level information from a mass of low-level details. (This talent, after all, is the hallmark of a computer scientist.)

The programs in this book appear in alphabetical order:

MMIX explains everything about the `MMIX` architecture.

MMIX-ARITH contains subroutines for 64-bit fixed and floating point arithmetic, using only 32-bit fixed point arithmetic.

MMIX-CONFIG processes configuration files for MMMIX.

MMIX-IO contains subroutines for the primitive input/output operations of a rudimentary operating system.

MMIX-MEM handles memory references of MMMIX in special cases associated with memory-mapped input/output.

MMIX-PIPE does the hard work of pipeline simulation.

MMIX-SIM is the program for the non-pipelined simulator.

MMIXAL is the assembly program.

MMMIX is the driver program for the meta-simulator.

MMOTYPE is a utility program that translates an `MMIX` object file into human-readable form.

The first of these, MMIX, is not actually a program, although it has been formatted as a `CWEB` document; it is a complete definition of `MMIX`, including the details of features that are used only by the operating system. It should be read first, but the other programs can be read in any order. (Actually MMIXAL or MMIX-SIM should probably be read next after MMIX, and MMIX-PIPE last. The program MMIX-SIM is the line-at-a-time simulator that is known simply as `mmix` after it has been compiled.)

Mini-indexes have been provided on each right-hand page of this book so that the programs can be read essentially as hypertext. Every identifier that is used on a two-page spread but defined on some other page is listed in the mini-index. For example, a mini-index entry such as '*oplus*: **octa** ( ), MMIX-ARITH §5' means that the identifier *oplus* denotes a function defined in section §5 of the MMIX-ARITH module, returning a value of type **octa**. A master index to all uses of all identifiers appears at the end of this book.

Happy hacking!

Donald E. Knuth
Cambridge, Massachusetts
17 October 1999

CONTENTS

Welcome to the revised printing of *MMIXware*, which incorporates hundreds of detailed changes suggested by readers of the original 1999 printing. I thank the staff at Springer for providing this opportunity to make an archival, corrected version of the entire text.

The current printing documents Version 1 of `MMIX`, and it corresponds to the programs of `mmix-20131017.tgz`. Version 1 is permanently frozen, and "bug-free by definition." All future developments can be accessed via the `MMIX` home page cited above in the README section (the "frontmatter").

Each of the following ten chapters begins on a left-hand page, and represents a component of the official `CWEB` source files for `MMIX` Version 1.

DEK, 17 October 2013

D.E. Knuth: MMIXware, LNCS 1750, p. 1, 2014.
DOI: 10.1007/3-540-46611-8_1

MMIX

1. Introduction to MMIX. Thirty-eight years have passed since the MIX computer was designed, and computer architecture has been converging during those years towards a rather different style of machine. Therefore it is time to replace MIX with a new computer that contains even less saturated fat than its predecessor.

Exercise 1.3.1–25 in the third edition of *Fundamental Algorithms* speaks of an extended MIX called MixMaster, which is upward compatible with the old version. But MixMaster itself is hopelessly obsolete; although it allows for several gigabytes of memory, we can't even use it with ASCII code to get lowercase letters. And ouch, the standard subroutine calling convention of MIX is irrevocably based on self-modifying code! Decimal arithmetic and self-modifying code were popular in 1962, but they sure have disappeared quickly as machines have gotten bigger and faster. A completely new design is called for, based on the principles of RISC architecture as expounded in *Computer Architecture* by Hennessy and Patterson (Morgan Kaufmann, 1996).

So here is MMIX, a computer that will totally replace MIX in the "ultimate" editions of *The Art of Computer Programming*, Volumes 1–3, and in the first editions of the remaining volumes. I must confess that I can hardly wait to own a computer like this.

How do you pronounce MMIX? I've been saying "em-mix" to myself, because the first 'M' represents a new millennium. Therefore I use the article "an" instead of "a" before the name MMIX in English phrases like "an MMIX simulator."

Incidentally, the *Dictionary of American Regional English* **3** (1996) lists "mommix" as a common dialect word used both as a noun and a verb; to mommix something means to botch it, to bollix it. Only time will tell whether I have mommixed the definition of MMIX.

2. The original MIX computer could be operated without an operating system; you could bootstrap it with punched cards or paper tape and do everything yourself. But nowadays such power is no longer in the hands of ordinary users. The MMIX hardware, like all other computing machines made today, relies on an operating system to get jobs started in their own address spaces and to provide I/O capabilities.

Whenever anybody has asked if I will be writing about operating systems, my reply has always been "Nix." Therefore the name of MMIX's operating system, NNIX, will come as no surprise. From time to time I will necessarily have to refer to things that NNIX does for its users, but I am unable to build NNIX myself. Life is too short. It would be wonderful if some expert in operating system design became inspired to write a book that explains exactly how to construct a nice, clean NNIX kernel for an MMIX chip.

3. I am deeply grateful to the many people who have helped me shape the behavior of MMIX. In particular, John Hennessy and (especially) Dick Sites have made significant contributions.

D.E. Knuth: MMIXware, LNCS 1750, pp. 2–61, 2014.
DOI: 10.1007/3-540-46611-8_2

4. A programmer's introduction to `MMIX` appears in "Volume 1, Fascicle 1," a booklet containing tutorial material that will ultimately appear in the fourth edition of *The Art of Computer Programming*. The description in the following sections is rather different, because we are concerned about a complete implementation, including all of the features used by the operating system and invisible to normal programs. Here it is important to emphasize exceptional cases that were glossed over in the tutorial, and to consider nitpicky details about things that might go wrong.

5. MMIX basics. `MMIX` is a 64-bit RISC machine with at least 256 general-purpose registers and a 64-bit address space. Every instruction is four bytes long and has the form

OP	X	Y	Z

The 256 possible OP codes fall into a dozen or so easily remembered categories; an instruction usually means, "Set register X to the result of Y OP Z." For example,

32	1	2	3

sets register 1 to the sum of registers 2 and 3. A few instructions combine the Y and Z bytes into a 16-bit YZ field; two of the jump instructions use a 24-bit XYZ field. But the three bytes X, Y, Z usually have three-pronged significance independent of each other.

Instructions are usually represented in a symbolic form corresponding to the `MMIX` assembly language, in which each operation code has a mnemonic name. For example, operation 32 is `ADD`, and the instruction above might be written '`ADD $1,$2,$3`'; a dollar sign '`$`' symbolizes a register number. In general, the instruction `ADD $X,$Y,$Z` is the operation of setting $\$X = \$Y + \$Z$. An assembly language instruction with two commas has three operand fields X, Y, Z; an instruction with one comma has two operand fields X, YZ; an instruction with no comma has one operand field, XYZ; an instruction with no operands has $X = Y = Z = 0$.

Most instructions have two forms, one in which the Z field stands for register \$Z, and one in which Z is an unsigned "immediate" constant. Thus, for example, the command '`ADD $X,$Y,$Z`' has a counterpart '`ADD $X,$Y,Z`', which sets $\$X = \$Y+Z$. Immediate constants are always nonnegative. In the descriptions below we will introduce such pairs of instructions by writing just '`ADD $X,$Y,$Z|Z`' instead of naming both cases explicitly.

The operation code for `ADD $X,$Y,$Z` is 32, but the operation code for `ADD $X,$Y,Z` is 33. The `MMIX` assembler chooses the correct code by noting whether the third argument is a register number or not.

Register numbers and constants can be given symbolic names; for example, the assembly language instruction '`x IS $1`' makes `x` an abbreviation for register number 1. Similarly, '`FIVE IS 5`' makes `FIVE` an abbreviation for the constant 5. After these abbreviations have been specified, the instruction `ADD x,x,FIVE` increases \$1 by 5, using opcode 33, while the instruction `ADD x,x,x` doubles \$1 using opcode 32. Symbolic names that stand for register numbers conventionally begin with a lowercase letter, while names that stand for constants conventionally begin with an uppercase letter. This convention is not actually enforced by the assembler, but it tends to reduce a programmer's confusion.

6. A *nybble* is a 4-bit quantity, often used to denote a decimal or hexadecimal digit. A *byte* is an 8-bit quantity, often used to denote an alphanumeric character in ASCII code. The Unicode standard extends ASCII to essentially all the world's languages by using 16-bit-wide characters called *wydes*. (Weight watchers know that two nybbles make one byte, but two bytes make one wyde.) In the discussion below we use the term *tetrabyte* or "tetra" for a 4-byte quantity, and the similar term *octabyte* or "octa" for an 8-byte quantity. Thus, a tetra is two wydes, an octa is two tetras; an octabyte has 64 bits. Each MMIX register can be thought of as containing one octabyte, or two tetras, or four wydes, or eight bytes, or sixteen nybbles.

When bytes, wydes, tetras, and octas represent numbers they are said to be either *signed* or *unsigned.* An unsigned byte is a number between 0 and $2^8-1 = 255$ inclusive; an unsigned wyde lies, similarly, between 0 and $2^{16} - 1 = 65535$; an unsigned tetra lies between 0 and $2^{32} - 1 = 4{,}294{,}967{,}295$; an unsigned octa lies between 0 and $2^{64} - 1 = 18{,}446{,}744{,}073{,}709{,}551{,}615$. Their signed counterparts use the conventions of two's complement notation, by subtracting respectively 2^8, 2^{16}, 2^{32}, or 2^{64} times the most significant bit. Thus, the unsigned bytes 128 through 255 are regarded as the numbers -128 through -1 when they are evaluated as signed bytes; a signed byte therefore lies between -128 and $+127$, inclusive. A signed wyde is a number between -32768 and $+32767$; a signed tetra lies between $-2{,}147{,}483{,}648$ and $+2{,}147{,}483{,}647$; a signed octa lies between $-9{,}223{,}372{,}036{,}854{,}775{,}808$ and $+9{,}223{,}372{,}036{,}854{,}775{,}807$.

The virtual memory of MMIX is an array M of 2^{64} bytes. If k is any unsigned octabyte, $M[k]$ is a 1-byte quantity. MMIX machines do not actually have such vast memories, but programmers can act as if 2^{64} bytes are indeed present, because MMIX provides address translation mechanisms by which an operating system can maintain this illusion.

We use the notation $M_{2^t}[k]$ to stand for a number consisting of 2^t consecutive bytes starting at location $k \wedge (2^{64} - 2^t)$. (The notation $k \wedge (2^{64} - 2^t)$ means that the least significant t bits of k are set to 0, and only the least 64 bits of the resulting address are retained. Similarly, the notation $k \vee (2^t - 1)$ means that the least significant t bits of k are set to 1.) All accesses to 2^t-byte quantities by MMIX are *aligned*, in the sense that the first byte is a multiple of 2^t.

Addressing is always "big-endian." In other words, the most significant (leftmost) byte of $M_{2^t}[k]$ is $M_1[k \wedge (2^{64} - 2^t)]$ and the least significant (rightmost) byte is $M_1[k \vee (2^t - 1)]$. We use the notation $s(M_{2^t}[k])$ when we want to regard this 2^t-byte number as a *signed* integer. Formally speaking, if $l = 2^t$,

$$s(M_l[k]) = \bigl(M_1[k\wedge(-l)]\, M_1[k\wedge(-l)+1] \,\ldots\, M_1[k\vee(l-1)]\bigr)_{256} - 2^{8l}[M_1[k\wedge(-l)] \geq 128].$$

7. Loading and storing. Several instructions can be used to get information from memory into registers. For example, the "load tetra unsigned" instruction `LDTU $1,$4,$5` puts the four bytes $M_4[\$4 + \$5]$ into register 1 as an unsigned integer; the most significant four bytes of register 1 are set to zero. The similar instruction `LDT $1,$4,$5`, "load tetra," sets $1 to the *signed* integer $s(M_4[\$4 + \$5])$. (Instructions generally treat numbers as signed unless the operation code specifically calls them unsigned.) In the signed case, the most significant four bytes of the register will be copies of the most significant bit of the tetrabyte loaded; thus they will be all 0s or all 1s, depending on whether the number is ≥ 0 or < 0.

• `LDB $X,$Y,$Z|Z` 'load byte'.
Byte $s(M[\$Y + \$Z])$ or $s(M[\$Y + Z])$ is loaded into register X as a signed number between -128 and $+127$, inclusive.

• `LDBU $X,$Y,$Z|Z` 'load byte unsigned'. Byte $M[\$Y + \$Z]$ or $M[\$Y + Z]$ is loaded into register X as an unsigned number between 0 and 255, inclusive.

• `LDW $X,$Y,$Z|Z` 'load wyde'.
Bytes $s(M_2[\$Y + \$Z])$ or $s(M_2[\$Y + Z])$ are loaded into register X as a signed number between -32768 and $+32767$, inclusive. As mentioned above, our notation $M_2[k]$ implies that the least significant bit of the address $\$Y + \$Z$ or $\$Y + Z$ is ignored and assumed to be 0.

• `LDWU $X,$Y,$Z|Z` 'load wyde unsigned'. Bytes $M_2[\$Y + \$Z]$ or $M_2[\$Y + Z]$ are loaded into register X as an unsigned number between 0 and 65535, inclusive.

• `LDT $X,$Y,$Z|Z` 'load tetra'.
Bytes $s(M_4[\$Y + \$Z])$ or $s(M_4[\$Y + Z])$ are loaded into register X as a signed number between $-2{,}147{,}483{,}648$ and $+2{,}147{,}483{,}647$, inclusive. As mentioned above, our notation $M_4[k]$ implies that the two least significant bits of the address $\$Y + \$Z$ or $\$Y + Z$ are ignored and assumed to be 0.

• `LDTU $X,$Y,$Z|Z` 'load tetra unsigned'.
Bytes $M_4[\$Y + \$Z]$ or $M_4[\$Y + Z]$ are loaded into register X as an unsigned number between 0 and 4,294,967,296, inclusive.

• `LDO $X,$Y,$Z|Z` 'load octa'.
Bytes $M_8[\$Y + \$Z]$ or $M_8[\$Y + Z]$ are loaded into register X. As mentioned above, our notation $M_8[k]$ implies that the three least significant bits of the address $\$Y + \$Z$ or $\$Y + Z$ are ignored and assumed to be 0.

• `LDOU $X,$Y,$Z|Z` 'load octa unsigned'.
Bytes $M_8[\$Y + \$Z]$ or $M_8[\$Y + Z]$ are loaded into register X. There is in fact no difference between the behavior of `LDOU` and `LDO`, since an octabyte can be regarded as either signed or unsigned. `LDOU` is included in `MMIX` just for completeness and consistency, in spite of the fact that a foolish consistency is the hobgoblin of little minds. (Niklaus Wirth made a strong plea for such consistency in his early critique of System/360; see *JACM* **15** (1967), 37–74.)

• `LDHT $X,$Y,$Z|Z` 'load high tetra'.
Bytes $M_4[\$Y+\$Z]$ or $M_4[\$Y+Z]$ are loaded into the most significant half of register X, and the least significant half is cleared to zero. (One use of "high tetra arithmetic"

is to detect overflow easily when tetrabytes are added or subtracted.)

• `LDA $X,$Y,$Z|Z` 'load address'.
The address $Y + $Z or $Y + Z is loaded into register X. This instruction is simply another name for the `ADDU` instruction discussed below; it can be used when the programmer is thinking of memory addresses instead of numbers. The `MMIX` assembler converts `LDA` into the same OP-code as `ADDU`.

8. Another family of instructions goes the other way, storing registers into memory. For example, the "store octa immediate" command `STO $3,$2,17` puts the current contents of register 3 into $M_8[\$2 + 17]$.

• `STB $X,$Y,$Z|Z` 'store byte'.
The least significant byte of register X is stored into byte M[$Y + $Z] or M[$Y + Z]. An integer overflow exception occurs if $X is not between −128 and +127. (We will discuss overflow and other kinds of exceptions later.)

• `STBU $X,$Y,$Z|Z` 'store byte unsigned'.
The least significant byte of register X is stored into byte M[$Y + $Z] or M[$Y + Z]. `STBU` instructions are the same as `STB` instructions, except that no test for overflow is made.

• `STW $X,$Y,$Z|Z` 'store wyde'.
The two least significant bytes of register X are stored into bytes $M_2[\$Y + \$Z]$ or $M_2[\$Y + Z]$. An integer overflow exception occurs if $X is not between −32768 and +32767.

• `STWU $X,$Y,$Z|Z` 'store wyde unsigned'.
The two least significant bytes of register X are stored into bytes $M_2[\$Y + \$Z]$ or $M_2[\$Y + Z]$. `STWU` instructions are the same as `STW` instructions, except that no test for overflow is made.

• `STT $X,$Y,$Z|Z` 'store tetra'.
The four least significant bytes of register X are stored into bytes $M_4[\$Y + \$Z]$ or $M_4[\$Y+Z]$. An integer overflow exception occurs if $X is not between −2,147,483,648 and +2,147,483,647.

• `STTU $X,$Y,$Z|Z` 'store tetra unsigned'.
The four least significant bytes of register X are stored into bytes $M_4[\$Y + \$Z]$ or $M_4[\$Y + Z]$. `STTU` instructions are the same as `STT` instructions, except that no test for overflow is made.

• `STO $X,$Y,$Z|Z` 'store octa'.
Register X is stored into bytes $M_8[\$Y + \$Z]$ or $M_8[\$Y + Z]$.

• `STOU $X,$Y,$Z|Z` 'store octa unsigned'.
Identical to `STO $X,$Y,$Z|Z`.

• `STCO X,$Y,$Z|Z` 'store constant octabyte'.
An octabyte whose value is the unsigned byte X is stored into $M_8[\$Y + \$Z]$ or $M_8[\$Y + Z]$.

• `STHT $X,$Y,$Z|Z` 'store high tetra'.
The most significant four bytes of register X are stored into $M_4[\$Y+\$Z]$ or $M_4[\$Y+Z]$.

9. Adding and subtracting. Once numbers are in registers, we can compute with them. Let's consider addition and subtraction first.

• `ADD $X,$Y,$Z|Z` 'add'.
The sum \$Y + \$Z or \$Y + Z is placed into register X using signed, two's complement arithmetic. An integer overflow exception occurs if the sum is $\geq 2^{63}$ or $< -2^{63}$. (We will discuss overflow and other kinds of exceptions later.)

• `ADDU $X,$Y,$Z|Z` 'add unsigned'.
The sum (\$Y + \$Z) mod 2^{64} or (\$Y + Z) mod 2^{64} is placed into register X. These instructions are the same as `ADD $X,$Y,$Z|Z` commands except that no test for overflow is made. (Overflow could be detected if desired by using the command `CMPU ovflo,$X,$Y` after addition, where `CMPU` means "compare unsigned"; see below.)

• `2ADDU $X,$Y,$Z|Z` 'times 2 and add unsigned'.
The sum (2\$Y + \$Z) mod 2^{64} or (2\$Y + Z) mod 2^{64} is placed into register X.

• `4ADDU $X,$Y,$Z|Z` 'times 4 and add unsigned'.
The sum (4\$Y + \$Z) mod 2^{64} or (4\$Y + Z) mod 2^{64} is placed into register X.

• `8ADDU $X,$Y,$Z|Z` 'times 8 and add unsigned'.
The sum (8\$Y + \$Z) mod 2^{64} or (8\$Y + Z) mod 2^{64} is placed into register X.

• `16ADDU $X,$Y,$Z|Z` 'times 16 and add unsigned'.
The sum (16\$Y + \$Z) mod 2^{64} or (16\$Y + Z) mod 2^{64} is placed into register X.

• `SUB $X,$Y,$Z|Z` 'subtract'.
The difference \$Y − \$Z or \$Y − Z is placed into register X using signed, two's complement arithmetic. An integer overflow exception occurs if the difference is $\geq 2^{63}$ or $< -2^{63}$.

• `SUBU $X,$Y,$Z|Z` 'subtract unsigned'.
The difference (\$Y − \$Z) mod 2^{64} or (\$Y − Z) mod 2^{64} is placed into register X. These two instructions are the same as `SUB $X,$Y,$Z|Z` except that no test for overflow is made.

• `NEG $X,Y,$Z|Z` 'negate'.
The value Y − \$Z or Y − Z is placed into register X using signed, two's complement arithmetic. An integer overflow exception occurs if the result is greater than $2^{63} - 1$. (Notice that in this case `MMIX` works with the "immediate" constant Y, not register Y. `NEG` commands are analogous to the immediate variants of other commands, because they save us from having to put one-byte constants into a register. When Y = 0, overflow occurs if and only if \$Z = -2^{63}. The instruction `NEG $X,1,2` has exactly the same effect as `NEG $X,0,1`.)

• `NEGU $X,Y,$Z|Z` 'negate unsigned'.
The value (Y − \$Z) mod 2^{64} or (Y − Z) mod 2^{64} is placed into register X. `NEGU` instructions are the same as `NEG` instructions, except that no test for overflow is made.

`CMPU`, §15.

10. Bit fiddling. Before looking at multiplication and division, which take longer than addition and subtraction, let's look at some of the other things that `MMIX` can do fast. There are eighteen instructions for bitwise logical operations on unsigned numbers.

• `AND $X,$Y,$Z|Z` 'bitwise and'.
Each bit of register Y is logically anded with the corresponding bit of register Z or of the constant Z, and the result is placed in register X. In other words, a bit of register X is set to 1 if and only if the corresponding bits of the operands are both 1; in symbols, $\$X = \$Y \wedge \$Z$ or $\$X = \$Y \wedge Z$. This means in particular that `AND $X,$Y,Z` always zeroes out the seven most significant bytes of register X, because 0s are prefixed to the constant byte Z.

• `OR $X,$Y,$Z|Z` 'bitwise or'.
Each bit of register Y is logically ored with the corresponding bit of register Z or of the constant Z, and the result is placed in register X. In other words, a bit of register X is set to 0 if and only if the corresponding bits of the operands are both 0; in symbols, $\$X = \$Y \vee \$Z$ or $\$X = \$Y \vee Z$.

In the special case $Z = 0$, the immediate variant of this command simply copies register Y to register X. The `MMIX` assembler allows us to write '`SET $X,$Y`' as a convenient abbreviation for '`OR $X,$Y,0`'.

• `XOR $X,$Y,$Z|Z` 'bitwise exclusive-or'.
Each bit of register Y is logically xored with the corresponding bit of register Z or of the constant Z, and the result is placed in register X. In other words, a bit of register X is set to 0 if and only if the corresponding bits of the operands are equal; in symbols, $\$X = \$Y \oplus \$Z$ or $\$X = \$Y \oplus Z$.

• `ANDN $X,$Y,$Z|Z` 'bitwise and-not'.
Each bit of register Y is logically anded with the complement of the corresponding bit of register Z or of the constant Z, and the result is placed in register X. In other words, a bit of register X is set to 1 if and only if the corresponding bit of register Y is 1 and the other corresponding bit is 0; in symbols, $\$X = \$Y \setminus \$Z$ or $\$X = \$Y \setminus Z$. (This is the *logical difference* operation; if the operands are bit strings representing sets, we are computing the elements that lie in one set but not the other.)

• `ORN $X,$Y,$Z|Z` 'bitwise or-not'.
Each bit of register Y is logically ored with the complement of the corresponding bit of register Z or of the constant Z, and the result is placed in register X. In other words, a bit of register X is set to 1 if and only if the corresponding bit of register Y is greater than or equal to the other corresponding bit; in symbols, $\$X = \$Y \vee \overline{\$Z}$ or $\$X = \$Y \vee \overline{Z}$. (This is the complement of $\$Z \setminus \$Y$ or $Z \setminus \$Y$.)

• `NAND $X,$Y,$Z|Z` 'bitwise not-and'.
Each bit of register Y is logically anded with the corresponding bit of register Z or of the constant Z, and the complement of the result is placed in register X. In other words, a bit of register X is set to 0 if and only if the corresponding bits of the operands are both 1; in symbols, $\$X = \$Y \barwedge \$Z$ or $\$X = \$Y \barwedge Z$.

• `NOR $X,$Y,$Z|Z` 'bitwise not-or'.
Each bit of register Y is logically ored with the corresponding bit of register Z or of the constant Z, and the complement of the result is placed in register X. In other words, a bit of register X is set to 1 if and only if the corresponding bits of the operands are both 0; in symbols, $\$X = \$Y \,\overline{\vee}\, \$Z$ or $\$X = \$Y \,\overline{\vee}\, Z$.

• `NXOR $X,$Y,$Z|Z` 'bitwise not-exclusive-or'.
Each bit of register Y is logically xored with the corresponding bit of register Z or of the constant Z, and the complement of the result is placed in register X. In other words, a bit of register X is set to 1 if and only if the corresponding bits of the operands are equal; in symbols, $\$X = \$Y \,\overline{\oplus}\, \$Z$ or $\$X = \$Y \,\overline{\oplus}\, Z$.

• `MUX $X,$Y,$Z|Z` 'bitwise multiplex'.
For each bit position j, the jth bit of register X is set either to bit j of register Y or to bit j of the other operand \$Z or Z, depending on whether bit j of the special *mask register* rM is 1 or 0: if M_j then Y_j else Z_j. In symbols, $\$X = (\$Y \wedge \mathrm{rM}) \vee (\$Z \wedge \overline{\mathrm{rM}})$ or $\$X = (\$Y \wedge \mathrm{rM}) \vee (Z \wedge \overline{\mathrm{rM}})$. (`MMIX` has several such special registers, associated with instructions that need more than two inputs or produce more than one output.)

11. Besides the eighteen bitwise operations, `MMIX` can also perform unsigned bytewise and biggerwise operations that are somewhat more exotic.

• `BDIF $X,$Y,$Z|Z` 'byte difference'.
For each byte position j, the jth byte of register X is set to byte j of register Y minus byte j of the other operand $Z or Z, unless that difference is negative; in the latter case, byte j of $X is set to zero.

• `WDIF $X,$Y,$Z|Z` 'wyde difference'.
For each wyde position j, the jth wyde of register X is set to wyde j of register Y minus wyde j of the other operand $Z or Z, unless that difference is negative; in the latter case, wyde j of $X is set to zero.

• `TDIF $X,$Y,$Z|Z` 'tetra difference'.
For each tetra position j, the jth tetra of register X is set to tetra j of register Y minus tetra j of the other operand $Z or Z, unless that difference is negative; in the latter case, tetra j of $X is set to zero.

• `ODIF $X,$Y,$Z|Z` 'octa difference'.
Register X is set to register Y minus the other operand $Z or Z, unless $Z or Z exceeds register Y; in the latter case, $X is set to zero. The operands are treated as unsigned integers.

The `BDIF` and `WDIF` commands are useful in applications to graphics or video; `TDIF` and `ODIF` are also present for reasons of consistency. For example, if `a` and `b` are registers containing 8-byte quantities, their bytewise maxima `c` and bytewise minima `d` are computed by

```
BDIF x,a,b; ADDU c,x,b; SUBU d,a,x;
```

similarly, the individual "pixel differences" `e`, namely the absolute values of the differences of corresponding bytes, are computed by

```
BDIF x,a,b; BDIF y,b,a; OR e,x,y.
```

To add individual bytes of `a` and `b` while clipping all sums to 255 if they don't fit in a single byte, one can say

```
NOR acomp,a,0; BDIF x,acomp,b; NOR clippedsums,x,0;
```

in other words, complement `a`, apply `BDIF`, and complement the result. The operations can also be used to construct efficient operations on strings of bytes or wydes.

Exercise: Implement a "nybble difference" instruction that operates in a similar way on sixteen nybbles at a time.

Answer: `AND x,a,m; AND y,b,m; ANDN xx,a,m; ANDN yy,b,m; BDIF x,x,y; BDIF xx,xx,yy; OR ans,x,xx` where register `m` contains the mask `#0f0f0f0f0f0f0f0f`.

(The `ANDN` operation can be regarded as a "bit difference" instruction that operates in a similar way on 64 bits at a time.)

12. Three more pairs of bit-fiddling instructions round out the collection of exotics.

• `SADD $X,$Y,$Z|Z` 'sideways add'.

Each bit of register Y is logically anded with the complement of the corresponding bit of register Z or of the constant Z, and the number of 1 bits in the result is placed in register X. In other words, register X is set to the number of bit positions in which register Y has a 1 and the other operand has a 0; in symbols, $\$X = \nu(\$Y \setminus \$Z)$ or $\$X = \nu(\$Y \setminus Z)$. When the second operand is zero this operation is sometimes called "population counting," because it counts the number of 1s in register Y.

• `MOR $X,$Y,$Z|Z` 'multiple or'.

Suppose the 64 bits of register Y are indexed as

$$y_{00}y_{01}\ldots y_{07}y_{10}y_{11}\ldots y_{17}\ldots y_{70}y_{71}\ldots y_{77};$$

in other words, y_{ij} is the jth bit of the ith byte, if we number the bits and bytes from 0 to 7 in big-endian fashion from left to right. Let the bits of the other operand, $Z or Z, be indexed similarly:

$$z_{00}z_{01}\ldots z_{07}z_{10}z_{11}\ldots z_{17}\ldots z_{70}z_{71}\ldots z_{77}.$$

The `MOR` operation replaces each bit x_{ij} of register X by the bit

$$y_{0j}z_{i0} \vee y_{1j}z_{i1} \vee \cdots \vee y_{7j}z_{i7}.$$

Thus, for example, if register Z contains the constant `#0102040810204080`, `MOR` reverses the order of the bytes in register Y, converting between little-endian and big-endian addressing. (The ith byte of $X depends on the bytes of $Y as specified by the ith byte of $Z or Z. If we regard 64-bit words as 8×8 Boolean matrices, with one byte per column, this operation computes the Boolean product $\$X = \$Y\,\$Z$ or $\$X = \$Y\,Z$. Alternatively, if we regard 64-bit words as 8×8 matrices with one byte per *row*, `MOR` computes the Boolean product $\$X = \$Z\,\$Y$ or $\$X = Z\,\$Y$ with operands in the opposite order. The immediate form `MOR $X,$Y,Z` always sets the leading seven bytes of register X to zero; the other byte is set to the bitwise or of whatever bytes of register Y are specified by the immediate operand Z.)

Exercise: Explain how to compute a mask `m` that is `#ff` in byte positions where `a` exceeds `b`, `#00` in all other bytes. Answer: `BDIF x,a,b; MOR m,minusone,x;` here `minusone` is a register consisting of all 1s. (Moreover, if we `AND` this result with `#8040201008040201`, then `MOR` with Z = 255, we get a one-byte encoding of `m`.)

• `MXOR $X,$Y,$Z|Z` 'multiple exclusive-or'.

This operation is like the Boolean multiplication just discussed, but exclusive-or is used to combine the bits. Thus we obtain a matrix product over the field of two elements instead of a Boolean matrix product. This operation can be used to construct hash functions, among many other things. (The hash functions aren't bad, but they are not "universal" in the sense of *Sorting and Searching*, exercise 6.4–72.)

13. Sixteen "immediate wyde" instructions are available for the common case that a 16-bit constant is needed. In this case the Y and Z fields of the instruction are regarded as a single 16-bit unsigned number YZ.

• `SETH $X,YZ` 'set to high wyde'; `SETMH $X,YZ` 'set to medium high wyde'; `SETML $X,YZ` 'set to medium low wyde'; `SETL $X,YZ` 'set to low wyde'.
The 16-bit unsigned number YZ is shifted left by either 48 or 32 or 16 or 0 bits, respectively, and placed into register X. Thus, for example, `SETML` inserts a given value into the second-least-significant wyde of register X and sets the other three wydes to zero.

• `INCH $X,YZ` 'increase by high wyde'; `INCMH $X,YZ` 'increase by medium high wyde'; `INCML $X,YZ` 'increase by medium low wyde'; `INCL $X,YZ` 'increase by low wyde'.
The 16-bit unsigned number YZ is shifted left by either 48 or 32 or 16 or 0 bits, respectively, and added to register X, ignoring overflow; the result is placed back into register X.

If YZ is the hexadecimal constant #8000, the command `INCH $X,YZ` complements the most significant bit of register X. We will see below that this can be used to negate a floating point number.

• `ORH $X,YZ` 'bitwise or with high wyde'; `ORMH $X,YZ` 'bitwise or with medium high wyde'; `ORML $X,YZ` 'bitwise or with medium low wyde'; `ORL $X,YZ` 'bitwise or with low wyde'.
The 16-bit unsigned number YZ is shifted left by either 48 or 32 or 16 or 0 bits, respectively, and ored with register X; the result is placed back into register X.

Notice that any desired 4-wyde constant `GH IJ KL MN` can be inserted into a register with a sequence of four instructions such as

```
SETH $X,GH; INCMH $X,IJ; INCML $X,KL; INCL $X,MN;
```

any of these `INC` instructions could also be replaced by `OR`.

• `ANDNH $X,YZ` 'bitwise and-not high wyde'; `ANDNMH $X,YZ` 'bitwise and-not medium high wyde'; `ANDNML $X,YZ` 'bitwise and-not medium low wyde'; `ANDNL $X,YZ` 'bitwise and-not low wyde'.
The 16-bit unsigned number YZ is shifted left by either 48 or 32 or 16 or 0 bits, respectively, then complemented and anded with register X; the result is placed back into register X.

If YZ is the hexadecimal constant #8000, the command `ANDNH $X,YZ` forces the most significant bit of register X to be 0. This can be used to compute the absolute value of a floating point number.

14. `MMIX` knows several ways to shift a register left or right by any number of bits.

• `SL $X,$Y,$Z|Z` 'shift left'.
The bits of register Y are shifted left by $Z or Z places, and 0s are shifted in from the right; the result is placed in register X. Register Y is treated as a signed number, but the second operand is treated as an unsigned number. The effect is the same as multiplication by $2^{\$Z}$ or by 2^{Z}; an integer overflow exception occurs if the result is $\geq 2^{63}$ or $< -2^{63}$. In particular, if the second operand is 64 or more, register X will become entirely zero, and integer overflow will be signaled unless register Y was zero.

• `SLU $X,$Y,$Z|Z` 'shift left unsigned'.
The bits of register Y are shifted left by \$Z or Z places, and 0s are shifted in from the right; the result is placed in register X. Both operands are treated as unsigned numbers. The `SLU` instructions are equivalent to `SL`, except that no test for overflow is made.

• `SR $X,$Y,$Z|Z` 'shift right'.
The bits of register Y are shifted right by \$Z or Z places, and copies of the leftmost bit (the sign bit) are shifted in from the left; the result is placed in register X. Register Y is treated as a signed number, but the second operand is treated as an unsigned number. The effect is the same as division by $2^{\$Z}$ or by 2^{Z} and rounding down. In particular, if the second operand is 64 or more, register X will become zero if \$Y was nonnegative, -1 if \$Y was negative.

• `SRU $X,$Y,$Z|Z` 'shift right unsigned'.
The bits of register Y are shifted right by \$Z or Z places, and 0s are shifted in from the left; the result is placed in register X. Both operands are treated as unsigned numbers. The effect is the same as unsigned division of a 64-bit number by $2^{\$Z}$ or by 2^{Z}; if the second operand is 64 or more, register X will become entirely zero.

15. Comparisons. Arithmetic and logical operations are nice, but computer programs also need to compare numbers and to change the course of a calculation depending on what they find. `MMIX` has four comparison instructions to facilitate such decision-making.

• `CMP $X,$Y,$Z|Z` 'compare'.
Register X is set to -1 if register Y is less than register Z or less than the unsigned immediate value Z, using the conventions of signed arithmetic; it is set to 0 if register Y is equal to register Z or equal to the unsigned immediate value Z; otherwise it is set to 1. In symbols, $\$X = [\$Y > \$Z] - [\$Y < \$Z]$ or $\$X = [\$Y > Z] - [\$Y < Z]$.

• `CMPU $X,$Y,$Z|Z` 'compare unsigned'.
Register X is set to -1 if register Y is less than register Z or less than the unsigned immediate value Z, using the conventions of unsigned arithmetic; it is set to 0 if register Y is equal to register Z or equal to the unsigned immediate value Z; otherwise it is set to 1. In symbols, $\$X = [\$Y > \$Z] - [\$Y < \$Z]$ or $\$X = [\$Y > Z] - [\$Y < Z]$.

16. There also are 32 conditional instructions, which choose quickly between two alternative courses of action.

• CSN $X,$Y,$Z|Z 'conditionally set if negative'.

If register Y is negative (namely if its most significant bit is 1), register X is set to the contents of register Z or to the unsigned immediate value Z. Otherwise nothing happens.

• CSZ $X,$Y,$Z|Z 'conditionally set if zero'.
• CSP $X,$Y,$Z|Z 'conditionally set if positive'.
• CSOD $X,$Y,$Z|Z 'conditionally set if odd'.
• CSNN $X,$Y,$Z|Z 'conditionally set if nonnegative'.
• CSNZ $X,$Y,$Z|Z 'conditionally set if nonzero'.
• CSNP $X,$Y,$Z|Z 'conditionally set if nonpositive'.
• CSEV $X,$Y,$Z|Z 'conditionally set if even'.

These instructions are entirely analogous to CSN, except that register X changes only if register Y is respectively zero, positive, odd, nonnegative, nonzero, nonpositive, or nonodd.

• ZSN $X,$Y,$Z|Z 'zero or set if negative'.

If register Y is negative (namely if its most significant bit is 1), register X is set to the contents of register Z or to the unsigned immediate value Z. Otherwise register X is set to zero.

• ZSZ $X,$Y,$Z|Z 'zero or set if zero'.
• ZSP $X,$Y,$Z|Z 'zero or set if positive'.
• ZSOD $X,$Y,$Z|Z 'zero or set if odd'.
• ZSNN $X,$Y,$Z|Z 'zero or set if nonnegative'.
• ZSNZ $X,$Y,$Z|Z 'zero or set if nonzero'.
• ZSNP $X,$Y,$Z|Z 'zero or set if nonpositive'.
• ZSEV $X,$Y,$Z|Z 'zero or set if even'.

These instructions are entirely analogous to ZSN, except that $X is set to $Z or Z if register Y is respectively zero, positive, odd, nonnegative, nonzero, nonpositive, or even; otherwise $X is set to zero.

Notice that the two instructions CMPU r,s,0 and ZSNZ r,s,1 have the same effect. So do the two instructions CSNP r,s,0 and ZSP r,s,r. So do AND r,s,1 and ZSOD r,s,1.

17. Branches and jumps. MMIX ordinarily executes instructions in sequence, proceeding from an instruction in tetrabyte $M_4[\lambda]$ to the instruction in $M_4[\lambda+4]$. But there are several ways to interrupt the normal flow of control, most of which use the Y and Z fields of an instruction as a combined 16-bit YZ field. For example, `BNZ $3,@+4000` (branch if nonzero) is typical: It means that control should skip ahead 1000 instructions to the command that appears 4000 bytes after the `BNZ`, if register 3 is not equal to zero.

There are eight branch-forward instructions, corresponding to the eight conditions in the `CS` and `ZS` commands that we discussed earlier. And there are eight similar branch-backward instructions; for example, `BOD $2,@-4000` (branch if odd) takes control to the instruction that appears 4000 bytes *before* this `BOD` command, if register 2 is odd. The numeric OP-code when branching backward is one greater than the OP-code when branching forward; the assembler takes care of this automatically, just as it takes cares of changing `ADD` from 32 to 33 when necessary.

Since branches are relative to the current location, the MMIX assembler treats branch instructions in a special way. Suppose a programmer writes '`BNZ $3,Case5`', where `Case5` is the address of an instruction in location l. If this instruction appears in location λ, the assembler first computes the displacement $\delta = \lfloor (l-\lambda)/4 \rfloor$. Then if δ is nonnegative, the quantity δ is placed in the YZ field of a `BNZ` command, and it should be less than 2^{16}; if δ is negative, the quantity $2^{16}+\delta$ is placed in the YZ field of a `BNZ` command with OP-code increased by 1, and δ should not be less than -2^{16}.

The symbol `@` used in our examples of `BNZ` and `BOD` above is interpreted by the assembler as an abbreviation for "the location of the current instruction." In the following notes we will define pairs of branch commands by writing, for example, '`BNZ $X,@+4*YZ[-262144]`'; this stands for a branch-forward command that branches to the current location plus four times YZ, as well as for a branch-backward command that branches to the current location plus four times (YZ − 65536).

- `BN $X,@+4*YZ[-262144]` 'branch if negative'.
- `BZ $X,@+4*YZ[-262144]` 'branch if zero'.
- `BP $X,@+4*YZ[-262144]` 'branch if positive'.
- `BOD $X,@+4*YZ[-262144]` 'branch if odd'.
- `BNN $X,@+4*YZ[-262144]` 'branch if nonnegative'.
- `BNZ $X,@+4*YZ[-262144]` 'branch if nonzero'.
- `BNP $X,@+4*YZ[-262144]` 'branch if nonpositive'.
- `BEV $X,@+4*YZ[-262144]` 'branch if even'.

If register X is respectively negative, zero, positive, odd, nonnegative, nonzero, nonpositive, or even, and if this instruction appears in memory location λ, the next instruction is taken from memory location $\lambda+4\mathrm{YZ}$ (branching forward) or $\lambda+4(\mathrm{YZ}-2^{16})$ (branching backward). Thus one can go from location λ to any location between $\lambda - 262{,}144$ and $\lambda + 262{,}140$, inclusive.

Sixteen additional branch instructions called *probable branches* are also provided. They have exactly the same meaning as ordinary branch instructions; for example, `PBOD $2,@-4000` and `BOD $2,@-4000` both go backward 4000 bytes if register 2 is odd. But they differ in running time: On some implementations of MMIX, a branch instruction takes longer when the branch is taken, while a probable branch takes longer when the branch is *not* taken. Thus programmers should use a `B` instruction when they think branching is relatively unlikely, but they should use `PB` when they expect branching to occur more often than not. Here is a list of the probable branch commands, for completeness:

- `PBN $X,@+4*YZ[-262144]` 'probable branch if negative'.
- `PBZ $X,@+4*YZ[-262144]` 'probable branch if zero'.
- `PBP $X,@+4*YZ[-262144]` 'probable branch if positive'.
- `PBOD $X,@+4*YZ[-262144]` 'probable branch if odd'.
- `PBNN $X,@+4*YZ[-262144]` 'probable branch if nonnegative'.
- `PBNZ $X,@+4*YZ[-262144]` 'probable branch if nonzero'.
- `PBNP $X,@+4*YZ[-262144]` 'probable branch if nonpositive'.
- `PBEV $X,@+4*YZ[-262144]` 'probable branch if even'.

18. Locations that are relative to the current instruction can be transformed into absolute locations with `GETA` commands.

- `GETA $X,@+4*YZ[-262144]` 'get address'.

The value $\lambda + 4\mathrm{YZ}$ or $\lambda + 4(\mathrm{YZ} - 2^{16})$ is placed in register X. (The assembly language conventions of branch instructions apply; for example, we can write '`GETA $X,Addr`'.)

19. `MMIX` also has unconditional jump instructions, which change the location of the next instruction no matter what.

- `JMP @+4*XYZ[-67108864]` 'jump'.

A `JMP` command treats bytes X, Y, and Z as an unsigned 24-bit integer XYZ. It allows a program to transfer control from location λ to any location between $\lambda - 67{,}108{,}864$ and $\lambda + 67{,}108{,}860$ inclusive, using relative addressing as in the `B` and `PB` commands.

- `GO $X,$Y,$Z|Z` 'go to location'.

`MMIX` takes its next instruction from location $\$Y + \$Z$ or $\$Y + Z$, and continues from there. Register X is set equal to $\lambda + 4$, the location of the instruction that would ordinarily have been executed next. (`GO` is similar to a jump, but it is not relative to the current location. Since `GO` has the same format as a load or store instruction, a loading routine can treat program labels with the same mechanism that is used to treat references to data.)

An old-fashioned type of subroutine linkage can be implemented by saying either '`GO r,subloc,0`' or '`GETA r,@+8; JMP Sub`' to enter a subroutine, then '`GO r,r,0`' to return. But subroutines are normally entered with the instructions `PUSHJ` or `PUSHGO`.

The two least significant bits of the address in a `GO` command are essentially ignored. They will, however, appear in the value of λ returned by `GETA` instructions, and in the return-jump register rJ after `PUSHJ` or `PUSHGO` instructions are performed, and in the where-interrupted register at the time of an interrupt. Therefore they could be used to send some kind of signal to a subroutine or (less likely) to an interrupt handler.

`PUSHGO`, §29. `PUSHJ`, §29.

20. Multiplication and division. Now for some instructions that make MMIX work harder.

• MUL $X,$Y,$Z|Z 'multiply'.

The signed product of the number in register Y by either the number in register Z or the unsigned byte Z replaces the contents of register X. An integer overflow exception can occur, as with ADD or SUB, if the result is less than -2^{63} or greater than $2^{63}-1$. (Immediate multiplication by powers of 2 can be done more rapidly with the SL instruction.)

• MULU $X,$Y,$Z|Z 'multiply unsigned'.

The lower 64 bits of the unsigned 128-bit product of register Y and either register Z or Z are placed in register X, and the upper 64 bits are placed in the special *himult register* rH. (Immediate multiplication by powers of 2 can be done more rapidly with the SLU instruction, if the upper half is not needed. Furthermore, an instruction like 4ADDU $X,$Y,$Y is faster than MULU $X,$Y,5.)

• `DIV $X,$Y,$Z|Z` 'divide'.
The signed quotient of the number in register Y divided by either the number in register Z or the unsigned byte Z replaces the contents of register X, and the signed remainder is placed in the special *remainder register* rR. An integer divide check exception occurs if the divisor is zero; in that case $X is set to zero and rR is set to $Y. An integer overflow exception occurs if the number -2^{63} is divided by -1; otherwise integer overflow is impossible. The quotient of y divided by z is defined to be $\lfloor y/z \rfloor$, and the remainder is defined to be $y - \lfloor y/z \rfloor z$ (also written $y \bmod z$). Thus, the remainder is either zero or has the sign of the divisor. Dividing by $z = 2^t$ gives exactly the same quotient as shifting right t via the `SR` command, and exactly the same remainder as anding with $z - 1$ via the `AND` command. Division of a positive 63-bit number by a positive constant can be accomplished more quickly by computing the upper half of a suitable unsigned product and shifting it right appropriately.

• `DIVU $X,$Y,$Z|Z` 'divide unsigned'.
The unsigned 128-bit number obtained by prefixing the special *dividend register* rD to the contents of register Y is divided either by the unsigned number in register Z or by the unsigned byte Z, and the quotient is placed in register X. The remainder is placed in the remainder register rR. However, if rD is greater than or equal to the divisor (and in particular if the divisor is zero), then $X is set to rD and rR is set to $Y. (Unsigned arithmetic never signals an exceptional condition, even when dividing by zero.) If rD is zero, unsigned division by $z = 2^t$ gives exactly the same quotient as shifting right t via the `SRU` command, and exactly the same remainder as anding with $z - 1$ via the `AND` command. Section 4.3.1 of *Seminumerical Algorithms* explains how to use unsigned division to obtain the quotient and remainder of extremely large numbers.

21. Floating point computations. Floating point arithmetic conforming to the famous IEEE/ANSI Standard 754 is provided for arbitrary 64-bit numbers. The IEEE standard refers to such numbers as "double format" quantities, but `MMIX` calls them simply floating point numbers because 64-bit quantities are the norm.

A positive floating point number has 53 bits of precision and can range from approximately 10^{-308} to 10^{308}. "Subnormal numbers" between 10^{-324} and 10^{-308} can also be represented, but with fewer bits of precision. Floating point numbers can be infinite, and they satisfy such identities as $1.0/\infty = +0.0$, $-2.8 \times \infty = -\infty$. Floating point quantities can also be "Not-a-Numbers" or NaNs, which are further classified into signaling NaNs and quiet NaNs.

Five kinds of exceptions can occur during floating point computations, and they each have code letters: Floating overflow (O) or underflow (U); floating divide by zero (Z); floating inexact (X); and floating invalid (I). For example, the multiplication of sufficiently small integers causes no exceptions, and the division of 91.0 by 13.0 is also exception-free, but the division 1.0/3.0 is inexact. The multiplication of extremely large or extremely small floating point numbers is inexact and it also causes overflow or underflow. Invalid results occur when taking the square root of a negative number; mathematicians can remember the I exception by relating it to the square root of -1.0. Invalid results also occur when trying to convert infinity or a quiet NaN to a fixed-point integer, or when any signaling NaN is encountered, or when mathematically undefined operations like $\infty - \infty$ or $0/0$ are requested. (Programmers can be sure that they have not erroneously used uninitialized floating point data if they initialize all their variables to signaling NaN values.)

Four different rounding modes for inexact results are available: round to nearest (and to even in case of ties); round off (toward zero); round up (toward $+\infty$); or round down (toward $-\infty$). `MMIX` has a special *arithmetic status register* rA that specifies the current rounding mode and the user's current preferences for exception handling.

IEEE standard arithmetic provides an excellent foundation for scientific calculations, and it will be thoroughly explained in the fourth edition of *Seminumerical Algorithms*, Section 4.2. For our present purposes, we need not study all the details; but we do need to specify `MMIX`'s behavior with respect to several things that are not completely defined by the standard. For example, the IEEE standard does not fully define the result of operations with NaNs.

When an octabyte represents a floating point number in `MMIX`'s registers, the leftmost bit is the sign; then come 11 bits for an exponent e; and the remaining 52 bits are the fraction part f. We regard e as an integer between 0 and $(11111111111)_2 = 2047$, and we regard f as a fraction between 0 and $(.111\ldots1)_2 = 1 - 2^{-52}$. Each octabyte has the following significance:

$$
\begin{aligned}
\pm 0.0, &\quad \text{if } e = f = 0 \text{ (zero)};\\
\pm 2^{-1022} f, &\quad \text{if } e = 0 \text{ and } f > 0 \text{ (subnormal)};\\
\pm 2^{e-1023}(1+f), &\quad \text{if } 0 < e < 2047 \text{ (normal)};\\
\pm\infty, &\quad \text{if } e = 2047 \text{ and } f = 0 \text{ (infinite)};\\
\pm \mathrm{NaN}(f), &\quad \text{if } e = 2047 \text{ and } 0 < f < 1/2 \text{ (signaling NaN)};\\
\pm \mathrm{NaN}(f), &\quad \text{if } e = 2047 \text{ and } f \ge 1/2 \text{ (quiet NaN)}.
\end{aligned}
$$

Notice that +0.0 is distinguished from −0.0; this fact is important for interval arithmetic.

Exercise: What 64 bits represent the floating point number 1.0? Answer: We want $e = 1023$ and $f = 0$, so the answer is #3ff0000000000000.

Exercise: What is the largest finite floating point number? Answer: We want $e = 2046$ and $f = 1 - 2^{-52}$, so the answer is #7fefffffffffffff $= 2^{1024} - 2^{971}$.

22. The seven IEEE floating point arithmetic operations (addition, subtraction, multiplication, division, remainder, square root, and nearest-integer) all share common features, called the *standard floating point conventions* in the discussion below: The operation is performed on floating point numbers found in two registers, \$Y and \$Z, except that square root and integerization involve only one operand. If neither input operand is a NaN, we first determine the exact result, then round it using the current rounding mode found in special register rA. Infinite results are exact and need no rounding. A floating overflow exception occurs if the rounded result is finite but needs an exponent greater than 2046. A floating underflow exception occurs if the rounded result needs an exponent less than 1 and either (i) the unrounded result cannot be represented exactly as a subnormal number or (ii) the "floating underflow trip" is enabled in rA. (Trips are discussed below.) NaNs are treated specially as follows: If either \$Y or \$Z is a signaling NaN, an invalid exception occurs and the NaN is quieted by adding 1/2 to its fraction part. Then if \$Z is a quiet NaN, the result is set to \$Z; otherwise if \$Y is a quiet NaN, the result is set to \$Y. (Registers \$Y and \$Z do not actually change.)

• `FADD $X,$Y,$Z` 'floating add'.
The floating point sum \$Y+\$Z is computed by the standard floating point conventions just described, and placed in register X. An invalid exception occurs if the sum is $(+\infty)+(-\infty)$ or $(-\infty)+(+\infty)$; in that case the result is NaN(1/2) with the sign of \$Z. If the sum is exactly zero and the current mode is not rounding-down, the result is +0.0 except that $(-0.0)+(-0.0)=-0.0$. If the sum is exactly zero and the current mode is rounding-down, the result is −0.0 except that $(+0.0)+(+0.0)=+0.0$. These rules for signed zeros turn out to be useful when doing interval arithmetic: If the lower bound of an interval is +0.0 or if the upper bound is −0.0, the interval does not contain zero, so the numbers in the interval have a known sign.

Floating point underflow cannot occur unless the U-trip has been enabled, because any underflowing result of floating point addition can be represented exactly as a subnormal number.

Silly but instructive exercise: Find all pairs of numbers (\$Y, \$Z) such that the commands `FADD $X,$Y,$Z` and `ADDU $X,$Y,$Z` both produce the same result in \$X (although `FADD` may cause floating exceptions). Answer: Of course \$Y or \$Z could be zero, if the other one is not a signaling NaN. Or one could be signaling and the other #0008000000000000. Other possibilities occur when they are both positive and less than #0010000000000001; or when one operand is #0000000000000001 and the other is an odd number between #0020000000000001 and #002ffffffffffffd inclusive (rounding to nearest). And still more surprising possibilities exist, such as #7f6001b4c67bc809 + #ff5ffb6a4534a3f7. All eight families of solutions will be revealed some day in the fourth edition of *Seminumerical Algorithms*.

• `FSUB $X,$Y,$Z` 'floating subtract'.
This instruction is equivalent to `FADD`, but with the sign of \$Z negated unless \$Z is a NaN.

• `FMUL $X,$Y,$Z` 'floating multiply'.
The floating point product $\$Y \times \$Z$ is computed by the standard floating point

conventions, and placed in register X. An invalid exception occurs if the product is $(\pm 0.0) \times (\pm\infty)$ or $(\pm\infty) \times (\pm 0.0)$; in that case the result is $\pm$NaN(1/2). No exception occurs for the product $(\pm\infty) \times (\pm\infty)$. If neither \$Y nor \$Z is a NaN, the sign of the result is the product of the signs of \$Y and \$Z.

• `FDIV $X,$Y,$Z` 'floating divide'.
The floating point quotient \$Y/\$Z is computed by the standard floating point conventions, and placed in \$X. A floating divide by zero exception occurs if the quotient is (normal or subnormal)/(± 0.0). An invalid exception occurs if the quotient is $(\pm 0.0)/(\pm 0.0)$ or $(\pm\infty)/(\pm\infty)$; in that case the result is $\pm$NaN(1/2). No exception occurs for the quotient $(\pm\infty)/(\pm 0.0)$. If neither \$Y nor \$Z is a NaN, the sign of the result is the product of the signs of \$Y and \$Z.

If a floating point number in register X is known to have an exponent between 2 and 2046, the instruction `INCH $X,#fff0` will divide it by 2.0.

• `FREM $X,$Y,$Z` 'floating remainder'.
The floating point remainder \$Y rem \$Z is computed by the standard floating point conventions, and placed in register X. (The IEEE standard defines the remainder to be \$Y $- n \times$ \$Z, where n is the nearest integer to \$Y/\$Z, and n is an even integer in case of ties. This is not the same as the remainder \$Y mod \$Z computed by `DIV` or `DIVU`.) A zero remainder has the sign of \$Y. An invalid exception occurs if \$Y is infinite and/or \$Z is zero; in that case the result is NaN(1/2) with the sign of \$Y.

• `FSQRT $X,$Z` 'floating square root'.
The floating point square root $\sqrt{\$Z}$ is computed by the standard floating point conventions, and placed in register X. An invalid exception occurs if \$Z is a negative number (either infinite, normal, or subnormal); in that case the result is $-$NaN(1/2). No exception occurs when taking the square root of -0.0 or $+\infty$. In all cases the sign of the result is the sign of \$Z.

The Y field of `FSQRT` can be used to specify a special rounding mode, as explained below.

• `FINT $X,$Z` 'floating integer'.
The floating point number in register Z is rounded (if necessary) to a floating point integer, using the current rounding mode, and placed in register X. Infinite values and quiet NaNs are not changed; signaling NaNs are treated as in the standard conventions. Floating point overflow and underflow exceptions cannot occur.

The Y field of `FINT` can be used to specify a special rounding mode, as explained below.

23. Besides doing arithmetic, we need to compare floating point numbers with each other, taking proper account of NaNs and the fact that -0.0 should be considered equal to $+0.0$. The following instructions are analogous to the comparison operators `CMP` and `CMPU` that we have used for integers.

• `FCMP $X,$Y,$Z` 'floating compare'.
Register X is set to -1 if $Y < $Z according to the conventions of floating point arithmetic, or to 1 if $Y > $Z according to those conventions. Otherwise it is set to 0. An invalid exception occurs if either $Y or $Z is a NaN; in such cases the result is zero.

• `FEQL $X,$Y,$Z` 'floating equal to'.
Register X is set to 1 if $Y = $Z according to the conventions of floating point arithmetic. Otherwise it is set to 0. The result is zero if either $Y or $Z is a NaN, even if a NaN is being compared with itself. However, no invalid exception occurs, not even when $Y or $Z is a signaling NaN. (Perhaps `MMIX` differs slightly from the IEEE standard in this regard, but programmers sometimes need to look at signaling NaNs without encountering side effects. Programmers who insist on raising an invalid exception whenever a signaling NaN is compared for floating equality should issue the instructions `FSUB $X,$Y,$Y; FSUB $X,$Z,$Z` just before saying `FEQL $X,$Y,$Z`.)

Suppose w, x, y, and z are unsigned 64-bit integers with $w < x < 2^{63} \le y < z$. Thus, the leftmost bits of w and x are 0, while the leftmost bits of y and z are 1. Then we have $w < x < y < z$ when these numbers are considered as unsigned integers, but $y < z < w < x$ when they are considered as signed integers, because y and z are negative. Furthermore, we have $z < y \le w < x$ when these same 64-bit quantities are considered to be floating point numbers, assuming that no NaNs are present, because the leftmost bit of a floating point number represents its sign and the remaining bits represent its magnitude. The case $y = w$ occurs in floating point comparison if and only if y is the representation of -0.0 and w is the representation of $+0.0$.

• `FUN $X,$Y,$Z` 'floating unordered'.
Register X is set to 1 if $Y and $Z are unordered according to the conventions of floating point arithmetic (namely, if either one is a NaN); otherwise register X is set to 0. No invalid exception occurs, not even when $Y or $Z is a signaling NaN.

The IEEE standard discusses 26 different possible relations on floating point numbers; `MMIX` implements 14 of them with single instructions, followed by a branch (or by a `ZS` to make a "pure" 0 or 1 result); all 26 can be evaluated with a sequence of at most four `MMIX` commands and a subsequent branch. The hardest case to handle is '?>=' (unordered or greater or equal, to be computed without exceptions), for which the following sequence makes $X ≥ 0 if and only if $Y ?>= $Z:

```
    FUN   $255,$Y,$Z
    BP    $255,1F      % skip ahead if unordered
    FCMP  $X,$Y,$Z     % $X=[$Y>$Z]-[$Y<$Z]; no exceptions will arise
 1H CSNZ  $X,$255,1    % $X=1 if unordered
```

24. Exercise: Suppose MMIX had no FINT instruction. Explain how to obtain the equivalent of FINT $X,$Z using other instructions. Your program should do the proper thing with respect to NaNs and exceptions. (For example, it should cause an invalid exception if and only if $Z is a signaling NaN; it should cause an inexact exception only if $Z needs to be rounded to another value.)

Answer: (The assembler prefixes hexadecimal constants by #.)

```
      SETH  $0,#4330 % $0=2^52
      SET   $1,$Z    % $1=$Z
      ANDNH $1,#8000 % $1=abs($Z)
      ANDN  $2,$Z,$1 % $2=signbit($Z)
      FUN   $3,$Z,$Z % $3=[$Z is a NaN]
      BNZ   $3,1F    % skip ahead if $Z is a NaN
      FCMP  $3,$1,$0 % $3=[abs($Z)>2^52]-[abs($Z)<2^52]
      CSNN  $0,$3,0  % set $0=0 if $3>=0
      OR    $0,$2,$0 % attach sign of $Z to $0
1H    FADD  $1,$Z,$0 % $1=$Z+$0
      FSUB  $1,$1,$0 % $X=$1-$0
      OR    $X,$1,$2 % make sure minus zero isn't lost
```

This program handles most cases of interest by adding and subtracting $\pm 2^{52}$ using floating point arithmetic. It would be incorrect to do this in all cases; for example, such addition/subtraction might fail to give the correct answer when $Z is a small negative quantity (if rounding toward zero), or when $Z is a number like $2^{105} + 2^{53}$ (if rounding to nearest).

25. `MMIX` goes beyond the IEEE standard to define additional relations between floating point numbers, as suggested by the theory in Section 4.2.2 of *Seminumerical Algorithms*. Given a nonnegative number ϵ, each normal floating point number $u = (f, e)$ has a *neighborhood*

$$N_\epsilon(u) = \{x \mid |x - u| \le 2^{e-1022}\epsilon\};$$

we also define $N_\epsilon(0) = \{0\}$, $N_\epsilon(u) = \{x \mid |x - u| \le 2^{-1021}\epsilon\}$ if u is subnormal; $N_\epsilon(\pm\infty) = \{\pm\infty\}$ if $\epsilon < 1$, $N_\epsilon(\pm\infty) = \{\text{everything except } \mp\infty\}$ if $1 \le \epsilon < 2$, $N_\epsilon(\pm\infty) = \{\text{everything}\}$ if $\epsilon \ge 2$. Then we write

$$\begin{aligned}
&u \prec v\ (\epsilon), \text{ if } u < N_\epsilon(v) \text{ and } N_\epsilon(u) < v;\\
&u \sim v\ (\epsilon), \text{ if } u \in N_\epsilon(v) \text{ or } v \in N_\epsilon(u);\\
&u \approx v\ (\epsilon), \text{ if } u \in N_\epsilon(v) \text{ and } v \in N_\epsilon(u);\\
&u \succ v\ (\epsilon), \text{ if } u > N_\epsilon(v) \text{ and } N_\epsilon(u) > v.
\end{aligned}$$

• **`FCMPE $X,$Y,$Z`** 'floating compare (with respect to epsilon)'.
Register X is set to -1 if $Y $\prec$ $Z (rE) according to the conventions of *Seminumerical Algorithms* as stated above; it is set to 1 if $Y $\succ$ $Z (rE) according to those conventions; otherwise it is set to 0. Here rE is a floating point number in the special *epsilon register*, which is used only by the floating point comparison operations `FCMPE`, `FEQLE`, and `FUNE`. An invalid exception occurs, and the result is zero, if any of $Y, $Z, or rE are NaN, or if rE is negative. If no such exception occurs, exactly one of the three conditions $Y $\prec$ $Z, $Y $\sim$ $Z, $Y $\succ$ $Z holds with respect to rE.

• **`FEQLE $X,$Y,$Z`** 'floating equivalent (with respect to epsilon)'.
Register X is set to 1 if $Y $\approx$ $Z (rE) according to the conventions of *Seminumerical Algorithms* as stated above; otherwise it is set to 0. An invalid exception occurs, and the result is zero, if any of $Y, $Z, or rE are NaN, or if rE is negative. Notice that the relation $Y $\approx$ $Z computed by `FEQLE` is stronger than the relation $Y $\sim$ $Z computed by `FCMPE`.

• **`FUNE $X,$Y,$Z`** 'floating unordered (with respect to epsilon)'.
Register X is set to 1 if $Y, $Z, or rE are exceptional as discussed for `FCMPE` and `FEQLE`; otherwise it is set to 0. No exceptions occur, even if $Y, $Z, or rE is a signaling NaN.

Exercise: What floating point numbers does `FCMPE` regard as $\sim$ 0.0 with respect to $\epsilon = 1/2$, when no exceptions arise? Answer: Zero, subnormal numbers, and normal numbers with $f = 0$. (The numbers similar to zero with respect to ϵ are zero, subnormal numbers with $f \le 2\epsilon$, normal numbers with $f \le 2\epsilon - 1$, and $\pm\infty$ if $\epsilon >= 1$.)

26. The IEEE standard also defines 32-bit floating point quantities, which it calls "single format" numbers. `MMIX` calls them *short floats*, and converts between 32-bit and 64-bit forms when such numbers are loaded from memory or stored into memory. A short float consists of a sign bit followed by an 8-bit exponent and a 23-bit fraction. After it has been loaded into one of `MMIX`'s registers, its 52-bit fraction part will have 29 trailing zero bits, and its exponent e will be one of the 256 values 0, $(01110000001)_2 = 897$, $(01110000010)_2 = 898$, $\ldots$, $(10001111110)_2 = 1150$, or 2047, unless it was subnormal; a subnormal short float loads into a normal number with $874 \le e \le 896$.

• `LDSF $X,$Y,$Z|Z` 'load short float'.
Register X is set to the 64-bit floating point number corresponding to the 32-bit floating point number represented by $M_4[\$Y + \$Z]$ or $M_4[\$Y + Z]$. No arithmetic exceptions occur, not even if a signaling NaN is loaded.

• `STSF $X,$Y,$Z|Z` 'store short float'.
The value obtained by rounding register X to a 32-bit floating point number is placed in $M_4[\$Y + \$Z]$ or $M_4[\$Y + Z]$. Rounding is done with the current rounding mode, in a manner exactly analogous to the standard conventions for rounding 64-bit results, except that the precision and exponent range are limited. In particular, floating overflow, underflow, and inexact exceptions might occur; a signaling NaN will trigger an invalid exception and it will become quiet. The fraction part of a NaN is truncated if necessary to a multiple of 2^{-23}, by ignoring the least significant 29 bits.

If we load any two short floats and operate on them once with either `FADD`, `FSUB`, `FMUL`, `FDIV`, `FREM`, `FSQRT`, or `FINT`, and if we then store the result as a short float, we obtain the results required by the IEEE standard for single format arithmetic, because the double format can be shown to have enough precision to avoid any problems of "double rounding." But programmers are usually better off sticking to 64-bit arithmetic unless they have a strong reason to emulate the precise behavior of a 32-bit computer; 32 bits do not offer much precision.

27. Of course we need to be able to go back and forth between integers and floating point values.

• `FIX $X,$Z` 'convert floating to fixed'.
The floating point number in register Z is converted to an integer as with the `FINT` instruction, and the resulting integer (mod 2^{64}) is placed in register X. An invalid exception occurs if $Z is infinite or a NaN; in that case $X is simply set equal to $Z. A float-to-fix exception occurs if the result is less than -2^{63} or greater than $2^{63} - 1$.

• `FIXU $X,$Z` 'convert floating to fixed unsigned'.
This instruction is identical to `FIX` except that no float-to-fix exception occurs.

• `FLOT $X,$Z|Z` 'convert fixed to floating'.
The integer in $Z or the immediate constant Z is converted to the nearest floating point value (using the current rounding mode) and placed in register X. A floating inexact exception occurs if rounding is necessary.

• `FLOTU $X,$Z|Z` 'convert fixed to floating unsigned'.
`FLOTU` is like `FLOT`, but $Z is treated as an unsigned integer.

• `SFLOT $X,$Z|Z` 'convert fixed to short float'; `SFLOTU $X,$Z|Z` 'convert fixed to short float unsigned'.
The `SFLOT` instructions are like the `FLOT` instructions, except that they round to a floating point number whose fraction part is a multiple of 2^{-23}. (Thus, the resulting value will not be changed by a "store short float" instruction.) Such conversions appear in `MMIX`'s repertoire only to establish complete conformance with the IEEE standard; a programmer needs them only when emulating a 32-bit machine.

28. Since the variants of `FIX` and `FLOT` involve only one input operand ($Z or Z), their Y field is normally zero. A programmer can, however, force the mode of rounding used with these commands by setting

$Y = 1$,	`ROUND_OFF`	(none);
$Y = 2$,	`ROUND_UP`	(away from zero);
$Y = 3$,	`ROUND_DOWN`	(toward zero);
$Y = 4$,	`ROUND_NEAR`	(to closest);

for example, the instruction `FLOTU $X,ROUND_OFF,$Z` will set the exponent e of register X to $1086 - l$ if $Z is a nonzero quantity with l leading zero bits. Thus we can count leading zeros by continuing with `SETL $0,1086`; `SR $X,$X,52`; `SUB $X,$0,$X`; `CSZ $X,$Z,64`.

The Y field can also be used in the same way to specify any desired rounding mode in the other floating point instructions that have only a single operand, namely `FSQRT` and `FINT`. An illegal instruction interrupt occurs if Y exceeds 4 in any of these commands.

29. Subroutine linkage. MMIX has several special operations designed to facilitate the process of calling and implementing subroutines. The key notion is the idea of a hardware-supported *register stack*, which can coexist with a software-supported stack of variables that are not maintained in registers. From a programmer's standpoint, MMIX maintains a potentially unbounded list $S[0]$, $S[1]$, ..., $S[\tau-1]$ of certain registers that are temporarily inaccessible; initially $\tau=0$. When a subroutine is entered, registers can be "pushed" on to the end of this list, increasing τ; when the subroutine has finished its execution, the registers are "popped" off again and τ decreases.

Our discussion so far has treated all 256 registers \$0, \$1, ..., \$255 as if they were alike. But in fact MMIX maintains two internal one-byte counters L and G, where $0 \le L \le G \le 256$, with the property that

registers 0, 1, ..., $L-1$ are "local";
registers L, $L+1$, ..., $G-1$ are "marginal";
registers G, $G+1$, ..., 255 are "global".

A marginal register is zero when its value is read.

The G counter is normally set to a fixed value once and for all when a program is loaded, thereby defining the number of program variables that will live entirely in registers rather than in memory during the course of execution. A programmer may, however, change G dynamically using the PUT instruction described below.

The L counter starts at 0. If an instruction places a value into a register that is currently marginal, namely a register x such that $L \le x < G$, the value of L will increase to $x+1$, and any newly local registers will be zero. For example, if $L=10$ and $G=200$, the instruction ADD \$5,\$15,1 would simply set \$5 to 1. But the instruction ADD \$15,\$5,\$200 would set \$10, \$11, ..., \$14 to zero, \$15 to \$5 + \$200, and L to 16. (The process of clearing registers and increasing L might take quite a few machine cycles in the worst case. We will see later that MMIX is able to take care of any such backlog [illegible] during [illegible] time.)

• PUSHJ \$X,@+4*YZ[−262144] 'push registers and jump'.
• PUSHGO \$X,\$Y,\$Z|Z 'push registers and go'.

Suppose first that $X < L$. Register X is set equal to the number X, then registers 0, 1, ..., X are pushed onto the register stack as described below. If this instruction is in location λ, the value $\lambda+4$ is placed into the special *return-jump register* rJ. Then control jumps to instruction $\lambda+4YZ$ or $\lambda+4YZ-262144$ or \$Y + \$Z or \$Y + Z, as in a JMP or GO command.

Pushing the first $X+1$ registers onto the stack means essentially that we set $S[\tau] \leftarrow \$0$, $S[\tau+1] \leftarrow \$1$, ..., $S[\tau+X] \leftarrow \$X$, $\tau \leftarrow \tau+X+1$, $\$0 \leftarrow \$(X+1)$, ..., $\$(L-X-2) \leftarrow \$(L-1)$, $L \leftarrow L-X-1$. For example, if $X=1$ and $L=5$, the current contents of \$0 and the number 1 are placed on the register stack, where they will be temporarily inaccessible. Then control jumps to a subroutine with L reduced to 3; the registers that we had been calling \$2, \$3, and \$4 appear as \$0, \$1, and \$2 to the subroutine.

If $L \le X < G$, the value of L increases to $X+1$ as described above; then the rules for $X < L$ apply.

29. Subroutine linkage. `MMIX` has several special operations designed to facilitate the process of calling and implementing subroutines. The key notion is the idea of a hardware-supported *register stack*, which can coexist with a software-supported stack of variables that are not maintained in registers. From a programmer's standpoint, `MMIX` maintains a potentially unbounded list $S[0]$, $S[1]$, ..., $S[\tau-1]$ of octabytes holding the contents of registers that are temporarily inaccessible; initially $\tau = 0$. When a subroutine is entered, registers can be "pushed" on to the end of this list, increasing τ; when the subroutine has finished its execution, the registers are "popped" off again and τ decreases.

Our discussion so far has treated all 256 registers \$0, \$1, ..., \$255 as if they were alike. But in fact, `MMIX` maintains two internal one-byte counters L and G, where $0 \le L \le G < 256$, with the property that

registers 0, 1, ..., $L-1$ are "local";
registers L, $L+1$, ..., $G-1$ are "marginal";
registers G, $G+1$, ..., 255 are "global."

A marginal register is zero when its value is read.

The G counter is normally set to a fixed value once and for all when a program is loaded, thereby defining the number of program variables that will live entirely in registers rather than in memory during the course of execution. A programmer may, however, change G dynamically using the `PUT` instruction described below.

The L counter starts at 0. If an instruction places a value into a register that is currently marginal, namely a register x such that $L \le x < G$, the value of L will increase to $x + 1$, and any newly local registers will be zero. For example, if $L = 10$ and $G = 200$, the instruction `ADD $5,$15,1` would simply set \$5 to 1. But the instruction `ADD $15,$5,$200` would set \$10, \$11, ..., \$14 to zero, \$15 to \$5 + \$200, and L to 16. (The process of clearing registers and increasing L might take quite a few machine cycles in the worst case. We will see later that `MMIX` is able to take care of any high-priority interrupts that might occur during this time.)

- `PUSHJ $X,@+4*YZ[-262144]` 'push registers and jump'.
- `PUSHGO $X,$Y,$Z|Z` 'push registers and go'.

Suppose first that $\mathrm{X} < L$. Register X is set equal to the number X, then registers 0, 1, ..., X are pushed onto the register stack as described below. If this instruction is in location λ, the value $\lambda + 4$ is placed into the special *return-jump register* rJ. Then control jumps to instruction $\lambda + 4\mathrm{YZ}$ or $\lambda + 4\mathrm{YZ} - 262144$ or $\$\mathrm{Y} + \$\mathrm{Z}$ or $\$\mathrm{Y} + \mathrm{Z}$, as in a `JMP` or `GO` command.

Pushing the first $\mathrm{X} + 1$ registers onto the stack means essentially that we set $S[\tau] \leftarrow \$0$, $S[\tau+1] \leftarrow \$1$, ..., $S[\tau + \mathrm{X}] \leftarrow \$\mathrm{X}$, $\tau \leftarrow \tau + \mathrm{X} + 1$, $\$0 \leftarrow \$(\mathrm{X}+1)$, ..., $\$(L - \mathrm{X} - 2) \leftarrow \$(L-1)$, $L \leftarrow L - \mathrm{X} - 1$. For example, if $\mathrm{X} = 1$ and $L = 5$, the current contents of \$0 and the number 1 are placed on the register stack, where they will be temporarily inaccessible. Then control jumps to a subroutine with L reduced to 3; the registers that we had been calling \$2, \$3, and \$4 appear as \$0, \$1, and \$2 to the subroutine.

If $L \le \mathrm{X} < G$, the value of L increases to $\mathrm{X} + 1$ as described above; then the rules for $\mathrm{X} < L$ apply.

If $X \geq G$ the actions are similar, except that *all* of the local registers $\$0, \ldots, \$(L-1)$ are placed on the register stack followed by the number L, and L is reset to zero. In particular, the instruction `PUSHGO $255,$Y,$Z` pushes all the local registers onto the stack and sets L to zero, regardless of the previous value of L.

We will see later that `MMIX` is able to achieve the effect of pushing and renaming local registers without actually doing very much work at all.

• `POP X,YZ` 'pop registers and return from subroutine'.
This command preserves X of the current local registers, undoes the effect of the most recent `PUSHJ` or `PUSHGO`, and jumps to the instruction in $M_4[4YZ + rJ]$. If $X > 0$, the value of $\$(X-1)$ goes into the "hole" position where `PUSHJ` or `PUSHGO` stored the number of registers previously pushed.

The formal details of `POP` are slightly complicated, but we will see that they make sense: If $X > L$, we first replace X by $L+1$. Then we set $x \leftarrow S[\tau-1] \bmod 256$; this is the effective value of the X field in the push instruction that is being undone. Stack position $S[\tau-1]$ is now set to $\$(X-1)$ if $0 < X \leq L$, otherwise it is set to zero. Then we essentially set $L \leftarrow \min(x+X, G)$, $\$(L-1) \leftarrow \$(L-x-2)$, ..., $\$(x+1) \leftarrow \$0$, $\$x \leftarrow S[\tau-1]$, ..., $\$0 \leftarrow S[\tau-x-1]$, $\tau \leftarrow \tau - x - 1$. The operating system should arrange things so that a memory-protection interrupt will occur if a program does more pops than pushes. (If $x > G$, these formulas don't make sense as written; we actually set $\$j \leftarrow S[\tau-x-1+j]$ for $L > j \geq 0$ in that rare case.)

Suppose, for example, that a subroutine has three input parameters ($\$0, \$1, \$2$) and produces two outputs ($\$0, \$1$). If the subroutine does not call any other subroutines, it can simply end with `POP 2,0`, because rJ will contain the return address. Otherwise it should begin by saving rJ, for example with the instruction `GET $4,rJ` if it will be using local registers \$0 through \$3, and it should use `PUSHJ $5` or `PUSHGO $5` when calling sub-subroutines; finally it should `PUT rJ,$4` before saying `POP 2,0`. To call the subroutine from another routine that has, say, 6 local registers, we would put the input arguments into \$7, \$8, and \$9, then issue the command `PUSHGO $6,base,Subr`; in due time the outputs of the subroutine will appear in \$7 and \$6.

Notice that the push and pop commands make use of a one-place "hole" in the register stack, between the registers that are pushed down and the registers that remain local. (The hole is position \$6 in the example just considered.) `MMIX` needs this hole position to remember the number of registers that are pushed down. A subroutine with no outputs ends with `POP 0,0` and the hole disappears (becomes marginal). A subroutine with one output \$0 ends with `POP 1,0` and the hole gets the former value of \$0. A subroutine with two outputs ($\$0, \$1$) ends with `POP 2,0` and the hole gets the former value of \$1; in this case, therefore, the relative order of the two outputs has been switched on the register stack. If a subroutine has, say, five outputs ($\$0, \ldots, \$4$), it ends with `POP 5,0` and \$4 goes into the hole position, where it is followed by ($\$0, \$1, \$2, \$3$). `MMIX` makes this curious permutation in the case of multiple outputs because the hole is most easily plugged by moving one value down (namely \$4) instead of by sliding each of five values down in the stack.

GET, §43. PUT, §43.

These conventions for parameter passing are admittedly a bit confusing in the general case, and I suppose people who use them extensively might someday find themselves talking about "the infamous `MMIX` register shuffle." However, there is good use for subroutines that convert a sequence of register contents like (x, a, b, c) into (f, a, b, c) where f is a function of a, b, and c but not x. Moreover, `PUSHGO` and `POP` can be implemented with great efficiency, and subroutine linkage tends to be a significant bottleneck when other conventions are used.

Information about a subroutine's calling conventions needs to be communicated to a debugger. That can readily be done at the same time as we inform the debugger about the symbolic names of addresses in memory.

A subroutine that uses 50 local registers will not function properly if it is called by a program that sets G less than 50. `MMIX` does not allow the value of G to become less than 32. Therefore any subroutine that avoids global registers and uses at most 32 local registers can be sure to work properly regardless of the current value of G.

The rules stated above imply that a `PUSHJ` or `PUSHGO` instruction with $\mathrm{X} = 255$ pushes all of the currently defined local registers onto the stack and sets L to zero. This makes G local registers available for use by the subroutine jumped to. If that subroutine later returns with `POP 0,0`, the former value of L and the former contents of \$0, ..., \$$(L-1)$ will be restored (assuming that G doesn't decrease).

A `POP` instruction with $\mathrm{X} = 255$ preserves all the local registers as outputs of the subroutine (provided that the total doesn't exceed G after popping), and puts zero into the hole (unless $L = G = 255$). The best policy, however, is almost always to use `POP` with a small value of X, and in general to keep the value of L as small as possible by decreasing it when registers are no longer active. A smaller value of L means that `MMIX` can change context more easily when switching from one process to another.

30. System considerations. High-performance implementations of `MMIX` gain speed by keeping *caches* of instructions and data that are likely to be needed as computation proceeds. [See M. V. Wilkes, *IEEE Transactions* **EC-14** (1965), 270–271; J. S. Liptay, *IBM System J.* **7** (1968), 15–21.] Careful programmers can make the computer run even faster by giving hints about how to maintain such caches.

• `LDUNC $X,$Y,$Z|Z` 'load octa uncached'.
These instructions, which have the same meaning as `LDO`, also inform the computer that the loaded octabyte (and its neighbors in a cache block) will probably not be read or written in the near future.

• `STUNC $X,$Y,$Z|Z` 'store octa uncached'.
These instructions, which have the same meaning as `STO`, also inform the computer that the stored octabyte (and its neighbors in a cache block) will probably not be read or written in the near future.

• `PRELD X,$Y,$Z|Z` 'preload data'.
These instructions have no effect on registers or memory, but they inform the computer that many of the X+1 bytes M[\$Y+\$Z] through M[\$Y+\$Z+X], or M[\$Y+Z] through M[\$Y+Z+X], will probably be loaded and/or stored in the near future. No protection failure occurs if the memory is not accessible.

• `PREGO X,$Y,$Z|Z` 'prefetch to go'.
These instructions have no effect on registers or memory, but they inform the computer that many of the X+1 bytes M[\$Y+\$Z] through M[\$Y+\$Z+X], or M[\$Y+Z] through M[\$Y+Z+X], will probably be used as instructions in the near future. No protection failure occurs if the memory is not accessible.

• `PREST X,$Y,$Z|Z` 'prestore data'.
These instructions have no effect on registers or memory if the computer has no data cache. But when such a cache exists, they inform the computer that all of the X+1 bytes M[\$Y+\$Z] through M[\$Y+\$Z+X], or M[\$Y+Z] through M[\$Y+Z+X], will definitely be stored in the near future before they are loaded. (Therefore it is permissible for the machine to ignore the present contents of those bytes. Also, if those bytes are being shared by several processors, the current processor should try to acquire exclusive access.) No protection failure occurs if the memory is not accessible.

• `SYNCD X,$Y,$Z|Z` 'synchronize data'.
When executed from nonnegative locations, these instructions have no effect on registers or memory if neither a write buffer nor a "write back" data cache are present. But when such a buffer or cache exists, they force the computer to make sure that all data for the $X+1$ bytes $M[\$Y+\$Z]$ through $M[\$Y+\$Z+X]$, or $M[\$Y+Z]$ through $M[\$Y+Z+X]$, will be present in memory. (Otherwise the result of a previous store instruction might appear only in the cache; the computer is being told that now is the time to write the information back, if it hasn't already been written. A program can use this feature before outputting directly from memory.) No protection failure occurs if the memory is not accessible.

The action is similar when `SYNCD` is executed from a negative address, but in this case the specified bytes are also removed from the data cache (and from a secondary cache, if present). The operating system can use this feature when a page of virtual memory is being swapped out, or when data is input directly into memory.

• `SYNCID X,$Y,$Z|Z` 'synchronize instructions and data'.
When executed from nonnegative locations these instructions have no effect on registers or memory if the computer has no instruction cache separate from a data cache. But when such a cache exists, they force the computer to make sure that the $X+1$ bytes $M[\$Y+\$Z]$ through $M[\$Y+\$Z+X]$, or $M[\$Y+Z]$ through $M[\$Y+Z+X]$, will be interpreted correctly if used as instructions before they are next modified. (Generally speaking, an `MMIX` program is not expected to store anything in memory locations that are also being used as instructions. Therefore `MMIX`'s instruction cache is allowed to become inconsistent with respect to its data cache. Programmers who insist on executing instructions that have been fabricated dynamically, for example when setting a breakpoint for debugging, must first `SYNCID` those instructions in order to guarantee that the intended results will be obtained.) A `SYNCID` command might be implemented in several ways; for example, the machine might update its instruction cache to agree with its data cache. A simpler solution, which is good enough because the need for `SYNCID` ought to be rare, removes instructions in the specified range from the instruction cache, if present, so that they will have to be fetched from memory the next time they are needed; in this case the machine also carries out the effect of a `SYNCD` command. No protection failure occurs if the memory is not accessible.

The behavior is more drastic, but faster, when `SYNCID` is executed from a negative location. Then all bytes in the specified range are simply removed from all caches, and the memory corresponding to any "dirty" cache blocks involving such bytes is *not* brought up to date. An operating system can use this version of the command when pages of virtual memory are being discarded (for example, when a program is being terminated).

31. `MMIX` is designed to work not only on a single processor but also in situations where several processors share a common memory. The following commands are useful for efficient operation in such circumstances.

• `CSWAP $X,$Y,$Z|Z` 'compare and swap octabytes'.
If the octabyte $M_8[\$Y+\$Z]$ or $M_8[\$Y+Z]$ is equal to the contents of the special *prediction register* rP, it is replaced in memory with the contents of register X, and

register X is set equal to 1. Otherwise the octabyte in memory replaces rP and register X is set to zero. This is an atomic (indivisible, uninterruptible) operation, useful for interprocess communication when independent computers are sharing the same memory.

The compare-and-swap operation was introduced by IBM in late models of the System/370 architecture, and it soon spread to several other machines. Significant ways to use it are discussed, for example, in section 7.2.3 of Harold Stone's *High-Performance Computer Architecture* (Reading, Massachusetts: Addison–Wesley, 1987), and in sections 8.2 and 8.3 of *Transaction Processing* by Jim Gray and Andreas Reuter (San Francisco: Morgan Kaufmann, 1993).

• `SYNC XYZ` 'synchronize'.
If XYZ = 0, the machine drains its pipeline (that is, it stalls until all preceding instructions have completed their activity). If XYZ = 1, the machine controls its actions less drastically, in such a way that all store instructions preceding this `SYNC` will be completed before all store instructions after it. If XYZ = 2, the machine controls its actions in such a way that all load instructions preceding this `SYNC` will be completed before all load instructions after it. If XYZ = 3, the machine controls its actions in such a way that all *load or store* instructions preceding this `SYNC` will be completed before all load or store instructions after it. If XYZ = 4, the machine goes into a power-saver mode, in which instructions may be executed more slowly (or not at all) until some kind of "wake-up" signal is received. If XYZ = 5, the machine empties its write buffer and cleans its data caches, if any (including a possible secondary cache); the caches retain their data, but the cache contents also appear in memory. If XYZ = 6, the machine clears its virtual address translation caches (see below). If XYZ = 7, the machine clears its instruction and data caches, discarding any information in the data caches that wasn't previously in memory. ("Clearing" is stronger than "cleaning"; a clear cache remembers nothing. Clearing is also faster, because it simply obliterates everything.) If XYZ > 7, an illegal instruction interrupt occurs.

Of course no `SYNC` is necessary between a command that loads from or stores into memory and a subsequent command that loads from or stores into exactly the same location. However, `SYNC` might be necessary in certain cases even on a one-processor system, because input/output processes take place in parallel with ordinary computation.

The cases XYZ > 3 are *privileged*, in the sense that only the operating system can use them. More precisely, if a `SYNC` command is encountered with XYZ = 4 or XYZ = 5 or XYZ = 6 or XYZ = 7, a "privileged instruction interrupt" occurs unless that interrupt is currently disabled. Only the operating system can disable interrupts (see below).

32. Trips and traps. Special register rA records the current status information about arithmetic exceptions. Its least significant byte contains eight "event" bits called DVWIOUZX from left to right, where D stands for integer divide check, V for integer overflow, W for float-to-fix overflow, I for invalid operation, O for floating overflow, U for floating underflow, Z for floating division by zero, and X for floating inexact. The next least significant byte of rA contains eight "enable" bits with the same names DVWIOUZX and the same meanings. When an exceptional condition occurs, there are two cases: If the corresponding enable bit is 0, the corresponding event bit is set to 1. But if the corresponding enable bit is 1, `MMIX` interrupts its current instruction stream and executes a special "exception handler." Thus, the event bits record exceptions that have not been "tripped."

Floating point overflow always causes two exceptions, O and X. (The strictest interpretation of the IEEE standard would raise exception X on overflow only if floating overflow is not enabled, but `MMIX` always considers an overflowed result to be inexact.) Floating point underflow always causes both U and X when underflow is not enabled, and it might cause both U and X when underflow is enabled. If both enable bits are set to 1 in such cases, the overflow or underflow handler is called and the inexact handler is ignored. All other types of exceptions arise one at a time, so there is no ambiguity about which exception handler should be invoked unless exceptions are raised by "ropcode 2" (see below); in general the first enabled exception in the list DVWIOUZX takes precedence.

What about the six high-order bytes of the status register rA? At present, only two of those 48 bits are defined; the others must be zero for compatibility with possible future extensions. The two bits corresponding to 2^{17} and 2^{16} in rA specify a rounding mode, as follows: 00 means round to nearest (the default); 01 means round off (toward zero); 10 means round up (toward positive infinity); and 11 means round down (toward negative infinity).

33. The execution of `MMIX` programs can be interrupted in several ways. We have just seen that arithmetic exceptions will cause interrupts if they are enabled; so will illegal or privileged instructions, or instructions that are emulated in software instead of provided by the hardware. Input/output operations or external timers are another common source of interrupts; the operating system knows how to deal with all gadgets that might be hooked up to an `MMIX` processor chip. Interrupts occur also when memory accesses fail—for example if memory is nonexistent or protected. Power failures that force the machine to use its backup battery power in order to keep running in an emergency, or hardware failures like parity errors, all must be handled as gracefully as possible.

Users can also force interrupts to happen by giving explicit `TRAP` or `TRIP` instructions:

• `TRAP X,Y,Z` 'trap'; `TRIP X,Y,Z` 'trip'.

Both of these instructions interrupt processing and transfer control to a handler. The difference between them is that `TRAP` is handled by the operating system but `TRIP` is handled by the user. More precisely, the X, Y, and Z fields of `TRAP` have special significance predefined by the operating system kernel. For example, a system call—

say an I/O command, or a command to allocate more memory—might be invoked by certain settings of X, Y, and Z. The X, Y, and Z fields of TRIP, on the other hand, are definable by users for their own applications, and users also define their own handlers. "Trip handler" programs invoked by TRIP are interruptible, but interrupts are normally inhibited while a TRAP is being serviced. Specific details about the precise actions of TRIP and TRAP appear below, together with the description of another command called RESUME that returns control from a handler to the interrupted program.

Only two variants of TRAP are predefined by the MMIX architecture: If $XYZ = 0$ in a TRAP command, a user process should terminate. If $XYZ = 1$, the operating system should provide default action for cases in which the user has not provided any handler for a particular kind of interrupt (see below).

A few additional variants of TRAP are predefined in the rudimentary operating system used with MMIX simulators. These variants, which allow simple input/output operations to be done, all have $X = 0$, and the Y field is a small positive constant. For example, $Y = 1$ invokes the Fopen routine, which opens a file. (See the program MMIX-SIM for full details.)

34. Non-catastrophic interrupts in `MMIX` are always *precise*, in the sense that all legal instructions before a certain point have effectively been executed, and no instructions after that point have yet been executed. The current instruction, which may or may not have been completed at the time of interrupt and which may or may not need to be resumed after the interrupt has been serviced, is put into the special *execution register* rX, and its operands (if any) are placed in special registers rY and rZ. The address of the following instruction is placed in the special *where-interrupted register* rW. The instruction in rX might not be the same as the instruction in location rW − 4; for example, it might be an instruction that branched or jumped to rW. It might also be an instruction inserted internally by the `MMIX` processor. (For example, the computer silently inserts an internal instruction that increases L before an instruction like `ADD $9,$1,$0` if L is currently less than 10. If an interrupt occurs, between the inserted instruction and the `ADD`, the instruction in rX will say `ADD`, because an internal instruction retains the identity of the actual command that spawned it; but rW will point to the *real* `ADD` command.)

When an instruction has the normal meaning "set \$X to the result of \$Y op \$Z" or "set \$X to the result of \$Y op Z," special registers rY and rZ will relate in the obvious way to the Y and Z operands of the instruction; but this is not always the case. For example, after an interrupted store instruction, the first operand rY will hold the virtual memory address (\$Y plus either \$Z or Z), and the second operand rZ will be the octabyte to be stored in memory (including bytes that have not changed, in cases like `STB`). In other cases the actual contents of rY and rZ are defined by each implementation of `MMIX`, and programmers should not rely on their significance.

Some instructions take an unpredictable and possibly long amount of time, so it may be necessary to interrupt them in progress. For example, the `FREM` instruction (floating point remainder) is extremely difficult to compute rapidly if its first operand has an exponent of 2046 and its second operand has an exponent of 1. In such cases the rY and rZ registers saved during an interrupt show the current state of the computation, not necessarily the original values of the operands. The value of rY rem rZ will still be the desired remainder, but rY may well have been reduced to a number that has an exponent closer to the exponent of rZ. After the interrupt has been processed, the remainder computation will continue where it left off. (Alternatively, an operation like `FREM` or even `FADD` might be implemented in software instead of hardware, as we will see later.)

Another example arises with an instruction like `PREST` (prestore), which can specify prestoring up to 256 bytes. An implementation of `MMIX` might choose to prestore only 32 or 64 bytes at a time, depending on the cache block size; then it can change the contents of rX to reflect the unfinished part of a partially completed `PREST` command.

Commands that decrease G, pop the stack, save the current context, or unsave an old context also are interruptible. Register rX is used to communicate information about partial completion in such a way that the interruption will be essentially "invisible" after a program is resumed.

35. Three kinds of interruption are possible: trips, forced traps, and dynamic traps. We will discuss each of these in turn.

A `TRIP` instruction puts itself into the right half of the execution register rX, and sets the 32 bits of the left half to #80000000. (Therefore rX is *negative*; this fact will tell the `RESUME` command not to `TRIP` again.) The special registers rY and rZ are set to the contents of the registers specified by the Y and Z fields of the `TRIP` command, namely $Y and $Z. Then $255 is placed into the special *bootstrap register* rB, and $255 is set to rJ. `MMIX` now takes its next instruction from virtual memory address 0.

Arithmetic exceptions interrupt the computation in essentially the same way as `TRIP`, if they are enabled. The only difference is that their handlers begin at the respective addresses 16, 32, 48, 64, 80, 96, 112, and 128, for exception bits D, V, W, I, O, U, Z, and X of rA; registers rY and rZ are set to the operands of the interrupted instruction as explained earlier.

A 16-byte block of memory is just enough for a sequence of commands like

```
PUSHJ 255,Handler; PUT rJ,$255; GET $255,rB; RESUME
```

which will invoke a user's handler. And if the user does not choose to provide a custom-designed handler, the operating system provides a default handler via the instructions

```
TRAP 1; GET $255,rB; RESUME.
```

A trip handler might simply record the fact that tripping occurred. But the handler for an arithmetic interrupt might want to change the default result of a computation. In such cases, the handler should place the desired substitute result into rZ, and it should change the most significant byte of rX from #80 to #02. This will have the desired effect, because of the rules of `RESUME` explained below, *unless* the exception occurred on a command like `STB` or `STSF`. (A bit more work is needed to alter the effect of a command that stores into memory.)

Instructions in *negative* virtual locations do not invoke trip handlers, either for `TRIP` or for arithmetic exceptions. Such instructions are reserved for the operating system, as we will see.

G, §29.
`RESUME`, §38.
`STB`, §8.
`STSF`, §26.

36. A `TRAP` instruction interrupts the computation essentially like `TRIP`, but with the following modifications: (i) the interrupt mask register rK is cleared to zero, thereby inhibiting interrupts; (ii) control jumps to virtual memory address rT, not zero; (iii) information is placed in a separate set of special registers rBB, rWW, rXX, rYY, and rZZ, instead of rB, rW, rX, rY, and rZ. (These special registers are needed because a trap might occur while processing a `TRIP`.)

Another kind of forced trap occurs on implementations of `MMIX` that emulate certain instructions in software rather than in hardware. Such instructions cause a `TRAP` even though their opcode is something else like `FREM` or `FADD` or `DIV`. The trap handler can tell what instruction to emulate by looking at the opcode, which appears in rXX. In such cases the left-hand half of rXX is set to #`02000000`; the handler emulating `FADD`, say, should compute the floating point sum of rYY and rZZ and place the result in rZZ. A subsequent `RESUME 1` will then place the value of rZZ in the proper register.

When a forced trap occurs on a store instruction because of memory protection failure, the settings of rYY and rZZ are undefined. They do not necessarily correspond to the virtual address rY and the octabyte to be stored rZ that are supplied to a trip handler after a tripped store instruction, because a forced trap aborts its instruction as soon as possible.

Implementations of `MMIX` might also emulate the process of virtual-address-to-physical-address translation described below, instead of providing for page table calculations in hardware. Then if, say, a `LDB` instruction does not know the physical memory address corresponding to a specified virtual address, it will cause a forced trap with the left half of rXX set to #`03000000` and with rYY set to the virtual address in question. The trap handler should place the physical page address into rZZ; then `RESUME 1` will complete the `LDB`.

37. The third and final kind of interrupt is called a *dynamic* trap. Such interruptions occur when one or more of the 64 bits in the special *interrupt request register* rQ have been set to 1, and when at least one corresponding bit of the special *interrupt mask register* rK is also equal to 1. The bit positions of rQ and rK have the general form

24	8	24	8
low-priority I/O	program	high-priority I/O	machine

where the 8-bit "program" bits are called `rwxnkbsp` and have the following meanings:

- `r` bit: instruction tries to load from a page without read permission;
- `w` bit: instruction tries to store to a page without write permission;
- `x` bit: instruction appears in a page without execute permission;
- `n` bit: instruction refers to a negative virtual address;
- `k` bit: instruction is privileged, for use by the "kernel" only;
- `b` bit: instruction breaks the rules of `MMIX`;
- `s` bit: instruction violates security (see below);
- `p` bit: instruction comes from a privileged (negative) virtual address.

Negative addresses are for the use of the operating system only; a security violation occurs if an instruction in a nonnegative address is executed without the `rwxnkbsp` bits of rK all set to 1. (In such cases the `s` bits of both rQ and rK are set to 1.)

The eight "machine" bits of rQ and rK represent the most urgent kinds of interrupts. The rightmost bit stands for power failure, the next for memory parity error, the next for nonexistent memory, the next for rebooting, etc. Interrupts that need especially quick service, like requests from a high-speed network, also are allocated bit positions near the right end. Low priority I/O devices like keyboards are assigned to bits at the left. The allocation of input/output devices to bit positions will differ from implementation to implementation, depending on what devices are available.

Once $\mathrm{rQ} \wedge \mathrm{rK}$ becomes nonzero, the machine waits briefly until it can give a precise interrupt. Then it proceeds as with a forced trap, except that it uses the special "dynamic trap address register" rTT instead of rT. The trap handler that begins at location rTT can figure out the reason for interrupt by examining $\mathrm{rQ} \wedge \mathrm{rK}$. (For example, after the instructions

```
GET $0,rQ; LDOU $1,savedK; AND $0,$0,$1; SUBU $1,$0,1;
SADD $2,$1,$0; ANDN $1,$0,$1
```

the highest-priority offending bit will be in \$1 and its position will be in \$2.)

If the interrupted instruction contributed 1s to any of the `rwxnkbsp` bits of rQ, the corresponding bits are set to 1 also in rXX. A dynamic trap handler might be able to use this information (although it should service higher-priority interrupts first if the right half of $\mathrm{rQ} \wedge \mathrm{rK}$ is nonzero).

The rules of `MMIX` are rigged so that only the operating system can execute instructions with interrupts suppressed. Therefore the operating system can in fact use instructions that would interrupt an ordinary program. Control of register rK turns out to be the ultimate privilege, and in a sense the only important one.

An instruction that causes a dynamic trap is usually executed before the interruption occurs. However, an instruction that traps with bits `x`, `k`, or `b` does nothing; a load instruction that traps with `r` or `n` loads zero; a store instruction that traps with any of `rwxnkbsp` stores nothing.

38. After a trip handler or trap handler has done its thing, it generally invokes the following command.

• `RESUME Z` 'resume after interrupt'; the X and Y fields must be zero.

If the Z field of this instruction is zero, `MMIX` will use the information found in special registers rW, rX, rY, and rZ to restart an interrupted computation. If the execution register rX is negative, it will be ignored and instructions will be executed starting at virtual address rW; otherwise the instruction in the right half of the execution register will be inserted into the program as if it had appeared in location $rW - 4$, subject to certain modifications that we will explain momentarily, and the *next* instruction will come from rW.

If the Z field of `RESUME` is 1 and if this instruction appears in a negative location, registers rWW, rXX, rYY, and rZZ are used instead of rW, rX, rY, and rZ. Also, just before resuming the computation, mask register rK is set to \$255 and \$255 is set to rBB. (Only the operating system gets to use this feature.)

An interrupt handler within the operating system might choose to allow itself to be interrupted. In such cases it should save the contents of rBB, rWW, rXX, rYY, and rZZ on some kind of stack, before making rK nonzero. Then, before resuming whatever caused the base level interrupt, it must again disable all interrupts; this can be done with `TRAP`, because the trap handler can tell from the virtual address in rWW that it has been invoked by the operating system. Once rK is again zero, the contents of rBB, rWW, rXX, rYY, and rZZ are restored from the stack, the outer level interrupt mask is placed in \$255, and `RESUME 1` finishes the job.

Values of Z greater than 1 are reserved for possible later definition. Therefore they cause an illegal instruction interrupt (that is, they set the '`b`' bit of rQ) in the present version of `MMIX`.

If the execution register rX is nonnegative, its leftmost byte controls the way its right-hand half will be inserted into the program. Let's call this byte the "ropcode." A ropcode of 0 simply inserts the instruction into the execution stream; a ropcode of 1 is similar, but it substitutes rY and rZ for the two operands, assuming that this makes sense for the operation considered.

Ropcode 2 inserts a command that sets \$X to rZ, where X is the second byte in the right half of rX. This ropcode is normally used with forced-trap emulations, so that the result of an emulated instruction is placed into the correct register. It also uses the third-from-left byte of rX to raise any or all of the arithmetic exceptions DVWIOUZX, at the same time as rZ is being placed in \$X. Emulated instructions and explicit `TRAP` commands can therefore cause overflow, say, just as ordinary instructions can. (Such new exceptions may, of course, spawn a trip interrupt, if any of the corresponding bits are enabled in rA.)

Finally, ropcode 3 is the same as ropcode 0, except that it also tells `MMIX` to treat rZ as the page table entry for the virtual address rY. (See the discussion of virtual address translation below.) Ropcodes greater than 3 are not permitted; moreover, only `RESUME 1` is allowed to use ropcode 3.

The ropcode rules in the previous paragraphs should of course be understood to involve rWW, rXX, rYY, and rZZ instead of rW, rX, rY, and rZ when the ropcode is seen by `RESUME 1`. Thus, in particular, ropcode 3 always applies to rYY and rZZ, never to rY and rZ.

Special restrictions must hold if resumption is to work properly: Ropcodes 0 and 3 must not insert a `RESUME` instruction; ropcode 1 must insert a "normal" instruction, namely one whose opcode begins with one of the hexadecimal digits `#0`, `#1`, `#2`, `#3`, `#6`, `#7`, `#C`, `#D`, or `#E`. (See the opcode chart below.) Some implementations may also allow ropcode 1 with `SYNCD[I]` and `SYNCID[I]`, so that those instructions can conveniently be interrupted. Moreover, the destination register \$X used with ropcode 1 or 2 must not be marginal. All of these restrictions hold automatically in normal use; they are relevant only if the programmer tries to do something tricky.

Notice that the slightly tricky sequence

```
LDA $0,Loc; PUT rW,$0; LDTU $1,Inst; PUT rX,$1; RESUME
```

will execute an almost arbitrary instruction `Inst` as if it had been in location `Loc-4`, and then will jump to location `Loc` (assuming that `Inst` doesn't branch elsewhere).

opcode chart, §51.
SYNCD, §30.
SYNCID, §30.
virtual addresses, §47.

39. Special registers. Quite a few special registers have been mentioned so far, and `MMIX` actually has even more. It is time now to enumerate them all, together with their internal code numbers:

rA, arithmetic status register [21];
rB, bootstrap register (trip) [0];
rC, continuation register [8];
rD, dividend register [1];
rE, epsilon register [2];
rF, failure location register [22];
rG, global threshold register [19];
rH, himult register [3];
rI, interval counter [12];
rJ, return-jump register [4];
rK, interrupt mask register [15];
rL, local threshold register [20];
rM, multiplex mask register [5];
rN, serial number [9];
rO, register stack offset [10];
rP, prediction register [23];
rQ, interrupt request register [16];
rR, remainder register [6];
rS, register stack pointer [11];
rT, trap address register [13];
rU, usage counter [17];
rV, virtual translation register [18];
rW, where-interrupted register (trip) [24];
rX, execution register (trip) [25];
rY, Y operand (trip) [26];
rZ, Z operand (trip) [27];
rBB, bootstrap register (trap) [7];
rTT, dynamic trap address register [14];
rWW, where-interrupted register (trap) [28];
rXX, execution register (trap) [29];
rYY, Y operand (trap) [30];
rZZ, Z operand (trap) [31];

In this list rG and rL are what we have been calling simply G and L; rC, rF, rI, rN, rO, rS, rU, and rV have not been mentioned before.

40. The *interval counter* rI decreases by 1 on every "clock pulse" of the `MMIX` processor. Thus if `MMIX` is running at 500 MHz, the interval counter decreases every 2 nanoseconds. It causes an *interval interrupt* when it reaches zero. Such interrupts can be extremely useful for "continuous profiling" as a means of studying the empirical running time of programs; see Jennifer M. Anderson, Lance M. Berc, Jeffrey Dean, Sanjay Ghemawat, Monika R. Henzinger, Shun-Tak A. Leung, Richard L. Sites,

Mark T. Vandevoorde, Carl A. Waldspurger, and William E. Weihl, *ACM Transactions on Computer Systems* **15** (1997), 357–390. The interval interrupt is achieved by setting the next-to-leftmost bit of the "machine" byte of rQ equal to 1; this is the seventh-least-significant bit.

The *usage counter* rU consists of three fields (u_p, u_m, u_c), called the usage pattern u_p, the usage mask u_m, and the usage count u_c. The most significant byte of rU is the usage pattern; the next most significant byte is the usage mask; and the remaining 48 bits are the usage count. Whenever an instruction whose $\mathrm{OP} \wedge u_m = u_p$ has been executed, the value of u_c increases by 1 (modulo 2^{47}). Thus, for example, the OP-code chart below implies that all instructions are counted if $u_p = u_m = 0$; all loads and stores are counted together with GO and PUSHGO if $u_p = (10000000)_2$ and $u_m = (11000000)_2$; all floating point instructions are counted together with fixed point multiplications and divisions if $u_p = 0$ and $u_m = (11100000)_2$; fixed point multiplications and divisions alone are counted if $u_p = (00011000)_2$ and $u_m = (11111000)_2$; completed subroutine calls are counted if $u_p = \mathtt{POP}$ and $u_m = (11111111)_2$. Instructions in negative locations, which belong to the operating system, are exceptional: They are included in the usage count only if the leading bit of u_c is 1.

Incidentally, the 64-bit counter rI can be implemented rather cheaply with only two levels of logic, using an old trick called "carry-save addition" [see, for example, G. Metze and J. E. Robertson, *Proc. International Conf. Information Processing* (Paris: 1959), 389–396]. One nice embodiment of this idea is to represent a binary number x in a redundant form as the difference $x' - x''$ of two binary numbers. Any two such numbers can be added without carry propagation as follows: Let

$$f(x,y,z) = (x \wedge \bar{y}) \vee (x \wedge z) \vee (\bar{y} \wedge z), \qquad g(x,y,z) = x \oplus y \oplus z.$$

Then it is easy to check that $x - y + z = 2f(x,y,z) - g(x,y,z)$; we need only verify this in the eight cases when x, y, and z are 0 or 1. Thus we can subtract 1 from a counter $x' - x''$ by setting

$$(x', x'') \leftarrow (f(x', x'', -1) \ll 1,\ g(x', x'', -1));$$

we can add 1 by setting $(x', x'') \leftarrow (g(x'', x', -1), f(x'', x', -1) \ll 1)$. The result is zero if and only if $x' = x''$. We need not actually compute the difference $x' - x''$ until we need to examine the register. The computation of $f(x,y,z)$ and $g(x,y,z)$ is particularly simple in the special cases $z = 0$ and $z = -1$. A similar trick works for rU, but extra care is needed in that case because several instructions might finish at the same time. (Thanks to Frank Yellin for his improvements to this paragraph.)

G, §29. *L*, §29. opcode chart, §51.

41. The special *serial number register* rN is permanently set to the time this particular instance of `MMIX` was created (measured as the number of seconds since 00:00:00 Greenwich Mean Time on 1 January 1970), in its five least significant bytes. The three most significant bytes are permanently set to the *version number* of the `MMIX` architecture that is being implemented together with two additional bytes that modify the version number. This quantity serves as an essentially unique identification number for each copy of `MMIX`.

Version 1.0.0 of the architecture is described in the present document. Version 1.0.1 is similar, but simplified to avoid the complications of pipelines and operating systems. Other versions may become necessary in the future.

42. The *register stack offset* rO and *register stack pointer* rS are especially interesting, because they are used to implement `MMIX`'s register stack $S[0]$, $S[1]$, $S[2]$, ...

The operating system initializes a register stack by assigning a large area of virtual memory to each running process, beginning at an address like `#6000000000000000`. If this starting address is σ, stack entry $S[k]$ will go into the octabyte $M_8[\sigma+8k]$. Stack underflow will be detected because the process does not have permission to read from $M[\sigma-1]$. Stack overflow will be detected because something will give out—either the user's budget or the user's patience or the user's swap space—long before 2^{61} bytes of virtual memory are filled by a register stack.

The `MMIX` hardware maintains the register stack by having two banks of 64-bit general-purpose registers, one for globals and one for locals. The global registers $g[32]$, $g[33]$, ..., $g[255]$ are used for register numbers that are $\geq G$ in `MMIX` commands; recall that G is always 32 or more. The local registers come from another array that contains 2^n registers for some n where $8 \leq n \leq 10$; for simplicity of exposition we will assume that there are exactly 512 local registers, but there may be only 256 or there may be 1024.

The local register slots $l[0]$, $l[1]$, ..., $l[511]$ act as a cyclic buffer with addresses that wrap around mod 512, so that $l[512] = l[0]$, $l[513] = l[1]$, etc. This buffer is divided into three parts by three pointers, which we will call α, β, and γ.

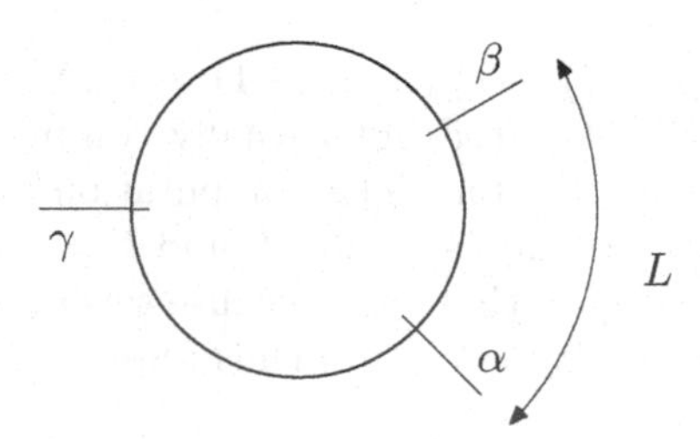

Registers $l[\alpha]$, $l[\alpha+1]$, ..., $l[\beta-1]$ are what program instructions currently call \$0, \$1, ..., $\$(L-1)$; registers $l[\beta]$, $l[\beta+1]$, ..., $l[\gamma-1]$ are currently unused; and registers $l[\gamma]$, $l[\gamma+1]$, ..., $l[\alpha-1]$ contain items of the register stack that have been pushed down but not yet stored in memory. Special register rS holds the virtual memory address where $l[\gamma]$ will be stored, if necessary. Special register rO holds the address where $l[\alpha]$ will be stored; this always equals 8τ plus the address of $S[0]$. We can deduce the values of α, β, and γ from the contents of rL, rO, and rS, because

$$\alpha = (\mathrm{rO}/8) \bmod 512, \qquad \beta = (\alpha + \mathrm{rL}) \bmod 512, \qquad \text{and} \qquad \gamma = (\mathrm{rS}/8) \bmod 512.$$

To maintain this situation we need to make sure that the pointers α, β, and γ never move past each other. A `PUSHJ` or `PUSHGO` operation simply advances α toward β, so it is very simple. The first part of a `POP` operation, which moves β toward α, is also very simple. But the next part of a `POP` requires α to move downward, and memory accesses might be required. `MMIX` will decrease rS by 8 (thereby decreasing γ by 1) and set $l[\gamma] \leftarrow M_8[\mathrm{rS}]$, one or more times if necessary, to keep α from decreasing past γ. Similarly, the operation of increasing L may cause `MMIX` to set $M_8[\mathrm{rS}] \leftarrow l[\gamma]$ and increase rS by 8 (thereby increasing γ by 1) one or more times, to keep β from increasing past γ. (Actually β is never allowed to increase to the point where it becomes *equal* to γ.) If many registers need to be loaded or stored at once, these operations are interruptible.

[A somewhat similar scheme was introduced by David R. Ditzel and H. R. McLellan in *SIGPLAN Notices* **17**, 4 (April 1982), 48–56, and incorporated in the so-called CRISP architecture developed at AT&T Bell Labs. An even more similar scheme was adopted in the late 1980s by Advanced Micro Devices, in the processors of their Am29000 series—a family of computers whose instructions have essentially the format 'OP X Y Z' used by `MMIX`.]

Limited versions of `MMIX`, having fewer registers, can also be envisioned. For example, we might have only 32 local registers $l[0]$, $l[1]$, ..., $l[31]$ and only 32 global registers $g[224]$, $g[225]$, ..., $g[255]$. Such a machine could run any `MMIX` program that maintains the inequalities $L < 32$ and $G \geq 224$.

43. Access to `MMIX`'s special registers is obtained via the `GET` and `PUT` commands.

• `GET $X,Z` 'get from special register'; the Y field must be zero.
Register X is set to the contents of the special register identified by its code number Z, using the code numbers listed earlier. An illegal instruction interrupt occurs if $Z \geq 32$.

Every special register is readable; `MMIX` does not keep secrets from an inquisitive user. But of course only the operating system is allowed to change registers like rK and rQ (the interrupt mask and request registers). And not even the operating system is allowed to change rN (the serial number) or the stack pointers rO and rS.

• `PUT X,$Z|Z` 'put into special register'; the Y field must be zero.
The special register identified by X is set to the contents of register Z or to the unsigned byte Z itself, if permissible. Some changes are, however, impermissible: Bits of rA that are always zero must remain zero; the leading seven bytes of rG and rL must remain zero, and rL must not exceed rG; special registers 9–11 (namely rN, rO, and rS) must not change; special registers 8 and 12–18 (namely rC, rI, rK, rQ, rT, rU, rV, and rTT) can be changed only if the privilege bit of rK is zero; and certain bits of rQ (depending on available hardware) might not allow software to change them from 0 to 1. Moreover, any bits of rQ that have changed from 0 to 1 since the most recent `GET x,rQ` will remain 1 after `PUT rQ,z`. The `PUT` command will not increase rL; it sets rL to the minimum of the current value and the new value. (A program should say `SETL $99,0` instead of `PUT rL,100` when rL is known to be less than 100.)

Impermissible `PUT` commands cause an illegal instruction interrupt, or (in the case of rC, rI, rK, rQ, rT, rU, rV, and rTT) a privileged operation interrupt.

• `SAVE $X,0` 'save process state'; `UNSAVE 0,$Z` 'restore process state'; the Y field must be 0, and so must the Z field of `SAVE`, the X field of `UNSAVE`.
The `SAVE` instruction stores all registers and special registers that might affect the computation of the currently running process. First the current local registers \$0, \$1, ..., $\$(L-1)$ are pushed down as in `PUSHGO $255`, and L is set to zero. Then the current global registers $\$G$, $\$(G+1)$, ..., \$255 are placed above them in the register stack; finally rB, rD, rE, rH, rJ, rM, rR, rP, rW, rX, rY, and rZ are placed at the very top, followed by registers rG and rA packed into eight bytes:

8	24	32
rG	0	rA

The address of the topmost octabyte is then placed in register X, which must be a global register. (This instruction is interruptible. If an interrupt occurs while the registers are being saved, we will have $\alpha = \beta = \gamma$ in the ring of local registers; thus rO will equal rS and rL will be zero. The interrupt handler essentially has a new register stack, starting on top of the partially saved context.) Immediately after a `SAVE` the values of rO and rS are equal to the location of the first byte following the stack just saved. The current register stack is effectively empty at this point; thus one shouldn't do a `POP` until this context or some other context has been unsaved.

The `UNSAVE` instruction goes the other way, restoring all the registers when given an address in register Z that was returned by a previous `SAVE`. Immediately after an `UNSAVE` the values of rO and rS will be equal. Like `SAVE`, this instruction is interruptible.

The operating system uses `SAVE` and `UNSAVE` to switch context between different processes. It can also use `UNSAVE` to establish suitable initial values of rO and rS. But a user program that knows what it is doing can in fact allocate its own register stack or stacks and do its own process switching.

Caution: `UNSAVE` is destructive, in the sense that a program can't reliably `UNSAVE` twice from the same saved context. Once an `UNSAVE` has been done, further operations are likely to change the memory record of what was saved. Moreover, an interrupt during the middle of an `UNSAVE` may have already clobbered some of the data in memory before the `UNSAVE` has completely finished, although the data will appear properly in all registers.

G, §29.
L, §29.
rO, §42.
rS, §42.

44. Virtual and physical addresses. Virtual 64-bit addresses are converted to physical addresses in a manner governed by the special *virtual translation register* rV. Thus M[A] really refers to m[ϕ(A)], where m is the physical memory array and $\phi(A)$ is determined by the physical mapping function ϕ. The details of this conversion are rather technical and of interest mainly to the operating system, but two simple rules are important to ordinary users:

• Negative addresses are mapped directly to physical addresses, by simply suppressing the sign bit:

$$\phi(A) = A + 2^{63} = A \land \texttt{\#7fffffffffffffff}, \qquad \text{if } A < 0.$$

All accesses to negative addresses are privileged, for use by the operating system only. (Thus, for example, the trap addresses in rT and rTT should be negative, because they are addresses inside the operating system.) Moreover, all physical addresses $\geq 2^{48}$ are intended for use by memory-mapped I/O devices; values read from or written to such locations are never placed in a cache.

• Nonnegative addresses belong to four *segments*, depending on whether the three leading bits are 000, 001, 010, or 011. These 2^{61}-byte segments are traditionally used for a program's text, data, dynamic memory, and register stack, respectively, but such conventions are not mandatory. There are four mappings ϕ_0, ϕ_1, ϕ_2, and ϕ_3 of 61-bit addresses into 48-bit physical memory space, one for each segment:

$$\phi(A) = \phi_{\lfloor A/2^{61}\rfloor}(A \bmod 2^{61}), \qquad \text{if } 0 \leq A < 2^{63}.$$

In general, the machine is able to access smaller addresses of a segment more efficiently than larger addresses. Thus a programmer should let each segment grow upward from zero, trying to keep any of the 61-bit addresses from becoming larger than necessary, although arbitrary addresses are legal.

45. Now it's time for the technical details of virtual address translation. The mappings ϕ_0, ϕ_1, ϕ_2, and ϕ_3 are defined by the following rules.

(1) The first two bytes of rV are four nybbles called b_1, b_2, b_3, b_4; we also define $b_0 = 0$. Segment i has at most $1024^{\,b_{i+1}-b_i}$ pages. In particular, segment i must have at most one page when $b_i = b_{i+1}$, and it must be entirely empty if $b_i > b_{i+1}$.

(2) The next byte of rV, s, specifies the current *page size*, which is 2^s bytes. We must have $s \geq 13$ (hence at least 8192 bytes per page). Values of s larger than, say, 20 or so are of use only in rather large programs that will reside in main memory for long periods of time, because memory protection and swapping are applied to entire pages. The maximum legal value of s is 48.

(3) The remaining five bytes of rV are a 27-bit *root location* r, a 10-bit *address space number* n, and a 3-bit *function field* f:

	4	4	4	4	8	27	10	3
rV =	b_1	b_2	b_3	b_4	s	r	n	f

Normally $f = 0$; if $f = 1$, virtual address translation will be done by software instead of hardware, and the b_1, b_2, b_3, b_4, and r fields of rV will be ignored by the hardware.

(Values of $f > 1$ are reserved for possible future use; if $f > 1$ when `MMIX` tries to translate an address, a memory-protection failure will occur.)

(4) Each page has an 8-byte *page table entry* (PTE), which looks like this:

	16	48 − s	s − 13	10	3
PTE =	x	a	y	n	p

Here x and y are ignored (thus they are usable for any purpose by the operating system); $2^s a$ is the physical address of byte 0 on the page; and n is the address space number (which must match the number in rV). The final three bits are the *protection bits* $p_r\,p_w\,p_x$; the user needs $p_r = 1$ to load from this page, $p_w = 1$ to store on this page, and $p_x = 1$ to execute instructions on this page. If n fails to match the number in rV, or if the appropriate protection bit is zero, a memory-protection fault occurs.

Page table entries should be writable only by the operating system. The 16 ignored bits of x imply that physical memory size is limited to 2^{48} bytes (namely 256 large terabytes); that should be enough capacity for awhile, if not for the entire new millennium.

(5) A given 61-bit address A belongs to page $\lfloor A/2^s \rfloor$ of its segment, and

$$\phi_i(A) = 2^s\,a + (A \bmod 2^s)$$

if a is the address in the PTE for page $\lfloor A/2^s \rfloor$ of segment i.

(6) Suppose $\lfloor A/2^s \rfloor$ is equal to $(a_4 a_3 a_2 a_1 a_0)_{1024}$ in the radix-1024 number system. In the common case $a_4 = a_3 = a_2 = a_1 = 0$, the PTE is simply the octabyte $\mathrm{m}_8[2^{13}(r + b_i) + 8a_0]$; this rule defines the mapping for the first 1024 pages. The next million or so pages are accessed through an auxiliary *page table pointer*

	1	50	10	3
PTP =	1	c	n	q

in $\mathrm{m}_8[2^{13}(r + b_i + 1) + 8a_1]$; here the sign must be 1 and the n-field must match rV, but the q bits are ignored. The desired PTE for page $(a_1 a_0)_{1024}$ is then in $\mathrm{m}_8[2^{13}c + 8a_0]$. The next billion or so pages, namely the pages $(a_2 a_1 a_0)_{1024}$ with $a_2 \neq 0$, are accessed similarly, through an auxiliary PTP at level two; and so on.

Notice that if $b_3 = b_4$, there is just one page in segment 3, and its PTE appears all alone in physical location $2^{13}(r + b_3)$. Otherwise the PTEs appear in 1024-octabyte blocks. We usually have $0 < b_1 < b_2 < b_3 < b_4$, but the null case $b_1 = b_2 = b_3 = b_4 = 0$ is worthy of mention: In this special case there is only one page, and the segment bits of a virtual address are ignored; the other $61 - s$ bits of each virtual address must be zero.

If $s = 13$, $b_1 = 3$, $b_2 = 2$, $b_3 = 1$, and $b_4 = 0$, there are at most 2^{30} pages of 8192 bytes each, all belonging to segment 0. This is essentially the virtual memory setup in the Alpha 21064 computers with DIGITAL UNIX™.

Several special cases have weird behavior, which probably isn't going to be useful. But I might as well mention them so that the flexibility of this scheme is clarified: If, for example, $b_1 = 2$, $b_2 = b_3 = 1$, and $b_4 = 5$, then $r + 1$ is used both for PTPs of segment 0 and PTEs of segment 2. And if $b_2 = b_3 < b_4$, then $r + b_2$ is used for the PTE of page 0 segments 2 and 3; page 1 of segment 2 is not allowed, but there is a page 1 in segment 3.

I know these rules look extremely complicated, and I sincerely wish I could have found an alternative that would be both simple and efficient in practice. I tried various schemes based on hashing, but came to the conclusion that "trie" methods such as those described here are better for this application. Indeed, the page tables in most contemporary computers are based on very similar ideas, but with significantly smaller virtual addresses and without the shortcut for small page numbers. I tried also to find formats for rV and the page tables that would match byte boundaries in a more friendly way, but the corresponding page sizes did not work well. Fortunately these grungy details are almost always completely hidden from ordinary users.

Stack overflow presents a potential problem: If γ increases to a virtual address on a new page for which there is no permission to write, the protection interrupt handler would have no stack space in which to work! Therefore `MMIX` has a *continuation register* rC, which contains the physical address of a "continuation page." Pushed-down information is written to the continuation page until `MMIX` comes to an instruction that is safely interruptible. Then a stack overflow interrupt occurs, and the operating system can restore order. The format of rC is just like an ordinary PTE entry, except that the n field is ignored.

46. Of course `MMIX` can't afford to perform a lengthy calculation of physical addresses every time it accesses memory. The machine therefore maintains a *translation cache* (TC), which contains the translations of recently accessed pages. (In fact, there usually are two such caches, one for instructions and one for data.) A TC holds a set of 64-bit translation keys

1	2	$61-s$	$s-13$	10	3
0	i	v	0	n	0

associated with 38-bit translations

$48-s$	$s-13$	3
a	0	p

representing the relevant parts of the PTE for page v of segment i. Different processes typically have different values of n, and possibly also different values of s. The operating system needs a way to keep such caches up to date when pages are being allocated, moved, swapped, or recycled. The operating system also likes to know which pages have been recently used. The `LDVTS` instructions facilitate such operations:

• `LDVTS $X,$Y,$Z|Z` 'load virtual translation status'.

The sum $\$Y + \$Z$ or $\$Y + Z$ should have the form of a translation cache key as above, except that the rightmost three bits need not be zero. If this key is present in a TC, the rightmost three bits replace the current protection code p; however, if p is thereby set to zero, the key is removed from the TC. Register X is set to 0 if the key was not present in any translation cache, or to 1 if the key was present in the TC for instructions, or to 2 if the key was present in the TC for data, or to 3 if the key was present in both. This instruction is for the operating system only. (Changes to the TC are not immediate; so `SYNC` and/or `SYNCD` ought to be done when appropriate, as discussed in MMIX-PIPE.)

47. We mentioned earlier that cheap versions of MMIX might calculate the physical addresses with software instead of hardware, using forced traps when the operating system needs to do page table calculations. Here is some code that could be used for such purposes; it defines the translation process precisely, given a nonnegative virtual address in register rYY. First we must unpack the fields of rV and compute the relevant base addresses for PTEs and PTPs:

```
GET     virt,rYY
GET     $7,rV              % $7=(virtual translation register)
SRU     $1,virt,61         % $1=i (segment number of virtual address)
SLU     $1,$1,2
NEG     $1,52,$1           % $1=52-4i
SRU     $1,$7,$1
SLU     $2,$1,4
SETL    $0,#f000
AND     $1,$1,$0           % $1=b[i]<<12
AND     $2,$2,$0           % $2=b[i+1]<<12
SLU     $3,$7,24
SRU     $3,$3,37
SLU     $3,$3,13           % $3=(r field of rV)
ORH     $3,#8000           % make $3 a physical address
2ADDU   base,$1,$3         % base=address of first page table
2ADDU   limit,$2,$3        % limit=address after last page table
SRU     s,$7,40
AND     s,s,#ff            % s=(s field of rV)
CMP     $0,s,13
BN      $0,Fail            % s must be 13 or more
CMP     $0,s,49
BNN     $0,Fail            % s must be 48 or less
SETH    mask,#8000
ORL     mask,#1ff8         % mask=(sign bit and n field)
ORH     $7,#8000           % set sign bit for PTP validation below
ANDNH   virt,#e000         % zero out the segment number
SRU     $0,virt,s          % $0=a4a3a2a1a0 (page number of virt)
ZSZ     $1,$0,1            % $1=[page number is zero]
ADD     limit,limit,$1     % increase limit if page number is zero
SETL    $6,#3ff
```

The next part of the routine finds the "digits" of the page number $(a_4a_3a_2a_1a_0)_{1024}$, from right to left:

```
CMP $5,base,limit; SRU $1,$0,10; PBZ $1,1F
AND $0,#3ff; INCL base,#2000
CMP $5,base,limit; SRU $2,$1,10; PBZ $2,2F
AND $1,#3ff; INCL base,#2000
CMP $5,base,limit; SRU $3,$2,10; PBZ $3,3F
AND $2,#3ff; INCL base,#2000
CMP $5,base,limit; SRU $4,$3,10; PBZ $4,4F
AND $3,#3ff; INCL base,#2000
```

Then the process cascades back through PTPs.

```
        CMP $5,base,limit
        BNN $5,Fail; 8ADDU $6,$4,base; LDO base,$6,0
        XOR $6,base,$7; AND $6,$6,mask; BNZ $6,Fail
        ANDNL base,#1fff
4H      BNN $5,Fail; 8ADDU $6,$3,base; LDO base,$6,0
        XOR $6,base,$7; AND $6,$6,mask; BNZ $6,Fail
        ANDNL base,#1fff
3H      BNN $5,Fail; 8ADDU $6,$2,base; LDO base,$6,0
        XOR $6,base,$7; AND $6,$6,mask; BNZ $6,Fail
        ANDNL base,#1fff
2H      BNN $5,Fail; 8ADDU $6,$1,base; LDO base,$6,0
        XOR $6,base,$7; AND $6,$6,mask; BNZ $6,Fail
```

Finally we obtain the PTE and communicate it to the machine. If errors have been detected, we set the translation to zero; actually any translation with permission bits zero would have the same effect.

```
        ANDNL  base,#1fff      % remove low 13 bits of PTP
1H      BNN    $5,Fail
        8ADDU  $6,$0,base
        LDO    base,$6,0       % base=PTE
        XOR    $6,base,$7
        ANDN   $6,$6,#7
        SLU    $6,$6,51
        PBZ    $6,Ready        % branch if n matches
Fail    SETL   base,0          % errors lead to PTE of zero
Ready   PUT    rZZ,base
        LDO    $255,IntMask    % load the desired setting of rK
        RESUME 1               % now the machine will digest the translation
```

All loads and stores in this program deal with negative virtual addresses. This effectively shuts off memory mapping and makes the page tables inaccessible to the user.

The program assumes that the ropcode in rXX is 3 (which it is when a forced trap is triggered by the need for virtual translation).

The translation from virtual pages to physical pages need not actually follow the rules for PTPs and PTEs; any other mapping could be substituted by operating systems with special needs. But people usually want compatibility between different implementations whenever possible. The only parts of rV that `MMIX` really needs are the s field, which defines page sizes, and the n field, which keeps TC entries of one process from being confused with the TC entries of another.

48. The complete instruction set. We have now described all of `MMIX`'s special registers—except one: The special *failure location register* rF is set to a physical memory address when a parity error or other memory fault occurs. (The instruction leading to this error will probably be long gone before such a fault is detected; for example, the machine might be trying to write old data from a cache in order to make room for new data. Thus there is generally no connection between the current virtual program location rW and the physical location of a memory error. But knowledge of the latter location can still be useful for hardware repair, or when an operating system is booting up.)

49. One additional instruction proves to be useful.

• `SWYM X,Y,Z` 'sympathize with your machinery'.

This command lubricates the disk drives, fans, magnetic tape drives, laser printers, scanners, and any other mechanical equipment hooked up to `MMIX`, if necessary. Fields X, Y, and Z are ignored.

The `SWYM` command was originally included in `MMIX`'s repertoire because machines occasionally need grease to keep in shape, just as human beings occasionally need to swim or do some other kind of exercise in order to maintain good muscle tone. But in fact, `SWYM` has turned out to be a "no-op," an instruction that does nothing at all; the hypothetical manufacturers of our hypothetical machine have pointed out that modern computer equipment is already well oiled and sealed for permanent use. Even so, a no-op instruction provides a good way for software to send signals to the hardware, for such things as scheduling the way instructions are issued on superscalar superpipelined buzzword-compliant machines. Software programs can also use no-ops to communicate with other programs like symbolic debuggers.

When a forced trap computes the translation rZZ of a virtual address rYY, ropcode 3 of `RESUME 1` will put (rYY, rZZ) into the TC for instructions if the opcode in rXX is `SWYM`; otherwise (rYY, rZZ) will be put into the TC for data.

50. The running time of `MMIX` programs depends to a great extent on changes in technology. `MMIX` is a mythical machine, but its mythical hardware exists in cheap, slow versions as well as in costly high-performance models. Details of running time usually depend on things like the amount of main memory available to implement virtual memory, as well as the sizes of caches and other buffers.

For practical purposes, the running time of an `MMIX` program can often be estimated satisfactorily by assigning a fixed cost to each operation, based on the approximate running time that would be obtained on a high-performance machine with lots of main memory; so that's what we will do. Each operation will be assumed to take an integer number of υ, where υ (pronounced "oops") is a unit that represents the clock cycle time in a pipelined implementation. The value of υ will probably decrease from year to year, but I'll keep calling it υ. The running time will also depend on the number of memory references or *mems* that a program uses; this is the number of load and store instructions. For example, each `LDO` (load octa) instruction will be assumed to cost $\mu+\upsilon$, where μ is the average cost of a memory reference. The total running time of a program might be reported as, say, $35\mu+1000\upsilon$, meaning 35 mems plus 1000 oops. The ratio μ/υ will probably increase with time, so mem-counting is likely to become increasingly important. [See the discussion of mems in *The Stanford GraphBase* (New York: ACM Press, 1994).]

Integer addition, subtraction, and comparison all take just $1v$. The same is true for `SET`, `GET`, `PUT`, `SYNC`, and `SWYM` instructions, as well as bitwise logical operations, shifts, relative jumps, comparisons, conditional assignments, and correctly predicted branches-not-taken or probable-branches-taken. Mispredicted branches or probable branches cost $3v$, and so do the `POP` and `GO` commands. Integer multiplication takes $10v$; integer division weighs in at $60v$. `TRAP`, `TRIP`, and `RESUME` cost $5v$ each.

Most floating point operations have a nominal running time of $4v$, although the comparison operators `FCMP`, `FEQL`, and `FUN` need only $1v$. `FDIV` and `FSQRT` cost $40v$ each. The actual running time of floating point computations will vary depending on the operands; for example, the machine might need one extra v for each subnormal input or output, and it might slow down greatly when trips are enabled. The `FREM` instruction might typically cost $(3+\delta)v$, where δ is the amount by which the exponent of the first operand exceeds the exponent of the second (or zero, if this amount is negative). A floating point operation might take only $1v$ if at least one of its operands is zero, infinity, or NaN. However, the fixed values stated at the beginning of this paragraph will be used for all seat-of-the-pants estimates of running time, since we want to keep the estimates as simple as possible without making them terribly out of line.

All load and store operations will be assumed to cost $\mu + v$, except that `CSWAP` costs $2\mu + 2v$. (This applies to all OP codes that begin with `#8`, `#9`, `#A`, and `#B`, except `#98`–`#9F` and `#B8`–`#BF`. It's best to keep the rules simple, because μ is just an approximate device for estimating average memory cost.) `SAVE` and `UNSAVE` are charged $20\mu + v$.

Of course we must remember that these numbers are very rough. We have not included the cost of fetching instructions from memory. Furthermore, an integer multiplication or division might have an effective cost of only $1v$, if the result is not needed while other numbers are being calculated. Only a detailed simulation can be expected to be truly realistic.

51. If you think that MMIX has plenty of operation codes, you are right; we have now described them all. Here is a chart that shows their numeric values:

	#0	#1	#2	#3	#4	#5	#6	#7	
#0x	TRAP	FCMP	FUN	FEQL	FADD	FIX	FSUB	FIXU	#0x
	FLOT[I]		FLOTU[I]		SFLOT[I]		SFLOTU[I]		
#1x	FMUL	FCMPE	FUNE	FEQLE	FDIV	FSQRT	FREM	FINT	#1x
	MUL[I]		MULU[I]		DIV[I]		DIVU[I]		
#2x	ADD[I]		ADDU[I]		SUB[I]		SUBU[I]		#2x
	2ADDU[I]		4ADDU[I]		8ADDU[I]		16ADDU[I]		
#3x	CMP[I]		CMPU[I]		NEG[I]		NEGU[I]		#3x
	SL[I]		SLU[I]		SR[I]		SRU[I]		
#4x	BN[B]		BZ[B]		BP[B]		BOD[B]		#4x
	BNN[B]		BNZ[B]		BNP[B]		BEV[B]		
#5x	PBN[B]		PBZ[B]		PBP[B]		PBOD[B]		#5x
	PBNN[B]		PBNZ[B]		PBNP[B]		PBEV[B]		
#6x	CSN[I]		CSZ[I]		CSP[I]		CSOD[I]		#6x
	CSNN[I]		CSNZ[I]		CSNP[I]		CSEV[I]		
#7x	ZSN[I]		ZSZ[I]		ZSP[I]		ZSOD[I]		#7x
	ZSNN[I]		ZSNZ[I]		ZSNP[I]		ZSEV[I]		
#8x	LDB[I]		LDBU[I]		LDW[I]		LDWU[I]		#8x
	LDT[I]		LDTU[I]		LDO[I]		LDOU[I]		
#9x	LDSF[I]		LDHT[I]		CSWAP[I]		LDUNC[I]		#9x
	LDVTS[I]		PRELD[I]		PREGO[I]		GO[I]		
#Ax	STB[I]		STBU[I]		STW[I]		STWU[I]		#Ax
	STT[I]		STTU[I]		STO[I]		STOU[I]		
#Bx	STSF[I]		STHT[I]		STCO[I]		STUNC[I]		#Bx
	SYNCD[I]		PREST[I]		SYNCID[I]		PUSHGO[I]		
#Cx	OR[I]		ORN[I]		NOR[I]		XOR[I]		#Cx
	AND[I]		ANDN[I]		NAND[I]		NXOR[I]		
#Dx	BDIF[I]		WDIF[I]		TDIF[I]		ODIF[I]		#Dx
	MUX[I]		SADD[I]		MOR[I]		MXOR[I]		
#Ex	SETH	SETMH	SETML	SETL	INCH	INCMH	INCML	INCL	#Ex
	ORH	ORMH	ORML	ORL	ANDNH	ANDNMH	ANDNML	ANDNL	
#Fx	JMP[B]		PUSHJ[B]		GETA[B]		PUT[I]		#Fx
	POP	RESUME	SAVE	UNSAVE	SYNC	SWYM	GET	TRIP	
	#8	#9	#A	#B	#C	#D	#E	#F	

The notation '[I]' indicates an operation with an "immediate" variant in which the Z field denotes a constant instead of a register number. Similarly, '[B]' indicates an operation with a "backward" variant in which a relative address has a negative displacement. Simulators and other programs that need to present MMIX instructions in symbolic form will say that opcode #20 is ADD while opcode #21 is ADDI; they will say that #F2 is PUSHJ while #F3 is PUSHJB. But the MMIX assembler uses only the forms ADD and PUSHJ, not ADDI or PUSHJB.

To read this chart, use the hexadecimal digits at the top, bottom, left, and right. For example, operation code A9 in hexadecimal notation appears in the lower part of the #Ax row and in the #1/#9 column; it is STTI, 'store tetrabyte immediate'.

MMIX-ARITH

1. Introduction. The subroutines below are used to simulate 64-bit MMIX arithmetic on an old-fashioned 32-bit computer—like the one the author had when he wrote MMIXAL and the first MMIX simulators in 1998 and 1999. All operations are fabricated from 32-bit arithmetic, including a full implementation of the IEEE floating point standard, assuming only that the C compiler has a 32-bit unsigned integer type.

Some day 64-bit machines will be commonplace and the awkward manipulations of the present program will look quite archaic. Interested readers who have such computers will be able to convert the code to a pure 64-bit form without difficulty, thereby obtaining much faster and simpler routines. Meanwhile, however, we can simulate the future and hope for continued progress.

This program module has a simple structure, intended to make it suitable for loading with MMIX simulators and assemblers.

```
#include <stdio.h>
#include <string.h>
#include <ctype.h>
  ⟨ Stuff for C preprocessor 2 ⟩
  typedef enum { false, true } bool;
  ⟨ Tetrabyte and octabyte type definitions 3 ⟩
  ⟨ Other type definitions 36 ⟩
  ⟨ Global variables 4 ⟩
  ⟨ Subroutines 5 ⟩
```

2. Subroutines of this program are declared first with a prototype, as in ANSI C, then with an old-style C function definition. Here are some preprocessor commands that make this work correctly with both new-style and old-style compilers.

```
⟨ Stuff for C preprocessor 2 ⟩ ≡
#ifdef __STDC__
#define ARGS(list) list
#else
#define ARGS(list) ()
#endif
```

This code is used in section 1.

3. The definition of type **tetra** should be changed, if necessary, so that it represents an unsigned 32-bit integer.

```
⟨ Tetrabyte and octabyte type definitions 3 ⟩ ≡
  typedef unsigned int tetra;
    /* for systems conforming to the LP-64 data model */
  typedef struct {
    tetra h, l;
  } octa;    /* two tetrabytes make one octabyte */
```

This code is used in section 1.

4. #define *sign_bit* ((**unsigned**) #80000000)

⟨ Global variables 4 ⟩ ≡

D.E. Knuth: MMIXware, LNCS 1750, pp. 62–109, 2014.
DOI: 10.1007/3-540-46611-8_3

```
octa zero_octa;       /* zero_octa.h = zero_octa.l = 0 */
octa neg_one = {-1, -1};     /* neg_one.h = neg_one.l = -1 */
octa inf_octa = {#7ff00000, 0};     /* floating point +∞ */
octa standard_NaN = {#7ff80000, 0};     /* floating point NaN(.5) */
```

See also sections 9, 30, 32, 69, and 75.

This code is used in section 1.

5. It's easy to add and subtract octabytes, if we aren't terribly worried about speed.

⟨ Subroutines 5 ⟩ ≡

```
octa oplus ARGS((octa, octa));
octa oplus(y, z)      /* compute y + z */
    octa y, z;
{ octa x;
  x.h = y.h + z.h; x.l = y.l + z.l;
  if (x.l < y.l) x.h++;
  return x;
}
octa ominus ARGS((octa, octa));
octa ominus(y, z)      /* compute y - z */
    octa y, z;
{ octa x;
  x.h = y.h - z.h; x.l = y.l - z.l;
  if (x.l > y.l) x.h--;
  return x;
}
```

See also sections 6, 7, 8, 12, 13, 24, 25, 26, 27, 28, 29, 31, 34, 37, 38, 39, 40, 41, 44, 46, 50, 54, 60, 61, 62, 68, 82, 85, 86, 88, 89, 91, and 93.

This code is used in section 1.

6. In the following subroutine, *delta* is a signed quantity that is assumed to fit in a signed tetrabyte.

⟨ Subroutines 5 ⟩ +≡

```
octa incr ARGS((octa, int));
octa incr(y, delta)      /* compute y + δ */
    octa y;
    int delta;
{ octa x;
  x.h = y.h; x.l = y.l + delta;
  if (delta ≥ 0) {
    if (x.l < y.l) x.h++;
  } else if (x.l > y.l) x.h--;
  return x;
}
```

__STDC__, Standard C.

7. Left and right shifts are only a bit more difficult.

```
⟨ Subroutines 5 ⟩ +≡
  octa shift_left ARGS((octa, int));
  octa shift_left(y, s)      /* shift left by s bits, where 0 ≤ s ≤ 64 */
      octa y;
      int s;
  {
    while (s ≥ 32) y.h = y.l, y.l = 0, s −= 32;
    if (s) { register tetra yhl = y.h ≪ s, ylh = y.l ≫ (32 − s);
      y.h = yhl + ylh; y.l ≪= s;
    }
    return y;
  }
  octa shift_right ARGS((octa, int, int));
  octa shift_right(y, s, u)      /* shift right, arithmetically if u = 0 */
      octa y;
      int s, u;
  {
    while (s ≥ 32) y.l = y.h, y.h = (u ? 0 : −(y.h ≫ 31)), s −= 32;
    if (s) { register tetra yhl = y.h ≪ (32 − s), ylh = y.l ≫ s;
      y.h = (u ? 0 : (−(y.h ≫ 31)) ≪ (32 − s)) + (y.h ≫ s); y.l = yhl + ylh;
    }
    return y;
  }
```

8. Multiplication. We need to multiply two unsigned 64-bit integers, obtaining an unsigned 128-bit product. It is easy to do this on a 32-bit machine by using Algorithm 4.3.1M of *Seminumerical Algorithms*, with $b = 2^{16}$.

The following subroutine returns the lower half of the product, and puts the upper half into a global octabyte called *aux*.

```
⟨Subroutines 5⟩ +≡
  octa omult ARGS((octa, octa));
  octa omult(y, z)
      octa y, z;
  {
    register int i, j, k;
    tetra u[4], v[4], w[8];
    register tetra t;
    octa acc;
    ⟨Unpack the multiplier and multiplicand to u and v 10⟩;
    for (j = 0; j < 4; j++) w[j] = 0;
    for (j = 0; j < 4; j++)
      if (¬v[j]) w[j + 4] = 0;
      else {
        for (i = k = 0; i < 4; i++) {
          t = u[i] * v[j] + w[i + j] + k;
          w[i + j] = t & #ffff, k = t ≫ 16;
        }
        w[j + 4] = k;
      }
    ⟨Pack w into the outputs aux and acc 11⟩;
    return acc;
  }
```

9. ⟨Global variables 4⟩ +≡

```
  octa aux;    /* secondary output of subroutines with multiple outputs */
  bool overflow;    /* set by certain subroutines for signed arithmetic */
```

10. ⟨Unpack the multiplier and multiplicand to *u* and *v* 10⟩ ≡

```
  u[3] = y.h ≫ 16, u[2] = y.h & #ffff, u[1] = y.l ≫ 16, u[0] = y.l & #ffff;
  v[3] = z.h ≫ 16, v[2] = z.h & #ffff, v[1] = z.l ≫ 16, v[0] = z.l & #ffff;
```

This code is used in section 8.

11. ⟨Pack *w* into the outputs *aux* and *acc* 11⟩ ≡

```
  aux.h = (w[7] ≪ 16) + w[6], aux.l = (w[5] ≪ 16) + w[4];
  acc.h = (w[3] ≪ 16) + w[2], acc.l = (w[1] ≪ 16) + w[0];
```

This code is used in section 8.

ARGS = macro ( ), §2.
bool: **enum**, §1.
h: **tetra**, §3.
l: **tetra**, §3.
octa = **struct**, §3.
tetra = **unsigned int**, §3.

12. Signed multiplication has the same lower half product as unsigned multiplication. The signed upper half product is obtained with at most two further subtractions, after which the result has overflowed if and only if the upper half is unequal to 64 copies of the sign bit in the lower half.

⟨ Subroutines 5 ⟩ +≡

```
octa signed_omult ARGS((octa, octa));
octa signed_omult(y, z)
    octa y, z;
{
  octa acc;
  acc = omult(y, z);
  if (y.h & sign_bit) aux = ominus(aux, z);
  if (z.h & sign_bit) aux = ominus(aux, y);
  overflow = (aux.h ≠ aux.l ∨ (aux.h ⊕ (aux.h ≫ 1) ⊕ (acc.h & sign_bit)));
  return acc;
}
```

13. Division. Long division of an unsigned 128-bit integer by an unsigned 64-bit integer is, of course, one of the most challenging routines needed for MMIX arithmetic. The following program, based on Algorithm 4.3.1D of *Seminumerical Algorithms*, computes octabytes q and r such that $(2^{64}x+y) = qz + r$ and $0 \le r < z$, given octabytes x, y, and z, assuming that $x < z$. (If $x \ge z$, it simply sets $q = x$ and $r = y$.) The quotient q is returned by the subroutine; the remainder r is stored in *aux*.

```
⟨ Subroutines 5 ⟩ +≡
  octa odiv ARGS((octa, octa, octa));
  octa odiv(x, y, z)
       octa x, y, z;
  {
    register int i, j, k, n, d;
    tetra u[8], v[4], q[4], mask, qhat, rhat, vh, vmh;
    register tetra t;
    octa acc;
    ⟨ Check that x < z; otherwise give trivial answer 14 ⟩;
    ⟨ Unpack the dividend and divisor to u and v 15 ⟩;
    ⟨ Determine the number of significant places n in the divisor v 16 ⟩;
    ⟨ Normalize the divisor 17 ⟩;
    for (j = 3; j ≥ 0; j−−) ⟨ Determine the quotient digit q[j] 20 ⟩;
    ⟨ Unnormalize the remainder 18 ⟩;
    ⟨ Pack q and u to acc and aux 19 ⟩;
    return acc;
  }
```

14. ⟨ Check that $x < z$; otherwise give trivial answer 14 ⟩ ≡

```
  if (x.h > z.h ∨ (x.h ≡ z.h ∧ x.l ≥ z.l)) {
    aux = y; return x;
  }
```

This code is used in section 13.

15. ⟨ Unpack the dividend and divisor to u and v 15 ⟩ ≡

```
  u[7] = x.h ≫ 16, u[6] = x.h & #ffff, u[5] = x.l ≫ 16, u[4] = x.l & #ffff;
  u[3] = y.h ≫ 16, u[2] = y.h & #ffff, u[1] = y.l ≫ 16, u[0] = y.l & #ffff;
  v[3] = z.h ≫ 16, v[2] = z.h & #ffff, v[1] = z.l ≫ 16, v[0] = z.l & #ffff;
```

This code is used in section 13.

16. ⟨ Determine the number of significant places n in the divisor v 16 ⟩ ≡

```
  for (n = 4; v[n − 1] ≡ 0; n−−) ;
```

This code is used in section 13.

17. We shift u and v left by d places, where d is chosen to make $2^{15} \le v_{n-1} < 2^{16}$.

⟨ Normalize the divisor 17 ⟩ ≡

```
vh = v[n − 1];
for (d = 0; vh < #8000; d++, vh <<= 1) ;
for (j = k = 0; j < n + 4; j++) {
   t = (u[j] << d) + k;
   u[j] = t & #ffff, k = t >> 16;
}
for (j = k = 0; j < n; j++) {
   t = (v[j] << d) + k;
   v[j] = t & #ffff, k = t >> 16;
}
vh = v[n − 1];
vmh = (n > 1 ? v[n − 2] : 0);
```

This code is used in section 13.

18. ⟨ Unnormalize the remainder 18 ⟩ ≡

```
mask = (1 << d) − 1;
for (j = 3; j ≥ n; j−−) u[j] = 0;
for (k = 0; j ≥ 0; j−−) {
   t = (k << 16) + u[j];
   u[j] = t >> d, k = t & mask;
}
```

This code is used in section 13.

19. ⟨ Pack q and u to *acc* and *aux* 19 ⟩ ≡

```
acc.h = (q[3] << 16) + q[2], acc.l = (q[1] << 16) + q[0];
aux.h = (u[3] << 16) + u[2], aux.l = (u[1] << 16) + u[0];
```

This code is used in section 13.

20. ⟨ Determine the quotient digit $q[j]$ 20 ⟩ ≡

```
{
   ⟨ Find the trial quotient, q̂ 21 ⟩;
   ⟨ Subtract b^j q̂v from u 22 ⟩;
   ⟨ If the result was negative, decrease q̂ by 1 23 ⟩;
   q[j] = qhat;
}
```

This code is used in section 13.

21. ⟨ Find the trial quotient, $\hat{q}$ 21 ⟩ ≡

```
t = (u[j + n] << 16) + u[j + n − 1];
qhat = t/vh, rhat = t − vh * qhat;
if (n > 1)
   while (qhat ≡ #10000 ∨ qhat * vmh > (rhat << 16) + u[j + n − 2]) {
      qhat−−, rhat += vh;
      if (rhat ≥ #10000) break;
   }
```

This code is used in section 20.

22. After this step, $u[j+n]$ will either equal k or $k-1$. The true value of u would be obtained by subtracting k from $u[j+n]$; but we don't have to fuss over $u[j+n]$, because it won't be examined later.

⟨ Subtract $b^j\hat{q}v$ from u 22 ⟩ ≡

```
for (i = k = 0; i < n; i++) {
   t = u[i + j] + #ffff0000 − k − qhat * v[i];
   u[i + j] = t & #ffff, k = #ffff − (t >> 16);
}
```

This code is used in section 20.

23. The correction here occurs only rarely, but it can be necessary—for example, when dividing the number #7fff800100000000 by #800080020005.

⟨ If the result was negative, decrease $\hat{q}$ by 1 23 ⟩ ≡

```
if (u[j + n] ≠ k) {
   qhat−−;
   for (i = k = 0; i < n; i++) {
      t = u[i + j] + v[i] + k;
      u[i + j] = t & #ffff, k = t >> 16;
   }
}
```

This code is used in section 20.

---

acc: **octa**, §13.
aux: **octa**, §9.
d: **register int**, §13.
h: **tetra**, §3.
i: **register int**, §13.
j: **register int**, §13.
k: **register int**, §13.
l: **tetra**, §3.
mask: **tetra**, §13.
n: **register int**, §13.
q: **tetra** [], §13.
qhat: **tetra**, §13.
rhat: **tetra**, §13.
t: **register tetra**, §13.
u: **tetra** [], §13.
v: **tetra** [], §13.
vh: **tetra**, §13.
vmh: **tetra**, §13.

24. Signed division can be reduced to unsigned division in a tedious but straightforward manner. We assume that the divisor isn't zero.

```
⟨ Subroutines 5 ⟩ +≡
  octa signed_odiv ARGS((octa, octa));
  octa signed_odiv(y, z)
      octa y, z;
  {
    octa yy, zz, q;
    register int sy, sz;
    if (y.h & sign_bit) sy = 2, yy = ominus(zero_octa, y);
    else sy = 0, yy = y;
    if (z.h & sign_bit) sz = 1, zz = ominus(zero_octa, z);
    else sz = 0, zz = z;
    q = odiv(zero_octa, yy, zz);
    overflow = false;
    switch (sy + sz) {
    case 2 + 1: aux = ominus(zero_octa, aux);
      if (q.h ≡ sign_bit) overflow = true;
    case 0 + 0: return q;
    case 2 + 0: if (aux.h ∨ aux.l) aux = ominus(zz, aux);
      goto negate_q;
    case 0 + 1: if (aux.h ∨ aux.l) aux = ominus(aux, zz);
    negate_q: if (aux.h ∨ aux.l) return ominus(neg_one, q);
      else return ominus(zero_octa, q);
    }
  }
```

25. Bit fiddling. The bitwise operators of MMIX are fairly easy to implement directly, but three of them occur often enough to deserve packaging as subroutines.

⟨ Subroutines 5 ⟩ +≡

```
octa oand ARGS((octa, octa));
octa oand(y, z)    /* compute y ∧ z */
    octa y, z;
{ octa x;
  x.h = y.h & z.h; x.l = y.l & z.l;
  return x;
}
octa oandn ARGS((octa, octa));
octa oandn(y, z)    /* compute y ∧ z̄ */
    octa y, z;
{ octa x;
  x.h = y.h & ~z.h; x.l = y.l & ~z.l;
  return x;
}
octa oxor ARGS((octa, octa));
octa oxor(y, z)    /* compute y ⊕ z */
    octa y, z;
{ octa x;
  x.h = y.h ⊕ z.h; x.l = y.l ⊕ z.l;
  return x;
}
```

ARGS = macro ( ), §2.
aux: **octa**, §9.
false = 0, §1.
h: **tetra**, §3.
l: **tetra**, §3.
neg_one: **octa**, §4.
octa = **struct**, §3.
odiv: **octa** ( ), §13.
ominus: **octa** ( ), §5.
overflow: **bool**, §9.
sign_bit = macro, §4.
true = 1, §1.
zero_octa: **octa**, §4.

26. Here's a fun way to count the number of bits in a tetrabyte. [This classical trick is called the "Gillies–Miller method for sideways addition" in *The Preparation of Programs for an Electronic Digital Computer* by Wilkes, Wheeler, and Gill, second edition (Reading, Mass.: Addison–Wesley, 1957), 191–193. Some of the tricks used here were suggested by Balbir Singh, Peter Rossmanith, and Stefan Schwoon.]

```
⟨ Subroutines 5 ⟩ +≡
  int count_bits ARGS((tetra));
  int count_bits(x)
      tetra x;
  {
    register int xx = x;
    xx = xx - ((xx >> 1) & #55555555);
    xx = (xx & #33333333) + ((xx >> 2) & #33333333);
    xx = (xx + (xx >> 4)) & #0f0f0f0f;
    xx = xx + (xx >> 8);
    return (xx + (xx >> 16)) & #ff;
  }
```

27. To compute the nonnegative byte differences of two given tetrabytes, we can carry out the following 20-step branchless computation:

```
⟨ Subroutines 5 ⟩ +≡
  tetra byte_diff ARGS((tetra, tetra));
  tetra byte_diff(y, z)
      tetra y, z;
  {
    register tetra d = (y & #00ff00ff) + #01000100 - (z & #00ff00ff);
    register tetra m = d & #01000100;
    register tetra x = d & (m - (m >> 8));
    d = ((y >> 8) & #00ff00ff) + #01000100 - ((z >> 8) & #00ff00ff);
    m = d & #01000100;
    return x + ((d & (m - (m >> 8))) << 8);
  }
```

28. To compute the nonnegative wyde differences of two tetrabytes, another trick leads to a 15-step branchless computation. (Research problem: Can *count_bits*, *byte_diff*, or *wyde_diff* be done with fewer operations?)

```
⟨ Subroutines 5 ⟩ +≡
  tetra wyde_diff ARGS((tetra, tetra));
  tetra wyde_diff(y, z)
      tetra y, z;
  {
    register tetra a = ((y >> 16) - (z >> 16)) & #10000;
    register tetra b = ((y & #ffff) - (z & #ffff)) & #10000;
    return y - (z ⊕ ((y ⊕ z) & (b - a - (b >> 16))));
  }
```

29. The last bitwise subroutine we need is the most interesting: It implements MMIX's MOR and MXOR operations.

```
⟨ Subroutines 5 ⟩ +≡
  octa bool_mult ARGS((octa, octa, bool));
  octa bool_mult(y, z, xor)
      octa y, z;      /* the operands */
      bool xor;       /* do we do xor instead of or? */
  {
    octa o, x;
    register tetra a, b, c;
    register int k;
    for (k = 0, o = y, x = zero_octa; o.h ∨ o.l; k++, o = shift_right(o, 8, 1))
      if (o.l & #ff) {
        a = ((z.h ≫ k) & #01010101) * #ff;
        b = ((z.l ≫ k) & #01010101) * #ff;
        c = (o.l & #ff) * #01010101;
        if (xor) x.h ⊕= a & c, x.l ⊕= b & c;
        else x.h |= a & c, x.l |= b & c;
      }
    return x;
  }
```

ARGS = macro ( ), §2.
bool: enum, §1.
h: tetra, §3.
l: tetra, §3.
octa = struct, §3.
shift_right: octa ( ), §7.
tetra = unsigned int, §3.
zero_octa: octa, §4.

30. Floating point packing and unpacking. Standard IEEE floating binary numbers pack a sign, exponent, and fraction into a tetrabyte or octabyte. In this section we consider basic subroutines that convert between IEEE format and the separate unpacked components.

```
#define ROUND_OFF 1
#define ROUND_UP 2
#define ROUND_DOWN 3
#define ROUND_NEAR 4
⟨ Global variables 4 ⟩ +≡
  int cur_round;    /* the current rounding mode */
```

31. The *fpack* routine takes an octabyte f, a raw exponent e, and a sign s, and packs them into the floating binary number that corresponds to $\pm 2^{e-1076} f$, using a given rounding mode. The value of f should satisfy $2^{54} \le f \le 2^{55}$.

Thus, for example, the floating binary number $+1.0$ = #3ff0000000000000 is obtained when $f = 2^{54}$, e = #3fe, and s = '+'. The raw exponent e is usually one less than the final exponent value; the leading bit of f is essentially added to the exponent. (This trick works nicely for subnormal numbers, when $e < 0$, or in cases where the value of f is rounded upwards to 2^{55}.)

Exceptional events are noted by oring appropriate bits into the global variable *exceptions*. Special considerations apply to underflow, which is not fully specified by Section 7.4 of the IEEE standard: Implementations of the standard are free to choose between two definitions of "tininess" and two definitions of "accuracy loss." MMIX determines tininess *after* rounding, hence a result with $e < 0$ is not necessarily tiny; MMIX treats accuracy loss as equivalent to inexactness. Thus, a result underflows if and only if it is tiny and either (i) it is inexact or (ii) the underflow trap is enabled. The *fpack* routine sets U_BIT in *exceptions* if and only if the result is tiny, X_BIT if and only if the result is inexact.

```
#define X_BIT (1 << 8)    /* floating inexact */
#define Z_BIT (1 << 9)    /* floating division by zero */
#define U_BIT (1 << 10)   /* floating underflow */
#define O_BIT (1 << 11)   /* floating overflow */
#define I_BIT (1 << 12)   /* floating invalid operation */
#define W_BIT (1 << 13)   /* float-to-fix overflow */
#define V_BIT (1 << 14)   /* integer overflow */
#define D_BIT (1 << 15)   /* integer divide check */
#define E_BIT (1 << 18)   /* external (dynamic) trap bit */
⟨ Subroutines 5 ⟩ +≡
  octa fpack ARGS((octa, int, char, int));
  octa fpack(f, e, s, r)
      octa f;    /* the normalized fraction part */
      int e;    /* the raw exponent */
      char s;    /* the sign */
      int r;    /* the rounding mode */
  {
    octa o;
    if (e > #7fd) e = #7ff, o = zero_octa;
```

```
  else {
    if (e < 0) {
      if (e < -54) o.h = 0, o.l = 1;
      else { octa oo;
        o = shift_right(f, -e, 1);
        oo = shift_left(o, -e);
        if (oo.l ≠ f.l ∨ oo.h ≠ f.h) o.l |= 1;      /* sticky bit */
      }
      e = 0;
    } else o = f;
  }
  ⟨Round and return the result 33⟩;
}
```

32. ⟨Global variables 4⟩ +≡

```
int exceptions;    /* bits possibly destined for rA */
```

33. Everything falls together so nicely here, it's almost too good to be true!

⟨Round and return the result 33⟩ ≡

```
if (o.l & 3) exceptions |= X_BIT;
switch (r) {
case ROUND_DOWN: if (s ≡ '-') o = incr(o, 3); break;
case ROUND_UP: if (s ≠ '-') o = incr(o, 3);
case ROUND_OFF: break;
case ROUND_NEAR: o = incr(o, o.l & 4 ? 2 : 1); break;
}
o = shift_right(o, 2, 1);
o.h += e ≪ 20;
if (o.h ≥ #7ff00000) exceptions |= O_BIT + X_BIT;      /* overflow */
else if (o.h < #100000) exceptions |= U_BIT;      /* tininess */
if (s ≡ '-') o.h |= sign_bit;
return o;
```

This code is used in section 31.

ARGS = macro ( ), §2.
h: **tetra**, §3.
incr: **octa** ( ), §6.
l: **tetra**, §3.
octa = **struct**, §3.
shift_left: **octa** ( ), §7.
shift_right: **octa** ( ), §7.
sign_bit = macro, §4.
zero_octa: **octa**, §4.

34. Similarly, *sfpack* packs a short float, from inputs having the same conventions as *fpack*.

```
⟨ Subroutines 5 ⟩ +≡
  tetra sfpack ARGS((octa, int, char, int));
  tetra sfpack(f, e, s, r)
      octa f;    /* the fraction part */
      int e;    /* the raw exponent */
      char s;    /* the sign */
      int r;    /* the rounding mode */
  {
    register tetra o;
    if (e > #47d) e = #47f, o = 0;
    else {
      o = shift_left(f, 3).h;
      if (f.l & #1ffffff) o |= 1;
      if (e < #380) {
        if (e < #380 − 25) o = 1;
        else { register tetra o0, oo;
          o0 = o;
          o = o ≫ (#380 − e);
          oo = o ≪ (#380 − e);
          if (oo ≠ o0) o |= 1;    /* sticky bit */
        }
        e = #380;
      }
    }
    ⟨ Round and return the short result 35 ⟩;
  }
```

35.
```
⟨ Round and return the short result 35 ⟩ ≡
  if (o & 3) exceptions |= X_BIT;
  switch (r) {
  case ROUND_DOWN: if (s ≡ '-') o += 3; break;
  case ROUND_UP: if (s ≠ '-') o += 3;
  case ROUND_OFF: break;
  case ROUND_NEAR: o += (o & 4 ? 2 : 1); break;
  }
  o = o ≫ 2;
  o += (e − #380) ≪ 23;
  if (o ≥ #7f800000) exceptions |= O_BIT + X_BIT;    /* overflow */
  else if (o < #100000) exceptions |= U_BIT;    /* tininess */
  if (s ≡ '-') o |= sign_bit;
  return o;
```

This code is used in section 34.

36. The *funpack* routine is, roughly speaking, the opposite of *fpack*. It takes a given floating point number x and separates out its fraction part f, exponent e, and sign s. It clears *exceptions* to zero. It returns the type of value found: *zro*, *num*, *inf*, or *nan*. When it returns *num*, it will have set *f*, *e*, and *s* to the values from which *fpack* would produce the original number *x* without exceptions.

```
#define zero_exponent (−1000)   /* zero is assumed to have this exponent */
⟨ Other type definitions 36 ⟩ ≡
  typedef enum {
    zro, num, inf, nan
  } ftype;
```

See also section 59.

This code is used in section 1.

37. ⟨ Subroutines 5 ⟩ +≡

```
  ftype funpack ARGS((octa, octa *, int *, char *));
  ftype funpack(x, f, e, s)
      octa x;    /* the given floating point value */
      octa *f;    /* address where the fraction part should be stored */
      int *e;    /* address where the exponent part should be stored */
      char *s;    /* address where the sign should be stored */
  {
    register int ee;
    exceptions = 0;
    *s = (x.h & sign_bit ? '-' : '+');
    *f = shift_left(x, 2);
    f→h &= #3fffff;
    ee = (x.h ≫ 20) & #7ff;
    if (ee) {
      *e = ee − 1;
      f→h |= #400000;
      return (ee < #7ff ? num : f→h ≡ #400000 ∧ ¬f→l ? inf : nan);
    }
    if (¬x.l ∧ ¬f→h) {
      *e = zero_exponent; return zro;
    }
    do { ee−−; *f = shift_left(*f, 1); } while (¬(f→h & #400000));
    *e = ee; return num;
  }
```

ARGS = macro ( ), §2.
exceptions: **int**, §32.
fpack: **octa** ( ), §31.
h: **tetra**, §3.
l: **tetra**, §3.
O_BIT = macro, §31.
octa = **struct**, §3.
ROUND_DOWN = 3, §30.
ROUND_NEAR = 4, §30.
ROUND_OFF = 1, §30.
ROUND_UP = 2, §30.
shift_left: **octa** ( ), §7.
sign_bit = macro, §4.
tetra = **unsigned int**, §3.
U_BIT = macro, §31.
X_BIT = macro, §31.

38. ⟨ Subroutines 5 ⟩ +≡

```
ftype sfunpack ARGS((tetra, octa *, int *, char *));
ftype sfunpack(x, f, e, s)
      tetra x;      /* the given floating point value */
      octa *f;      /* address where the fraction part should be stored */
      int *e;       /* address where the exponent part should be stored */
      char *s;      /* address where the sign should be stored */
{
   register int ee;
   exceptions = 0;
   *s = (x & sign_bit ? '-' : '+');
   f→h = (x ≫ 1) & #3fffff, f→l = x ≪ 31;
   ee = (x ≫ 23) & #ff;
   if (ee) {
      *e = ee + #380 − 1;
      f→h |= #400000;
      return (ee < #ff ? num : (x & #7fffffff) ≡ #7f800000 ? inf : nan);
   }
   if (¬(x & #7fffffff)) {
      *e = zero_exponent; return zro;
   }
   do { ee−−; *f = shift_left(*f, 1); } while (¬(f→h & #400000));
   *e = ee + #380; return num;
}
```

39. Since MMIX downplays 32-bit operations, it uses *sfpack* and *sfunpack* only when loading and storing short floats, or when converting from fixed point to floating point.

⟨ Subroutines 5 ⟩ +≡

```
octa load_sf ARGS((tetra));
octa load_sf(z)
      tetra z;      /* 32 bits to be loaded into a 64-bit register */
{
   octa f, x; int e; char s; ftype t;
   t = sfunpack(z, &f, &e, &s);
   switch (t) {
   case zro: x = zero_octa; break;
   case num: return fpack(f, e, s, ROUND_OFF);
   case inf: x = inf_octa; break;
   case nan: x = shift_right(f, 2, 1); x.h |= #7ff00000; break;
   }
   if (s ≡ '-') x.h |= sign_bit;
   return x;
}
```

40. ⟨ Subroutines 5 ⟩ +≡

```
tetra store_sf ARGS((octa));
tetra store_sf(x)
    octa x;    /* 64 bits to be loaded into a 32-bit word */
{
  octa f; tetra z; int e; char s; ftype t;
  t = funpack(x, &f, &e, &s);
  switch (t) {
  case zro: z = 0; break;
  case num: return sfpack(f, e, s, cur_round);
  case inf: z = #7f800000; break;
  case nan: if (¬(f.h & #200000)) {
      f.h |= #200000; exceptions |= I_BIT;    /* NaN was signaling */
    }
    z = #7f800000 | (f.h ≪ 1) | (f.l ≫ 31); break;
  }
  if (s ≡ '-') z |= sign_bit;
  return z;
}
```

ARGS = macro ( ), §2.
cur_round: **int**, §30.
exceptions: **int**, §32.
fpack: **octa** ( ), §31.
ftype = **enum**, §36.
funpack: **ftype** ( ), §37.
h: **tetra**, §3.
I_BIT = macro, §31.
inf = 2, §36.
inf_octa: **octa**, §4.
l: **tetra**, §3.
nan = 3, §36.
num = 1, §36.
octa = **struct**, §3.
ROUND_OFF = 1, §30.
sfpack: **tetra** ( ), §34.
shift_left: **octa** ( ), §7.
shift_right: **octa** ( ), §7.
sign_bit = macro, §4.
tetra = **unsigned int**, §3.
zero_exponent = macro, §36.
zero_octa: **octa**, §4.
zro = 0, §36.

41. Floating multiplication and division. The hardest fixed point operations were multiplication and division; but these two operations are the *easiest* to implement in floating point arithmetic, once their fixed point counterparts are available.

```
⟨ Subroutines 5 ⟩ +≡
  octa fmult ARGS((octa, octa));
  octa fmult(y, z)
      octa y, z;
  {
    ftype yt, zt;
    int ye, ze;
    char ys, zs;
    octa x, xf, yf, zf;
    register int xe;
    register char xs;
    yt = funpack(y, &yf, &ye, &ys);
    zt = funpack(z, &zf, &ze, &zs);
    xs = ys + zs − '+';      /* will be '-' when the result is negative */
    switch (4 * yt + zt) {
    ⟨ The usual NaN cases 42 ⟩;
    case 4 * zro + zro: case 4 * zro + num: case 4 * num + zro: x = zero_octa; break;
    case 4 * num + inf: case 4 * inf + num: case 4 * inf + inf: x = inf_octa; break;
    case 4 * zro + inf: case 4 * inf + zro: x = standard_NaN;
      exceptions |= I_BIT; break;
    case 4 * num + num: ⟨ Multiply nonzero numbers and return 43 ⟩;
    }
    if (xs ≡ '-') x.h |= sign_bit;
    return x;
  }
```

42. ⟨ The usual NaN cases 42 ⟩ ≡

```
case 4 * nan + nan: if (¬(y.h & #80000)) exceptions |= I_BIT;      /* y is signaling */
case 4 * zro + nan: case 4 * num + nan: case 4 * inf + nan:
  if (¬(z.h & #80000)) exceptions |= I_BIT, z.h |= #80000;
  return z;
case 4 * nan + zro: case 4 * nan + num: case 4 * nan + inf:
  if (¬(y.h & #80000)) exceptions |= I_BIT, y.h |= #80000;
  return y;
```

This code is used in sections 41, 44, 46, and 93.

43. ⟨ Multiply nonzero numbers and **return** 43 ⟩ ≡

```
  xe = ye + ze − #3fd;      /* the raw exponent */
  x = omult(yf, shift_left(zf, 9));
  if (aux.h ≥ #400000) xf = aux;
  else xf = shift_left(aux, 1), xe−−;
  if (x.h ∨ x.l) xf.l |= 1;      /* adjust the sticky bit */
  return fpack(xf, xe, xs, cur_round);
```

This code is used in section 41.

44. ⟨Subroutines 5⟩ +≡

```
octa fdivide ARGS((octa, octa));
octa fdivide(y, z)
    octa y, z;
{
  ftype yt, zt;
  int ye, ze;
  char ys, zs;
  octa x, xf, yf, zf;
  register int xe;
  register char xs;

  yt = funpack(y, &yf, &ye, &ys);
  zt = funpack(z, &zf, &ze, &zs);
  xs = ys + zs - '+';      /* will be '-' when the result is negative */
  switch (4 * yt + zt) {
  ⟨The usual NaN cases 42⟩;
  case 4 * zro + inf: case 4 * zro + num: case 4 * num + inf: x = zero_octa; break;
  case 4 * num + zro: exceptions |= Z_BIT;
  case 4 * inf + num: case 4 * inf + zro: x = inf_octa; break;
  case 4 * zro + zro: case 4 * inf + inf: x = standard_NaN;
    exceptions |= I_BIT; break;
  case 4 * num + num: ⟨Divide nonzero numbers and return 45⟩;
  }
  if (xs ≡ '-') x.h |= sign_bit;
  return x;
}
```

45. ⟨Divide nonzero numbers and **return** 45⟩ ≡

```
  xe = ye - ze + #3fd;      /* the raw exponent */
  xf = odiv(yf, zero_octa, shift_left(zf, 9));
  if (xf.h ≥ #800000) {
    aux.l |= xf.l & 1;
    xf = shift_right(xf, 1, 1);
    xe++;
  }
  if (aux.h ∨ aux.l) xf.l |= 1;      /* adjust the sticky bit */
  return fpack(xf, xe, xs, cur_round);
```

This code is used in section 44.

ARGS = macro ( ), §2.
aux: **octa**, §9.
cur_round: **int**, §30.
exceptions: **int**, §32.
fpack: **octa** ( ), §31.
ftype = **enum**, §36.
funpack: **ftype** ( ), §37.
h: **tetra**, §3.
I_BIT = macro, §31.
inf = 2, §36.
inf_octa: **octa**, §4.
l: **tetra**, §3.
nan = 3, §36.
num = 1, §36.
octa = **struct**, §3.
odiv: **octa** ( ), §13.
omult: **octa** ( ), §8.
shift_left: **octa** ( ), §7.
shift_right: **octa** ( ), §7.
sign_bit = macro, §4.
standard_NaN: **octa**, §4.
y: **octa**, §46.
y: **octa**, §93.
z: **octa**, §46.
z: **octa**, §93.
Z_BIT = macro, §31.
zero_octa: **octa**, §4.
zro = 0, §36.

46. Floating addition and subtraction. Now for the bread-and-butter operation, the sum of two floating point numbers. It is not terribly difficult, but many cases need to be handled carefully.

```
⟨Subroutines 5⟩ +≡
  octa fplus ARGS((octa, octa));
  octa fplus(y, z)
      octa y, z;
  {
    ftype yt, zt;
    int ye, ze;
    char ys, zs;
    octa x, xf, yf, zf;
    register int xe, d;
    register char xs;
    yt = funpack(y, &yf, &ye, &ys);
    zt = funpack(z, &zf, &ze, &zs);
    switch (4 * yt + zt) {
    ⟨The usual NaN cases 42⟩;
    case 4 * zro + num: return fpack(zf, ze, zs, ROUND_OFF); break;
        /* may underflow */
    case 4 * num + zro: return fpack(yf, ye, ys, ROUND_OFF); break;
        /* may underflow */
    case 4 * inf + inf: if (ys ≠ zs) {
        exceptions |= I_BIT; x = standard_NaN; xs = zs; break;
      }
    case 4 * num + inf: case 4 * zro + inf: x = inf_octa; xs = zs; break;
    case 4 * inf + num: case 4 * inf + zro: x = inf_octa; xs = ys; break;
    case 4 * num + num: if (y.h ≠ (z.h ⊕ #80000000) ∨ y.l ≠ z.l)
        ⟨Add nonzero numbers and return 47⟩;
    case 4 * zro + zro: x = zero_octa;
      xs = (ys ≡ zs ? ys : cur_round ≡ ROUND_DOWN ? '-' : '+'); break;
    }
    if (xs ≡ '-') x.h |= sign_bit;
    return x;
  }
```

47. ⟨Add nonzero numbers and **return** 47⟩ ≡

```
  { octa o, oo;
    if (ye < ze ∨ (ye ≡ ze ∧ (yf.h < zf.h ∨ (yf.h ≡ zf.h ∧ yf.l < zf.l))))
      ⟨Exchange y with z 48⟩;
    d = ye − ze;
    xs = ys, xe = ye;
    if (d) ⟨Adjust for difference in exponents 49⟩;
    if (ys ≡ zs) {
      xf = oplus(yf, zf);
      if (xf.h ≥ #800000) xe++, d = xf.l & 1, xf = shift_right(xf, 1, 1), xf.l |= d;
    } else {
      xf = ominus(yf, zf);
      if (xf.h ≥ #800000) xe++, d = xf.l & 1, xf = shift_right(xf, 1, 1), xf.l |= d;
```

```
    else while (xf.h < #400000) xe--, xf = shift_left(xf, 1);
  }
  return fpack(xf, xe, xs, cur_round);
}
```

This code is used in section 46.

48. ⟨ Exchange y with z 48 ⟩ ≡

```
{
  o = yf, yf = zf, zf = o;
  d = ye, ye = ze, ze = d;
  d = ys, ys = zs, zs = d;
}
```

This code is used in sections 47 and 51.

49. Proper rounding requires two bits to the right of the fraction delivered to *fpack*. The first is the true next bit of the result; the other is a "sticky" bit, which is nonzero if any further bits of the true result are nonzero. Sticky rounding to an integer takes x into the number $\lfloor x/2 \rfloor + \lceil x/2 \rceil$.

Some subtleties need to be observed here, in order to prevent the sticky bit from being shifted left. If we did not shift *yf* left 1 before shifting *zf* to the right, an incorrect answer would be obtained in certain cases—for example, if $yf = 2^{54}$, $zf = 2^{54} + 2^{53} - 1$, $d = 52$.

⟨ Adjust for difference in exponents 49 ⟩ ≡

```
{
  if (d ≤ 2) zf = shift_right(zf, d, 1);        /* exact result */
  else if (d > 53) zf.h = 0, zf.l = 1;          /* tricky but OK */
  else {
    if (ys ≠ zs) d--, xe--, yf = shift_left(yf, 1);
    o = zf;
    zf = shift_right(o, d, 1);
    oo = shift_left(zf, d);
    if (oo.l ≠ o.l ∨ oo.h ≠ o.h) zf.l |= 1;
  }
}
```

This code is used in section 47.

ARGS = macro ( ), §2.
cur_round: **int**, §30.
exceptions: **int**, §32.
fpack: **octa** ( ), §31.
ftype = **enum**, §36.
funpack: **ftype** ( ), §37.
h: **tetra**, §3.
I_BIT = macro, §31.
inf = 2, §36.
inf_octa: **octa**, §4.
l: **tetra**, §3.
num = 1, §36.
octa = **struct**, §3.
ominus: **octa** ( ), §5.
oplus: **octa** ( ), §5.
ROUND_DOWN = 3, §30.
ROUND_OFF = 1, §30.
shift_left: **octa** ( ), §7.
shift_right: **octa** ( ), §7.
sign_bit = macro, §4.
standard_NaN: **octa**, §4.
zero_octa: **octa**, §4.
zro = 0, §36.

50. The comparison of floating point numbers with respect to ϵ shares some of the characteristics of floating point addition/subtraction. In some ways it is simpler, and in other ways it is more difficult; we might as well deal with it now.

Subroutine *fepscomp*(y, z, e, s) returns 2 if y, z, or e is a NaN or e is negative. It returns 1 if $s = 0$ and $y \approx z\ (e)$ or if $s \neq 0$ and $y \sim z\ (e)$, as defined in Section 4.2.2 of *Seminumerical Algorithms*; otherwise it returns 0.

```
⟨ Subroutines 5 ⟩ +≡
  int fepscomp ARGS((octa, octa, octa, int));
  int fepscomp(y, z, e, s)
      octa y, z, e;    /* the operands */
      int s;    /* test similarity? */
  {
    octa yf, zf, ef, o, oo;
    int ye, ze, ee;
    char ys, zs, es;
    register int yt, zt, et, d;
    et = funpack(e, &ef, &ee, &es);
    if (es ≡ '-') return 2;
    switch (et) {
    case nan: return 2;
    case inf: ee = 10000;
    case num: case zro: break;
    }
    yt = funpack(y, &yf, &ye, &ys);
    zt = funpack(z, &zf, &ze, &zs);
    switch (4 * yt + zt) {
    case 4 * nan + nan: case 4 * nan + inf: case 4 * nan + num: case 4 * nan + zro:
      case 4 * inf + nan: case 4 * num + nan: case 4 * zro + nan: return 2;
    case 4 * inf + inf: return (ys ≡ zs ∨ ee ≥ 1023);
    case 4 * inf + num: case 4 * inf + zro: case 4 * num + inf: case 4 * zro + inf:
      return (s ∧ ee ≥ 1022);
    case 4 * zro + zro: return 1;
    case 4 * zro + num: case 4 * num + zro: if (¬s) return 0;
    case 4 * num + num: break;
    }
    ⟨ Compare two numbers with respect to epsilon and return 51 ⟩;
  }
```

51. The relation $y \approx z\ (\epsilon)$ reduces to $y \sim z\ (\epsilon/2^d)$, if d is the difference between the larger and smaller exponents of y and z.

```
⟨ Compare two numbers with respect to epsilon and return 51 ⟩ ≡
  ⟨ Unsubnormalize y and z, if they are subnormal 52 ⟩;
  if (ye < ze ∨ (ye ≡ ze ∧ (yf.h < zf.h ∨ (yf.h ≡ zf.h ∧ yf.l < zf.l))))
    ⟨ Exchange y with z 48 ⟩;
  if (ze ≡ zero_exponent) ze = ye;
  d = ye − ze;
  if (¬s) ee −= d;
  if (ee ≥ 1023) return 1;    /* if ε ≥ 2, z ∈ N_ε(y) */
```

```
⟨ Compute the difference of fraction parts, o 53 ⟩;
if (¬o.h ∧ ¬o.l) return 1;
if (ee < 968) return 0;      /* if y ≠ z and ε < 2^-54, y ≁ z */
if (ee ≥ 1021) ef = shift_left(ef, ee − 1021);
else ef = shift_right(ef, 1021 − ee, 1);
return o.h < ef.h ∨ (o.h ≡ ef.h ∧ o.l ≤ ef.l);
```

This code is used in section 50.

52. ⟨ Unsubnormalize y and z, if they are subnormal 52 ⟩ ≡

```
if (ye < 0 ∧ yt ≠ zro) yf = shift_left(y, 2), ye = 0;
if (ze < 0 ∧ zt ≠ zro) zf = shift_left(z, 2), ze = 0;
```

This code is used in section 51.

53. At this point $y \sim z$ if and only if

$$yf + (-1)^{[ys=zs]} zf / 2^d \le 2^{ee-1021} ef = 2^{55}\epsilon.$$

We need to evaluate this relation without overstepping the bounds of our simulated 64-bit registers.

When $d > 2$, the difference of fraction parts might not fit exactly in an octabyte; in that case the numbers are not similar unless $\epsilon > 3/8$, and we replace the difference by the ceiling of the true result. When $\epsilon < 1/8$, our program essentially replaces $2^{55}\epsilon$ by $\lfloor 2^{55}\epsilon \rfloor$. These truncations are not needed simultaneously. Therefore the logic is justified by the facts that, if n is an integer, we have $x \le n$ if and only if $\lceil x \rceil \le n$; $n \le x$ if and only if $n \le \lfloor x \rfloor$. (Notice that the concept of "sticky bit" is *not* appropriate here.)

⟨ Compute the difference of fraction parts, o 53 ⟩ ≡

```
if (d > 54) o = zero_octa, oo = zf;
else o = shift_right(zf, d, 1), oo = shift_left(o, d);
if (oo.h ≠ zf.h ∨ oo.l ≠ zf.l) {      /* truncated result, hence d > 2 */
  if (ee < 1020) return 0;      /* difference is too large for similarity */
  o = incr(o, ys ≡ zs ? 0 : 1);      /* adjust for ceiling */
}
o = (ys ≡ zs ? ominus(yf, o) : oplus(yf, o));
```

This code is used in section 51.

ARGS = macro ( ), §2.
funpack: **ftype** ( ), §37.
h: **tetra**, §3.
incr: **octa** ( ), §6.
inf = 2, §36.
l: **tetra**, §3.
nan = 3, §36.
num = 1, §36.
octa = **struct**, §3.
ominus: **octa** ( ), §5.
oplus: **octa** ( ), §5.
shift_left: **octa** ( ), §7.
shift_right: **octa** ( ), §7.
zero_exponent = macro, §36.
zero_octa: **octa**, §4.
zro = 0, §36.

54. Floating point output conversion. The *print_float* routine converts an octabyte to a floating decimal representation that will be input as precisely the same value.

```
⟨ Subroutines 5 ⟩ +≡
  static void bignum_times_ten ARGS((bignum *));
  static void bignum_dec ARGS((bignum *, bignum *, tetra));
  static int bignum_compare ARGS((bignum *, bignum *));
  void print_float ARGS((octa));
  void print_float(x)
       octa x;
  {
    ⟨ Local variables for print_float 56 ⟩;
    if (x.h & sign_bit) printf("-");
    ⟨ Extract the exponent e and determine the fraction interval [f .. g] or (f .. g) 55 ⟩;
    ⟨ Store f and g as multiprecise integers 63 ⟩;
    ⟨ Compute the significant digits s and decimal exponent e 64 ⟩;
    ⟨ Print the significant digits with proper context 67 ⟩;
  }
```

55. One way to visualize the problem being solved here is to consider the vastly simpler case in which there are only 2-bit exponents and 2-bit fractions. Then the sixteen possible 4-bit combinations have the following interpretations:

0000	$[0\,..\,0.125]$
0001	$(0.125\,..\,0.375)$
0010	$[0.375\,..\,0.625]$
0011	$(0.625\,..\,0.875)$
0100	$[0.875\,..\,1.125]$
0101	$(1.125\,..\,1.375)$
0110	$[1.375\,..\,1.625]$
0111	$(1.625\,..\,1.875)$
1000	$[1.875\,..\,2.25]$
1001	$(2.25\,..\,2.75)$
1010	$[2.75\,..\,3.25]$
1011	$(3.25\,..\,3.75)$
1100	$[3.75\,..\,\infty]$
1101	$\mathrm{NaN}(0\,..\,0.375)$
1110	$\mathrm{NaN}[0.375\,..\,0.625]$
1111	$\mathrm{NaN}(0.625\,..\,1)$

Notice that the interval is closed, $[f\,..\,g]$, when the fraction part is even; it is open, $(f\,..\,g)$, when the fraction part is odd. The printed outputs for these sixteen values, if we actually were dealing with such short exponents and fractions, would be `0.`, `.2`, `.5`, `.7`, `1.`, `1.2`, `1.5`, `1.7`, `2.`, `2.5`, `3.`, `3.5`, `Inf`, `NaN.2`, `NaN`, `NaN.8`, respectively.

```
⟨ Extract the exponent e and determine the fraction interval [f .. g] or (f .. g) 55 ⟩ ≡
  f = shift_left(x, 1);
  e = f.h ≫ 21;
```

```
  f.h &= #1fffff;
  if (¬f.h ∧ ¬f.l) ⟨Handle the special case when the fraction part is zero 57⟩
  else {
    g = incr(f, 1);
    f = incr(f, −1);
    if (¬e) e = 1;    /* subnormal */
    else if (e ≡ #7ff) {
      printf("NaN");
      if (g.h ≡ #100000 ∧ g.l ≡ 1) return;    /* the "standard" NaN */
      e = #3ff;    /* extreme NaNs come out OK even without adjusting f or g */
    } else f.h |= #200000, g.h |= #200000;
  }
```

This code is used in section 54.

56. ⟨Local variables for *print_float* 56⟩ ≡

```
  octa f, g;    /* lower and upper bounds on the fraction part */
  register int e;    /* exponent part */
  register int j, k;    /* all purpose indices */
```

See also section 66.

This code is used in section 54.

57. The transition points between exponents correspond to powers of 2. At such points the interval extends only half as far to the left of that power of 2 as it does to the right. For example, in the 4-bit minifloat numbers considered above, case 1000 corresponds to the interval [1.875 .. 2.25].

⟨Handle the special case when the fraction part is zero 57⟩ ≡

```
  {
    if (¬e) {
      printf("0."); return;
    }
    if (e ≡ #7ff) {
      printf("Inf"); return;
    }
    e−−;
    f.h = #3fffff, f.l = #ffffffff;
    g.h = #400000, g.l = 2;
  }
```

This code is used in section 55.

ARGS = macro ( ), §2.
bignum = **struct**, §59.
h: **tetra**, §3.
incr: **octa** ( ), §6.
l: **tetra**, §3.
octa = **struct**, §3.
printf: **int** ( ), <stdio.h>.
s: **char** [ ], §66.
shift_left: **octa** ( ), §7.
sign_bit = macro, §4.
tetra = **unsigned int**, §3.

58. We want to find the "simplest" value in the interval corresponding to the given number, in the sense that it has fewest significant digits when expressed in decimal notation. Thus, for example, if the floating point number can be described by a relatively short string such as '`.1`' or '`37e100`', we want to discover that representation.

The basic idea is to generate the decimal representations of the two endpoints of the interval, outputting the leading digits where both endpoints agree, then making a final decision at the first place where they disagree.

The "simplest" value is not always unique. For example, in the case of 4-bit minifloat numbers we could represent the bit pattern 0001 as either `.2` or `.3`, and we could represent 1001 in five equally short ways: `2.3` or `2.4` or `2.5` or `2.6` or `2.7`. The algorithm below tries to choose the middle possibility in such cases.

[A solution to the analogous problem for fixed-point representations, without the additional complication of round-to-even, was used by the author in the program for TeX; see *Beauty is Our Business* (Springer, 1990), 233–242.]

Suppose we are given two fractions f and g, where $0 \le f < g < 1$, and we want to compute the shortest decimal in the closed interval $[f \mathinner{.\,.} g]$. If $f = 0$, we are done. Otherwise let $10f = d + f'$ and $10g = e + g'$, where $0 \le f' < 1$ and $0 \le g' < 1$. If $d < e$, we can terminate by outputting any of the digits $d + 1$, $\ldots$, e; otherwise we output the common digit $d = e$, and repeat the process on the fractions $0 \le f' < g' < 1$. A similar procedure works with respect to the open interval $(f \mathinner{.\,.} g)$.

59. The program below carries out the stated algorithm by using multiprecision arithmetic on 77-place integers with 28 bits each. This choice facilitates multiplication by 10, and allows us to deal with the whole range of floating binary numbers using fixed point arithmetic. We keep track of the leading and trailing digit positions so that trivial operations on zeros are avoided.

If f points to a **bignum**, its radix-2^{28} digits are $f\to dat[0]$ through $f\to dat[76]$, from most significant to least significant. We assume that all digit positions are zero unless they lie in the subarray between indices $f\to a$ and $f\to b$, inclusive. Furthermore, both $f\to dat[f\to a]$ and $f\to dat[f\to b]$ are nonzero, unless $f\to a = f\to b = bignum\_prec - 1$.

The **bignum** data type can be used with any radix less than 2^{32}; we will use it later with radix 10^9. The *dat* array is made large enough to accommodate both applications.

```
#define bignum_prec 157    /* would be 77 if we cared only about print_float */

⟨ Other type definitions 36 ⟩ +≡
  typedef struct {
    int a;    /* index of the most significant digit */
    int b;    /* index of the least significant digit; must be ≥ a */
    tetra dat[bignum_prec];    /* the digits; undefined except between a and b */
  } bignum;
```

60. Here, for example, is how we go from f to $10f$, assuming that overflow will not occur and that the radix is 2^{28}:

```
⟨ Subroutines 5 ⟩ +≡
  static void bignum_times_ten(f)
      bignum *f;
  {
    register tetra *p, *q;
    register tetra x, carry;
    for (p = &f→dat[f→b], q = &f→dat[f→a], carry = 0; p ≥ q; p−−) {
      x = *p * 10 + carry;
      *p = x & #fffffff;
      carry = x ≫ 28;
    }
    *p = carry;
    if (carry) f→a−−;
    if (f→dat[f→b] ≡ 0 ∧ f→b > f→a) f→b−−;
  }
```

61. And here is how we test whether $f < g$, $f = g$, or $f > g$, using any radix whatever:

```
⟨ Subroutines 5 ⟩ +≡
  static int bignum_compare(f, g)
      bignum *f, *g;
  {
    register tetra *p, *pp, *q, *qq;
    if (f→a ≠ g→a) return f→a > g→a ? −1 : 1;
    pp = &f→dat[f→b], qq = &g→dat[g→b];
    for (p = &f→dat[f→a], q = &g→dat[g→a]; p ≤ pp; p++, q++) {
      if (*p ≠ *q) return *p < *q ? −1 : 1;
      if (q ≡ qq) return p < pp;
    }
    return −1;
  }
```

print_float: **void** (), §54. **tetra** = **unsigned int**, §3.

62. The following subroutine subtracts g from f, assuming that $f \ge g > 0$ and using a given radix.

```
⟨ Subroutines 5 ⟩ +≡
  static void bignum_dec(f, g, r)
      bignum *f, *g;
      tetra r;    /* the radix */
  {
    register tetra *p, *q, *qq;
    register int x, borrow;
    while (g→b > f→b) f→dat[++f→b] = 0;
    qq = &g→dat[g→a];
    for (p = &f→dat[g→b], q = &g→dat[g→b], borrow = 0; q ≥ qq; p--, q--) {
      x = *p − *q − borrow;
      if (x ≥ 0) borrow = 0, *p = x;
      else borrow = 1, *p = x + r;
    }
    for ( ; borrow; p--)
      if (*p) borrow = 0, *p = *p − 1;
      else *p = r − 1;
    while (f→dat[f→a] ≡ 0) {
      if (f→a ≡ f→b) {    /* the result is zero */
        f→a = f→b = bignum_prec − 1, f→dat[bignum_prec − 1] = 0;
        return;
      }
      f→a++;
    }
    while (f→dat[f→b] ≡ 0) f→b--;
  }
```

63. Armed with these subroutines, we are ready to solve the problem. The first task is to put the numbers into **bignum** form. If the exponent is e, the number destined for digit $dat[k]$ will consist of the rightmost 28 bits of the given fraction after it has been shifted right $c - e - 28k$ bits, for some constant c. We choose c so that, when e has its maximum value #7ff, the leading digit will go into position $dat[1]$, and so that when the number to be printed is exactly 1 the integer part of g will also be exactly 1.

```
#define magic_offset 2112    /* the constant c that makes it work */
#define origin 37    /* the radix point follows dat[37] */

⟨ Store f and g as multiprecise integers 63 ⟩ ≡
  k = (magic_offset − e)/28;
  ff.dat[k − 1] = shift_right(f, magic_offset + 28 − e − 28 * k, 1).l & #ffffff;
  gg.dat[k − 1] = shift_right(g, magic_offset + 28 − e − 28 * k, 1).l & #ffffff;
  ff.dat[k] = shift_right(f, magic_offset − e − 28 * k, 1).l & #ffffff;
  gg.dat[k] = shift_right(g, magic_offset − e − 28 * k, 1).l & #ffffff;
  ff.dat[k + 1] = shift_left(f, e + 28 * k − (magic_offset − 28)).l & #ffffff;
  gg.dat[k + 1] = shift_left(g, e + 28 * k − (magic_offset − 28)).l & #ffffff;
  ff.a = (ff.dat[k − 1] ? k − 1 : k);
  ff.b = (ff.dat[k + 1] ? k + 1 : k);
```

```
  gg.a = (gg.dat[k − 1] ? k − 1 : k);
  gg.b = (gg.dat[k + 1] ? k + 1 : k);
```

This code is used in section 54.

64. If e is sufficiently small, the fractions f and g will be less than 1, and we can use the stated algorithm directly. Of course, if e is extremely small, a lot of leading zeros need to be lopped off; in the worst case, we may have to multiply f and g by 10 more than 300 times. But hey, we don't need to do that extremely often, and computers are pretty fast nowadays.

In the small-exponent case, the computation always terminates before f becomes zero, because the interval endpoints are fractions with denominator 2^t for some $t > 50$.

The invariant relations $ff.dat[ff.a] \neq 0$ and $gg.dat[gg.a] \neq 0$ are not maintained by the computation here, when $ff.a = origin$ or $gg.a = origin$. But no harm is done, because *bignum_compare* is not used.

```
⟨ Compute the significant digits s and decimal exponent e 64 ⟩ ≡
  if (e > #401) ⟨ Compute the significant digits in the large-exponent case 65 ⟩
  else {     /* if e ≤ #401 we have gg.a ≥ origin and gg.dat[origin] ≤ 8 */
    if (ff.a > origin) ff.dat[origin] = 0;
    for (e = 1, p = s; gg.a > origin ∨ ff.dat[origin] ≡ gg.dat[origin]; ) {
      if (gg.a > origin) e−−;
      else *p++ = ff.dat[origin] + '0', ff.dat[origin] = 0, gg.dat[origin] = 0;
      bignum_times_ten(&ff);
      bignum_times_ten(&gg);
    }
    *p++ = ((ff.dat[origin] + 1 + gg.dat[origin]) ≫ 1) + '0';     /* the middle digit */
  }
  *p = '\0';     /* terminate the string s */
```

This code is used in section 54.

---

a: **int**, §59.
b: **int**, §59.
bignum = **struct**, §59.
bignum_compare: **static int** ( ), §61.
bignum_prec = 157, §59.
bignum_times_ten: **static void** ( ), §60.
dat: **tetra** [ ], §59.
e: **register int**, §56.
f: **octa**, §56.
ff: **bignum**, §66.
g: **octa**, §56.
gg: **bignum**, §66.
k: **register int**, §56.
l: **tetra**, §3.
p: **register char** *, §66.
s: **char** [ ], §66.
shift_left: **octa** ( ), §7.
shift_right: **octa** ( ), §7.
tetra = **unsigned int**, §3.

65. When e is large, we use the stated algorithm by considering f and g to be fractions whose denominator is a power of 10.

An interesting case arises when the number to be converted is #44ada56a4b0835bf, since the interval turns out to be

$$(69999999999999991611392 \;..\; 70000000000000000000000).$$

If this were a closed interval, we could simply give the answer 7e22; but the number 7e22 actually corresponds to #44ada56a4b0835c0 because of the round-to-even rule. Therefore the correct answer is, say, 6.9999999999999995e22. This example shows that we need a slightly different strategy in the case of open intervals; we cannot simply look at the first position in which the endpoints have different decimal digits. Therefore we change the invariant relation to $0 \le f < g \le 1$, when open intervals are involved, and we do not terminate the process when $f = 0$ or $g = 1$.

```
⟨ Compute the significant digits in the large-exponent case 65 ⟩ ≡
  { register int open = x.l & 1;
    tt.dat[origin] = 10;
    tt.a = tt.b = origin;
    for (e = 1; bignum_compare(&gg, &tt) ≥ open; e++) bignum_times_ten(&tt);
    p = s;
    while (1) {
      bignum_times_ten(&ff);
      bignum_times_ten(&gg);
      for (j = '0'; bignum_compare(&ff, &tt) ≥ 0; j++)
        bignum_dec(&ff, &tt, #10000000), bignum_dec(&gg, &tt, #10000000);
      if (bignum_compare(&gg, &tt) ≥ open) break;
      *p++ = j;
      if (ff.a ≡ bignum_prec − 1 ∧ ¬open) goto done;      /* f = 0 in a closed interval */
    }
    for (k = j; bignum_compare(&gg, &tt) ≥ open; k++)
      bignum_dec(&gg, &tt, #10000000);
    *p++ = (j + 1 + k) ≫ 1;      /* the middle digit */
  done: ;
  }
```

This code is used in section 64.

66. The length of string s will be at most 17. For if f and g agree to 17 places, we have $g/f < 1 + 10^{-16}$; but the ratio g/f is always $\ge (1 + 2^{-52} + 2^{-53})/(1 + 2^{-52} - 2^{-53}) > 1 + 2 \times 10^{-16}$.

```
⟨ Local variables for print_float 56 ⟩ +≡
  bignum ff, gg;      /* fractions or numerators of fractions */
  bignum tt;      /* power of ten (used as the denominator) */
  char s[18];
  register char *p;
```

67. At this point the significant digits are in string s, and $s[0] \neq$ '0'. If we put a decimal point at the left of s, the result should be multiplied by 10^e.

We prefer the output '300.' to the form '3e2', and we prefer '.03' to '3e-2'. In general, the output will use an explicit exponent only if the alternative would take more than 18 characters.

```
⟨Print the significant digits with proper context 67⟩ ≡
  if (e > 17 ∨ e < (int) strlen(s) − 17)
     printf("%c%s%se%d", s[0], (s[1] ? "." : ""), s + 1, e − 1);
  else if (e < 0) printf(".%0*d%s", −e, 0, s);
  else if (strlen(s) ≥ e) printf("%.*s.%s", e, s, s + e);
  else printf("%s%0*d.", s, e − (int) strlen(s), 0);
```

This code is used in section 54.

---

a: **int**, §59.
b: **int**, §59.
bignum = **struct**, §59.
bignum_compare: **static int** ( ), §61.
bignum_dec: **static void** ( ), §62.
bignum_prec = 157, §59.
bignum_times_ten: **static void** ( ), §60.
dat: **tetra** [ ], §59.
e: **register int**, §56.
j: **register int**, §56.
k: **register int**, §56.
l: **tetra**, §3.
origin = 37, §63.
print_float: **void** ( ), §54.
printf: **int** ( ), <stdio.h>.
strlen: **size_t** ( ), <string.h>.
x: **octa**, §54.

68. Floating point input conversion. Going the other way, we want to be able to convert a given decimal number into its floating binary equivalent. The following syntax is supported:

⟨digit⟩ ⟶ `0` | `1` | `2` | `3` | `4` | `5` | `6` | `7` | `8` | `9`
⟨digit string⟩ ⟶ ⟨digit⟩ | ⟨digit string⟩⟨digit⟩
⟨decimal string⟩ ⟶ ⟨digit string⟩`.` | `.`⟨digit string⟩ |
  ⟨digit string⟩`.`⟨digit string⟩
⟨optional sign⟩ ⟶ ⟨empty⟩ | `+` | `-`
⟨exponent⟩ ⟶ `e`⟨optional sign⟩⟨digit string⟩
⟨optional exponent⟩ ⟶ ⟨empty⟩ | ⟨exponent⟩
⟨floating magnitude⟩ ⟶ ⟨digit string⟩⟨exponent⟩ |
  ⟨decimal string⟩⟨optional exponent⟩ |
  `Inf` | `NaN` | `NaN.`⟨digit string⟩
⟨floating constant⟩ ⟶ ⟨optional sign⟩⟨floating magnitude⟩
⟨decimal constant⟩ ⟶ ⟨optional sign⟩⟨digit string⟩

For example, '`-3.`' is the floating constant #`c008000000000000`; '`1e3`' and '`1000`' are both equivalent to #`408f400000000000`; '`NaN`' and '`+NaN.5`' are both equivalent to #`7ff8000000000000`.

The *scan_const* routine looks at a given string and finds the longest initial substring that matches the syntax of either ⟨decimal constant⟩ or ⟨floating constant⟩. It puts the corresponding value into the global octabyte variable *val*; it also puts the position of the first unscanned character in the global pointer variable *next_char*. It returns 1 if a floating constant was found, 0 if a decimal constant was found, -1 if nothing was found. A decimal constant that doesn't fit in an octabyte is computed modulo 2^{64}.

The value of *exceptions* set by *scan_const* is not necessarily correct.

```
⟨Subroutines 5⟩ +≡
  static void bignum_double ARGS((bignum *));
  int scan_const ARGS((char *));
  int scan_const(s)
      char *s;
  {
    ⟨Local variables for scan_const 70⟩;
    val.h = val.l = 0;
    p = s;
    if (*p ≡ '+' ∨ *p ≡ '-') sign = *p++; else sign = '+';
    if (strncmp(p, "NaN", 3) ≡ 0) NaN = true, p += 3;
    else NaN = false;
    if ((isdigit(*p) ∧ ¬NaN) ∨ (*p ≡ '.' ∧ isdigit(*(p + 1))))
      ⟨Scan a number and return 73⟩;
    if (NaN) ⟨Return the standard NaN 71⟩;
    if (strncmp(p, "Inf", 3) ≡ 0) ⟨Return infinity 72⟩;
  no_const_found: next_char = s; return -1;
  }
```

69. ⟨Global variables 4⟩ +≡

```
  octa val;        /* value returned by scan_const */
  char *next_char;     /* pointer returned by scan_const */
```

70. ⟨ Local variables for *scan_const* 70 ⟩ ≡

```
register char *p, *q;  /* for string manipulations */
register bool NaN;  /* are we processing a NaN? */
int sign;  /* '+' or '-' */
```

See also sections 76 and 81.

This code is used in section 68.

71. ⟨ Return the standard NaN 71 ⟩ ≡

```
{
  next_char = p;
  val.h = #600000, exp = #3fe;
  goto packit;
}
```

This code is used in section 68.

72. ⟨ Return infinity 72 ⟩ ≡

```
{
  next_char = p + 3;
  goto make_it_infinite;
}
```

This code is used in section 68.

ARGS = macro ( ), §2.
bignum = **struct**, §59.
bool: **enum**, §1.
exceptions: **int**, §32.
exp: **register int**, §76.
false = 0, §1.
h: **tetra**, §3.
isdigit: **int** ( ), <ctype.h>.
l: **tetra**, §3.
make_it_infinite: label, §79.
octa = **struct**, §3.
packit: label, §78.
strncmp: **int** ( ), <string.h>.
true = 1, §1.

73. We saw above that a string of at most 17 digits is enough to characterize a floating point number, for purposes of output. But a much longer buffer for digits is needed when we're doing input. For example, consider the borderline quantity $(1 + 2^{-53})/2^{1022}$; its decimal expansion, when written out exactly, is a number with more than 750 significant digits: `2.2250738585...8125e-308`. If *any one* of those digits is increased, or if additional nonzero digits are added as in `2.2250738585...81250000001e-308`, the rounded value is supposed to change from `#0010000000000000` to `#0010000000000001`.

We assume here that the user prefers a perfectly correct answer to a speedy almost-correct one, so we implement the most general case.

```
⟨ Scan a number and return 73 ⟩ ≡
  {
    for (q = buf0, dec_pt = (char *) 0; isdigit(*p); p++) {
      val = oplus(val, shift_left(val, 2));      /* multiply by 5 */
      val = incr(shift_left(val, 1), *p − '0');
      if (q > buf0 ∨ *p ≠ '0')
        if (q < buf_max) *q++ = *p;
        else if (*(q − 1) ≡ '0') *(q − 1) = *p;
    }
    if (NaN) *q++ = '1';
    if (*p ≡ '.') ⟨ Scan a fraction part 74 ⟩;
    next_char = p;
    exp = 0;
    if (*p ≡ 'e' ∧ ¬NaN) ⟨ Scan an exponent 77 ⟩;
    if (dec_pt) ⟨ Return a floating point constant 78 ⟩;
    if (sign ≡ '-') val = ominus(zero_octa, val);
    return 0;
  }
```

This code is used in section 68.

74. ⟨ Scan a fraction part 74 ⟩ ≡

```
  {
    dec_pt = q;
    p++;
    for (zeros = 0; isdigit(*p); p++)
      if (*p ≡ '0' ∧ q ≡ buf0) zeros++;
      else if (q < buf_max) *q++ = *p;
      else if (*(q − 1) ≡ '0') *(q − 1) = *p;
  }
```

This code is used in section 73.

75. The buffer needs room for eight digits of padding at the left, followed by up to $1022 + 53 - 307$ significant digits, followed by a "sticky" digit at position $buf\_max - 1$, and eight more digits of padding.

```
#define buf0 (buf + 8)
#define buf_max (buf + 777)
⟨ Global variables 4 ⟩ +≡
  static char buf[785] = "00000000";      /* where we put significant input digits */
```

76. ⟨ Local variables for *scan_const* 70 ⟩ +≡

```
register char *dec_pt;   /* position of decimal point in buf */
register int exp;   /* scanned exponent; later used for raw binary exponent */
register int zeros;   /* leading zeros removed after decimal point */
```

77. Here we don't advance *next_char* and force a decimal point until we know that a syntactically correct exponent exists.

The code here will convert extra-large inputs like '9e+9999999999999999' into ∞ and extra-small inputs into zero. Strange inputs like '-00.0e9999999' must also be accommodated. (But we *don't* try to deliver precise answers when there are a billion or more leading zeros.)

⟨ Scan an exponent 77 ⟩ ≡

```
{ register char exp_sign;
  p++;
  if (*p ≡ '+' ∨ *p ≡ '-') exp_sign = *p++; else exp_sign = '+';
  if (isdigit(*p)) {
    for (exp = *p++ − '0'; isdigit(*p); p++)
      if (exp < 100000000) exp = 10 * exp + *p − '0';
    if (¬dec_pt) dec_pt = q, zeros = 0;
    if (exp_sign ≡ '-') exp = −exp;
    next_char = p;
  }
}
```

This code is used in section 73.

78. ⟨ Return a floating point constant 78 ⟩ ≡

```
{
  ⟨ Move the digits from buf to ff 79 ⟩;
  ⟨ Determine the binary fraction and binary exponent 83 ⟩;
packit: ⟨ Pack and round the answer 84 ⟩;
  return 1;
}
```

This code is used in section 73.

---

ff: **bignum**, §81.
incr: **octa** ( ), §6.
isdigit: **int** ( ), <ctype.h>.
NaN: **register bool**, §70.
next_char: **char** ∗, §69.
ominus: **octa** ( ), §5.
oplus: **octa** ( ), §5.
p: **register char** ∗, §70.
q: **register char** ∗, §70.
scan_const: **int** ( ), §68.
shift_left: **octa** ( ), §7.
sign: **int**, §70.
val: **octa**, §69.
zero_octa: **octa**, §4.

79. Now we get ready to compute the binary fraction bits, by putting the scanned input digits into a multiprecision fixed-point accumulator *ff* that spans the full necessary range. After this step, the number that we want to convert to floating binary will appear in *ff.dat*[*ff.a*], *ff.dat*[*ff.a* + 1], ..., *ff.dat*[*ff.b*]. The radix-10^9 digit in *ff*[36 − *k*] is understood to be multiplied by 10^{9k}, for $36 \ge k \ge -120$.

```
⟨ Move the digits from buf to ff 79 ⟩ ≡
  x = buf + 341 + zeros − dec_pt − exp;
  if (q ≡ buf0 ∨ x ≥ 1413) {
  make_it_zero: exp = −99999; goto packit;
  }
  if (x < 0) {
  make_it_infinite: exp = 99999; goto packit;
  }
  ff.a = x/9;
  for (p = q; p < q + 8; p++) *p = '0';      /* pad with trailing zeros */
  q = q − 1 − (q + 341 + zeros − dec_pt − exp) % 9;      /* compute stopping place in buf */
  for (p = buf0 − x % 9, k = ff.a; p ≤ q ∧ k ≤ 156; p += 9, k++)
    ⟨ Put the 9-digit number *p ... *(p + 8) into ff.dat[k] 80 ⟩;
  ff.b = k − 1;
  for (x = 0; p ≤ q; p += 9)
    if (strncmp(p, "000000000", 9) ≠ 0) x = 1;
  ff.dat[156] += x;      /* nonzero digits that fall off the right are sticky */
  while (ff.dat[ff.b] ≡ 0) ff.b−−;
```

This code is used in section 78.

80.
```
⟨ Put the 9-digit number *p ... *(p + 8) into ff.dat[k] 80 ⟩ ≡
  {
    for (x = *p − '0', pp = p + 1; pp < p + 9; pp++) x = 10 * x + *pp − '0';
    ff.dat[k] = x;
  }
```

This code is used in section 79.

81.
```
⟨ Local variables for scan_const 70 ⟩ +≡
  register int k, x;
  register char *pp;
  bignum ff, tt;
```

82. Here's a subroutine that is dual to *bignum_times_ten*. It changes *f* to 2*f*, assuming that overflow will not occur and that the radix is 10^9.

```
⟨ Subroutines 5 ⟩ +≡
  static void bignum_double(f)
      bignum *f;
  {
    register tetra *p, *q;
    register int x, carry;
    for (p = &f→dat[f→b], q = &f→dat[f→a], carry = 0; p ≥ q; p−−) {
      x = *p + *p + carry;
      if (x ≥ 1000000000) carry = 1, *p = x − 1000000000;
      else carry = 0, *p = x;
```

```
    }
    *p = carry;
    if (carry) f->a--;
    if (f->dat[f->b] ≡ 0 ∧ f->b > f->a) f->b--;
  }
```

83. ⟨ Determine the binary fraction and binary exponent 83 ⟩ ≡

```
  val = zero_octa;
  if (ff.a > 36) {
    for (exp = #3fe; ff.a > 36; exp--) bignum_double(&ff);
    for (k = 54; k; k--) {
      if (ff.dat[36]) {
        if (k ≥ 32) val.h |= 1 ≪ (k - 32); else val.l |= 1 ≪ k;
        ff.dat[36] = 0;
        if (ff.b ≡ 36) break;      /* break if ff now zero */
      }
      bignum_double(&ff);
    }
  } else {
    tt.a = tt.b = 36, tt.dat[36] = 2;
    for (exp = #3fe; bignum_compare(&ff, &tt) ≥ 0; exp++) bignum_double(&tt);
    for (k = 54; k; k--) {
      bignum_double(&ff);
      if (bignum_compare(&ff, &tt) ≥ 0) {
        if (k ≥ 32) val.h |= 1 ≪ (k - 32); else val.l |= 1 ≪ k;
        bignum_dec(&ff, &tt, 1000000000);
        if (ff.a ≡ bignum_prec - 1) break;      /* break if ff now zero */
      }
    }
  }
  if (k ≡ 0) val.l |= 1;      /* add sticky bit if ff nonzero */
```

This code is used in section 78.

---

a: **int**, §59.
b: **int**, §59.
bignum = **struct**, §59.
bignum_compare: **static int** ( ), §61.
bignum_dec: **static void** ( ), §62.
bignum_prec = 157, §59.
bignum_times_ten: **static void** ( ), §60.
buf: **static char** [ ], §75.
buf0 = macro, §75.
dat: **tetra** [ ], §59.
dec_pt: **register char** ∗, §76.
exp: **register int**, §76.
h: **tetra**, §3.
l: **tetra**, §3.
p: **register char** ∗, §70.
packit: label, §78.
q: **register char** ∗, §70.
scan_const: **int** ( ), §68.
strncmp: **int** ( ), <string.h>.
tetra = **unsigned int**, §3.
val: **octa**, §69.
zero_octa: **octa**, §4.
zeros: **register int**, §76.

84. We need to be careful that the input '`NaN.99999999999999999999`' doesn't get rounded up; it is supposed to yield #`7fffffffffffffff`.

Although the input '`NaN.0`' is illegal, strictly speaking, we silently convert it to #`7ff0000000000001`—a number that would be output as '`NaN.0000000000000002`'.

⟨ Pack and round the answer 84 ⟩ ≡

```
val = fpack(val, exp, sign, ROUND_NEAR);
if (NaN) {
  if ((val.h & #7fffffff) ≡ #40000000) val.h |= #7fffffff, val.l = #ffffffff;
  else if ((val.h & #7fffffff) ≡ #3ff00000 ∧ ¬val.l) val.h |= #40000000, val.l = 1;
  else val.h |= #40000000;
}
```

This code is used in section 78.

85. Floating point remainders. In this section we implement the remainder of the floating point operations—one of which happens to be the operation of taking the remainder.

The easiest task remaining is to compare two floating point quantities. Routine *fcomp* returns −1 if $y < z$, 0 if $y = z$, +1 if $y > z$, and +2 if y and z are unordered.

```
⟨ Subroutines 5 ⟩ +≡
  int fcomp ARGS((octa, octa));
  int fcomp(y, z)
      octa y, z;
  {
    ftype yt, zt;
    int ye, ze;
    char ys, zs;
    octa yf, zf;
    register int x;
    yt = funpack(y, &yf, &ye, &ys);
    zt = funpack(z, &zf, &ze, &zs);
    switch (4 * yt + zt) {
    case 4 * nan + nan: case 4 * zro + nan: case 4 * num + nan: case 4 * inf + nan:
      case 4 * nan + zro: case 4 * nan + num: case 4 * nan + inf: return 2;
    case 4 * zro + zro: return 0;
    case 4 * zro + num: case 4 * num + zro: case 4 * zro + inf: case 4 * inf + zro:
      case 4 * num + num: case 4 * num + inf: case 4 * inf + num: case 4 * inf + inf:
      if (ys ≠ zs) x = 1;
      else if (y.h > z.h) x = 1;
      else if (y.h < z.h) x = −1;
      else if (y.l > z.l) x = 1;
      else if (y.l < z.l) x = −1;
      else return 0;
      break;
    }
    return (ys ≡ '-' ? −x : x);
  }
```

ARGS = macro ( ), §2.
exp: **register int**, §76.
fpack: **octa** ( ), §31.
ftype = **enum**, §36.
funpack: **ftype** ( ), §37.
h: **tetra**, §3.
inf = 2, §36.
l: **tetra**, §3.
NaN: **register bool**, §70.
nan = 3, §36.
num = 1, §36.
octa = **struct**, §3.
ROUND_NEAR = 4, §30.
sign: **int**, §70.
val: **octa**, §69.
zro = 0, §36.

86. Several MMIX operations act on a single floating point number and accept an arbitrary rounding mode. For example, consider the operation of rounding to the nearest floating point integer:

```
⟨Subroutines 5⟩ +≡
  octa fintegerize ARGS((octa, int));
  octa fintegerize(z, r)
       octa z;      /* the operand */
       int r;      /* the rounding mode */
  {
    ftype zt;
    int ze;
    char zs;
    octa xf, zf;
    zt = funpack(z, &zf, &ze, &zs);
    if (¬r) r = cur_round;
    switch (zt) {
    case nan: if (¬(z.h & #80000)) { exceptions |= I_BIT; z.h |= #80000; }
    case inf: case zro: return z;
    case num: ⟨Integerize and return 87⟩;
    }
  }
```

87. ⟨Integerize and **return** 87⟩ ≡

```
  if (ze ≥ 1074) return fpack(zf, ze, zs, ROUND_OFF);      /* already an integer */
  if (ze ≤ 1020) xf.h = 0, xf.l = 1;
  else { octa oo;
    xf = shift_right(zf, 1074 − ze, 1);
    oo = shift_left(xf, 1074 − ze);
    if (oo.l ≠ zf.l ∨ oo.h ≠ zf.h) xf.l |= 1;      /* sticky bit */
  }
  switch (r) {
  case ROUND_DOWN: if (zs ≡ '-') xf = incr(xf, 3); break;
  case ROUND_UP: if (zs ≠ '-') xf = incr(xf, 3);
  case ROUND_OFF: break;
  case ROUND_NEAR: xf = incr(xf, xf.l & 4 ? 2 : 1); break;
  }
  xf.l &= #fffffffc;
  if (ze ≥ 1022) return fpack(shift_left(xf, 1074 − ze), ze, zs, ROUND_OFF);
  if (xf.l) xf.h = #3ff00000, xf.l = 0;
  if (zs ≡ '-') xf.h |= sign_bit;
  return xf;
```

This code is used in section 86.

88. To convert floating point to fixed point, we use *fixit*.

```
⟨ Subroutines 5 ⟩ +≡
  octa fixit ARGS((octa, int));
  octa fixit(z, r)
      octa z;    /* the operand */
      int r;    /* the rounding mode */
  {
    ftype zt;
    int ze;
    char zs;
    octa zf, o;
    zt = funpack(z, &zf, &ze, &zs);
    if (¬r) r = cur_round;
    switch (zt) {
    case nan: case inf: exceptions |= I_BIT; return z;
    case zro: return zero_octa;
    case num: if (funpack(fintegerize(z, r), &zf, &ze, &zs) ≡ zro) return zero_octa;
      if (ze ≤ 1076) o = shift_right(zf, 1076 − ze, 1);
      else {
        if (ze > 1085 ∨ (ze ≡ 1085 ∧ (zf.h > #400000 ∨
              (zf.h ≡ #400000 ∧ (zf.l ∨ zs ≠ '-'))))) exceptions |= W_BIT;
        if (ze ≥ 1140) return zero_octa;
        o = shift_left(zf, ze − 1076);
      }
      return (zs ≡ '-' ? ominus(zero_octa, o) : o);
    }
  }
```

ARGS = macro ( ), §2.
cur_round: **int**, §30.
exceptions: **int**, §32.
fpack: **octa** ( ), §31.
ftype = **enum**, §36.
funpack: **ftype** ( ), §37.
h: **tetra**, §3.
I_BIT = macro, §31.
incr: **octa** ( ), §6.
inf = 2, §36.
l: **tetra**, §3.
nan = 3, §36.
num = 1, §36.
octa = **struct**, §3.
ominus: **octa** ( ), §5.
ROUND_DOWN = 3, §30.
ROUND_NEAR = 4, §30.
ROUND_OFF = 1, §30.
ROUND_UP = 2, §30.
shift_left: **octa** ( ), §7.
shift_right: **octa** ( ), §7.
sign_bit = macro, §4.
W_BIT = macro, §31.
zero_octa: **octa**, §4.
zro = 0, §36.

89. Going the other way, we can specify not only a rounding mode but whether the given fixed point octabyte is signed or unsigned, and whether the result should be rounded to short precision.

```
⟨ Subroutines 5 ⟩ +≡
  octa floatit ARGS((octa, int, int, int));
  octa floatit(z, r, u, p)
      octa z;     /* octabyte to float */
      int r;      /* rounding mode */
      int u;      /* unsigned? */
      int p;      /* short precision? */
  {
    int e; char s;
    register int t;

    exceptions = 0;
    if (¬z.h ∧ ¬z.l) return zero_octa;
    if (¬r) r = cur_round;
    if (¬u ∧ (z.h & sign_bit)) s = '-', z = ominus(zero_octa, z); else s = '+';
    e = 1076;
    while (z.h < #400000) e--, z = shift_left(z, 1);
    while (z.h ≥ #800000) {
      e++;
      t = z.l & 1;
      z = shift_right(z, 1, 1);
      z.l |= t;
    }
    if (p) ⟨ Convert to short float 90 ⟩;
    return fpack(z, e, s, r);
  }
```

90.

```
⟨ Convert to short float 90 ⟩ ≡
  {
    register int ex; register tetra t;

    t = sfpack(z, e, s, r);
    ex = exceptions;
    sfunpack(t, &z, &e, &s);
    exceptions = ex;
  }
```

This code is used in section 89.

91. The square root operation is more interesting.

```
⟨ Subroutines 5 ⟩ +≡
  octa froot ARGS((octa, int));
  octa froot(z, r)
      octa z;     /* the operand */
      int r;      /* the rounding mode */
  {
    ftype zt;
    int ze;
```

```
  char zs;
  octa x, xf, rf, zf;
  register int xe, k;
  if (¬r) r = cur_round;
  zt = funpack(z, &zf, &ze, &zs);
  if (zs ≡ '-' ∧ zt ≠ zro) exceptions |= I_BIT, x = standard_NaN;
  else switch (zt) {
    case nan: if (¬(z.h & #80000)) exceptions |= I_BIT, z.h |= #80000;
      return z;
    case inf: case zro: x = z; break;
    case num: ⟨Take the square root and return 92⟩;
    }
  if (zs ≡ '-') x.h |= sign_bit;
  return x;
}
```

92. The square root can be found by an adaptation of the old pencil-and-paper method. If $n = \lfloor\sqrt{s}\rfloor$, where s is an integer, we have $s = n^2 + r$ where $0 \le r \le 2n$; this invariant can be maintained if we replace s by $4s + (0,1,2,3)$ and n by $2n + (0,1)$. The following code implements this idea with $2n$ in *xf* and r in *rf*. (It could easily be made to run about twice as fast.)

```
⟨Take the square root and return 92⟩ ≡
  xf.h = 0, xf.l = 2;
  xe = (ze + #3fe) ≫ 1;
  if (ze & 1) zf = shift_left(zf, 1);
  rf.h = 0, rf.l = (zf.h ≫ 22) − 1;
  for (k = 53; k; k−−) {
    rf = shift_left(rf, 2); xf = shift_left(xf, 1);
    if (k ≥ 43) rf = incr(rf, (zf.h ≫ (2 ∗ (k − 43))) & 3);
    else if (k ≥ 27) rf = incr(rf, (zf.l ≫ (2 ∗ (k − 27))) & 3);
    if ((rf.l > xf.l ∧ rf.h ≥ xf.h) ∨ rf.h > xf.h) {
      xf.l++; rf = ominus(rf, xf); xf.l++;
    }
  }
  if (rf.h ∨ rf.l) xf.l++;    /∗ sticky bit ∗/
  return fpack(xf, xe, '+', r);
```

This code is used in section 91.

ARGS = macro ( ), §2.
cur_round: **int**, §30.
exceptions: **int**, §32.
fpack: **octa** ( ), §31.
ftype = **enum**, §36.
funpack: **ftype** ( ), §37.
h: **tetra**, §3.
I_BIT = macro, §31.
incr: **octa** ( ), §6.
inf = 2, §36.
l: **tetra**, §3.
nan = 3, §36.
num = 1, §36.
octa = **struct**, §3.
ominus: **octa** ( ), §5.
sfpack: **tetra** ( ), §34.
sfunpack: **ftype** ( ), §38.
shift_left: **octa** ( ), §7.
shift_right: **octa** ( ), §7.
sign_bit = macro, §4.
standard_NaN: **octa**, §4.
tetra = **unsigned int**, §3.
zero_octa: **octa**, §4.
zro = 0, §36.

93. And finally, the genuine floating point remainder. Subroutine *fremstep* either calculates $y \operatorname{rem} z$ or reduces y to a smaller number having the same remainder with respect to z. In the latter case the `E_BIT` is set in *exceptions*. A third parameter, *delta*, gives a decrease in exponent that is acceptable for incomplete results; if *delta* is sufficiently large, say 2500, the correct result will always be obtained in one step of *fremstep*.

```
⟨ Subroutines 5 ⟩ +≡
  octa fremstep ARGS((octa, octa, int));
  octa fremstep(y, z, delta)
      octa y, z;
      int delta;
  {
    ftype yt, zt;
    int ye, ze;
    char xs, ys, zs;
    octa x, xf, yf, zf;
    register int xe, thresh, odd;
    yt = funpack(y, &yf, &ye, &ys);
    zt = funpack(z, &zf, &ze, &zs);
    switch (4 * yt + zt) {
    ⟨ The usual NaN cases 42 ⟩;
    case 4 * zro + zro: case 4 * num + zro: case 4 * inf + zro: case 4 * inf + num:
      case 4 * inf + inf: x = standard_NaN;
      exceptions |= I_BIT; break;
    case 4 * zro + num: case 4 * zro + inf: case 4 * num + inf: return y;
    case 4 * num + num: ⟨ Remainderize nonzero numbers and return 94 ⟩;
    zero_out: x = zero_octa;
    }
    if (ys ≡ '-') x.h |= sign_bit;
    return x;
  }
```

94. If there's a huge difference in exponents and the remainder is nonzero, this computation will take a long time. One could compute $(2^n y) \operatorname{rem} z$ much more quickly for large n by using $O(\log n)$ multiplications modulo z, but the floating remainder operation isn't important enough to justify such expensive hardware.

Results of floating remainder are always exact, so the rounding mode is immaterial.

```
⟨ Remainderize nonzero numbers and return 94 ⟩ ≡
  odd = 0;     /* will be 1 if we've subtracted an odd multiple of z from y */
  thresh = ye − delta;
  if (thresh < ze) thresh = ze;
  while (ye ≥ thresh) ⟨ Reduce (ye, yf) by a multiple of zf; goto zero_out if the
          remainder is zero, goto try_complement if appropriate 95 ⟩;
  if (ye ≥ ze) {
    exceptions |= E_BIT; return fpack(yf, ye, ys, ROUND_OFF);
  }
  if (ye < ze − 1) return fpack(yf, ye, ys, ROUND_OFF);
  yf = shift_right(yf, 1, 1);
```

```
try_complement: xf = ominus(zf, yf), xe = ze, xs = '+' + '-' - ys;
  if (xf.h > yf.h ∨ (xf.h ≡ yf.h ∧ (xf.l > yf.l ∨ (xf.l ≡ yf.l ∧ ¬odd)))) xf = yf, xs = ys;
  while (xf.h < #400000) xe--, xf = shift_left(xf, 1);
  return fpack(xf, xe, xs, ROUND_OFF);
```

This code is used in section 93.

95. Here we are careful not to change the sign of y, because a remainder of 0 is supposed to inherit the original sign of y.

```
⟨Reduce (ye, yf) by a multiple of zf; goto zero_out if the remainder is zero, goto
      try_complement if appropriate 95⟩ ≡
  {
    if (yf.h ≡ zf.h ∧ yf.l ≡ zf.l) goto zero_out;
    if (yf.h < zf.h ∨ (yf.h ≡ zf.h ∧ yf.l < zf.l)) {
      if (ye ≡ ze) goto try_complement;
      ye--, yf = shift_left(yf, 1);
    }
    yf = ominus(yf, zf);
    if (ye ≡ ze) odd = 1;
    while (yf.h < #400000) ye--, yf = shift_left(yf, 1);
  }
```

This code is used in section 94.

ARGS = macro ( ), §2.
E_BIT = macro, §31.
exceptions: **int**, §32.
fpack: **octa** ( ), §31.
ftype = **enum**, §36.
funpack: **ftype** ( ), §37.
h: **tetra**, §3.
I_BIT = macro, §31.
inf = 2, §36.
l: **tetra**, §3.
num = 1, §36.
octa = **struct**, §3.
ominus: **octa** ( ), §5.
ROUND_OFF = 1, §30.
shift_left: **octa** ( ), §7.
shift_right: **octa** ( ), §7.
sign_bit = macro, §4.
standard_NaN: **octa**, §4.
zero_octa: **octa**, §4.
zro = 0, §36.

96. Names of the sections.

⟨ Subroutines 5, 6, 7, 8, 12, 13, 24, 25, 26, 27, 28, 29, 31, 34, 37, 38, 39, 40, 41, 44, 46, 50, 54, 60, 61, 62, 68, 82, 85, 86, 88, 89, 91, 93 ⟩ Used in section 1.
⟨ Subtract $b^j \hat{q} v$ from u 22 ⟩ Used in section 20.
⟨ Take the square root and **return** 92 ⟩ Used in section 91.
⟨ Tetrabyte and octabyte type definitions 3 ⟩ Used in section 1.
⟨ The usual NaN cases 42 ⟩ Used in sections 41, 44, 46, and 93.
⟨ Unnormalize the remainder 18 ⟩ Used in section 13.
⟨ Unpack the dividend and divisor to u and v 15 ⟩ Used in section 13.
⟨ Unpack the multiplier and multiplicand to u and v 10 ⟩ Used in section 8.
⟨ Unsubnormalize y and z, if they are subnormal 52 ⟩ Used in section 51.

MMIX-CONFIG

1. Input format. Configuration files allow this simulator to adapt itself to infinitely many possible combinations of hardware features. The purpose of the present module is to read a configuration file, check it for validity, and set up the relevant data structures.

All data in a configuration file consists simply of *tokens* separated by one or more units of white space, where a "token" is any sequence of nonspace characters that doesn't contain a percent sign. Percent signs and anything following them on a line are ignored; this convention allows a user to include comments in the file. Here's a simple (but weird) example:

```
% Silly configuration
writebuffer 200
memaddresstime 100
Dcache associativity 4 lru
Dcache blocksize 1024
unit ODD 5555555555555555555555555555555555555555555555555555555555555555
unit EVEN aaaaaaaaaaaaaaaaaaaaaaaaaaaaaaaaaaaaaaaaaaaaaaaaaaaaaaaaaaaaaaaa
div 40 30 20  % three-stage divide
```

It means that (1) the write buffer has capacity for 200 octabytes; (2) the memory bus takes 100 cycles to process an address; (3) there's a D-cache, in which each set has 4 blocks and the replacement policy is least-recently-used; (4) each block in the D-cache has 1024 bytes; (5) there are two functional units, one for all the odd-numbered opcodes and one for all the rest; (6) the division instructions take three pipeline stages, spending 40 cycles in the first stage, 30 in the second, and 20 in the last; (7) all other parameters have default values.

2. Four kinds of specifications can appear in a configuration file, according to the following syntax:

⟨ specification ⟩ ⟶ ⟨ PV spec ⟩ | ⟨ cache spec ⟩ | ⟨ pipe spec ⟩ | ⟨ functional spec ⟩
⟨ PV spec ⟩ ⟶ ⟨ parameter ⟩⟨ decimal value ⟩
⟨ cache spec ⟩ ⟶ ⟨ cache name ⟩⟨ cache parameter ⟩⟨ decimal value ⟩⟨ policy ⟩
⟨ pipe spec ⟩ ⟶ ⟨ operation ⟩⟨ pipeline times ⟩
⟨ functional spec ⟩ ⟶ `unit` ⟨ name ⟩⟨ 64 hexadecimal digits ⟩

3. A ⟨ PV spec ⟩ simply assigns a given value to a given parameter. The possibilities for ⟨ parameter ⟩ are as follows:

- `fetchbuffer` (default 4), maximum instructions in the fetch buffer; must be ≥ 1.
- `writebuffer` (default 2), maximum octabytes in the write buffer; must be ≥ 1.
- `reorderbuffer` (default 5), maximum instructions issued but not committed; must be ≥ 1.
- `renameregs` (default 5), maximum partial results in the reorder buffer; must be ≥ 1.

D.E. Knuth: MMIXware, LNCS 1750, pp. 110–137, 2014.
DOI: 10.1007/3-540-46611-8_4

- `memslots` (default 2), maximum store instructions in the reorder buffer; must be ≥ 1.
- `localregs` (default 256), number of local registers in ring; must be 256, 512, or 1024.
- `fetchmax` (default 2), maximum instructions fetched per cycle; must be ≥ 1.
- `dispatchmax` (default 1), maximum instructions issued per cycle; must be ≥ 1.
- `peekahead` (default 1), maximum lookahead for jumps per cycle.
- `commitmax` (default 1), maximum instructions committed per cycle; must be ≥ 1.
- `fremmax` (default 1), maximum reductions in `FREM` computation per cycle; must be ≥ 1.
- `denin` (default 1), extra cycles taken if a floating point input is subnormal.
- `denout` (default 1), extra cycles taken if a floating point result is subnormal.
- `writeholdingtime` (default 0), minimum number of cycles for data to remain in the write buffer.
- `memaddresstime` (default 20), cycles to process memory address; must be ≥ 1.
- `memreadtime` (default 20), cycles to read one memory busload; must be ≥ 1.
- `memwritetime` (default 20), cycles to write one memory busload; must be ≥ 1.
- `membusbytes` (default 8), number of bytes per memory busload; must be a power of 2 that is 8 or more.
- `branchpredictbits` (default 0), number of bits in each branch prediction table entry; must be ≤ 8.
- `branchaddressbits` (default 0), number of bits in instruction address used to index the branch prediction table.
- `branchhistorybits` (default 0), number of bits in branch history used to index the branch prediction table.
- `branchdualbits` (default 0), number of bits of instruction-address-xor-branch-history used to index the branch prediction table.
- `hardwarepagetable` (default 1), is zero if page table calculations must be emulated by the operating system.
- `disablesecurity` (default 0), is 1 if the hot-seat security checks are turned off. This option is used only for testing purposes; it means that the '`s`' interrupt will not occur, and the '`p`' interrupt will be signaled only when going from a nonnegative location to a negative one.
- `memchunksmax` (default 1000), maximum number of 2^{16}-byte chunks of simulated memory; must be ≥ 1.
- `hashprime` (default 2003), prime number used to address simulated memory; must exceed `memchunksmax`, preferably by a factor of about 2.

The values of `memchunksmax` and `hashprime` affect only the speed of the simulator, not its results—unless a very huge program is being simulated. The stated defaults for `memchunksmax` and `hashprime` should be adequate for almost all applications.

4. A ⟨ cache spec ⟩ assigns a given value to a parameter affecting one of five possible caches:

⟨ cache spec ⟩ ⟶ ⟨ cache name ⟩⟨ cache parameter ⟩⟨ decimal value ⟩⟨ policy ⟩
⟨ cache name ⟩ ⟶ `ITcache` | `DTcache` | `Icache` | `Dcache` | `Scache`
⟨ policy ⟩ ⟶ ⟨ empty ⟩ | `random` | `serial` | `pseudolru` | `lru`

The possibilities for ⟨ cache parameter ⟩ are as follows:

- `associativity` (default 1), number of cache blocks per cache set; must be a power of 2. (A cache with associativity 1 is said to be "direct-mapped.")
- `blocksize` (default 8), number of bytes per cache block; must be a power of 2, at least equal to the granularity, and at most equal to 8192. The blocksize of `ITcache` and `DTcache` must be 8.
- `setsize` (default 1), number of sets of cache blocks; must be a power of 2. (A cache with set size 1 is said to be "fully associative.")
- `granularity` (default 8), number of bytes per "dirty bit," used to remember which items of data have changed since they were read from memory; must be a power of 2 and at least 8. The granularity must be 8 if `writeallocate` is 0.
- `victimsize` (default 0), number of cache blocks in the victim buffer, which holds blocks removed from the main cache sets; must be zero or a power of 2.
- `writeback` (default 0), is 1 in a "write-back" cache, which holds dirty data as long as possible; is 0 in a "write-through" cache, which cleans all data as soon as possible.
- `writeallocate` (default 0), is 1 in a "write-allocate" cache, which remembers all recently written data; is 0 in a "write-around" cache, which doesn't make space for newly written data that fails to hit an existing cache block.
- `accesstime` (default 1), number of cycles to query the cache; must be ≥ 1. (Hits in the S-cache actually require *twice* the accesstime, once to query the tag and once to transmit the data.)
- `copyintime` (default 1), number of cycles to move a cache block from its input buffer into the cache proper; must be ≥ 1.
- `copyouttime` (default 1), number of cycles to move a cache block from the cache proper to its output buffer; must be ≥ 1.
- `ports` (default 1), number of processes that can simultaneous query the cache; must be ≥ 1.

The ⟨ policy ⟩ parameter should be nonempty only on cache specifications for parameters `associativity` and `victimsize`. If no replacement policy is specified, `random` is the default. All four policies are equivalent when the `associativity` or `victimsize` is 1; `pseudolru` is equivalent to `lru` when the `associativity` or `victimsize` is 2.

The `granularity`, `writeback`, `writeallocate`, and `copyouttime` parameters affect the performance only of the D-cache and S-cache; the other three caches are read-only, so they never need to write their data.

The `ports` parameter affects the performance of the D-cache and DT-cache, and (if the `PREGO` command is used) the performance of the I-cache and IT-cache. The S-cache accommodates only one process at a time, regardless of the number of specified ports.

Only the translation caches (the IT-cache and DT-cache) are present by default. But if any specifications are given for, say, an I-cache, all of the unspecified I-cache parameters take their default values.

The existence of an S-cache (secondary cache) implies the existence of both I-cache and D-cache (primary caches for instructions and data). The block size of the secondary cache must not be less than the block size of the primary caches. The secondary cache must have the same granularity as the D-cache.

5. A ⟨ pipe spec ⟩ governs the execution time of potentially slow operations.

⟨ pipe spec ⟩ ⟶ ⟨ operation ⟩⟨ pipeline times ⟩
⟨ pipeline times ⟩ ⟶ ⟨ decimal value ⟩ | ⟨ pipeline times ⟩⟨ decimal value ⟩

Here the ⟨ operation ⟩ is one of the following:

- `mul0` through `mul8` (default 10); the values for `mul`j refer to products in which the second operand is less than 2^{8j}, where j is as small as possible. Thus, for example, `mul1` applies to nonzero one-byte multipliers.
- `div` (default 60); this applies to integer division, signed and unsigned.
- `sh` (default 1); this applies to left and right shifts, signed and unsigned.
- `mux` (default 1); the multiplex operator.
- `sadd` (default 1); the sideways addition operator.
- `mor` (default 1); the boolean matrix multiplication operators `MOR` and `MXOR`.
- `fadd` (default 4); floating point addition and subtraction.
- `fmul` (default 4); floating point multiplication.
- `fdiv` (default 40); floating point division.
- `fsqrt` (default 40); floating point square root.
- `fint` (default 4); floating point integerization.
- `fix` (default 2); conversion from floating to fixed, signed and unsigned.
- `flot` (default 2); conversion from fixed to floating, signed and unsigned.
- `feps` (default 4); floating comparison with respect to epsilon.

In each case one can specify a sequence of pipeline stages, with a positive number of cycles to be spent in each stage. For example, a specification like '`fmul 3 1`' would say that a functional unit that supports `FMUL` takes a total of four cycles to compute the floating point product in two stages; it can start working on a second product after three cycles have gone by.

If a floating point operation has a subnormal input, `denin` is added to the time for the first stage. If a floating point operation has a subnormal result, `denout` is added to the time for the last stage.

6. The fourth and final kind of specification defines a functional unit:

$$\langle\,\text{functional spec}\,\rangle \longrightarrow \texttt{unit}\ \langle\,\text{name}\,\rangle\langle\,\text{64 hexadecimal digits}\,\rangle$$

The symbolic name should be at most fifteen characters long. The 64 hexadecimal digits contain 256 bits, with '1' for each supported opcode; the most significant (leftmost) bit is for opcode 0 (`TRAP`), and the least significant bit is for opcode 255 (`TRIP`).

For example, we can define a load/store unit (which handles register/memory operations), a multiplication unit (which handles fixed and floating point multiplication), a boolean unit (which handles only bitwise operations), and a more general arithmetic-logical unit, as follows:

```
unit LSU 00000000000000000000000000000000fffffffcfffffffc0000000000000000
unit MUL 000080f000000000000000000000000000000000000000000000000000000000
unit BIT 000000000000000000000000000000000000000000000000ffff00ff00ff0000
unit ALU f0000000ffffffffffffffffffffffff0000000300000003ffffffffffffffff
```

The order in which units are specified is important, because `MMIX`'s dispatcher will try to match each instruction with the first functional unit that supports its opcode. Therefore it is best to list more specialized units (like the `BIT` unit in this example) before more general ones; this lets the specialized units have first chance at the instructions they can handle.

There can be any number of functional units, having possibly identical specifications. One should, however, give each unit a unique name (e.g., `ALU1` and `ALU2` if there are two arithmetic-logical units), since these names are used in diagnostic messages.

Opcodes that aren't supported by any specified unit will cause an emulation trap.

7. Full details about the significance of all these parameters can be found in the `mmix-pipe` module, which defines and discusses the data structures that need to be configured and initialized.

Of course the specifications in a configuration file needn't make any sense, nor need they be practically achievable. We could, for example, specify a unit that handles only the two opcodes `NXOR` and `DIVUI`; we could specify 1-cycle division but pipelined 100-cycle shifts, or 1-cycle memory access but 100-cycle cache access. We could create a thousand rename registers and issue a hundred instructions per cycle, etc. Some combinations of parameters are clearly ridiculous.

But there remain a huge number of possibilities of interest, especially as technology continues to evolve. By experimenting with configurations that are extreme by present-day standards, we can see how much might be gained if the corresponding hardware could be built economically.

8. Basic input/output. Let's get ready to program the *MMIX_config* subroutine by building some simple infrastructure. First we need some macros to print error messages.

```
#define errprint0(f) fprintf(stderr, f)
#define errprint1(f, a) fprintf(stderr, f, a)
#define errprint2(f, a, b) fprintf(stderr, f, a, b)
#define errprint3(f, a, b, c) fprintf(stderr, f, a, b, c)
#define panic(x) { x; errprint0("!\n"); exit(-1); }
```

9. And we need a place to look at the input.

```
#define BUF_SIZE 100    /* we don't need long lines */

⟨ Global variables 9 ⟩ ≡
  FILE *config_file;    /* input comes from here */
  char buffer[BUF_SIZE];    /* input lines go here */
  char token[BUF_SIZE];    /* and tokens are copied to here */
  char *buf_pointer = buffer;    /* this is our current position */
  bool token_prescanned;    /* does token contain the next token already? */
```

See also sections 15 and 28.

This code is used in section 38.

---

bool = **enum**, MMIX-PIPE §11. **FILE**, <stdio.h>. *MMIX_config*: **void** ( ), §38.
exit: **void** ( ), <stdlib.h>. *fprintf*: **int** ( ), <stdio.h>. *stderr*: **FILE** *, <stdio.h>.

10. The *get_token* routine copies the next token of input into the *token* buffer. After the input has ended, a final '`end`' is appended.

```
⟨ Subroutines 10 ⟩ ≡
  static void get_token ARGS((void));
  static void get_token()    /* set token to the next token of the configuration file */
  {
    register char *p, *q;
    if (token_prescanned) {
      token_prescanned = false; return;
    }
    while (1) {    /* scan past white space */
      if (*buf_pointer ≡ '\0' ∨ *buf_pointer ≡ '\n' ∨ *buf_pointer ≡ '%') {
        if (¬fgets(buffer, BUF_SIZE, config_file)) {
          strcpy(token, "end"); return;
        }
        if (strlen(buffer) ≡ BUF_SIZE − 1 ∧ buffer[BUF_SIZE − 2] ≠ '\n')
          panic(errprint1("config␣file␣line␣too␣long:␣`%s...'", buffer));
        buf_pointer = buffer;
      } else if (¬isspace(*buf_pointer)) break;
      else buf_pointer++;
    }
    for (p = buf_pointer, q = token; ¬isspace(*p) ∧ *p ≠ '%'; p++, q++) *q = *p;
    buf_pointer = p; *q = '\0';
    return;
  }
```

See also sections 11, 16, 22, 23, 30, and 31.

This code is used in section 38.

11. The *get_int* routine is called when we wish to input a decimal value. It returns −1 if the next token isn't a string of decimal digits.

```
⟨ Subroutines 10 ⟩ +≡
  static int get_int ARGS((void));
  static int get_int()
  { int v;
    char *p;
    get_token();
    for (p = token, v = 0; *p ≥ '0' ∧ *p ≤ '9'; p++) v = 10 * v + *p − '0';
    if (*p) return −1;
    return v;
  }
```

12. A simple data structure makes it fairly easy to deal with parameter/value specifications.

```
⟨ Type definitions 12 ⟩ ≡
  typedef struct {
    char name[20];   /* symbolic name */
    int *v;   /* internal name */
    int defval;   /* default value */
    int minval, maxval;   /* minimum and maximum legal values */
    bool power_of_two;   /* must it be a power of two? */
  } pv_spec;
```

See also sections 13 and 14.

This code is used in section 38.

13. Cache parameters are a bit more difficult, but still not bad.

```
⟨ Type definitions 12 ⟩ +≡
  typedef enum {
    assoc, blksz, setsz, gran, vctsz, wrb, wra, acctm, citm, cotm, prts
  } c_param;
  typedef struct {
    char name[20];   /* symbolic name */
    c_param v;   /* internal code */
    int defval;   /* default value */
    int minval, maxval;   /* minimum and maximum legal values */
    bool power_of_two;   /* must it be a power of two? */
  } cpv_spec;
```

14. Operation codes are the easiest of all.

```
⟨ Type definitions 12 ⟩ +≡
  typedef struct {
    char name[8];   /* symbolic name */
    internal_opcode v;   /* internal code */
    int defval;   /* default value */
  } op_spec;
```

ARGS = macro ( ), MMIX-PIPE §6.
bool = **enum**, MMIX-PIPE §11.
buf_pointer: **char** *, §9.
BUF_SIZE = 100, §9.
buffer: **char** [], §9.
config_file: **FILE** *, §9.
errprint1 = macro ( ), §8.
false = 0, MMIX-PIPE §11.
fgets: **char** *(), <stdio.h>.
internal_opcode = **enum**, MMIX-PIPE §49.
isspace: **int** ( ), <ctype.h>.
panic = macro ( ), §8.
strcpy: **char** *(), <string.h>.
strlen: **size_t** ( ), <string.h>.
token: **char** [], §9.
token_prescanned: **bool**, §9.

15. Most of the parameters are external variables that are declared in the header file `mmix-pipe.h`; but some are private to this module. Here we define the main tables used below.

⟨ Global variables 9 ⟩ +≡

```
int fetch_buf_size, write_buf_size, reorder_buf_size, mem_bus_bytes, hardware_PT;
int max_cycs = 60;
pv_spec PV[] = {
{"fetchbuffer", &fetch_buf_size, 4, 1, INT_MAX, false},
{"writebuffer", &write_buf_size, 2, 1, INT_MAX, false},
{"reorderbuffer", &reorder_buf_size, 5, 1, INT_MAX, false},
{"renameregs", &max_rename_regs, 5, 1, INT_MAX, false},
{"memslots", &max_mem_slots, 2, 1, INT_MAX, false},
{"localregs", &lring_size, 256, 256, 1024, true},
{"fetchmax", &fetch_max, 2, 1, INT_MAX, false},
{"dispatchmax", &dispatch_max, 1, 1, INT_MAX, false},
{"peekahead", &peekahead, 1, 0, INT_MAX, false},
{"commitmax", &commit_max, 1, 1, INT_MAX, false},
{"fremmax", &frem_max, 1, 1, INT_MAX, false},
{"denin", &denin_penalty, 1, 0, INT_MAX, false},
{"denout", &denout_penalty, 1, 0, INT_MAX, false},
{"writeholdingtime", &holding_time, 0, 0, INT_MAX, false},
{"memaddresstime", &mem_addr_time, 20, 1, INT_MAX, false},
{"memreadtime", &mem_read_time, 20, 1, INT_MAX, false},
{"memwritetime", &mem_write_time, 20, 1, INT_MAX, false},
{"membusbytes", &mem_bus_bytes, 8, 8, INT_MAX, true},
{"branchpredictbits", &bp_n, 0, 0, 8, false},
{"branchaddressbits", &bp_a, 0, 0, 32, false},
{"branchhistorybits", &bp_b, 0, 0, 32, false},
{"branchdualbits", &bp_c, 0, 0, 32, false},
{"hardwarepagetable", &hardware_PT, 1, 0, 1, false},
{"disablesecurity", (int *) &security_disabled, 0, 0, 1, false},
{"memchunksmax", &mem_chunks_max, 1000, 1, INT_MAX, false},
{"hashprime", &hash_prime, 2003, 2, INT_MAX, false}};
cpv_spec CPV[] = {{"associativity", assoc, 1, 1, INT_MAX, true},
{"blocksize", blksz, 8, 8, 8192, true},
{"setsize", setsz, 1, 1, INT_MAX, true},
{"granularity", gran, 8, 8, 8192, true},
{"victimsize", vctsz, 0, 0, INT_MAX, true},
{"writeback", wrb, 0, 0, 1, false},
{"writeallocate", wra, 0, 0, 1, false},
{"accesstime", acctm, 1, 1, INT_MAX, false},
{"copyintime", citm, 1, 1, INT_MAX, false},
{"copyouttime", cotm, 1, 1, INT_MAX, false},
{"ports", prts, 1, 1, INT_MAX, false}};
op_spec OP[] = {{"mul0", mul0, 10}, {"mul1", mul1, 10}, {"mul2", mul2, 10}, {"mul3",
    mul3, 10}, {"mul4", mul4, 10}, {"mul5", mul5, 10}, {"mul6", mul6, 10}, {"mul7",
    mul7, 10}, {"mul8", mul8, 10},
    {"div", div, 60}, {"sh", sh, 1}, {"mux", mux, 1}, {"sadd", sadd, 1}, {"mor", mor, 1},
```

```
    {"fadd",fadd,4},{"fmul",fmul,4},{"fdiv",fdiv,40},{"fsqrt",fsqrt,40},
    {"fint",fint,4},
    {"fix",fix,2},{"flot",flot,2},{"feps",feps,4}};
int PV_size, CPV_size, OP_size;     /* the number of entries in PV, CPV, OP */
```

acctm = 7, §13.
assoc = 0, §13.
blksz = 1, §13.
bp_a: **int**, MMIX-PIPE §150.
bp_b: **int**, MMIX-PIPE §150.
bp_c: **int**, MMIX-PIPE §150.
bp_n: **int**, MMIX-PIPE §150.
citm = 8, §13.
commit_max: **int**, MMIX-PIPE §59.
cotm = 9, §13.
cpv_spec = **struct**, §13.
denin_penalty: **int**, MMIX-PIPE §349.
denout_penalty: **int**, MMIX-PIPE §349.
dispatch_max: **int**, MMIX-PIPE §59.
div = 9, MMIX-PIPE §49.
fadd = 14, MMIX-PIPE §49.
false = 0, MMIX-PIPE §11.
fdiv = 16, MMIX-PIPE §49.
feps = 21, MMIX-PIPE §49.
fetch_max: **int**, MMIX-PIPE §59.
fint = 18, MMIX-PIPE §49.
fix = 19, MMIX-PIPE §49.
flot = 20, MMIX-PIPE §49.
fmul = 15, MMIX-PIPE §49.
frem_max: **int**, MMIX-PIPE §349.
fsqrt = 17, MMIX-PIPE §49.
gran = 3, §13.
hash_prime: **int**, MMIX-PIPE §207.
holding_time: **int**, MMIX-PIPE §247.
INT_MAX = macro, <limits.h>.
lring_size: **int**, MMIX-PIPE §86.
max_mem_slots: **int**, MMIX-PIPE §86.
max_rename_regs: **int**, MMIX-PIPE §86.
mem_addr_time: **int**, MMIX-PIPE §214.
mem_chunks_max: **int**, MMIX-PIPE §207.
mem_read_time: **int**, MMIX-PIPE §214.
mem_write_time: **int**, MMIX-PIPE §214.
mor = 13, MMIX-PIPE §49.
mul0 = 0, MMIX-PIPE §49.
mul1 = 1, MMIX-PIPE §49.
mul2 = 2, MMIX-PIPE §49.
mul3 = 3, MMIX-PIPE §49.
mul4 = 4, MMIX-PIPE §49.
mul5 = 5, MMIX-PIPE §49.
mul6 = 6, MMIX-PIPE §49.
mul7 = 7, MMIX-PIPE §49.
mul8 = 8, MMIX-PIPE §49.
mux = 11, MMIX-PIPE §49.
op_spec = **struct**, §14.
peekahead: **int**, MMIX-PIPE §59.
prts = 10, §13.
pv_spec = **struct**, §12.
sadd = 12, MMIX-PIPE §49.
security_disabled: **bool**, MMIX-PIPE §66.
setsz = 2, §13.
sh = 10, MMIX-PIPE §49.
true = 1, MMIX-PIPE §11.
vctsz = 4, §13.
wra = 6, §13.
wrb = 5, §13.

16. The *new_cache* routine creates a **cache** structure with default values. (These default values are "hard-wired" into the program, not actually read from the *CPV* table.)

```
⟨ Subroutines 10 ⟩ +≡
  static cache *new_cache ARGS((char *));
  static cache *new_cache(name)
      char *name;
  { register cache *c = (cache *) calloc(1, sizeof(cache));
    if (¬c) panic(errprint1("Can't␣allocate␣%s", name));
    c→aa = 1;     /* default associativity, should equal CPV[0].defval */
    c→bb = 8;     /* default blocksize */
    c→cc = 1;     /* default setsize */
    c→gg = 8;     /* default granularity */
    c→vv = 0;     /* default victimsize */
    c→repl = random;     /* default replacement policy */
    c→vrepl = random;     /* default victim replacement policy */
    c→mode = 0;     /* default mode is write-through and write-around */
    c→access_time = c→copy_in_time = c→copy_out_time = 1;
    c→filler.ctl = &(c→filler_ctl);
    c→filler_ctl.ptr_a = (void *) c;
    c→filler_ctl.go.o.l = 4;
    c→flusher.ctl = &(c→flusher_ctl);
    c→flusher_ctl.ptr_a = (void *) c;
    c→flusher_ctl.go.o.l = 4;
    c→ports = 1;
    c→name = name;
    return c;
  }
```

17. ⟨ Initialize to defaults 17 ⟩ ≡

```
  PV_size = (sizeof PV)/sizeof(pv_spec);
  CPV_size = (sizeof CPV)/sizeof(cpv_spec);
  OP_size = (sizeof OP)/sizeof(op_spec);
  ITcache = new_cache("ITcache");
  DTcache = new_cache("DTcache");
  Icache = Dcache = Scache = Λ;
  for (j = 0; j < PV_size; j++) *(PV[j].v) = PV[j].defval;
  for (j = 0; j < OP_size; j++) {
    pipe_seq[OP[j].v][0] = OP[j].defval;
    pipe_seq[OP[j].v][1] = 0;     /* one stage */
  }
```

This code is used in section 38.

18. Reading the specs. Before we're ready to process the configuration file, we need to count the number of functional units, so that we know how much space to allocate for them.

A special background unit is always provided, just to make sure that TRAP and TRIP instructions are handled by somebody.

```
⟨ Count and allocate the functional units 18 ⟩ ≡
  funit_count = 0;
  while (strcmp(token, "end") ≠ 0) {
    get_token();
    if (strcmp(token, "unit") ≡ 0) {
      funit_count++;
      get_token(); get_token();   /* a unit might be named unit or end */
    }
  }
  funit = (func *) calloc(funit_count + 1, sizeof(func));
  if (¬funit) panic(errprint0("Can't␣allocate␣the␣functional␣units"));
  strcpy(funit[funit_count].name, "%%");
  funit[funit_count].ops[0] = #80000000;   /* TRAP */
  funit[funit_count].ops[7] = #1;   /* TRIP */
```

This code is used in section 38.

aa: **int**, MMIX-PIPE §167.
access_time: **int**, MMIX-PIPE §167.
ARGS = macro ( ), MMIX-PIPE §6.
bb: **int**, MMIX-PIPE §167.
cache = **struct**, MMIX-PIPE §167.
calloc: **void** *( ), <stdlib.h>.
cc: **int**, MMIX-PIPE §167.
copy_in_time: **int**, MMIX-PIPE §167.
copy_out_time: **int**, MMIX-PIPE §167.
CPV: **cpv_spec** [ ], §15.
CPV_size: **int**, §15.
cpv_spec = **struct**, §13.
ctl: **control** *, MMIX-PIPE §23.
Dcache: **cache** *, MMIX-PIPE §168.
defval: **int**, §14.
defval: **int**, §12.
DTcache: **cache** *, MMIX-PIPE §168.
errprint0 = macro ( ), §8.
errprint1 = macro ( ), §8.
filler: **coroutine**, MMIX-PIPE §167.
filler_ctl: **control**, MMIX-PIPE §167.
flusher: **coroutine**, MMIX-PIPE §167.
flusher_ctl: **control**, MMIX-PIPE §167.
func: **struct**, MMIX-PIPE §76.
funit: **func** *, MMIX-PIPE §77.
funit_count: **int**, MMIX-PIPE §77.
get_token: **static void** ( ), §10.
gg: **int**, MMIX-PIPE §167.
go = 72, MMIX-PIPE §49.
Icache: **cache** *, MMIX-PIPE §168.
ITcache: **cache** *, MMIX-PIPE §168.
j: **register int**, §38.
l: **tetra**, MMIX-PIPE §17.
mode: **int**, MMIX-PIPE §167.
name: **char** *, MMIX-PIPE §167.
name: **char** [ ], MMIX-PIPE §76.
o: **octa**, MMIX-PIPE §40.
OP: **op_spec** [ ], §15.
OP_size: **int**, §15.
op_spec = **struct**, §14.
ops: **tetra** [ ], MMIX-PIPE §76.
panic = macro ( ), §8.
pipe_seq: **unsigned char** [ ][ ], MMIX-PIPE §136.
ports: **int**, MMIX-PIPE §167.
ptr_a: **void** *, MMIX-PIPE §44.
PV: **pv_spec** [ ], §15.
PV_size: **int**, §15.
pv_spec = **struct**, §12.
random = 0, MMIX-PIPE §164.
repl: **replace_policy**, MMIX-PIPE §167.
Scache: **cache** *, MMIX-PIPE §168.
strcmp: **int** ( ), <string.h>.
strcpy: **char** *( ), <string.h>.
token: **char** [ ], §9.
v: **internal_opcode**, §14.
v: **int** *, §12.
vrepl: **replace_policy**, MMIX-PIPE §167.
vv: **int**, MMIX-PIPE §167.

19. Now we can read the specifications and obey them. This program doesn't bother to be very tolerant of errors, nor does it try to be very efficient.

Incidentally, the specifications don't have to be broken into individual lines in any meaningful way. We simply read them token by token.

```
⟨ Record all the specs 19 ⟩ ≡
  rewind(config_file);
  funit_count = 0;
  token[0] = '\0';
  while (strcmp(token, "end") ≠ 0) {
    get_token();
    if (strcmp(token, "end") ≡ 0) break;
    ⟨ If token is a parameter name, process a PV spec 20 ⟩;
    ⟨ If token is a cache name, process a cache spec 21 ⟩;
    ⟨ If token is an operation name, process a pipe spec 24 ⟩;
    if (strcmp(token, "unit") ≡ 0) ⟨ Process a functional spec 25 ⟩;
    panic(errprint1("Configuration␣syntax␣error:␣Specification␣can't␣start␣with␣\
        `%s'", token));
  }
```

This code is used in section 38.

20. ⟨ If *token* is a parameter name, process a PV spec 20 ⟩ ≡

```
  for (j = 0; j < PV_size; j++)
    if (strcmp(token, PV[j].name) ≡ 0) {
      n = get_int();
      if (n < PV[j].minval)
        panic(errprint2("Configuration␣error:␣%s␣must␣be␣>=␣%d", PV[j].name,
            PV[j].minval));
      if (n > PV[j].maxval)
        panic(errprint2("Configuration␣error:␣%s␣must␣be␣<=␣%d", PV[j].name,
            PV[j].maxval));
      if (PV[j].power_of_two ∧ (n & (n − 1)))
        panic(errprint1("Configuration␣error:␣%s␣must␣be␣a␣power␣of␣2",
            PV[j].name));
      *(PV[j].v) = n;
      break;
    }
  if (j < PV_size) continue;
```

This code is used in section 19.

21. ⟨ If *token* is a cache name, process a cache spec 21 ⟩ ≡

```
if (strcmp(token, "ITcache") ≡ 0) {
  pcs(ITcache); continue;
} else if (strcmp(token, "DTcache") ≡ 0) {
  pcs(DTcache); continue;
} else if (strcmp(token, "Icache") ≡ 0) {
  if (¬Icache) Icache = new_cache("Icache");
  pcs(Icache); continue;
} else if (strcmp(token, "Dcache") ≡ 0) {
  if (¬Dcache) Dcache = new_cache("Dcache");
  pcs(Dcache); continue;
} else if (strcmp(token, "Scache") ≡ 0) {
  if (¬Icache) Icache = new_cache("Icache");
  if (¬Dcache) Dcache = new_cache("Dcache");
  if (¬Scache) Scache = new_cache("Scache");
  pcs(Scache); continue;
}
```

This code is used in section 19.

22. ⟨ Subroutines 10 ⟩ +≡

```
static void ppol ARGS((replace_policy *));
static void ppol(rr)    /* subroutine to scan for a replacement policy */
    replace_policy *rr;
{
  get_token();
  if (strcmp(token, "random") ≡ 0) *rr = random;
  else if (strcmp(token, "serial") ≡ 0) *rr = serial;
  else if (strcmp(token, "pseudolru") ≡ 0) *rr = pseudo_lru;
  else if (strcmp(token, "lru") ≡ 0) *rr = lru;
  else token_prescanned = true;    /* oops, we should rescan that token */
}
```

ARGS = macro ( ), MMIX-PIPE §6.
config_file: **FILE** ∗, §9.
Dcache: **cache** ∗, MMIX-PIPE §168.
DTcache: **cache** ∗, MMIX-PIPE §168.
errprint1 = macro ( ), §8.
errprint2 = macro ( ), §8.
funit_count: **int**, MMIX-PIPE §77.
get_int: **static int** ( ), §11.
get_token: **static void** ( ), §10.
Icache: **cache** ∗, MMIX-PIPE §168.
ITcache: **cache** ∗, MMIX-PIPE §168.
j: **register int**, §38.
lru = 3, MMIX-PIPE §164.
maxval: **int**, §12.
minval: **int**, §12.
n: **register int**, §38.
name: **char** [ ], §12.
new_cache: **static cache** ∗( ), §16.
panic = macro ( ), §8.
pcs: **static void** ( ), §23.
power_of_two: **bool**, §12.
pseudo_lru = 2, MMIX-PIPE §164.
PV: **pv_spec** [ ], §15.
PV_size: **int**, §15.
random = 0, MMIX-PIPE §164.
replace_policy = **enum**, MMIX-PIPE §164.
rewind: **void** ( ), <stdio.h>.
Scache: **cache** ∗, MMIX-PIPE §168.
serial = 1, MMIX-PIPE §164.
strcmp: **int** ( ), <string.h>.
token: **char** [ ], §9.
token_prescanned: **bool**, §9.
true = 1, MMIX-PIPE §11.
v: **int** ∗, §12.

23. ⟨Subroutines 10⟩ +≡

```
static void pcs ARGS((cache *));
static void pcs(c)      /* subroutine to process a cache spec */
    cache *c;
{
  register int j, n;
  get_token();
  for (j = 0; j < CPV_size; j++)
    if (strcmp(token, CPV[j].name) ≡ 0) break;
  if (j ≡ CPV_size) panic(errprint1("Configuration␣syntax␣error:␣`%s'␣isn't␣\
        a␣cache␣parameter␣name", token));
  n = get_int();
  if (n < CPV[j].minval)
    panic(errprint2("Configuration␣error:␣%s␣must␣be␣>=␣%d", CPV[j].name,
        CPV[j].minval));
  if (n > CPV[j].maxval)
    panic(errprint2("Configuration␣error:␣%s␣must␣be␣<=␣%d", CPV[j].name,
        CPV[j].maxval));
  if (CPV[j].power_of_two ∧ (n & (n − 1)))
    panic(errprint1("Configuration␣error:␣%s␣must␣be␣power␣of␣2", CPV[j].name));
  switch (CPV[j].v) {
  case assoc: c→aa = n; ppol(&(c→repl)); break;
  case blksz: c→bb = n; break;
  case setsz: c→cc = n; break;
  case gran: c→gg = n; break;
  case vctsz: c→vv = n; ppol(&(c→vrepl)); break;
  case wrb: c→mode = (c→mode & ~WRITE_BACK) + n * WRITE_BACK; break;
  case wra: c→mode = (c→mode & ~WRITE_ALLOC) + n * WRITE_ALLOC; break;
  case acctm: if (n > max_cycs) max_cycs = n;
    c→access_time = n; break;
  case citm: if (n > max_cycs) max_cycs = n;
    c→copy_in_time = n; break;
  case cotm: if (n > max_cycs) max_cycs = n;
    c→copy_out_time = n; break;
  case prts: c→ports = n; break;
  }
}
```

24. ⟨If *token* is an operation name, process a pipe spec 24⟩ ≡

```
for (j = 0; j < OP_size; j++)
  if (strcmp(token, OP[j].name) ≡ 0) {
    for (i = 0; ; i++) {
      n = get_int();
      if (n < 0) break;
      if (n ≡ 0) panic(errprint0("Configuration␣error:␣Pipeline␣cycles␣mu\
          st␣be␣positive"));
      if (n > 255)
        panic(errprint0("Configuration␣error:␣Pipeline␣cycles␣must␣be␣<=␣255"));
      if (n > max_cycs) max_cycs = n;
```

```
        if (i ≥ pipe_limit)
          panic(errprint1("Configuration␣error:␣More␣than␣%d␣pipeline␣stages",
                pipe_limit));
        pipe_seq[OP[j].v][i] = n;
      }
      token_prescanned = true;
      break;
    }
  if (j < OP_size) continue;
```

This code is used in section 19.

---

aa: **int**, MMIX-PIPE §167.
access_time: **int**, MMIX-PIPE §167.
acctm = 7, §13.
ARGS = macro ( ), MMIX-PIPE §6.
assoc = 0, §13.
bb: **int**, MMIX-PIPE §167.
blksz = 1, §13.
cache = **struct**, MMIX-PIPE §167.
cc: **int**, MMIX-PIPE §167.
citm = 8, §13.
copy_in_time: **int**, MMIX-PIPE §167.
copy_out_time: **int**, MMIX-PIPE §167.
cotm = 9, §13.
CPV: **cpv_spec** [], §15.
CPV_size: **int**, §15.
errprint0 = macro ( ), §8.
errprint1 = macro ( ), §8.
errprint2 = macro ( ), §8.
get_int: **static int** ( ), §11.
get_token: **static void** ( ), §10.
gg: **int**, MMIX-PIPE §167.
gran = 3, §13.
i: **register int**, §38.
j: **register int**, §38.
max_cycs: **int**, §15.
maxval: **int**, §13.
minval: **int**, §13.
mode: **int**, MMIX-PIPE §167.
n: **register int**, §38.
name: **char** [], §13.
name: **char** [], §14.
OP: **op_spec** [], §15.
OP_size: **int**, §15.
panic = macro ( ), §8.
pipe_limit = 90, MMIX-PIPE §136.
pipe_seq: **unsigned char** [][], MMIX-PIPE §136.
ports: **int**, MMIX-PIPE §167.
power_of_two: **bool**, §13.
ppol: **static void** ( ), §22.
prts = 10, §13.
repl: **replace_policy**, MMIX-PIPE §167.
setsz = 2, §13.
strcmp: **int** ( ), `<string.h>`.
token: **char** [], §9.
token_prescanned: **bool**, §9.
true = 1, MMIX-PIPE §11.
v: **c_param**, §13.
v: **internal_opcode**, §14.
vctsz = 4, §13.
vrepl: **replace_policy**, MMIX-PIPE §167.
vv: **int**, MMIX-PIPE §167.
wra = 6, §13.
wrb = 5, §13.
WRITE_ALLOC = 2, MMIX-PIPE §166.
WRITE_BACK = 1, MMIX-PIPE §166.

25. ⟨ Process a functional spec 25 ⟩ ≡

```
{
  get_token();
  if (strlen(token) > 15)
    panic(errprint1("Configuration␣error:␣`%s'␣is␣more␣than␣15␣characters␣long",
        token));
  strcpy(funit[funit_count].name, token);
  get_token();
  if (strlen(token) ≠ 64)
    panic(errprint1("Configuration␣error:␣unit␣%s␣doesn't␣ha\
        ve␣64␣hex␣digit␣specs", funit[funit_count].name));
  for (i = j = n = 0; j < 64; j++) {
    if (token[j] ≥ '0' ∧ token[j] ≤ '9') n = (n ≪ 4) + (token[j] − '0');
    else if (token[j] ≥ 'a' ∧ token[j] ≤ 'f') n = (n ≪ 4) + (token[j] − 'a' + 10);
    else if (token[j] ≥ 'A' ∧ token[j] ≤ 'F') n = (n ≪ 4) + (token[j] − 'A' + 10);
    else
      panic(errprint1("Configuration␣error:␣`%c'␣is␣not␣a␣hex␣digit", token[j]));
    if ((j & #7) ≡ #7) funit[funit_count].ops[i++] = n, n = 0;
  }
  funit_count++;
  continue;
}
```

This code is used in section 19.

26. Checking and allocating. The battle is only half over when we've absorbed all the data of the configuration file. We still must check for interactions between different quantities, and we must allocate space for cache blocks, coroutines, etc.

One of the most difficult tasks facing us is to determine the maximum number of pipeline stages needed by each functional unit. Let's tackle that first.

```
⟨ Allocate coroutines in each functional unit 26 ⟩ ≡
  ⟨ Build table of pipeline stages needed for each opcode 27 ⟩;
  for (j = 0; j ≤ funit_count; j++) {
    ⟨ Determine the number of stages, n, needed by funit[j] 29 ⟩;
    funit[j].k = n;
    funit[j].co = (coroutine *) calloc(n, sizeof(coroutine));
    for (i = 0; i < n; i++) {
      funit[j].co[i].name = funit[j].name;
      funit[j].co[i].stage = i + 1;
    }
  }
```

This code is used in section 38.

27.
```
⟨ Build table of pipeline stages needed for each opcode 27 ⟩ ≡
  for (j = div; j ≤ max_pipe_op; j++) int_stages[j] = strlen(pipe_seq[j]);
  for ( ; j ≤ max_real_command; j++) int_stages[j] = 1;
  for (j = mul0, n = 0; j ≤ mul8; j++)
    if (strlen(pipe_seq[j]) > n) n = strlen(pipe_seq[j]);
  int_stages[mul] = n;
  int_stages[ld] = int_stages[st] = int_stages[frem] = 2;
  for (j = 0; j < 256; j++) stages[j] = int_stages[int_op[j]];
```

This code is used in section 26.

---

calloc: **void** *( ), <stdlib.h>.
co: **coroutine** *, MMIX-PIPE §76.
coroutine = **struct**, MMIX-PIPE §23.
div = 9, MMIX-PIPE §49.
errprint1 = macro ( ), §8.
frem = 25, MMIX-PIPE §49.
funit: **func** *, MMIX-PIPE §77.
funit_count: **int**, MMIX-PIPE §77.
get_token: **static void** ( ), §10.
i: **register int**, §38.
int_op: **internal_opcode** [ ], §28.
int_stages: **int** [ ], §28.
j: **register int**, §38.
k: **int**, MMIX-PIPE §76.
ld = 56, MMIX-PIPE §49.
max_pipe_op = *feps*, MMIX-PIPE §49.
max_real_command = *trip*, MMIX-PIPE §49.
mul = 26, MMIX-PIPE §49.
mul0 = 0, MMIX-PIPE §49.
mul8 = 8, MMIX-PIPE §49.
n: **register int**, §38.
name: **char** [ ], MMIX-PIPE §76.
ops: **tetra** [ ], MMIX-PIPE §76.
panic = macro ( ), §8.
pipe_seq: **unsigned char** [ ][ ], MMIX-PIPE §136.
st = 63, MMIX-PIPE §49.
stage: **int**, MMIX-PIPE §23.
stages: **int** [ ], §28.
strcpy: **char** *( ), <string.h>.
strlen: **size_t** ( ), <string.h>.
token: **char** [ ], §9.

28. The *int_op* conversion table is similar to the *internal_op* array of the *MMIX_run* routine, but it replaces *divu* by *div*, *fsub* by *fadd*, etc.

⟨ Global variables 9 ⟩ +≡

```
internal_opcode int_op[256] = {
trap, fcmp, funeq, funeq, fadd, fix, fadd, fix,
flot, flot, flot, flot, flot, flot, flot, flot,
fmul, feps, feps, feps, fdiv, fsqrt, frem, fint,
mul, mul, mul, mul, div, div, div, div,
add, add, addu, addu, sub, sub, subu, subu,
addu, addu, addu, addu, addu, addu, addu, addu,
cmp, cmp, cmpu, cmpu, sub, sub, subu, subu,
sh, sh, sh, sh, sh, sh, sh, sh,
br, br, br, br, br, br, br, br,
br, br, br, br, br, br, br, br,
pbr, pbr, pbr, pbr, pbr, pbr, pbr, pbr,
pbr, pbr, pbr, pbr, pbr, pbr, pbr, pbr,
cset, cset, cset, cset, cset, cset, cset, cset,
cset, cset, cset, cset, cset, cset, cset, cset,
zset, zset, zset, zset, zset, zset, zset, zset,
zset, zset, zset, zset, zset, zset, zset, zset,
ld, ld, ld, ld, ld, ld, ld, ld,
ld, ld, ld, ld, ld, ld, ld, ld,
ld, ld, ld, ld, ld, ld, ld, ld,
ld, ld, ld, ld, prego, prego, go, go,
st, st, st, st, st, st, st, st,
st, st, st, st, st, st, st, st,
st, st, st, st, st, st, st, st,
st, st, st, st, st, st, pushgo, pushgo,
or, or, orn, orn, nor, nor, xor, xor,
and, and, andn, andn, nand, nand, nxor, nxor,
bdif, bdif, wdif, wdif, tdif, tdif, odif, odif,
mux, mux, sadd, sadd, mor, mor, mor, mor,
set, set, set, set, addu, addu, addu, addu,
or, or, or, or, andn, andn, andn, andn,
noop, noop, pushj, pushj, set, set, put, put,
pop, resume, save, unsave, sync, noop, get, trip};
int int_stages[max_real_command + 1];   /* stages as function of internal_opcode */
int stages[256];   /* stages as function of mmix_opcode */
```

29. ⟨ Determine the number of stages, n, needed by *funit*[*j*] 29 ⟩ ≡

```
for (i = n = 0; i < 256; i++)
  if (((funit[j].ops[i >> 5] << (i & #1f)) & #80000000) ∧ stages[i] > n) n = stages[i];
if (n ≡ 0) panic(errprint1("Configuration␣error:␣unit␣%s␣doesn't␣do␣anything",
      funit[j].name));
```

This code is used in section 26.

30. The next hardest thing on our agenda is to set up the cache structure fields that depend on the parameters. For example, although we have defined the parameter in the *bb* field (the block size), we also need to compute the *b* field (log of the block size), and we must create the cache blocks themselves.

```
⟨ Subroutines 10 ⟩ +≡
  static int lg ARGS((int));
  static int lg(n)      /* compute binary logarithm */
      int n;
  { register int j, l;
    for (j = n, l = 0; j; j >>= 1) l++;
    return l − 1;
  }
```


add = 29, MMIX-PIPE §49.
addu = 30, MMIX-PIPE §49.
and = 37, MMIX-PIPE §49.
andn = 38, MMIX-PIPE §49.
ARGS = macro ( ), MMIX-PIPE §6.
b: **int**, MMIX-PIPE §167.
bb: **int**, MMIX-PIPE §167.
bdif = 48, MMIX-PIPE §49.
br = 69, MMIX-PIPE §49.
cmp = 46, MMIX-PIPE §49.
cmpu = 47, MMIX-PIPE §49.
cset = 53, MMIX-PIPE §49.
div = 9, MMIX-PIPE §49.
divu = 28, MMIX-PIPE §49.
errprint1 = macro ( ), §8.
fadd = 14, MMIX-PIPE §49.
fcmp = 22, MMIX-PIPE §49.
fdiv = 16, MMIX-PIPE §49.
feps = 21, MMIX-PIPE §49.
fint = 18, MMIX-PIPE §49.
fix = 19, MMIX-PIPE §49.
flot = 20, MMIX-PIPE §49.
fmul = 15, MMIX-PIPE §49.
frem = 25, MMIX-PIPE §49.
fsqrt = 17, MMIX-PIPE §49.
fsub = 24, MMIX-PIPE §49.
funeq = 23, MMIX-PIPE §49.
funit: **func** ∗, MMIX-PIPE §77.
get = 54, MMIX-PIPE §49.
go = 72, MMIX-PIPE §49.
i: **register int**, §38.
internal_op: **internal_opcode** [ ], MMIX-PIPE §51.
internal_opcode = **enum**, MMIX-PIPE §49.
j: **register int**, §38.
ld = 56, MMIX-PIPE §49.
max_real_command = *trip*, MMIX-PIPE §49.
mmix_opcode = **enum**, MMIX-PIPE §47.
MMIX_run: **void** ( ), MMIX-PIPE §10.
mor = 13, MMIX-PIPE §49.
mul = 26, MMIX-PIPE §49.
mux = 11, MMIX-PIPE §49.
n: **register int**, §38.
name: **char** [ ], MMIX-PIPE §76.
nand = 39, MMIX-PIPE §49.
noop = 81, MMIX-PIPE §49.
nor = 36, MMIX-PIPE §49.
nxor = 41, MMIX-PIPE §49.
odif = 51, MMIX-PIPE §49.
ops: **tetra** [ ], MMIX-PIPE §76.
or = 34, MMIX-PIPE §49.
orn = 35, MMIX-PIPE §49.
panic = macro ( ), §8.
pbr = 70, MMIX-PIPE §49.
pop = 75, MMIX-PIPE §49.
prego = 73, MMIX-PIPE §49.
pushgo = 74, MMIX-PIPE §49.
pushj = 71, MMIX-PIPE §49.
put = 55, MMIX-PIPE §49.
resume = 76, MMIX-PIPE §49.
sadd = 12, MMIX-PIPE §49.
save = 77, MMIX-PIPE §49.
set: **cacheset** ∗, MMIX-PIPE §167.
sh = 10, MMIX-PIPE §49.
st = 63, MMIX-PIPE §49.
sub = 31, MMIX-PIPE §49.
subu = 32, MMIX-PIPE §49.
sync = 79, MMIX-PIPE §49.
tdif = 50, MMIX-PIPE §49.
trap = 82, MMIX-PIPE §49.
trip = 83, MMIX-PIPE §49.
unsave = 78, MMIX-PIPE §49.
wdif = 49, MMIX-PIPE §49.
xor = 40, MMIX-PIPE §49.
zset = 52, MMIX-PIPE §49.

31. ⟨ Subroutines 10 ⟩ +≡

```
static void alloc_cache ARGS((cache *, char *));
static void alloc_cache(c, name)
    cache *c;
    char *name;
{ register int j, k;
  if (c→bb < c→gg) panic(errprint1("Configuration␣error:␣blocksize␣of␣%s␣is\
      ␣less␣than␣granularity", name));
  if (name[1] ≡ 'T' ∧ c→bb ≠ 8)
    panic(errprint1("Configuration␣error:␣blocksize␣of␣%s␣must␣be␣8", name));
  c→a = lg(c→aa);
  c→b = lg(c→bb);
  c→c = lg(c→cc);
  c→g = lg(c→gg);
  c→v = lg(c→vv);
  c→tagmask = −(1 ≪ (c→b + c→c));
  if (c→a + c→b + c→c ≥ 32)
    panic(errprint1("Configuration␣error:␣%s␣has␣>=␣4␣gigabytes␣of␣data",
        name));
  if (c→gg ≠ 8 ∧ ¬(c→mode & WRITE_ALLOC)) panic(errprint2("Configuration␣error\
      :␣%s␣does␣write-around␣with␣granularity␣%d", name, c→gg));
  ⟨ Allocate the cache sets for cache c 32 ⟩;
  if (c→vv) ⟨ Allocate the victim cache for cache c 33 ⟩;
  c→inbuf.dirty = (char *) calloc(c→bb ≫ c→g, sizeof(char));
  if (¬c→inbuf.dirty)
    panic(errprint1("Can't␣allocate␣dirty␣bits␣for␣inbuffer␣of␣%s", name));
  c→inbuf.data = (octa *) calloc(c→bb ≫ 3, sizeof(octa));
  if (¬c→inbuf.data)
    panic(errprint1("Can't␣allocate␣data␣for␣inbuffer␣of␣%s", name));
  c→outbuf.dirty = (char *) calloc(c→bb ≫ c→g, sizeof(char));
  if (¬c→outbuf.dirty)
    panic(errprint1("Can't␣allocate␣dirty␣bits␣for␣outbuffer␣of␣%s", name));
  c→outbuf.data = (octa *) calloc(c→bb ≫ 3, sizeof(octa));
  if (¬c→outbuf.data)
    panic(errprint1("Can't␣allocate␣data␣for␣outbuffer␣of␣%s", name));
  if (name[0] ≠ 'S') ⟨ Allocate reader coroutines for cache c 34 ⟩;
}
```

32. **#define** *sign_bit* #80000000

⟨ Allocate the cache sets for cache c 32 ⟩ ≡

```
c→set = (cacheset *) calloc(c→cc, sizeof(cacheset));
if (¬c→set) panic(errprint1("Can't␣allocate␣cache␣sets␣for␣%s", name));
for (j = 0; j < c→cc; j++) {
  c→set[j] = (cacheblock *) calloc(c→aa, sizeof(cacheblock));
  if (¬c→set[j])
    panic(errprint2("Can't␣allocate␣cache␣blocks␣for␣set␣%d␣of␣%s", j, name));
  for (k = 0; k < c→aa; k++) {
    c→set[j][k].tag.h = sign_bit;    /* invalid tag */
    c→set[j][k].dirty = (char *) calloc(c→bb ≫ c→g, sizeof(char));
```

```
      if (¬c→set[j][k].dirty)
        panic(errprint3("Can't␣allocate␣dirty␣bits␣for␣block␣%d␣of␣set␣%d␣of␣%s",
            k, j, name));
      c→set[j][k].data = (octa *) calloc(c→bb ≫ 3, sizeof(octa));
      if (¬c→set[j][k].data)
        panic(errprint3("Can't␣allocate␣data␣for␣block␣%d␣of␣set␣%d␣of␣%s", k, j,
            name));
    }
  }
```

This code is used in section 31.

33. ⟨ Allocate the victim cache for cache *c* 33 ⟩ ≡

```
  {
    c→victim = (cacheblock *) calloc(c→vv, sizeof(cacheblock));
    if (¬c→victim)
      panic(errprint1("Can't␣allocate␣blocks␣for␣victim␣cache␣of␣%s", name));
    for (k = 0; k < c→vv; k++) {
      c→victim[k].tag.h = sign_bit;      /* invalid tag */
      c→victim[k].dirty = (char *) calloc(c→bb ≫ c→g, sizeof(char));
      if (¬c→victim[k].dirty)
        panic(errprint2("Can't␣allocate␣dirty␣bits␣for␣block␣%d␣\
            of␣victim␣cache␣of␣%s", k, name));
      c→victim[k].data = (octa *) calloc(c→bb ≫ 3, sizeof(octa));
      if (¬c→victim[k].data)
        panic(errprint2("Can't␣allocate␣data␣for␣block␣%d␣of␣victim␣cache␣of␣%s",
            k, name));
    }
  }
```

This code is used in section 31.

---

a: **int**, MMIX-PIPE §167.
aa: **int**, MMIX-PIPE §167.
ARGS = macro ( ), MMIX-PIPE §6.
b: **int**, MMIX-PIPE §167.
bb: **int**, MMIX-PIPE §167.
cache = **struct**, MMIX-PIPE §167.
calloc: **void** *( ), <stdlib.h>.
cc: **int**, MMIX-PIPE §167.
data: **octa** *, MMIX-PIPE §167.
dirty: **char** *, MMIX-PIPE §167.
errprint1 = macro ( ), §8.
errprint2 = macro ( ), §8.
errprint3 = macro ( ), §8.
g: **int**, MMIX-PIPE §167.
gg: **int**, MMIX-PIPE §167.
h: **tetra**, MMIX-PIPE §17.
inbuf: **cacheblock**, MMIX-PIPE §167.
lg: **static int** ( ), §30.
mode: **int**, MMIX-PIPE §167.
octa = **struct**, MMIX-PIPE §17.
outbuf: **cacheblock**, MMIX-PIPE §167.
panic = macro ( ), §8.
set: **cacheset** *, MMIX-PIPE §167.
tag: **octa**, MMIX-PIPE §167.
tagmask: **int**, MMIX-PIPE §167.
v: **int**, MMIX-PIPE §167.
victim: **cacheset**, MMIX-PIPE §167.
vv: **int**, MMIX-PIPE §167.
WRITE_ALLOC = 2, MMIX-PIPE §166.

34. ⟨ Allocate reader coroutines for cache c 34 ⟩ ≡

```
{
  c→reader = (coroutine *) calloc(c→ports, sizeof(coroutine));
  if (¬c→reader) panic(errprint1("Can't␣allocate␣readers␣for␣%s", name));
  for (j = 0; j < c→ports; j++) {
    c→reader[j].stage = vanish;
    c→reader[j].name = (name[0] ≡ 'D' ? (name[1] ≡ 'T' ? "DTreader" : "Dreader") :
        (name[1] ≡ 'T' ? "ITreader" : "Ireader"));
  }
}
```

This code is used in section 31.

35. ⟨ Allocate the caches 35 ⟩ ≡

```
alloc_cache(ITcache, "ITcache");
ITcache→filler.name = "ITfiller"; ITcache→filler.stage = fill_from_virt;
alloc_cache(DTcache, "DTcache");
DTcache→filler.name = "DTfiller"; DTcache→filler.stage = fill_from_virt;
if (Icache) {
  alloc_cache(Icache, "Icache");
  Icache→filler.name = "Ifiller"; Icache→filler.stage = fill_from_mem;
}
if (Dcache) {
  alloc_cache(Dcache, "Dcache");
  Dcache→filler.name = "Dfiller"; Dcache→filler.stage = fill_from_mem;
  Dcache→flusher.name = "Dflusher"; Dcache→flusher.stage = flush_to_mem;
}
if (Scache) {
  alloc_cache(Scache, "Scache");
  if (Scache→bb < Icache→bb) panic(errprint0("Configuration␣error\
        :␣Scache␣blocks␣smaller␣than␣Icache␣blocks"));
  if (Scache→bb < Dcache→bb) panic(errprint0("Configuration␣error\
        :␣Scache␣blocks␣smaller␣than␣Dcache␣blocks"));
  if (Scache→gg ≠ Dcache→gg) panic(errprint0("Configuration␣error\
        :␣Scache␣granularity␣differs␣from␣the␣Dcache"));
  Icache→filler.stage = fill_from_S;
  Dcache→filler.stage = fill_from_S; Dcache→flusher.stage = flush_to_S;
  Scache→filler.name = "Sfiller"; Scache→filler.stage = fill_from_mem;
  Scache→flusher.name = "Sflusher"; Scache→flusher.stage = flush_to_mem;
}
```

This code is used in section 38.

36. Now we are nearly done. The only nontrivial task remaining is to allocate the ring of queues for coroutine scheduling; for this we need to determine the maximum waiting time that will occur between scheduler and schedulee.

⟨ Allocate the scheduling queue 36 ⟩ ≡

```
bus_words = mem_bus_bytes ≫ 3;
j = (mem_read_time < mem_write_time ? mem_write_time : mem_read_time);
n = 1;
if (Scache ∧ Scache→bb > n) n = Scache→bb;
```

```
if (Icache ∧ Icache→bb > n) n = Icache→bb;
if (Dcache ∧ Dcache→bb > n) n = Dcache→bb;
n = mem_addr_time + ((int)(n + bus_words − 1)/bus_words) * j;
if (n > max_cycs) max_cycs = n;     /* now max_cycs bounds the waiting time */
ring_size = max_cycs + 1;
ring = (coroutine *) calloc(ring_size, sizeof(coroutine));
if (¬ring) panic(errprint0("Can't␣allocate␣the␣scheduling␣ring"));
{ register coroutine *p;
  for (p = ring; p < ring + ring_size; p++) {
    p→name = "";     /* header nodes are nameless */
    p→stage = max_stage;
  }
}
```

This code is used in section 38.

alloc_cache: **static void** ( ), §31.
bb: **int**, MMIX-PIPE §167.
bus_words: **int**, MMIX-PIPE §214.
c: **cache** *, §31.
calloc: **void** *( ), <stdlib.h>.
coroutine = **struct**, MMIX-PIPE §23.
Dcache: **cache** *, MMIX-PIPE §168.
DTcache: **cache** *, MMIX-PIPE §168.
errprint0 = macro ( ), §8.
errprint1 = macro ( ), §8.
fill_from_mem = 95, MMIX-PIPE §129.
fill_from_S = 94, MMIX-PIPE §129.
fill_from_virt = 93, MMIX-PIPE §129.
filler: **coroutine**, MMIX-PIPE §167.
flush_to_mem = 97, MMIX-PIPE §129.
flush_to_S = 96, MMIX-PIPE §129.
flusher: **coroutine**, MMIX-PIPE §167.
gg: **int**, MMIX-PIPE §167.
Icache: **cache** *, MMIX-PIPE §168.
ITcache: **cache** *, MMIX-PIPE §168.
j: **register int**, §31.
j: **register int**, §38.
max_cycs: **int**, §15.
max_stage = 99, MMIX-PIPE §129.
mem_addr_time: **int**, MMIX-PIPE §214.
mem_bus_bytes: **int**, §15.
mem_read_time: **int**, MMIX-PIPE §214.
mem_write_time: **int**, MMIX-PIPE §214.
n: **register int**, §38.
name: **char** *, §31.
name: **char** *, MMIX-PIPE §23.
panic = macro ( ), §8.
ports: **int**, MMIX-PIPE §167.
reader: **coroutine** *, MMIX-PIPE §167.
ring: **coroutine** *, MMIX-PIPE §29.
ring_size: **int**, MMIX-PIPE §29.
Scache: **cache** *, MMIX-PIPE §168.
stage: **int**, MMIX-PIPE §23.
vanish = 98, MMIX-PIPE §129.

37. ⟨ Touch up last-minute trivia 37 ⟩ ≡

```
if (hash_prime ≤ mem_chunks_max)
  panic(errprint0("Configuration␣error:␣hashprime␣must␣exceed␣memchunksmax"));
mem_hash = (chunknode *) calloc(hash_prime + 1, sizeof(chunknode));
if (¬mem_hash) panic(errprint0("Can't␣allocate␣the␣hash␣table"));
mem_hash[0].chunk = (octa *) calloc(1 ≪ 13, sizeof(octa));
if (¬mem_hash[0].chunk) panic(errprint0("Can't␣allocate␣chunk␣0"));
mem_hash[hash_prime].chunk = (octa *) calloc(1 ≪ 13, sizeof(octa));
if (¬mem_hash[hash_prime].chunk) panic(errprint0("Can't␣allocate␣0␣chunk"));
mem_chunks = 1;
fetch_bot = (fetch *) calloc(fetch_buf_size + 1, sizeof(fetch));
if (¬fetch_bot) panic(errprint0("Can't␣allocate␣the␣fetch␣buffer"));
fetch_top = fetch_bot + fetch_buf_size;
reorder_bot = (control *) calloc(reorder_buf_size + 1, sizeof(control));
if (¬reorder_bot) panic(errprint0("Can't␣allocate␣the␣reorder␣buffer"));
reorder_top = reorder_bot + reorder_buf_size;
wbuf_bot = (write_node *) calloc(write_buf_size + 1, sizeof(write_node));
if (¬wbuf_bot) panic(errprint0("Can't␣allocate␣the␣write␣buffer"));
wbuf_top = wbuf_bot + write_buf_size;
if (bp_n ≡ 0) bp_table = Λ;
else {      /* a branch prediction table is desired */
  if (bp_a + bp_b + bp_c ≥ 31) panic(errprint0("Configuration␣error\
        :␣Branch␣table␣has␣>=␣2␣gigabytes␣of␣data"));
  bp_table = (char *) calloc(1 ≪ (bp_a + bp_b + bp_c), sizeof(char));
  if (¬bp_table) panic(errprint0("Can't␣allocate␣the␣branch␣table"));
}
l = (specnode *) calloc(lring_size, sizeof(specnode));
if (¬l) panic(errprint0("Can't␣allocate␣local␣registers"));
j = bus_words;
if (Icache ∧ (Icache→bb ≫ 3) > j) j = Icache→bb ≫ 3;
fetched = (octa *) calloc(j, sizeof(octa));
if (¬fetched) panic(errprint0("Can't␣allocate␣prefetch␣buffer"));
dispatch_stat = (int *) calloc(dispatch_max + 1, sizeof(int));
if (¬dispatch_stat) panic(errprint0("Can't␣allocate␣dispatch␣counts"));
no_hardware_PT = 1 − hardware_PT;
```

This code is used in section 38.

38. Putting it all together. Here then is the desired configuration subroutine.

```
#include <stdio.h>     /* fopen, fgets, sscanf, rewind */
#include <stdlib.h>     /* calloc, exit */
#include <ctype.h>     /* isspace */
#include <string.h>     /* strcpy, strlen, strcmp */
#include <limits.h>     /* INT_MAX */
#include "mmix-pipe.h"
  ⟨Type definitions 12⟩
  ⟨Global variables 9⟩
  ⟨Subroutines 10⟩
  void MMIX_config(filename)
       char *filename;
  { register int i, j, n;
    config_file = fopen(filename, "r");
    if (¬config_file) panic(errprint1("Can't␣open␣configuration␣file␣%s", filename));
    ⟨Initialize to defaults 17⟩;
    ⟨Count and allocate the functional units 18⟩;
    ⟨Record all the specs 19⟩;
    ⟨Allocate coroutines in each functional unit 26⟩;
    ⟨Allocate the caches 35⟩;
    ⟨Allocate the scheduling queue 36⟩;
    ⟨Touch up last-minute trivia 37⟩;
  }
```


bb: **int**, MMIX-PIPE §167.
bp_a: **int**, MMIX-PIPE §150.
bp_b: **int**, MMIX-PIPE §150.
bp_c: **int**, MMIX-PIPE §150.
bp_n: **int**, MMIX-PIPE §150.
bp_table: **char** *, MMIX-PIPE §150.
bus_words: **int**, MMIX-PIPE §214.
calloc: **void** *(), <stdlib.h>.
chunk: **octa** *, MMIX-PIPE §206.
chunknode = **struct**, MMIX-PIPE §206.
config_file: **FILE** *, §9.
control = **struct**, MMIX-PIPE §44.
dispatch_max: **int**, MMIX-PIPE §59.
dispatch_stat: **int** *, MMIX-PIPE §66.
errprint0 = macro (), §8.
errprint1 = macro (), §8.
exit: **void** (), <stdlib.h>.
fetch = **struct**, MMIX-PIPE §68.
fetch_bot: **fetch** *, MMIX-PIPE §69.
fetch_buf_size: **int**, §15.
fetch_top: **fetch** *, MMIX-PIPE §69.
fetched: **octa** *, MMIX-PIPE §284.
fgets: **char** *(), <stdio.h>.
fopen: **FILE** *(), <stdio.h>.
hardware_PT: **int**, §15.
hash_prime: **int**, MMIX-PIPE §207.
Icache: **cache** *, MMIX-PIPE §168.
INT_MAX = macro, <limits.h>.
isspace: **int** (), <ctype.h>.
l: **specnode** *, MMIX-PIPE §86.
lring_size: **int**, MMIX-PIPE §86.
mem_chunks: **int**, MMIX-PIPE §207.
mem_chunks_max: **int**, MMIX-PIPE §207.
mem_hash: **chunknode** *, MMIX-PIPE §207.
no_hardware_PT: **bool**, MMIX-PIPE §242.
octa = **struct**, MMIX-PIPE §17.
panic = macro (), §8.
reorder_bot: **control** *, MMIX-PIPE §60.
reorder_buf_size: **int**, §15.
reorder_top: **control** *, MMIX-PIPE §60.
rewind: **void** (), <stdio.h>.
specnode = **struct**, MMIX-PIPE §40.
sscanf: **int** (), <stdio.h>.
strcmp: **int** (), <string.h>.
strcpy: **char** *(), <string.h>.
strlen: **size_t** (), <string.h>.
wbuf_bot: **write_node** *, MMIX-PIPE §247.
wbuf_top: **write_node** *, MMIX-PIPE §247.
write_buf_size: **int**, §15.
write_node = **struct**, MMIX-PIPE §246.

39. Names of the sections.

⟨ Allocate coroutines in each functional unit 26 ⟩ Used in section 38.
⟨ Allocate reader coroutines for cache c 34 ⟩ Used in section 31.
⟨ Allocate the cache sets for cache c 32 ⟩ Used in section 31.
⟨ Allocate the caches 35 ⟩ Used in section 38.
⟨ Allocate the scheduling queue 36 ⟩ Used in section 38.
⟨ Allocate the victim cache for cache c 33 ⟩ Used in section 31.
⟨ Build table of pipeline stages needed for each opcode 27 ⟩ Used in section 26.
⟨ Count and allocate the functional units 18 ⟩ Used in section 38.
⟨ Determine the number of stages, n, needed by *funit*[j] 29 ⟩ Used in section 26.
⟨ Global variables 9, 15, 28 ⟩ Used in section 38.
⟨ If *token* is a cache name, process a cache spec 21 ⟩ Used in section 19.
⟨ If *token* is a parameter name, process a PV spec 20 ⟩ Used in section 19.
⟨ If *token* is an operation name, process a pipe spec 24 ⟩ Used in section 19.
⟨ Initialize to defaults 17 ⟩ Used in section 38.
⟨ Process a functional spec 25 ⟩ Used in section 19.
⟨ Record all the specs 19 ⟩ Used in section 38.
⟨ Subroutines 10, 11, 16, 22, 23, 30, 31 ⟩ Used in section 38.
⟨ Touch up last-minute trivia 37 ⟩ Used in section 38.
⟨ Type definitions 12, 13, 14 ⟩ Used in section 38.

MMIX-IO

1. Introduction. This program module contains brute-force implementations of the ten input/output primitives defined at the beginning of MMIX-SIM. The subroutines are grouped here as a separate package, because they are intended to be loaded with the pipeline simulator as well as with the simple simulator.

```
⟨Preprocessor macros 2⟩
⟨Type definitions 3⟩
⟨External subroutines 4⟩
⟨Global variables 6⟩
⟨Subroutines 7⟩
```

2. Of course we include standard C library routines, and we set things up to accommodate older versions of C.

```
⟨Preprocessor macros 2⟩ ≡
#include <stdio.h>
#include <stdlib.h>
#ifdef __STDC__
#define ARGS(list) list
#else
#define ARGS(list) ()
#endif
#ifndef FILENAME_MAX
#define FILENAME_MAX 256
#endif
#ifndef SEEK_SET
#define SEEK_SET 0
#endif
#ifndef SEEK_END
#define SEEK_END 2
#endif
```

This code is used in section 1.

3. The unsigned 32-bit type **tetra** must agree with its definition in the simulators.

```
⟨Type definitions 3⟩ ≡
  typedef unsigned int tetra;
  typedef struct {
    tetra h, l;
  } octa;      /* two tetrabytes make one octabyte */
```

See also section 5.

This code is used in section 1.

4. Three basic subroutines are used to get strings from the simulated memory and to put strings into that memory. These subroutines are defined appropriately in each simulator. We also use a few subroutines and constants defined in MMIX-ARITH.

```
⟨External subroutines 4⟩ ≡
  extern char stdin_chr ARGS((void));
  extern int mmgetchars ARGS((char *buf, int size, octa addr, int stop));
```

D.E. Knuth: MMIXware, LNCS 1750, pp. 138–147, 2014.
DOI: 10.1007/3-540-46611-8_5

```
extern void mmputchars ARGS((unsigned char *buf, int size, octa addr));
extern octa oplus ARGS((octa, octa));
extern octa ominus ARGS((octa, octa));
extern octa incr ARGS((octa, int));
extern octa zero_octa;    /* zero_octa.h = zero_octa.l = 0 */
extern octa neg_one;    /* neg_one.h = neg_one.l = -1 */
```

This code is used in section 1.

5. Each possible handle has a file pointer and a current mode.

```
⟨ Type definitions 3 ⟩ +≡
  typedef struct {
    FILE *fp;    /* file pointer */
    int mode;    /* [read OK] + 2[write OK] + 4[binary] + 8[readwrite] */
  } sim_file_info;
```

6. ⟨ Global variables 6 ⟩ ≡

```
  sim_file_info sfile[256];
```

See also sections 9 and 24.

This code is used in section 1.

7. The first three handles are initially open.

```
⟨ Subroutines 7 ⟩ ≡
  void mmix_io_init ARGS((void));
  void mmix_io_init()
  {
    sfile[0].fp = stdin, sfile[0].mode = 1;
    sfile[1].fp = stdout, sfile[1].mode = 2;
    sfile[2].fp = stderr, sfile[2].mode = 2;
  }
```

See also sections 8, 10, 11, 12, 14, 16, 18, 19, 20, 21, 22, and 23.

This code is used in section 1.

__STDC__, Standard C.
FILE, <stdio.h>.
FILENAME_MAX = macro, <stdio.h>.
incr: **octa** ( ), MMIX-ARITH §6.
mmgetchars: **int** ( ), MMIX-SIM §114.
mmgetchars: **int** ( ), MMIX-PIPE §381.
mmputchars: **void** ( ), MMIX-SIM §117.
mmputchars: **void** ( ), MMIX-PIPE §384.
neg_one: **octa**, MMIX-ARITH §4.
ominus: **octa** ( ), MMIX-ARITH §5.
oplus: **octa** ( ), MMIX-ARITH §5.
SEEK_END = macro, <stdio.h>.
SEEK_SET = macro, <stdio.h>.
stderr: **FILE** *, <stdio.h>.
stdin: **FILE** *, <stdio.h>.
stdin_chr: **char** ( ), MMIX-SIM §120.
stdin_chr: **char** ( ), MMIX-PIPE §387.
stdout: **FILE** *, <stdio.h>.
zero_octa: **octa**, MMIX-ARITH §4.

8. The only tricky thing about these routines is that we want to protect the standard input, output, and error streams from being preempted.

```
⟨Subroutines 7⟩ +≡
  octa mmix_fopen ARGS((unsigned char, octa, octa));
  octa mmix_fopen(handle, name, mode)
       unsigned char handle;
       octa name, mode;
  {
    char name_buf[FILENAME_MAX];
    if (mode.h ∨ mode.l > 4) goto abort;
    if (mmgetchars(name_buf, FILENAME_MAX, name, 0) ≡ FILENAME_MAX) goto abort;
    if (sfile[handle].mode ≠ 0 ∧ handle > 2) fclose(sfile[handle].fp);
    sfile[handle].fp = fopen(name_buf, mode_string[mode.l]);
    if (¬sfile[handle].fp) goto abort;
    sfile[handle].mode = mode_code[mode.l];
    return zero_octa;     /* success */
  abort: sfile[handle].mode = 0;
    return neg_one;     /* failure */
  }
```

9. ⟨Global variables 6⟩ +≡

```
  char *mode_string[] = {"r", "w", "rb", "wb", "w+b"};
  int mode_code[] = {#1, #2, #5, #6, #f};
```

10. If the simulator is being used interactively, we can avoid competition for *stdin* by substituting another file.

```
⟨Subroutines 7⟩ +≡
  void mmix_fake_stdin ARGS((FILE *));
  void mmix_fake_stdin(f)
       FILE *f;
  {
    sfile[0].fp = f;     /* f should be open in mode "r" */
  }
```

11. ⟨Subroutines 7⟩ +≡

```
  octa mmix_fclose ARGS((unsigned char));
  octa mmix_fclose(handle)
       unsigned char handle;
  {
    if (sfile[handle].mode ≡ 0) return neg_one;
    if (handle > 2 ∧ fclose(sfile[handle].fp) ≠ 0) return neg_one;
    sfile[handle].mode = 0;
    return zero_octa;     /* success */
  }
```

12. ⟨ Subroutines 7 ⟩ +≡

```
octa mmix_fread ARGS((unsigned char, octa, octa));
octa mmix_fread(handle, buffer, size)
    unsigned char handle;
    octa buffer, size;
{
  register unsigned char *buf;
  register int n;
  octa o;

  o = neg_one;
  if (¬(sfile[handle].mode & #1)) goto done;
  if (sfile[handle].mode & #8) sfile[handle].mode &= ~#2;
  if (size.h) goto done;
  buf = (unsigned char *) calloc(size.l, sizeof(char));
  if (¬buf) goto done;
  ⟨ Read n ≤ size.l characters into buf 13 ⟩;
  mmputchars(buf, n, buffer);
  free(buf);
  o.h = 0, o.l = n;
done: return ominus(o, size);
}
```

13. ⟨ Read n ≤ size.l characters into buf 13 ⟩ ≡

```
if (sfile[handle].fp ≡ stdin) {
  register unsigned char *p;

  for (p = buf, n = size.l; p < buf + n; p++) *p = stdin_chr();
}
else {
  clearerr(sfile[handle].fp);
  n = fread(buf, 1, size.l, sfile[handle].fp);
  if (ferror(sfile[handle].fp)) {
    free(buf);
    goto done;
  }
}
```

This code is used in section 12.

ARGS = macro ( ), §2.
calloc: **void** *( ), <stdlib.h>.
clearerr: **void** ( ), <stdio.h>.
fclose: **int** ( ), <stdio.h>.
ferror: **int** ( ), <stdio.h>.
FILE, <stdio.h>.
FILENAME_MAX = macro, <stdio.h>.
fopen: **FILE** *( ), <stdio.h>.
fp: **FILE** *, §5.
fread: **size_t** ( ), <stdio.h>.
free: **void** ( ), <stdlib.h>.
h: **tetra**, §3.
l: **tetra**, §3.
mmgetchars: **int** ( ), MMIX-SIM §114.
mmgetchars: **int** ( ), MMIX-PIPE §381.
mmputchars: **void** ( ), MMIX-SIM §117.
mmputchars: **void** ( ), MMIX-PIPE §384.
mode: **int**, §5.
neg_one: **octa**, MMIX-ARITH §4.
octa = **struct**, §3.
ominus: **octa** ( ), MMIX-ARITH §5.
sfile: **sim_file_info** [ ], §6.
stdin: **FILE** *, <stdio.h>.
stdin_chr: **char** ( ), MMIX-SIM §120.
stdin_chr: **char** ( ), MMIX-PIPE §387.
zero_octa: **octa**, MMIX-ARITH §4.

14. ⟨ Subroutines 7 ⟩ +≡

```
octa mmix_fgets ARGS((unsigned char, octa, octa));
octa mmix_fgets(handle, buffer, size)
    unsigned char handle;
    octa buffer, size;
{
  char buf[256];
  register int n, s;
  register char *p;
  octa o;
  int eof = 0;
  if (¬(sfile[handle].mode & #1)) return neg_one;
  if (¬size.l ∧ ¬size.h) return neg_one;
  if (sfile[handle].mode & #8) sfile[handle].mode &= ~#2;
  size = incr(size, −1);
  o = zero_octa;
  while (1) {
    ⟨ Read n < 256 characters into buf 15 ⟩;
    mmputchars((unsigned char *) buf, n + 1, buffer);
    o = incr(o, n);
    size = incr(size, −n);
    if ((n ∧ buf[n − 1] ≡ '\n') ∨ (¬size.l ∧ ¬size.h) ∨ eof) return o;
    buffer = incr(buffer, n);
  }
}
```

15. ⟨ Read $n < 256$ characters into *buf* 15 ⟩ ≡

```
s = 255;
if (size.l < s ∧ ¬size.h) s = size.l;
if (sfile[handle].fp ≡ stdin)
  for (p = buf, n = 0; n < s; ) {
    *p = stdin_chr();
    n++;
    if (*p++ ≡ '\n') break;
  }
else {
  if (¬fgets(buf, s + 1, sfile[handle].fp)) return neg_one;
  eof = feof(sfile[handle].fp);
  for (p = buf, n = 0; n < s; ) {
    if (¬*p ∧ eof) break;
    n++;
    if (*p++ ≡ '\n') break;
  }
}
*p = '\0';
```

This code is used in section 14.

16. The routines that deal with wyde characters might need to be changed on a system that is little-endian; the author wishes good luck to whoever has to do this. MMIX is always big-endian, but external files prepared on random operating systems might be backwards.

```
⟨Subroutines 7⟩ +≡
  octa mmix_fgetws ARGS((unsigned char, octa, octa));
  octa mmix_fgetws(handle, buffer, size)
      unsigned char handle;
      octa buffer, size;
  {
    char buf[256];
    register int n, s;
    register char *p;
    octa o;
    int eof = 0;
    if (¬(sfile[handle].mode & #1)) return neg_one;
    if (¬size.l ∧ ¬size.h) return neg_one;
    if (sfile[handle].mode & #8) sfile[handle].mode &= ~#2;
    buffer.l &= −2;
    size = incr(size, −1);
    o = zero_octa;
    while (1) {
      ⟨Read n < 128 wyde characters into buf 17⟩;
      mmputchars((unsigned char *) buf, 2 * n + 2, buffer);
      o = incr(o, n);
      size = incr(size, −n);
      if ((n ∧ buf[2 * n − 1] ≡ '\n' ∧ buf[2 * n − 2] ≡ 0) ∨ (¬size.l ∧ ¬size.h) ∨ eof)
        return o;
      buffer = incr(buffer, 2 * n);
    }
  }
```

ARGS = macro ( ), §2.
feof: **int** ( ), <stdio.h>.
fgets: **char** *( ), <stdio.h>.
fp: **FILE** *, §5.
h: **tetra**, §3.
incr: **octa** ( ), MMIX-ARITH §6.
l: **tetra**, §3.
mmputchars: **void** ( ), MMIX-SIM §117.
mmputchars: **void** ( ), MMIX-PIPE §384.
mode: **int**, §5.
neg_one: **octa**, MMIX-ARITH §4.
octa = **struct**, §3.
sfile: **sim_file_info** [ ], §6.
stdin: **FILE** *, <stdio.h>.
stdin_chr: **char** ( ), MMIX-SIM §120.
stdin_chr: **char** ( ), MMIX-PIPE §387.
zero_octa: **octa**, MMIX-ARITH §4.

17. ⟨ Read $n < 128$ wyde characters into *buf* 17 ⟩ ≡

```
s = 127;
if (size.l < s ∧ ¬size.h) s = size.l;
if (sfile[handle].fp ≡ stdin)
   for (p = buf, n = 0; n < s; ) {
      *p++ = stdin_chr(); *p++ = stdin_chr();
      n++;
      if (*(p − 1) ≡ '\n' ∧ *(p − 2) ≡ 0) break;
   }
else
   for (p = buf, n = 0; n < s; ) {
      if (fread(p, 1, 2, sfile[handle].fp) ≠ 2) {
         eof = feof(sfile[handle].fp);
         if (¬eof) return neg_one;
         break;
      }
      n++, p += 2;
      if (*(p − 1) ≡ '\n' ∧ *(p − 2) ≡ 0) break;
   }
*p = *(p + 1) = '\0';
```

This code is used in section 16.

18. ⟨ Subroutines 7 ⟩ +≡

```
octa mmix_fwrite ARGS((unsigned char, octa, octa));
octa mmix_fwrite(handle, buffer, size)
      unsigned char handle;
      octa buffer, size;
{
   char buf[256];
   register int n;
   if (¬(sfile[handle].mode & #2)) return ominus(zero_octa, size);
   if (sfile[handle].mode & #8) sfile[handle].mode &= ∼#1;
   while (1) {
      if (size.h ∨ size.l ≥ 256) n = mmgetchars(buf, 256, buffer, −1);
      else n = mmgetchars(buf, size.l, buffer, −1);
      size = incr(size, −n);
      if (fwrite(buf, 1, n, sfile[handle].fp) ≠ n) return ominus(zero_octa, size);
      fflush(sfile[handle].fp);
      if (¬size.l ∧ ¬size.h) return zero_octa;
      buffer = incr(buffer, n);
   }
}
```

19. ⟨ Subroutines 7 ⟩ +≡

```
octa mmix_fputs ARGS((unsigned char, octa));
octa mmix_fputs(handle, string)
      unsigned char handle;
      octa string;
{
```

```
    char buf[256];
    register int n;
    octa o;
    o = zero_octa;
    if (¬(sfile[handle].mode & #2)) return neg_one;
    if (sfile[handle].mode & #8) sfile[handle].mode &= ~#1;
    while (1) {
      n = mmgetchars(buf, 256, string, 0);
      if (fwrite(buf, 1, n, sfile[handle].fp) ≠ n) return neg_one;
      o = incr(o, n);
      if (n < 256) {
        fflush(sfile[handle].fp);
        return o;
      }
      string = incr(string, n);
    }
  }
```

20. ⟨ Subroutines 7 ⟩ +≡

```
  octa mmix_fputws ARGS((unsigned char, octa));
  octa mmix_fputws(handle, string)
      unsigned char handle;
      octa string;
  {
    char buf[256];
    register int n;
    octa o;
    o = zero_octa;
    if (¬(sfile[handle].mode & #2)) return neg_one;
    if (sfile[handle].mode & #8) sfile[handle].mode &= ~#1;
    while (1) {
      n = mmgetchars(buf, 256, string, 1);
      if (fwrite(buf, 1, n, sfile[handle].fp) ≠ n) return neg_one;
      o = incr(o, n ≫ 1);
      if (n < 256) {
        fflush(sfile[handle].fp);
        return o;
      }
      string = incr(string, n);
    }
  }
```

ARGS = macro ( ), §2.
buf: **char** [ ], §16.
eof: **int**, §16.
feof: **int** ( ), <stdio.h>.
fflush: **int** ( ), <stdio.h>.
fp: **FILE** ∗, §5.
fread: **size_t** ( ), <stdio.h>.
fwrite: **size_t** ( ), <stdio.h>.
h: **tetra**, §3.
handle: **unsigned char**, §16.
incr: **octa** ( ), MMIX-ARITH §6.
l: **tetra**, §3.
mmgetchars: **int** ( ), MMIX-SIM §114.
mmgetchars: **int** ( ), MMIX-PIPE §381.
mode: **int**, §5.
n: **register int**, §16.
neg_one: **octa**, MMIX-ARITH §4.
octa = **struct**, §3.
ominus: **octa** ( ), MMIX-ARITH §5.
p: **register char** ∗, §16.
s: **register int**, §16.
sfile: **sim_file_info** [ ], §6.
size: **octa**, §16.
stdin: **FILE** ∗, <stdio.h>.
stdin_chr: **char** ( ), MMIX-SIM §120.
stdin_chr: **char** ( ), MMIX-PIPE §387.
zero_octa: **octa**, MMIX-ARITH §4.

21. **#define** *sign_bit* ((**unsigned**) #80000000)

```
⟨ Subroutines 7 ⟩ +≡
  octa mmix_fseek ARGS((unsigned char, octa));
  octa mmix_fseek(handle, offset)
      unsigned char handle;
      octa offset;
  {
    if (¬(sfile[handle].mode & #4)) return neg_one;
    if (sfile[handle].mode & #8) sfile[handle].mode = #f;
    if (offset.h & sign_bit) {
      if (offset.h ≠ #ffffffff ∨ ¬(offset.l & sign_bit)) return neg_one;
      if (fseek(sfile[handle].fp, (int) offset.l + 1, SEEK_END) ≠ 0) return neg_one;
    } else {
      if (offset.h ∨ (offset.l & sign_bit)) return neg_one;
      if (fseek(sfile[handle].fp, (int) offset.l, SEEK_SET) ≠ 0) return neg_one;
    }
    return zero_octa;
  }
```

22. ⟨ Subroutines 7 ⟩ +≡

```
  octa mmix_ftell ARGS((unsigned char));
  octa mmix_ftell(handle)
      unsigned char handle;
  {
    register long x;
    octa o;
    if (¬(sfile[handle].mode & #4)) return neg_one;
    x = ftell(sfile[handle].fp);
    if (x < 0) return neg_one;
    o.h = 0, o.l = x;
    return o;
  }
```

23. One last subroutine belongs here, just in case the user has modified the standard error handle.

```
⟨ Subroutines 7 ⟩ +≡
  void print_trip_warning ARGS((int, octa));
  void print_trip_warning(n, loc)
      int n;
      octa loc;
  {
    if (sfile[2].mode & #2) fprintf(sfile[2].fp, "Warning:␣%s␣at␣location␣%08x%08x\n",
          trip_warning[n], loc.h, loc.l);
  }
```

24. ⟨ Global variables 6 ⟩ +≡

```
  char *trip_warning[] = {"TRIP", "integer␣divide␣check", "integer␣overflow",
      "float-to-fix␣overflow", "invalid␣floating␣point␣operation",
      "floating␣point␣overflow", "floating␣point␣underflow",
      "floating␣point␣division␣by␣zero", "floating␣point␣inexact"};
```

25. Names of the sections.

⟨ External subroutines 4 ⟩ Used in section 1.
⟨ Global variables 6, 9, 24 ⟩ Used in section 1.
⟨ Preprocessor macros 2 ⟩ Used in section 1.
⟨ Read $n < 128$ wyde characters into *buf* 17 ⟩ Used in section 16.
⟨ Read $n < 256$ characters into *buf* 15 ⟩ Used in section 14.
⟨ Read $n \le size.l$ characters into *buf* 13 ⟩ Used in section 12.
⟨ Subroutines 7, 8, 10, 11, 12, 14, 16, 18, 19, 20, 21, 22, 23 ⟩ Used in section 1.
⟨ Type definitions 3, 5 ⟩ Used in section 1.

ARGS = macro ( ), §2.
fp: **FILE** ∗, §5.
fprintf: **int** ( ), <stdio.h>.
fseek: **int** ( ), <stdio.h>.
ftell: **long** ( ), <stdio.h>.
h: **tetra**, §3.
l: **tetra**, §3.
mode: **int**, §5.
neg_one: **octa**, MMIX-ARITH §4.
octa = **struct**, §3.
SEEK_END = macro, <stdio.h>.
SEEK_SET = macro, <stdio.h>.
sfile: **sim_file_info** [ ], §6.
zero_octa: **octa**, MMIX-ARITH §4.

MMIX-MEM

1. Memory-mapped input and output. This module supplies procedures for reading from and writing to MMIX memory addresses that exceed 48 bits. Such addresses are used by the operating system for input and output, so they require special treatment. At present only dummy versions of these routines are implemented. Users who need nontrivial versions of *spec_read* and/or *spec_write* should prepare their own and link them with the rest of the simulator.

Many I/O devices communicate via bytes or wydes or tetras instead of octabytes. So these prototype routines have a *size* parameter, to distinguish between the various kinds of quantities that MMIX wants to read from and write to the memory-mapped addresses.

```
#include <stdio.h>
#include "mmix-pipe.h"     /* header file for all modules */
  extern octa read_hex();     /* found in the main program module */
  static char buf[20];
  static char *kind[] = {"byte", "wyde", "tetra", "octa"};
  extern octa shift_left ARGS((octa y, int s));     /* y ≪ s, 0 ≤ s ≤ 64 */
  extern octa shift_right ARGS((octa y, int s, int u));     /* y ≫ s, signed if ¬u */
```

2. If the *interactive_read_bit* of the *verbose* control is set, the user is supposed to supply values dynamically. Otherwise zero is read.

```
  octa spec_read ARGS((octa, int));
  octa spec_read(addr, size)
      octa addr;
      int size;
  {
    octa val;
    size &= #3, addr.l &= −(1 ≪ size);
    if (verbose & interactive_read_bit) {
      printf("**␣Read␣%s␣from␣loc␣%08x%08x:␣", kind[size], addr.h, addr.l);
      fgets(buf, 20, stdin);
      val = read_hex(buf);
    }
    else val.l = val.h = 0;
    switch (size) {
    case 0: val.l &= #ff;
    case 1: val.l &= #ffff;
    case 2: val.h = 0;
    case 3: break;
    }
    if (verbose & show_spec_bit) {
      printf("␣␣␣(spec_read␣");
      switch (size) {
      case 0: printf("%02x", val.l); break;
      case 1: printf("%04x", val.l); break;
      case 2: printf("%08x", val.l); break;
      case 3: printf("%08x%08x", val.h, val.l); break;
```

D.E. Knuth: MMIXware, LNCS 1750, pp. 148–149, 2014.
DOI: 10.1007/3-540-46611-8_6

```
    }
    printf(" from %08x%08x at time %d)\n", addr.h, addr.l, ticks.l);
  }
  return shift_left(val, (8 - (1 << size) - (addr.l & 7)) << 3);
}
```

3. The default *spec_write* just reports its arguments, without actually writing anything.

```
void spec_write ARGS((octa, octa, int));
void spec_write(addr, val, size)
    octa addr, val;
    int size;
{
  if (verbose & show_spec_bit) {
    size &= #3, addr.l &= -(1 << size);
    val = shift_right(val, (8 - (1 << size) - (addr.l & 7)) << 3, 1);
    printf("   (spec_write ");
    switch (size) {
    case 0: printf("%02x", val.l); break;
    case 1: printf("%04x", val.l); break;
    case 2: printf("%08x", val.l); break;
    case 3: printf("%08x%08x", val.h, val.l); break;
    }
    printf(" to %08x%08x at time %d)\n", addr.h, addr.l, ticks.l);
  }
}
```

4. Incidentally, the combined address a and size s could be transmitted in 64 bits of an actual memory bus, because a is always a multiple of 2^s that is less than 2^{63}. Thus (a, s) can be packed neatly into the 64-bit number $2a + 2^s$. (Think about it.)

ARGS = macro, MMIX-PIPE §6.
fgets: **char** *( ), <stdio.h>.
h: **tetra**, MMIX-PIPE §17.
interactive_read_bit = 1 ≪ 5, MMIX-PIPE §8.
l: **tetra**, MMIX-PIPE §17.
octa = **struct**, MMIX-PIPE §17.
printf: **int** ( ), <stdio.h>.
read_hex: **octa** ( ), MMMIX §17.
shift_left: **octa** ( ), MMIX-ARITH §7.
shift_right: **octa** ( ), MMIX-ARITH §7.
show_spec_bit = 1 ≪ 6, MMIX-PIPE §8.
stdin: **FILE** *, <stdio.h>.
ticks: **Extern octa**, MMIX-PIPE §87.
verbose: **int**, MMIX-PIPE §4.

MMIX-PIPE

1. Introduction. This program is the heart of the meta-simulator for the ultra-configurable `MMIX` pipeline: It defines the *MMIX_run* routine, which does most of the work. Another routine, *MMIX_init*, is also defined here, and so is a header file called `mmix_pipe.h`. The header file is used by the main routine and by other routines like *MMIX_config*, which are compiled separately.

Readers of this program should be familiar with the explanation of `MMIX` architecture as presented in the main program module for MMMIX.

A lot of subtle things can happen when instructions are executed in parallel. Therefore this simulator ranks among the most interesting and instructive programs in the author's experience. The author has tried his best to make everything correct ... but the chances for error are great. Anyone who discovers a bug is therefore urged to report it as soon as possible; please see `http://mmix.cs.hm.edu/bugs/` for instructions.

It sort of boggles the mind when one realizes that the present program might someday be translated by a C compiler for `MMIX` and used to simulate *itself.*

2. This high-performance prototype of `MMIX` achieves its efficiency by means of "pipelining," a technique of overlapping that is explained for the related `DLX` computer in Chapter 3 of Hennessy & Patterson's book *Computer Architecture* (second edition). Other techniques such as "dynamic scheduling" and "multiple issue," explained in Chapter 4 of that book, are used too.

One good way to visualize the procedure is to imagine that somebody has organized a high-tech car repair shop according to similar principles. There are eight independent functional units, which we can think of as eight groups of auto mechanics, each specializing in a particular task; each group has its own workspace with room to deal with one car at a time. Group F (the "fetch" group) is in charge of rounding up customers and getting them to enter the assembly-line garage in an orderly fashion. Group D (the "decode and dispatch" group) does the initial vehicle inspection and writes up an order that explains what kind of servicing is required. The vehicles go next to one of the four "execution" groups: Group X handles routine maintenance, while groups XF, XM, and XD are specialists in more complex tasks that tend to take longer. (The XF people are good at floating the points, while the XM and XD groups are experts in multilink suspensions and differentials.) When the relevant X group has finished its work, cars drive to M station, where they send or receive messages and possibly pay money to members of the "memory" group. Finally all necessary parts are installed by members of group W, the "write" group, and the car leaves the shop. Everything is tightly organized so that in most cases the cars move in synchronized fashion from station to station, at regular 100-nanocentury intervals.

In a similar way, most `MMIX` instructions can be handled in a five-stage pipeline, F–D–X–M–W, with X replaced by XF for floating-point addition or conversion, or by XM for multiplication, or by XD for division or square root. Each stage ideally takes one clock cycle, although XF, XM, and (especially) XD are slower. If the instructions enter in a suitable pattern, we might see one instruction being fetched, another being decoded, and up to four being executed, while another is accessing memory, and yet

D.E. Knuth: MMIXware, LNCS 1750, pp. 150–331, 2014.
DOI: 10.1007/3-540-46611-8_7

another is finishing up by writing new information into registers; all this is going on simultaneously during one clock cycle. Pipelining with eight separate stages might therefore make the machine run up to 8 times as fast as it could if each instruction were being dealt with individually and without overlap. (Well, perfect speedup turns out to be impossible, because of the shared M and W stages; the theory of knapsack programming, to be discussed in Section 7.7 of *The Art of Computer Programming*, tells us that the maximal achievable speedup is at most $8-1/p-1/q-1/r$ when XF, XM, and XD have delays bounded by p, q, and r cycles. But we can achieve a factor of more than 7 if we are very lucky.)

Consider, for example, the `ADD` instruction. This instruction enters the computer's processing unit in F stage, taking only one clock cycle if it is in the cache of instructions recently seen. Then the D stage recognizes the command as an `ADD` and acquires the current values of \$Y and \$Z; meanwhile, of course, another instruction is being fetched by F. On the next clock cycle, the X stage adds the values together. This prepares the way for the M stage to watch for overflow and to get ready for any exceptional action that might be needed with respect to the settings of special register rA. Finally, on the fifth clock cycle, the sum is either written into \$X or the trip handler for integer overflow is invoked. Although this process has taken five clock cycles (that is, 5υ), the net increase in running time has been only 1υ.

Of course congestion can occur, inside a computer as in a repair shop. For example, auto parts might not be readily available; or a car might have to sit in D station while waiting to move to XM, thereby blocking somebody else from moving from F to D. Sometimes there won't necessarily be a steady stream of customers. In such cases the employees in some parts of the shop will occasionally be idle. But we assume that they always do their jobs as fast as possible, given the sequence of customers that they encounter. With a clever person setting up appointments—translation: with a clever programmer and/or compiler arranging `MMIX` instructions—the organization can often be expected to run at nearly peak capacity.

In fact, this program is designed for experiments with many kinds of pipelines, potentially using additional functional units (such as several independent X groups), and potentially fetching, dispatching, and executing several nonconflicting instructions simultaneously. Such complications make this program more difficult than a simple pipeline simulator would be, but they also make it a lot more instructive because we can get a better understanding of the issues involved if we are required to treat them in greater generality.

MMIX_config: **void** (), MMIX-CONFIG §38. *MMIX_init*: **void** (), §10. *MMIX_run*: **void** (), §10.

3. Here's the overall structure of the present program module.

```
#include <stdio.h>
#include <stdlib.h>
#include <math.h>
#include "abstime.h"
  ⟨ Preprocessor definitions ⟩
  ⟨ Header definitions 6 ⟩
  ⟨ Type definitions 11 ⟩
  ⟨ Global variables 20 ⟩
  ⟨ External variables 4 ⟩
  ⟨ Internal prototypes 13 ⟩
  ⟨ External prototypes 9 ⟩
  ⟨ Subroutines 14 ⟩
  ⟨ External routines 10 ⟩
```

4. The identifier **Extern** is used in MMIX-PIPE to declare variables that are accessed in other modules. Actually all appearances of '**Extern**' are defined to be blank here, but '**Extern**' will become '**extern**' in the header file.

```
#define Extern        /* blank for us, extern for them */
  format Extern extern
```

```
⟨ External variables 4 ⟩ ≡
  Extern int verbose;      /* controls the level of diagnostic output */
```

See also sections 29, 59, 60, 66, 69, 77, 86, 87, 98, 115, 136, 150, 168, 207, 211, 214, 242, 247, 284, and 349.

This code is used in sections 3 and 5.

5. The header file repeats the basic definitions and declarations.

```
⟨ mmix-pipe.h 5 ⟩ ≡
#define Extern extern
  ⟨ Header definitions 6 ⟩
  ⟨ Type definitions 11 ⟩
  ⟨ External variables 4 ⟩
  ⟨ External prototypes 9 ⟩
```

6. Subroutines of this program are declared first with a prototype, as in ANSI C, then with an old-style C function definition. The following preprocessor commands make this work correctly with both new-style and old-style compilers.

```
⟨ Header definitions 6 ⟩ ≡
#ifdef __STDC__
#define ARGS(list) list
#else
#define ARGS(list) ()
#endif
```

See also sections 7, 8, 52, 57, 129, and 166.

This code is used in sections 3 and 5.

7. Some of the names that are natural for this program are in conflict with library names on at least one of the host computers in the author's tests. So we bypass the library names here.

⟨ Header definitions 6 ⟩ +≡
```
#define random my_random
#define fsqrt my_fsqrt
#define div my_div
```

8. The amount of verbosity depends on the following bit codes.

⟨ Header definitions 6 ⟩ +≡
```
#define issue_bit (1 << 0)
    /* show control blocks when issued, deissued, committed */
#define pipe_bit (1 << 1) /* show the pipeline and locks on every cycle */
#define coroutine_bit (1 << 2) /* show the coroutines when started on every cycle */
#define schedule_bit (1 << 3) /* show the coroutines when scheduled */
#define uninit_mem_bit (1 << 4)
    /* complain when reading from an uninitialized chunk of memory */
#define interactive_read_bit (1 << 5)
    /* prompt user when reading from I/O location */
#define show_spec_bit (1 << 6)
    /* display special read/write transactions as they happen */
#define show_pred_bit (1 << 7) /* display branch prediction details */
#define show_wholecache_bit (1 << 8)
    /* display cache blocks even when their key tag is invalid */
```

9. The *MMIX_init*( ) routine should be called exactly once, after *MMIX_config*( ) has done its work but before the simulator starts to execute any programs. Then *MMIX_run*( ) can be called as often as the user likes.

⟨ External prototypes 9 ⟩ ≡
```
Extern void MMIX_init ARGS((void));
Extern void MMIX_run ARGS((int cycs, octa breakpoint));
```

See also sections 38, 161, 175, 178, 180, 209, 212, and 252.

This code is used in sections 3 and 5.

__STDC__, Standard C.
MMIX_config: **void** ( ), MMIX-CONFIG §38.
MMIX_init: **void** ( ), §10.
MMIX_run: **void** ( ), §10.
octa = **struct**, §17.

10. ⟨ External routines 10 ⟩ ≡

```
void MMIX_init()
{
  register int i, j;
  ⟨ Initialize everything 22 ⟩;
}

void MMIX_run(cycs, breakpoint)
    int cycs;
    octa breakpoint;
{
  ⟨ Local variables 12 ⟩;
  while (cycs) {
    if (verbose & (issue_bit | pipe_bit | coroutine_bit | schedule_bit))
      printf("***␣Cycle␣%d\n", ticks.l);
    ⟨ Perform one machine cycle 64 ⟩;
    if (verbose & pipe_bit) {
      print_pipe(); print_locks();
    }
    if (breakpoint_hit ∨ halted) {
      if (breakpoint_hit)
        printf("Breakpoint␣instruction␣fetched␣at␣time␣%d\n", ticks.l − 1);
      if (halted) printf("Halted␣at␣time␣%d\n", ticks.l − 1);
      break;
    }
    cycs−−;
  }
cease: ;
}
```

See also sections 39, 162, 176, 179, 181, 210, 213, and 253.

This code is used in section 3.

11. ⟨ Type definitions 11 ⟩ ≡

```
typedef enum {
  false, true, wow
} bool;     /* slightly extended booleans */
```

See also sections 17, 23, 37, 40, 44, 68, 76, 164, 167, 206, 246, and 371.

This code is used in sections 3 and 5.

12. ⟨ Local variables 12 ⟩ ≡

```
register int i, j, m;
bool breakpoint_hit = false;
bool halted = false;
```

See also sections 124 and 258.

This code is used in section 10.

13. Error messages that abort this program are called panic messages. The macro called *confusion* will never be needed unless this program is internally inconsistent.

```
#define errprint0(f) fprintf(stderr,f)
#define errprint1(f,a) fprintf(stderr,f,a)
#define errprint2(f,a,b) fprintf(stderr,f,a,b)
#define panic(x) { errprint0("Panic: "); x; errprint0("!\n"); expire(); }
#define confusion(m) errprint1("This can't happen: %s",m)
```

```
⟨ Internal prototypes 13 ⟩ ≡
  static void expire ARGS((void));
```

See also sections 18, 24, 27, 30, 32, 34, 42, 45, 55, 62, 72, 90, 92, 94, 96, 156, 158, 169, 171, 173, 182, 184, 186, 188, 190, 192, 195, 198, 200, 202, 204, 240, 250, 254, and 377.

This code is used in section 3.

14.
```
⟨ Subroutines 14 ⟩ ≡
  static void expire()      /* the last gasp before dying */
  {
    if (ticks.h) errprint2("(Clock time is %dH+%d.)\n", ticks.h, ticks.l);
    else errprint1("(Clock time is %d.)\n", ticks.l);
    exit(−2);
  }
```

See also sections 19, 21, 25, 28, 31, 33, 35, 43, 46, 56, 63, 73, 91, 93, 95, 97, 157, 159, 170, 172, 174, 183, 185, 187, 189, 191, 193, 196, 199, 201, 203, 205, 208, 241, 251, 255, 378, 379, 381, 384, and 387.

This code is used in section 3.

15. The data structures of this program are not precisely equivalent to logical gates that could be implemented directly in silicon; we will use data structures and algorithms appropriate to the C programming language. For example, we'll use pointers and arrays, instead of buses and ports and latches. However, the net effect of our data structures and algorithms is intended to be equivalent to the net effect of a silicon implementation. The methods used below are essentially equivalent to those used in real machines today, except that diagnostic facilities are added so that we can readily watch what is happening.

Each functional unit in the MMIX pipeline is programmed here as a coroutine in C. At every clock cycle, we will call on each active coroutine to do one phase of its operation; in terms of the repair-station analogy described in the main program, this corresponds to getting each group of auto mechanics to do one unit of operation on a car. The coroutines are performed sequentially, although a real pipeline would have them act in parallel. We will not "cheat" by letting one coroutine access a value early in its cycle that another one computes late in its cycle, unless computer hardware could "cheat" in an equivalent way.

ARGS = macro, §6.
coroutine_bit = 1 ≪ 2, §8.
exit: **void** (), <stdlib.h>.
fprintf: **int** (), <stdio.h>.
h: **tetra**, §17.
issue_bit = 1 ≪ 0, §8.
l: **tetra**, §17.
octa = **struct**, §17.
pipe_bit = 1 ≪ 1, §8.
print_locks: **void** (), §39.
print_pipe: **void** (), §253.
printf: **int** (), <stdio.h>.
schedule_bit = 1 ≪ 3, §8.
stderr: **FILE** *, <stdio.h>.
ticks: **Extern octa**, §87.
verbose: **int**, §4.

16. Low-level routines. Where should we begin? It is tempting to start with a global view of the simulator and then to break it down into component parts. But that task is too daunting, because there are so many unknowns about what basic ingredients ought to be combined when we construct the larger components. So let us look first at the primitive operations on which the superstructure will be built. Once we have created some infrastructure, we'll be able to proceed with confidence to the larger tasks ahead.

17. This program for the 64-bit MMIX architecture is based on 32-bit integer arithmetic, because nearly every computer available to the author at the time of writing (1998–1999) was limited in that way. Details of the basic arithmetic appear in a separate program module called MMIX-ARITH, because the same routines are needed also for the assembler and for the non-pipelined simulator. The definition of type **tetra** should be changed, if necessary, to conform with the definitions found there.

```
⟨ Type definitions 11 ⟩ +≡
  typedef unsigned int tetra;
    /* for systems conforming to the LP-64 data model */
  typedef struct {
    tetra h, l;
  } octa;      /* two tetrabytes make one octabyte */
```

18. ⟨ Internal prototypes 13 ⟩ +≡

```
  static void print_octa ARGS((octa));
```

19. ⟨ Subroutines 14 ⟩ +≡

```
  static void print_octa(o)
        octa o;
  {
    if (o.h) printf("%x%08x", o.h, o.l); else printf("%x", o.l);
  }
```

20. ⟨ Global variables 20 ⟩ ≡

```
  extern octa zero_octa;     /* zero_octa.h = zero_octa.l = 0 */
  extern octa neg_one;     /* neg_one.h = neg_one.l = −1 */
  extern octa aux;     /* auxiliary output of a subroutine */
  extern bool overflow;     /* set by certain subroutines for signed arithmetic */
  extern int exceptions;     /* bits set by floating point operations */
  extern int cur_round;     /* the current rounding mode */
```

See also sections 36, 41, 48, 50, 51, 53, 54, 65, 70, 78, 83, 88, 99, 107, 127, 148, 154, 194, 230, 235, 238, 248, 285, 303, 305, 315, 374, 376, and 388.

This code is used in section 3.

21. Most of the subroutines in MMIX-ARITH return an octabyte as a function of two octabytes; for example, *oplus*(y, z) returns the sum of octabytes y and z. Multiplication returns the high half of a product in the global variable *aux*; division returns the remainder in *aux*.

```
⟨ Subroutines 14 ⟩ +≡
  extern octa oplus ARGS((octa y, octa z));     /* unsigned y + z */
  extern octa ominus ARGS((octa y, octa z));     /* unsigned y − z */
```

```
extern octa incr ARGS((octa y, int delta));   /* unsigned y + δ (δ is signed) */
extern octa oand ARGS((octa y, octa z));   /* y ∧ z */
extern octa oandn ARGS((octa y, octa z));   /* y ∧ z̄ */
extern octa shift_left ARGS((octa y, int s));   /* y ≪ s, 0 ≤ s ≤ 64 */
extern octa shift_right ARGS((octa y, int s, int u));   /* y ≫ s, signed if ¬u */
extern octa omult ARGS((octa y, octa z));   /* unsigned (aux, x) = y × z */
extern octa signed_omult ARGS((octa y, octa z));
  /* signed x = y × z, setting overflow */
extern octa odiv ARGS((octa x, octa y, octa z));
  /* unsigned (x, y)/z; aux = (x, y) mod z */
extern octa signed_odiv ARGS((octa y, octa z));
  /* signed y/z, when z ≠ 0; aux = y mod z */
extern int count_bits ARGS((tetra z));   /* x = ν(z) */
extern tetra byte_diff ARGS((tetra y, tetra z));   /* half of BDIF */
extern tetra wyde_diff ARGS((tetra y, tetra z));   /* half of WDIF */
extern octa bool_mult ARGS((octa y, octa z, bool xor));   /* MOR or MXOR */
extern octa load_sf ARGS((tetra z));   /* load short float */
extern tetra store_sf ARGS((octa x));   /* store short float */
extern octa fplus ARGS((octa y, octa z));   /* floating point x = y ⊕ z */
extern octa fmult ARGS((octa y, octa z));   /* floating point x = y ⊗ z */
extern octa fdivide ARGS((octa y, octa z));   /* floating point x = y ⊘ z */
extern octa froot ARGS((octa, int));   /* floating point x = √z */
extern octa fremstep ARGS((octa y, octa z, int delta));
  /* floating point x rem z = y rem z */
extern octa fintegerize ARGS((octa z, int mode));   /* floating point x = round(z) */
extern int fcomp ARGS((octa y, octa z));
  /* −1, 0, 1, or 2 if y < z, y = z, y > z, y ∥ z */
extern int fepscomp ARGS((octa y, octa z, octa eps, int sim));
  /* x = sim? [y ∼ z (ε)] : [y ≈ z (ε)] */
extern octa floatit ARGS((octa z, int mode, int unsgnd, int shrt));
  /* fix to float */
extern octa fixit ARGS((octa z, int mode));   /* float to fix */
```

ARGS = macro, §6.
aux: **octa**, MMIX-ARITH §4.
bool = **enum**, §11.
bool_mult: **octa** ( ), MMIX-ARITH §29.
byte_diff: **tetra** ( ), MMIX-ARITH §27.
count_bits: **int** ( ), MMIX-ARITH §26.
cur_round: **int**, MMIX-ARITH §30.
exceptions: **int**, MMIX-ARITH §32.
fcomp: **int** ( ), MMIX-ARITH §85.
fdivide: **octa** ( ), MMIX-ARITH §44.
fepscomp: **int** ( ), MMIX-ARITH §50.
fintegerize: **octa** ( ), MMIX-ARITH §86.
fixit: **octa** ( ), MMIX-ARITH §88.
floatit: **octa** ( ), MMIX-ARITH §89.
fmult: **octa** ( ), MMIX-ARITH §41.
fplus: **octa** ( ), MMIX-ARITH §46.
fremstep: **octa** ( ), MMIX-ARITH §93.
froot: **octa** ( ), MMIX-ARITH §91.
incr: **octa** ( ), MMIX-ARITH §6.
load_sf: **octa** ( ), MMIX-ARITH §39.
neg_one: **octa**, MMIX-ARITH §4.
oand: **octa** ( ), MMIX-ARITH §25.
oandn: **octa** ( ), MMIX-ARITH §25.
odiv: **octa** ( ), MMIX-ARITH §13.
ominus: **octa** ( ), MMIX-ARITH §5.
omult: **octa** ( ), MMIX-ARITH §8.
oplus: **octa** ( ), MMIX-ARITH §5.
overflow: **bool**, MMIX-ARITH §4.
printf: **int** ( ), <stdio.h>.
shift_left: **octa** ( ), MMIX-ARITH §7.
shift_right: **octa** ( ), MMIX-ARITH §7.
signed_odiv: **octa** ( ), MMIX-ARITH §24.
signed_omult: **octa** ( ), MMIX-ARITH §12.
store_sf: **tetra** ( ), MMIX-ARITH §40.
wyde_diff: **tetra** ( ), MMIX-ARITH §28.
zero_octa: **octa**, MMIX-ARITH §4.

22. We had better check that our 32-bit assumption holds.

⟨ Initialize everything 22 ⟩ ≡

```
if (shift_left(neg_one, 1).h ≠ #ffffffff)
  panic(errprint0("Incorrect␣implementation␣of␣type␣tetra"));
```

See also sections 26, 61, 71, 79, 89, 116, 128, 153, 231, 236, 249, and 286.

This code is used in section 10.

23. Coroutines. As stated earlier, this program can be regarded as a system of interacting coroutines. Coroutines—sometimes called threads—are more or less independent processes that share and pass data and control back and forth. They correspond to the individual workers in an organization.

We don't need the full power of recursive coroutines, in which new threads are spawned dynamically and have independent stacks for computation; we are, after all, simulating a fixed piece of hardware. The total number of coroutines we deal with is established once and for all by the *MMIX_config* routine, and each coroutine has a fixed amount of local data.

The simulation operates one clock tick at a time, by executing all coroutines scheduled for time t before advancing to time $t+1$. The coroutines at time t may decide to become dormant or they may reschedule themselves and/or other coroutines for future times.

Each coroutine has a symbolic *name* for diagnostic purposes (e.g., `ALU1`); a nonnegative *stage* number (e.g., 2 for the second stage of a pipeline); a pointer to the next coroutine scheduled at the same time (or Λ if the coroutine is unscheduled); a pointer to a lock variable (or Λ if no lock is currently relevant); and a reference to a control block containing the data to be processed.

```
⟨Type definitions 11⟩ +≡
  typedef struct coroutine_struct {
    char *name;    /* symbolic identification of a coroutine */
    int stage;    /* its rank */
    struct coroutine_struct *next;    /* its successor */
    struct coroutine_struct **lockloc;    /* what it might be locking */
    struct control_struct *ctl;    /* its data */
  } coroutine;
```

24.
```
⟨Internal prototypes 13⟩ +≡
  static void print_coroutine_id ARGS((coroutine *));
  static void errprint_coroutine_id ARGS((coroutine *));
```

`ARGS` = macro, §6.
control_struct: **struct**, §44.
errprint0 = macro ( ), §13.
h: **tetra**, §17.
MMIX_config: **void** ( ), MMIX-CONFIG §38.
neg_one: **octa**, MMIX-ARITH §4.
panic = macro ( ), §13.
shift_left: **octa** ( ), MMIX-ARITH §7.

25. ⟨ Subroutines 14 ⟩ +≡

```
static void print_coroutine_id(c)
    coroutine *c;
{
  if (c) printf("%s:%d", c->name, c->stage);
  else printf("??");
}
static void errprint_coroutine_id(c)
    coroutine *c;
{
  if (c) errprint2("%s:%d", c->name, c->stage);
  else errprint0("??");
}
```

26. Coroutine control is masterminded by a ring of queues, one each for times t, $t+1$, ..., $t + ring\_size - 1$, when t is the current clock time.

All scheduling is first-come-first-served, except that coroutines with higher *stage* numbers have priority. We want to process the later stages of a pipeline first, in this sequential implementation, for the same reason that a car must drive from M station into W station before another car can enter M station.

Each queue is a circular list of **coroutine** nodes, linked together by their *next* fields. A list head h with $stage = max\_stage$ comes at the end and the beginning of the queue. (All *stage* numbers of legitimate coroutines are less than *max_stage*.) The queued items are *h→next*, *h→next→next*, etc., from back to front, and we have $c\to stage \le c\to next\to stage$ unless $c = h$.

Initially all queues are empty.

⟨ Initialize everything 22 ⟩ +≡

```
{ register coroutine *p;
  for (p = ring; p < ring + ring_size; p++) p->next = p;
}
```

27. To schedule a coroutine c with positive delay $d < ring\_size$, we call the function *schedule*(c, d, s). (The s parameter is used only if scheduling is being logged; it does not affect the computation, but we will generally set s to the state at which the scheduled coroutine will begin.)

⟨ Internal prototypes 13 ⟩ +≡

```
static void schedule ARGS((coroutine *, int, int));
```

28. ⟨ Subroutines 14 ⟩ +≡

```
static void schedule(c, d, s)
    coroutine *c;
    int d, s;
{
  register int tt = (cur_time + d) % ring_size;
  register coroutine *p = &ring[tt];   /* start at the list head */
  if (d ≤ 0 ∨ d ≥ ring_size)   /* do a sanity check */
    panic(confusion("Scheduling␣"); errprint_coroutine_id(c);
        errprint1("␣with␣delay␣%d", d));
```

```
    while (p->next->stage < c->stage) p = p->next;
    c->next = p->next;
    p->next = c;
    if (verbose & schedule_bit) {
      printf(" scheduling "); print_coroutine_id(c);
      printf(" at time %d, state %d\n", ticks.l + d, s);
    }
  }
```

29. ⟨ External variables 4 ⟩ +≡

```
  Extern int ring_size;    /* set by MMIX_config, must be sufficiently large */
  Extern coroutine *ring;
  Extern int cur_time;
```

30. The all-important *ctl* field of a coroutine, which contains the data being manipulated, will be explained below. One of its key components is the *state* field, which helps to specify the next actions the coroutine will perform. When we schedule a coroutine for a new task, we often want it to begin in state 0.

⟨ Internal prototypes 13 ⟩ +≡

```
  static void startup ARGS((coroutine *, int));
```

31. ⟨ Subroutines 14 ⟩ +≡

```
  static void startup(c, d)
      coroutine *c;
      int d;
  {
    c->ctl->state = 0;
    schedule(c, d, 0);
  }
```

ARGS = macro, §6.
confusion = macro ( ), §13.
coroutine = **struct**, §23.
ctl: **control** *, §23.
errprint0 = macro ( ), §13.
errprint1 = macro ( ), §13.
errprint2 = macro ( ), §13.
Extern = macro, §4.
l: **tetra**, §17.
max_stage = 99, §129.
MMIX_config: **void** ( ), MMIX-CONFIG §38.
name: **char** *, §23.
next: **coroutine** *, §23.
panic = macro ( ), §13.
printf: **int** ( ), <stdio.h>.
schedule_bit = 1 ≪ 3, §8.
stage: **int**, §23.
state: **int**, §44.
ticks: **Extern octa**, §87.
verbose: **int**, §4.

32. The following routine removes a coroutine from whatever queue it's in. The case $c\to next = c$ is also permitted; such a self-loop can occur when a coroutine goes to sleep and expects to be awakened (that is, scheduled) by another coroutine. Sleeping coroutines have important data in their *ctl* field; they are therefore quite different from unscheduled or "unemployed" coroutines, which have $c\to next = \Lambda$. An unemployed coroutine is not assumed to have any valid data in its *ctl* field.

```
⟨ Internal prototypes 13 ⟩ +≡
  static void unschedule ARGS((coroutine *));
```

33. ⟨ Subroutines 14 ⟩ +≡

```
  static void unschedule(c)
      coroutine *c;
  { register coroutine *p;
    if (c→next) {
      for (p = c; p→next ≠ c; p = p→next) ;
      p→next = c→next;
      c→next = Λ;
      if (verbose & schedule_bit) {
        printf("␣unscheduling␣"); print_coroutine_id(c); printf("\n");
      }
    }
  }
```

34. When it is time to process all coroutines that have queued up for a particular time t, we empty the queue called $ring[t]$ and link its items in the opposite order (from front to back). The following subroutine uses the well known algorithm discussed in exercise 2.2.3–7 of *The Art of Computer Programming*.

```
⟨ Internal prototypes 13 ⟩ +≡
  static coroutine *queuelist ARGS((int));
```

35. ⟨ Subroutines 14 ⟩ +≡

```
  static coroutine *queuelist(t)
      int t;
  { register coroutine *p, *q = &sentinel, *r;
    for (p = ring[t].next; p ≠ &ring[t]; p = r) {
      r = p→next;
      p→next = q;
      q = p;
    }
    ring[t].next = &ring[t];
    sentinel.next = q;
    return q;
  }
```

36. ⟨ Global variables 20 ⟩ +≡

```
  coroutine sentinel;    /* dummy coroutine at origin of circular list */
```

37. Coroutines often start working on tasks that are *speculative*, in the sense that we want certain results to be ready if they prove to be useful; we understand that speculative computations might not actually be needed. Therefore a coroutine might need to be aborted before it has finished its work.

All coroutines must be written in such a way that important data structures remain intact even when the coroutine is abruptly terminated. In particular, we need to be sure that "locks" on shared resources are restored to an unlocked state when a coroutine holding the lock is aborted.

A **lockvar** variable is Λ when it is unlocked; otherwise it points to the coroutine responsible for unlocking it.

```
#define set_lock(c, l)
        { l = c; (c)→lockloc = &(l); }
#define release_lock(c, l)
        { l = Λ; (c)→lockloc = Λ; }
```

⟨Type definitions 11⟩ +≡

```
  typedef coroutine *lockvar;
```

38. ⟨External prototypes 9⟩ +≡

```
  Extern void print_locks ARGS((void));
```

39. ⟨External routines 10⟩ +≡

```
  void print_locks()
  {
    print_cache_locks(ITcache);
    print_cache_locks(DTcache);
    print_cache_locks(Icache);
    print_cache_locks(Dcache);
    print_cache_locks(Scache);
    if (mem_lock) printf("mem locked by %s:%d\n", mem_lock→name, mem_lock→stage);
    if (dispatch_lock)
      printf("dispatch locked by %s:%d\n", dispatch_lock→name, dispatch_lock→stage);
    if (wbuf_lock) printf("head of write buffer locked by %s:%d\n", wbuf_lock→name,
          wbuf_lock→stage);
    if (clean_lock)
      printf("cleaner locked by %s:%d\n", clean_lock→name, clean_lock→stage);
    if (speed_lock) printf("write buffer flush locked by %s:%d\n", speed_lock→name,
          speed_lock→stage);
  }
```

ARGS = macro, §6.
clean_lock: **lockvar**, §230.
coroutine = **struct**, §23.
ctl: **control** *, §23.
Dcache: **cache** *, §168.
dispatch_lock: **lockvar**, §65.
DTcache: **cache** *, §168.
Extern = macro, §4.
Icache: **cache** *, §168.
ITcache: **cache** *, §168.
lockloc: **coroutine** **, §23.
mem_lock: **lockvar**, §214.
name: **char** *, §23.
next: **coroutine** *, §23.
print_cache_locks: **static void** (), §174.
print_coroutine_id: **static void** (), §25.
printf: **int** (), <stdio.h>.
ring: **coroutine** *, §29.
Scache: **cache** *, §168.
schedule_bit = 1 ≪ 3, §8.
speed_lock: **lockvar**, §247.
stage: **int**, §23.
verbose: **int**, §4.
wbuf_lock: **lockvar**, §247.

40. Many of the quantities we deal with are speculative values that might not yet have been certified as part of the "real" calculation; in fact, they might not yet have been calculated.

A **spec** consists of a 64-bit quantity o and a pointer p to a **specnode**. The value o is meaningful only if the pointer p is Λ; otherwise p points to a source of further information.

A **specnode** is a 64-bit quantity o together with links to other **specnode**s that are above it or below it in a doubly linked list. An additional *known* bit tells whether the o field has been calculated. There also is a 64-bit *addr* field, to identify the list and give further information. A **specnode** list keeps track of speculative values related to a specific register or to all of main memory; we will discuss such lists in detail later.

```
⟨ Type definitions 11 ⟩ +≡
  typedef struct {
    octa o;
    struct specnode_struct *p;
  } spec;

  typedef struct specnode_struct {
    octa o;
    bool known;
    octa addr;
    struct specnode_struct *up, *down;
  } specnode;
```

41. ⟨ Global variables 20 ⟩ +≡

```
  spec zero_spec;    /* zero_spec.o.h = zero_spec.o.l = 0 and zero_spec.p = Λ */
```

42. ⟨ Internal prototypes 13 ⟩ +≡

```
  static void print_spec ARGS((spec));
```

43. ⟨ Subroutines 14 ⟩ +≡

```
  static void print_spec(s)
      spec s;
  {
    if (¬s.p) print_octa(s.o);
    else {
      printf(">"); print_specnode_id(s.p→addr);
    }
  }

  static void print_specnode(s)
      specnode s;
  {
    if (s.known) { print_octa(s.o); printf("!"); }
    else if (s.o.h ∨ s.o.l) { print_octa(s.o); printf("?"); }
    else printf("?");
    print_specnode_id(s.addr);
  }
```

ARGS = macro, §6.
bool = **enum**, §11.
h: **tetra**, §17.
l: **tetra**, §17.
octa = **struct**, §17.
print_octa: **static void** ( ), §19.
print_specnode_id: **static void** ( ), §91.
printf: **int** ( ), <stdio.h>.

44. The analog of an automobile in our simulator is a block of data called **control**, which represents all the relevant facts about an `MMIX` instruction. We can think of it as the work order attached to a car's windshield. Each group of employees updates the work order as the car moves through the shop.

A **control** record contains the original location of an instruction, and its four bytes OP X Y Z. An instruction has up to four inputs, which are **spec** records called y, z, b and ra; it also has up to three outputs, which are **specnode** records called x, a, and rl. (We usually don't mention the special input ra or the special output rl, which refer to `MMIX`'s internal registers rA and rL.) For example, the main inputs to a `DIVU` command are \$Y, \$Z, and rD; the outputs are the quotient \$X and the remainder rR. The inputs to a `STO` command are \$Y, \$Z, and \$X; there is one "output," and the field $x.addr$ will be set to the physical address of the memory location corresponding to virtual address \$Y + \$Z.

Each **control** block also points to the coroutine that owns it, if any. And it has various other fields that contain other tidbits of information; for example, we have already mentioned the *state* field, which often governs a coroutine's actions. The i field, which contains an internal operation code number, is generally used together with *state* to switch between alternative computational steps. If, for example, the *op* field is `SUB` or `SUBI` or `NEG` or `NEGI`, the internal opcode i will be simply *sub*. We shall define all the fields of **control** records now and discuss them later.

An actual hardware implementation of `MMIX` wouldn't need all the information we are putting into a **control** block. Some of that information would typically be latched between stages of a pipeline; other portions would probably appear in so-called "rename registers." We simulate rename registers only indirectly, by counting how many registers of that kind would be in use if we were mimicking low-level hardware details more precisely. The *go* field is a **specnode** for convenience in programming, although we use only its *known* and *o* subfields. It generally contains the address of the subsequent instruction.

```
⟨Type definitions 11⟩ +≡
  ⟨Declare mmix_opcode and internal_opcode 47⟩
  typedef struct control_struct {
    octa loc;   /* virtual address where an instruction originated */
    mmix_opcode op; unsigned char xx, yy, zz;
      /* the original instruction bytes */
    spec y, z, b, ra;   /* inputs */
    specnode x, a, go, rl;   /* outputs */
    coroutine *owner;   /* a coroutine whose ctl this is */
    internal_opcode i;   /* internal opcode */
    int state;   /* internal mindset */
    bool usage;   /* should rU be increased? */
    bool need_b;   /* should we stall until b.p ≡ Λ? */
    bool need_ra;   /* should we stall until ra.p ≡ Λ? */
    bool ren_x;   /* does x correspond to a rename register? */
    bool mem_x;   /* does x correspond to a memory write? */
    bool ren_a;   /* does a correspond to a rename register? */
    bool set_l;   /* does rl correspond to a new value of rL? */
```

```
  bool interim;      /* does this instruction need to be reissued on interrupt? */
  bool stack_alert;     /* is there potential for stack overflow? */
  unsigned int arith_exc;      /* arithmetic exceptions for event bits of rA */
  unsigned int hist;     /* history bits for use in branch prediction */
  int denin, denout;     /* execution time penalties for subnormal handling */
  octa cur_O, cur_S;     /* speculative rO and rS before this instruction */
  unsigned int interrupt;      /* does this instruction generate an interrupt? */
  void *ptr_a, *ptr_b, *ptr_c;      /* generic pointers for miscellaneous use */
} control;
```

addr: **octa**, §40.
bool = **enum**, §11.
coroutine = **struct**, §23.
ctl: **control** ∗, §23.
internal_opcode = **enum**, §49.
known: **bool**, §40.
mmix_opcode = **enum**, §47.
o: **octa**, §40.
octa = **struct**, §17.
p: **specnode** ∗, §40.
spec = **struct**, §40.
specnode = **struct**, §40.
sub = 31, §49.

45. ⟨ Internal prototypes 13 ⟩ +≡

```
static void print_control_block ARGS((control *));
```

46. ⟨ Subroutines 14 ⟩ +≡

```
static void print_control_block(c)
    control *c;
{
  octa default_go;
  if (c→loc.h ∨ c→loc.l ∨ c→op ∨ c→xx ∨ c→yy ∨ c→zz ∨ c→owner) {
    print_octa(c→loc);
    printf(":␣%02x%02x%02x%02x(%s)", c→op, c→xx, c→yy, c→zz, internal_op_name[c→i]);
  }
  if (c→usage) printf("*");
  if (c→interim) printf("+");
  if (c→y.o.h ∨ c→y.o.l ∨ c→y.p) { printf("␣y="); print_spec(c→y); }
  if (c→z.o.h ∨ c→z.o.l ∨ c→z.p) { printf("␣z="); print_spec(c→z); }
  if (c→b.o.h ∨ c→b.o.l ∨ c→b.p ∨ c→need_b) {
    printf("␣b="); print_spec(c→b);
    if (c→need_b) printf("*");
  }
  if (c→need_ra) { printf("␣rA="); print_spec(c→ra); }
  if (c→ren_x ∨ c→mem_x) { printf("␣x="); print_specnode(c→x); }
  else if (c→x.o.h ∨ c→x.o.l) {
    printf("␣x="); print_octa(c→x.o); printf("%c", c→x.known ? '!' : '?');
  }
  if (c→ren_a) { printf("␣a="); print_specnode(c→a); }
  if (c→set_l) { printf("␣rL="); print_specnode(c→rl); }
  if (c→interrupt) { printf("␣int="); print_bits(c→interrupt); }
  if (c→arith_exc) { printf("␣exc="); print_bits(c→arith_exc ≪ 8); }
  default_go = incr(c→loc, 4);
  if (c→go.o.l ≠ default_go.l ∨ c→go.o.h ≠ default_go.h) {
    printf("␣->"); print_octa(c→go.o);
  }
  if (verbose & show_pred_bit) printf("␣hist=%x", c→hist);
  if (c→i ≡ pop) {
    printf("␣rS=");
    print_octa(c→cur_S);
    printf("␣rO=");
    print_octa(c→cur_O);
  }
  printf("␣state=%d", c→state);
}
```

47. Lists. Here is a (boring) list of all the MMIX opcodes, in order.

⟨ Declare **mmix_opcode** and **internal_opcode** 47 ⟩ ≡

```
typedef enum {
  TRAP,FCMP,FUN,FEQL,FADD,FIX,FSUB,FIXU,
  FLOT,FLOTI,FLOTU,FLOTUI,SFLOT,SFLOTI,SFLOTU,SFLOTUI,
  FMUL,FCMPE,FUNE,FEQLE,FDIV,FSQRT,FREM,FINT,
  MUL,MULI,MULU,MULUI,DIV,DIVI,DIVU,DIVUI,
  ADD,ADDI,ADDU,ADDUI,SUB,SUBI,SUBU,SUBUI,
  IIADDU,IIADDUI,IVADDU,IVADDUI,VIIIADDU,VIIIADDUI,XVIADDU,XVIADDUI,
  CMP,CMPI,CMPU,CMPUI,NEG,NEGI,NEGU,NEGUI,
  SL,SLI,SLU,SLUI,SR,SRI,SRU,SRUI,
  BN,BNB,BZ,BZB,BP,BPB,BOD,BODB,
  BNN,BNNB,BNZ,BNZB,BNP,BNPB,BEV,BEVB,
  PBN,PBNB,PBZ,PBZB,PBP,PBPB,PBOD,PBODB,
  PBNN,PBNNB,PBNZ,PBNZB,PBNP,PBNPB,PBEV,PBEVB,
  CSN,CSNI,CSZ,CSZI,CSP,CSPI,CSOD,CSODI,
  CSNN,CSNNI,CSNZ,CSNZI,CSNP,CSNPI,CSEV,CSEVI,
  ZSN,ZSNI,ZSZ,ZSZI,ZSP,ZSPI,ZSOD,ZSODI,
  ZSNN,ZSNNI,ZSNZ,ZSNZI,ZSNP,ZSNPI,ZSEV,ZSEVI,
  LDB,LDBI,LDBU,LDBUI,LDW,LDWI,LDWU,LDWUI,
  LDT,LDTI,LDTU,LDTUI,LDO,LDOI,LDOU,LDOUI,
  LDSF,LDSFI,LDHT,LDHTI,CSWAP,CSWAPI,LDUNC,LDUNCI,
  LDVTS,LDVTSI,PRELD,PRELDI,PREGO,PREGOI,GO,GOI,
  STB,STBI,STBU,STBUI,STW,STWI,STWU,STWUI,
  STT,STTI,STTU,STTUI,STO,STOI,STOU,STOUI,
  STSF,STSFI,STHT,STHTI,STCO,STCOI,STUNC,STUNCI,
  SYNCD,SYNCDI,PREST,PRESTI,SYNCID,SYNCIDI,PUSHGO,PUSHGOI,
  OR,ORI,ORN,ORNI,NOR,NORI,XOR,XORI,
  AND,ANDI,ANDN,ANDNI,NAND,NANDI,NXOR,NXORI,
  BDIF,BDIFI,WDIF,WDIFI,TDIF,TDIFI,ODIF,ODIFI,
  MUX,MUXI,SADD,SADDI,MOR,MORI,MXOR,MXORI,
  SETH,SETMH,SETML,SETL,INCH,INCMH,INCML,INCL,
  ORH,ORMH,ORML,ORL,ANDNH,ANDNMH,ANDNML,ANDNL,
  JMP,JMPB,PUSHJ,PUSHJB,GETA,GETAB,PUT,PUTI,
  POP,RESUME,SAVE,UNSAVE,SYNC,SWYM,GET,TRIP
} mmix_opcode;
```

See also section 49.

This code is used in section 44.

48. ⟨ Global variables 20 ⟩ +≡

```
char *opcode_name[] = {"TRAP","FCMP","FUN","FEQL","FADD","FIX","FSUB","FIXU",
"FLOT","FLOTI","FLOTU","FLOTUI","SFLOT","SFLOTI","SFLOTU","SFLOTUI",
"FMUL","FCMPE","FUNE","FEQLE","FDIV","FSQRT","FREM","FINT",
"MUL","MULI","MULU","MULUI","DIV","DIVI","DIVU","DIVUI",
"ADD","ADDI","ADDU","ADDUI","SUB","SUBI","SUBU","SUBUI",
"2ADDU","2ADDUI","4ADDU","4ADDUI","8ADDU","8ADDUI","16ADDU","16ADDUI",
"CMP","CMPI","CMPU","CMPUI","NEG","NEGI","NEGU","NEGUI",
"SL","SLI","SLU","SLUI","SR","SRI","SRU","SRUI",
"BN","BNB","BZ","BZB","BP","BPB","BOD","BODB",
"BNN","BNNB","BNZ","BNZB","BNP","BNPB","BEV","BEVB",
"PBN","PBNB","PBZ","PBZB","PBP","PBPB","PBOD","PBODB",
"PBNN","PBNNB","PBNZ","PBNZB","PBNP","PBNPB","PBEV","PBEVB",
"CSN","CSNI","CSZ","CSZI","CSP","CSPI","CSOD","CSODI",
"CSNN","CSNNI","CSNZ","CSNZI","CSNP","CSNPI","CSEV","CSEVI",
"ZSN","ZSNI","ZSZ","ZSZI","ZSP","ZSPI","ZSOD","ZSODI",
"ZSNN","ZSNNI","ZSNZ","ZSNZI","ZSNP","ZSNPI","ZSEV","ZSEVI",
"LDB","LDBI","LDBU","LDBUI","LDW","LDWI","LDWU","LDWUI",
"LDT","LDTI","LDTU","LDTUI","LDO","LDOI","LDOU","LDOUI",
"LDSF","LDSFI","LDHT","LDHTI","CSWAP","CSWAPI","LDUNC","LDUNCI",
"LDVTS","LDVTSI","PRELD","PRELDI","PREGO","PREGOI","GO","GOI",
"STB","STBI","STBU","STBUI","STW","STWI","STWU","STWUI",
"STT","STTI","STTU","STTUI","STO","STOI","STOU","STOUI",
"STSF","STSFI","STHT","STHTI","STCO","STCOI","STUNC","STUNCI",
"SYNCD","SYNCDI","PREST","PRESTI","SYNCID","SYNCIDI","PUSHGO","PUSHGOI",
"OR","ORI","ORN","ORNI","NOR","NORI","XOR","XORI",
"AND","ANDI","ANDN","ANDNI","NAND","NANDI","NXOR","NXORI",
"BDIF","BDIFI","WDIF","WDIFI","TDIF","TDIFI","ODIF","ODIFI",
"MUX","MUXI","SADD","SADDI","MOR","MORI","MXOR","MXORI",
"SETH","SETMH","SETML","SETL","INCH","INCMH","INCML","INCL",
"ORH","ORMH","ORML","ORL","ANDNH","ANDNMH","ANDNML","ANDNL",
"JMP","JMPB","PUSHJ","PUSHJB","GETA","GETAB","PUT","PUTI",
"POP","RESUME","SAVE","UNSAVE","SYNC","SWYM","GET","TRIP"};
```

49. And here is a (likewise boring) list of all the internal opcodes. The smallest numbers, less than or equal to *max_pipe_op*, correspond to operations for which arbitrary pipeline delays can be configured with *MMIX_config*. The largest numbers, greater than *max_real_command*, correspond to internally generated operations that have no official OP code; for example, there are internal operations to shift the γ pointer in the register stack, and to compute page table entries.

```
⟨ Declare mmix_opcode and internal_opcode 47 ⟩ +≡
#define max_pipe_op feps
#define max_real_command trip
  typedef enum {
    mul0,    /* multiplication by zero */
    mul1, mul2, mul3, mul4, mul5, mul6, mul7, mul8,
      /* multiplication by 1–8, 9–16, ..., 57–64 bits */
    div,    /* DIV[U][I] */
    sh,    /* S[L,R][U][I] */
    mux,    /* MUX[I] */
    sadd,    /* SADD[I] */
    mor,    /* M[X]OR[I] */
    fadd,    /* FADD, FSUB */
    fmul,    /* FMUL */
    fdiv,    /* FDIV */
    fsqrt,    /* FSQRT */
    fint,    /* FINT */
    fix,    /* FIX[U] */
    flot,    /* [S]FLOT[U][I] */
    feps,    /* FCMPE, FUNE, FEQLE */
    fcmp,    /* FCMP */
    funeq,    /* FUN, FEQL */
    fsub,    /* FSUB */
    frem,    /* FREM */
    mul,    /* MUL[I] */
    mulu,    /* MULU[I] */
    divu,    /* DIVU[I] */
    add,    /* ADD[I] */
    addu,    /* [2,4,8,16,]ADDU[I], INC[M][H,L] */
    sub,    /* SUB[I], NEG[I] */
    subu,    /* SUBU[I], NEGU[I] */
    set,    /* SET[M][H,L], GETA[B] */
    or,    /* OR[I], OR[M][H,L] */
    orn,    /* ORN[I] */
    nor,    /* NOR[I] */
    and,    /* AND[I] */
    andn,    /* ANDN[I], ANDN[M][H,L] */
    nand,    /* NAND[I] */
    xor,    /* XOR[I] */
    nxor,    /* NXOR[I] */
    shlu,    /* SLU[I] */
    shru,    /* SRU[I] */
```

```
  shl,   /* SL[I] */
  shr,   /* SR[I] */
  cmp,   /* CMP[I] */
  cmpu,   /* CMPU[I] */
  bdif,   /* BDIF[I] */
  wdif,   /* WDIF[I] */
  tdif,   /* TDIF[I] */
  odif,   /* ODIF[I] */
  zset,   /* ZS[N][N,Z,P][I], ZSEV[I], ZSOD[I] */
  cset,   /* CS[N][N,Z,P][I], CSEV[I], CSOD[I] */
  get,   /* GET */
  put,   /* PUT[I] */
  ld,   /* LD[B,W,T,O][U][I], LDHT[I], LDSF[I] */
  ldptp,   /* load page table pointer */
  ldpte,   /* load page table entry */
  ldunc,   /* LDUNC[I] */
  ldvts,   /* LDVTS[I] */
  preld,   /* PRELD[I] */
  prest,   /* PREST[I] */
  st,   /* STO[U][I], STCO[I], STUNC[I] */
  syncd,   /* SYNCD[I] */
  syncid,   /* SYNCID[I] */
  pst,   /* ST[B,W,T][U][I], STHT[I] */
  stunc,   /* STUNC[I], in write buffer */
  cswap,   /* CSWAP[I] */
  br,   /* B[N][N,Z,P][B] */
  pbr,   /* PB[N][N,Z,P][B] */
  pushj,   /* PUSHJ[B] */
  go,   /* GO[I] */
  prego,   /* PREGO[I] */
  pushgo,   /* PUSHGO[I] */
  pop,   /* POP */
  resume,   /* RESUME */
  save,   /* SAVE */
  unsave,   /* UNSAVE */
  sync,   /* SYNC */
  jmp,   /* JMP[B] */
  noop,   /* SWYM */
  trap,   /* TRAP */
  trip,   /* TRIP */
  incgamma,   /* increase γ pointer */
  decgamma,   /* decrease γ pointer */
  incrl,   /* increase rL and β */
  sav,   /* intermediate stage of SAVE */
  unsav,   /* intermediate stage of UNSAVE */
  resum   /* intermediate stage of RESUME */
} internal_opcode;
```

MMIX_config: **void** (), MMIX-CONFIG §38.

50. ⟨ Global variables 20 ⟩ +≡

```
char *internal_op_name[] = {"mul0", "mul1", "mul2", "mul3", "mul4", "mul5", "mul6",
    "mul7", "mul8", "div", "sh", "mux", "sadd", "mor", "fadd", "fmul", "fdiv",
    "fsqrt", "fint", "fix", "flot", "feps", "fcmp", "funeq", "fsub", "frem", "mul",
    "mulu", "divu", "add", "addu", "sub", "subu", "set", "or", "orn", "nor", "and",
    "andn", "nand", "xor", "nxor", "shlu", "shru", "shl", "shr", "cmp", "cmpu",
    "bdif", "wdif", "tdif", "odif", "zset", "cset", "get", "put", "ld", "ldptp",
    "ldpte", "ldunc", "ldvts", "preld", "prest", "st", "syncd", "syncid", "pst",
    "stunc", "cswap", "br", "pbr", "pushj", "go", "prego", "pushgo", "pop", "resume",
    "save", "unsave", "sync", "jmp", "noop", "trap", "trip", "incgamma", "decgamma",
    "incrl", "sav", "unsav", "resum"};
```

51. We need a table to convert the external opcodes to internal ones.

⟨ Global variables 20 ⟩ +≡

```
internal_opcode internal_op[256] = {
trap, fcmp, funeq, funeq, fadd, fix, fsub, fix,
flot, flot, flot, flot, flot, flot, flot, flot,
fmul, feps, feps, feps, fdiv, fsqrt, frem, fint,
mul, mul, mulu, mulu, div, div, divu, divu,
add, add, addu, addu, sub, sub, subu, subu,
addu, addu, addu, addu, addu, addu, addu, addu,
cmp, cmp, cmpu, cmpu, sub, sub, subu, subu,
shl, shl, shlu, shlu, shr, shr, shru, shru,
br, br, br, br, br, br, br, br,
br, br, br, br, br, br, br, br,
pbr, pbr, pbr, pbr, pbr, pbr, pbr, pbr,
pbr, pbr, pbr, pbr, pbr, pbr, pbr, pbr,
cset, cset, cset, cset, cset, cset, cset, cset,
cset, cset, cset, cset, cset, cset, cset, cset,
zset, zset, zset, zset, zset, zset, zset, zset,
zset, zset, zset, zset, zset, zset, zset, zset,
ld, ld, ld, ld, ld, ld, ld, ld,
ld, ld, ld, ld, ld, ld, ld, ld,
ld, ld, ld, ld, cswap, cswap, ldunc, ldunc,
ldvts, ldvts, preld, preld, prego, prego, go, go,
pst, pst, pst, pst, pst, pst, pst, pst,
pst, pst, pst, pst, st, st, st, st,
pst, pst, pst, pst, st, st, st, st,
syncd, syncd, prest, prest, syncid, syncid, pushgo, pushgo,
or, or, orn, orn, nor, nor, xor, xor,
and, and, andn, andn, nand, nand, nxor, nxor,
bdif, bdif, wdif, wdif, tdif, tdif, odif, odif,
mux, mux, sadd, sadd, mor, mor, mor, mor,
set, set, set, set, addu, addu, addu, addu,
or, or, or, or, andn, andn, andn, andn,
jmp, jmp, pushj, pushj, set, set, put, put,
pop, resume, save, unsave, sync, noop, get, trip};
```

52. While we're into boring lists, we might as well define all the special register numbers, together with an inverse table for use in diagnostic outputs. These codes have been designed so that special registers 0–7 are unencumbered, 9–11 can't be `PUT` by anybody, 8 and 12–18 can't be `PUT` by the user. Pipeline delays might occur when `GET` is applied to special registers 21–31 or when `PUT` is applied to special registers 8 or 15–20. The `SAVE` and `UNSAVE` commands store and restore special registers 0–6 and 23–27.

⟨ Header definitions 6 ⟩ +≡

```
#define rA 21   /* arithmetic status register */
#define rB 0    /* bootstrap register (trip) */
#define rC 8    /* continuation register */
#define rD 1    /* dividend register */
#define rE 2    /* epsilon register */
#define rF 22   /* failure location register */
#define rG 19   /* global threshold register */
#define rH 3    /* himult register */
#define rI 12   /* interval counter */
#define rJ 4    /* return-jump register */
#define rK 15   /* interrupt mask register */
#define rL 20   /* local threshold register */
#define rM 5    /* multiplex mask register */
#define rN 9    /* serial number */
#define rO 10   /* register stack offset */
#define rP 23   /* prediction register */
#define rQ 16   /* interrupt request register */
#define rR 6    /* remainder register */
#define rS 11   /* register stack pointer */
#define rT 13   /* trap address register */
#define rU 17   /* usage counter */
#define rV 18   /* virtual translation register */
#define rW 24   /* where-interrupted register (trip) */
#define rX 25   /* execution register (trip) */
#define rY 26   /* Y operand (trip) */
#define rZ 27   /* Z operand (trip) */
#define rBB 7   /* bootstrap register (trap) */
#define rTT 14  /* dynamic trap address register */
#define rWW 28  /* where-interrupted register (trap) */
#define rXX 29  /* execution register (trap) */
#define rYY 30  /* Y operand (trap) */
#define rZZ 31  /* Z operand (trap) */
```

53. ⟨ Global variables 20 ⟩ +≡

```
char *special_name[32] = {"rB", "rD", "rE", "rH", "rJ", "rM", "rR", "rBB", "rC", "rN",
    "rO", "rS", "rI", "rT", "rTT", "rK", "rQ", "rU", "rV", "rG", "rL", "rA", "rF", "rP",
    "rW", "rX", "rY", "rZ", "rWW", "rXX", "rYY", "rZZ"};
```

54. Here are the bit codes that affect trips and traps. The first eight cases also apply to the upper half of rQ; the next eight apply to rA.

```
#define P_BIT (1 << 0)   /* instruction in privileged location */
```

```
#define S_BIT (1 << 1)   /* security violation */
#define B_BIT (1 << 2)   /* instruction breaks the rules */
#define K_BIT (1 << 3)   /* instruction for kernel only */
#define N_BIT (1 << 4)   /* virtual translation bypassed */
#define PX_BIT (1 << 5)   /* permission lacking to execute from page */
#define PW_BIT (1 << 6)   /* permission lacking to write on page */
#define PR_BIT (1 << 7)   /* permission lacking to read from page */
#define PROT_OFFSET 5   /* distance from PR_BIT to protection code position */
#define X_BIT (1 << 8)   /* floating inexact */
#define Z_BIT (1 << 9)   /* floating division by zero */
#define U_BIT (1 << 10)   /* floating underflow */
#define O_BIT (1 << 11)   /* floating overflow */
#define I_BIT (1 << 12)   /* floating invalid operation */
#define W_BIT (1 << 13)   /* float-to-fix overflow */
#define V_BIT (1 << 14)   /* integer overflow */
#define D_BIT (1 << 15)   /* integer divide check */
#define H_BIT (1 << 16)   /* trip handler bit */
#define F_BIT (1 << 17)   /* forced trap bit */
#define E_BIT (1 << 18)   /* external (dynamic) trap bit */
⟨Global variables 20⟩ +≡
  char bit_code_map[] = "EFHDVWIOUZXrwxnkbsp";
```

55. ⟨Internal prototypes 13⟩ +≡

```
  static void print_bits ARGS((int));
```

56. ⟨Subroutines 14⟩ +≡

```
  static void print_bits(x)
      int x;
  {
    register int b, j;
    for (j = 0, b = E_BIT; (x & (b + b − 1)) ∧ b; j++, b >>= 1)
      if (x & b) printf("%c", bit_code_map[j]);
  }
```

57. The lower half of rQ holds external interrupts of highest priority. Most of them are implementation-dependent, but a few are defined in general.

```
⟨Header definitions 6⟩ +≡
#define POWER_FAILURE (1 << 0)   /* try to shut down calmly and quickly */
#define PARITY_ERROR (1 << 1)   /* try to save the file systems */
#define NONEXISTENT_MEMORY (1 << 2)   /* a memory address can't be used */
#define REBOOT_SIGNAL (1 << 4)   /* it's time to start over */
#define INTERVAL_TIMEOUT (1 << 6)   /* the timer register, rI, has reached zero */
#define STACK_OVERFLOW (1 << 7)   /* data has been stored on the rC page */
```

ARGS = macro, §6. *printf*: **int** ( ), <stdio.h>.

58. Dynamic speculation. Now that we understand some basic low-level structures, we're ready to look at the larger picture.

This simulator is based on the idea of "dynamic scheduling with register renaming," as introduced in the 1960s by R. M. Tomasulo [*IBM Journal of Research and Development* **11** (1967), 25–33]. Moreover, the dynamic scheduling method is extended here to "speculative execution," as implemented in several processors of the 1990s and described in section 4.6 of Hennessy and Patterson's *Computer Architecture*, second edition (1995). The essential idea is to keep track of the pipeline contents by recording all dependencies between unfinished computations in a queue called the *reorder buffer*. An entry in the reorder buffer might, for example, correspond to an instruction that adds together two numbers whose values are still being computed; those numbers have been allocated space in earlier positions of the reorder buffer. The addition will take place as soon as both of its operands are known, but the sum won't be written immediately into the destination register. It will stay in the reorder buffer until reaching the *hot seat* at the front of the queue. Finally, the addition leaves the hot seat and is said to be *committed*.

Some instructions in the reorder buffer may in fact be executed only on speculation, meaning that they won't really be called for unless a prior branch instruction has the predicted outcome. Indeed, we can say that all instructions not yet in the hot seat are being executed speculatively, because an external interrupt might occur at any time and change the entire course of computation. Organizing the pipeline as a reorder buffer allows us to look ahead and keep busy computing values that have a good chance of being needed later, instead of waiting for slow instructions or slow memory references to be completed.

The reorder buffer is in fact a queue of **control** records, conceptually forming part of a circle of such records inside the simulator, corresponding to all instructions that have been dispatched or *issued* but not yet committed, in strict program order.

The best way to get an understanding of speculative execution is perhaps to imagine that the reorder buffer is large enough to hold hundreds of instructions in various stages of execution, and to think of an implementation of `MMIX` that has dozens of functional units—more than would ever actually be built into a chip. Then one can readily visualize the kinds of control structures and checks that must be made to ensure correct execution. Without such a broad viewpoint, a programmer or hardware designer will be inclined to think only of the simple cases and to devise algorithms that lack the proper generality. Thus we have a somewhat paradoxical situation in which a difficult general problem turns out to be easier to solve than its simpler special cases, because it enforces clarity of thinking.

Instructions that have completed execution and have not yet been committed are analogous to cars that have gone through our hypothetical repair shop and are waiting for their owners to pick them up. However, all analogies break down, and the world of automobiles does not have a natural counterpart for the notion of speculative execution. That notion corresponds roughly to situations in which people are led to believe that their cars need a new piece of equipment, but they suddenly change their mind once they see the price tag, and they insist on having the equipment removed even after it has been partially or completely installed.

Speculatively executed instructions might make no sense: They might divide by zero or refer to protected memory areas, etc. Such anomalies are not considered catastrophic or even exceptional until the instruction reaches the hot seat.

The person who designs a computer with speculative execution is an optimist, who has faith that the vast majority of the machine's predictions will come true. The person who designs a reliable implementation of such a computer is a pessimist, who understands that all predictions might come to naught. The pessimist does, however, take pains to optimize the cases that do turn out well.

59. Let's consider what happens to a single instruction, say `ADD $1,$2,$3`, as it travels through the pipeline in a normal situation. The first time this instruction is encountered, it is placed into the I-cache (that is, the instruction cache), so that we won't have to access memory when we need to perform it again. We will assume for simplicity in this discussion that each I-cache access takes one clock cycle, although other possibilities are allowed by *MMIX_config*.

Suppose the simulated machine fetches the example `ADD` instruction at time 1000. Fetching is done by a coroutine whose *stage* number is 0. A cache block typically contains 8 or 16 instructions. The fetch unit of our machine is able to fetch up to *fetch_max* instructions on each clock cycle and place them in the fetch buffer, provided that there is room in the buffer and that all the instructions belong to the same cache block.

The dispatch unit of our simulator is able to issue up to *dispatch_max* instructions on each clock cycle and move them from the fetch buffer to the reorder buffer, provided that functional units are available for those instructions and there is room in the reorder buffer. A functional unit that handles `ADD` is usually called an ALU (arithmetic logic unit), and our simulated machine might have several of them. If they aren't all stalled in stage 1 of their pipelines, and if the reorder buffer isn't full, and if the machine isn't in the process of deissuing instructions that were mispredicted, and if fewer than *dispatch_max* instructions are ahead of the `ADD` in the fetch buffer, and if all such prior instructions can be issued without using up all the free ALUs, our `ADD` instruction will be issued at time 1001. (In fact, all of these conditions are usually true.)

We assume that $\mathrm{L} > 3$, so that \$1, \$2, and \$3 are local registers. For simplicity we'll assume in fact that the register stack is empty, so that the `ADD` instruction is supposed to set $\mathrm{l}[1] \leftarrow \mathrm{l}[2] + \mathrm{l}[3]$. The operands l[2] and l[3] might not be known at time 1001; they are **spec** values, which might point to **specnode** entries in the reorder buffer for previous instructions whose destinations are l[2] and l[3]. The dispatcher fills the next available control block of the reorder buffer with information for the `ADD`, containing appropriate **spec** values corresponding to l[2] and l[3] in its y and z fields. The x field of this control block will be inserted into a doubly linked list of **specnode** records, corresponding to l[1] and to all instructions in the reorder buffer that have l[1] as a destination. The boolean value $x.known$ will be set to *false*, meaning that this speculative value still needs to be computed. Subsequent instructions that need l[1] as a source will point to x, if they are issued before the sum $x.o$ has been computed. Double linking is used in the **specnode** list because the `ADD` instruction might be cancelled before it is finally committed; thus deletions might occur at either end of the list for l[1].

At time 1002, the ALU handling the `ADD` will stall if its inputs y and z are not both known (namely if $y.p \neq \Lambda$ or $z.p \neq \Lambda$). In fact, it will also stall if its third input rA is not known; the current speculative value of rA, except for its event bits, is represented in the *ra* field of the control block, and we must have $ra.p \equiv \Lambda$. In such a case the ALU will look to see if the **spec** values pointed to by $y.p$ and/or $z.p$ and/or $ra.p$ become defined on this clock cycle, and it will update its own input values accordingly.

But let's assume that y, z, and ra are already known at time 1002. Then $x.o$ will be set to $y.o + z.o$ and $x.known$ will become *true*. This will make the result destined for l[1] available to be used in other commands at time 1003.

If no overflow occurs when adding $y.o$ to $z.o$, the *interrupt* and *arith_exc* fields of the control block for `ADD` are set to zero. But when overflow does occur (shudder), there are two cases, based on the V-enable bit of rA, which is found in field $b.o$ of the control block. If this bit is 0, the V-bit of the *arith_exc* field in the control block is set to 1; the *arith_exc* field will be ored into rA when the `ADD` instruction is eventually committed. But if the V-enable bit is 1, the trip handler should be called, interrupting the normal sequence. In such a case, the *interrupt* field of the control block is set to specify a trip, and the fetcher and dispatcher are told to forget what they have been doing; all instructions following the `ADD` in the reorder buffer must now be deissued. The virtual starting address of the overflow trip handler, namely location 32, is hastily passed to the fetch routine, and instructions will be fetched from that location as soon as possible. (Of course the overflow and the trip handler are still speculative until the `ADD` instruction is committed. Other exceptional conditions might cause the `ADD` itself to be terminated before it gets to the hot seat. But the pipeline keeps charging ahead, always trying to guess the most probable outcome.)

The commission unit of this simulator is able to commit and/or deissue up to *commit_max* instructions on each clock cycle. With luck, fewer than *commit_max* instructions will be ahead of our `ADD` instruction at time 1003, and they will all be completed normally. Then l[1] can be set to $x.o$, and the event bits of rA can be updated from *arith_exc*, and the `ADD` command can pass through the hot seat and out of the reorder buffer.

```
⟨ External variables 4 ⟩ +≡
  Extern int fetch_max, dispatch_max, peekahead, commit_max;
    /* limits on instructions that can be handled per clock cycle */
```

---

arith_exc: **unsigned int**, §44.
b: **spec**, §44.
Extern = macro, §4.
false = 0, §11.
interrupt: **unsigned int**, §44.
known: **bool**, §40.
MMIX_config: **void** (), MMIX-CONFIG §38.
o: **octa**, §40.
p: **specnode** *, §40.
ra: **spec**, §44.
stage: **int**, §23.
true = 1, §11.
x: **specnode**, §44.
y: **spec**, §44.
z: **spec**, §44.

60. The instruction currently occupying the hot seat is the only issued-but-not-yet-committed instruction that is guaranteed to be truly essential to the machine's computation. All other instructions in the reorder buffer are being executed on speculation; if they prove to be needed, well and good, but we might want to jettison them all if, say, an external interrupt occurs.

Thus all instructions that change the global state in complicated ways—like `LDVTS`, which changes the virtual address translation caches—are performed only when they reach the hot seat. Fortunately the vast majority of instructions are sufficiently simple that we can deal with them more efficiently while other computations are taking place.

In this implementation the reorder buffer is simply housed in an array of control records. The first array element is *reorder_bot*, and the last is *reorder_top*. Variable *hot* points to the control block in the hot seat, and $hot - 1$ to its predecessor, etc. Variable *cool* points to the next control block that will be filled in the reorder buffer. If $hot \equiv cool$ the reorder buffer is empty; otherwise it contains the control records hot, $hot - 1$, ..., $cool + 1$, except of course that we wrap around from *reorder_bot* to *reorder_top* when moving down in the buffer.

```
⟨External variables 4⟩ +≡
  Extern control *reorder_bot, *reorder_top;
    /* least and greatest entries in the ring containing the reorder buffer */
  Extern control *hot, *cool;    /* front and rear of the reorder buffer */
  Extern control *old_hot;    /* value of hot at beginning of cycle */
  Extern int deissues;    /* the number of instructions that need to be deissued */
```

61. ⟨Initialize everything 22⟩ +≡

```
  hot = cool = reorder_top; deissues = 0;
```

62. ⟨Internal prototypes 13⟩ +≡

```
  static void print_reorder_buffer ARGS((void));
```

63. ⟨Subroutines 14⟩ +≡

```
  static void print_reorder_buffer()
  {
    printf("Reorder␣buffer");
    if (hot ≡ cool) printf("␣(empty)\n");
    else { register control *p;
      if (deissues) printf("␣(%d␣to␣be␣deissued)", deissues);
      if (doing_interrupt) printf("␣(interrupt␣state␣%d)", doing_interrupt);
      printf(":\n");
      for (p = hot; p ≠ cool; p = (p ≡ reorder_bot ? reorder_top : p − 1)) {
        print_control_block(p);
        if (p→owner) {
          printf("␣"); print_coroutine_id(p→owner);
        }
        printf("\n");
      }
    }
    printf("␣%d␣available␣rename␣register%s,␣%d␣memory␣slot%s\n", rename_regs,
        rename_regs ≠ 1 ? "s" : "", mem_slots, mem_slots ≠ 1 ? "s" : "");
  }
```

64. Here is an overview of what happens on each clock cycle.

```
⟨ Perform one machine cycle 64 ⟩ ≡
  {
    ⟨ Check for external interrupt 314 ⟩;
    dispatch_count = 0;
    old_hot = hot;      /* remember the hot seat position at beginning of cycle */
    old_tail = tail;    /* remember the fetch buffer contents at beginning of cycle */
    suppress_dispatch = (deissues ∨ dispatch_lock);
    if (doing_interrupt) ⟨ Perform one cycle of the interrupt preparations 318 ⟩
    else ⟨ Commit and/or deissue up to commit_max instructions 67 ⟩;
    ⟨ Execute all coroutines scheduled for the current time 125 ⟩;
    if (¬suppress_dispatch) ⟨ Dispatch one cycle's worth of instructions 74 ⟩;
    ticks = incr(ticks, 1);    /* and the beat moves on */
    dispatch_stat[dispatch_count]++;
  }
```

This code is used in section 10.

65. ⟨ Global variables 20 ⟩ +≡

```
  int dispatch_count;      /* how many dispatched on this cycle */
  bool suppress_dispatch;      /* should dispatching be bypassed? */
  int doing_interrupt;      /* how many cycles of interrupt preparations remain */
  lockvar dispatch_lock;      /* lock to prevent instruction issues */
```

66. ⟨ External variables 4 ⟩ +≡

```
  Extern int *dispatch_stat;      /* how often did we dispatch 0, 1, ... instructions? */
  Extern bool security_disabled;      /* omit security checks for testing purposes? */
```

ARGS = macro, §6.
bool = **enum**, §11.
commit_max: **int**, §59.
control = **struct**, §44.
Extern = macro, §4.
incr: **octa** ( ), MMIX-ARITH §6.
lockvar = **coroutine** ∗, §37.
mem_slots: **int**, §86.
old_tail: **fetch** ∗, §70.
owner: **coroutine** ∗, §44.
print_control_block: **static void** ( ), §46.
print_coroutine_id: **static void** ( ), §25.
printf: **int** ( ), <stdio.h>.
rename_regs: **int**, §86.
tail: **fetch** ∗, §69.
ticks: **Extern octa**, §87.

67. ⟨ Commit and/or deissue up to *commit_max* instructions 67 ⟩ ≡

```
{
  for (m = commit_max; m > 0 ∧ deissues > 0; m--)
    ⟨ Deissue the coolest instruction 145 ⟩;
  for ( ; m > 0; m--) {
    if (hot ≡ cool) break;     /* reorder buffer is empty */
    if (¬security_disabled) ⟨ Check for security violation, break if so 149 ⟩;
    if (hot→owner) break;     /* hot seat instruction isn't finished */
    ⟨ Commit the hottest instruction, or break if it's not ready 146 ⟩;
    i = hot→i;
    if (hot ≡ reorder_bot) hot = reorder_top;
    else hot--;
    if (i ≡ resum) break;     /* allow the resumed instruction to see the new rK */
  }
}
```

This code is used in section 64.

68. The dispatch stage. It would be nice to present the parts of this simulator by dealing with the fetching, dispatching, executing, and committing stages in that order. After all, instructions are first fetched, then dispatched, then executed, and finally committed. However, the fetch stage depends heavily on difficult questions of memory management that are best deferred until we have looked at the simpler parts of simulation. Therefore we will take our initial plunge into the details of this program by looking first at the dispatch phase, assuming that instructions have somehow appeared magically in the fetch buffer.

The fetch buffer, like the circular priority queue of all coroutines and the circular queue used for the reorder buffer, lives in an array that is best regarded as a ring of elements. The elements are structures of type **fetch**, which have five fields: A 32-bit *inst*, which is an MMIX instruction; a 64-bit *loc*, which is the virtual address of that instruction; an *interrupt* field, which is nonzero if, for example, the protection bits in the relevant page table entry for this address do not permit execution access; a boolean *noted* field, which becomes *true* after the dispatch unit has peeked at the instruction to see whether it is a jump or probable branch; and a *hist* field, which records the recent branch history. (The least significant bits of *hist* correspond to the most recent branches.)

```
⟨ Type definitions 11 ⟩ +≡
  typedef struct {
    octa loc;    /* virtual address of instruction */
    tetra inst;    /* the instruction itself */
    unsigned int interrupt;    /* bit codes that might cause interruption */
    bool noted;    /* have we peeked at this instruction? */
    unsigned int hist;    /* if we peeked, this was the peek_hist */
  } fetch;
```

69. The oldest and youngest entries in the fetch buffer are pointed to by *head* and *tail*, just as the oldest and youngest entries in the reorder buffer are called *hot* and *cool*. The fetch coroutine will be adding entries at the *tail* position, which starts at *old_tail* when a cycle begins, in parallel with the actions simulated by the dispatcher. Therefore the dispatcher is allowed to look only at instructions in *head*, $head - 1$, ..., $old\_tail + 1$, although a few more recently fetched instructions will usually be present in the fetch buffer by the time this part of the program is executed.

```
⟨ External variables 4 ⟩ +≡
  Extern fetch *fetch_bot, *fetch_top;
    /* least and greatest entries in the ring containing the fetch buffer */
  Extern fetch *head, *tail;    /* front and rear of the fetch buffer */
```

---

bool = **enum**, §11.
commit_max: **int**, §59.
cool: **control** ∗, §60.
deissues: **int**, §60.
Extern = macro, §4.
hot: **control** ∗, §60.
i: **internal_opcode**, §44.
i: **register int**, §12.
m: **register int**, §12.
octa = **struct**, §17.
old_tail: **fetch** ∗, §70.
owner: **coroutine** ∗, §44.
peek_hist: **unsigned int**, §99.
reorder_bot: **control** ∗, §60.
reorder_top: **control** ∗, §60.
resum = 89, §49.
security_disabled: **bool**, §66.
tetra = **unsigned int**, §17.
true = 1, §11.

70. ⟨ Global variables 20 ⟩ +≡

```
fetch *old_tail;    /* rear of the fetch buffer available on the current cycle */
```

71.

```
#define UNKNOWN_SPEC ((specnode *) 1)
```

⟨ Initialize everything 22 ⟩ +≡

```
head = tail = fetch_top;
inst_ptr.p = UNKNOWN_SPEC;
```

72. ⟨ Internal prototypes 13 ⟩ +≡

```
static void print_fetch_buffer ARGS((void));
```

73. ⟨ Subroutines 14 ⟩ +≡

```
static void print_fetch_buffer()
{
  printf("Fetch␣buffer");
  if (head ≡ tail) printf("␣(empty)\n");
  else { register fetch *p;
    if (resuming) printf("␣(resumption␣state␣%d)", resuming);
    printf(":\n");
    for (p = head; p ≠ tail; p = (p ≡ fetch_bot ? fetch_top : p − 1)) {
      print_octa(p→loc);
      printf(":␣%08x(%s)", p→inst, opcode_name[p→inst ≫ 24]);
      if (p→interrupt) print_bits(p→interrupt);
      if (p→noted) printf("*");
      printf("\n");
    }
  }
  printf("Instruction␣pointer␣is␣");
  if (inst_ptr.p ≡ Λ) print_octa(inst_ptr.o);
  else {
    printf("waiting␣for␣");
    if (inst_ptr.p ≡ UNKNOWN_SPEC) printf("dispatch");
    else if (inst_ptr.p→addr.h ≡ (tetra) −1)
      print_coroutine_id(((control *) inst_ptr.p→up)→owner);
    else print_specnode_id(inst_ptr.p→addr);
  }
  printf("\n");
}
```

74. The best way to understand the dispatching process is once again to "think big," by imagining a huge fetch buffer and the potential ability to issue dozens of instructions per cycle, although the actual numbers are typically quite small.

If the fetch buffer is not empty after *dispatch_max* instructions have been dispatched, the dispatcher also looks at up to *peekahead* further instructions to see if they are jumps or other commands that change the flow of control. Much of this action would happen in parallel on a real machine, but our simulator works sequentially.

In the following program, *true_head* records the head of the fetch buffer as instructions are actually dispatched, while *head* refers to the position currently being examined (possibly peeking into the future).

If the fetch buffer is empty at the beginning of the current clock cycle, a "dispatch bypass" allows the dispatcher to issue the first instruction that enters the fetch buffer on this cycle. Otherwise the dispatcher is restricted to previously fetched instructions.

⟨ Dispatch one cycle's worth of instructions 74 ⟩ ≡
  { **register fetch** *$*true\_head$, $*new\_head$;
    $true\_head = head$;
    if ($head \equiv old\_tail \land head \neq tail$) $old\_tail = (head \equiv fetch\_bot\ ?\ fetch\_top : head - 1)$;
    $peek\_hist = cool\_hist$;
    for ($j = 0$; $j < dispatch\_max + peekahead$; j++)
      ⟨ Look at the *head* instruction, and try to dispatch it if $j < dispatch\_max$ 75 ⟩;
    $head = true\_head$;
  }

This code is used in section 64.

addr: **octa**, §40.
ARGS = macro, §6.
control = **struct**, §44.
cool_hist: **unsigned int**, §99.
dispatch_max: **int**, §59.
fetch = **struct**, §68.
fetch_bot: **fetch** *, §69.
fetch_top: **fetch** *, §69.
h: **tetra**, §17.
head: **fetch** *, §69.
inst: **tetra**, §68.
inst_ptr: **spec**, §284.
interrupt: **unsigned int**, §68.
j: **register int**, §12.
loc: **octa**, §68.
noted: **bool**, §68.
o: **octa**, §40.
opcode_name: **char** *[], §48.
owner: **coroutine** *, §44.
p: **specnode** *, §40.
peek_hist: **unsigned int**, §99.
peekahead: **int**, §59.
print_bits: **static void** ( ), §56.
print_coroutine_id: **static void** ( ), §25.
print_octa: **static void** ( ), §19.
print_specnode_id: **static void** ( ), §91.
printf: **int** ( ), <stdio.h>.
resuming: **int**, §78.
specnode = **struct**, §40.
tail: **fetch** *, §69.
tetra = **unsigned int**, §17.
up: **specnode** *, §40.

75. ⟨ Look at the *head* instruction, and try to dispatch it if $j < dispatch\_max$ 75 ⟩ ≡

```
{
  register mmix_opcode op;
  register int yz, f;
  register bool freeze_dispatch = false;
  register func *u = Λ;
  if (head ≡ old_tail) break;     /* fetch buffer empty */
  if (head ≡ fetch_bot) new_head = fetch_top; else new_head = head - 1;
  op = head→inst ≫ 24; yz = head→inst & #ffff;
  ⟨ Determine the flags, f, and the internal opcode, i 80 ⟩;
  ⟨ Install default fields in the cool block 100 ⟩;
  if (f & rel_addr_bit) ⟨ Convert relative address to absolute address 84 ⟩;
  if (head→noted) peek_hist = head→hist;
  else ⟨ Redirect the fetch if control changes at this inst 85 ⟩;
  if (j ≥ dispatch_max ∨ dispatch_lock ∨ nullifying) {
    head = new_head; continue;     /* can't dispatch, but can peek ahead */
  }
  if (cool ≡ reorder_bot) new_cool = reorder_top; else new_cool = cool - 1;
  ⟨ Dispatch an instruction to the cool block if possible, otherwise goto stall 101 ⟩;
  ⟨ Assign a functional unit if available, otherwise goto stall 82 ⟩;
  ⟨ Check for sufficient rename registers and memory slots, or goto stall 111 ⟩;
  if ((op & #e0) ≡ #40) ⟨ Record the result of branch prediction 152 ⟩;
  ⟨ Issue the cool instruction 81 ⟩;
  cool = new_cool; cool_O = new_O; cool_S = new_S;
  cool_hist = peek_hist; continue;
stall: ⟨ Undo data structures set prematurely in the cool block and break 123 ⟩;
}
```

This code is used in section 74.

76. An instruction can be dispatched only if a functional unit is available to handle it. A functional unit consists of a 256-bit vector that specifies a subset of MMIX's opcodes, and an array of coroutines for the pipeline stages. There are k coroutines in the array, where k is the maximum number of stages needed by any of the opcodes supported.

```
⟨ Type definitions 11 ⟩ +≡
typedef struct func_struct {
  char name[16];     /* symbolic designation */
  tetra ops[8];     /* big-endian bitmap for the opcodes supported */
  int k;     /* number of pipeline stages */
  coroutine *co;     /* pointer to the first of k consecutive coroutines */
} func;
```

77. ⟨ External variables 4 ⟩ +≡

```
Extern func *funit;     /* pointer to array of functional units */
Extern int funit_count;     /* the number of functional units */
```

78. It is convenient to have a 256-bit vector of all the supported opcodes, because we need to shut off a lot of special actions when an opcode is not supported.

```
⟨ Global variables 20 ⟩ +≡
  control *new_cool;   /* the reorder position following cool */
  int resuming;   /* set nonzero if resuming an interrupted instruction */
  tetra support[8];   /* big-endian bitmap for all opcodes supported */
```

79.

```
⟨ Initialize everything 22 ⟩ +≡
  { register func *u;
    for (u = funit; u ≤ funit + funit_count; u++)
      for (i = 0; i < 8; i++) support[i] |= u→ops[i];
  }
```

80.

```
#define sign_bit ((unsigned) #80000000)

⟨ Determine the flags, f, and the internal opcode, i 80 ⟩ ≡
  if (¬(support[op ≫ 5] & (sign_bit ≫ (op & 31)))) {
      /* oops, this opcode isn't supported by any functional unit */
    f = flags[TRAP], i = trap;
  } else f = flags[op], i = internal_op[op];
  if (i ≡ trip ∧ (head→loc.h & sign_bit)) f = 0, i = noop;
```

This code is used in section 75.

---

bool = **enum**, §11.
control = **struct**, §44.
cool: **control** ∗, §60.
cool_hist: **unsigned int**, §99.
cool_O: **octa**, §98.
cool_S: **octa**, §98.
coroutine = **struct**, §23.
dispatch_lock: **lockvar**, §65.
dispatch_max: **int**, §59.
Extern = macro, §4.
false = 0, §11.
fetch_bot: **fetch** ∗, §69.
fetch_top: **fetch** ∗, §69.
flags: **unsigned char** [], §83.
h: **tetra**, §17.
head: **fetch** ∗, §69.
hist: **unsigned int**, §68.
i: **register int**, §12.
i: **register int**, §10.
inst: **tetra**, §68.
internal_op: **internal_opcode** [], §51.
j: **register int**, §12.
loc: **octa**, §68.
mmix_opcode = **enum**, §47.
new_head: **register fetch** ∗, §74.
new_O: **octa**, §99.
new_S: **octa**, §99.
noop = 81, §49.
noted: **bool**, §68.
nullifying: **bool**, §315.
old_tail: **fetch** ∗, §70.
peek_hist: **unsigned int**, §99.
rel_addr_bit = #40, §83.
reorder_bot: **control** ∗, §60.
reorder_top: **control** ∗, §60.
tetra = **unsigned int**, §17.
trap = 82, §49.
TRAP = #00, §47.
trip = 83, §49.

81. ⟨ Issue the *cool* instruction 81 ⟩ ≡

```
if (cool→interim) {
  cool→usage = false;
  if (cool→op ≡ SAVE) ⟨ Get ready for the next step of SAVE 341 ⟩
  else if (cool→op ≡ UNSAVE) ⟨ Get ready for the next step of UNSAVE 335 ⟩
  else if (cool→i ≡ preld ∨ cool→i ≡ prest)
    ⟨ Get ready for the next step of PRELD or PREST 228 ⟩
  else if (cool→i ≡ prego) ⟨ Get ready for the next step of PREGO 229 ⟩
}
else if (cool→i ≤ max_real_command) {
  if ((flags[cool→op] & ctl_change_bit) ∨ cool→i ≡ pbr)
    if (inst_ptr.p ≡ Λ ∧ (inst_ptr.o.h & sign_bit) ∧ ¬(cool→loc.h & sign_bit) ∧ cool→i ≠ trap)
      cool→interrupt |= P_BIT;     /* jumping from nonnegative to negative */
  true_head = head = new_head;     /* delete instruction from fetch buffer */
  resuming = 0;
}
if (freeze_dispatch) set_lock(u→co, dispatch_lock);
cool→owner = u→co; u→co→ctl = cool;
startup(u→co, 1);     /* schedule execution of the new inst */
if (verbose & issue_bit) {
  printf("Issuing␣"); print_control_block(cool);
  printf("␣"); print_coroutine_id(u→co); printf("\n");
}
dispatch_count++;
```

This code is used in section 75.

82. We assign the first functional unit that supports *op* and is totally unoccupied, if possible; otherwise we assign the first functional unit that supports *op* and has stage 1 unoccupied.

⟨ Assign a functional unit if available, otherwise **goto** *stall* 82 ⟩ ≡

```
{ register int t = op ≫ 5, b = sign_bit ≫ (op & 31);
  if (cool→i ≡ trap ∧ op ≠ TRAP) {     /* opcode needs to be emulated */
    u = funit + funit_count;     /* this unit supports just TRIP and TRAP */
    goto unit_found;
  }
  for (u = funit; u ≤ funit + funit_count; u++)
    if (u→ops[t] & b) {
      for (i = 0; i < u→k; i++)
        if (u→co[i].next) goto unit_busy;
      goto unit_found;
    unit_busy: ;
    }
  for (u = funit; u < funit + funit_count; u++)
    if ((u→ops[t] & b) ∧ (u→co→next ≡ Λ)) goto unit_found;
  goto stall;     /* all units for this op are busy */
}
unit_found:
```

This code is used in section 75.

co: **coroutine** $*$, §76.
cool: **control** $*$, §60.
ctl: **control** $*$, §23.
ctl_change_bit = #80, §83.
dispatch_count: **int**, §65.
dispatch_lock: **lockvar**, §65.
false = 0, §11.
flags: **unsigned char** [ ], §83.
freeze_dispatch: **register bool**, §75.
funit: **func** $*$, §77.
funit_count: **int**, §77.
h: **tetra**, §17.
head: **fetch** $*$, §69.
i: **internal_opcode**, §44.
i: **register int**, §12.
inst_ptr: **spec**, §284.
interim: **bool**, §44.
interrupt: **unsigned int**, §44.
issue_bit = $1 \ll 0$, §8.
k: **int**, §76.
loc: **octa**, §44.
max_real_command = *trip*, §49.
new_head: **register fetch** $*$, §74.
next: **coroutine** $*$, §23.
o: **octa**, §40.
op: **mmix_opcode**, §44.
op: **register mmix_opcode**, §75.
ops: **tetra** [ ], §76.
owner: **coroutine** $*$, §44.
p: **specnode** $*$, §40.
`P_BIT` = $1 \ll 0$, §54.
pbr = 70, §49.
prego = 73, §49.
preld = 61, §49.
prest = 62, §49.
print_control_block: **static void** ( ), §46.
print_coroutine_id: **static void** ( ), §25.
printf: **int** ( ), <stdio.h>.
resuming: **int**, §78.
`SAVE` = #fa, §47.
set_lock = macro ( ), §37.
sign_bit = macro, §80.
stall: label, §75.
startup: **static void** ( ), §31.
trap = 82, §49.
`TRAP` = #00, §47.
true_head: **register fetch** $*$, §74.
u: **register func** $*$, §75.
`UNSAVE` = #fb, §47.
usage: **bool**, §44.
verbose: **int**, §4.

83. The *flags* table records special properties of each operation code in binary notation: #1 means Z is an immediate value, #2 means rZ is a source operand, #4 means Y is an immediate value, #8 means rY is a source operand, #10 means rX is a source operand, #20 means rX is a destination, #40 means YZ is part of a relative address, #80 means the control changes at this point.

```
#define X_is_dest_bit #20
#define rel_addr_bit #40
#define ctl_change_bit #80
⟨ Global variables 20 ⟩ +≡
  unsigned char flags[256] = {#8a, #2a, #2a, #2a, #2a, #26, #2a, #26,        /* TRAP, ... */
    #26, #25, #26, #25, #26, #25, #26, #25,       /* FLOT, ... */
    #2a, #2a, #2a, #2a, #2a, #26, #2a, #26,       /* FMUL, ... */
    #2a, #29, #2a, #29, #2a, #29, #2a, #29,       /* MUL, ... */
    #2a, #29, #2a, #29, #2a, #29, #2a, #29,       /* ADD, ... */
    #2a, #29, #2a, #29, #2a, #29, #2a, #29,       /* 2ADDU, ... */
    #2a, #29, #2a, #29, #26, #25, #26, #25,       /* CMP, ... */
    #2a, #29, #2a, #29, #2a, #29, #2a, #29,       /* SL, ... */
    #50, #50, #50, #50, #50, #50, #50, #50,       /* BN, ... */
    #50, #50, #50, #50, #50, #50, #50, #50,       /* BNN, ... */
    #50, #50, #50, #50, #50, #50, #50, #50,       /* PBN, ... */
    #50, #50, #50, #50, #50, #50, #50, #50,       /* PBNN, ... */
    #3a, #39, #3a, #39, #3a, #39, #3a, #39,       /* CSN, ... */
    #3a, #39, #3a, #39, #3a, #39, #3a, #39,       /* CSNN, ... */
    #2a, #29, #2a, #29, #2a, #29, #2a, #29,       /* ZSN, ... */
    #2a, #29, #2a, #29, #2a, #29, #2a, #29,       /* ZSNN, ... */
    #2a, #29, #2a, #29, #2a, #29, #2a, #29,       /* LDB, ... */
    #2a, #29, #2a, #29, #2a, #29, #2a, #29,       /* LDT, ... */
    #2a, #29, #2a, #29, #3a, #39, #2a, #29,       /* LDSF, ... */
    #2a, #29, #0a, #09, #0a, #09, #aa, #a9,       /* LDVTS, ... */
    #1a, #19, #1a, #19, #1a, #19, #1a, #19,       /* STB, ... */
    #1a, #19, #1a, #19, #1a, #19, #1a, #19,       /* STT, ... */
    #1a, #19, #1a, #19, #0a, #09, #1a, #19,       /* STSF, ... */
    #0a, #09, #0a, #09, #0a, #09, #aa, #a9,       /* SYNCD, ... */
    #2a, #29, #2a, #29, #2a, #29, #2a, #29,       /* OR, ... */
    #2a, #29, #2a, #29, #2a, #29, #2a, #29,       /* AND, ... */
    #2a, #29, #2a, #29, #2a, #29, #2a, #29,       /* BDIF, ... */
    #2a, #29, #2a, #29, #2a, #29, #2a, #29,       /* MUX, ... */
    #20, #20, #20, #20, #30, #30, #30, #30,       /* SETH, ... */
    #30, #30, #30, #30, #30, #30, #30, #30,       /* ORH, ... */
    #c0, #c0, #e0, #e0, #60, #60, #02, #01,       /* JMP, ... */
    #80, #80, #00, #02, #01, #00, #20, #8a};      /* POP, ... */
```

84. ⟨ Convert relative address to absolute address 84 ⟩ ≡

```
{
  if (i ≡ jmp) yz = head→inst & #ffffff;
  if (op & 1) yz −= (i ≡ jmp ? #1000000 : #10000);
  cool→y.o = incr(head→loc, 4), cool→y.p = Λ;
  cool→z.o = incr(head→loc, yz ≪ 2), cool→z.p = Λ;
}
```

This code is used in section 75.

85. The location of the next instruction to be fetched is in a **spec** variable called *inst_ptr*. A slightly tricky optimization of the POP instruction is made in the common case that the speculative value of rJ is known.

⟨ Redirect the fetch if control changes at this inst 85 ⟩ ≡

```
{ register int predicted = 0;
  if ((op & #e0) ≡ #40) ⟨ Predict a branch outcome 151 ⟩;
  head→noted = true;
  head→hist = peek_hist;
  if (predicted ∨ (f & ctl_change_bit) ∨ (i ≡ syncid ∧ ¬(cool→loc.h & sign_bit))) {
    old_tail = tail = new_head;   /* discard all remaining fetches */
    ⟨ Restart the fetch coroutine 287 ⟩;
    switch (i) {
    case jmp: case br: case pbr: case pushj: inst_ptr = cool→z; break;
    case pop: if (g[rJ].up→known ∧ j < dispatch_max ∧ ¬dispatch_lock ∧ ¬nullifying) {
        inst_ptr.o = incr(g[rJ].up→o, yz ≪ 2), inst_ptr.p = Λ; break;
      }   /* otherwise fall through, will wait on cool→go */
    case go: case pushgo: case trap: case resume: case syncid:
      inst_ptr.p = UNKNOWN_SPEC; break;
    case trip: inst_ptr = zero_spec; break;
    }
  }
}
```

This code is used in section 75.

---

br = 69, §49.
cool: **control** ∗, §60.
dispatch_lock: **lockvar**, §65.
dispatch_max: **int**, §59.
f: **register int**, §75.
g: **specnode** [ ], §86.
go = 72, §49.
go: **specnode**, §44.
h: **tetra**, §17.
head: **fetch** ∗, §69.
hist: **unsigned int**, §68.
i: **register int**, §12.
incr: **octa** ( ), MMIX-ARITH §6.
inst: **tetra**, §68.
inst_ptr: **spec**, §284.
j: **register int**, §12.
jmp = 80, §49.
known: **bool**, §40.
loc: **octa**, §68.
loc: **octa**, §44.
new_head: **register fetch** ∗, §74.
noted: **bool**, §68.
nullifying: **bool**, §315.
o: **octa**, §40.
old_tail: **fetch** ∗, §70.
op: **register mmix_opcode**, §75.
p: **specnode** ∗, §40.
pbr = 70, §49.
peek_hist: **unsigned int**, §99.
pop = 75, §49.
pushgo = 74, §49.
pushj = 71, §49.
resume = 76, §49.
rJ = 4, §52.
sign_bit = macro, §80.
syncid = 65, §49.
tail: **fetch** ∗, §69.
trap = 82, §49.
trip = 83, §49.
true = 1, §11.
UNKNOWN_SPEC = macro, §71.
up: **specnode** ∗, §40.
y: **spec**, §44.
yz: **register int**, §75.
z: **spec**, §44.
zero_spec: **spec**, §41.

86. At any given time the simulated machine is in two main states, the "hot state" corresponding to instructions that have been committed and the "cool state" corresponding to all the speculative changes currently being considered. The dispatcher works with cool instructions and puts them into the reorder buffer, where they gradually get warmer and warmer. Intermediate instructions, between *hot* and *cool*, have intermediate temperatures.

A machine register like l[101] or g[250] is represented by a specnode whose *o* field is the current hot value of the register. If the *up* and *down* fields of this specnode point to the node itself, the hot and cool values of the register are identical. Otherwise *up* and *down* are pointers to the coolest and hottest ends of a doubly linked list of specnodes, representing intermediate speculative values (sometimes called "rename registers"). The rename registers are implemented as the *x* or *a* specnodes inside control blocks, for speculative instructions that use this register as a destination. Speculative instructions that use the register as a source operand point to the next-hottest specnode on the list, until the value becomes known. The doubly linked list of specnodes is an input-restricted deque: A node is inserted at the cool end when the dispatcher issues an instruction with this register as destination; a node is removed from the cool end if an instruction needs to be deissued; a node is removed from the hot end when an instruction is committed.

The special registers rA, rB, ... occupy the same array as the global registers g[32], g[33], ... For example, rB is internally the same as g[0], because $rB = 0$.

⟨ External variables 4 ⟩ +≡
```
Extern specnode g[256];   /* global registers and special registers */
Extern specnode *l;   /* the ring of local registers */
Extern int lring_size;
  /* the number of on-chip local registers (must be a power of 2) */
Extern int max_rename_regs, max_mem_slots;   /* capacity of reorder buffer */
Extern int rename_regs, mem_slots;   /* currently unused capacity */
```

87. Special register rC was the clock in the original definition of MMIX. But now the clock is just an external variable, called *ticks*.

⟨ External variables 4 ⟩ +≡
```
Extern octa ticks;   /* the internal clock */
```

88. ⟨ Global variables 20 ⟩ +≡
```
int lring_mask;   /* for calculations modulo lring_size */
```

89. The *addr* fields in the specnode lists for registers are used to identify that register in diagnostic messages. Such addresses are negative; memory addresses are positive.

All registers are initially zero except rG, which is initially 255, and rN, which has a constant value identifying the time of compilation. (The macro ABSTIME is defined externally in the file abstime.h, which should have just been created by ABSTIME; ABSTIME is a trivial program that computes the value of the standard library function *time*(Λ). We assume that this number, which is the number of seconds in the "UNIX epoch," is less than 2^{32}. Beware: Our assumption will fail in February of 2106.)

```
#define VERSION 1   /* version of the MMIX architecture that we support */
```

```
#define SUBVERSION 0      /* secondary byte of version number */
#define SUBSUBVERSION 0      /* further qualification to version number */
⟨Initialize everything 22⟩ +≡
  rename_regs = max_rename_regs;
  mem_slots = max_mem_slots;
  lring_mask = lring_size − 1;
  for (j = 0; j < 256; j++) {
    g[j].addr.h = sign_bit, g[j].addr.l = j, g[j].known = true;
    g[j].up = g[j].down = &g[j];
  }
  g[rG].o.l = 255;
  g[rN].o.h = (VERSION ≪ 24) + (SUBVERSION ≪ 16) + (SUBSUBVERSION ≪ 8);
  g[rN].o.l = ABSTIME;      /* see comment and warning above */
  for (j = 0; j < lring_size; j++) {
    l[j].addr.h = sign_bit, l[j].addr.l = 256 + j, l[j].known = true;
    l[j].up = l[j].down = &l[j];
  }
```

90. ⟨Internal prototypes 13⟩ +≡

```
  static void print_specnode_id ARGS((octa));
```

91. ⟨Subroutines 14⟩ +≡

```
  static void print_specnode_id(a)
      octa a;
  {
    if (a.h ≡ sign_bit) {
      if (a.l < 32) printf(special_name[a.l]);
      else if (a.l < 256) printf("g[%d]", a.l);
      else printf("l[%d]", a.l − 256);
    } else if (a.h ≠ (tetra) −1) {
      printf("m["); print_octa(a); printf("]");
    }
  }
```


a: **specnode**, §44.
ABSTIME = macro, abstime.h.
addr: **octa**, §40.
ARGS = macro, §6.
cool: **control** *, §60.
down: **specnode** *, §40.
Extern = macro, §4.
h: **tetra**, §17.
hot: **control** *, §60.
j: **register int**, §10.
known: **bool**, §40.
l: **tetra**, §17.
o: **octa**, §40.
octa = **struct**, §17.
print_octa: **static void** ( ), §19.
printf: **int** ( ), <stdio.h>.
rB = 0, §52.
rG = 19, §52.
rN = 9, §52.
sign_bit = macro, §80.
special_name: **char** *[ ], §53.
specnode = **struct**, §40.
tetra = **unsigned int**, §17.
time: **time_t** ( ), <time.h>.
true = 1, §11.
up: **specnode** *, §40.
x: **specnode**, §44.

92. The *specval* subroutine produces a **spec** corresponding to the currently coolest value of a given local or global register.

⟨Internal prototypes 13⟩ +≡
```
static spec specval ARGS((specnode *));
```

93. ⟨Subroutines 14⟩ +≡
```
static spec specval(r)
    specnode *r;
{ spec res;
  if (r→up→known) res.o = r→up→o, res.p = Λ;
  else res.p = r→up;
  return res;
}
```

94. The *spec_install* subroutine introduces a new speculative value at the cool end of a given doubly linked list.

⟨Internal prototypes 13⟩ +≡
```
static void spec_install ARGS((specnode *, specnode *));
```

95. ⟨Subroutines 14⟩ +≡
```
static void spec_install(r, t)      /* insert t into list r */
    specnode *r, *t;
{
  t→up = r→up;
  t→up→down = t;
  r→up = t;
  t→down = r;
  t→addr = r→addr;
}
```

96. Conversely, *spec_rem* takes such a value out.

⟨Internal prototypes 13⟩ +≡
```
static void spec_rem ARGS((specnode *));
```

97. ⟨Subroutines 14⟩ +≡
```
static void spec_rem(t)      /* remove t from its list */
    specnode *t;
{ register specnode *u = t→up, *d = t→down;
  u→down = d; d→up = u;
}
```

98. Some special registers are so central to MMIX's operation, they are carried along with each control block in the reorder buffer instead of being treated as source and destination registers of each instruction. For example, the register stack pointers rO and rS are treated in this way. The normal specnodes for rO and rS, namely $g[rO]$ and $g[rS]$, are not actually used; the cool values are called *cool_O* and *cool_S*. (Actually *cool_O* and *cool_S* correspond to the register values divided by 8, since rO and rS are always multiples of 8.)

The arithmetic status register, rA, is also treated specially. Its event bits are kept up to date only at the "hot" end, by accumulating values of *arith_exc*; an instruction to GET the value of rA will be executed only in the hot seat. The other bits of rA, which are needed to control trip handlers and floating point rounding, are treated in the normal way.

```
⟨External variables 4⟩ +≡
  Extern octa cool_O, cool_S;    /* values of rO, rS before the cool instruction */
```

99. ⟨Global variables 20⟩ +≡

```
  int cool_L, cool_G;    /* values of rL and rG before the cool instruction */
  unsigned int cool_hist, peek_hist;    /* history bits for branch prediction */
  octa new_O, new_S;    /* values of rO, rS after cool */
```

---

addr: **octa**, §40.
ARGS = macro, §6.
arith_exc: **unsigned int**, §44.
cool: **control** *, §60.
down: **specnode** *, §40.
Extern = macro, §4.
g: **specnode** [], §86.
known: **bool**, §40.
o: **octa**, §40.
octa = **struct**, §17.
p: **specnode** *, §40.
rO = 10, §52.
rS = 11, §52.
spec = **struct**, §40.
specnode = **struct**, §40.
up: **specnode** *, §40.

100. ⟨ Install default fields in the *cool* block 100 ⟩ ≡

```
cool→op = op; cool→i = i;
cool→xx = (head→inst ≫ 16) & #ff; cool→yy = (head→inst ≫ 8) & #ff;
cool→zz = (head→inst) & #ff;
cool→loc = head→loc;
cool→y = cool→z = cool→b = cool→ra = zero_spec;
cool→x.o = cool→a.o = cool→rl.o = zero_octa;
cool→x.known = false;
cool→x.up = Λ;
cool→a.known = false;
cool→a.up = Λ;
cool→rl.known = true;
cool→rl.up = Λ;
cool→need_b = cool→need_ra = cool→ren_x = cool→mem_x = cool→ren_a = cool→set_l = false;
cool→arith_exc = cool→denin = cool→denout = 0;
if ((head→loc.h & sign_bit) ∧ ¬(g[rU].o.h & #8000)) cool→usage = false;
else cool→usage = ((op & (g[rU].o.h ≫ 16)) ≡ g[rU].o.h ≫ 24 ? true : false);
new_O = cool→cur_O = cool_O; new_S = cool→cur_S = cool_S;
cool→interrupt = head→interrupt;
cool→hist = peek_hist;
cool→go.o = incr(cool→loc, 4);
cool→go.known = false, cool→go.addr.h = −1, cool→go.up = (specnode *) cool;
cool→interim = cool→stack_alert = false;
```

This code is used in section 75.

101. ⟨ Dispatch an instruction to the *cool* block if possible, otherwise **goto** *stall* 101 ⟩ ≡

```
if (new_cool ≡ hot) goto stall;    /* reorder buffer is full */
⟨ Make sure cool_L and cool_G are up to date 102 ⟩;
⟨ Install the operand fields of the cool block 103 ⟩;
if (f & X_is_dest_bit) ⟨ Install register X as the destination, or insert an internal
        command and goto dispatch_done if X is marginal 110 ⟩;
switch (i) {
  ⟨ Special cases of instruction dispatch 117 ⟩
default: break;
}
dispatch_done:
```

This code is used in section 75.

102. The UNSAVE operation begins by loading register rG from memory. We don't really need to know the value of rG until twelve other registers have been unsaved, so we aren't fussy about it here.

⟨ Make sure *cool_L* and *cool_G* are up to date 102 ⟩ ≡

```
if (¬g[rL].up→known) goto stall;
cool_L = g[rL].up→o.l;
if (¬g[rG].up→known ∧ ¬(op ≡ UNSAVE ∧ cool→xx ≡ 1)) goto stall;
cool_G = g[rG].up→o.l;
```

This code is used in section 101.

103. ⟨ Install the operand fields of the *cool* block 103 ⟩ ≡

```
if (resuming) ⟨ Insert special operands when resuming an interrupted operation 324 ⟩
else {
  if (f & #10) ⟨ Set cool→b from register X 106 ⟩
  if (third_operand[op] ∧ (cool→i ≠ trap))
     ⟨ Set cool→b and/or cool→ra from special register 108 ⟩;
  if (f & #1) cool→z.o.l = cool→zz;
  else if (f & #2) ⟨ Set cool→z from register Z 104 ⟩
  else if ((op & #f0) ≡ #e0) ⟨ Set cool→z as an immediate wyde 109 ⟩;
  if (f & #4) cool→y.o.l = cool→yy;
  else if (f & #8) ⟨ Set cool→y from register Y 105 ⟩
}
```

This code is used in section 101.

104. ⟨ Set *cool→z* from register Z 104 ⟩ ≡

```
{
  if (cool→zz ≥ cool_G) cool→z = specval(&g[cool→zz]);
  else if (cool→zz < cool_L) cool→z = specval(&l[(cool_O.l + cool→zz) & lring_mask]);
}
```

This code is used in section 103.

105. ⟨ Set *cool→y* from register Y 105 ⟩ ≡

```
{
  if (cool→yy ≥ cool_G) cool→y = specval(&g[cool→yy]);
  else if (cool→yy < cool_L) cool→y = specval(&l[(cool_O.l + cool→yy) & lring_mask]);
}
```

This code is used in section 103.

---

a: **specnode**, §44.
addr: **octa**, §40.
arith_exc: **unsigned int**, §44.
b: **spec**, §44.
cool: **control** ∗, §60.
cool_G: **int**, §99.
cool_L: **int**, §99.
cool_O: **octa**, §98.
cool_S: **octa**, §98.
cur_O: **octa**, §44.
cur_S: **octa**, §44.
denin: **int**, §44.
denout: **int**, §44.
f: **register int**, §75.
false = 0, §11.
g: **specnode** [ ], §86.
go: **specnode**, §44.
h: **tetra**, §17.
head: **fetch** ∗, §69.
hist: **unsigned int**, §44.
hot: **control** ∗, §60.
i: **internal_opcode**, §44.
i: **register int**, §12.
incr: **octa** ( ), MMIX-ARITH §6.
inst: **tetra**, §68.
interim: **bool**, §44.
interrupt: **unsigned int**, §68.
interrupt: **unsigned int**, §44.
known: **bool**, §40.
l: **tetra**, §17.
l: **specnode** ∗, §86.
loc: **octa**, §44.
loc: **octa**, §68.
lring_mask: **int**, §88.
mem_x: **bool**, §44.
need_b: **bool**, §44.
need_ra: **bool**, §44.
new_cool: **control** ∗, §78.
new_O: **octa**, §99.
new_S: **octa**, §99.
o: **octa**, §40.
op: **register mmix_opcode**, §75.
op: **mmix_opcode**, §44.
peek_hist: **unsigned int**, §99.
ra: **spec**, §44.
ren_a: **bool**, §44.
ren_x: **bool**, §44.
resuming: **int**, §78.
rG = 19, §52.
rl: **specnode**, §44.
rL = 20, §52.
rU = 17, §52.
set_l: **bool**, §44.
sign_bit = macro, §80.
specnode = **struct**, §40.
specval: **static spec** ( ), §93.
stack_alert: **bool**, §44.
stall: label, §75.
third_operand: **unsigned char** [ ], §107.
trap = 82, §49.
true = 1, §11.
UNSAVE = #fb, §47.
up: **specnode** ∗, §40.
usage: **bool**, §44.
x: **specnode**, §44.
X_is_dest_bit = #20, §83.
xx: **unsigned char**, §44.
y: **spec**, §44.
yy: **unsigned char**, §44.
z: **spec**, §44.
zero_octa: **octa**, MMIX-ARITH §4.
zero_spec: **spec**, §41.
zz: **unsigned char**, §44.

106. ⟨ Set *cool→b* from register X 106 ⟩ ≡

```
{
  if (cool→xx ≥ cool_G) cool→b = specval(&g[cool→xx]);
  else if (cool→xx < cool_L) cool→b = specval(&l[(cool_O.l + cool→xx) & lring_mask]);
  if (f & rel_addr_bit) cool→need_b = true;     /* br, pbr */
}
```

This code is used in section 103.

107. If an operation requires a special register as third operand, that register is listed in the *third_operand* table.

⟨ Global variables 20 ⟩ +≡

```
unsigned char third_operand[256] = {
0, rA, 0, 0, rA, rA, rA, rA,     /* TRAP, ... */
rA, rA, rA, rA, rA, rA, rA, rA,     /* FLOT, ... */
rA, rE, rE, rE, rA, rA, rA, rA,     /* FMUL, ... */
rA, rA, 0, 0, rA, rA, rD, rD,     /* MUL, ... */
rA, rA, 0, 0, rA, rA, 0, 0,     /* ADD, ... */
0, 0, 0, 0, 0, 0, 0, 0,     /* 2ADDU, ... */
0, 0, 0, 0, rA, rA, 0, 0,     /* CMP, ... */
rA, rA, 0, 0, 0, 0, 0, 0,     /* SL, ... */
0, 0, 0, 0, 0, 0, 0, 0,     /* BN, ... */
0, 0, 0, 0, 0, 0, 0, 0,     /* BNN, ... */
0, 0, 0, 0, 0, 0, 0, 0,     /* PBN, ... */
0, 0, 0, 0, 0, 0, 0, 0,     /* PBNN, ... */
0, 0, 0, 0, 0, 0, 0, 0,     /* CSN, ... */
0, 0, 0, 0, 0, 0, 0, 0,     /* CSNN, ... */
0, 0, 0, 0, 0, 0, 0, 0,     /* ZSN, ... */
0, 0, 0, 0, 0, 0, 0, 0,     /* ZSNN, ... */
0, 0, 0, 0, 0, 0, 0, 0,     /* LDB, ... */
0, 0, 0, 0, 0, 0, 0, 0,     /* LDT, ... */
0, 0, 0, 0, 0, 0, 0, 0,     /* LDSF, ... */
0, 0, 0, 0, 0, 0, 0, 0,     /* LDVTS, ... */
rA, rA, 0, 0, rA, rA, 0, 0,     /* STB, ... */
rA, rA, 0, 0, 0, 0, 0, 0,     /* STT, ... */
rA, rA, 0, 0, 0, 0, 0, 0,     /* STSF, ... */
0, 0, 0, 0, 0, 0, 0, 0,     /* SYNCD, ... */
0, 0, 0, 0, 0, 0, 0, 0,     /* OR, ... */
0, 0, 0, 0, 0, 0, 0, 0,     /* AND, ... */
0, 0, 0, 0, 0, 0, 0, 0,     /* BDIF, ... */
rM, rM, 0, 0, 0, 0, 0, 0,     /* MUX, ... */
0, 0, 0, 0, 0, 0, 0, 0,     /* SETH, ... */
0, 0, 0, 0, 0, 0, 0, 0,     /* ORH, ... */
0, 0, 0, 0, 0, 0, 0, 0,     /* JMP, ... */
rJ, 0, 0, 0, 0, 0, 0, 255};     /* POP, ... */
```

108. The *cool→b* field is busy in operations like STB or STSF, which need rA. So we use *cool→ra* instead, when rA is needed.

⟨ Set *cool→b* and/or *cool→ra* from special register 108 ⟩ ≡

```
{
  if (third_operand[op] ≡ rA ∨ third_operand[op] ≡ rE)
    cool→need_ra = true, cool→ra = specval(&g[rA]);
  if (third_operand[op] ≠ rA)
    cool→need_b = true, cool→b = specval(&g[third_operand[op]]);
}
```

This code is used in section 103.

109. ⟨ Set *cool→z* as an immediate wyde 109 ⟩ ≡

```
{
  switch (op & 3) {
  case 0: cool→z.o.h = yz ≪ 16; break;
  case 1: cool→z.o.h = yz; break;
  case 2: cool→z.o.l = yz ≪ 16; break;
  case 3: cool→z.o.l = yz; break;
  }
  if (i ≠ set) {    /* register X should also be the Y operand */
    cool→y = cool→b;
    cool→b = zero_spec;
  }
}
```

This code is used in section 103.

b: **spec**, §44.
br = 69, §49.
cool: **control** *, §60.
cool_G: **int**, §99.
cool_L: **int**, §99.
cool_O: **octa**, §98.
f: **register int**, §75.
g: **specnode** [], §86.
h: **tetra**, §17.
i: **register int**, §12.
l: **specnode** *, §86.
l: **tetra**, §17.
lring_mask: **int**, §88.
need_b: **bool**, §44.
need_ra: **bool**, §44.
o: **octa**, §40.
op: **register mmix_opcode**, §75.
pbr = 70, §49.
rA = 21, §52.
ra: **spec**, §44.
rD = 1, §52.
rE = 2, §52.
rel_addr_bit = #40, §83.
rJ = 4, §52.
rM = 5, §52.
set = 33, §49.
specval: **static spec** (), §93.
true = 1, §11.
xx: **unsigned char**, §44.
y: **spec**, §44.
yz: **register int**, §75.
z: **spec**, §44.
zero_spec: **spec**, §41.

110. ⟨ Install register X as the destination, or insert an internal command and **goto** *dispatch_done* if X is marginal 110 ⟩ ≡

```
{
  if (cool→xx ≥ cool_G) {
    if (i ≠ pushgo ∧ i ≠ pushj ∧ i ≠ cswap)
      cool→ren_x = true, spec_install(&g[cool→xx], &cool→x);
  } else if (cool→xx < cool_L) {
    if (i ≠ cswap)
      cool→ren_x = true, spec_install(&l[(cool_O.l + cool→xx) & lring_mask], &cool→x);
  } else {    /* we need to increase L before issuing head→inst */
  increase_L: if (((cool_S.l − cool_O.l − cool_L − 1) & lring_mask) ≡ 0)
      ⟨ Insert an instruction to advance gamma 113 ⟩
    else ⟨ Insert an instruction to advance beta and L 112 ⟩;
  }
}
```

This code is used in section 101.

111. ⟨ Check for sufficient rename registers and memory slots, or **goto** *stall* 111 ⟩ ≡

```
  if (rename_regs < cool→ren_x + cool→ren_a) goto stall;
  if (cool→mem_x)
    if (mem_slots) mem_slots−−; else goto stall;
  rename_regs −= cool→ren_x + cool→ren_a;
```

This code is used in section 75.

112. The *incrl* instruction advances β and rL by 1 at a time when we know that $\beta \neq \gamma$, in the ring of local registers.

⟨ Insert an instruction to advance beta and L 112 ⟩ ≡

```
{
  cool→i = incrl;
  spec_install(&l[(cool_O.l + cool_L) & lring_mask], &cool→x);
  cool→need_b = cool→need_ra = false;
  cool→y = cool→z = zero_spec;
  cool→x.known = true;    /* cool→x.o = zero_octa */
  spec_install(&g[rL], &cool→rl);
  cool→rl.o.l = cool_L + 1;
  cool→ren_x = cool→set_l = true;
  op = SETH;    /* this instruction to be handled by the simplest units */
  cool→interim = true;
  goto dispatch_done;
}
```

This code is used in section 110.

113. The *incgamma* instruction advances γ and rS by storing an octabyte from the local register ring to virtual memory location $cool\_S \ll 3$.

⟨ Insert an instruction to advance gamma 113 ⟩ ≡

```
{
  cool→need_b = cool→need_ra = false;
  cool→i = incgamma;
  new_S = incr(cool_S, 1);
```

```
    cool→b = specval(&l[cool_S.l & lring_mask]);
    cool→y.p = Λ, cool→y.o = shift_left(cool_S, 3);
    cool→z = zero_spec;
    cool→mem_x = true, spec_install(&mem, &cool→x);
    op = STOU;      /* this instruction needs to be handled by load/store unit */
    cool→interim = true;
    cool→stack_alert = ¬(cool→y.o.h & sign_bit);
    goto dispatch_done;
  }
```

This code is used in sections 110, 119, and 337.

---

b: **spec**, §44.
cool: **control** ∗, §60.
cool_G: **int**, §99.
cool_L: **int**, §99.
cool_O: **octa**, §98.
cool_S: **octa**, §98.
cswap = 68, §49.
dispatch_done: label, §101.
false = 0, §11.
g: **specnode** [ ], §86.
h: **tetra**, §17.
head: **fetch** ∗, §69.
i: **register int**, §12.
i: **internal_opcode**, §44.
incgamma = 84, §49.
incr: **octa** ( ), MMIX-ARITH §6.
incrl = 86, §49.
inst: **tetra**, §68.
interim: **bool**, §44.
known: **bool**, §40.
l: **specnode** ∗, §86.
l: **tetra**, §17.
lring_mask: **int**, §88.
mem: **specnode**, §115.
mem_slots: **int**, §86.
mem_x: **bool**, §44.
need_b: **bool**, §44.
need_ra: **bool**, §44.
new_S: **octa**, §99.
o: **octa**, §40.
op: **register mmix_opcode**, §75.
p: **specnode** ∗, §40.
pushgo = 74, §49.
pushj = 71, §49.
ren_a: **bool**, §44.
ren_x: **bool**, §44.
rename_regs: **int**, §86.
rl: **specnode**, §44.
rL = 20, §52.
set_l: **bool**, §44.
SETH = #e0, §47.
shift_left: **octa** ( ), MMIX-ARITH §7.
sign_bit = macro, §80.
spec_install: **static void** ( ), §95.
specval: **static spec** ( ), §93.
stack_alert: **bool**, §44.
stall: label, §75.
STOU = #ae, §47.
true = 1, §11.
x: **specnode**, §44.
xx: **unsigned char**, §44.
y: **spec**, §44.
z: **spec**, §44.
zero_octa: **octa**, MMIX-ARITH §4.
zero_spec: **spec**, §41.

114. The *decgamma* instruction decreases γ and rS by loading an octabyte from virtual memory location $(cool\_S - 1) \ll 3$ into the local register ring. The value of β may need to be decreased too (by decreasing rL).

⟨ Insert an instruction to decrease gamma 114 ⟩ ≡

```
{
  if (cool_O.l + cool_L ≡ cool_S.l + lring_size) {     /* don't let γ pass β */
    if (cool→i ≡ pop ∧ cool→xx ≡ cool_L ∧ cool_L > 1) {
      cool→i = or;     /* we'll preserve the main result by moving it down */
      head→inst −= #10000;     /* decrease X field of POP in fetch buffer */
      op = OR;
      cool→y = specval(&l[(cool_O.l + cool→xx − 1) & lring_mask]);
      spec_install(&l[(cool_O.l + cool→xx − 2) & lring_mask], &cool→x);
    } else {     /* decrease rL by 1 */
      spec_install(&g[rL], &cool→rl); cool→rl.o.l = cool_L − 1; cool→set_l = true;
    }
  }
  if (cool→i ≠ or) {
    cool→i = decgamma;
    new_S = incr(cool_S, −1);
    cool→y.p = Λ, cool→y.o = shift_left(new_S, 3);
    spec_install(&l[new_S.l & lring_mask], &cool→x);
    op = LDOU;     /* this instruction needs to be handled by load/store unit */
    cool→ptr_a = (void *) mem.up;
  }
  cool→z = cool→b = zero_spec; cool→need_b = false; cool→ren_x = cool→interim = true;
  goto dispatch_done;
}
```

This code is used in section 120.

115. Storing into memory requires a doubly linked data list of specnodes like the lists we use for local and global registers. In this case the head of the list is called *mem*, and the *addr* fields are physical addresses in memory.

⟨ External variables 4 ⟩ +≡

```
Extern specnode mem;
```

116. The *addr* field of a memory specnode is all 1s until the physical address has been computed.

⟨ Initialize everything 22 ⟩ +≡

```
mem.addr.h = mem.addr.l = −1;
mem.up = mem.down = &mem;
```

117. The CSWAP operation is treated as a partial store, with \$X as a secondary output. Partial store (*pst*) commands read an octabyte from memory before they write it.

⟨ Special cases of instruction dispatch 117 ⟩ ≡

```
case cswap: cool→ren_a = true;
  spec_install(cool→xx ≥ cool_G ? &g[cool→xx] : &l[(cool_O.l + cool→xx) & lring_mask],
      &cool→a);
```

```
cool→i = pst;
case st: if ((op & #fe) ≡ STCO) cool→b.o.l = cool→xx;
case pst: cool→mem_x = true, spec_install(&mem, &cool→x); break;
case ld: case ldunc: cool→ptr_a = (void *) mem.up; break;
```

See also sections 118, 119, 120, 121, 122, 227, 312, 322, 332, 337, 347, and 355.

This code is used in section 101.

118. When new data is PUT into special registers 8 or 15–20 (namely rC, rK, rQ, rU, rV, rG, or rL) it can affect many things. Therefore we stop issuing further instructions until such PUTs are committed. Moreover, we will see later that such drastic PUTs defer execution until they reach the hot seat.

```
⟨ Special cases of instruction dispatch 117 ⟩ +≡
case put: if (cool→yy ≠ 0 ∨ cool→xx ≥ 32) goto illegal_inst;
  if (cool→xx ≥ 8) {
    if (cool→xx ≤ 11 ∧ cool→xx ≠ 8) goto illegal_inst;
    if (cool→xx ≤ 18 ∧ ¬(cool→loc.h & sign_bit)) goto privileged_inst;
  }
  if (cool→xx ≡ 8 ∨ (cool→xx ≥ 15 ∧ cool→xx ≤ 20)) freeze_dispatch = true;
  cool→ren_x = true, spec_install(&g[cool→xx], &cool→x); break;
case get: if (cool→yy ∨ cool→zz ≥ 32) goto illegal_inst;
  if (cool→zz ≡ rO) cool→z.o = shift_left(cool_O, 3);
  else if (cool→zz ≡ rS) cool→z.o = shift_left(cool_S, 3);
  else cool→z = specval(&g[cool→zz]); break;
illegal_inst: cool→interrupt |= B_BIT; goto noop_inst;
case ldvts: if (cool→loc.h & sign_bit) break;
privileged_inst: cool→interrupt |= K_BIT;
noop_inst: cool→i = noop; break;
```

---

a: **specnode**, §44.
addr: **octa**, §40.
b: **spec**, §44.
B_BIT = 1 ≪ 2, §54.
cool: **control** ∗, §60.
cool_G: **int**, §99.
cool_L: **int**, §99.
cool_O: **octa**, §98.
cool_S: **octa**, §98.
cswap = 68, §49.
decgamma = 85, §49.
dispatch_done: label, §101.
down: **specnode** ∗, §40.
Extern = macro, §4.
false = 0, §11.
freeze_dispatch: **register bool**, §75.
g: **specnode** [ ], §86.
get = 54, §49.
h: **tetra**, §17.
head: **fetch** ∗, §69.
i: **internal_opcode**, §44.
incr: **octa** ( ), MMIX-ARITH §6.
inst: **tetra**, §68.
interim: **bool**, §44.
interrupt: **unsigned int**, §44.
K_BIT = 1 ≪ 3, §54.
l: **specnode** ∗, §86.
l: **tetra**, §17.
ld = 56, §49.
LDOU = #8e, §47.
ldunc = 59, §49.
ldvts = 60, §49.
loc: **octa**, §44.
lring_mask: **int**, §88.
lring_size: **int**, §86.
mem_x: **bool**, §44.
need_b: **bool**, §44.
new_S: **octa**, §99.
noop = 81, §49.
o: **octa**, §40.
op: **register mmix_opcode**, §75.
OR = #c0, §47.
or = 34, §49.
p: **specnode** ∗, §40.
pop = 75, §49.
pst = 66, §49.
ptr_a: **void** ∗, §44.
put = 55, §49.
ren_a: **bool**, §44.
ren_x: **bool**, §44.
rl: **specnode**, §44.
rL = 20, §52.
rO = 10, §52.
rS = 11, §52.
set_l: **bool**, §44.
shift_left: **octa** ( ), MMIX-ARITH §7.
sign_bit = macro, §80.
spec_install: **static void** ( ), §95.
specnode = **struct**, §40.
specval: **static spec** ( ), §93.
st = 63, §49.
STCO = #b4, §47.
true = 1, §11.
up: **specnode** ∗, §40.
x: **specnode**, §44.
xx: **unsigned char**, §44.
y: **spec**, §44.
yy: **unsigned char**, §44.
z: **spec**, §44.
zero_spec: **spec**, §41.
zz: **unsigned char**, §44.

119. A PUSHGO instruction with X ≥ G causes L to increase momentarily by 1, even if L = G. But the value of L will be decreased before the PUSHGO is complete, so it will never actually exceed G. Moreover, we needn't insert an *incrl* command.

```
⟨ Special cases of instruction dispatch 117 ⟩ +≡
case pushgo: inst_ptr.p = &cool→go;
case pushj:
  { register int x = cool→xx;
    if (x ≥ cool_G) {
      if (((cool_S.l − cool_O.l − cool_L − 1) & lring_mask) ≡ 0)
        ⟨ Insert an instruction to advance gamma 113 ⟩
      x = cool_L; cool_L++;
      cool→ren_x = true, spec_install(&l[(cool_O.l + x) & lring_mask], &cool→x);
    }
    cool→x.known = true, cool→x.o.h = 0, cool→x.o.l = x;
    cool→ren_a = true, spec_install(&g[rJ], &cool→a);
    cool→a.known = true, cool→a.o = incr(cool→loc, 4);
    cool→set_l = true, spec_install(&g[rL], &cool→rl); cool→rl.o.l = cool_L − x − 1;
    new_O = incr(cool_O, x + 1);
  } break;
case syncid: if (cool→loc.h & sign_bit) break;
case go: inst_ptr.p = &cool→go; break;
```

120. We need to know the topmost "hidden" element of the register stack when a POP instruction is dispatched. This element is usually present in the local register ring, unless $\gamma = \alpha$.

Once it is known, let x be its least significant byte. We will be decreasing rO by $x + 1$, so we may have to decrease γ repeatedly in order to maintain the condition rS ≤ rO.

```
⟨ Special cases of instruction dispatch 117 ⟩ +≡
case pop: if (cool→xx ∧ cool_L ≥ cool→xx)
    cool→y = specval(&l[(cool_O.l + cool→xx − 1) & lring_mask]);
pop_unsave: if (cool_S.l ≡ cool_O.l) ⟨ Insert an instruction to decrease gamma 114 ⟩;
  { register tetra x;
    register int new_L;
    register specnode *p = l[(cool_O.l − 1) & lring_mask].up;
    if (p→known) x = (p→o.l) & #ff; else goto stall;
    if ((tetra)(cool_O.l − cool_S.l) ≤ x) ⟨ Insert an instruction to decrease gamma 114 ⟩;
    new_O = incr(cool_O, −x − 1);
    if (cool→i ≡ pop) new_L = x + (cool→xx ≤ cool_L ? cool→xx : cool_L + 1); else new_L = x;
    if (new_L > cool_G) new_L = cool_G;
    if (x < new_L) cool→ren_x = true, spec_install(&l[(cool_O.l − 1) & lring_mask], &cool→x);
    cool→set_l = true, spec_install(&g[rL], &cool→rl); cool→rl.o.l = new_L;
    if (cool→i ≡ pop) {
      cool→z.o.l = yz ≪ 2;
      if (inst_ptr.p ≡ UNKNOWN_SPEC ∧ new_head ≡ tail) inst_ptr.p = &cool→go;
    }
    break;
  }
```

121. ⟨ Special cases of instruction dispatch 117 ⟩ +≡

```
case mulu: cool→ren_a = true, spec_install(&g[rH], &cool→a); break;
case div: case divu: cool→ren_a = true, spec_install(&g[rR], &cool→a); break;
```

122. It's tempting to say that we could avoid taking up space in the reorder buffer when no operation needs to be done. A `JMP` instruction qualifies as a no-op in this sense, because the change of control occurs before the execution stage. However, even a no-op might have to be counted in the usage register rU, so it might get into the execution stage for that reason. A no-op can also cause a protection interrupt, if it appears in a negative location. Even more importantly, a program might get into a loop that consists entirely of jumps and no-ops; then we wouldn't be able to interrupt it, because the interruption mechanism needs to find the current location in the reorder buffer! At least one functional unit therefore needs to provide explicit support for `JMP`, `JMPB`, and `SWYM`.

The `SWYM` instruction with `F_BIT` set is a special case: This is a request from the fetch coroutine for an update to the IT-cache, when the page table method isn't implemented in hardware.

⟨ Special cases of instruction dispatch 117 ⟩ +≡

```
case noop: if (cool→interrupt & F_BIT) {
    cool→go.o = cool→y.o = cool→loc; inst_ptr = specval(&g[rT]);
  }
  break;
```

123. ⟨ Undo data structures set prematurely in the *cool* block and **break** 123 ⟩ ≡

```
  if (cool→ren_x ∨ cool→mem_x) spec_rem(&cool→x);
  if (cool→ren_a) spec_rem(&cool→a);
  if (cool→set_l) spec_rem(&cool→rl);
  if (inst_ptr.p ≡ &cool→go) inst_ptr.p = UNKNOWN_SPEC;
  break;
```

This code is used in section 75.

a: **specnode**, §44.
cool: **control** ∗, §60.
cool_G: **int**, §99.
cool_L: **int**, §99.
cool_O: **octa**, §98.
cool_S: **octa**, §98.
div = 9, §49.
divu = 28, §49.
`F_BIT` = 1 ≪ 17, §54.
g: **specnode** [ ], §86.
go = 72, §49.
go: **specnode**, §44.
h: **tetra**, §17.
i: **internal_opcode**, §44.
incr: **octa** ( ), MMIX-ARITH §6.
incrl = 86, §49.
inst_ptr: **spec**, §284.
interrupt: **unsigned int**, §44.
known: **bool**, §40.
l: **specnode** ∗, §86.
l: **tetra**, §17.
loc: **octa**, §44.
lring_mask: **int**, §88.
mem_x: **bool**, §44.
mulu = 27, §49.
new_head: **register fetch** ∗, §74.
new_O: **octa**, §99.
noop = 81, §49.
o: **octa**, §40.
p: **specnode** ∗, §40.
pop = 75, §49.
pushgo = 74, §49.
pushj = 71, §49.
ren_a: **bool**, §44.
ren_x: **bool**, §44.
rH = 3, §52.
rJ = 4, §52.
rl: **specnode**, §44.
rL = 20, §52.
rR = 6, §52.
rT = 13, §52.
set_l: **bool**, §44.
sign_bit = macro, §80.
spec_install: **static void** ( ), §95.
spec_rem: **static void** ( ), §97.
specnode = **struct**, §40.
specval: **static spec** ( ), §93.
stall: label, §75.
syncid = 65, §49.
tail: **fetch** ∗, §69.
tetra = **unsigned int**, §17.
true = 1, §11.
`UNKNOWN_SPEC` = macro, §71.
up: **specnode** ∗, §40.
x: **specnode**, §44.
xx: **unsigned char**, §44.
y: **spec**, §44.
yz: **register int**, §75.
z: **spec**, §44.

124. The execution stages. MMIX's *raison d'être* is its ability to execute instructions. So now we want to simulate the behavior of its functional units.

Each coroutine scheduled for action at the current tick of the clock has a *stage* number corresponding to a particular subset of the MMIX hardware. For example, the coroutines with *stage* = 2 are the second stages in the pipelines of the functional units. A coroutine with *stage* = 0 works in the fetch unit. Several artificially large stage numbers are used to control special coroutines that do things like write data from buffers into memory.

In this program the current coroutine of interest is called *self*; hence *self→stage* is the current stage number of interest. Another key variable, *self→ctl*, is called *data*; this is the control block being operated on by the current coroutine. We typically are simulating an operation in which *data→x* is being computed as a function of *data→y* and *data→z*. The *data* record has many fields, as described earlier when we defined **control** structures; for example, *data→owner* is the same as *self*, during the execution stage, if it is nonnull.

This part of the simulator is written as if each functional unit is able to handle all 256 operations. In practice, of course, a functional unit tends to be much more specialized; the actual specialization is governed by the dispatcher, which issues an instruction only to a functional unit that supports it. Once an instruction has been dispatched, however, we can simulate it most easily if we imagine that its functional unit is universal.

Coroutines with higher *stage* numbers are processed first. The three most important variables that govern a coroutine's behavior, once *self→stage* is given, are the external operation code *data→op*, the internal operation code *data→i*, and the value of *data→state*. We typically have *data→state* = 0 when a coroutine is first fired up.

```
⟨ Local variables 12 ⟩ +≡
  register coroutine *self;      /* the current coroutine being executed */
  register control *data;       /* the control block of the current coroutine */
```

125. When a coroutine has done all it wants to on a single cycle, it says **goto** *done*. It will not be scheduled to do any further work unless the *schedule* routine has been called since it began execution. The *wait* macro is a convenient way to say "Please schedule me to resume again at the current *data→state*" after a specified time; for example, *wait*(1) will restart a coroutine on the next clock tick.

```
#define wait(t)  { schedule(self, t, data→state); goto done; }
#define pass_after(t)  schedule(self + 1, t, data→state)
#define sleep  { self→next = self; goto done; }      /* wait forever */
#define awaken(c, t)  schedule(c, t, c→ctl→state)
```

```
⟨Execute all coroutines scheduled for the current time 125⟩ ≡
  cur_time++; if (cur_time ≡ ring_size) cur_time = 0;
  for (self = queuelist(cur_time); self ≠ &sentinel; self = sentinel.next) {
    sentinel.next = self→next; self→next = Λ;      /* unschedule this coroutine */
    data = self→ctl;
    if (verbose & coroutine_bit) {
      printf("␣running␣"); print_coroutine_id(self); printf("␣");
      print_control_block(data); printf("\n");
    }
    switch (self→stage) {
    case 0: ⟨Simulate an action of the fetch coroutine 288⟩;
    case 1: ⟨Simulate the first stage of an execution pipeline 130⟩;
    default: ⟨Simulate later stages of an execution pipeline 135⟩;
    ⟨Cases for control of special coroutines 126⟩;
    }
  terminate: if (self→lockloc) *(self→lockloc) = Λ, self→lockloc = Λ;
  done: ;
  }
```

This code is used in section 64.

126. A special coroutine whose *stage* number is *vanish* simply goes away at its scheduled time.

```
⟨Cases for control of special coroutines 126⟩ ≡
case vanish: goto terminate;
```

See also sections 215, 217, 222, 224, 232, 237, and 257.

This code is used in section 125.

127. ⟨Global variables 20⟩ +≡

```
  coroutine mem_locker;      /* trivial coroutine that vanishes */
  coroutine Dlocker;      /* another */
  control vanish_ctl;      /* such coroutines share a common control block */
```

---

control = **struct**, §44.
coroutine = **struct**, §23.
coroutine_bit = 1 ≪ 2, §8.
ctl: **control** *, §23.
cur_time: **int**, §29.
i: **internal_opcode**, §44.
lockloc: **coroutine** **, §23.
next: **coroutine** *, §23.
op: **mmix_opcode**, §44.
owner: **coroutine** *, §44.
print_control_block: **static void** (), §46.
print_coroutine_id: **static void** (), §25.
printf: **int** (), <stdio.h>.
queuelist: **static coroutine** *(), §35.
ring_size: **int**, §29.
schedule: **static void** (), §28.
sentinel: **coroutine**, §36.
stage: **int**, §23.
state: **int**, §44.
vanish = 98, §129.
verbose: **int**, §4.
x: **specnode**, §44.
y: **spec**, §44.
z: **spec**, §44.

128. ⟨ Initialize everything 22 ⟩ +≡

```
mem_locker.name = "Locker";
mem_locker.ctl = &vanish_ctl;
mem_locker.stage = vanish;
Dlocker.name = "Dlocker";
Dlocker.ctl = &vanish_ctl;
Dlocker.stage = vanish;
vanish_ctl.go.o.l = 4;
for (j = 0; j < DTcache→ports; j++) DTcache→reader[j].ctl = &vanish_ctl;
if (Dcache)
  for (j = 0; j < Dcache→ports; j++) Dcache→reader[j].ctl = &vanish_ctl;
for (j = 0; j < ITcache→ports; j++) ITcache→reader[j].ctl = &vanish_ctl;
if (Icache)
  for (j = 0; j < Icache→ports; j++) Icache→reader[j].ctl = &vanish_ctl;
```

129. Here is a list of the *stage* numbers for special coroutines to be defined below.

⟨ Header definitions 6 ⟩ +≡

```
#define max_stage 99    /* exceeds all stage numbers */
#define vanish 98    /* special coroutine that just goes away */
#define flush_to_mem 97    /* coroutine for flushing from a cache to memory */
#define flush_to_S 96    /* coroutine for flushing from a cache to the S-cache */
#define fill_from_mem 95    /* coroutine for filling a cache from memory */
#define fill_from_S 94    /* coroutine for filling a cache from the S-cache */
#define fill_from_virt 93    /* coroutine for filling a translation cache */
#define write_from_wbuf 92    /* coroutine for emptying the write buffer */
#define cleanup 91    /* coroutine for cleaning the caches */
```

130. At the very beginning of stage 1, a functional unit will stall if necessary until its operands are available. As soon as the operands are all present, the *state* is set nonzero and execution proper begins.

⟨ Simulate the first stage of an execution pipeline 130 ⟩ ≡

```
switch1: switch (data→state) {
  case 0: ⟨ Wait for input data if necessary; set state = 1 if it's there 131 ⟩;
  case 1: ⟨ Begin execution of an operation 132 ⟩;
  case 2: ⟨ Pass data to the next stage of the pipeline 134 ⟩;
  case 3: ⟨ Finish execution of an operation 144 ⟩;
    ⟨ Special cases for states in the first stage 266 ⟩;
}
```

This code is used in section 125.

131. If some of our input data has been computed by another coroutine on the current cycle, we grab it now but wait for the next cycle. (An actual machine wouldn't have latched the data until then.)

⟨ Wait for input data if necessary; set *state* = 1 if it's there 131 ⟩ ≡

```
j = 0;
if (data→y.p) {
  j++;
  if (data→y.p→known) data→y.o = data→y.p→o, data→y.p = Λ;
  else j += 10;
}
if (data→z.p) {
  j++;
  if (data→z.p→known) data→z.o = data→z.p→o, data→z.p = Λ;
  else j += 10;
}
if (data→b.p) {
  if (data→need_b) j++;
  if (data→b.p→known) data→b.o = data→b.p→o, data→b.p = Λ;
  else if (data→need_b) j += 10;
}
if (data→ra.p) {
  if (data→need_ra) j++;
  if (data→ra.p→known) data→ra.o = data→ra.p→o, data→ra.p = Λ;
  else if (data→need_ra) j += 10;
}
if (j < 10) data→state = 1;
if (j) wait(1);    /* otherwise we fall through to case 1 */
```

This code is used in section 130.

b: **spec**, §44.
ctl: **control** ∗, §23.
data: **register control** ∗, §124.
Dcache: **cache** ∗, §168.
Dlocker: **coroutine**, §127.
DTcache: **cache** ∗, §168.
go: **specnode**, §44.
Icache: **cache** ∗, §168.
ITcache: **cache** ∗, §168.
j: **register int**, §10.
j: **register int**, §12.
known: **bool**, §40.
l: **tetra**, §17.
mem_locker: **coroutine**, §127.
name: **char** ∗, §23.
need_b: **bool**, §44.
need_ra: **bool**, §44.
o: **octa**, §40.
p: **specnode** ∗, §40.
ports: **int**, §167.
ra: **spec**, §44.
reader: **coroutine** ∗, §167.
stage: **int**, §23.
state: **int**, §44.
vanish_ctl: **control**, §127.
wait = macro ( ), §125.
y: **spec**, §44.
z: **spec**, §44.

132. Simple register-to-register instructions like `ADD` are assumed to take just one cycle, but others like `FADD` almost certainly require more time. This simulator can be configured so that `FADD` might take, say, four pipeline stages of one cycle each $(1+1+1+1)$, or two pipeline stages of two cycles each $(2+2)$, or a single unpipelined stage lasting four cycles (4), etc. In any case the simulator computes the results now, for simplicity, placing them in *data→x* and possibly also in *data→a* and/or *data→interrupt*. The results will not be officially made *known* until the proper time.

```
⟨ Begin execution of an operation 132 ⟩ ≡
  switch (data→i) {
    ⟨ Cases to compute the results of register-to-register operation 137 ⟩;
    ⟨ Cases to compute the virtual address of a memory operation 265 ⟩;
    ⟨ Cases for stage 1 execution 155 ⟩;
  }
  ⟨ Set things up so that the results become known when they should 133 ⟩;
```

This code is used in section 130.

133. If the internal opcode *data→i* is *max_pipe_op* or less, a special pipeline sequence like $1+1+1+1$ or $2+2$ or $15+10$, etc., has been configured. Otherwise we assume that the pipeline sequence is simply 1.

Suppose the pipeline sequence is $t_1 + t_2 + \cdots + t_k$. Each t_j is positive and less than 256, so we represent the sequence as a string *pipe_seq*[*data→i*] of unsigned "characters," terminated by 0. Given such a string, we want to do the following: Wait $(t_1 - 1)$ cycles and pass *data* to stage 2; wait t_2 cycles and pass *data* to stage 3; ...; wait t_{k-1} cycles and pass *data* to stage k; wait t_k cycles and make the results *known*.

The value of *denin* is added to t_1; the value of *denout* is added to t_k.

```
⟨ Set things up so that the results become known when they should 133 ⟩ ≡
  data→state = 3;
  if (data→i ≤ max_pipe_op) { register unsigned char *s = pipe_seq[data→i];
    j = s[0] + data→denin;
    if (s[1]) data→state = 2;      /* more than one stage */
    else j += data→denout;
    if (j > 1) wait(j − 1);
  }
  goto switch1;
```

This code is used in section 132.

134. When we're in stage j, the coroutine for stage $j+1$ of the same functional unit is *self* $+ 1$.

```
⟨ Pass data to the next stage of the pipeline 134 ⟩ ≡
pass_data: if ((self + 1)→next) wait(1);     /* stall if the next stage is occupied */
  { register unsigned char *s = pipe_seq[data→i];
    j = s[self→stage];
    if (s[self→stage + 1] ≡ 0) j += data→denout, data→state = 3;
          /* the next stage is the last */
    pass_after(j);
  }
passit: (self + 1)→ctl = data;
```

```
  data→owner = self + 1;
  goto done;
```

This code is used in section 130.

135. ⟨ Simulate later stages of an execution pipeline 135 ⟩ ≡

```
switch2: if (data→b.p ∧ data→b.p→known) data→b.o = data→b.p→o, data→b.p = Λ;
  switch (data→state) {
  case 0: panic(confusion("switch2"));
  case 1: ⟨ Begin execution of a stage-two operation 351 ⟩;
  case 2: goto pass_data;
  case 3: goto fin_ex;
    ⟨ Special cases for states in later stages 272 ⟩;
  }
```

This code is used in section 125.

136. The default pipeline times use only one stage; they can be overridden by *MMIX_config*. The total number of stages supported by this simulator is limited to 90, since it must never interfere with the *stage* numbers for special coroutines defined below. (The author doesn't feel guilty about making this restriction.)

⟨ External variables 4 ⟩ +≡

```
#define pipe_limit 90
  Extern unsigned char pipe_seq[max_pipe_op + 1][pipe_limit + 1];
```

137. The simplest of all register-to-register operations is *set*, which occurs for commands like `SETH` as well as for commands like `GETA`. (We might as well start with the easy cases and work our way up.)

⟨ Cases to compute the results of register-to-register operation 137 ⟩ ≡

```
case set: data→x.o = data→z.o; break;
```

See also sections 138, 139, 140, 141, 142, 143, 343, 344, 345, 346, 348, and 350.

This code is used in section 132.

---

a: **specnode**, §44.
b: **spec**, §44.
confusion = macro ( ), §13.
ctl: **control** *, §23.
data: **register control** *, §124.
denin: **int**, §44.
denout: **int**, §44.
done: label, §125.
Extern = macro, §4.
fin_ex: label, §144.
i: **internal_opcode**, §44.
interrupt: **unsigned int**, §44.
j: **register int**, §12.
known: **bool**, §40.
max_pipe_op = *feps*, §49.
MMIX_config: **void** ( ), MMIX-CONFIG §38.
next: **coroutine** *, §23.
o: **octa**, §40.
owner: **coroutine** *, §44.
p: **specnode** *, §40.
panic = macro ( ), §13.
pass_after = macro ( ), §125.
self: **register coroutine** *, §124.
set = 33, §49.
stage: **int**, §23.
state: **int**, §44.
switch1: label, §130.
wait = macro ( ), §125.
x: **specnode**, §44.
z: **spec**, §44.

138. Here are the basic boolean operations, which account for 24 of MMIX's 256 opcodes.

⟨Cases to compute the results of register-to-register operation 137⟩ $+\equiv$
case *or*: $data\to x.o.h = data\to y.o.h \mid data\to z.o.h$;
  $data\to x.o.l = data\to y.o.l \mid data\to z.o.l$;
  break;
case *orn*: $data\to x.o.h = data\to y.o.h \mid \sim data\to z.o.h$;
  $data\to x.o.l = data\to y.o.l \mid \sim data\to z.o.l$;
  break;
case *nor*: $data\to x.o.h = \sim(data\to y.o.h \mid data\to z.o.h)$;
  $data\to x.o.l = \sim(data\to y.o.l \mid data\to z.o.l)$;
  break;
case *and*: $data\to x.o.h = data\to y.o.h \,\&\, data\to z.o.h$;
  $data\to x.o.l = data\to y.o.l \,\&\, data\to z.o.l$;
  break;
case *andn*: $data\to x.o.h = data\to y.o.h \,\&\, \sim data\to z.o.h$;
  $data\to x.o.l = data\to y.o.l \,\&\, \sim data\to z.o.l$;
  break;
case *nand*: $data\to x.o.h = \sim(data\to y.o.h \,\&\, data\to z.o.h)$;
  $data\to x.o.l = \sim(data\to y.o.l \,\&\, data\to z.o.l)$;
  break;
case *xor*: $data\to x.o.h = data\to y.o.h \oplus data\to z.o.h$;
  $data\to x.o.l = data\to y.o.l \oplus data\to z.o.l$;
  break;
case *nxor*: $data\to x.o.h = data\to y.o.h \oplus \sim data\to z.o.h$;
  $data\to x.o.l = data\to y.o.l \oplus \sim data\to z.o.l$;
  break;

139. The implementation of ADDU is only slightly more difficult. It would be trivial except for the fact that internal opcode *addu* is used not only for the ADDU[I] and INC[M][H,L] operations, in which we simply want to add $data\to y.o$ to $data\to z.o$, but also for operations like 4ADDU.

⟨Cases to compute the results of register-to-register operation 137⟩ $+\equiv$
case *addu*: $data\to x.o = oplus((data\to op \,\&\, \#\texttt{f8}) \equiv \#28\ ?$
    $shift\_left(data\to y.o, 1 + ((data\to op \gg 1) \,\&\, \#3)) : data\to y.o, data\to z.o)$;
  break;
case *subu*: $data\to x.o = ominus(data\to y.o, data\to z.o)$; **break**;

140. Signed addition and subtraction produce the same results as their unsigned counterparts, but overflow must also be detected. Overflow occurs when adding y to z if and only if y and z have the same sign but their sum has a different sign. Overflow occurs in the calculation $x = y - z$ if and only if it occurs in the calculation $y = x + z$.

⟨Cases to compute the results of register-to-register operation 137⟩ $+\equiv$
case *add*: $data\to x.o = oplus(data\to y.o, data\to z.o)$;
  if $(((data\to y.o.h \oplus data\to z.o.h) \,\&\, sign\_bit) \equiv 0 \wedge ((data\to y.o.h \oplus data\to x.o.h) \,\&\, sign\_bit) \neq 0)$
    $data\to interrupt \mid=$ V_BIT;
  break;

case *sub*: $data\to x.o = ominus(data\to y.o, data\to z.o)$;
  if $(((data\to x.o.h \oplus data\to z.o.h)\ \&\ sign\_bit) \equiv 0 \land ((data\to y.o.h \oplus data\to x.o.h)\ \&\ sign\_bit) \neq 0)$
    $data\to interrupt$ |= V_BIT;
  break;

141. The shift commands might take more than one cycle, or they might even be pipelined, if the default value of *pipe_seq*[*sh*] is changed. But we compute shifts all at once here, because other parts of the simulator will take care of the pipeline timing. (Notice that *shlu* is changed to *sh*, for this reason. Similar changes to the internal op codes are made for other operators below.)

#define *shift_amt* $(data\to z.o.h \lor data\to z.o.l \geq 64\ ?\ 64 : data\to z.o.l)$

⟨ Cases to compute the results of register-to-register operation 137 ⟩ +≡
case *shlu*: $data\to x.o = shift\_left(data\to y.o, shift\_amt)$; $data\to i = sh$; **break**;
case *shl*: $data\to x.o = shift\_left(data\to y.o, shift\_amt)$; $data\to i = sh$;
  { **octa** *tmpo*;
    $tmpo = shift\_right(data\to x.o, shift\_amt, 0)$;
    if $(tmpo.h \neq data\to y.o.h \lor tmpo.l \neq data\to y.o.l)$ $data\to interrupt$ |= V_BIT;
  } **break**;
case *shru*: $data\to x.o = shift\_right(data\to y.o, shift\_amt, 1)$; $data\to i = sh$; **break**;
case *shr*: $data\to x.o = shift\_right(data\to y.o, shift\_amt, 0)$; $data\to i = sh$; **break**;

142. The MUX operation has three operands, namely *data*→*y*, *data*→*z*, and *data*→*b*; the third operand is the current (speculative) value of rM, the special mask register. Otherwise MUX is unexceptional.

⟨ Cases to compute the results of register-to-register operation 137 ⟩ +≡
case *mux*: $data\to x.o.h = (data\to y.o.h\ \&\ data\to b.o.h) + (data\to z.o.h\ \&\ {\sim}data\to b.o.h)$;
  $data\to x.o.l = (data\to y.o.l\ \&\ data\to b.o.l) + (data\to z.o.l\ \&\ {\sim}data\to b.o.l)$;
  break;

---

add = 29, §49.
addu = 30, §49.
and = 37, §49.
andn = 38, §49.
b: **spec**, §44.
data: **register control** *, §124.
h: **tetra**, §17.
i: **internal_opcode**, §44.
interrupt: **unsigned int**, §44.
l: **tetra**, §17.
mux = 11, §49.
nand = 39, §49.
nor = 36, §49.
nxor = 41, §49.
o: **octa**, §40.
octa = **struct**, §17.
ominus: **octa** ( ), MMIX-ARITH §5.
op: **mmix_opcode**, §44.
oplus: **octa** ( ), MMIX-ARITH §5.
or = 34, §49.
orn = 35, §49.
pipe_seq: **unsigned char** [ ][ ], §136.
sh = 10, §49.
shift_left: **octa** ( ), MMIX-ARITH §7.
shift_right: **octa** ( ), MMIX-ARITH §7.
shl = 44, §49.
shlu = 42, §49.
shr = 45, §49.
shru = 43, §49.
sign_bit = macro, §80.
sub = 31, §49.
subu = 32, §49.
V_BIT = 1 ≪ 14, §54.
x: **specnode**, §44.
xor = 40, §49.
y: **spec**, §44.
z: **spec**, §44.

143. Comparisons are a breeze.

⟨ Cases to compute the results of register-to-register operation 137 ⟩ +≡
case *cmp*: **if** ((*data*→*y.o.h* & *sign_bit*) > (*data*→*z.o.h* & *sign_bit*)) **goto** *cmp_neg*;
  if ((*data*→*y.o.h* & *sign_bit*) < (*data*→*z.o.h* & *sign_bit*)) **goto** *cmp_pos*;
case *cmpu*: **if** (*data*→*y.o.h* < *data*→*z.o.h*) **goto** *cmp_neg*;
  if (*data*→*y.o.h* > *data*→*z.o.h*) **goto** *cmp_pos*;
  if (*data*→*y.o.l* < *data*→*z.o.l*) **goto** *cmp_neg*;
  if (*data*→*y.o.l* > *data*→*z.o.l*) **goto** *cmp_pos*;
cmp_zero: **break**;   /* *data*→*x* is zero */
cmp_pos: *data*→*x.o.l* = 1; **break**;   /* *data*→*x.o.h* is zero */
cmp_neg: *data*→*x.o* = *neg_one*; **break**;

144. The other operations will be deferred until later, now that we understand the basic ideas. But one more piece of code ought to be written before we move on, because it completes the execution stage for the simple cases already considered.

The *ren_x* and *ren_a* fields tell us whether the *x* and/or *a* fields contain valid information that should become officially known.

⟨ Finish execution of an operation 144 ⟩ ≡
fin_ex: **if** (*data*→*ren_x*) *data*→*x.known* = *true*;
  else if (*data*→*mem_x*) {
    data→*x.known* = *true*;
    if (¬(*data*→*x.addr.h* & #`ffff0000`)) *data*→*x.addr.l* &= −8;
  }
  if (*data*→*ren_a*) *data*→*a.known* = *true*;
  if (*data*→*loc.h* & *sign_bit*) *data*→*ra.o.l* = 0;
    /* no trips enabled for the operating system */
  if (*data*→*interrupt* & #**ffff**) ⟨ Handle interrupt at end of execution stage 307 ⟩;
die: *data*→*owner* = Λ; **goto** *terminate*;   /* this coroutine now fades away */

This code is used in section 130.

145. The commission/deissue stage. Control blocks leave the reorder buffer either at the hot end (when they're committed) or at the cool end (when they're deissued). We hope most of them are committed, but from time to time our speculation is incorrect and we must deissue a sequence of instructions that prove to be unwanted. Deissuing must take priority over committing, because the dispatcher cannot do anything until the machine's cool state has stabilized.

Deissuing changes the cool state by undoing the most recently issued instructions, in reverse order. Committing changes the hot state by doing the least recently issued instructions, in their original order. Both operations are similar, so we assume that they take the same time; at most *commit_max* instructions are deissued and/or committed on each clock cycle.

```
⟨ Deissue the coolest instruction 145 ⟩ ≡
  {
    cool = (cool ≡ reorder_top ? reorder_bot : cool + 1);
    if (verbose & issue_bit) {
      printf("Deissuing␣"); print_control_block(cool);
      if (cool→owner) { printf("␣"); print_coroutine_id(cool→owner); }
      printf("\n");
    }
    if (cool→ren_x) rename_regs++, spec_rem(&cool→x);
    if (cool→ren_a) rename_regs++, spec_rem(&cool→a);
    if (cool→mem_x) mem_slots++, spec_rem(&cool→x);
    if (cool→set_l) spec_rem(&cool→rl);
    if (cool→owner) {
      if (cool→owner→lockloc) *(cool→owner→lockloc) = Λ, cool→owner→lockloc = Λ;
      if (cool→owner→next) unschedule(cool→owner);
    }
    cool_O = cool→cur_O; cool_S = cool→cur_S;
    deissues--;
  }
```

This code is used in section 67.

a: **specnode**, §44.
addr: **octa**, §40.
cmp = 46, §49.
cmpu = 47, §49.
commit_max: **int**, §59.
cool: **control** ∗, §60.
cool_O: **octa**, §98.
cool_S: **octa**, §98.
cur_O: **octa**, §44.
cur_S: **octa**, §44.
data: **register control** ∗, §124.
deissues: **int**, §60.
h: **tetra**, §17.
interrupt: **unsigned int**, §44.
issue_bit = 1 ≪ 0, §8.
known: **bool**, §40.
l: **tetra**, §17.
loc: **octa**, §44.
lockloc: **coroutine** ∗∗, §23.
mem_slots: **int**, §86.
mem_x: **bool**, §44.
neg_one: **octa**, MMIX-ARITH §4.
next: **coroutine** ∗, §23.
o: **octa**, §40.
owner: **coroutine** ∗, §44.
print_control_block: **static void** ( ), §46.
print_coroutine_id: **static void** ( ), §25.
printf: **int** ( ), <stdio.h>.
ra: **spec**, §44.
ren_a: **bool**, §44.
ren_x: **bool**, §44.
rename_regs: **int**, §86.
reorder_bot: **control** ∗, §60.
reorder_top: **control** ∗, §60.
rl: **specnode**, §44.
set_l: **bool**, §44.
sign_bit = macro, §80.
spec_rem: **static void** ( ), §97.
terminate: label, §125.
true = 1, §11.
unschedule: **static void** ( ), §33.
verbose: **int**, §4.
x: **specnode**, §44.
y: **spec**, §44.
z: **spec**, §44.

146. ⟨ Commit the hottest instruction, or **break** if it's not ready 146 ⟩ ≡

```
{
  if (nullifying) ⟨ Nullify the hottest instruction 147 ⟩
  else {
    if (hot→i ≡ get ∧ hot→zz ≡ rQ) new_Q = oandn(g[rQ].o, hot→x.o);
    else if (hot→i ≡ put ∧ hot→xx ≡ rQ) hot→x.o.h |= new_Q.h, hot→x.o.l |= new_Q.l;
    if (hot→mem_x) ⟨ Commit to memory if possible, otherwise break 256 ⟩;
    if (hot→stack_alert) stack_overflow = true;
    else if (stack_overflow ∧ ¬hot→interim) {
      g[rQ].o.l |= STACK_OVERFLOW, new_Q.l |= STACK_OVERFLOW, stack_overflow = false;
      if (verbose & issue_bit) {
        printf("␣setting␣rQ="); print_octa(g[rQ].o); printf("\n");
      }
    }
    if (verbose & issue_bit) {
      printf("Committing␣"); print_control_block(hot); printf("\n");
    }
    if (hot→ren_x) rename_regs++, hot→x.up→o = hot→x.o, spec_rem(&(hot→x));
    if (hot→ren_a) rename_regs++, hot→a.up→o = hot→a.o, spec_rem(&(hot→a));
    if (hot→set_l) hot→rl.up→o = hot→rl.o, spec_rem(&(hot→rl));
    if (hot→arith_exc) g[rA].o.l |= hot→arith_exc;
    if (hot→usage) {
      g[rU].o.l++; if (g[rU].o.l ≡ 0) {
        g[rU].o.h++; if ((g[rU].o.h & #7fff) ≡ 0) g[rU].o.h −= #8000;
      }
    }
  }
  if (hot→interrupt ≥ H_BIT) ⟨ Begin an interruption and break 317 ⟩;
}
```

This code is used in section 67.

147. A load or store instruction is "nullified" if it is about to be captured by a trap interrupt. In such cases it will be the only item in the reorder buffer; thus nullifying is sort of a cross between deissuing and committing. (It is important to have stopped dispatching when nullification is necessary, because instructions such as *incgamma* and *decgamma* change rS, and we need to change it back when an unexpected interruption occurs.)

⟨ Nullify the hottest instruction 147 ⟩ ≡

```
{
  if (verbose & issue_bit) {
    printf("Nullifying␣"); print_control_block(hot); printf("\n");
  }
  if (hot→ren_x) rename_regs++, spec_rem(&hot→x);
  if (hot→ren_a) rename_regs++, spec_rem(&hot→a);
  if (hot→mem_x) mem_slots++, spec_rem(&hot→x);
  if (hot→set_l) spec_rem(&hot→rl);
  cool_O = hot→cur_O, cool_S = hot→cur_S;
  nullifying = false;
```

```
}
```

This code is used in section 146.

148. Interrupt bits in rQ might be lost if they are set between a GET and a PUT. Therefore we don't allow PUT to zero out bits that have become 1 since the most recently committed GET.

```
⟨ Global variables 20 ⟩ +≡
  octa new_Q;    /* when rQ increases in any bit position, so should this */
  bool stack_overflow;    /* stack overflow not yet reported */
```

a: **specnode**, §44.
arith_exc: **unsigned int**, §44.
bool = **enum**, §11.
cool_O: **octa**, §98.
cool_S: **octa**, §98.
cur_O: **octa**, §44.
cur_S: **octa**, §44.
decgamma = 85, §49.
false = 0, §11.
g: **specnode** [ ], §86.
get = 54, §49.
h: **tetra**, §17.
H_BIT = 1 ≪ 16, §54.
hot: **control** *, §60.
i: **internal_opcode**, §44.
incgamma = 84, §49.
interim: **bool**, §44.
interrupt: **unsigned int**, §44.
issue_bit = 1 ≪ 0, §8.
l: **tetra**, §17.
mem_slots: **int**, §86.
mem_x: **bool**, §44.
nullifying: **bool**, §315.
o: **octa**, §40.
oandn: **octa** ( ), MMIX-ARITH §25.
octa = **struct**, §17.
print_control_block: **static void** ( ), §46.
print_octa: **static void** ( ), §19.
printf: **int** ( ), <stdio.h>.
put = 55, §49.
rA = 21, §52.
ren_a: **bool**, §44.
ren_x: **bool**, §44.
rename_regs: **int**, §86.
rl: **specnode**, §44.
rQ = 16, §52.
rU = 17, §52.
set_l: **bool**, §44.
spec_rem: **static void** ( ), §97.
stack_alert: **bool**, §44.
STACK_OVERFLOW = 1 ≪ 7, §57.
true = 1, §11.
up: **specnode** *, §40.
usage: **bool**, §44.
verbose: **int**, §4.
x: **specnode**, §44.
xx: **unsigned char**, §44.
zz: **unsigned char**, §44.

149. An instruction will not be committed immediately if it violates the basic security rule of MMIX: An instruction in a nonnegative location should not be performed unless all eight of the internal interrupts have been enabled in the interrupt mask register rK. Conversely, an instruction in a negative location should not be performed if the P_BIT is enabled in rK.

Such instructions take one extra cycle before they are committed. The nonnegative-location case turns on the S_BIT of both rK and rQ, leading to an immediate interrupt (unless the current instruction is *trap*, *put*, or *resume*).

```
⟨ Check for security violation, break if so 149 ⟩ ≡
  {
    if (hot→loc.h & sign_bit) {
      if ((g[rK].o.h & P_BIT) ∧ ¬(hot→interrupt & P_BIT)) {
        hot→interrupt |= P_BIT;
        g[rQ].o.h |= P_BIT;
        new_Q.h |= P_BIT;
        if (verbose & issue_bit) {
          printf(" setting rQ="); print_octa(g[rQ].o); printf("\n");
        }
        break;
      }
    } else if ((g[rK].o.h & #ff) ≠ #ff ∧ ¬(hot→interrupt & S_BIT)) {
      hot→interrupt |= S_BIT;
      g[rQ].o.h |= S_BIT;
      new_Q.h |= S_BIT;
      g[rK].o.h |= S_BIT;
      if (verbose & issue_bit) {
        printf(" setting rQ="); print_octa(g[rQ].o);
        printf(", rK="); print_octa(g[rK].o); printf("\n");
      }
      break;
    }
  }
```

This code is used in section 67.

150. Branch prediction. An MMIX programmer distinguishes statically between "branches" and "probable branches," but many modern computers attempt to do better by implementing dynamic branch prediction. (See, for example, section 4.3 of Hennessy and Patterson's *Computer Architecture*, second edition.) Experience has shown that dynamic branch prediction can significantly improve the performance of speculative execution, by reducing the number of instructions that need to be deissued.

This simulator has an optional *bp_table* containing 2^{a+b+c} entries of n bits each, where n is between 1 and 8. Usually n is 1 or 2 in practice, but 8 bits are allocated per entry for convenience in this program. The *bp_table* is consulted and updated on every branch instruction (every B or PB instruction, but not JMP), for advice on past history of similar situations. It is indexed by the a least significant bits of the address of the instruction, the b most recent bits of global branch history, and the next c bits of both address and history (exclusive-ored).

A *bp_table* entry begins at zero and is regarded as a signed n-bit number. If it is nonnegative, we will follow the prediction in the instruction, namely to predict a branch taken only in the PB case. If it is negative, we will predict the opposite of the instruction's recommendation. The n-bit number is increased (if possible) if the instruction's prediction was correct, decreased (if possible) if the instruction's prediction was incorrect.

(Incidentally, a large value of n is not necessarily a good idea. For example, if $n = 8$ the machine might need 128 steps to recognize that a branch taken the first 150 times is not taken the next 150 times. And if we modify the update criteria to avoid this problem, we obtain a scheme that is rarely better than a simple scheme with smaller n.)

The values a, b, c, and n in this discussion are called *bp_a*, *bp_b*, *bp_c*, and *bp_n* in the program.

⟨ External variables 4 ⟩ +≡
```
Extern int bp_a, bp_b, bp_c, bp_n;    /* parameters for branch prediction */
Extern char *bp_table;    /* either Λ or an array of 2^{a+b+c} items */
```

Extern = macro, §4.
g: **specnode** [], §86.
h: **tetra**, §17.
hot: **control** *, §60.
interrupt: **unsigned int**, §44.
issue_bit = 1 ≪ 0, §8.
loc: **octa**, §44.
new_Q: **octa**, §148.
o: **octa**, §40.
P_BIT = 1 ≪ 0, §54.
print_octa: **static void** ( ), §19.
printf: **int** ( ), <stdio.h>.
put = 55, §49.
resume = 76, §49.
rK = 15, §52.
rQ = 16, §52.
S_BIT = 1 ≪ 1, §54.
sign_bit = macro, §80.
trap = 82, §49.
verbose: **int**, §4.

151. Branch prediction is made when we are either about to issue an instruction or peeking ahead. We look at the *bp_table*, but we don't want to update it yet.

```
⟨ Predict a branch outcome 151 ⟩ ≡
  {
    predicted = op & #10;      /* start with the instruction's recommendation */
    if (bp_table) { register int h;
      m = ((head→loc.l & bp_cmask) ≪ bp_b) + (head→loc.l & bp_amask);
      m = ((cool_hist & bp_bcmask) ≪ bp_a) ⊕ (m ≫ 2);
      h = bp_table[m];
      if (h & bp_npower) predicted ⊕= #10;
    }
    if (predicted) peek_hist = (peek_hist ≪ 1) + 1;
    else peek_hist ≪= 1;
  }
```

This code is used in section 85.

152. We update the *bp_table* when an instruction is issued. And we store the opposite table value in *cool→x.o.l*, just in case our prediction turns out to be wrong.

```
⟨ Record the result of branch prediction 152 ⟩ ≡
  if (bp_table) { register int reversed, h, h_up, h_down;
    reversed = op & #10;
    if (peek_hist & 1) reversed ⊕= #10;
    m = ((head→loc.l & bp_cmask) ≪ bp_b) + (head→loc.l & bp_amask);
    m = ((cool_hist & bp_bcmask) ≪ bp_a) ⊕ (m ≫ 2);
    h = bp_table[m];
    h_up = (h + 1) & bp_nmask; if (h_up ≡ bp_npower) h_up = h;
    if (h ≡ bp_npower) h_down = h; else h_down = (h − 1) & bp_nmask;
    if (reversed) {
      bp_table[m] = h_down, cool→x.o.l = h_up;
      cool→i = pbr + br − cool→i;      /* reverse the sense */
      bp_rev_stat++;
    } else {
      bp_table[m] = h_up, cool→x.o.l = h_down;      /* go with the flow */
      bp_ok_stat++;
    }
    if (verbose & show_pred_bit) {
      printf("␣predicting␣"); print_octa(cool→loc);
      printf("␣%s;␣bp[%x]=%d\n", reversed ? "NG" : "OK", m,
          bp_table[m] − ((bp_table[m] & bp_npower) ≪ 1));
    }
    cool→x.o.h = m;
  }
```

This code is used in section 75.

153. The calculations in the previous sections need several precomputed constants, depending on the parameters a, b, c, and n.

⟨Initialize everything 22⟩ +≡
```
bp_amask = ((1 ≪ bp_a) − 1) ≪ 2;   /* least a bits of instruction address */
bp_cmask = ((1 ≪ bp_c) − 1) ≪ (bp_a + 2);   /* the next c address bits */
bp_bcmask = (1 ≪ (bp_b + bp_c)) − 1;   /* least b + c bits of history info */
bp_nmask = (1 ≪ bp_n) − 1;   /* least significant n bits */
bp_npower = 1 ≪ (bp_n − 1);   /* 2^{n−1}, the sign bit of an n-bit number */
```

154. ⟨Global variables 20⟩ +≡
```
int bp_amask, bp_cmask, bp_bcmask, bp_nmask, bp_npower;
int bp_rev_stat, bp_ok_stat;   /* how often we overrode and agreed */
int bp_bad_stat, bp_good_stat;   /* how often we failed and succeeded */
```

155. After a branch or probable branch instruction has been issued and the value of the relevant register has been computed in the reorder buffer as *data→b.o*, we're ready to determine if the prediction was correct or not.

⟨Cases for stage 1 execution 155⟩ ≡
```
case br: case pbr: j = register_truth(data→b.o, data→op);
  if (j) data→go.o = data→z.o; else data→go.o = data→y.o;
  if (j ≡ (data→i ≡ pbr)) bp_good_stat++;
  else {   /* oops, misprediction */
    bp_bad_stat++;
    ⟨Recover from incorrect branch prediction 160⟩;
  }
  goto fin_ex;
```
See also sections 313, 325, 327, 328, 329, 331, and 356.

This code is used in section 132.

b: **spec**, §44.
bp_a: **int**, §150.
bp_b: **int**, §150.
bp_c: **int**, §150.
bp_n: **int**, §150.
bp_table: **char** ∗, §150.
br = 69, §49.
cool: **control** ∗, §60.
cool_hist: **unsigned int**, §99.
data: **register control** ∗, §124.
fin_ex: label, §144.
go: **specnode**, §44.
h: **tetra**, §17.
head: **fetch** ∗, §69.
i: **internal_opcode**, §44.
j: **register int**, §12.
l: **tetra**, §17.
loc: **octa**, §68.
loc: **octa**, §44.
m: **register int**, §12.
o: **octa**, §40.
op: **register mmix_opcode**, §75.
op: **mmix_opcode**, §44.
pbr = 70, §49.
peek_hist: **unsigned int**, §99.
predicted: **register int**, §85.
print_octa: **static void** ( ), §19.
printf: **int** ( ), <stdio.h>.
register_truth: **static int** ( ), §157.
show_pred_bit = 1 ≪ 7, §8.
verbose: **int**, §4.
x: **specnode**, §44.
y: **spec**, §44.
z: **spec**, §44.

156. The *register_truth* subroutine is used by B, PB, CS, and ZS commands to decide whether an octabyte satisfies the conditions of the opcode, *data→op*.

⟨ Internal prototypes 13 ⟩ +≡

```
static int register_truth ARGS((octa, mmix_opcode));
```

157. ⟨ Subroutines 14 ⟩ +≡

```
static int register_truth(o, op)
     octa o;
     mmix_opcode op;
{ register int b;
  switch ((op >> 1) & #3) {
  case 0: b = o.h >> 31; break;     /* negative? */
  case 1: b = (o.h ≡ 0 ∧ o.l ≡ 0); break;     /* zero? */
  case 2: b = (o.h < sign_bit ∧ (o.h ∨ o.l)); break;     /* positive? */
  case 3: b = o.l & #1; break;     /* odd? */
  }
  if (op & #8) return b ⊕ 1;
  else return b;
}
```

158. The *issued_between* subroutine determines how many speculative instructions were issued between a given control block in the reorder buffer and the current *cool* pointer, when *cc* = *cool*.

⟨ Internal prototypes 13 ⟩ +≡

```
static int issued_between ARGS((control *, control *));
```

159. ⟨ Subroutines 14 ⟩ +≡

```
static int issued_between(c, cc)
     control *c, *cc;
{
  if (c > cc) return c − 1 − cc;
  return (c − reorder_bot) + (reorder_top − cc);
}
```

160. If more than one functional unit is able to process branch instructions and if two of them simultaneously discover misprediction, or if misprediction is detected by one unit just as another unit is generating an interrupt, we assume that an arbitration takes place so that only the hottest one actually deissues the cooler instructions.

Changes to the *bp_table* aren't undone when they were made on speculation in an instruction being deissued; nor do we worry about cases where the same *bp_table* entry is being updated by two or more active coroutines. After all, the *bp_table* is just a heuristic, not part of the real computation. We correct the *bp_table* only if we discover that a prediction was wrong, so that we will be less likely to make the same mistake later.

⟨ Recover from incorrect branch prediction 160 ⟩ ≡

```
i = issued_between(data, cool);
if (i < deissues) goto die;
deissues = i;
old_tail = tail = head; resuming = 0;     /* clear the fetch buffer */
```

```
⟨ Restart the fetch coroutine 287 ⟩;
inst_ptr.o = data→go.o, inst_ptr.p = Λ;
if (¬(data→loc.h & sign_bit)) {
  if (inst_ptr.o.h & sign_bit) data→interrupt |= P_BIT;
  else data→interrupt &= ∼P_BIT;
}
if (bp_table) {
  bp_table[data→x.o.h] = data→x.o.l;      /* this is what we should have stored */
  if (verbose & show_pred_bit) {
    printf("␣mispredicted␣"); print_octa(data→loc);
    printf(";␣bp[%x]=%d\n", data→x.o.h, data→x.o.l − ((data→x.o.l & bp_npower) ≪ 1));
  }
}
cool_hist = (j ? (data→hist ≪ 1) + 1 : data→hist ≪ 1);
```

This code is used in section 155.

161. ⟨ External prototypes 9 ⟩ +≡

```
Extern void print_stats ARGS((void));
```

162. ⟨ External routines 10 ⟩ +≡

```
void print_stats()
{
  register int j;
  if (bp_table)
    printf("Predictions:␣%d␣in␣agreement,␣%d␣in␣opposition;␣%d␣good,␣%d␣bad\n",
        bp_ok_stat, bp_rev_stat, bp_good_stat, bp_bad_stat);
  else printf("Predictions:␣%d␣good,␣%d␣bad\n", bp_good_stat, bp_bad_stat);
  printf("Instructions␣issued␣per␣cycle:\n");
  for (j = 0; j ≤ dispatch_max; j++) printf("␣␣%d␣␣␣%d\n", j, dispatch_stat[j]);
}
```

ARGS = macro, §6.
bp_bad_stat: **int**, §154.
bp_good_stat: **int**, §154.
bp_npower: **int**, §154.
bp_ok_stat: **int**, §154.
bp_rev_stat: **int**, §154.
bp_table: **char** ∗, §150.
control = **struct**, §44.
cool: **control** ∗, §60.
cool_hist: **unsigned int**, §99.
data: **register control** ∗, §124.
deissues: **int**, §60.
die: label, §144.
dispatch_max: **int**, §59.
dispatch_stat: **int** ∗, §66.
Extern = macro, §4.
go: **specnode**, §44.
h: **tetra**, §17.
head: **fetch** ∗, §69.
hist: **unsigned int**, §44.
i: **register int**, §12.
inst_ptr: **spec**, §284.
interrupt: **unsigned int**, §44.
j: **register int**, §12.
l: **tetra**, §17.
loc: **octa**, §44.
mmix_opcode = **enum**, §47.
o: **octa**, §40.
octa = **struct**, §17.
old_tail: **fetch** ∗, §70.
op: **mmix_opcode**, §44.
p: **specnode** ∗, §40.
P_BIT = 1 ≪ 0, §54.
print_octa: **static void** ( ), §19.
printf: **int** ( ), <stdio.h>.
reorder_bot: **control** ∗, §60.
reorder_top: **control** ∗, §60.
resuming: **int**, §78.
show_pred_bit = 1 ≪ 7, §8.
sign_bit = macro, §80.
tail: **fetch** ∗, §69.
verbose: **int**, §4.
x: **specnode**, §44.

163. Cache memory. It's time now to consider MMIX's MMU, the memory management unit. This part of the machine deals with the critical problem of getting data to and from the computational units. In a RISC architecture all interaction between main memory and the computer registers is specified by load and store instructions; thus memory accesses are much easier to deal with than they would be on a machine with more complex kinds of interaction. But memory management is still difficult, if we want to do it well, because main memory typically operates at a much slower speed than the registers do. High-speed implementations of MMIX introduce intermediate "caches" of storage in order to keep the most important data accessible, and cache maintenance can be complicated when all the details are taken into account. (See, for example, Chapter 5 of Hennessy and Patterson's *Computer Architecture*, second edition.)

This simulator can be configured to have up to three auxiliary caches between registers and memory: An I-cache for instructions, a D-cache for data, and an S-cache for both instructions and data. The S-cache, also called a *secondary cache*, is supported only if both I-cache and D-cache are present. Arbitrary access times for each cache can be specified independently; we might assume, for example, that data items in the I-cache or D-cache can be sent to a register in one or two clock cycles, but the access time for the S-cache might be say 5 cycles, and main memory might require 20 cycles or more. Our speculative pipeline can have many functional units handling load and store instructions, but only one load or store instruction can be updating the D-cache or S-cache or main memory at a time. (However, the D-cache can have several read ports; furthermore, data might be passing between the S-cache and memory while other data is passing between the reorder buffer and the D-cache.)

Besides the optional I-cache, D-cache, and S-cache, there are required caches called the IT-cache and DT-cache, for translation of virtual addresses to physical addresses. A translation cache is often called a "translation lookaside buffer" or TLB; but we call it a cache since it is implemented in nearly the same way as an I-cache.

164. Consider a cache that has blocks of 2^b bytes each and associativity 2^a; here $b \geq 3$ and $a \geq 0$. The I-cache, D-cache, and S-cache are addressed by 48-bit physical addresses, as if they were part of main memory; but the IT and DT caches are addressed by 64-bit keys, obtained from a virtual address by blanking out the lower s bits and inserting the value of n, where the page size s and the process number n are found in rV. We will consider all caches to be addressed by 64-bit keys, so that both cases are handled with the same basic methods.

Given a 64-bit key, we ignore the low-order b bits and use the next c bits to address the *cache set*; then the remaining $64 - b - c$ bits should match one of 2^a *tags* in that set. The case $a = 0$ corresponds to a so-called *direct-mapped* cache; the case $c = 0$ corresponds to a so-called *fully associative* cache. With 2^c sets of 2^a blocks each, and 2^b bytes per block, the cache contains 2^{a+b+c} bytes of data, in addition to the space needed for tags. Translation caches have $b = 3$ and they also usually have $c = 0$.

If a tag matches the specified bits, we "hit" in the cache and can use and/or update the data found there. Otherwise we "miss," and we probably want to replace one of the cache blocks by the block containing the item sought. The item chosen for replacement is called a *victim*. The choice of victim is forced when the cache is direct-mapped, but four strategies for victim selection are available when we must choose from among 2^a entries for $a > 0$:

• "Random" selection chooses the victim by extracting the least significant a bits of the clock.

• "Serial" selection chooses $0, 1, \ldots, 2^a - 1, 0, 1, \ldots, 2^a - 1, 0, \ldots$ on successive trials.

• "LRU (Least Recently Used)" selection chooses the victim that ranks last if items are ranked inversely to the time that has elapsed since their previous use.

• "Pseudo-LRU" selection chooses the victim by a rough approximation to LRU that is simpler to implement in hardware. It requires a bit table $r_1 \ldots r_{2^a-1}$. Whenever we use an item with binary address $(i_1 \ldots i_a)_2$ in the set, we adjust the bit table as follows:

$$r_1 \leftarrow 1 - i_1, \quad r_{1i_1} \leftarrow 1 - i_2, \quad \ldots, \quad r_{1i_1 \ldots i_{a-1}} \leftarrow 1 - i_a;$$

here the subscripts on r are binary numbers. (For example, when $a = 3$, the use of element $(010)_2$ sets $r_1 \leftarrow 1$, $r_{10} \leftarrow 0$, $r_{101} \leftarrow 1$, where r_{101} means the same as r_5.) To select a victim, we start with $l \leftarrow 1$ and then repeatedly set $l \leftarrow 2l + r_l$, a times; then we choose element $l - 2^a$. When $a = 1$, this scheme is equivalent to LRU. When $a = 2$, this scheme was implemented in the Intel 80486 chip.

⟨ Type definitions 11 ⟩ +≡
  typedef enum {
    random, *serial*, *pseudo_lru*, *lru*
  } **replace_policy**;

165. A cache might also include a "victim" area, which contains the last 2^v victim blocks removed from the main cache area. The victim area can be searched in parallel with the specified cache set, thereby increasing the chance of a hit without making the search go slower. Each of the three replacement policies can be used also in the victim cache.

166. A cache also has a *granularity* 2^g, where $b \ge g \ge 3$. This means that we maintain, for each cache block, a set of 2^{b-g} "dirty bits," which identify the 2^g-byte groups that have possibly changed since they were last read from memory. Thus if $g = b$, an entire cache block is either dirty or clean; if $g = 3$, the dirtiness of each octabyte is maintained separately.

Two policies are available when new data is written into all or part of a cache block. We can *write-through*, meaning that we send all new data to memory immediately and never mark anything dirty; or we can *write-back*, meaning that we update the memory from the cache only when absolutely necessary. Furthermore we can *write-allocate*, meaning that we keep the new data in the cache, even if the cache block being written has to be fetched first because of a miss; or we can *write-around*, meaning that we keep the new data only if it was part of an existing cache block.

(In this discussion, "memory" is shorthand for "the next level of the memory hierarchy"; if there is an S-cache, the I-cache and D-cache write new data to the S-cache, not directly to memory. The I-cache, IT-cache, and DT-cache are read-only, so they do not need the facilities discussed in this section. Moreover, the D-cache and S-cache can be assumed to have the same granularity.)

```
⟨Header definitions 6⟩ +≡
#define WRITE_BACK 1    /* use this if not write-through */
#define WRITE_ALLOC 2   /* use this if not write-around */
```

167. We have seen that many flavors of cache can be simulated. They are represented by **cache** structures, containing arrays of **cacheset** structures that contain arrays of **cacheblock** structures for the individual blocks. We use a full byte to store each *dirty* bit, and we use full integer words to store *rank* fields for LRU processing, etc.; memory economy is less important than simplicity in this simulator.

```
⟨Type definitions 11⟩ +≡
  typedef struct {
    octa tag;    /* bits of key not included in the cache block address */
    char *dirty;    /* array of 2^(g-b) dirty bits, one per granule */
    octa *data;    /* array of 2^(b-3) octabytes, the data in a cache block */
    int rank;    /* auxiliary information for non-random policies */
  } cacheblock;

  typedef cacheblock *cacheset;    /* array of 2^a or 2^v blocks */

  typedef struct {
    int a, b, c, g, v;
      /* lg of associativity, blocksize, setsize, granularity, and victimsize */
    int aa, bb, cc, gg, vv;
      /* associativity, blocksize, setsize, granularity, and victimsize (all powers of 2) */
    int tagmask;    /* -2^(b+c) */
    replace_policy repl, vrepl;    /* how to choose victims and victim-victims */
    int mode;    /* optional WRITE_BACK and/or WRITE_ALLOC */
    int access_time;    /* cycles to know if there's a hit */
    int copy_in_time;    /* cycles to copy a new block into the cache */
    int copy_out_time;    /* cycles to copy an old block from the cache */
    cacheset *set;    /* array of 2^c sets of arrays of cache blocks */
    cacheset victim;    /* the victim cache, if present */
```

```
    coroutine filler;    /* a coroutine for copying new blocks into the cache */
    control filler_ctl;    /* its control block */
    coroutine flusher;    /* a coroutine for writing dirty old data from the cache */
    control flusher_ctl;    /* its control block */
    cacheblock inbuf;    /* filling comes from here */
    cacheblock outbuf;    /* flushing goes to here */
    lockvar lock;    /* nonzero when the cache is being changed significantly */
    lockvar fill_lock;    /* nonzero when filler should pass data back */
    int ports;    /* how many coroutines can be reading the cache? */
    coroutine *reader;
      /* array of coroutines that might be reading simultaneously */
    char *name;    /* "Icache", for example */
  } cache;
```

168. ⟨ External variables 4 ⟩ +≡

```
  Extern cache *Icache, *Dcache, *Scache, *ITcache, *DTcache;
```

169. Now we are ready to define some basic subroutines for cache maintenance. Let's begin with a trivial routine that tests if a given cache block is dirty.

⟨ Internal prototypes 13 ⟩ +≡

```
  static bool is_dirty ARGS((cache *, cacheblock *));
```

170. ⟨ Subroutines 14 ⟩ +≡

```
  static bool is_dirty(c, p)
       cache *c;    /* the cache containing it */
       cacheblock *p;    /* a cache block */
  {
    register int j;
    register char *d = p->dirty;
    for (j = 0; j < c->bb; d++, j += c->gg)
      if (*d) return true;
    return false;
  }
```

ARGS = macro, §6.
bool = **enum**, §11.
control = **struct**, §44.
coroutine = **struct**, §23.
Extern = macro, §4.
false = 0, §11.
lockvar = **coroutine** *, §37.
octa = **struct**, §17.
random = 0, §164.
replace_policy = **enum**, §164.
true = 1, §11.

171. For diagnostic purposes we might want to display an entire cache block.

```
⟨ Internal prototypes 13 ⟩ +≡
  static void print_cache_block ARGS((cacheblock, cache *));
```

172.
```
⟨ Subroutines 14 ⟩ +≡
  static void print_cache_block(p, c)
      cacheblock p;
      cache *c;
  { register int i, j, b = c→bb ≫ 3, g = c→gg ≫ 3;
    printf("%08x%08x:␣", p.tag.h, p.tag.l);
    for (i = j = 0; j < b; j++, i += ((j & (g − 1)) ? 0 : 1))
      printf("%08x%08x%c", p.data[j].h, p.data[j].l, p.dirty[i] ? '*' : '␣');
    printf("␣(%d)\n", p.rank);
  }
```

173.
```
⟨ Internal prototypes 13 ⟩ +≡
  static void print_cache_locks ARGS((cache *));
```

174.
```
⟨ Subroutines 14 ⟩ +≡
  static void print_cache_locks(c)
      cache *c;
  {
    if (c) {
      if (c→lock) printf("%s␣locked␣by␣%s:%d\n", c→name, c→lock→name, c→lock→stage);
      if (c→fill_lock)
        printf("%sfill␣locked␣by␣%s:%d\n", c→name, c→fill_lock→name, c→fill_lock→stage);
    }
  }
```

175. The *print_cache* routine prints the entire contents of a cache. This can be a huge amount of data, but it can be very useful when debugging. Fortunately, the task of debugging favors the use of small caches, since interesting cases arise more often when a cache is fairly small.

```
⟨ External prototypes 9 ⟩ +≡
  Extern void print_cache ARGS((cache *, bool));
```

176.
```
⟨ External routines 10 ⟩ +≡
  void print_cache(c, dirty_only)
      cache *c;
      bool dirty_only;
  {
    if (c) { register int i, j;
      printf("%s␣of␣%s:", dirty_only ? "Dirty␣blocks" : "Contents", c→name);
      if (c→filler.next) {
        printf("␣(filling␣");
        print_octa(c→name[1] ≡ 'T' ? c→filler_ctl.y.o : c→filler_ctl.z.o);
        printf(")");
      }
      if (c→flusher.next) {
        printf("␣(flushing␣");
```

```
        print_octa(c->outbuf.tag);
        printf(")");
      }
      printf("\n");
      ⟨ Print all of c's cache blocks 177 ⟩;
    }
  }
```

177. We don't print the cache blocks that have an invalid tag, unless requested to be verbose.

```
⟨ Print all of c's cache blocks 177 ⟩ ≡
  for (i = 0; i < c->cc; i++)
    for (j = 0; j < c->aa; j++)
      if ((¬(c->set[i][j].tag.h & sign_bit) ∨ (verbose & show_wholecache_bit)) ∧
            (¬dirty_only ∨ is_dirty(c, &c->set[i][j]))) {
        printf("[%d][%d]␣", i, j);
        print_cache_block(c->set[i][j], c);
      }
  for (j = 0; j < c->vv; j++)
    if ((¬(c->victim[j].tag.h & sign_bit) ∨ (verbose & show_wholecache_bit)) ∧
          (¬dirty_only ∨ is_dirty(c, &c->victim[j]))) {
      printf("V[%d]␣", j);
      print_cache_block(c->victim[j], c);
    }
```

This code is used in section 176.

---

aa: **int**, §167.
ARGS = macro, §6.
bb: **int**, §167.
bool = **enum**, §11.
cache = **struct**, §167.
cacheblock = **struct**, §167.
cc: **int**, §167.
data: **octa** ∗, §167.
dirty: **char** ∗, §167.
Extern = macro, §4.
fill_lock: **lockvar**, §167.
filler: **coroutine**, §167.
filler_ctl: **control**, §167.
flusher: **coroutine**, §167.
gg: **int**, §167.
h: **tetra**, §17.
is_dirty: **static bool** ( ), §170.
l: **tetra**, §17.
lock: **lockvar**, §167.
name: **char** ∗, §167.
next: **coroutine** ∗, §23.
o: **octa**, §40.
outbuf: **cacheblock**, §167.
print_octa: **static void** ( ), §19.
printf: **int** ( ), <stdio.h>.
rank: **int**, §167.
set: **cacheset** ∗, §167.
show_wholecache_bit = 1 ≪ 8, §8.
sign_bit = macro, §80.
stage: **int**, §23.
tag: **octa**, §167.
verbose: **int**, §4.
victim: **cacheset**, §167.
vv: **int**, §167.
y: **spec**, §44.
z: **spec**, §44.

178. The *clean_block* routine simply initializes a given cache block.

⟨ External prototypes 9 ⟩ +≡

```
Extern void clean_block ARGS((cache *, cacheblock *));
```

179. ⟨ External routines 10 ⟩ +≡

```
void clean_block(c, p)
    cache *c;
    cacheblock *p;
{
  register int j;
  p->tag.h = sign_bit, p->tag.l = 0;
  for (j = 0; j < c->bb >> 3; j++) p->data[j] = zero_octa;
  for (j = 0; j < c->bb >> c->g; j++) p->dirty[j] = false;
}
```

180. The *zap_cache* routine invalidates all tags of a given cache, effectively restoring it to its initial condition.

⟨ External prototypes 9 ⟩ +≡

```
Extern void zap_cache ARGS((cache *));
```

181. We clear the *dirty* entries here, just to be tidy, although they could actually be left in arbitrary condition when the tags are invalid.

⟨ External routines 10 ⟩ +≡

```
void zap_cache(c)
    cache *c;
{
  register int i, j;
  for (i = 0; i < c->cc; i++)
    for (j = 0; j < c->aa; j++) {
      clean_block(c, &(c->set[i][j]));
    }
  for (j = 0; j < c->vv; j++) {
    clean_block(c, &(c->victim[j]));
  }
}
```

182. The *get_reader* subroutine finds the index of an available reader coroutine for a given cache, or returns a negative value if no readers are available.

⟨ Internal prototypes 13 ⟩ +≡

```
static int get_reader ARGS((cache *));
```

183. ⟨ Subroutines 14 ⟩ +≡

```
static int get_reader(c)
    cache *c;
{ register int j;
  for (j = 0; j < c->ports; j++)
    if (c->reader[j].next ≡ Λ) return j;
  return -1;
}
```

184. The subroutine *copy_block*(c, p, cc, pp) copies the dirty items from block p of cache c into block pp of cache cc, assuming that the destination cache has a sufficiently large block size. (In other words, we assume that $cc\to b \ge c\to b$.) We also assume that both blocks have compatible tags, and that both caches have the same granularity.

```
⟨Internal prototypes 13⟩ +≡
  static void copy_block ARGS((cache *, cacheblock *, cache *, cacheblock *));
```

185.
```
⟨Subroutines 14⟩ +≡
  static void copy_block(c, p, cc, pp)
      cache *c, *cc;
      cacheblock *p, *pp;
  {
    register int j, jj, i, ii, lim;
    register int off = p→tag.l & (cc→bb − 1);
    if (c→g ≠ cc→g ∨ p→tag.h ≠ pp→tag.h ∨ p→tag.l − off ≠ pp→tag.l)
      panic(confusion("copy block"));
    for (j = 0, jj = off ≫ c→g; j < c→bb ≫ c→g; j++, jj++)
      if (p→dirty[j]) {
        pp→dirty[jj] = true;
        for (i = j ≪ (c→g − 3), ii = jj ≪ (c→g − 3), lim = (j + 1) ≪ (c→g − 3); i < lim;
              i++, ii++) pp→data[ii] = p→data[i];
      }
  }
```

aa: **int**, §167.
ARGS = macro, §6.
b: **int**, §167.
bb: **int**, §167.
cache = **struct**, §167.
cacheblock = **struct**, §167.
cc: **int**, §167.
confusion = macro ( ), §13.
data: **octa** ∗, §167.
dirty: **char** ∗, §167.
Extern = macro, §4.
false = 0, §11.
g: **int**, §167.
h: **tetra**, §17.
l: **tetra**, §17.
next: **coroutine** ∗, §23.
panic = macro ( ), §13.
ports: **int**, §167.
reader: **coroutine** ∗, §167.
set: **cacheset** ∗, §167.
sign_bit = macro, §80.
tag: **octa**, §167.
true = 1, §11.
victim: **cacheset**, §167.
vv: **int**, §167.
zero_octa: **octa**, MMIX-ARITH §4.

186. The *choose_victim* subroutine selects the victim to be replaced when we need to change a cache set. We need only one bit of the *rank* fields to implement the r table when *policy* = *pseudo_lru*, and we don't need *rank* at all when *policy* = *random*. Of course we use an a-bit counter to implement *policy* = *serial*. In the other case, *policy* = *lru*, we need an a-bit *rank* field; the least recently used entry has rank 0, and the most recently used entry has rank $2^a - 1 = aa - 1$.

```
⟨Internal prototypes 13⟩ +≡
  static cacheblock *choose_victim ARGS((cacheset, int, replace_policy));
```

187. ⟨Subroutines 14⟩ +≡

```
static cacheblock *choose_victim(s, aa, policy)
    cacheset s;
    int aa;    /* setsize */
    replace_policy policy;
{
  register cacheblock *p;
  register int l, m;
  switch (policy) {
  case random: return &s[ticks.l & (aa − 1)];
  case serial: l = s[0].rank; s[0].rank = (l + 1) & (aa − 1); return &s[l];
  case lru:
    for (p = s; p < s + aa; p++)
      if (p→rank ≡ 0) return p;
    panic(confusion("lru␣victim"));    /* what happened? nobody has rank zero */
  case pseudo_lru:
    for (l = 1, m = aa ≫ 1; m; m ≫= 1) l = l + l + s[l].rank;
    return &s[l − aa];
  }
}
```

188. The *note_usage* subroutine updates the *rank* entries to record the fact that a particular block in a cache set is now being used.

```
⟨Internal prototypes 13⟩ +≡
  static void note_usage ARGS((cacheblock *, cacheset, int, replace_policy));
```

189. ⟨Subroutines 14⟩ +≡

```
static void note_usage(l, s, aa, policy)
    cacheblock *l;    /* a cache block that's probably worth preserving */
    cacheset s;    /* the set that contains l */
    int aa;    /* setsize */
    replace_policy policy;
{
  register cacheblock *p;
  register int j, m, r;
  if (aa ≡ 1 ∨ policy ≤ serial) return;
  if (policy ≡ lru) {
    r = l→rank;
    for (p = s; p < s + aa; p++)
      if (p→rank > r) p→rank−−;
```

```
      l→rank = aa − 1;
    }
    else {  /* policy ≡ pseudo_lru */
      r = l − s;
      for (j = 1, m = aa ≫ 1; m; m ≫= 1)
        if (r & m) s[j].rank = 0, j = j + j + 1;
        else s[j].rank = 1, j = j + j;
    }
    return;
  }
```

190. The *demote_usage* subroutine is sort of the opposite of *note_usage*; it changes the rank of a given block to *least* recently used.

```
⟨ Internal prototypes 13 ⟩ +≡
  static void demote_usage ARGS((cacheblock *, cacheset, int, replace_policy));
```

191. ⟨ Subroutines 14 ⟩ +≡

```
  static void demote_usage(l, s, aa, policy)
      cacheblock *l;   /* a cache block we probably don't need */
      cacheset s;   /* the set that contains l */
      int aa;   /* setsize */
      replace_policy policy;
  {
    register cacheblock *p;
    register int j, m, r;
    if (aa ≡ 1 ∨ policy ≤ serial) return;
    if (policy ≡ lru) {
      r = l→rank;
      for (p = s; p < s + aa; p++)
        if (p→rank < r) p→rank++;
      l→rank = 0;
    }
    else {   /* policy ≡ pseudo_lru */
      r = l − s;
      for (j = 1, m = aa ≫ 1; m; m ≫= 1)
        if (r & m) s[j].rank = 1, j = j + j + 1;
        else s[j].rank = 0, j = j + j;
    }
    return;
  }
```

---

aa: **int**, §167.
ARGS = macro, §6.
cacheblock = **struct**, §167.
cacheset = **cacheblock** *, §167.
confusion = macro ( ), §13.
lru = 3, §164.
panic = macro ( ), §13.
pseudo_lru = 2, §164.
random = 0, §164.
rank: **int**, §167.
replace_policy = **enum**, §164.
serial = 1, §164.
ticks: **Extern octa**, §87.

192. The *cache_search* routine looks for a given key α in a given cache, and returns a cache block if there's a hit; otherwise it returns Λ. If the search hits, the set in which the block was found is stored in global variable *hit_set*. Notice that we need to check more bits of the tag when we search in the victim area.

```
#define cache_addr(c, alf)  c→set[(alf.l & ~(c→tagmask)) ≫ c→b]
⟨Internal prototypes 13⟩ +≡
  static cacheblock *cache_search ARGS((cache *, octa));
```

193. ⟨Subroutines 14⟩ +≡

```
  static cacheblock *cache_search(c, alf)
      cache *c;      /* the cache to be searched */
      octa alf;      /* the key */
  {
    register cacheset s;
    register cacheblock *p;
    s = cache_addr(c, alf);     /* the set corresponding to alf */
    for (p = s; p < s + c→aa; p++)
      if (((p→tag.l ⊕ alf.l) & c→tagmask) ≡ 0 ∧ p→tag.h ≡ alf.h) goto hit;
    s = c→victim;
    if (¬s) return Λ;     /* cache miss, and no victim area */
    for (p = s; p < s + c→vv; p++)
      if (((p→tag.l ⊕ alf.l) & (−c→bb)) ≡ 0 ∧ p→tag.h ≡ alf.h) goto hit;
    return Λ;     /* double miss */
  hit: hit_set = s; return p;
  }
```

194. ⟨Global variables 20⟩ +≡

```
  cacheset hit_set;
```

195. If p = *cache_search*(*c*, *alf*) hits and if we call *use_and_fix*(*c*, *p*) immediately afterwards, cache *c* is updated to record the usage of key *alf*. A hit in the victim area moves the cache block to the main area, unless the *filler* routine of cache *c* is active. A pointer to the (possibly moved) cache block is returned.

```
⟨Internal prototypes 13⟩ +≡
  static cacheblock *use_and_fix ARGS((cache *, cacheblock *));
```

196. ⟨Subroutines 14⟩ +≡

```
  static cacheblock *use_and_fix(c, p)
      cache *c;
      cacheblock *p;
  {
    if (hit_set ≠ c→victim) note_usage(p, hit_set, c→aa, c→repl);
    else {
      note_usage(p, hit_set, c→vv, c→vrepl);     /* found in victim cache */
      if (¬c→filler.next) {
        register cacheset s = cache_addr(c, p→tag);
        register cacheblock *q = choose_victim(s, c→aa, c→repl);
        note_usage(q, s, c→aa, c→repl);
        ⟨Swap cache blocks p and q 197⟩;
```

```
        return q;
      }
    }
    return p;
  }
```

197. We can simply permute the pointers inside the cacheblock structures of a cache, instead of copying the data, if we are careful not to let any of those pointers escape into other data structures.

```
⟨ Swap cache blocks p and q 197 ⟩ ≡
  {
    octa t;
    register char *d = p→dirty;
    register octa *dd = p→data;
    t = p→tag; p→tag = q→tag; q→tag = t;
    p→dirty = q→dirty; q→dirty = d;
    p→data = q→data; q→data = dd;
  }
```

This code is used in sections 196 and 205.

198. The *demote_and_fix* routine is analogous to *use_and_fix*, except that we don't want to promote the data we found.

```
⟨ Internal prototypes 13 ⟩ +≡
  static cacheblock *demote_and_fix ARGS((cache *, cacheblock *));
```

199.
```
⟨ Subroutines 14 ⟩ +≡
  static cacheblock *demote_and_fix(c, p)
      cache *c;
      cacheblock *p;
  {
    if (hit_set ≠ c→victim) demote_usage(p, hit_set, c→aa, c→repl);
    else demote_usage(p, hit_set, c→vv, c→vrepl);
    return p;
  }
```

aa: **int**, §167.
ARGS = macro, §6.
b: **int**, §167.
bb: **int**, §167.
cache = **struct**, §167.
cacheblock = **struct**, §167.
cacheset = **cacheblock** ∗, §167.
choose_victim: **static cacheblock** ∗( ), §187.
data: **octa** ∗, §167.
demote_usage: **static void** ( ), §191.
dirty: **char** ∗, §167.
filler: **coroutine**, §167.
h: **tetra**, §17.
l: **tetra**, §17.
next: **coroutine** ∗, §23.
note_usage: **static void** ( ), §189.
octa = **struct**, §17.
p: **register cacheblock** ∗, §205.
q: **register cacheblock** ∗, §205.
repl: **replace_policy**, §167.
set: **cacheset** ∗, §167.
tag: **octa**, §167.
tagmask: **int**, §167.
victim: **cacheset**, §167.
vrepl: **replace_policy**, §167.
vv: **int**, §167.

200. The subroutine *load_cache*(c,p) is called at a moment when *c→lock* has been set and *c→inbuf* has been filled with clean data to be placed in the cache block p.

⟨ Internal prototypes 13 ⟩ +≡
```
static void load_cache ARGS((cache *, cacheblock *));
```

201. ⟨ Subroutines 14 ⟩ +≡
```
static void load_cache(c, p)
    cache *c; cacheblock *p;
{
  register int i;
  register octa *d;
  for (i = 0; i < c->bb >> c->g; i++) p->dirty[i] = false;
  d = p->data; p->data = c->inbuf.data; c->inbuf.data = d;
  p->tag = c->inbuf.tag;
  hit_set = cache_addr(c, p->tag); use_and_fix(c, p);    /* p not moved */
}
```

202. The subroutine *flush_cache*$(c,p,keep)$ is called at a "quiet" moment when *c→flusher.next* $= \Lambda$. It puts cache block p into *c→outbuf* and fires up the *c→flusher* coroutine, which will take care of sending the data to lower levels of the memory hierarchy. Cache block p is also marked clean.

⟨ Internal prototypes 13 ⟩ +≡
```
static void flush_cache ARGS((cache *, cacheblock *, bool));
```

203. ⟨ Subroutines 14 ⟩ +≡
```
static void flush_cache(c, p, keep)
    cache *c;
    cacheblock *p;    /* a block inside cache c */
    bool keep;    /* should we preserve the data in p? */
{
  register octa *d;
  register char *dd;
  register int j;
  c->outbuf.tag = p->tag;
  if (keep) for (j = 0; j < c->bb >> 3; j++) c->outbuf.data[j] = p->data[j];
  else d = c->outbuf.data, c->outbuf.data = p->data, p->data = d;
  dd = c->outbuf.dirty, c->outbuf.dirty = p->dirty, p->dirty = dd;
  for (j = 0; j < c->bb >> c->g; j++) p->dirty[j] = false;
  startup(&c->flusher, c->copy_out_time);    /* will not be aborted */
}
```

204. The *alloc_slot* routine is called when we wish to put new information into a cache after a cache miss. It returns a pointer to a cache block in the main area where the new information should be put. The tag of that cache block is invalidated; the calling routine should take care of filling it and giving it a valid tag in due time. The cache's *filler* routine should not be active when *alloc_slot* is called.

Inserting new information might also require writing old information into the next level of the memory hierarchy, if the block being replaced is dirty. This routine returns

Λ in such cases if the cache is flushing a previously discarded block. Otherwise it schedules the *flusher* coroutine.

This routine returns Λ also if the given key happens to be in the cache. Such cases are rare, but the following scenario shows that they aren't impossible: Suppose the DT-cache access time is 5, the D-cache access time is 1, and two processes simultaneously look for the same physical address. One process hits in DT-cache but misses in D-cache, waiting 5 cycles before trying *alloc_slot* in the D-cache; meanwhile the other process missed in D-cache but didn't need to use the DT-cache, so it might have updated the D-cache.

A key value is never negative. Therefore we can invalidate the tag in the chosen slot by forcing it to be negative.

```
⟨ Internal prototypes 13 ⟩ +≡
  static cacheblock *alloc_slot ARGS((cache *, octa));
```

205. ⟨ Subroutines 14 ⟩ +≡

```
static cacheblock *alloc_slot(c, alf)
    cache *c;
    octa alf;    /* key that probably isn't in the cache */
{
  register cacheset s;
  register cacheblock *p, *q;
  if (cache_search(c, alf)) return Λ;
  if (c→flusher.next ∧ c→outbuf.tag.h ≡ alf.h ∧ ¬((c→outbuf.tag.l ⊕ alf.l) & c→tagmask))
    return Λ;
  s = cache_addr(c, alf);    /* the set corresponding to alf */
  if (c→victim) p = choose_victim(c→victim, c→vv, c→vrepl);
  else p = choose_victim(s, c→aa, c→repl);
  if (is_dirty(c, p)) {
    if (c→flusher.next) return Λ;
    flush_cache(c, p, false);
  }
  if (c→victim) {
    q = choose_victim(s, c→aa, c→repl); ⟨ Swap cache blocks p and q 197 ⟩;
    q→tag.h |= sign_bit;    /* invalidate the tag */
    return q;
  }
  p→tag.h |= sign_bit; return p;
}
```

aa: **int**, §167.
ARGS = macro, §6.
bb: **int**, §167.
bool = **enum**, §11.
cache = **struct**, §167.
cache_addr = macro ( ), §192.
cache_search: **static cacheblock** *( ), §193.
cacheblock = **struct**, §167.
cacheset = **cacheblock** *, §167.
choose_victim: **static cacheblock** *( ), §187.
copy_out_time: **int**, §167.
data: **octa** *, §167.
dirty: **char** *, §167.
false = 0, §11.
filler: **coroutine**, §167.
flusher: **coroutine**, §167.
g: **int**, §167.
h: **tetra**, §17.
hit_set: **cacheset**, §194.
inbuf: **cacheblock**, §167.
is_dirty: **static bool** ( ), §170.
l: **tetra**, §17.
lock: **lockvar**, §167.
next: **coroutine** *, §23.
octa = **struct**, §17.
outbuf: **cacheblock**, §167.
repl: **replace_policy**, §167.
sign_bit = macro, §80.
startup: **static void** ( ), §31.
tag: **octa**, §167.
tagmask: **int**, §167.
use_and_fix: **static cacheblock** *( ), §196.
victim: **cacheset**, §167.
vrepl: **replace_policy**, §167.
vv: **int**, §167.

206. Simulated memory. How should we deal with the potentially gigantic memory of MMIX? We can't simply declare an array m that has 2^{48} bytes. (Indeed, up to 2^{63} bytes are needed, if we consider also the physical addresses $\geq 2^{48}$ that are reserved for memory-mapped input/output.)

We could regard memory as a special kind of cache, in which every access is required to hit. For example, such an "M-cache" could be fully associative, with 2^a blocks each having a different tag; simulation could proceed until more than $2^a - 1$ tags are required. But then the predefined value of a might well be so large that the sequential search of our *cache_search* routine would be too slow.

Instead, we will allocate memory in chunks of 2^{16} bytes at a time, as needed, and we will use hashing to search for the relevant chunk whenever a physical address is given. If the address is 2^{48} or greater, special routines called *spec_read* and *spec_write*, supplied by the user, will be called upon to do the reading or writing. Otherwise the 48-bit address consists of a 32-bit *chunk address* and a 16-bit *chunk offset*.

Chunk addresses that are not used take no space in this simulator. But if, say, 1000 such patterns occur, the simulator will dynamically allocate approximately 65MB for the portions of main memory that are used. Parameter *mem_chunks_max* specifies the largest number of different chunk addresses that are supported. This parameter does not constrain the range of simulated physical addresses, which cover the entire 256 large-terabyte range permitted by MMIX.

⟨ Type definitions 11 ⟩ +≡
```
typedef struct {
  tetra tag;     /* 32-bit chunk address */
  octa *chunk;   /* either Λ or an array of 2^13 octabytes */
} chunknode;
```

207. The parameter *hash_prime* should be a prime number larger than the parameter *mem_chunks_max*, preferably more than twice as large but not much bigger than that. The default values *mem_chunks_max* = 1000 and *hash_prime* = 2003 are set by *MMIX_config* unless the user specifies otherwise.

⟨ External variables 4 ⟩ +≡
```
Extern int mem_chunks;   /* this many chunks are allocated so far */
Extern int mem_chunks_max;   /* up to this many different chunks per run */
Extern int hash_prime;   /* larger than mem_chunks_max, but not enormous */
Extern chunknode *mem_hash;   /* the simulated main memory */
```

208. The separately compiled procedures *spec_read*( ) and *spec_write*( ) have the same calling conventions as the general procedures *mem_read*( ) and *mem_write*( ), but with an additional *size* parameter, which specifies that $1 \ll size$ bytes should be read or written.

⟨ Subroutines 14 ⟩ +≡
```
extern octa spec_read ARGS((octa addr, int size));   /* for memory mapped I/O */
extern void spec_write ARGS((octa addr, octa val, int size));   /* likewise */
```

209. If the program tries to read from a chunk that hasn't been allocated, the value zero is returned, optionally with a comment to the user.

Chunk address 0 is always allocated first. Then we can assume that a matching chunk tag implies a nonnull *chunk* pointer.

This routine sets *last_h* to the chunk found, so that we can rapidly read other words that we know must belong to the same chunk. For this purpose it is convenient to let *mem_hash*[*hash_prime*] be a chunk full of zeros, representing uninitialized memory.

```
⟨External prototypes 9⟩ +≡
  Extern octa mem_read ARGS((octa addr));
```

210. ⟨External routines 10⟩ +≡

```
  octa mem_read(addr)
      octa addr;
  {
    register tetra off, key;
    register int h;
    off = (addr.l & #ffff) ≫ 3;
    key = (addr.l & #ffff0000) + addr.h;
    for (h = key % hash_prime; mem_hash[h].tag ≠ key; h--) {
      if (mem_hash[h].chunk ≡ Λ) {
        if (verbose & uninit_mem_bit)
          errprint2("uninitialized␣memory␣read␣at␣%08x%08x", addr.h, addr.l);
        h = hash_prime; break;      /* zero will be returned */
      }
      if (h ≡ 0) h = hash_prime;
    }
    last_h = h;
    return mem_hash[h].chunk[off];
  }
```

211. ⟨External variables 4⟩ +≡

```
  Extern int last_h;     /* the hash index that was most recently correct */
```

ARGS = macro, §6.
cache_search: **static cacheblock** ∗( ), §193.
errprint2 = macro ( ), §13.
Extern = macro, §4.
h: **tetra**, §17.
l: **tetra**, §17.
mem_write: **void** ( ), §213.
MMIX_config: **void** ( ), MMIX-CONFIG §38.
octa = **struct**, §17.
spec_read: **octa** ( ), MMIX-MEM §2.
spec_write: ( ), MMIX-MEM §3.
tetra = **unsigned int**, §17.
uninit_mem_bit = 1 ≪ 4, §8.
verbose: **int**, §4.

212. ⟨External prototypes 9⟩ +≡

```
Extern void mem_write ARGS((octa addr, octa val));
```

213. ⟨External routines 10⟩ +≡

```
void mem_write(addr, val)
    octa addr, val;
{
  register tetra off, key;
  register int h;
  off = (addr.l & #ffff) >> 3;
  key = (addr.l & #ffff0000) + addr.h;
  for (h = key % hash_prime; mem_hash[h].tag ≠ key; h--) {
    if (mem_hash[h].chunk ≡ Λ) {
      if (++mem_chunks > mem_chunks_max)
        panic(errprint1("More␣than␣%d␣memory␣chunks␣are␣needed",
            mem_chunks_max));
      mem_hash[h].chunk = (octa *) calloc(1 << 13, sizeof(octa));
      if (mem_hash[h].chunk ≡ Λ)
        panic(errprint1("I␣can't␣allocate␣memory␣chunk␣number␣%d", mem_chunks));
      mem_hash[h].tag = key;
      break;
    }
    if (h ≡ 0) h = hash_prime;
  }
  last_h = h;
  mem_hash[h].chunk[off] = val;
}
```

214. The memory is characterized by several parameters, depending on the characteristics of the memory bus being simulated. Let *bus_words* be the number of octabytes read or written simultaneously (usually *bus_words* is 1 or 2; it must be a power of 2). The number of clock cycles needed to read or write $c * bus\_words$ octabytes that all belong to the same cache block is assumed to be $mem\_addr\_time + c * mem\_read\_time$ or $mem\_addr\_time + c * mem\_write\_time$, respectively.

⟨External variables 4⟩ +≡

```
Extern int mem_addr_time;   /* cycles to transmit an address on memory bus */
Extern int bus_words;   /* width of memory bus, in octabytes */
Extern int mem_read_time;   /* cycles to read from main memory */
Extern int mem_write_time;   /* cycles to write to main memory */
Extern lockvar mem_lock;   /* is nonnull when the bus is busy */
```

215. One of the principal ways to write memory is to invoke a *flush_to_mem* coroutine, which is the *Scache→flusher* if there is an S-cache, or the *Dcache→flusher* if there is a D-cache but no S-cache.

When such a coroutine is started, its *data→ptr_a* will be *Scache* or *Dcache*. The data to be written will just have been copied to the cache's *outbuf*.

```
⟨ Cases for control of special coroutines 126 ⟩ +≡
case flush_to_mem:
  { register cache *c = (cache *) data→ptr_a;
    switch (data→state) {
    case 0: if (mem_lock) wait(1);
      data→state = 1;
    case 1: set_lock(self, mem_lock);
      data→state = 2;
      ⟨ Write the dirty data of c→outbuf and wait for the bus 216 ⟩;
    case 2: goto terminate;     /* this frees mem_lock and c→outbuf */
    }
  }
```

216. ⟨ Write the dirty data of c→outbuf and wait for the bus 216 ⟩ ≡

```
  {
    register int off, last_off, count, first, ii;
    register int del = c→gg ≫ 3;     /* octabytes per granule */
    octa addr;
    addr = c→outbuf.tag; off = (addr.l & #ffff) ≫ 3;
    for (i = j = 0, first = 1, count = 0; j < c→bb ≫ c→g; j++) {
      ii = i + del;
      if (¬c→outbuf.dirty[j]) i = ii, off += del, addr.l += del ≪ 3;
      else while (i < ii) {
          if (first) {
            count++; last_off = off; first = 0;
            mem_write(addr, c→outbuf.data[i]);
          } else {
            if ((off ⊕ last_off) & (−bus_words)) count++;
            last_off = off;
            mem_hash[last_h].chunk[off] = c→outbuf.data[i];
          }
          i++; off++; addr.l += 8;
        }
    }
    wait(mem_addr_time + count * mem_write_time);
  }
```

This code is used in section 215.

ARGS = macro, §6.
bb: **int**, §167.
cache = **struct**, §167.
calloc: **void** *(), `<stdlib.h>`.
chunk: **octa** *, §206.
data: **register control** *, §124.
data: **octa** *, §167.
Dcache: **cache** *, §168.
dirty: **char** *, §167.
errprint1 = macro ( ), §13.
Extern = macro, §4.
flush_to_mem = 97, §129.
flusher: **coroutine**, §167.
g: **int**, §167.
gg: **int**, §167.
h: **tetra**, §17.
hash_prime: **int**, §207.
i: **register int**, §12.
j: **register int**, §12.
l: **tetra**, §17.
last_h: **int**, §211.
lockvar = **coroutine** *, §37.
mem_chunks: **int**, §207.
mem_chunks_max: **int**, §207.
mem_hash: **chunknode** *, §207.
octa = **struct**, §17.
outbuf: **cacheblock**, §167.
panic = macro ( ), §13.
ptr_a: **void** *, §44.
Scache: **cache** *, §168.
self: **register coroutine** *, §124.
set_lock = macro ( ), §37.
state: **int**, §44.
tag: **tetra**, §206.
tag: **octa**, §167.
terminate: label, §125.
tetra = **unsigned int**, §17.
wait = macro ( ), §125.

217. Cache transfers. We have seen that the *Dcache→flusher* sends data directly to the main memory if there is no S-cache. But if both D-cache and S-cache exist, the *Dcache→flusher* is a more complicated coroutine of type *flush_to_S*. In this case we need to deal with the fact that the S-cache blocks might be larger than the D-cache blocks; furthermore, the S-cache might have a write-around and/or write-through policy, etc. But one simplifying fact does help us: We know that the flusher coroutine will not be aborted until it has run to completion.

Some machines, such as the Alpha 21164, have an additional cache between the S-cache and memory, called the B-cache (the "backup cache"). A B-cache could be simulated by extending the logic used here; but such extensions of the present program are left to the interested reader.

```
⟨ Cases for control of special coroutines 126 ⟩ +≡
case flush_to_S:
  { register cache *c = (cache *) data→ptr_a;
    register int block_diff = Scache→bb − c→bb;

    p = (cacheblock *) data→ptr_b;
    switch (data→state) {
    case 0: if (Scache→lock) wait(1);
      data→state = 1;
    case 1: set_lock(self, Scache→lock);
      data→ptr_b = (void *) cache_search(Scache, c→outbuf.tag);
      if (data→ptr_b) data→state = 4;
      else if (Scache→mode & WRITE_ALLOC) data→state = (block_diff ? 2 : 3);
      else data→state = 6;
      wait(Scache→access_time);
    case 2: ⟨ Fill Scache→inbuf with clean memory data 219 ⟩;
    case 3: ⟨ Allocate a slot p in the S-cache 218 ⟩;
      if (block_diff) ⟨ Copy Scache→inbuf to slot p 220 ⟩;
    case 4: copy_block(c, &(c→outbuf), Scache, p);
      hit_set = cache_addr(Scache, c→outbuf.tag); use_and_fix(Scache, p);
        /* p not moved */
      data→state = 5; wait(Scache→copy_in_time);
    case 5: if ((Scache→mode & WRITE_BACK) ≡ 0) {      /* write-through */
        if (Scache→flusher.next) wait(1);
        flush_cache(Scache, p, true);
      }
      goto terminate;
    case 6: ⟨ Handle write-around when flushing to the S-cache 221 ⟩;
    }
  }
```

218. ⟨ Allocate a slot *p* in the S-cache 218 ⟩ ≡

```
  if (Scache→filler.next) wait(1);      /* perhaps an unnecessary precaution? */
  p = alloc_slot(Scache, c→outbuf.tag);
  if (¬p) wait(1);
  data→ptr_b = (void *) p;
  p→tag = c→outbuf.tag; p→tag.l = c→outbuf.tag.l & (−Scache→bb);
```

This code is used in section 217.

219. We only need to read *block_diff* bytes, but it's easier to read them all and to charge only for reading the ones we needed.

⟨ Fill *Scache→inbuf* with clean memory data 219 ⟩ ≡

```
{ register int count = block_diff >> 3;
  register int off, delay;
  octa addr;
  if (mem_lock) wait(1);
  addr.h = c→outbuf.tag.h; addr.l = c→outbuf.tag.l & -Scache→bb;
  off = (addr.l & #ffff) >> 3;
  for (j = 0; j < Scache→bb >> 3; j++)
    if (j ≡ 0) Scache→inbuf.data[j] = mem_read(addr);
    else Scache→inbuf.data[j] = mem_hash[last_h].chunk[j + off];
  set_lock(&mem_locker, mem_lock);
  delay = mem_addr_time + (int)((count + bus_words - 1)/(bus_words)) * mem_read_time;
  startup(&mem_locker, delay);
  data→state = 3; wait(delay);
}
```

This code is used in section 217.

220. ⟨ Copy *Scache→inbuf* to slot *p* 220 ⟩ ≡

```
{
  register octa *d = p→data;
  p→data = Scache→inbuf.data; Scache→inbuf.data = d;
}
```

This code is used in section 217.

221. Here we assume that the granularity is 8.

⟨ Handle write-around when flushing to the S-cache 221 ⟩ ≡

```
if (Scache→flusher.next) wait(1);
Scache→outbuf.tag.h = c→outbuf.tag.h;
Scache→outbuf.tag.l = c→outbuf.tag.l & (−Scache→bb);
for (j = 0; j < Scache→bb ≫ Scache→g; j++) Scache→outbuf.dirty[j] = false;
copy_block(c, &(c→outbuf), Scache, &(Scache→outbuf));
startup(&Scache→flusher, Scache→copy_out_time);
goto terminate;
```

This code is used in section 217.

222. The S-cache gets new data from memory by invoking a *fill_from_mem* coroutine; the I-cache or D-cache may also invoke a *fill_from_mem* coroutine, if there is no S-cache. When such a coroutine is invoked, it holds *mem_lock*, and its caller has gone to sleep. A physical memory address is given in *data→z.o*, and *data→ptr_a* specifies either *Icache*, *Dcache*, or *Scache*. Furthermore, *data→ptr_b* specifies a block within that cache, determined by the *alloc_slot* routine. The coroutine simulates reading the contents of the specified memory location, places the result in the *x.o* field of its caller's control block, and wakes up the caller. It proceeds to fill the cache's *inbuf* and, ultimately, the specified cache block, before waking the caller again.

Let c = *data→ptr_a*. The caller is then *c→fill_lock*, if this variable is nonnull. However, the caller might not wish to be awoken or to receive the data (for example, if it has been aborted). In such cases *c→fill_lock* will be Λ; the filling action continues without the wakeup calls. If c = *Scache*, the S-cache will be locked and the caller will not have been aborted.

⟨ Cases for control of special coroutines 126 ⟩ +≡

```
case fill_from_mem:
  { register cache *c = (cache *) data→ptr_a;
    register coroutine *cc = c→fill_lock;

    switch (data→state) {
    case 0: data→x.o = mem_read(data→z.o);
      if (cc) {
        cc→ctl→x.o = data→x.o; awaken(cc, mem_read_time);
      }
      data→state = 1;
      ⟨ Read data into c→inbuf and wait for the bus 223 ⟩;
    case 1: release_lock(self, mem_lock); data→state = 2;
    case 2: if (c ≠ Scache) {
        if (c→lock) wait(1);
        set_lock(self, c→lock);
      }
      if (cc) awaken(cc, c→copy_in_time);      /* the second wakeup call */
      load_cache(c, (cacheblock *) data→ptr_b);
      data→state = 3; wait(c→copy_in_time);
    case 3: goto terminate;
    }
  }
```

223. If *c*'s cache size is no larger than the memory bus, we wait an extra cycle, so that there will be two wakeup calls.

⟨ Read data into *c*→*inbuf* and wait for the bus 223 ⟩ ≡

```
{
  register int count, off;
  c→inbuf.tag = data→z.o; c→inbuf.tag.l &= −c→bb;
  count = c→bb ≫ 3, off = (c→inbuf.tag.l & #ffff) ≫ 3;
  for (i = 0; i < count; i++, off++) c→inbuf.data[i] = mem_hash[last_h].chunk[off];
  if (count ≤ bus_words) wait(1 + mem_read_time)
  else wait((int)(count / bus_words) ∗ mem_read_time);
}
```

This code is used in section 222.

---

alloc_slot: **static cacheblock** ∗( ), §205.
awaken = macro ( ), §125.
bb: **int**, §167.
bus_words: **int**, §214.
c: **register cache** ∗, §217.
cache = **struct**, §167.
cacheblock = **struct**, §167.
chunk: **octa** ∗, §206.
copy_block: **static void** ( ), §185.
copy_in_time: **int**, §167.
copy_out_time: **int**, §167.
coroutine = **struct**, §23.
ctl: **control** ∗, §23.
data: **register control** ∗, §124.
data: **octa** ∗, §167.
Dcache: **cache** ∗, §168.
dirty: **char** ∗, §167.
false = 0, §11.
fill_from_mem = 95, §129.
fill_lock: **lockvar**, §167.
flusher: **coroutine**, §167.
g: **int**, §167.
h: **tetra**, §17.
i: **register int**, §12.
Icache: **cache** ∗, §168.
inbuf: **cacheblock**, §167.
j: **register int**, §12.
l: **tetra**, §17.
last_h: **int**, §211.
load_cache: **static void** ( ), §201.
lock: **lockvar**, §167.
mem_hash: **chunknode** ∗, §207.
mem_lock: **lockvar**, §214.
mem_read: **octa** ( ), §210.
mem_read_time: **int**, §214.
next: **coroutine** ∗, §23.
o: **octa**, §40.
outbuf: **cacheblock**, §167.
ptr_a: **void** ∗, §44.
ptr_b: **void** ∗, §44.
release_lock = macro ( ), §37.
Scache: **cache** ∗, §168.
self: **register coroutine** ∗, §124.
set_lock = macro ( ), §37.
startup: **static void** ( ), §31.
state: **int**, §44.
tag: **octa**, §167.
terminate: label, §125.
wait = macro ( ), §125.
x: **specnode**, §44.
z: **spec**, §44.

224. The *fill_from_S* coroutine has the same conventions as *fill_from_mem*, except that the data comes directly from the S-cache if it is present there. This is the *filler* coroutine for the I-cache and D-cache if an S-cache is present.

```
⟨ Cases for control of special coroutines 126 ⟩ +≡
case fill_from_S:
  { register cache *c = (cache *) data→ptr_a;
    register coroutine *cc = c→fill_lock;
    p = (cacheblock *) data→ptr_c;
    switch (data→state) {
    case 0: p = cache_search(Scache, data→z.o);
      if (p) goto S_non_miss;
      data→state = 1;
    case 1: ⟨ Start the S-cache filler 225 ⟩;
      data→state = 2; sleep;
    case 2: if (cc) {
          cc→ctl→x.o = data→x.o;      /* this data has been supplied by Scache→filler */
          awaken(cc, Scache→access_time);      /* we propagate it back */
      }
      data→state = 3; sleep;      /* when we awake, the S-cache will have our data */
    S_non_miss: if (cc) {
          cc→ctl→x.o = p→data[(data→z.o.l & (Scache→bb − 1)) ≫ 3];
          awaken(cc, Scache→access_time);
      }
    case 3: ⟨ Copy data from p into c→inbuf 226 ⟩;
      data→state = 4; wait(Scache→access_time);
    case 4: Scache→lock = Λ;      /* we had been holding that lock */
      data→state = 5;
    case 5: if (c→lock) wait(1);
      set_lock(self, c→lock);
      load_cache(c, (cacheblock *) data→ptr_b);
      data→state = 6; wait(c→copy_in_time);
    case 6: if (cc) awaken(cc, 1);      /* second wakeup call */
      goto terminate;
    }
  }
```

225. We are already holding the *Scache→lock*, but we're about to take on the *Scache→fill_lock* too (with the understanding that one is "stronger" than the other). For a short time the *Scache→lock* will point to us but we will point to *Scache→fill_lock*; this will not cause difficulty, because the present coroutine is not abortable.

```
⟨ Start the S-cache filler 225 ⟩ ≡
  if (Scache→filler.next ∨ mem_lock) wait(1);
  p = alloc_slot(Scache, data→z.o);
  if (¬p) wait(1);
  set_lock(&Scache→filler, mem_lock);
  set_lock(self, Scache→fill_lock);
  data→ptr_c = Scache→filler_ctl.ptr_b = (void *) p;
  Scache→filler_ctl.z.o = data→z.o;
  startup(&Scache→filler, mem_addr_time);
```

This code is used in section 224.

226. The S-cache blocks might be wider than the blocks of the I-cache or D-cache, so the copying in this step isn't quite trivial.

```
⟨ Copy data from p into c→inbuf 226 ⟩ ≡
  { register int off;
    c→inbuf.tag = data→z.o; c→inbuf.tag.l &= −c→bb;
    for (j = 0, off = (c→inbuf.tag.l & (Scache→bb − 1)) ≫ 3; j < c→bb ≫ 3; j++, off++)
      c→inbuf.data[j] = p→data[off];
    release_lock(self, Scache→fill_lock);
    set_lock(self, Scache→lock);
  }
```

This code is used in section 224.

---

access_time: **int**, §167.
alloc_slot: **static cacheblock** *( ), §205.
awaken = macro ( ), §125.
bb: **int**, §167.
cache = **struct**, §167.
cache_search: **static cacheblock** *( ), §193.
cacheblock = **struct**, §167.
copy_in_time: **int**, §167.
coroutine = **struct**, §23.
ctl: **control** *, §23.
data: **octa** *, §167.
data: **register control** *, §124.
fill_from_mem = 95, §129.
fill_from_S = 94, §129.
fill_lock: **lockvar**, §167.
filler: **coroutine**, §167.
filler_ctl: **control**, §167.
inbuf: **cacheblock**, §167.
j: **register int**, §12.
l: **tetra**, §17.
load_cache: **static void** ( ), §201.
lock: **lockvar**, §167.
mem_addr_time: **int**, §214.
mem_lock: **lockvar**, §214.
next: **coroutine** *, §23.
o: **octa**, §40.
p: **register cacheblock** *, §258.
ptr_a: **void** *, §44.
ptr_b: **void** *, §44.
ptr_c: **void** *, §44.
release_lock = macro ( ), §37.
Scache: **cache** *, §168.
self: **register coroutine** *, §124.
set_lock = macro ( ), §37.
sleep = macro, §125.
startup: **static void** ( ), §31.
state: **int**, §44.
tag: **octa**, §167.
terminate: label, §125.
wait = macro ( ), §125.
x: **specnode**, §44.
z: **spec**, §44.

227. The instruction `PRELD X,$Y,$Z` generates $\lfloor X/2^b \rfloor$ commands if there are 2^b bytes per block in the D-cache. These commands will try to preload blocks $\$Y + \$Z$, $\$Y + \$Z + 2^b$, $\ldots$, into the cache if it is not too busy.

Similar considerations apply to the instructions `PREGO X,$Y,$Z` and `PREST X,$Y,$Z`.

⟨ Special cases of instruction dispatch 117 ⟩ +≡
case *preld*: **case** *prest*: **if** (¬*Dcache*) **goto** *noop_inst*;
  if (*cool*→*xx* ≥ *Dcache*→*bb*) *cool*→*interim* = *true*;
  cool→*ptr_a* = (**void** ∗) *mem.up*; **break**;
case *prego*: **if** (¬*Icache*) **goto** *noop_inst*;
  if (*cool*→*xx* ≥ *Icache*→*bb*) *cool*→*interim* = *true*;
  cool→*ptr_a* = (**void** ∗) *mem.up*; **break**;

228. If the block size is 64, a command like `PREST 200,$Y,$Z` is actually issued as four commands `PREST 200,$Y,$Z; PREST 191,$Y,$Z; PREST 127,$Y,$Z; PREST 63,$Y,$Z`. An interruption will then be able to resume properly. In the pipeline, the instruction `PREST 200,$Y,$Z` is considered to affect bytes $\$Y + \$Z + 192$ through $\$Y + \$Z + 200$, or fewer bytes if $\$Y + \$Z$ is not a multiple of 64. (Remember that these instructions are only hints; we act on them only if it is reasonably convenient to do so.)

⟨ Get ready for the next step of `PRELD` or `PREST` 228 ⟩ ≡
  head→*inst* = (*head*→*inst* & ∼((*Dcache*→*bb* − 1) ≪ 16)) − #10000;

This code is used in section 81.

229. ⟨ Get ready for the next step of `PREGO` 229 ⟩ ≡
  head→*inst* = (*head*→*inst* & ∼((*Icache*→*bb* − 1) ≪ 16)) − #10000;

This code is used in section 81.

230. Another coroutine, called *cleanup*, is occasionally called into action to remove dirty data from the D-cache and S-cache. If it is invoked by starting in state 0, with its *i* field set to *sync*, it will clean everything. It can also be invoked in state 4, with its *i* field set to *syncd* and with a physical address in its *z.o* field; then it simply makes sure that no D-cache or S-cache blocks associated with that address are dirty.

Field *x.o.h* should be set to zero if items are expected to remain in the cache after being cleaned; otherwise field *x.o.h* should be set to *sign_bit*.

The coroutine that invokes *cleanup* should hold *clean_lock*. If that coroutine dies, because of an interruption, the *cleanup* coroutine will terminate prematurely.

We assume that the D-cache and S-cache have some sort of way to identify their first dirty block, if any, in *access_time* cycles.

⟨ Global variables 20 ⟩ +≡
  coroutine *clean_co*;
  control *clean_ctl*;
  lockvar *clean_lock*;

231. ⟨ Initialize everything 22 ⟩ +≡
  clean_co.ctl = &*clean_ctl*;
  clean_co.name = "Clean";
  clean_co.stage = *cleanup*;
  clean_ctl.go.o.l = 4;

232. ⟨ Cases for control of special coroutines 126 ⟩ +≡
case *cleanup*: *p* = (**cacheblock** ∗) *data*→*ptr_b*;
  switch (*data*→*state*) {
    ⟨ Cases 0 through 4, for the D-cache 233 ⟩;
    ⟨ Cases 5 through 9, for the S-cache 234 ⟩;
  case 10: **goto** *terminate*;
  }

---

access_time: **int**, §167.
bb: **int**, §167.
cacheblock = **struct**, §167.
cleanup = 91, §129.
control = **struct**, §44.
cool: **control** ∗, §60.
coroutine = **struct**, §23.
ctl: **control** ∗, §23.
data: **register control** ∗, §124.
Dcache: **cache** ∗, §168.
go: **specnode**, §44.
h: **tetra**, §17.
head: **fetch** ∗, §69.
i: **register int**, §12.
Icache: **cache** ∗, §168.
inst: **tetra**, §68.
interim: **bool**, §44.
l: **tetra**, §17.
lockvar = **coroutine** ∗, §37.
mem: **specnode**, §115.
name: **char** ∗, §23.
noop_inst: label, §118.
o: **octa**, §40.
p: **register cacheblock** ∗, §258.
prego = 73, §49.
preld = 61, §49.
prest = 62, §49.
ptr_a: **void** ∗, §44.
ptr_b: **void** ∗, §44.
sign_bit = macro, §80.
stage: **int**, §23.
state: **int**, §44.
sync = 79, §49.
syncd = 64, §49.
terminate: label, §125.
true = 1, §11.
up: **specnode** ∗, §40.
x: **specnode**, §44.
xx: **unsigned char**, §44.
z: **spec**, §44.

233. ⟨ Cases 0 through 4, for the D-cache 233 ⟩ ≡

```
case 0: if (Dcache→lock ∨ (j = get_reader(Dcache) < 0)) wait(1);
  startup(&Dcache→reader[j], Dcache→access_time);
  set_lock(self, Dcache→lock);
  i = j = 0;
Dclean_loop: p = (i < Dcache→cc ? &(Dcache→set[i][j]) : &(Dcache→victim[j]));
  if (p→tag.h & sign_bit) goto Dclean_inc;
  if (¬is_dirty(Dcache, p)) {
    p→tag.h |= data→x.o.h; goto Dclean_inc;
  }
  data→y.o.h = i, data→y.o.l = j;
Dclean: data→state = 1; data→ptr_b = (void *) p; wait(Dcache→access_time);
case 1: if (Dcache→flusher.next) wait(1);
  flush_cache(Dcache, p, data→x.o.h ≡ 0);
  p→tag.h |= data→x.o.h;
  release_lock(self, Dcache→lock);
  data→state = 2; wait(Dcache→copy_out_time);
case 2: if (¬clean_lock) goto done;    /* premature termination */
  if (Dcache→flusher.next) wait(1);
  if (data→i ≠ sync) goto Sprep;
  data→state = 3;
case 3: if (Dcache→lock ∨ (j = get_reader(Dcache) < 0)) wait(1);
  startup(&Dcache→reader[j], Dcache→access_time);
  set_lock(self, Dcache→lock);
  i = data→y.o.h, j = data→y.o.l;
Dclean_inc: j++;
  if (i < Dcache→cc ∧ j ≡ Dcache→aa) j = 0, i++;
  if (i ≡ Dcache→cc ∧ j ≡ Dcache→vv) {
    data→state = 5; wait(Dcache→access_time);
  }
  goto Dclean_loop;
case 4: if (Dcache→lock ∨ (j = get_reader(Dcache) < 0)) wait(1);
  startup(&Dcache→reader[j], Dcache→access_time);
  set_lock(self, Dcache→lock);
  p = cache_search(Dcache, data→z.o);
  if (p) {
    demote_and_fix(Dcache, p);
    if (is_dirty(Dcache, p)) goto Dclean;
  }
  data→state = 9; wait(Dcache→access_time);
```

This code is used in section 232.

234. ⟨ Cases 5 through 9, for the S-cache 234 ⟩ ≡

```
case 5: if (self→lockloc) *(self→lockloc) = Λ, self→lockloc = Λ;
  if (¬Scache) goto done;
  if (Scache→lock) wait(1);
  set_lock(self, Scache→lock);
  i = j = 0;
Sclean_loop: p = (i < Scache→cc ? &(Scache→set[i][j]) : &(Scache→victim[j]));
```

```
  if (p→tag.h & sign_bit) goto Sclean_inc;
  if (¬is_dirty(Scache, p)) {
    p→tag.h |= data→x.o.h; goto Sclean_inc;
  }
  data→y.o.h = i, data→y.o.l = j;
Sclean: data→state = 6; data→ptr_b = (void *) p; wait(Scache→access_time);
case 6: if (Scache→flusher.next) wait(1);
  flush_cache(Scache, p, data→x.o.h ≡ 0);
  p→tag.h |= data→x.o.h;
  release_lock(self, Scache→lock);
  data→state = 7; wait(Scache→copy_out_time);
case 7: if (¬clean_lock) goto done;    /* premature termination */
  if (Scache→flusher.next) wait(1);
  if (data→i ≠ sync) goto done;
  data→state = 8;
case 8: if (Scache→lock) wait(1);
  set_lock(self, Scache→lock);
  i = data→y.o.h, j = data→y.o.l;
Sclean_inc: j++;
  if (i < Scache→cc ∧ j ≡ Scache→aa) j = 0, i++;
  if (i ≡ Scache→cc ∧ j ≡ Scache→vv) {
    data→state = 10; wait(Scache→access_time);
  }
  goto Sclean_loop;
Sprep: data→state = 9;
case 9: if (self→lockloc) release_lock(self, Dcache→lock);
  if (¬Scache) goto done;
  if (Scache→lock) wait(1);
  set_lock(self, Scache→lock);
  p = cache_search(Scache, data→z.o);
  if (p) {
    demote_and_fix(Scache, p);
    if (is_dirty(Scache, p)) goto Sclean;
  }
  data→state = 10; wait(Scache→access_time);
```

This code is used in section 232.

---

aa: **int**, §167.
access_time: **int**, §167.
cache_search: **static cacheblock** *(), §193.
cc: **int**, §167.
clean_lock: **lockvar**, §230.
copy_out_time: **int**, §167.
data: **register control** *, §124.
Dcache: **cache** *, §168.
demote_and_fix: **static cacheblock** *(), §199.
done: label, §125.
flush_cache: **static void** (), §203.
flusher: **coroutine**, §167.
get_reader: **static int** (), §183.
h: **tetra**, §17.
i: **internal_opcode**, §44.
i: **register int**, §12.
is_dirty: **static bool** (), §170.
j: **register int**, §12.
l: **tetra**, §17.
lock: **lockvar**, §167.
lockloc: **coroutine** **, §23.
next: **coroutine** *, §23.
o: **octa**, §40.
p: **register cacheblock** *, §258.
ptr_b: **void** *, §44.
reader: **coroutine** *, §167.
release_lock = macro (), §37.
Scache: **cache** *, §168.
self: **register coroutine** *, §124.
set: **cacheset** *, §167.
set_lock = macro (), §37.
sign_bit = macro, §80.
startup: **static void** (), §31.
state: **int**, §44.
sync = 79, §49.
tag: **octa**, §167.
victim: **cacheset**, §167.
vv: **int**, §167.
wait = macro (), §125.
x: **specnode**, §44.
y: **spec**, §44.
z: **spec**, §44.

235. Virtual address translation. Special arrays of coroutines and control blocks come into play when we need to implement MMIX's rather complicated page table mechanism for virtual address translation. In effect, we have up to ten control blocks *outside* of the reorder buffer that are capable of executing instructions just as if they were part of that buffer. The "opcodes" of these non-abortable instructions are special internal operations called *ldptp* and *ldpte*, for loading page table pointers and page table entries.

Suppose, for example, that we need to translate a virtual address for the DT-cache in which the virtual page address $(a_4a_3a_2a_1a_0)_{1024}$ of segment i has $a_4 = a_3 = 0$ and $a_2 \neq 0$. Then the rules say that we should first find a page table pointer p_2 in physical location $2^{13}(r + b_i + 2) + 8a_2$, then another page table pointer p_1 in location $p_2 + 8a_1$, and finally the page table entry p_0 in location $p_1 + 8a_0$. The simulator achieves this by setting up three coroutines c_0, c_1, c_2 whose control blocks correspond to the pseudo-instructions

LDPTP x,[$2^{63} + 2^{13}(r + b_i + 2)$],$8a_2$
LDPTP x,x,$8a_1$
LDPTE x,x,$8a_0$

where x is a hidden internal register and the other quantities are immediate values. Slight changes to the normal functionality of LDO give us the actions needed to implement LDPTP and LDPTE. Coroutine c_j corresponds to the instruction that involves a_j and computes p_j; when c_0 has computed its value p_0, we know how to translate the original virtual address.

The LDPTP and LDPTE commands return zero if their y operand is zero or if the page table does not properly match rV.

```
#define LDPTP PREGO   /* internally this won't cause confusion */
#define LDPTE GO
```

⟨ Global variables 20 ⟩ +≡

```
  control IPTctl[5], DPTctl[5];     /* control blocks for I and D page translation */
  coroutine IPTco[10], DPTco[10];     /* each coroutine is a two-stage pipeline */
  char *IPTname[5] = {"IPT0","IPT1","IPT2","IPT3","IPT4"};
  char *DPTname[5] = {"DPT0","DPT1","DPT2","DPT3","DPT4"};
```

236. ⟨ Initialize everything 22 ⟩ +≡

```
for (j = 0; j < 5; j++) {
  DPTco[2 * j].ctl = &DPTctl[j]; IPTco[2 * j].ctl = &IPTctl[j];
  if (j > 0) DPTctl[j].op = IPTctl[j].op = LDPTP, DPTctl[j].i = IPTctl[j].i = ldptp;
  else DPTctl[0].op = IPTctl[0].op = LDPTE, DPTctl[0].i = IPTctl[0].i = ldpte;
  IPTctl[j].loc = DPTctl[j].loc = neg_one;
  IPTctl[j].go.o = DPTctl[j].go.o = incr(neg_one, 4);
  IPTctl[j].ptr_a = DPTctl[j].ptr_a = (void *) &mem;
  IPTctl[j].ren_x = DPTctl[j].ren_x = true;
  IPTctl[j].x.addr.h = DPTctl[j].x.addr.h = -1;
  IPTco[2 * j].stage = DPTco[2 * j].stage = 1;
  IPTco[2 * j + 1].stage = DPTco[2 * j + 1].stage = 2;
  IPTco[2 * j].name = IPTco[2 * j + 1].name = IPTname[j];
  DPTco[2 * j].name = DPTco[2 * j + 1].name = DPTname[j];
}
ITcache→filler_ctl.ptr_c = (void *) &IPTco[0];
DTcache→filler_ctl.ptr_c = (void *) &DPTco[0];
```

---

addr: **octa**, §40.
control = **struct**, §44.
coroutine = **struct**, §23.
ctl: **control** ∗, §23.
DTcache: **cache** ∗, §168.
filler_ctl: **control**, §167.
GO = #9e, §47.
go: **specnode**, §44.
h: **tetra**, §17.
i: **internal_opcode**, §44.
incr: **octa** ( ), MMIX-ARITH §6.
ITcache: **cache** ∗, §168.
j: **register int**, §10.
ldpte = 58, §49.
ldptp = 57, §49.
loc: **octa**, §44.
mem: **specnode**, §115.
name: **char** ∗, §23.
neg_one: **octa**, MMIX-ARITH §4.
o: **octa**, §40.
op: **mmix_opcode**, §44.
PREGO = #9c, §47.
ptr_a: **void** ∗, §44.
ptr_c: **void** ∗, §44.
ren_x: **bool**, §44.
stage: **int**, §23.
true = 1, §11.
x: **specnode**, §44.

237. Page table calculations are invoked by a coroutine of type *fill_from_virt*, which is used to fill the IT-cache or DT-cache. The calling conventions of *fill_from_virt* are analogous to those of *fill_from_mem* or *fill_from_S*: A virtual address is supplied in *data→y.o*, and *data→ptr_a* points to a cache (*ITcache* or *DTcache*), while *data→ptr_b* is a block in that cache. We wake up the caller, who holds the cache's *fill_lock*, as soon as the translation of the given address has been calculated, unless the caller has been aborted. (No second wakeup call is necessary.)

```
⟨ Cases for control of special coroutines 126 ⟩ +≡
case fill_from_virt:
  { register cache *c = (cache *) data→ptr_a;
    register coroutine *cc = c→fill_lock;
    register coroutine *co = (coroutine *) data→ptr_c;
      /* &IPTco[0] or &DPTco[0] */
    octa aaaaa;

    switch (data→state) {
    case 0: ⟨ Start up auxiliary coroutines to compute the page table entry 243 ⟩;
      data→state = 1;
    case 1: if (data→b.p) {
        if (data→b.p→known) data→b.o = data→b.p→o, data→b.p = Λ;
        else wait(1);
      }
      ⟨ Compute the new entry for c→inbuf and give the caller a sneak preview 245 ⟩;
      data→state = 2;
    case 2: if (c→lock) wait(1);
      set_lock(self, c→lock);
      load_cache(c, (cacheblock *) data→ptr_b);
      data→state = 3; wait(c→copy_in_time);
    case 3: data→b.o = zero_octa; goto terminate;
    }
  }
```

238. The current contents of rV, the special virtual translation register, are kept unpacked in several global variables *page_r*, *page_s*, etc., for convenience. Whenever rV changes, we recompute all these variables.

```
⟨ Global variables 20 ⟩ +≡
  int page_n;      /* the 10-bit n field of rV, times 8 */
  int page_r;      /* the 27-bit r field of rV */
  int page_s;      /* the 8-bit s field of rV */
  int page_f;      /* the 3-bit f field of rV */
  int page_b[5];     /* the 4-bit b fields of rV; page_b[0] = 0 */
  octa page_mask;      /* the least significant s bits */
  bool page_bad = true;      /* does rV violate the rules? */
```

239. ⟨ Update the *page* variables 239 ⟩ ≡

```
  { octa rv;

    rv = data→z.o;
    page_f = rv.l & 7, page_bad = (page_f > 1);
    page_n = rv.l & #1ff8;
```

```
    rv = shift_right(rv, 13, 1);
    page_r = rv.l & #7fffff;
    rv = shift_right(rv, 27, 1);
    page_s = rv.l & #ff;
    if (page_s < 13 ∨ page_s > 48) page_bad = true;
    else if (page_s < 32) page_mask.h = 0, page_mask.l = (1 ≪ page_s) − 1;
    else page_mask.h = (1 ≪ (page_s − 32)) − 1, page_mask.l = #ffffffff;
    page_b[4] = (rv.l ≫ 8) & #f;
    page_b[3] = (rv.l ≫ 12) & #f;
    page_b[2] = (rv.l ≫ 16) & #f;
    page_b[1] = (rv.l ≫ 20) & #f;
  }
```

This code is used in section 329.

240. Here's how we compute a tag of the IT-cache or DT-cache from a virtual address, and how we compute a physical address from a translation found in the cache.

```
#define trans_key(addr) incr(oandn(addr, page_mask), page_n)
⟨Internal prototypes 13⟩ +≡
  static octa phys_addr ARGS((octa, octa));
```

241. ⟨Subroutines 14⟩ +≡

```
  static octa phys_addr(virt, trans)
      octa virt, trans;
  { octa t;
    t = oandn(trans, page_mask);   /* zero out the ynp fields of a PTE */
    return oplus(t, oand(virt, page_mask));
  }
```

242. Cheap (and slow) versions of MMIX leave the page table calculations to software. If the global variable *no_hardware_PT* is set true, *fill_from_virt* begins its actions in state 1, not state 0. (See the RESUME_TRANS operation.)

```
⟨External variables 4⟩ +≡
  Extern bool no_hardware_PT;
```

ARGS = macro, §6.
b: **spec**, §44.
b, MMIX-DOC §45.
bool = **enum**, §11.
cache = **struct**, §167.
cacheblock = **struct**, §167.
copy_in_time: **int**, §167.
coroutine = **struct**, §23.
data: **register control** ∗, §124.
DPTco: **coroutine** [ ], §235.
DTcache: **cache** ∗, §168.
Extern = macro, §4.
f: **register int**, §75.
fill_from_mem = 95, §129.
fill_from_S = 94, §129.
fill_from_virt = 93, §129.
fill_lock: **lockvar**, §167.
h: **tetra**, §17.
inbuf: **cacheblock**, §167.
incr: **octa** ( ), MMIX-ARITH §6.
IPTco: **coroutine** [ ], §235.
ITcache: **cache** ∗, §168.
known: **bool**, §40.
l: **tetra**, §17.
load_cache: **static void** ( ), §201.
lock: **lockvar**, §167.
n, MMIX-DOC §45.
o: **octa**, §40.
oand: **octa** ( ), MMIX-ARITH §25.
oandn: **octa** ( ), MMIX-ARITH §25.
octa = **struct**, §17.
oplus: **octa** ( ), MMIX-ARITH §5.
p: **specnode** ∗, §40.
ptr_a: **void** ∗, §44.
ptr_b: **void** ∗, §44.
ptr_c: **void** ∗, §44.
r, MMIX-DOC §45.
RESUME_TRANS = 3, §320.
s, MMIX-DOC §45.
self: **register coroutine** ∗, §124.
set_lock = macro ( ), §37.
shift_right: **octa** ( ), MMIX-ARITH §7.
state: **int**, §44.
terminate: label, §125.
true = 1, §11.
wait = macro ( ), §125.
y: **spec**, §44.
z: **spec**, §44.
zero_octa: **octa**, MMIX-ARITH §4.

243. Note: The operating system is supposed to ensure that changes to the page table entries do not appear in the pipeline when a translation cache is being updated. The internal `LDPTP` and `LDPTE` instructions use only the "hot state" of the memory system.

```
⟨ Start up auxiliary coroutines to compute the page table entry 243 ⟩ ≡
  aaaaa = data→y.o;
  i = aaaaa.h ≫ 29;    /* the segment number */
  aaaaa.h &= #1fffffff;    /* the address within segment i */
  aaaaa = shift_right(aaaaa, page_s, 1);    /* the page address */
  for (j = 0; aaaaa.l ≠ 0 ∨ aaaaa.h ≠ 0; j++) {
    co[2 * j].ctl→z.o.h = 0, co[2 * j].ctl→z.o.l = (aaaaa.l & #3ff) ≪ 3;
    aaaaa = shift_right(aaaaa, 10, 1);
  }
  if (page_b[i + 1] < page_b[i] + j)    /* address too large */
    ;    /* nothing needs to be done, since data→b.o is zero */
  else {
    if (j ≡ 0) j = 1, co[0].ctl→z.o = zero_octa;
    ⟨ Issue j pseudo-instructions to compute a page table entry 244 ⟩;
  }
```

This code is used in section 237.

244. The first stage of coroutine c_j is $co[2*j]$. It will pass the jth control block to the second stage, $co[2*j+1]$, which will load page table information from memory (or hopefully from the D-cache).

```
⟨ Issue j pseudo-instructions to compute a page table entry 244 ⟩ ≡
  j--;
  aaaaa.l = page_r + page_b[i] + j;
  co[2 * j].ctl→y.p = Λ;
  co[2 * j].ctl→y.o = shift_left(aaaaa, 13);
  co[2 * j].ctl→y.o.h += sign_bit;
  for ( ; ; j--) {
    co[2 * j].ctl→x.o = zero_octa; co[2 * j].ctl→x.known = false;
    co[2 * j].ctl→owner = &co[2 * j];
    startup(&co[2 * j], 1);
    if (j ≡ 0) break;
    co[2 * (j − 1)].ctl→y.p = &co[2 * j].ctl→x;
  }
  data→b.p = &co[0].ctl→x;
```

This code is used in section 243.

245. At this point the translation of the given virtual address *data→y.o* is the octabyte *data→b.o*. Its least significant three bits are the protection code $p = p_r p_w p_x$; its page address field is scaled by 2^s. It is entirely zero, including the protection bits, if there was a page table failure.

The *z* field of the caller receives this translation.

⟨ Compute the new entry for *c→inbuf* and give the caller a sneak preview 245 ⟩ ≡

```
c→inbuf.tag = trans_key(data→y.o);
c→inbuf.data[0] = data→b.o;
if (cc) {
    cc→ctl→z.o = data→b.o;
    awaken(cc, 1);
}
```

This code is used in section 237.

---

aaaaa: **octa**, §237.
awaken = macro ( ), §125.
b: **spec**, §44.
c: **register cache** ∗, §237.
cc: **register coroutine** ∗, §237.
co: **register coroutine** ∗, §237.
ctl: **control** ∗, §23.
data: **register control** ∗, §124.
data: **octa** ∗, §167.
false = 0, §11.
h: **tetra**, §17.
i: **register int**, §12.
inbuf: **cacheblock**, §167.
j: **register int**, §12.
known: **bool**, §40.
l: **tetra**, §17.
o: **octa**, §40.
owner: **coroutine** ∗, §44.
p: **specnode** ∗, §40.
page_b: **int** [ ], §238.
page_r: **int**, §238.
page_s: **int**, §238.
shift_left: **octa** ( ), MMIX-ARITH §7.
shift_right: **octa** ( ), MMIX-ARITH §7.
sign_bit = macro, §80.
startup: **static void** ( ), §31.
tag: **octa**, §167.
trans_key = macro ( ), §240.
x: **specnode**, §44.
y: **spec**, §44.
z: **spec**, §44.
zero_octa: **octa**, MMIX-ARITH §4.

246. The write buffer. The dispatcher has arranged things so that speculative stores into memory are recorded in a doubly linked list leading upward from *mem*. When such instructions finally are committed, they enter the "write buffer," which holds octabytes that are ready to be written into designated physical memory addresses (or into the D-cache and/or S-cache). The "hot state" of the computation is reflected not only by the registers and caches but also by the instructions that are pending in the write buffer.

```
⟨ Type definitions 11 ⟩ +≡
  typedef struct {
    octa o;   /* data to be stored */
    octa addr;   /* its physical address */
    tetra stamp;   /* when last committed (mod 2^32) */
    internal_opcode i;   /* is this write special? */
    int size;   /* parameter for spec_write */
  } write_node;
```

247. We represent the buffer in the usual way as a circular list, with elements *write_tail* + 1, *write_tail* + 2, . . . , *write_head*.

The data will sit at least *holding_time* cycles before it leaves the write buffer. This speeds things up when different fields of the same octabyte are being stored by different instructions.

```
⟨ External variables 4 ⟩ +≡
  Extern write_node *wbuf_bot, *wbuf_top;
    /* least and greatest write buffer nodes */
  Extern write_node *write_head, *write_tail;
    /* front and rear of the write buffer */
  Extern lockvar wbuf_lock;   /* is the data in write_head being written? */
  Extern int holding_time;   /* minimum holding time */
  Extern lockvar speed_lock;   /* should we ignore holding_time? */
```

248.
```
⟨ Global variables 20 ⟩ +≡
  coroutine write_co;   /* coroutine that empties the write buffer */
  control write_ctl;   /* its control block */
```

249.
```
⟨ Initialize everything 22 ⟩ +≡
  write_co.ctl = &write_ctl;
  write_co.name = "Write";
  write_co.stage = write_from_wbuf;
  write_ctl.ptr_a = (void *) &mem;
  write_ctl.go.o.l = 4;
  startup(&write_co, 1);
  write_head = write_tail = wbuf_top;
```

250.
```
⟨ Internal prototypes 13 ⟩ +≡
  static void print_write_buffer ARGS((void));
```

251.
```
⟨ Subroutines 14 ⟩ +≡
  static void print_write_buffer()
  {
    printf("Write␣buffer");
```

```
  if (write_head ≡ write_tail) printf("␣(empty)\n");
  else { register write_node *p;
    printf(":\n");
    for (p = write_head; p ≠ write_tail; p = (p ≡ wbuf_bot ? wbuf_top : p − 1)) {
      printf("m["); print_octa(p→addr); printf("]="); print_octa(p→o);
      if (p→i ≡ stunc) printf("␣unc");
      else if (p→i ≡ sync) printf("␣sync");
      printf("␣(age␣%d)\n", ticks.l − p→stamp);
    }
  }
}
```

252. The entire present state of the pipeline computation can be visualized by printing first the write buffer, then the reorder buffer, then the fetch buffer. This shows the progression of results from oldest to youngest, from sizzling hot to ice cold.

```
⟨ External prototypes 9 ⟩ +≡
  Extern void print_pipe ARGS((void));
```

253.
```
⟨ External routines 10 ⟩ +≡
  void print_pipe()
  {
    print_write_buffer();
    print_reorder_buffer();
    print_fetch_buffer();
  }
```

ARGS = macro, §6.
control = **struct**, §44.
coroutine = **struct**, §23.
ctl: **control** ∗, §23.
Extern = macro, §4.
go: **specnode**, §44.
internal_opcode = **enum**, §49.
l: **tetra**, §17.
lockvar = **coroutine** ∗, §37.
mem: **specnode**, §115.
name: **char** ∗, §23.
o: **octa**, §40.
octa = **struct**, §17.
print_fetch_buffer: **static void** ( ), §73.
print_octa: **static void** ( ), §19.
print_reorder_buffer: **static void** ( ), §63.
printf: **int** ( ), <stdio.h>.
ptr_a: **void** ∗, §44.
spec_write: **extern void** ( ), §208.
stage: **int**, §23.
startup: **static void** ( ), §31.
stunc = 67, §49.
sync = 79, §49.
tetra = **unsigned int**, §17.
ticks: **Extern octa**, §87.
write_from_wbuf = 92, §129.

254. The *write_search* routine looks to see if any instructions ahead of a given place in the *mem* list of the reorder buffer are storing into a given physical address, or if there's a pending instruction in the write buffer for that address. If so, it returns a pointer to the value to be written. If not, it returns Λ. If the answer is currently unknown, because at least one possibly relevant physical address has not yet been computed, the subroutine returns the special code value DUNNO.

The search starts at the *x.up* field of a control block for a store instruction, otherwise at the *ptr_a* field of the control block, unless *ptr_a* points to a committed instruction.

The *i* field in the write buffer is usually *st* or *pst*, inherited from a store or partial store command. It may also be *sync* (from SYNC 1 or SYNC 3) or *stunc* (from STUNC).

```
#define DUNNO ((octa *) 1)    /* an impossible non-Λ pointer */

⟨Internal prototypes 13⟩ +≡
  static octa *write_search ARGS((control *, octa));
```

255. ⟨Subroutines 14⟩ +≡

```
  static octa *write_search(ctl, addr)
      control *ctl;
      octa addr;
  { register specnode *p = (ctl→mem_x ? ctl→x.up : (specnode *) ctl→ptr_a);
    register write_node *q = write_tail;
    addr.l &= −8;
    if (p ≡ &mem) goto qloop;
    if (p > &hot→x ∧ ctl ≤ hot) goto qloop;    /* already committed */
    if (p < &ctl→x ∧ (ctl ≤ hot ∨ p > &hot→x)) goto qloop;
    for ( ; p ≠ &mem; p = p→up) {
      if (p→addr.h ≡ (tetra) −1) return DUNNO;
      if ((p→addr.l & −8) ≡ addr.l ∧ p→addr.h ≡ addr.h)
        return (p→known ? &(p→o) : DUNNO);
    }
  qloop: for ( ; ; ) {
      if (q ≡ write_head) return Λ;
      if (q ≡ wbuf_top) q = wbuf_bot; else q++;
      if (q→addr.l ≡ addr.l ∧ q→addr.h ≡ addr.h) return &(q→o);
    }
  }
```

256. When we're committing new data to memory, we can update an existing item in the write buffer if it has the same physical address, unless that item is already in the process of being written out. Increasing the value of *holding_time* will increase the chance that this economy is possible, but it will also increase the number of buffered items when writes are to different locations.

A store instruction that sets any of the eight interrupt bits rwxnkbsp will not affect memory, even if it doesn't cause an interrupt.

When "store" is followed by "store uncached" at the same address, or vice versa, we believe the most recent hint.

```
⟨Commit to memory if possible, otherwise break 256⟩ ≡
  { register write_node *q = write_tail;
```

```
    if (hot→interrupt & (F_BIT + #ff)) goto done_with_write;
    if (hot→x.addr.h & #ffff0000) {
      if (hot→op ≥ STB ∧ hot→op < STSF) q→size = (hot→op & #f) ≫ 2;
      else if (hot→op ≥ STSF ∧ hot→op < STCO) q→size = 2;
      else q→size = 3;
    }
    if (hot→i ≠ sync)
      for ( ; ; ) {
        if (q ≡ write_head) break;
        if (q ≡ wbuf_top) q = wbuf_bot; else q++;
        if (q→i ≡ sync) break;
        if (q→addr.l ≡ hot→x.addr.l ∧ q→addr.h ≡ hot→x.addr.h ∧ (q ≠
              write_head ∨ ¬wbuf_lock)) goto addr_found;
      }
    { register write_node *p = (write_tail ≡ wbuf_bot ? wbuf_top : write_tail − 1);
      if (p ≡ write_head) break;        /* the write buffer is full */
      q = write_tail; write_tail = p;
      q→addr = hot→x.addr;
    }
  addr_found: q→o = hot→x.o;
    q→stamp = ticks.l;
    q→i = hot→i;
  done_with_write: spec_rem(&(hot→x));
    mem_slots++;
  }
```

This code is used in section 146.

---

addr: **octa**, §246.
addr: **octa**, §40.
ARGS = macro, §6.
control = **struct**, §44.
F_BIT = 1 ≪ 17, §54.
h: **tetra**, §17.
holding_time: **int**, §247.
hot: **control** ∗, §60.
i: **internal_opcode**, §246.
i: **internal_opcode**, §44.
interrupt: **unsigned int**, §44.
known: **bool**, §40.
l: **tetra**, §17.
mem: **specnode**, §115.
mem_slots: **int**, §86.
mem_x: **bool**, §44.
o: **octa**, §246.
o: **octa**, §40.
octa = **struct**, §17.
op: **mmix_opcode**, §44.
pst = 66, §49.
ptr_a: **void** ∗, §44.
size: **int**, §246.
spec_rem: **static void** ( ), §97.
specnode = **struct**, §40.
st = 63, §49.
stamp: **tetra**, §246.
STB = #a0, §47.
STCO = #b4, §47.
STSF = #b0, §47.
stunc = 67, §49.
sync = 79, §49.
tetra = **unsigned int**, §17.
ticks: **Extern octa**, §87.
up: **specnode** ∗, §40.
wbuf_bot: **write_node** ∗, §247.
wbuf_lock: **lockvar**, §247.
wbuf_top: **write_node** ∗, §247.
write_head: **write_node** ∗, §247.
write_node = **struct**, §246.
write_tail: **write_node** ∗, §247.
x: **specnode**, §44.

257. A special coroutine whose duty is to empty the write buffer is always active. It holds the *wbuf_lock* while it is writing the contents of *write_head*. It holds *Dcache→fill_lock* while waiting for the D-cache to fill a block.

```
⟨ Cases for control of special coroutines 126 ⟩ +≡
case write_from_wbuf: p = (cacheblock *) data→ptr_b;
  switch (data→state) {
  case 4: ⟨ Forward the new data past the D-cache if it is write-through 263 ⟩;
    data→state = 5;
  case 5: if (write_head ≡ wbuf_bot) write_head = wbuf_top; else write_head−−;
  write_restart: data→state = 0;
  case 0: if (self→lockloc) *(self→lockloc) = Λ, self→lockloc = Λ;
    if (write_head ≡ write_tail) wait(1);      /* write buffer is empty */
    if (write_head→i ≡ sync) ⟨ Ignore the item in write_head 264 ⟩;
    if (write_head→addr.h & #ffff0000) goto mem_direct;
    if (ticks.l − write_head→stamp < holding_time ∧ ¬speed_lock) wait(1);
        /* data too raw */
    if (¬Dcache) goto mem_direct;      /* not cached */
    if (Dcache→lock ∨ (j = get_reader(Dcache) < 0)) wait(1);      /* D-cache busy */
    startup(&Dcache→reader[j], Dcache→access_time);
    ⟨ Write the data into the D-cache and set state = 4, if there's a cache hit 262 ⟩;
    data→state = ((Dcache→mode & WRITE_ALLOC) ∧ write_head→i ≠ stunc ? 1 : 3);
    wait(Dcache→access_time);
  case 1: ⟨ Try to put the contents of location write_head→addr into the D-cache 261 ⟩;
    data→state = 2; sleep;
  case 2: data→state = 0; sleep;      /* wake up when the D-cache has the block */
  case 3: ⟨ Handle write-around when writing to the D-cache 259 ⟩;
  mem_direct: ⟨ Write directly from write_head to memory 260 ⟩;
  }
```

258.
```
⟨ Local variables 12 ⟩ +≡
  register cacheblock *p, *q;
```

259. The granularity is guaranteed to be 8 in write-around mode (see *MMIX_config*). Although an uncached store will not be stored in the D-cache (unless it hits in the D-cache), it will go into a secondary cache.

```
⟨ Handle write-around when writing to the D-cache 259 ⟩ ≡
  if (Dcache→flusher.next) wait(1);
  Dcache→outbuf.tag.h = write_head→addr.h;
  Dcache→outbuf.tag.l = write_head→addr.l & (−Dcache→bb);
  for (j = 0; j < Dcache→bb ≫ Dcache→g; j++) Dcache→outbuf.dirty[j] = false;
  Dcache→outbuf.data[(write_head→addr.l & (Dcache→bb − 1)) ≫ 3] = write_head→o;
  Dcache→outbuf.dirty[(write_head→addr.l & (Dcache→bb − 1)) ≫ Dcache→g] = true;
  set_lock(self, wbuf_lock);
  startup(&Dcache→flusher, Dcache→copy_out_time);
  data→state = 5; wait(Dcache→copy_out_time);
```
This code is used in section 257.

260. ⟨ Write directly from *write_head* to memory 260 ⟩ ≡

```
if (mem_lock) wait(1);
set_lock(self, wbuf_lock);
set_lock(&mem_locker, mem_lock);   /* a coroutine of type vanish */
startup(&mem_locker, mem_addr_time + mem_write_time);
if (write_head->addr.h & #ffff0000)
  spec_write(write_head->addr, write_head->o, write_head->size);
else mem_write(write_head->addr, write_head->o);
data->state = 5; wait(mem_addr_time + mem_write_time);
```

This code is used in section 257.

261. A subtlety needs to be mentioned here: While we're trying to update the D-cache, another instruction might be filling the same cache block (although not because of the same physical address). Therefore we **goto** *write_restart* here instead of saying *wait*(1).

⟨ Try to put the contents of location *write_head*→*addr* into the D-cache 261 ⟩ ≡

```
if (Dcache->filler.next) goto write_restart;
if ((Scache ∧ Scache->lock) ∨ (¬Scache ∧ mem_lock)) goto write_restart;
p = alloc_slot(Dcache, write_head->addr);
if (¬p) goto write_restart;
if (Scache) set_lock(&Dcache->filler, Scache->lock)
else set_lock(&Dcache->filler, mem_lock);
set_lock(self, Dcache->fill_lock);
data->ptr_b = Dcache->filler_ctl.ptr_b = (void *) p;
Dcache->filler_ctl.z.o = write_head->addr;
startup(&Dcache->filler, Scache ? Scache->access_time : mem_addr_time);
```

This code is used in section 257.

---

access_time: **int**, §167.
addr: **octa**, §246.
alloc_slot: **static cacheblock** *( ), §205.
bb: **int**, §167.
cacheblock = **struct**, §167.
copy_out_time: **int**, §167.
data: **register control** *, §124.
data: **octa** *, §167.
Dcache: **cache** *, §168.
dirty: **char** *, §167.
false = 0, §11.
fill_lock: **lockvar**, §167.
filler: **coroutine**, §167.
filler_ctl: **control**, §167.
flusher: **coroutine**, §167.
g: **int**, §167.
get_reader: **static int** ( ), §183.
h: **tetra**, §17.
holding_time: **int**, §247.
i: **internal_opcode**, §246.
j: **register int**, §12.
l: **tetra**, §17.
lock: **lockvar**, §167.
lockloc: **coroutine** **, §23.
mem_addr_time: **int**, §214.
mem_lock: **lockvar**, §214.
mem_locker: **coroutine**, §127.
mem_write: **void** ( ), §213.
mem_write_time: **int**, §214.
MMIX_config: **void** ( ), MMIX-CONFIG §38.
mode: **int**, §167.
next: **coroutine** *, §23.
o: **octa**, §246.
o: **octa**, §40.
outbuf: **cacheblock**, §167.
p: **register write_node** *, §256.
ptr_b: **void** *, §44.
reader: **coroutine** *, §167.
Scache: **cache** *, §168.
self: **register coroutine** *, §124.
set_lock = macro ( ), §37.
size: **int**, §246.
sleep = macro, §125.
spec_write: **extern void** ( ), §208.
speed_lock: **lockvar**, §247.
stamp: **tetra**, §246.
startup: **static void** ( ), §31.
state: **int**, §44.
stunc = 67, §49.
sync = 79, §49.
tag: **octa**, §167.
ticks: **Extern octa**, §87.
true = 1, §11.
vanish = 98, §129.
wait = macro ( ), §125.
wbuf_bot: **write_node** *, §247.
wbuf_lock: **lockvar**, §247.
wbuf_top: **write_node** *, §247.
WRITE_ALLOC = 2, §166.
write_from_wbuf = 92, §129.
write_head: **write_node** *, §247.
write_tail: **write_node** *, §247.
z: **spec**, §44.

262. Here it is assumed that *Dcache→access_time* is enough to search the D-cache and update one octabyte in case of a hit. The D-cache is not locked, since other coroutines that might be simultaneously reading the D-cache are not going to use the octabyte that changes. Perhaps the simulator is being too lenient here.

⟨ Write the data into the D-cache and set *state* = 4, if there's a cache hit 262 ⟩ ≡

```
p = cache_search(Dcache, write_head→addr);
if (p) {
  p = use_and_fix(Dcache, p);
  set_lock(self, wbuf_lock);
  data→ptr_b = (void *) p;
  p→data[(write_head→addr.l & (Dcache→bb − 1)) ≫ 3] = write_head→o;
  p→dirty[(write_head→addr.l & (Dcache→bb − 1)) ≫ Dcache→g] = true;
  data→state = 4; wait(Dcache→access_time);
}
```

This code is used in section 257.

263. ⟨ Forward the new data past the D-cache if it is write-through 263 ⟩ ≡

```
if ((Dcache→mode & WRITE_BACK) ≡ 0) {   /* write-through */
  if (Dcache→flusher.next) wait(1);
  flush_cache(Dcache, p, true);
}
```

This code is used in section 257.

264. ⟨ Ignore the item in *write_head* 264 ⟩ ≡

```
{
  set_lock(self, wbuf_lock);
  data→state = 5;
  wait(1);
}
```

This code is used in section 257.

---

access_time: **int**, §167.
addr: **octa**, §246.
bb: **int**, §167.
cache_search: **static cacheblock** ∗( ), §193.
data: **octa** ∗, §167.
data: **register control** ∗, §124.
Dcache: **cache** ∗, §168.
dirty: **char** ∗, §167.
flush_cache: **static void** ( ), §203.
flusher: **coroutine**, §167.
g: **int**, §167.
l: **tetra**, §17.
mode: **int**, §167.
next: **coroutine** ∗, §23.
o: **octa**, §246.
p: **register cacheblock** ∗, §258.
ptr_b: **void** ∗, §44.
self: **register coroutine** ∗, §124.
set_lock = macro ( ), §37.
state: **int**, §44.
true = 1, §11.
use_and_fix: **static cacheblock** ∗( ), §196.
wait = macro ( ), §125.
wbuf_lock: **lockvar**, §247.
`WRITE_BACK` = 1, §166.
write_head: **write_node** ∗, §247.

265. Loading and storing. A RISC machine is often said to have a "load/store architecture," perhaps because loading and storing are among the most difficult things a RISC machine is called upon to do.

We want memory accesses to be efficient, so we try to access the D-cache at the same time as we are translating a virtual address via the DT-cache. Usually we hit in both caches, but numerous cases must be dealt with when we miss. Is there an elegant way to handle all the contingencies? Alas, the author of this program was unable to think of anything better than to throw lots of code at the problem — knowing full well that such a spaghetti-like approach is fraught with possibilities for error.

Instructions like LDO x, y, z operate in two pipeline stages. The first stage computes the virtual address $y + z$, waiting if necessary until y and z are both known; then it starts to access the necessary caches. In the second stage we ascertain the corresponding physical address and hopefully find the data in the cache (or in the speculative *mem* list or the write buffer).

An instruction like STB x, y, z shares some of the computation of LDO x, y, z, because only one byte is being stored but the other seven bytes must be found in the cache. In this case, however, x is treated as an input, and *mem* is the output. The second stage of a store command can begin even though x is not known during the first stage.

Here's what we do at the beginning of stage 1.

```
#define ld_st_launch 7
            /* state when load/store command has its memory address */

⟨ Cases to compute the virtual address of a memory operation 265 ⟩ ≡
case preld: case prest: case prego:
  data→z.o = incr(data→z.o, data→xx & −(data→i ≡ prego ? Icache : Dcache)→bb);
    /* (I hope the adder is fast enough) */
case ld: case ldunc: case ldvts: case st: case pst: case syncd: case syncid:
  start_ld_st: data→y.o = oplus(data→y.o, data→z.o);
  data→state = ld_st_launch; goto switch1;
case ldptp: case ldpte: if (data→y.o.h) goto start_ld_st;
  data→x.o = zero_octa; data→x.known = true; goto die;      /* page table fault */
```

This code is used in section 132.

```
266. #define PRW_BITS (data→i < st ? PR_BIT : data→i ≡ pst ? PR_BIT + PW_BIT :
            (data→i ≡ syncid ∧ (data→loc.h & sign_bit)) ? 0 : PW_BIT)

⟨ Special cases for states in the first stage 266 ⟩ ≡
case ld_st_launch: if ((self + 1)→next) wait(1);     /* second stage must be clear */
  ⟨ Handle special cases for operations like prego and ldvts 289 ⟩;
  if (data→y.o.h & sign_bit) ⟨ Do load/store stage 1 with known physical address 271 ⟩;
  if (page_bad) {
    if (data→i < preld ∨ data→i ≡ st ∨ data→i ≡ pst) data→interrupt |= PRW_BITS;
    goto fin_ex;
  }
  if (DTcache→lock ∨ (j = get_reader(DTcache)) < 0) wait(1);
  startup(&DTcache→reader[j], DTcache→access_time);
  ⟨ Look up the address in the DT-cache, and also in the D-cache if possible 267 ⟩;
```

pass_after(*DTcache*→*access_time*); **goto** *passit*;

See also sections 310, 326, 360, and 363.

This code is used in section 130.

267. When stage 2 of a load/store command begins, the state will depend on what transpired in stage 1. For example, *data*→*state* will be *DT_miss* if the virtual address key can't be found in the DT-cache; then stage 2 will have to compute the physical address the hard way.

The *data*→*state* will be *DT_hit* if the physical address is known via the DT-cache, but the data may or may not be in the D-cache. The *data*→*state* will be *hit_and_miss* if the DT-cache hits and the D-cache doesn't. And *data*→*state* will be *ld_ready* if *data*→*x.o* is the desired octabyte (for example, if both caches hit).

```
#define DT_miss 10 /* second stage state when DT-cache doesn't hold the key */
#define DT_hit 11 /* second stage state when physical address is known */
#define hit_and_miss 12 /* second stage state when D-cache misses */
#define ld_ready 13 /* second stage state when data has been read */
#define st_ready 14 /* second stage state when data needn't be read */
#define prest_win 15 /* second stage state when we can fill a block with zeroes */
```

⟨Look up the address in the DT-cache, and also in the D-cache if possible 267⟩ ≡

```
  p = cache_search(DTcache, trans_key(data→y.o));
  if (¬Dcache ∨ Dcache→lock ∨ (j = get_reader(Dcache)) < 0 ∨ (data→i ≥ st ∧ data→i ≤ syncid))
    ⟨Do load/store stage 1 without D-cache lookup 270⟩;
  startup(&Dcache→reader[j], Dcache→access_time);
  if (p) ⟨Do a simultaneous lookup in the D-cache 268⟩
  else data→state = DT_miss;
```

This code is used in section 266.

access_time: **int**, §167.
bb: **int**, §167.
cache_search: **static cacheblock** *( ), §193.
data: **register control** *, §124.
Dcache: **cache** *, §168.
die: label, §144.
DTcache: **cache** *, §168.
fin_ex: label, §144.
get_reader: **static int** ( ), §183.
h: **tetra**, §17.
i: **internal_opcode**, §44.
Icache: **cache** *, §168.
incr: **octa** ( ), MMIX-ARITH §6.
interrupt: **unsigned int**, §44.
j: **register int**, §12.
known: **bool**, §40.
ld = 56, §49.
ldpte = 58, §49.
ldptp = 57, §49.
ldunc = 59, §49.
ldvts = 60, §49.
loc: **octa**, §44.
lock: **lockvar**, §167.
mem: **specnode**, §115.
next: **coroutine** *, §23.
o: **octa**, §40.
oplus: **octa** ( ), MMIX-ARITH §5.
p: **register cacheblock** *, §258.
page_bad: **bool**, §238.
pass_after = macro ( ), §125.
passit: label, §134.
PR_BIT = 1 ≪ 7, §54.
prego = 73, §49.
preld = 61, §49.
prest = 62, §49.
pst = 66, §49.
PW_BIT = 1 ≪ 6, §54.
reader: **coroutine** *, §167.
self: **register coroutine** *, §124.
sign_bit = macro, §80.
st = 63, §49.
startup: **static void** ( ), §31.
state: **int**, §44.
switch1: label, §130.
syncd = 64, §49.
syncid = 65, §49.
trans_key = macro ( ), §240.
true = 1, §11.
wait = macro ( ), §125.
x: **specnode**, §44.
xx: **unsigned char**, §44.
y: **spec**, §44.
z: **spec**, §44.
zero_octa: **octa**, MMIX-ARITH §4.

268. We assume that it is possible to look up a virtual address in the DT-cache at the same time as we look for a corresponding physical address in the D-cache, provided that the lower $b + c$ bits of the two addresses are the same. (They will always be the same if $b + c \le page\_s$; otherwise the operating system can try to make them the same by "page coloring" whenever possible.) If both caches hit, the physical address is known in max(*DTcache→access_time*, *Dcache→access_time*) cycles.

If the lower $b + c$ bits of the virtual and physical addresses differ, the machine will not know this until the DT-cache has hit. Therefore we simulate the operation of accessing the D-cache, but we go to *DT_hit* instead of to *hit_and_miss* because the D-cache will experience a spurious miss.

```
#define max(x, y) ((x) < (y) ? (y) : (x))

⟨Do a simultaneous lookup in the D-cache 268⟩ ≡
  { octa *m;
    p = use_and_fix(DTcache, p), data→z.o = p→data[0];
    ⟨Check the protection bits and get the physical address 269⟩;
    m = write_search(data, data→z.o);
    if (m ≡ DUNNO) data→state = DT_hit;
    else if (m) data→x.o = *m, data→state = ld_ready;
    else if (Dcache→b + Dcache→c > page_s ∧
            ((data→y.o.l ⊕ data→z.o.l) & ((Dcache→bb ≪ Dcache→c) − (1 ≪ page_s))))
      data→state = DT_hit;   /* spurious D-cache lookup */
    else {
      q = cache_search(Dcache, data→z.o);
      if (q) {
        if (data→i ≡ ldunc) q = demote_and_fix(Dcache, q);
        else q = use_and_fix(Dcache, q);
        data→x.o = q→data[(data→z.o.l & (Dcache→bb − 1)) ≫ 3];
        data→state = ld_ready;
      } else data→state = hit_and_miss;
    }
    pass_after(max(DTcache→access_time, Dcache→access_time));
    goto passit;
  }
```

This code is used in section 267.

269. The protection bits $p_r p_w p_x$ in a translation cache are shifted four positions right from the interrupt codes PR_BIT, PW_BIT, PX_BIT. If the data is protected, we abort the load/store operation immediately; this protects the privacy of other users.

```
⟨ Check the protection bits and get the physical address 269 ⟩ ≡
  if (data→stack_alert) {
    if (data→z.o.l & (PW_BIT ≫ PROT_OFFSET)) data→stack_alert = false;
    else data→z.o = g[rC].o;      /* use the continuation page for stack overflow */
  }
  j = PRW_BITS;
  if (((data→z.o.l ≪ PROT_OFFSET) & j) ≠ j) {
    if (data→i ≡ syncd ∨ data→i ≡ syncid) goto sync_check;
    if (data→i ≠ preld ∧ data→i ≠ prest)
      data→interrupt |= j & ∼(data→z.o.l ≪ PROT_OFFSET);
    data→stack_alert = false;
    goto fin_ex;
  }
  data→z.o = phys_addr(data→y.o, data→z.o);
```

This code is used in sections 268, 270, and 272.

270.

```
⟨ Do load/store stage 1 without D-cache lookup 270 ⟩ ≡
  { octa *m;
    if (p) {
      p = use_and_fix(DTcache, p), data→z.o = p→data[0];
      ⟨ Check the protection bits and get the physical address 269 ⟩;
      if (data→i ≥ st ∧ data→i ≤ syncid) data→state = st_ready;
      else {
        m = write_search(data, data→z.o);
        if (m ∧ m ≠ DUNNO) data→x.o = *m, data→state = ld_ready;
        else data→state = DT_hit;
      }
    } else data→state = DT_miss;
    pass_after(DTcache→access_time); goto passit;
  }
```

This code is used in section 267.

---

access_time: **int**, §167.
b: **int**, §167.
bb: **int**, §167.
c: **int**, §167.
cache_search: **static cacheblock** *(), §193.
data: **octa** *, §167.
data: **register control** *, §124.
Dcache: **cache** *, §168.
demote_and_fix: **static cacheblock** *(), §199.
DT_hit = 11, §267.
DT_miss = 10, §267.
DTcache: **cache** *, §168.
DUNNO = macro, §254.
false = 0, §11.
fin_ex: label, §144.
g: **int**, §167.
hit_and_miss = 12, §267.
i: **internal_opcode**, §44.
interrupt: **unsigned int**, §44.
j: **register int**, §12.
l: **tetra**, §17.
ld_ready = 13, §267.
ldunc = 59, §49.
o: **octa**, §40.
octa = **struct**, §17.
p: **register cacheblock** *, §258.
page_s: **int**, §238.
pass_after = macro ( ), §125.
passit: label, §134.
phys_addr: **static octa** ( ), §241.
PR_BIT = 1 ≪ 7, §54.
preld = 61, §49.
prest = 62, §49.
PROT_OFFSET = 5, §54.
PRW_BITS = macro, §266.
PW_BIT = 1 ≪ 6, §54.
PX_BIT = 1 ≪ 5, §54.
q: **register cacheblock** *, §258.
rC = 8, §52.
st = 63, §49.
st_ready = 14, §267.
stack_alert: **bool**, §44.
state: **int**, §44.
sync_check: label, §370.
syncd = 64, §49.
syncid = 65, §49.
use_and_fix: **static cacheblock** *(), §196.
write_search: **static octa** *(), §255.
x: **specnode**, §44.
y: **spec**, §44.
z: **spec**, §44.

271. ⟨ Do load/store stage 1 with known physical address 271 ⟩ ≡

```
{ octa *m;
  if (¬(data→loc.h & sign_bit)) {
    if (data→i ≡ syncd ∨ data→i ≡ syncid) goto sync_check;
    if (data→i ≠ preld ∧ data→i ≠ prest) data→interrupt |= N_BIT;
    goto fin_ex;
  }
  data→z.o = data→y.o; data→z.o.h −= sign_bit;
  if (data→z.o.h & #ffff0000) {
    switch (data→i) {
    case ldvts: case preld: case prest: case prego: case syncd: case syncid:
      goto fin_ex;
    case ld: case ldunc: if (mem_lock) wait(1);
      if (data→op < LDSF) i = (data→op & #f) ≫ 2;
      else if (data→op < CSWAP) i = 2;
      else i = 3;
      data→x.o = spec_read(data→z.o, i);
      goto make_ld_ready;
    case pst:
      if ((data→op ⊕ CSWAP) ≤ 1) {
        data→x.o = spec_read(data→z.o, 3); goto make_ld_ready;
      }
      data→x.o = zero_octa;
    case st: data→state = st_ready; pass_after(1); goto passit;
    }
  } else if (data→i ≥ st ∧ data→i ≤ syncid) {
    data→state = st_ready; pass_after(1); goto passit;
  }
  m = write_search(data, data→z.o);
  if (m) {
    if (m ≡ DUNNO) data→state = DT_hit;
    else data→x.o = *m, data→state = ld_ready;
    pass_after(1); goto passit;
  } else if (¬Dcache) {
    if (mem_lock) wait(1);
    data→x.o = mem_read(data→z.o);
  make_ld_ready: set_lock(&mem_locker, mem_lock);
    data→state = ld_ready;
    startup(&mem_locker, mem_addr_time + mem_read_time);
    pass_after(mem_addr_time + mem_read_time); goto passit;
  }
  if (Dcache→lock ∨ (j = get_reader(Dcache)) < 0) {
    data→state = DT_hit; pass_after(1); goto passit;
  }
  startup(&Dcache→reader[j], Dcache→access_time);
  q = cache_search(Dcache, data→z.o);
  if (q) {
    if (data→i ≡ ldunc) q = demote_and_fix(Dcache, q);
    else q = use_and_fix(Dcache, q);
```

```
      data→x.o = q→data[(data→z.o.l & (Dcache→bb − 1)) ≫ 3];
      data→state = ld_ready;
    } else data→state = hit_and_miss;
    pass_after(Dcache→access_time); goto passit;
  }
```

This code is used in section 266.

access_time: **int**, §167.
bb: **int**, §167.
cache_search: **static cacheblock** ∗( ), §193.
CSWAP = #94, §47.
data: **octa** ∗, §167.
data: **register control** ∗, §124.
Dcache: **cache** ∗, §168.
demote_and_fix: **static cacheblock** ∗( ), §199.
DT_hit = 11, §267.
DUNNO = macro, §254.
fin_ex: label, §144.
get_reader: **static int** ( ), §183.
h: **tetra**, §17.
hit_and_miss = 12, §267.
i: **internal_opcode**, §44.
interrupt: **unsigned int**, §44.
j: **register int**, §12.
l: **tetra**, §17.
ld = 56, §49.
ld_ready = 13, §267.
LDSF = #90, §47.
ldunc = 59, §49.
ldvts = 60, §49.
loc: **octa**, §44.
lock: **lockvar**, §167.
mem_addr_time: **int**, §214.
mem_lock: **lockvar**, §214.
mem_locker: **coroutine**, §127.
mem_read: **octa** ( ), §210.
mem_read_time: **int**, §214.
N_BIT = 1 ≪ 4, §54.
o: **octa**, §40.
octa = **struct**, §17.
op: **mmix_opcode**, §44.
pass_after = macro ( ), §125.
passit: label, §134.
prego = 73, §49.
preld = 61, §49.
prest = 62, §49.
pst = 66, §49.
q: **register cacheblock** ∗, §258.
reader: **coroutine** ∗, §167.
set_lock = macro ( ), §37.
sign_bit = macro, §80.
spec_read: **extern octa** ( ), §208.
st = 63, §49.
st_ready = 14, §267.
startup: **static void** ( ), §31.
state: **int**, §44.
sync_check: label, §370.
syncd = 64, §49.
syncid = 65, §49.
use_and_fix: **static cacheblock** ∗( ), §196.
wait = macro ( ), §125.
write_search: **static octa** ∗( ), §255.
x: **specnode**, §44.
y: **spec**, §44.
z: **spec**, §44.
zero_octa: **octa**, MMIX-ARITH §4.

272. The program for the second stage is, likewise, rather long-winded, yet quite similar to the cache manipulations we have already seen several times.

Several instructions might be trying to fill the DT-cache for the same page. (A similar situation faced us in the *write_from_wbuf* coroutine.) The second stage therefore needs to do some translation cache searching just as the first stage did. In this stage, however, we don't go all out for speed, because DT-cache misses are rare.

```
#define DT_retry 8
        /* second stage state when DT-cache should be searched again */
#define got_DT 9
        /* second stage state when DT-cache entry has been computed */

⟨ Special cases for states in later stages 272 ⟩ ≡
square_one: data→state = DT_retry;
case DT_retry: if (DTcache→lock ∨ (j = get_reader(DTcache)) < 0) wait(1);
  startup(&DTcache→reader[j], DTcache→access_time);
  p = cache_search(DTcache, trans_key(data→y.o));
  if (p) {
    p = use_and_fix(DTcache, p), data→z.o = p→data[0];
    ⟨ Check the protection bits and get the physical address 269 ⟩;
    if (data→i ≥ st ∧ data→i ≤ syncid) data→state = st_ready;
    else data→state = DT_hit;
  } else data→state = DT_miss;
  wait(DTcache→access_time);
case DT_miss: if (DTcache→filler.next)
    if (data→i ≡ preld ∨ data→i ≡ prest) goto fin_ex; else goto square_one;
  if (no_hardware_PT ∨ page_f)
    if (data→i ≡ preld ∨ data→i ≡ prest) goto fin_ex; else goto emulate_virt;
  p = alloc_slot(DTcache, trans_key(data→y.o));
  if (¬p) goto square_one;
  data→ptr_b = DTcache→filler_ctl.ptr_b = (void *) p;
  DTcache→filler_ctl.y.o = data→y.o;
  set_lock(self, DTcache→fill_lock);
  startup(&DTcache→filler, 1);
  data→state = got_DT;
  if (data→i ≡ preld ∨ data→i ≡ prest) goto fin_ex; else sleep;
case got_DT: release_lock(self, DTcache→fill_lock);
  ⟨ Check the protection bits and get the physical address 269 ⟩;
  if (data→i ≥ st ∧ data→i ≤ syncid) goto finish_store;
      /* otherwise we fall through to ld_retry below */
```

See also sections 273, 276, 279, 280, 299, 311, 354, 364, and 370.

This code is used in section 135.

273. The second stage might also want to fill the D-cache (and perhaps the S-cache) as we get the data.

Several load instructions might be trying to fill the same cache block. So we should go back and look in the D-cache again if we miss and cannot allocate a slot immediately.

A PRELD or PREST instruction, which is just a "hint," doesn't do anything more if the caches are already busy.

```
⟨Special cases for states in later stages 272⟩ +≡
ld_retry: data→state = DT_hit;
case DT_hit: if (data→i ≡ preld ∨ data→i ≡ prest) goto fin_ex;
  ⟨Check for a hit in pending writes 278⟩;
  if ((data→z.o.h & #ffff0000) ∨ ¬Dcache)
    ⟨Do load/store stage 2 without D-cache lookup 277⟩;
  if (Dcache→lock ∨ (j = get_reader(Dcache)) < 0) wait(1);
  startup(&Dcache→reader[j], Dcache→access_time);
  q = cache_search(Dcache, data→z.o);
  if (q) {
    if (data→i ≡ ldunc) q = demote_and_fix(Dcache, q);
    else q = use_and_fix(Dcache, q);
    data→x.o = q→data[(data→z.o.l & (Dcache→bb − 1)) ≫ 3];
    data→state = ld_ready;
  } else data→state = hit_and_miss;
  wait(Dcache→access_time);
case hit_and_miss: if (data→i ≡ ldunc) goto avoid_D;
  ⟨Try to get the contents of location data→z.o in the D-cache 274⟩;
```

---

access_time: **int**, §167.
alloc_slot: **static cacheblock** *(), §205.
avoid_D: label, §277.
bb: **int**, §167.
cache_search: **static cacheblock** *(), §193.
data: **octa** *, §167.
data: **register control** *, §124.
Dcache: **cache** *, §168.
demote_and_fix: **static cacheblock** *(), §199.
DT_hit = 11, §267.
DT_miss = 10, §267.
DTcache: **cache** *, §168.
emulate_virt: label, §310.
fill_lock: **lockvar**, §167.
filler: **coroutine**, §167.
filler_ctl: **control**, §167.
fin_ex: label, §144.
finish_store: label, §280.
get_reader: **static int** (), §183.
h: **tetra**, §17.
hit_and_miss = 12, §267.
i: **internal_opcode**, §44.
j: **register int**, §12.
l: **tetra**, §17.
ld_ready = 13, §267.
ldunc = 59, §49.
lock: **lockvar**, §167.
next: **coroutine** *, §23.
no_hardware_PT: **bool**, §242.
o: **octa**, §40.
p: **register cacheblock** *, §258.
page_f: **int**, §238.
preld = 61, §49.
prest = 62, §49.
ptr_b: **void** *, §44.
q: **register cacheblock** *, §258.
reader: **coroutine** *, §167.
release_lock = macro (), §37.
self: **register coroutine** *, §124.
set_lock = macro (), §37.
sleep = macro, §125.
st = 63, §49.
st_ready = 14, §267.
startup: **static void** (), §31.
state: **int**, §44.
syncid = 65, §49.
trans_key = macro (), §240.
use_and_fix: **static cacheblock** *(), §196.
wait = macro (), §125.
write_from_wbuf = 92, §129.
x: **specnode**, §44.
y: **spec**, §44.
z: **spec**, §44.

274. ⟨ Try to get the contents of location *data→z.o* in the D-cache 274 ⟩ ≡

```
⟨ Check for prest with a fully spanned cache block 275 ⟩;
if (Dcache→filler.next) goto ld_retry;
if ((Scache ∧ Scache→lock) ∨ (¬Scache ∧ mem_lock)) goto ld_retry;
q = alloc_slot(Dcache, data→z.o);
if (¬q) goto ld_retry;
if (Scache) set_lock(&Dcache→filler, Scache→lock)
else set_lock(&Dcache→filler, mem_lock);
set_lock(self, Dcache→fill_lock);
data→ptr_b = Dcache→filler_ctl.ptr_b = (void *) q;
Dcache→filler_ctl.z.o = data→z.o;
startup(&Dcache→filler, Scache ? Scache→access_time : mem_addr_time);
data→state = ld_ready;
if (data→i ≡ preld ∨ data→i ≡ prest) goto fin_ex; else sleep;
```

This code is used in section 273.

275. If a *prest* instruction makes it to the hot seat, we have been assured by the user of PREST that the current values of bytes in virtual addresses *data→y.o* − (*data→xx* & −*Dcache→bb*) through *data→y.o* + (*data→xx* & (*Dcache→bb* − 1)) are irrelevant. Hence we can pretend that we know they are zero. This is advantageous if it saves us from filling a cache block from the S-cache or from memory.

⟨ Check for *prest* with a fully spanned cache block 275 ⟩ ≡

```
if (data→i ≡ prest ∧
      (data→xx ≥ Dcache→bb ∨ ((data→y.o.l & (Dcache→bb − 1)) ≡ 0)) ∧
      ((data→y.o.l + (data→xx & (Dcache→bb − 1)) + 1) ⊕ data→y.o.l) ≥ Dcache→bb)
   goto prest_span;
```

This code is used in section 274.

276. ⟨ Special cases for states in later stages 272 ⟩ +≡

```
prest_span: data→state = prest_win;
case prest_win: if (data ≠ old_hot ∨ Dlocker.next) wait(1);
  if (Dcache→lock) goto fin_ex;
  q = alloc_slot(Dcache, data→z.o);      /* OK if Dcache→filler is busy */
  if (q) {
    clean_block(Dcache, q);
    q→tag = data→z.o; q→tag.l &= −Dcache→bb;
    set_lock(&Dlocker, Dcache→lock);
    startup(&Dlocker, Dcache→copy_in_time);
  }
  goto fin_ex;
```

277. ⟨ Do load/store stage 2 without D-cache lookup 277 ⟩ ≡

```
{
avoid_D: if (mem_lock) wait(1);
    set_lock(&mem_locker, mem_lock);
    startup(&mem_locker, mem_addr_time + mem_read_time);
    data→x.o = mem_read(data→z.o);
    data→state = ld_ready; wait(mem_addr_time + mem_read_time);
}
```

This code is used in section 273.

278. ⟨ Check for a hit in pending writes 278 ⟩ ≡

```
{
  octa *m = write_search(data, data→z.o);
  if (m ≡ DUNNO) wait(1);
  if (m) {
    data→x.o = *m;
    data→state = ld_ready;
    wait(1);
  }
}
```

This code is used in section 273.

---

access_time: **int**, §167.
alloc_slot: **static cacheblock** *(), §205.
bb: **int**, §167.
clean_block: **void** (), §179.
copy_in_time: **int**, §167.
data: **register control** *, §124.
Dcache: **cache** *, §168.
Dlocker: **coroutine**, §127.
DUNNO = macro, §254.
fill_lock: **lockvar**, §167.
filler: **coroutine**, §167.
filler_ctl: **control**, §167.
fin_ex: label, §144.
i: **internal_opcode**, §44.
l: **tetra**, §17.
ld_ready = 13, §267.
ld_retry: label, §273.
lock: **lockvar**, §167.
mem_addr_time: **int**, §214.
mem_lock: **lockvar**, §214.
mem_locker: **coroutine**, §127.
mem_read: **octa** (), §210.
mem_read_time: **int**, §214.
next: **coroutine** *, §23.
o: **octa**, §40.
octa = **struct**, §17.
old_hot: **control** *, §60.
preld = 61, §49.
prest = 62, §49.
prest_win = 15, §267.
ptr_b: **void** *, §44.
q: **register cacheblock** *, §258.
Scache: **cache** *, §168.
self: **register coroutine** *, §124.
set_lock = macro (), §37.
sleep = macro, §125.
startup: **static void** (), §31.
state: **int**, §44.
tag: **octa**, §167.
wait = macro (), §125.
write_search: **static octa** *(), §255.
x: **specnode**, §44.
xx: **unsigned char**, §44.
y: **spec**, §44.
z: **spec**, §44.

279. The requested octabyte will arrive sooner or later in *data→x.o*. Then a load instruction is almost done, except that we might need to massage the input a little bit.

```
⟨ Special cases for states in later stages 272 ⟩ +≡
case ld_ready: if (self→lockloc) *(self→lockloc) = Λ, self→lockloc = Λ;
  if (data→i ≥ st) goto finish_store;
  switch (data→op ≫ 1) {
  case LDB ≫ 1: case LDBU ≫ 1: j = (data→z.o.l & #7) ≪ 3; i = 56; goto fin_ld;
  case LDW ≫ 1: case LDWU ≫ 1: j = (data→z.o.l & #6) ≪ 3; i = 48; goto fin_ld;
  case LDT ≫ 1: case LDTU ≫ 1: j = (data→z.o.l & #4) ≪ 3; i = 32;
  fin_ld: data→x.o = shift_right(shift_left(data→x.o, j), i, data→op & #2);
  default: goto fin_ex;
  case LDHT ≫ 1: if (data→z.o.l & 4) data→x.o.h = data→x.o.l;
    data→x.o.l = 0; goto fin_ex;
  case LDSF ≫ 1: if (data→z.o.l & 4) data→x.o.h = data→x.o.l;
    if ((data→x.o.h & #7f800000) ≡ 0 ∧ (data→x.o.h & #7fffff)) {
      data→x.o = load_sf(data→x.o.h);
      data→state = 3; wait(denin_penalty);
    }
    else data→x.o = load_sf(data→x.o.h); goto fin_ex;
  case LDPTP ≫ 1: if ((data→x.o.h & sign_bit) ≡ 0 ∨ (data→x.o.l & #1ff8) ≠ page_n)
      data→x.o = zero_octa;
    else data→x.o.l &= −(1 ≪ 13);
    goto fin_ex;
  case LDPTE ≫ 1: if ((data→x.o.l & #1ff8) ≠ page_n) data→x.o = zero_octa;
    else data→x.o = incr(oandn(data→x.o, page_mask), data→x.o.l & #7);
    data→x.o.h &= #ffff; goto fin_ex;
  case UNSAVE ≫ 1: ⟨ Handle an internal UNSAVE when it's time to load 336 ⟩;
  }
```

280.
```
⟨ Special cases for states in later stages 272 ⟩ +≡
finish_store: data→state = st_ready;
case st_ready: switch (data→i) {
  case st: case pst: ⟨ Finish a store command 281 ⟩;
  case syncd: data→b.o.l = (Dcache ? Dcache→bb : 8192); goto do_syncd;
  case syncid: data→b.o.l = (Icache ? Icache→bb : 8192);
    if (Dcache ∧ Dcache→bb < data→b.o.l) data→b.o.l = Dcache→bb;
    goto do_syncid;
  }
```

281. Store instructions have an extra complication, because some of them need to check for overflow.

```
⟨ Finish a store command 281 ⟩ ≡
  data→x.addr = data→z.o;
  if (data→b.p) wait(1);
  switch (data→op ≫ 1) {
  case STUNC ≫ 1: data→i = stunc;
  default: data→x.o = data→b.o; goto fin_ex;
  case STSF ≫ 1: set_round; data→b.o.h = store_sf(data→b.o);
```

```
    data→interrupt |= exceptions;
    if ((data→b.o.h & #7f800000) ≡ 0 ∧ (data→b.o.h & #7fffff)) {
      if (data→z.o.l & 4) data→x.o.l = data→b.o.h;
      else data→x.o.h = data→b.o.h;
      data→state = 3; wait(denout_penalty);
    }
  case STHT ≫ 1: if (data→z.o.l & 4) data→x.o.l = data→b.o.h;
    else data→x.o.h = data→b.o.h;
    goto fin_ex;
  case STB ≫ 1: case STBU ≫ 1: j = (data→z.o.l & #7) ≪ 3; i = 56; goto fin_st;
  case STW ≫ 1: case STWU ≫ 1: j = (data→z.o.l & #6) ≪ 3; i = 48; goto fin_st;
  case STT ≫ 1: case STTU ≫ 1: j = (data→z.o.l & #4) ≪ 3; i = 32;
  fin_st: ⟨Insert data→b.o into the proper field of data→x.o, checking for arithmetic
        exceptions if signed 282⟩;
    goto fin_ex;
  case CSWAP ≫ 1: ⟨Finish a CSWAP 283⟩;
  case SAVE ≫ 1: ⟨Handle an internal SAVE when it's time to store 342⟩;
  }
```

This code is used in section 280.

addr: **octa**, §40.
b: **spec**, §44.
bb: **int**, §167.
CSWAP = #94, §47.
data: **register control** ∗, §124.
Dcache: **cache** ∗, §168.
denin_penalty: **int**, §349.
denout_penalty: **int**, §349.
do_syncd: label, §364.
do_syncid: label, §364.
exceptions: **int**, MMIX-ARITH §32.
fin_ex: label, §144.
h: **tetra**, §17.
i: **register int**, §12.
i: **internal_opcode**, §44.
Icache: **cache** ∗, §168.
incr: **octa** ( ), MMIX-ARITH §6.
interrupt: **unsigned int**, §44.
j: **register int**, §12.
l: **tetra**, §17.
ld_ready = 13, §267.
LDB = #80, §47.
LDBU = #82, §47.
LDHT = #92, §47.
LDPTE = macro, §235.
LDPTP = macro, §235.
LDSF = #90, §47.
LDT = #88, §47.
LDTU = #8a, §47.
LDW = #84, §47.
LDWU = #86, §47.
load_sf: **octa** ( ), MMIX-ARITH §39.
lockloc: **coroutine** ∗∗, §23.
o: **octa**, §40.
oandn: **octa** ( ), MMIX-ARITH §25.
op: **mmix_opcode**, §44.
p: **specnode** ∗, §40.
page_mask: **octa**, §238.
page_n: **int**, §238.
pst = 66, §49.
SAVE = #fa, §47.
self: **register coroutine** ∗, §124.
set_round = macro, §346.
shift_left: **octa** ( ), MMIX-ARITH §7.
shift_right: **octa** ( ), MMIX-ARITH §7.
sign_bit = macro, §80.
st = 63, §49.
st_ready = 14, §267.
state: **int**, §44.
STB = #a0, §47.
STBU = #a2, §47.
STHT = #b2, §47.
store_sf: **tetra** ( ), MMIX-ARITH §40.
STSF = #b0, §47.
STT = #a8, §47.
STTU = #aa, §47.
stunc = 67, §49.
STUNC = #b6, §47.
STW = #a4, §47.
STWU = #a6, §47.
syncd = 64, §49.
syncid = 65, §49.
UNSAVE = #fb, §47.
wait = macro ( ), §125.
x: **specnode**, §44.
z: **spec**, §44.
zero_octa: **octa**, MMIX-ARITH §4.

282. ⟨ Insert *data→b.o* into the proper field of *data→x.o*, checking for arithmetic exceptions if signed 282 ⟩ ≡

```
{
  octa mask;
  if (¬(data→op & 2)) { octa before, after;
    before = data→b.o; after = shift_right(shift_left(data→b.o, i), i, 0);
    if (before.l ≠ after.l ∨ before.h ≠ after.h) data→interrupt |= V_BIT;
  }
  mask = shift_right(shift_left(neg_one, i), j, 1);
  data→b.o = shift_right(shift_left(data→b.o, i), j, 1);
  data→x.o.h ⊕= mask.h & (data→x.o.h ⊕ data→b.o.h);
  data→x.o.l ⊕= mask.l & (data→x.o.l ⊕ data→b.o.l);
}
```

This code is used in section 281.

283. The CSWAP operation has four inputs ($X, $Y, $Z, rP) as well as three outputs ($X, M_8[A], rP). To keep from exceeding the capacity of the control blocks in our pipeline, we wait until this instruction reaches the hot seat, thereby allowing us non-speculative access to rP.

⟨ Finish a CSWAP 283 ⟩ ≡

```
  if (data ≠ old_hot) wait(1);
  if (data→x.o.h ≡ g[rP].o.h ∧ data→x.o.l ≡ g[rP].o.l) {
    data→a.o.l = 1;     /* data→a.o.h is zero */
    data→x.o = data→b.o;
  } else {
    g[rP].o = data→x.o;     /* data→a.o is zero */
    if (verbose & issue_bit) {
      printf("␣setting␣rP="); print_octa(g[rP].o); printf("\n");
    }
  }
  data→i = cswap;     /* cosmetic change, affects the trace output only */
  goto fin_ex;
```

This code is used in section 281.

284. The fetch stage. Now that we've mastered the most difficult memory operations, we can relax and apply our knowledge to the slightly simpler task of filling the fetch buffer. Fetching is like loading/storing, except that we use the I-cache instead of the D-cache. It's slightly simpler because the I-cache is read-only. Further simplifications would be possible if there were no `PREGO` instruction, because there is only one fetch unit. However, we want to implement `PREGO` with reasonable efficiency, in order to see if that instruction is worthwhile; so we include the complications of simultaneous I-cache and IT-cache readers, which we have already implemented for the D-cache and DT-cache.

The fetch coroutine is always present, as the one and only coroutine with *stage* number zero.

In normal circumstances, the fetch coroutine accesses a cache block containing the instruction whose virtual address is given by *inst_ptr* (the instruction pointer), and transfers up to *fetch_max* instructions from that block to the fetch buffer. Complications arise if the instruction isn't in the cache, or if we can't translate the virtual address because of a miss in the IT-cache. Moreover, *inst_ptr* is a **spec** variable whose value might not even be known; if *inst_ptr.p* is nonnull, we don't know what to fetch.

⟨ External variables 4 ⟩ +≡
  Extern spec *inst_ptr*; /* the instruction pointer (aka program counter) */
  Extern octa **fetched*; /* buffer for incoming instructions */

285. The fetch coroutine usually begins a cycle in state *fetch_ready*, with the most recently fetched octabytes in positions *fetch_lo*, *fetch_lo* + 1, ..., *fetch_hi* − 1 of a buffer called *fetched*. Once that buffer has been exhausted, the coroutine reverts to state 0; with luck, the buffer might have more data by the time the next cycle rolls around.

⟨ Global variables 20 ⟩ +≡
  int *fetch_lo*, *fetch_hi*; /* the active region of that buffer */
  coroutine *fetch_co*;
  control *fetch_ctl*;

---

a: **specnode**, §44.
b: **spec**, §44.
control = **struct**, §44.
coroutine = **struct**, §23.
cswap = 68, §49.
data: **register control** *, §124.
Extern = macro, §4.
fetch_max: **int**, §59.
fetch_ready = 23, §291.
fin_ex: label, §144.
g: **specnode** [ ], §86.
h: **tetra**, §17.
i: **register int**, §12.
i: **internal_opcode**, §44.
interrupt: **unsigned int**, §44.
issue_bit = 1 ≪ 0, §8.
j: **register int**, §12.
l: **tetra**, §17.
neg_one: **octa**, MMIX-ARITH §4.
o: **octa**, §40.
octa = **struct**, §17.
old_hot: **control** *, §60.
op: **mmix_opcode**, §44.
p: **specnode** *, §40.
print_octa: **static void** ( ), §19.
printf: **int** ( ), `<stdio.h>`.
rP = 23, §52.
shift_left: **octa** ( ), MMIX-ARITH §7.
shift_right: **octa** ( ), MMIX-ARITH §7.
spec = **struct**, §40.
stage: **int**, §23.
`V_BIT` = 1 ≪ 14, §54.
verbose: **int**, §4.
wait = macro ( ), §125.
x: **specnode**, §44.

286. ⟨ Initialize everything 22 ⟩ +≡

```
fetch_co.ctl = &fetch_ctl;
fetch_co.name = "Fetch";
fetch_ctl.go.o.l = 4;
startup(&fetch_co, 1);
```

287. ⟨ Restart the fetch coroutine 287 ⟩ ≡

```
if (fetch_co.lockloc) *(fetch_co.lockloc) = Λ, fetch_co.lockloc = Λ;
unschedule(&fetch_co);
startup(&fetch_co, 1);
```

This code is used in sections 85, 160, 308, 309, and 316.

288. Some of the actions here are done not only by the fetcher but also by the first and second stages of a *prego* operation.

```
#define wait_or_pass(t)
        if (data→i ≡ prego) { pass_after(t); goto passit; }
        else wait(t)
```

⟨ Simulate an action of the fetch coroutine 288 ⟩ ≡

```
switch0: switch (data→state) {
  new_fetch: data→state = 0;
  case 0: ⟨ Wait, if necessary, until the instruction pointer is known 290 ⟩;
    data→y.o = inst_ptr.o;
    data→state = 1; data→interrupt = 0; data→x.o = data→z.o = zero_octa;
  case 1: start_fetch: if (data→y.o.h & sign_bit)
      ⟨ Begin fetch with known physical address 296 ⟩;
    if (page_bad) goto bad_fetch;
    if (ITcache→lock ∨ (j = get_reader(ITcache)) < 0) wait(1);
    startup(&ITcache→reader[j], ITcache→access_time);
    ⟨ Look up the address in the IT-cache, and also in the I-cache if possible 291 ⟩;
    wait_or_pass(ITcache→access_time);
    ⟨ Other cases for the fetch coroutine 298 ⟩
}
```

This code is used in section 125.

289. ⟨ Handle special cases for operations like *prego* and *ldvts* 289 ⟩ ≡

```
if (data→i ≡ prego) goto start_fetch;
```

See also section 352.

This code is used in section 266.

290. ⟨ Wait, if necessary, until the instruction pointer is known 290 ⟩ ≡

```
if (inst_ptr.p) {
  if (inst_ptr.p ≠ UNKNOWN_SPEC ∧ inst_ptr.p→known)
    inst_ptr.o = inst_ptr.p→o, inst_ptr.p = Λ;
  wait(1);
}
```

This code is used in section 288.

291. **#define** *got_IT* 19 /* *state* when IT-cache entry has been computed */
#define *IT_miss* 20 /* *state* when IT-cache doesn't hold the key */
#define *IT_hit* 21 /* *state* when physical instruction address is known */
#define *Ihit_and_miss* 22 /* *state* when I-cache misses */
#define *fetch_ready* 23 /* *state* when instructions have been read */
#define *got_one* 24 /* *state* when a "preview" octabyte is ready */

⟨ Look up the address in the IT-cache, and also in the I-cache if possible 291 ⟩ ≡

```
p = cache_search(ITcache, trans_key(data→y.o));
if (¬Icache ∨ Icache→lock ∨ (j = get_reader(Icache)) < 0)
   ⟨ Begin fetch without I-cache lookup 295 ⟩;
startup(&Icache→reader[j], Icache→access_time);
if (p) ⟨ Do a simultaneous lookup in the I-cache 292 ⟩
else data→state = IT_miss;
```

This code is used in section 288.

---

access_time: **int**, §167.
bad_fetch: label, §301.
cache_search: **static cacheblock** *(), §193.
ctl: **control** *, §23.
data: **register control** *, §124.
fetch_co: **coroutine**, §285.
fetch_ctl: **control**, §285.
get_reader: **static int** (), §183.
go: **specnode**, §44.
h: **tetra**, §17.
i: **internal_opcode**, §44.
Icache: **cache** *, §168.
inst_ptr: **spec**, §284.
interrupt: **unsigned int**, §44.
ITcache: **cache** *, §168.
j: **register int**, §12.
known: **bool**, §40.
l: **tetra**, §17.
ldvts = 60, §49.
lock: **lockvar**, §167.
lockloc: **coroutine** **, §23.
name: **char** *, §23.
o: **octa**, §40.
p: **specnode** *, §40.
p: **register cacheblock** *, §258.
page_bad: **bool**, §238.
pass_after = macro (), §125.
passit: label, §134.
prego = 73, §49.
reader: **coroutine** *, §167.
sign_bit = macro, §80.
startup: **static void** (), §31.
state: **int**, §44.
trans_key = macro (), §240.
UNKNOWN_SPEC = macro, §71.
unschedule: **static void** (), §33.
wait = macro (), §125.
x: **specnode**, §44.
y: **spec**, §44.
z: **spec**, §44.
zero_octa: **octa**, MMIX-ARITH §4.

292. We assume that it is possible to look up a virtual address in the IT-cache at the same time as we look for a corresponding physical address in the I-cache, provided that the lower $b+c$ bits of the two addresses are the same. (See the remarks about "page coloring," when we made similar assumptions about the DT-cache and D-cache.)

```
⟨ Do a simultaneous lookup in the I-cache 292 ⟩ ≡
  {
    ⟨ Update IT-cache usage and check the protection bits 293 ⟩;
    data→z.o = phys_addr(data→y.o, p→data[0]);
    if (Icache→b + Icache→c > page_s ∧
          ((data→y.o.l ⊕ data→z.o.l) & ((Icache→bb ≪ Icache→c) − (1 ≪ page_s))))
      data→state = IT_hit;     /* spurious I-cache lookup */
    else {
      q = cache_search(Icache, data→z.o);
      if (q) {
        q = use_and_fix(Icache, q);
        ⟨ Copy the data from block q to fetched 294 ⟩;
        data→state = fetch_ready;
      } else data→state = Ihit_and_miss;
    }
    wait_or_pass(max(ITcache→access_time, Icache→access_time));
  }
```

This code is used in section 291.

293. ⟨ Update IT-cache usage and check the protection bits 293 ⟩ ≡

```
  p = use_and_fix(ITcache, p);
  if (¬(p→data[0].l & (PX_BIT ≫ PROT_OFFSET))) goto bad_fetch;
```

This code is used in sections 292 and 295.

294. At this point *inst_ptr.o* equals *data→y.o*.

```
⟨ Copy the data from block q to fetched 294 ⟩ ≡
  if (data→i ≠ prego) {
    for (j = 0; j < Icache→bb ≫ 3; j++) fetched[j] = q→data[j];
    fetch_lo = (inst_ptr.o.l & (Icache→bb − 1)) ≫ 3;
    fetch_hi = Icache→bb ≫ 3;
  }
```

This code is used in sections 292 and 296.

295. ⟨ Begin fetch without I-cache lookup 295 ⟩ ≡

```
  {
    if (p) {
      ⟨ Update IT-cache usage and check the protection bits 293 ⟩;
      data→z.o = phys_addr(data→y.o, p→data[0]);
      data→state = IT_hit;
    } else data→state = IT_miss;
    wait_or_pass(ITcache→access_time);
  }
```

This code is used in section 291.

296. ⟨ Begin fetch with known physical address 296 ⟩ ≡

```
{
   if (data→i ≡ prego ∧ ¬(data→loc.h & sign_bit)) goto fin_ex;
   data→z.o = data→y.o; data→z.o.h −= sign_bit;
 known_phys: if (data→z.o.h & #ffff0000) goto bad_fetch;
   if (¬Icache) ⟨ Read from memory into fetched 297 ⟩;
   if (Icache→lock ∨ (j = get_reader(Icache)) < 0) {
      data→state = IT_hit; wait_or_pass(1);
   }
   startup(&Icache→reader[j], Icache→access_time);
   q = cache_search(Icache, data→z.o);
   if (q) {
      q = use_and_fix(Icache, q);
      ⟨ Copy the data from block q to fetched 294 ⟩;
      data→state = fetch_ready;
   } else data→state = Ihit_and_miss;
   wait_or_pass(Icache→access_time);
}
```

This code is used in section 288.

access_time: **int**, §167.
b: **int**, §167.
bad_fetch: label, §301.
bb: **int**, §167.
c: **int**, §167.
cache_search: **static cacheblock** ∗(), §193.
data: **octa** ∗, §167.
data: **register control** ∗, §124.
fetch_hi: **int**, §285.
fetch_lo: **int**, §285.
fetch_ready = 23, §291.
fetched: **octa** ∗, §284.
fin_ex: label, §144.
get_reader: **static int** (), §183.
h: **tetra**, §17.
i: **internal_opcode**, §44.
Icache: **cache** ∗, §168.
Ihit_and_miss = 22, §291.
inst_ptr: **spec**, §284.
IT_hit = 21, §291.
IT_miss = 20, §291.
ITcache: **cache** ∗, §168.
j: **register int**, §12.
l: **tetra**, §17.
loc: **octa**, §44.
lock: **lockvar**, §167.
max = macro (), §268.
o: **octa**, §40.
p: **register cacheblock** ∗, §258.
page_s: **int**, §238.
phys_addr: **static octa** (), §241.
prego = 73, §49.
PROT_OFFSET = 5, §54.
PX_BIT = 1 ≪ 5, §54.
q: **register cacheblock** ∗, §258.
reader: **coroutine** ∗, §167.
sign_bit = macro, §80.
startup: **static void** (), §31.
state: **int**, §44.
use_and_fix: **static cacheblock** ∗(), §196.
wait_or_pass = macro (), §288.
y: **spec**, §44.
z: **spec**, §44.

297. ⟨ Read from memory into *fetched* 297 ⟩ ≡

```
{ octa addr;
  addr = data→z.o;
  if (mem_lock) wait(1);
  set_lock(&mem_locker, mem_lock);
  startup(&mem_locker, mem_addr_time + mem_read_time);
  addr.l &= −(bus_words ≪ 3);
  fetched[0] = mem_read(addr);
  for (j = 1; j < bus_words; j++)
    fetched[j] = mem_hash[last_h].chunk[((addr.l & #ffff) ≫ 3) + j];
  fetch_lo = (data→z.o.l ≫ 3) & (bus_words − 1); fetch_hi = bus_words;
  data→state = fetch_ready;
  wait(mem_addr_time + mem_read_time);
}
```

This code is used in section 296.

298. ⟨ Other cases for the fetch coroutine 298 ⟩ ≡

```
case IT_miss: if (ITcache→filler.next)
    if (data→i ≡ prego) goto fin_ex; else wait(1);
  if (no_hardware_PT ∨ page_f) ⟨ Insert dummy instruction for page table emulation 302 ⟩;
  p = alloc_slot(ITcache, trans_key(data→y.o));
  if (¬p)    /* hey, it was present after all */
    if (data→i ≡ prego) goto fin_ex; else goto new_fetch;
  data→ptr_b = ITcache→filler_ctl.ptr_b = (void *) p;
  ITcache→filler_ctl.y.o = data→y.o;
  set_lock(self, ITcache→fill_lock);
  startup(&ITcache→filler, 1);
  data→state = got_IT;
  if (data→i ≡ prego) goto fin_ex; else sleep;
case got_IT: release_lock(self, ITcache→fill_lock);
  if (¬(data→z.o.l & (PX_BIT ≫ PROT_OFFSET))) goto bad_fetch;
  data→z.o = phys_addr(data→y.o, data→z.o);
fetch_retry: data→state = IT_hit;
case IT_hit: if (data→i ≡ prego) goto fin_ex; else goto known_phys;
case Ihit_and_miss: ⟨ Try to get the contents of location data→z.o in the I-cache 300 ⟩;
```

See also section 301.

This code is used in section 288.

299. ⟨ Special cases for states in later stages 272 ⟩ +≡

```
case IT_miss: case Ihit_and_miss: case IT_hit: case fetch_ready: goto switch0;
```

300. ⟨ Try to get the contents of location *data→z.o* in the I-cache 300 ⟩ ≡

```
if (Icache→filler.next) goto fetch_retry;
if ((Scache ∧ Scache→lock) ∨ (¬Scache ∧ mem_lock)) goto fetch_retry;
q = alloc_slot(Icache, data→z.o);
if (¬q) goto fetch_retry;
if (Scache) set_lock(&Icache→filler, Scache→lock)
else set_lock(&Icache→filler, mem_lock);
set_lock(self, Icache→fill_lock);
data→ptr_b = Icache→filler_ctl.ptr_b = (void *) q;
Icache→filler_ctl.z.o = data→z.o;
startup(&Icache→filler, Scache ? Scache→access_time : mem_addr_time);
data→state = got_one;
if (data→i ≡ prego) goto fin_ex; else sleep;
```

This code is used in section 298.

access_time: **int**, §167.
alloc_slot: **static cacheblock** *(), §205.
bad_fetch: label, §301.
bus_words: **int**, §214.
chunk: **octa** *, §206.
data: **register control** *, §124.
fetch_hi: **int**, §285.
fetch_lo: **int**, §285.
fetch_ready = 23, §291.
fetched: **octa** *, §284.
fill_lock: **lockvar**, §167.
filler: **coroutine**, §167.
filler_ctl: **control**, §167.
fin_ex: label, §144.
got_IT = 19, §291.
got_one = 24, §291.
i: **internal_opcode**, §44.
Icache: **cache** *, §168.
Ihit_and_miss = 22, §291.
IT_hit = 21, §291.
IT_miss = 20, §291.
ITcache: **cache** *, §168.
j: **register int**, §12.
known_phys: label, §296.
l: **tetra**, §17.
last_h: **int**, §211.
lock: **lockvar**, §167.
mem_addr_time: **int**, §214.
mem_hash: **chunknode** *, §207.
mem_lock: **lockvar**, §214.
mem_locker: **coroutine**, §127.
mem_read: **octa** (), §210.
mem_read_time: **int**, §214.
new_fetch: label, §288.
next: **coroutine** *, §23.
no_hardware_PT: **bool**, §242.
o: **octa**, §40.
octa = **struct**, §17.
p: **register cacheblock** *, §258.
page_f: **int**, §238.
phys_addr: **static octa** (), §241.
prego = 73, §49.
PROT_OFFSET = 5, §54.
ptr_b: **void** *, §44.
PX_BIT = 1 ≪ 5, §54.
q: **register cacheblock** *, §258.
release_lock = macro (), §37.
Scache: **cache** *, §168.
self: **register coroutine** *, §124.
set_lock = macro (), §37.
sleep = macro, §125.
startup: **static void** (), §31.
state: **int**, §44.
switch0: label, §288.
trans_key = macro (), §240.
wait = macro (), §125.
y: **spec**, §44.
z: **spec**, §44.

301. The I-cache filler will wake us up with the octabyte we want, before it has filled the entire cache block. In that case we can fetch one or two instructions before the rest of the block has been loaded.

```
⟨Other cases for the fetch coroutine 298⟩ +≡
bad_fetch: if (data→i ≡ prego) goto fin_ex;
  data→interrupt |= PX_BIT;
swym_one: fetched[0].h = fetched[0].l = SWYM ≪ 24;
  goto fetch_one;
case got_one: fetched[0] = data→x.o;      /* a "preview" of the new cache data */
fetch_one: fetch_lo = 0; fetch_hi = 1;
  data→state = fetch_ready;
case fetch_ready: if (self→lockloc) *(self→lockloc) = Λ, self→lockloc = Λ;
  if (data→i ≡ prego) goto fin_ex;
  for (j = 0; j < fetch_max; j++) {
    register fetch *new_tail;
    if (tail ≡ fetch_bot) new_tail = fetch_top;
    else new_tail = tail − 1;
    if (new_tail ≡ head) break;      /* fetch buffer is full */
    ⟨Install a new instruction into the tail position 304⟩;
    tail = new_tail;
    if (sleepy) {
      sleepy = false; sleep;
    }
    inst_ptr.o = incr(inst_ptr.o, 4);
    if (fetch_lo ≡ fetch_hi) goto new_fetch;
  }
  wait(1);
```

302.

```
⟨Insert dummy instruction for page table emulation 302⟩ ≡
  {
    if (cache_search(ITcache, trans_key(inst_ptr.o))) goto new_fetch;
    data→interrupt |= F_BIT;
    sleepy = true;
    goto swym_one;
  }
```

This code is used in section 298.

303.

```
⟨Global variables 20⟩ +≡
  bool sleepy;      /* have we just emitted the page table emulation call? */
```

304. At this point we check for egregiously invalid instructions. (Sometimes the dispatcher will actually allow such instructions to occupy the fetch buffer, for internally generated commands.)

⟨Install a new instruction into the *tail* position 304⟩ ≡

```
tail→loc = inst_ptr.o;
if (inst_ptr.o.l & 4) tail→inst = fetched[fetch_lo++].l;
else tail→inst = fetched[fetch_lo].h;
tail→interrupt = data→interrupt;
i = tail→inst >> 24;
if (i ≥ RESUME ∧ i ≤ SYNC ∧ (tail→inst & bad_inst_mask[i − RESUME]))
  tail→interrupt |= B_BIT;
tail→noted = false;
if (inst_ptr.o.l ≡ breakpoint.l ∧ inst_ptr.o.h ≡ breakpoint.h) breakpoint_hit = true;
```

This code is used in section 301.

305. The commands RESUME, SAVE, UNSAVE, and SYNC should not have nonzero bits in the positions defined here.

⟨Global variables 20⟩ +≡

```
int bad_inst_mask[4] = {#fffffe, #ffff, #ffff00, #fffff8};
```

B_BIT = 1 ≪ 2, §54.
bool = **enum**, §11.
breakpoint: **octa**, §10.
breakpoint_hit: **bool**, §12.
cache_search: **static cacheblock** ∗(), §193.
data: **register control** ∗, §124.
F_BIT = 1 ≪ 17, §54.
false = 0, §11.
fetch = **struct**, §68.
fetch_bot: **fetch** ∗, §69.
fetch_hi: **int**, §285.
fetch_lo: **int**, §285.
fetch_max: **int**, §59.
fetch_ready = 23, §291.
fetch_top: **fetch** ∗, §69.
fetched: **octa** ∗, §284.
fin_ex: label, §144.
got_one = 24, §291.
h: **tetra**, §17.
head: **fetch** ∗, §69.
i: **internal_opcode**, §44.
i: **register int**, §12.
incr: **octa** (), MMIX-ARITH §6.
inst: **tetra**, §68.
inst_ptr: **spec**, §284.
interrupt: **unsigned int**, §44.
interrupt: **unsigned int**, §68.
ITcache: **cache** ∗, §168.
j: **register int**, §12.
l: **tetra**, §17.
loc: **octa**, §68.
lockloc: **coroutine** ∗∗, §23.
new_fetch: label, §288.
noted: **bool**, §68.
o: **octa**, §40.
prego = 73, §49.
PX_BIT = 1 ≪ 5, §54.
RESUME = #f9, §47.
self: **register coroutine** ∗, §124.
sleep = macro, §125.
state: **int**, §44.
SWYM = #fd, §47.
SYNC = #fc, §47.
tail: **fetch** ∗, §69.
trans_key = macro (), §240.
true = 1, §11.
wait = macro (), §125.
x: **specnode**, §44.

306. Interrupts. The scariest thing about the design of a pipelined machine is the existence of interrupts, which disrupt the smooth flow of a computation in ways that are difficult to anticipate. Fortunately, however, the discipline of a reorder buffer, which forces instructions to be committed in order, allows us to deal with interrupts in a fairly natural way. Our solution to the problems of dynamic scheduling and speculative execution therefore solves the interrupt problem as well.

MMIX has three kinds of interrupts, which show up as bit codes in the *interrupt* field when an instruction is ready to be committed: H_BIT invokes a trip handler, for TRIP instructions and arithmetic exceptions; F_BIT invokes a forced-trap handler, for TRAP instructions and unimplemented instructions that need to be emulated in software; E_BIT invokes a dynamic-trap handler, for external interrupts like I/O signals or for internal interrupts caused by improper instructions. In all three cases, the pipeline control has already been redirected to fetch new instructions starting at the correct handler address by the time an interrupted instruction is ready to be committed.

307. Most instructions come to the following part of the program, if they have finished execution with any 1s among the eight trip bits or the eight trap bits.

If the trip bits aren't all zero, we want to update the event bits of rA, or perform an enabled trip handler, or both. If the trap bits are nonzero, we need to hold onto them until we get to the hot seat, when they will be joined with the bits of rQ and probably cause an interrupt. A load or store instruction with nonzero trap bits will be nullified, not committed.

Underflow that is exact and not enabled is ignored, in accordance with the IEEE standard conventions. (This applies also to underflow triggered by RESUME_SET.)

#define *is_load_store*(*i*) $(i \ge ld \wedge i \le cswap)$

⟨Handle interrupt at end of execution stage 307⟩ ≡

```
{
  if ((data→interrupt & #ff) ∧ is_load_store(data→i)) goto state_5;
  j = data→interrupt & #ff00;
  data→interrupt −= j;
  if ((j & (U_BIT + X_BIT)) ≡ U_BIT ∧ ¬(data→ra.o.l & U_BIT)) j &= ∼U_BIT;
  data→arith_exc = (j & ∼data→ra.o.l) ≫ 8;
  if (j & data→ra.o.l) ⟨Prepare for exceptional trip handler 308⟩;
  if (data→interrupt & #ff) goto state_5;
}
```

This code is used in section 144.

308. Since execution is speculative, an exceptional condition might not be part of the "real" computation. Indeed, the present coroutine might have already been deissued.

⟨ Prepare for exceptional trip handler 308 ⟩ ≡

```
{
  i = issued_between(data, cool);
  if (i < deissues) goto die;
  deissues = i;
  old_tail = tail = head; resuming = 0;     /* clear the fetch buffer */
  ⟨ Restart the fetch coroutine 287 ⟩;
  cool_hist = data→hist;
  for (i = j & data→ra.o.l, m = 16; ¬(i & D_BIT); i <<= 1, m += 16) ;
  data→arith_exc |= (j & ~(#10000 >> (m >> 4))) >> 8;
    /* trips taken are not logged as events */
  data→go.o.h = 0, data→go.o.l = m;
  inst_ptr.o = data→go.o, inst_ptr.p = Λ;
  data→interrupt |= H_BIT;
  goto state_4;
}
```

This code is used in section 307.

309. ⟨ Prepare to emulate the page translation 309 ⟩ ≡

```
i = issued_between(data, cool);
if (i < deissues) goto die;
deissues = i;
old_tail = tail = head; resuming = 0;     /* clear the fetch buffer */
⟨ Restart the fetch coroutine 287 ⟩;
cool_hist = data→hist;
inst_ptr.p = UNKNOWN_SPEC;
data→interrupt |= F_BIT;
```

This code is used in section 310.

---

arith_exc: **unsigned int**, §44.
cool: **control** ∗, §60.
cool_hist: **unsigned int**, §99.
cswap = 68, §49.
D_BIT = 1 ≪ 15, §54.
data: **register control** ∗, §124.
deissues: **int**, §60.
die: label, §144.
E_BIT = 1 ≪ 18, §54.
F_BIT = 1 ≪ 17, §54.
go: **specnode**, §44.
h: **tetra**, §17.
H_BIT = 1 ≪ 16, §54.
head: **fetch** ∗, §69.
hist: **unsigned int**, §44.
i: **internal_opcode**, §44.
i: **register int**, §12.
inst_ptr: **spec**, §284.
interrupt: **unsigned int**, §44.
issued_between: **static int** ( ), §159.
j: **register int**, §12.
l: **tetra**, §17.
ld = 56, §49.
m: **register int**, §12.
o: **octa**, §40.
old_tail: **fetch** ∗, §70.
p: **specnode** ∗, §40.
ra: **spec**, §44.
RESUME_SET = 2, §320.
resuming: **int**, §78.
state_4: label, §310.
state_5: label, §310.
tail: **fetch** ∗, §69.
U_BIT = 1 ≪ 10, §54.
UNKNOWN_SPEC = macro, §71.
X_BIT = 1 ≪ 8, §54.

310. We need to stop dispatching when calling a trip handler from within the reorder buffer, lest we issue an instruction that uses $g[255]$ or rB as an operand.

```
⟨ Special cases for states in the first stage 266 ⟩ +≡
emulate_virt: ⟨ Prepare to emulate the page translation 309 ⟩;
state_4: data→state = 4;
case 4: if (dispatch_lock) wait(1);
  set_lock(self, dispatch_lock);
state_5: data→state = 5;
case 5: if (data ≠ old_hot) wait(1);
  if ((data→interrupt & F_BIT) ∧ data→i ≠ trap) {
    inst_ptr.o = g[rT].o, inst_ptr.p = Λ;
    if (is_load_store(data→i)) nullifying = true;
  }
  if (data→interrupt & #ff) {
    g[rQ].o.h |= data→interrupt & #ff;
    new_Q.h |= data→interrupt & #ff;
    if (verbose & issue_bit) {
      printf("␣setting␣rQ="); print_octa(g[rQ].o); printf("\n");
    }
  }
  goto die;
```

311. The instructions of the previous section appear in the switch for coroutine stage 1 only. We need to use them also in later stages.

```
⟨ Special cases for states in later stages 272 ⟩ +≡
case 4: goto state_4;
case 5: goto state_5;
```

312.

```
⟨ Special cases of instruction dispatch 117 ⟩ +≡
case trap: if ((flags[op] & X_is_dest_bit) ∧ cool→xx < cool_G ∧ cool→xx ≥ cool_L)
    goto increase_L;
  if (¬g[rT].up→known ∨ ¬g[rJ].up→known) goto stall;
  inst_ptr = specval(&g[rT]);      /* traps and emulated ops */
  cool→need_b = true, cool→b = specval(&g[255]);
case trip:
  if (¬g[rJ].up→known) goto stall;
  cool→ren_x = true, spec_install(&g[255], &cool→x);
  cool→x.known = true, cool→x.o = g[rJ].up→o;
  if (i ≡ trip) cool→go.o = zero_octa;
  cool→ren_a = true, spec_install(&g[i ≡ trap ? rBB : rB], &cool→a); break;
```

313.

```
⟨ Cases for stage 1 execution 155 ⟩ +≡
case trap: data→interrupt |= F_BIT; data→a.o = data→b.o; goto fin_ex;
case trip: data→interrupt |= H_BIT; data→a.o = data→b.o; goto fin_ex;
```

314. The following check is performed at the beginning of every cycle. An instruction in the hot seat can be externally interrupted only if it is ready to be committed and not already marked for tripping or trapping.

⟨ Check for external interrupt 314 ⟩ ≡

```
g[rI].o = incr(g[rI].o, −1);
if (g[rI].o.l ≡ 0 ∧ g[rI].o.h ≡ 0) {
   g[rQ].o.l |= INTERVAL_TIMEOUT, new_Q.l |= INTERVAL_TIMEOUT;
   if (verbose & issue_bit) {
      printf("␣setting␣rQ="); print_octa(g[rQ].o); printf("\n");
   }
}
trying_to_interrupt = false;
if (((g[rQ].o.h & g[rK].o.h) ∨ (g[rQ].o.l & g[rK].o.l)) ∧ cool ≠ hot ∧
        ¬(hot→interrupt & (E_BIT + F_BIT + H_BIT)) ∧ ¬doing_interrupt ∧
        ¬(hot→i ≡ resum)) {
   if (hot→owner) trying_to_interrupt = true;
   else {
      hot→interrupt |= E_BIT;
      ⟨ Deissue all but the hottest command 316 ⟩;
      inst_ptr.o = g[rTT].o; inst_ptr.p = Λ;
   }
}
```

This code is used in section 64.

315. ⟨ Global variables 20 ⟩ +≡

```
bool trying_to_interrupt;     /* encouraging interruptible operations to pause */
bool nullifying;    /* stopping dispatch to nullify a load/store command */
```

316. It's possible that the command in the hot seat has been deissued, but only if the simulator has done so at the user's request. Otherwise the test '$i \ge deissues$' here will always succeed.

The value of *cool_hist* becomes flaky here. We could try to keep it strictly up to date, but the unpredictable nature of external interrupts suggests that we are better off leaving it alone. (It's only a heuristic for branch prediction, and a sufficiently strong prediction will survive one-time glitches due to interrupts.)

```
⟨ Deissue all but the hottest command 316 ⟩ ≡
  i = issued_between(hot, cool);
  if (i ≥ deissues) {
    deissues = i;
    tail = head; resuming = 0;      /* clear the fetch buffer */
    ⟨ Restart the fetch coroutine 287 ⟩;
    if (is_load_store(hot→i)) nullifying = true;
  }
```

This code is used in section 314.

317. Even though an interrupted instruction has officially been either "committed" or "nullified," it stays in the hot seat for two or three extra cycles, while we save enough of the machine state to resume the computation later.

```
⟨ Begin an interruption and break 317 ⟩ ≡
  {
    if (¬(hot→interrupt & H_BIT)) g[rK].o = zero_octa;      /* trap */
    if (((hot→interrupt & H_BIT) ∧ hot→i ≠ trip) ∨
          ((hot→interrupt & F_BIT) ∧ hot→i ≠ trap) ∨
          (hot→interrupt & E_BIT)) doing_interrupt = 3, suppress_dispatch = true;
    else doing_interrupt = 2;     /* trip or trap started by dispatcher */
    break;
  }
```

This code is used in section 146.

318. If a memory failure occurs, we should set rF here, either in case 2 or case 1. The simulator doesn't do anything with rF at present.

```
⟨ Perform one cycle of the interrupt preparations 318 ⟩ ≡
  switch (doing_interrupt−−) {
  case 3: ⟨ Set resumption registers (rB, $255) or (rBB, $255) 319 ⟩; break;
  case 2: ⟨ Set resumption registers (rW, rX) or (rWW, rXX) 320 ⟩; break;
  case 1: ⟨ Set resumption registers (rY, rZ) or (rYY, rZZ) 321 ⟩;
    if (hot ≡ reorder_bot) hot = reorder_top; else hot−−;
    break;
  }
```

This code is used in section 64.

319. ⟨Set resumption registers (rB, $255) or (rBB, $255) 319⟩ ≡

```
j = hot→interrupt & H_BIT;
g[j ? rB : rBB].o = g[255].o;
g[255].o = g[rJ].o;
if (verbose & issue_bit) {
  if (j) {
    printf("␣setting␣rB="); print_octa(g[rB].o);
  } else {
    printf("␣setting␣rBB="); print_octa(g[rBB].o);
  }
  printf(",␣$255="); print_octa(g[255].o); printf("\n");
}
```

This code is used in section 318.

---

cool: **control** ∗, §60.
cool_hist: **unsigned int**, §99.
deissues: **int**, §60.
doing_interrupt: **int**, §65.
E_BIT = 1 ≪ 18, §54.
F_BIT = 1 ≪ 17, §54.
g: **specnode** [], §86.
H_BIT = 1 ≪ 16, §54.
head: **fetch** ∗, §69.
hot: **control** ∗, §60.
i: **internal_opcode**, §44.
i: **register int**, §12.
interrupt: **unsigned int**, §44.
is_load_store = macro ( ), §307.
issue_bit = 1 ≪ 0, §8.
issued_between: **static int** ( ), §159.
j: **register int**, §12.
nullifying: **bool**, §315.
o: **octa**, §40.
print_octa: **static void** ( ), §19.
printf: **int** ( ), <stdio.h>.
rB = 0, §52.
rBB = 7, §52.
reorder_bot: **control** ∗, §60.
reorder_top: **control** ∗, §60.
resuming: **int**, §78.
rJ = 4, §52.
rK = 15, §52.
suppress_dispatch: **bool**, §65.
tail: **fetch** ∗, §69.
trap = 82, §49.
trip = 83, §49.
true = 1, §11.
verbose: **int**, §4.
zero_octa: **octa**, MMIX-ARITH §4.

320. Here's where we manufacture the "ropcodes" for resumption.

```
#define RESUME_AGAIN 0   /* repeat the command in rX as if in location rW − 4 */
#define RESUME_CONT 1   /* same, but substitute rY and rZ for operands */
#define RESUME_SET 2   /* set register $X to rZ */
#define RESUME_TRANS 3
        /* install (rY, rZ) into IT-cache or DT-cache, then RESUME_AGAIN */
#define pack_bytes(a, b, c, d) ((((((unsigned)(a) ≪ 8) + (b)) ≪ 8) + (c)) ≪ 8) + (d)
⟨ Set resumption registers (rW, rX) or (rWW, rXX) 320 ⟩ ≡
  j = pack_bytes(hot→op, hot→xx, hot→yy, hot→zz);
  if (hot→interrupt & H_BIT) {   /* trip */
    g[rW].o = incr(hot→loc, 4);
    g[rX].o.h = sign_bit, g[rX].o.l = j;
    if (verbose & issue_bit) {
      printf("␣setting␣rW="); print_octa(g[rW].o);
      printf(",␣rX="); print_octa(g[rX].o); printf("\n");
    }
  } else {   /* trap */
    g[rWW].o = hot→go.o;
    g[rXX].o.l = j;
    if (hot→interrupt & F_BIT) {   /* forced */
      if (hot→i ≠ trap) j = RESUME_TRANS;   /* emulate page translation */
      else if (hot→op ≡ TRAP) j = #80;   /* TRAP */
      else if (flags[internal_op[hot→op]] & X_is_dest_bit) j = RESUME_SET;
          /* emulation */
      else j = #80;   /* emulation when r[X] is not a destination */
    } else {   /* dynamic */
      if (hot→interim)
        j = (hot→i ≡ frem ∨ hot→i ≡ syncd ∨ hot→i ≡ syncid ? RESUME_CONT : RESUME_AGAIN);
      else if (is_load_store(hot→i)) j = RESUME_AGAIN;
      else j = #80;   /* normal external interruption */
    }
    g[rXX].o.h = (j ≪ 24) + (hot→interrupt & #ff);
    if (verbose & issue_bit) {
      printf("␣setting␣rWW="); print_octa(g[rWW].o);
      printf(",␣rXX="); print_octa(g[rXX].o); printf("\n");
    }
  }
```

This code is used in section 318.

321. ⟨ Set resumption registers (rY, rZ) or (rYY, rZZ) 321 ⟩ ≡

```
j = hot→interrupt & H_BIT;
if ((hot→interrupt & F_BIT) ∧ hot→op ≡ SWYM) g[rYY].o = hot→go.o;
else g[j ? rY : rYY].o = hot→y.o;
if (hot→i ≡ st ∨ hot→i ≡ pst) g[j ? rZ : rZZ].o = hot→x.o;
else g[j ? rZ : rZZ].o = hot→z.o;
if (verbose & issue_bit) {
  if (j) {
    printf("␣setting␣rY="); print_octa(g[rY].o);
    printf(",␣rZ="); print_octa(g[rZ].o); printf("\n");
  } else {
    printf("␣setting␣rYY="); print_octa(g[rYY].o);
    printf(",␣rZZ="); print_octa(g[rZZ].o); printf("\n");
  }
}
```

This code is used in section 318.

F_BIT = 1 ≪ 17, §54.
flags: **unsigned char** [], §83.
frem = 25, §49.
g: **specnode** [], §86.
go: **specnode**, §44.
h: **tetra**, §17.
H_BIT = 1 ≪ 16, §54.
hot: **control** ∗, §60.
i: **internal_opcode**, §44.
incr: **octa** ( ), MMIX-ARITH §6.
interim: **bool**, §44.
internal_op: **internal_opcode** [], §51.
interrupt: **unsigned int**, §44.
is_load_store = macro ( ), §307.
issue_bit = 1 ≪ 0, §8.
j: **register int**, §12.
l: **tetra**, §17.
loc: **octa**, §44.
o: **octa**, §40.
op: **mmix_opcode**, §44.
print_octa: **static void** ( ), §19.
printf: **int** ( ), <stdio.h>.
pst = 66, §49.
rW = 24, §52.
rWW = 28, §52.
rX = 25, §52.
rXX = 29, §52.
rY = 26, §52.
rYY = 30, §52.
rZ = 27, §52.
rZZ = 31, §52.
sign_bit = macro, §80.
st = 63, §49.
SWYM = #fd, §47.
syncd = 64, §49.
syncid = 65, §49.
TRAP = #00, §47.
trap = 82, §49.
verbose: **int**, §4.
x: **specnode**, §44.
X_is_dest_bit = #20, §83.
xx: **unsigned char**, §44.
y: **spec**, §44.
yy: **unsigned char**, §44.
z: **spec**, §44.
zz: **unsigned char**, §44.

322. Whew; we've successfully interrupted the computation. The remaining task is to restart it again, as transparently as possible.

The RESUME instruction waits for the pipeline to drain, because it has to do such drastic things. For example, an interrupt may be occurring at this very moment, changing the registers needed for resumption.

```
⟨Special cases of instruction dispatch 117⟩ +≡
case resume: if (cool ≠ old_hot) goto stall;
  inst_ptr = specval(&g[cool→zz ? rWW : rW]);
  if (¬(cool→loc.h & sign_bit)) {
    if (cool→zz) cool→interrupt |= K_BIT;
    else if (inst_ptr.o.h & sign_bit) cool→interrupt |= P_BIT;
  }
  if (cool→interrupt) {
    inst_ptr.o = incr(cool→loc, 4); cool→i = noop;
  } else {
    cool→go.o = inst_ptr.o;
    if (cool→zz) {
      ⟨Magically do an I/O operation, if cool→loc is rT 372⟩;
      cool→ren_a = true, spec_install(&g[rK], &cool→a);
      cool→a.known = true, cool→a.o = g[255].o;
      cool→ren_x = true, spec_install(&g[255], &cool→x);
      cool→x.known = true, cool→x.o = g[rBB].o;
    }
    cool→b = specval(&g[cool→zz ? rXX : rX]);
    if (¬(cool→b.o.h & sign_bit)) ⟨Resume an interrupted operation 323⟩;
  } break;
```

323. Here we set *cool*→*i* = *resum*, since we want to issue another instruction after the RESUME itself.

The restrictions on inserted instructions are designed to ensure that those instructions will be the very next ones issued. (If, for example, an *incgamma* instruction were necessary, it might cause a page fault and we'd lose the operand values for RESUME_SET or RESUME_CONT.)

A subtle point arises here: If RESUME_TRANS is being used to compute the page translation of virtual address zero, we don't want to execute the dummy SWYM instruction from virtual address −4! So we avoid the SWYM altogether.

```
⟨Resume an interrupted operation 323⟩ ≡
  {
    cool→xx = cool→b.o.h ≫ 24, cool→i = resum;
    head→loc = incr(inst_ptr.o, −4);
    switch (cool→xx) {
    case RESUME_SET: cool→b.o.l = (SETH ≪ 24) + (cool→b.o.l & #ff0000);
      head→interrupt |= cool→b.o.h & #ff00;
      resuming = 2;
    case RESUME_CONT: resuming += 1 + cool→zz;
      if (((cool→b.o.l ≫ 24) & #fa) ≠ #b8) {     /* not syncd or syncid */
        m = cool→b.o.l ≫ 28;
        if ((1 ≪ m) & #8f30) goto bad_resume;
```

```
        m = (cool→b.o.l ≫ 16) & #ff;
        if (m ≥ cool_L ∧ m < cool_G) goto bad_resume;
      }
    case RESUME_AGAIN: resume_again: head→inst = cool→b.o.l;
      m = head→inst ≫ 24;
      if (m ≡ RESUME) goto bad_resume;      /* avoid uninterruptible loop */
      if (¬cool→zz ∧ m > RESUME ∧ m ≤ SYNC ∧ (head→inst & bad_inst_mask[m − RESUME]))
        head→interrupt |= B_BIT;
      head→noted = false; break;
    case RESUME_TRANS: if (cool→zz) {
        cool→y = specval(&g[rYY]), cool→z = specval(&g[rZZ]);
        if ((cool→b.o.l ≫ 24) ≠ SWYM) goto resume_again;
        cool→i = resume; break;     /* see "subtle point" above */
      }
    default: bad_resume: cool→interrupt |= B_BIT, cool→i = noop;
      resuming = 0; break;
    }
  }
```

This code is used in section 322.

a: **specnode**, §44.
b: **spec**, §44.
B_BIT = 1 ≪ 2, §54.
bad_inst_mask: **int** [ ], §305.
cool: **control** *, §60.
cool_G: **int**, §99.
cool_L: **int**, §99.
false = 0, §11.
g: **specnode** [ ], §86.
go: **specnode**, §44.
h: **tetra**, §17.
head: **fetch** *, §69.
i: **internal_opcode**, §44.
incgamma = 84, §49.
incr: **octa** ( ), MMIX-ARITH §6.
inst: **tetra**, §68.
inst_ptr: **spec**, §284.
interrupt: **unsigned int**, §44.
interrupt: **unsigned int**, §68.
K_BIT = 1 ≪ 3, §54.
known: **bool**, §40.
l: **tetra**, §17.
loc: **octa**, §44.
loc: **octa**, §68.
m: **register int**, §12.
noop = 81, §49.
noted: **bool**, §68.
o: **octa**, §40.
old_hot: **control** *, §60.
P_BIT = 1 ≪ 0, §54.
rBB = 7, §52.
ren_a: **bool**, §44.
ren_x: **bool**, §44.
resum = 89, §49.
resume = 76, §49.
RESUME = #f9, §47.
RESUME_AGAIN = 0, §320.
RESUME_CONT = 1, §320.
RESUME_SET = 2, §320.
RESUME_TRANS = 3, §320.
resuming: **int**, §78.
rK = 15, §52.
rW = 24, §52.
rWW = 28, §52.
rX = 25, §52.
rXX = 29, §52.
rYY = 30, §52.
rZZ = 31, §52.
SETH = #e0, §47.
sign_bit = macro, §80.
spec_install: **static void** ( ), §95.
specval: **static spec** ( ), §93.
stall: label, §75.
SWYM = #fd, §47.
SYNC = #fc, §47.
syncd = 64, §49.
syncid = 65, §49.
true = 1, §11.
x: **specnode**, §44.
xx: **unsigned char**, §44.
y: **spec**, §44.
z: **spec**, §44.
zz: **unsigned char**, §44.

324. ⟨ Insert special operands when resuming an interrupted operation 324 ⟩ ≡

```
{
  if (resuming & 1) {
    cool→y = specval(&g[rY]);
    cool→z = specval(&g[rZ]);
  } else {
    cool→y = specval(&g[rYY]);
    cool→z = specval(&g[rZZ]);
  }
  if (resuming ≥ 3) {    /* RESUME_SET */
    cool→need_ra = true, cool→ra = specval(&g[rA]);
  }
  cool→usage = false;
}
```

This code is used in section 103.

325. **#define** *do_resume_trans* 17
/* *state* for performing RESUME_TRANS actions */

⟨ Cases for stage 1 execution 155 ⟩ +≡

```
case resume: case resum: if (data→xx ≠ RESUME_TRANS) goto fin_ex;
  data→ptr_a = (void *)((data→b.o.l ≫ 24) ≡ SWYM ? ITcache : DTcache);
  data→state = do_resume_trans;
  data→z.o = incr(oandn(data→z.o, page_mask), data→z.o.l & 7);
  data→z.o.h &= #ffff;
  goto resume_trans;
```

326. ⟨ Special cases for states in the first stage 266 ⟩ +≡

```
case do_resume_trans: resume_trans:
  { register cache *c = (cache *) data→ptr_a;
    if (c→lock) wait(1);
    if (c→filler.next) wait(1);
    p = alloc_slot(c, trans_key(data→y.o));
    if (p) {
      c→filler_ctl.ptr_b = (void *) p;
      c→filler_ctl.y.o = data→y.o;
      c→filler_ctl.b.o = data→z.o;
      c→filler_ctl.state = 1;
      schedule(&c→filler, c→access_time, 1);
    }
    goto fin_ex;
  }
```

327. Administrative operations. The internal instructions that handle the register stack simply reduce to things we already know how to do. (Well, the internal instructions for saving and unsaving do sometimes lead to special cases, based on *data→op*; for the most part, though, the necessary mechanisms are already present.)

⟨ Cases for stage 1 execution 155 ⟩ +≡
case *noop*: **if** (*data→interrupt* & F_BIT) **goto** *emulate_virt*;
case *incrl*: **case** *unsave*: **goto** *fin_ex*;
case *jmp*: **case** *pushj*: *data→go.o* = *data→z.o*;
  goto *fin_ex*;
case *sav*: **if** (¬(*data→mem_x*)) **goto** *fin_ex*;
case *incgamma*: **case** *save*: *data→i* = *st*;
  goto *switch1*;
case *decgamma*: **case** *unsav*: *data→i* = *ld*;
  goto *switch1*;

328. We can GET special registers ≥ 21 (that is, rA, rF, rP, rW–rZ, or rWW–rZZ) only in the hot seat, because those registers are implicit outputs of many instructions. The same applies to rK, since it is changed by TRAP and by emulated instructions. Likewise, rQ must not be prematurely gotten.

⟨ Cases for stage 1 execution 155 ⟩ +≡
case *get*: **if** (*data→zz* ≥ 21 ∨ *data→zz* ≡ *rK* ∨ *data→zz* ≡ *rQ*) {
    if (*data* ≠ *old_hot*) *wait*(1);
    data→z.o = *g*[*data→zz*].*o*;
  }
  data→x.o = *data→z.o*; **goto** *fin_ex*;

---

access_time: **int**, §167.
alloc_slot: **static cacheblock** ∗( ), §205.
b: **spec**, §44.
cache = **struct**, §167.
cool: **control** ∗, §60.
data: **register control** ∗, §124.
decgamma = 85, §49.
DTcache: **cache** ∗, §168.
emulate_virt: label, §310.
F_BIT = 1 ≪ 17, §54.
false = 0, §11.
filler: **coroutine**, §167.
filler_ctl: **control**, §167.
fin_ex: label, §144.
g: **specnode** [ ], §86.
get = 54, §49.
go: **specnode**, §44.
h: **tetra**, §17.
i: **internal_opcode**, §44.
incgamma = 84, §49.
incr: **octa** ( ), MMIX-ARITH §6.
incrl = 86, §49.
interrupt: **unsigned int**, §44.
ITcache: **cache** ∗, §168.
jmp = 80, §49.
l: **tetra**, §17.
ld = 56, §49.
lock: **lockvar**, §167.
mem_x: **bool**, §44.
need_ra: **bool**, §44.
next: **coroutine** ∗, §23.
noop = 81, §49.
o: **octa**, §40.
oandn: **octa** ( ), MMIX-ARITH §25.
old_hot: **control** ∗, §60.
op: **mmix_opcode**, §44.
p: **register cacheblock** ∗, §258.
page_mask: **octa**, §238.
ptr_a: **void** ∗, §44.
ptr_b: **void** ∗, §44.
pushj = 71, §49.
rA = 21, §52.
ra: **spec**, §44.
resum = 89, §49.
resume = 76, §49.
RESUME_SET = 2, §320.
RESUME_TRANS = 3, §320.
resuming: **int**, §78.
rK = 15, §52.
rQ = 16, §52.
rY = 26, §52.
rYY = 30, §52.
rZ = 27, §52.
rZZ = 31, §52.
sav = 87, §49.
save = 77, §49.
schedule: **static void** ( ), §28.
specval: **static spec** ( ), §93.
st = 63, §49.
state: **int**, §44.
switch1: label, §130.
SWYM = #fd, §47.
trans_key = macro ( ), §240.
true = 1, §11.
unsav = 88, §49.
unsave = 78, §49.
usage: **bool**, §44.
wait = macro ( ), §125.
x: **specnode**, §44.
xx: **unsigned char**, §44.
y: **spec**, §44.
z: **spec**, §44.
zz: **unsigned char**, §44.

329. A PUT is, similarly, delayed in the cases that hold *dispatch_lock*. This program does not restrict the 1 bits that might be PUT into rQ, although the contents of that register can have drastic implications.

```
⟨ Cases for stage 1 execution 155 ⟩ +≡
case put: if (data→xx ≡ 8 ∨ (data→xx ≥ 15 ∧ data→xx ≤ 20)) {
    if (data ≠ old_hot) wait(1);
    switch (data→xx) {
    case rV: ⟨ Update the page variables 239 ⟩; break;
    case rQ: new_Q.h |= data→z.o.h & ~g[rQ].o.h; new_Q.l |= data→z.o.l & ~g[rQ].o.l;
      data→z.o.l |= new_Q.l; data→z.o.h |= new_Q.h; break;
    case rL: if (data→z.o.h ≠ 0) data→z.o.h = 0, data→z.o.l = g[rL].o.l;
      else if (data→z.o.l > g[rL].o.l) data→z.o.l = g[rL].o.l;
    default: break;
    case rG: ⟨ Update rG 330 ⟩; break;
    }
  } else if (data→xx ≡ rA ∧ (data→z.o.h ≠ 0 ∨ data→z.o.l ≥ #40000))
    data→interrupt |= B_BIT, data→z.o.h = 0, data→z.o.l &= #3ffff;
  data→x.o = data→z.o; goto fin_ex;
```

330. When rG decreases, we assume that up to *commit_max* marginal registers can be zeroed during each clock cycle. (Remember that we're currently in the hot seat, and holding *dispatch_lock*.)

```
⟨ Update rG 330 ⟩ ≡
  if (data→z.o.h ≠ 0 ∨ data→z.o.l ≥ 256 ∨ data→z.o.l < g[rL].o.l ∨ data→z.o.l < 32)
    data→interrupt |= B_BIT, data→z.o = g[rG].o;
  else if (data→z.o.l < g[rG].o.l) {
    data→interim = true;    /* potentially interruptible */
    for (j = 0; j < commit_max; j++) {
      g[rG].o.l−−;
      g[g[rG].o.l].o = zero_octa;
      if (data→z.o.l ≡ g[rG].o.l) break;
    }
    if (j ≡ commit_max) {
      if (¬trying_to_interrupt) wait(1);
    } else data→interim = false;
  }
```

This code is used in section 329.

331. Computed jumps put the desired destination address into the *go* field.

```
⟨ Cases for stage 1 execution 155 ⟩ +≡
case go: data→x.o = data→go.o; goto add_go;
case pop: data→x.o = data→y.o;
  data→y.o = data→b.o;    /* move rJ to y field */
case pushgo: add_go: data→go.o = oplus(data→y.o, data→z.o);
  if ((data→go.o.h & sign_bit) ∧ ¬(data→loc.h & sign_bit)) data→interrupt |= P_BIT;
  data→go.known = true; goto fin_ex;
```

332. The instruction `UNSAVE` z generates a sequence of internal instructions that accomplish the actual unsaving. This sequence is controlled by the instruction currently in the fetch buffer, which changes its X and Y fields until all global registers have been loaded. The first instructions of the sequence are `UNSAVE` $0,0,z$; `UNSAVE` $1,rZ,z-8$; `UNSAVE` $1,rY,z-16$; ...; `UNSAVE` $1,rB,z-96$; `UNSAVE` $2,255,z-104$; `UNSAVE` $2,254,z-112$; etc. If an interrupt occurs before these instructions have all been committed, the execution register will contain enough information to restart the process.

After the global registers have all been loaded, `UNSAVE` continues by acting rather like `POP`. An interrupt occurring during this last stage will find rS < rO; a context switch might then take us back to restoring the local registers again. But no information will be lost, even though the register from which we began unsaving has long since been replaced.

```
⟨Special cases of instruction dispatch 117⟩ +≡
case unsave: if (cool→interrupt & B_BIT) cool→i = noop;
  else {
    cool→interim = true;
    op = LDOU;    /* this instruction needs to be handled by load/store unit */
    cool→i = unsav;
    switch (cool→xx) {
    case 0: if (cool→z.p) goto stall;
      ⟨Set up the first phase of unsaving 334⟩; break;
    case 1: case 2: ⟨Generate an instruction to unsave g[yy] 333⟩; break;
    case 3: cool→i = unsave, cool→interim = false, op = UNSAVE;
      goto pop_unsave;
    default: cool→interim = false, cool→i = noop, cool→interrupt |= B_BIT; break;
    }
  }
  break;    /* this takes us to dispatch_done */
```

---

b: **spec**, §44.
B_BIT = 1 ≪ 2, §54.
commit_max: **int**, §59.
cool: **control** *, §60.
data: **register control** *, §124.
dispatch_done: label, §101.
dispatch_lock: **lockvar**, §65.
false = 0, §11.
fin_ex: label, §144.
g: **specnode** [], §86.
go = 72, §49.
go: **specnode**, §44.
h: **tetra**, §17.
i: **internal_opcode**, §44.
interim: **bool**, §44.
interrupt: **unsigned int**, §44.
j: **register int**, §12.
known: **bool**, §40.
l: **tetra**, §17.
LDOU = #8e, §47.
loc: **octa**, §44.
new_Q: **octa**, §148.
noop = 81, §49.
o: **octa**, §40.
old_hot: **control** *, §60.
op: **mmix_opcode**, §44.
oplus: **octa** (), MMIX-ARITH §5.
p: **specnode** *, §40.
P_BIT = 1 ≪ 0, §54.
pop = 75, §49.
pop_unsave: label, §120.
pushgo = 74, §49.
put = 55, §49.
rA = 21, §52.
rG = 19, §52.
rL = 20, §52.
rQ = 16, §52.
rV = 18, §52.
sign_bit = macro, §80.
stall: label, §75.
true = 1, §11.
trying_to_interrupt: **bool**, §315.
unsav = 88, §49.
UNSAVE = #fb, §47.
unsave = 78, §49.
wait = macro (), §125.
x: **specnode**, §44.
xx: **unsigned char**, §44.
y: **spec**, §44.
yy: **unsigned char**, §44.
z: **spec**, §44.
zero_octa: **octa**, MMIX-ARITH §4.

333. ⟨ Generate an instruction to unsave g[yy] 333 ⟩ ≡

```
cool→ren_x = true, spec_install(&g[cool→yy], &cool→x);
new_O = new_S = incr(cool_O, −1);
cool→z.o = shift_left(new_O, 3);
cool→ptr_a = (void *) mem.up;
```

This code is used in section 332.

334. ⟨ Set up the first phase of unsaving 334 ⟩ ≡

```
cool→ren_x = true, spec_install(&g[rG], &cool→x);
cool→ren_a = true, spec_install(&g[rA], &cool→a);
new_O = new_S = shift_right(cool→z.o, 3, 1);
cool→set_l = true, spec_install(&g[rL], &cool→rl);
cool→ptr_a = (void *) mem.up;
```

This code is used in section 332.

335. ⟨ Get ready for the next step of UNSAVE 335 ⟩ ≡

```
switch (cool→xx) {
case 0: head→inst = pack_bytes(UNSAVE, 1, rZ, 0); break;
case 1: if (cool→yy ≡ rP) head→inst = pack_bytes(UNSAVE, 1, rR, 0);
  else if (cool→yy ≡ 0) head→inst = pack_bytes(UNSAVE, 2, 255, 0);
  else head→inst = pack_bytes(UNSAVE, 1, cool→yy − 1, 0); break;
case 2: if (cool→yy ≡ cool_G) head→inst = pack_bytes(UNSAVE, 3, 0, 0);
  else head→inst = pack_bytes(UNSAVE, 2, cool→yy − 1, 0); break;
}
```

This code is used in section 81.

336. ⟨ Handle an internal UNSAVE when it's time to load 336 ⟩ ≡

```
if (data→xx ≡ 0) {
  data→a.o = data→x.o; data→a.o.h &= #ffffff;      /* unsaved rA */
  data→x.o.l = data→x.o.h ≫ 24; data→x.o.h = 0;    /* unsaved rG */
  if (data→a.o.h ∨ (data→a.o.l & #fffc0000)) {
    data→a.o.h = 0, data→a.o.l &= #3ffff; data→interrupt |= B_BIT;
  }
  if (data→x.o.l < 32) {
    data→x.o.l = 32; data→interrupt |= B_BIT;
  }
}
goto fin_ex;
```

This code is used in section 279.

337. Of course SAVE is handled essentially like UNSAVE, but backwards.

⟨ Special cases of instruction dispatch 117 ⟩ +≡

```
case save: if (cool→xx < cool_G) cool→interrupt |= B_BIT;
  if (cool→interrupt & B_BIT) cool→i = noop;
  else if (((cool_S.l − cool_O.l − cool_L − 1) & lring_mask) ≡ 0)
    ⟨ Insert an instruction to advance gamma 113 ⟩
  else {
    cool→interim = true;
    cool→i = sav;
    switch (cool→zz) {
```

```
    case 0: ⟨Set up the first phase of saving 338⟩; break;
    case 1: if (cool_O.l ≠ cool_S.l) ⟨Insert an instruction to advance gamma 113⟩
      cool→zz = 2; cool→yy = cool_G;
    case 2: case 3: ⟨Generate an instruction to save g[yy] 339⟩; break;
    default: cool→interim = false, cool→i = noop, cool→interrupt |= B_BIT; break;
    }
  }
  break;
```

338. If an interrupt occurs during the first phase, say between two *incgamma* instructions, the value *cool→zz* = 1 will get things restarted properly. (Indeed, if context is saved and unsaved during the interrupt, many *incgamma* instructions may no longer be necessary.)

```
⟨Set up the first phase of saving 338⟩ ≡
  cool→zz = 1;
  cool→ren_x = true, spec_install(&l[(cool_O.l + cool_L) & lring_mask], &cool→x);
  cool→x.known = true, cool→x.o.h = 0, cool→x.o.l = cool_L;
  cool→set_l = true, spec_install(&g[rL], &cool→rl);
  new_O = incr(cool_O, cool_L + 1);
```

This code is used in section 337.

339. ⟨Generate an instruction to save *g*[*yy*] 339⟩ ≡

```
  op = STOU;    /* this instruction needs to be handled by load/store unit */
  cool→mem_x = true, spec_install(&mem, &cool→x);
  cool→z.o = shift_left(cool_O, 3);
  new_O = new_S = incr(cool_O, 1);
  if (cool→zz ≡ 3 ∧ cool→yy > rZ) ⟨Do the final SAVE 340⟩
  else cool→b = specval(&g[cool→yy]);
```

This code is used in section 337.

340. The final SAVE instruction not only stores rG and rA, it also places the final address in global register X.

```
⟨ Do the final SAVE 340 ⟩ ≡
  {
    cool→i = save;
    cool→interim = false;
    cool→ren_a = true, spec_install(&g[cool→xx], &cool→a);
  }
```

This code is used in section 339.

341.
```
⟨ Get ready for the next step of SAVE 341 ⟩ ≡
  switch (cool→zz) {
  case 1: head→inst = pack_bytes(SAVE, cool→xx, 0, 1); break;
  case 2: if (cool→yy ≡ 255) head→inst = pack_bytes(SAVE, cool→xx, 0, 3);
    else head→inst = pack_bytes(SAVE, cool→xx, cool→yy + 1, 2); break;
  case 3: if (cool→yy ≡ rR) head→inst = pack_bytes(SAVE, cool→xx, rP, 3);
    else head→inst = pack_bytes(SAVE, cool→xx, cool→yy + 1, 3); break;
  }
```

This code is used in section 81.

342.
```
⟨ Handle an internal SAVE when it's time to store 342 ⟩ ≡
  {
    if (data→interim) data→x.o = data→b.o;
    else {
      if (data ≠ old_hot) wait(1);      /* we need the hottest value of rA */
      data→x.o.h = g[rG].o.l ≪ 24;
      data→x.o.l = g[rA].o.l;
      data→a.o = data→y.o;
    }
    goto fin_ex;
  }
```

This code is used in section 281.

343. More register-to-register ops. Now that we've finished most of the hard stuff, we can relax and fill in the holes that we left in the all-register parts of the execution stages.

First let's complete the fixed point arithmetic operations, by dispensing with multiplication and division.

```
⟨ Cases to compute the results of register-to-register operation 137 ⟩ +≡
case mulu: data→x.o = omult(data→y.o, data→z.o);
  data→a.o = aux;
  goto quantify_mul;
case mul: data→x.o = signed_omult(data→y.o, data→z.o);
  if (overflow) data→interrupt |= V_BIT;
quantify_mul: aux = data→z.o;
  for (j = mul0; aux.l ∨ aux.h; j++) aux = shift_right(aux, 8, 1);
  data→i = j; break;      /* j is mul0 or mul1 or ... or mul8 */
case divu: data→x.o = odiv(data→b.o, data→y.o, data→z.o);
  data→a.o = aux; data→i = div; break;
case div: if (data→z.o.l ≡ 0 ∧ data→z.o.h ≡ 0) {
    data→interrupt |= D_BIT; data→a.o = data→y.o;
    data→i = set;      /* divide by zero needn't wait in the pipeline */
  } else {
    data→x.o = signed_odiv(data→y.o, data→z.o);
    if (overflow) data→interrupt |= V_BIT;
    data→a.o = aux;
  } break;
```


a: **specnode**, §44.
aux: **octa**, MMIX-ARITH §4.
b: **spec**, §44.
cool: **control** ∗, §60.
D_BIT = 1 ≪ 15, §54.
data: **register control** ∗, §124.
div = 9, §49.
divu = 28, §49.
false = 0, §11.
fin_ex: label, §144.
g: **specnode** [], §86.
h: **tetra**, §17.
head: **fetch** ∗, §69.
i: **internal_opcode**, §44.
inst: **tetra**, §68.
interim: **bool**, §44.
interrupt: **unsigned int**, §44.
j: **register int**, §12.
l: **tetra**, §17.
mul = 26, §49.
mul0 = 0, §49.
mul1 = 1, §49.
mul8 = 8, §49.
mulu = 27, §49.
o: **octa**, §40.
odiv: **octa** (), MMIX-ARITH §13.
old_hot: **control** ∗, §60.
omult: **octa** (), MMIX-ARITH §8.
overflow: **bool**, MMIX-ARITH §4.
pack_bytes = macro (), §320.
rA = 21, §52.
ren_a: **bool**, §44.
rG = 19, §52.
rP = 23, §52.
rR = 6, §52.
save = 77, §49.
SAVE = #fa, §47.
set = 33, §49.
shift_right: **octa** (), MMIX-ARITH §7.
signed_odiv: **octa** (), MMIX-ARITH §24.
signed_omult: **octa** (), MMIX-ARITH §12.
spec_install: **static void** (), §95.
true = 1, §11.
V_BIT = 1 ≪ 14, §54.
wait = macro (), §125.
x: **specnode**, §44.
xx: **unsigned char**, §44.
y: **spec**, §44.
yy: **unsigned char**, §44.
z: **spec**, §44.
zz: **unsigned char**, §44.

344. Next let's polish off the bitwise and bytewise operations.

```
⟨ Cases to compute the results of register-to-register operation 137 ⟩ +≡
case sadd:
  data→x.o.l = count_bits(data→y.o.h & ~data→z.o.h) + count_bits(data→y.o.l & ~data→z.o.l);
  break;
case mor: data→x.o = bool_mult(data→y.o, data→z.o, data→op & #2); break;
case bdif: data→x.o.h = byte_diff(data→y.o.h, data→z.o.h);
  data→x.o.l = byte_diff(data→y.o.l, data→z.o.l); break;
case wdif: data→x.o.h = wyde_diff(data→y.o.h, data→z.o.h);
  data→x.o.l = wyde_diff(data→y.o.l, data→z.o.l); break;
case tdif: if (data→y.o.h > data→z.o.h) data→x.o.h = data→y.o.h − data→z.o.h;
tdif_l: if (data→y.o.l > data→z.o.l) data→x.o.l = data→y.o.l − data→z.o.l; break;
case odif: if (data→y.o.h > data→z.o.h) data→x.o = ominus(data→y.o, data→z.o);
  else if (data→y.o.h ≡ data→z.o.h) goto tdif_l;
  break;
```

345. The conditional set (CS) instructions are, rather surprisingly, more difficult to implement than the zero set (ZS) instructions, although the ZS instructions do more. The reason is that dynamic instruction dependencies are more complicated with CS. Consider, for example, the instructions

```
LDO x,a,b;   FDIV y,c,d;   CSZ y,x,0;   INCL y,1.
```

If the value of x is zero, the INCL instruction need not wait for the division to be completed. (We do not, however, abort the division in such a case; it might invoke a trip handler, or change the inexact bit, etc. Our policy is to treat common cases efficiently and to treat all cases correctly, but not to treat all cases with maximum efficiency.)

```
⟨ Cases to compute the results of register-to-register operation 137 ⟩ +≡
case zset: if (register_truth(data→y.o, data→op)) data→x.o = data→z.o;
      /* otherwise data→x.o is already zero */
  goto fin_ex;
case cset: if (register_truth(data→y.o, data→op)) data→x.o = data→z.o, data→b.p = Λ;
  else if (data→b.p ≡ Λ) data→x.o = data→b.o;
  else {
    data→state = 0; data→need_b = true; goto switch1;
  } break;
```

346. Floating point computations are mostly handled by the routines in MMIX-ARITH, which record anomalous events in the global variable *exceptions*. But we consider the operation trivial if an input is infinite or NaN; and we may need to increase the execution time when subnormals are present.

```
#define ROUND_OFF 1
#define ROUND_UP 2
#define ROUND_DOWN 3
#define ROUND_NEAR 4
#define is_subnormal(x) ((x.h & #7ff00000) ≡ 0 ∧ ((x.h & #fffff) ∨ x.l))
#define is_trivial(x) ((x.h & #7ff00000) ≡ #7ff00000)
#define set_round cur_round = (data→ra.o.l < #10000 ? ROUND_NEAR : data→ra.o.l ≫ 16)
```

```
⟨ Cases to compute the results of register-to-register operation 137 ⟩ +≡
case fadd: set_round; data→x.o = fplus(data→y.o, data→z.o);
fin_bflot: if (is_subnormal(data→y.o)) data→denin = denin_penalty;
fin_uflot: if (is_subnormal(data→x.o)) data→denout = denout_penalty;
fin_flot: if (is_subnormal(data→z.o)) data→denin = denin_penalty;
  data→interrupt |= exceptions;
  if (is_trivial(data→y.o) ∨ is_trivial(data→z.o)) goto fin_ex;
  if (data→i ≡ fsqrt ∧ (data→z.o.h & sign_bit)) goto fin_ex;
  break;
case fsub: data→a.o = data→z.o;
  if (fcomp(data→z.o, zero_octa) ≠ 2) data→a.o.h ⊕= sign_bit;
  set_round; data→x.o = fplus(data→y.o, data→a.o);
  data→i = fadd;      /* use pipeline times for addition */
  goto fin_bflot;
case fmul: set_round; data→x.o = fmult(data→y.o, data→z.o); goto fin_bflot;
case fdiv: set_round; data→x.o = fdivide(data→y.o, data→z.o); goto fin_bflot;
case fsqrt: set_round; data→x.o = froot(data→z.o, data→y.o.l); goto fin_uflot;
case fint: set_round; data→x.o = fintegerize(data→z.o, data→y.o.l); goto fin_uflot;
case fix: set_round; data→x.o = fixit(data→z.o, data→y.o.l);
  if (data→op & #2) exceptions &= ~W_BIT;      /* unsigned case doesn't overflow */
  goto fin_flot;
case flot: set_round; data→x.o = floatit(data→z.o, data→y.o.l, data→op & #2, data→op & #4);
  data→interrupt |= exceptions; break;
```

347. ⟨ Special cases of instruction dispatch 117 ⟩ +≡

```
case fsqrt: case fint: case fix: case flot: if (cool→y.o.l > 4) goto illegal_inst;
  break;
```

---

a: **specnode**, §44.
b: **spec**, §44.
bdif = 48, §49.
bool_mult: **octa** ( ), MMIX-ARITH §29.
byte_diff: **tetra** ( ), MMIX-ARITH §27.
cool: **control** *, §60.
count_bits: **int** ( ), MMIX-ARITH §26.
cset = 53, §49.
cur_round: **int**, MMIX-ARITH §30.
data: **register control** *, §124.
denin: **int**, §44.
denin_penalty: **int**, §349.
denout: **int**, §44.
denout_penalty: **int**, §349.
exceptions: **int**, MMIX-ARITH §32.
fadd = 14, §49.
fcomp: **int** ( ), MMIX-ARITH §85.
fdiv = 16, §49.
fdivide: **octa** ( ), MMIX-ARITH §44.
fin_ex: label, §144.
fint = 18, §49.
fintegerize: **octa** ( ), MMIX-ARITH §86.
fix = 19, §49.
fixit: **octa** ( ), MMIX-ARITH §88.
floatit: **octa** ( ), MMIX-ARITH §89.
flot = 20, §49.
fmul = 15, §49.
fmult: **octa** ( ), MMIX-ARITH §41.
fplus: **octa** ( ), MMIX-ARITH §46.
froot: **octa** ( ), MMIX-ARITH §91.
fsqrt = 17, §49.
fsub = 24, §49.
h: **tetra**, §17.
i: **internal_opcode**, §44.
illegal_inst: label, §118.
interrupt: **unsigned int**, §44.
l: **tetra**, §17.
mor = 13, §49.
need_b: **bool**, §44.
o: **octa**, §40.
odif = 51, §49.
ominus: **octa** ( ), MMIX-ARITH §5.
op: **mmix_opcode**, §44.
p: **specnode** *, §40.
ra: **spec**, §44.
register_truth: **static int** ( ), §157.
sadd = 12, §49.
sign_bit = macro, §80.
state: **int**, §44.
switch1: label, §130.
tdif = 50, §49.
true = 1, §11.
W_BIT = 1 ≪ 13, §54.
wdif = 49, §49.
wyde_diff: **tetra** ( ), MMIX-ARITH §28.
x: **specnode**, §44.
y: **spec**, §44.
z: **spec**, §44.
zero_octa: **octa**, MMIX-ARITH §4.
zset = 52, §49.

348. ⟨ Cases to compute the results of register-to-register operation 137 ⟩ +≡

```
case feps: j = fepscomp(data→y.o, data→z.o, data→b.o, data→op ≠ FEQLE);
  if (j ≡ 2) data→i = fcmp;
  else if (is_subnormal(data→y.o) ∨ is_subnormal(data→z.o)) data→denin = denin_penalty;
  switch (data→op) {
  case FUNE: if (j ≡ 2) goto cmp_pos; else goto cmp_zero;
  case FEQLE: goto cmp_fin;
  case FCMPE: if (j) goto cmp_zero_or_invalid;
  }
case fcmp: j = fcomp(data→y.o, data→z.o);
  if (j < 0) goto cmp_neg;
cmp_fin: if (j ≡ 1) goto cmp_pos;
cmp_zero_or_invalid: if (j ≡ 2) data→interrupt |= I_BIT;
  goto cmp_zero;
case funeq: if (fcomp(data→y.o, data→z.o) ≡ (data→op ≡ FUN ? 2 : 0)) goto cmp_pos;
  else goto cmp_zero;
```

349. ⟨ External variables 4 ⟩ +≡

```
  Extern int frem_max;
  Extern int denin_penalty, denout_penalty;
```

350. The floating point remainder operation is especially interesting because it can be interrupted when it's in the hot seat.

⟨ Cases to compute the results of register-to-register operation 137 ⟩ +≡

```
case frem: if (is_trivial(data→y.o) ∨ is_trivial(data→z.o)) {
      data→x.o = fremstep(data→y.o, data→z.o, 2500);
      data→interrupt |= exceptions; goto fin_ex;
  }
  if ((self + 1)→next) wait(1);
  data→interim = true;
  j = 1;
  if (is_subnormal(data→y.o) ∨ is_subnormal(data→z.o)) j += denin_penalty;
  pass_after(j);
  goto passit;
```

351. ⟨ Begin execution of a stage-two operation 351 ⟩ ≡

```
j = 1;
if (data→i ≡ frem) {
  data→x.o = fremstep(data→y.o, data→z.o, frem_max);
  if (exceptions & E_BIT) {
    data→y.o = data→x.o;
    if (trying_to_interrupt ∧ data ≡ old_hot) goto fin_ex;
  } else {
    data→state = 3;
    data→interim = false;
    data→interrupt |= exceptions;
    if (is_subnormal(data→x.o)) j += denout_penalty;
  }
  wait(j);
}
```

This code is used in section 135.

---

b: **spec**, §44.
cmp_neg: label, §143.
cmp_pos: label, §143.
cmp_zero: label, §143.
data: **register control** ∗, §124.
denin: **int**, §44.
E_BIT = 1 ≪ 18, §54.
exceptions: **int**, MMIX-ARITH §32.
Extern = macro, §4.
false = 0, §11.
fcmp = 22, §49.
FCMPE = #11, §47.
fcomp: **int** ( ), MMIX-ARITH §85.
feps = 21, §49.
fepscomp: **int** ( ), MMIX-ARITH §50.
FEQLE = #13, §47.
fin_ex: label, §144.
frem = 25, §49.
fremstep: **octa** ( ), MMIX-ARITH §93.
FUN = #02, §47.
FUNE = #12, §47.
funeq = 23, §49.
i: **internal_opcode**, §44.
I_BIT = 1 ≪ 12, §54.
interim: **bool**, §44.
interrupt: **unsigned int**, §44.
is_subnormal = macro ( ), §346.
is_trivial = macro ( ), §346.
j: **register int**, §12.
next: **coroutine** ∗, §23.
o: **octa**, §40.
old_hot: **control** ∗, §60.
op: **mmix_opcode**, §44.
pass_after = macro ( ), §125.
passit: label, §134.
self: **register coroutine** ∗, §124.
state: **int**, §44.
true = 1, §11.
trying_to_interrupt: **bool**, §315.
wait = macro ( ), §125.
x: **specnode**, §44.
y: **spec**, §44.
z: **spec**, §44.

352. System operations. Finally we need to implement some operations for the operating system; then the hardware simulation will be done!

A `LDVTS` instruction is delayed until it reaches the hot seat, because it changes the IT and DT caches. The operating system should use `SYNC` after `LDVTS` if the effects are needed immediately; the system is also responsible for ensuring that the page table permission bits agree with the `LDVTS` permission bits when the latter are nonzero. (Also, if write permission is taken away from a page, the operating system must have previously used `SYNCD` to write out any dirty bytes that might have been cached from that page; `SYNCD` will be inoperative after write permission goes away.)

```
⟨Handle special cases for operations like prego and ldvts 289⟩ +≡
  if (data→i ≡ ldvts) ⟨Do stage 1 of LDVTS 353⟩;
```

353.

```
⟨Do stage 1 of LDVTS 353⟩ ≡
  {
    if (data ≠ old_hot) wait(1);
    if (DTcache→lock ∨ (j = get_reader(DTcache)) < 0) wait(1);
    startup(&DTcache→reader[j], DTcache→access_time);
    data→z.o.h = 0, data→z.o.l = data→y.o.l & #7;
    p = cache_search(DTcache, data→y.o);      /* N.B.: Not trans_key(data→y.o) */
    if (p) {
      data→x.o.l = 2;
      if (data→z.o.l) {
        p = use_and_fix(DTcache, p);
        p→data[0].l = (p→data[0].l & −8) + data→z.o.l;
      } else {
        p = demote_and_fix(DTcache, p);
        p→tag.h |= sign_bit;      /* invalidate the tag */
      }
    }
    pass_after(DTcache→access_time); goto passit;
  }
```

This code is used in section 352.

354.

```
⟨Special cases for states in later stages 272⟩ +≡
case ld_st_launch: if (ITcache→lock ∨ (j = get_reader(ITcache)) < 0) wait(1);
  startup(&ITcache→reader[j], ITcache→access_time);
  p = cache_search(ITcache, data→y.o);      /* N.B.: Not trans_key(data→y.o) */
  if (p) {
    data→x.o.l |= 1;
    if (data→z.o.l) {
      p = use_and_fix(ITcache, p);
      p→data[0].l = (p→data[0].l & −8) + data→z.o.l;
    } else {
      p = demote_and_fix(ITcache, p);
      p→tag.h |= sign_bit;      /* invalidate the tag */
    }
  }
  data→state = 3; wait(ITcache→access_time);
```

355. The SYNC operation interacts with the pipeline in interesting ways. SYNC 0 and SYNC 4 are the simplest; they just lock the dispatch and wait until they get to the hot seat, after which the pipeline has drained. SYNC 1 and SYNC 3 put a "barrier" into the write buffer so that subsequent store instructions will not merge with previous stores. SYNC 2 and SYNC 3 lock the dispatch until all previous load instructions have left the pipeline. SYNC 5, SYNC 6, and SYNC 7 remove things from caches once they get to the hot seat.

```
⟨ Special cases of instruction dispatch 117 ⟩ +≡
case sync: if (cool→zz > 3) {
    if (¬(cool→loc.h & sign_bit)) goto privileged_inst;
    if (cool→zz ≡ 4) freeze_dispatch = true;
  } else {
    if (cool→zz ≠ 1) freeze_dispatch = true;
    if (cool→zz & 1) cool→mem_x = true, spec_install(&mem, &cool→x);
  } break;
```

356.

```
⟨ Cases for stage 1 execution 155 ⟩ +≡
case sync: switch (data→zz) {
  case 0: case 4: if (data ≠ old_hot) wait(1);
    halted = (data→zz ≠ 0); goto fin_ex;
  case 2: case 3: ⟨ Wait if there's an unfinished load ahead of us 357 ⟩;
    release_lock(self, dispatch_lock);
  case 1: data→x.addr = zero_octa; goto fin_ex;
  case 5: if (data ≠ old_hot) wait(1);
    ⟨ Clean the data caches 361 ⟩;
  case 6: if (data ≠ old_hot) wait(1);
    ⟨ Zap the translation caches 358 ⟩;
  case 7: if (data ≠ old_hot) wait(1);
    ⟨ Zap the instruction and data caches 359 ⟩;
  }
```

---

access_time: **int**, §167.
addr: **octa**, §40.
cache_search: **static cacheblock** *(), §193.
cool: **control** *, §60.
data: **register control** *, §124.
data: **octa** *, §167.
demote_and_fix: **static cacheblock** *(), §199.
dispatch_lock: **lockvar**, §65.
DTcache: **cache** *, §168.
fin_ex: label, §144.
freeze_dispatch: **register bool**, §75.
get_reader: **static int** (), §183.
h: **tetra**, §17.
halted: **bool**, §12.
i: **internal_opcode**, §44.
ITcache: **cache** *, §168.
j: **register int**, §12.
l: **tetra**, §17.
ld_st_launch = 7, §265.
ldvts = 60, §49.
loc: **octa**, §44.
lock: **lockvar**, §167.
mem: **specnode**, §115.
mem_x: **bool**, §44.
o: **octa**, §40.
old_hot: **control** *, §60.
p: **register cacheblock** *, §258.
pass_after = macro (), §125.
passit: label, §134.
prego = 73, §49.
privileged_inst: label, §118.
reader: **coroutine** *, §167.
release_lock = macro (), §37.
self: **register coroutine** *, §124.
sign_bit = macro, §80.
spec_install: **static void** (), §95.
startup: **static void** (), §31.
state: **int**, §44.
sync = 79, §49.
tag: **octa**, §167.
trans_key = macro (), §240.
true = 1, §11.
use_and_fix: **static cacheblock** *(), §196.
wait = macro (), §125.
x: **specnode**, §44.
y: **spec**, §44.
z: **spec**, §44.
zero_octa: **octa**, MMIX-ARITH §4.
zz: **unsigned char**, §44.

357. ⟨ Wait if there's an unfinished load ahead of us 357 ⟩ ≡

```
{
  register control *cc;
  for (cc = data; cc ≠ hot; ) {
    cc = (cc ≡ reorder_top ? reorder_bot : cc + 1);
    if (cc→owner ∧ (cc→i ≡ ld ∨ cc→i ≡ ldunc ∨ cc→i ≡ pst)) wait(1);
  }
}
```

This code is used in section 356.

358. Perhaps the delay should be longer here.

⟨ Zap the translation caches 358 ⟩ ≡

```
  if (DTcache→lock ∨ (j = get_reader(DTcache)) < 0) wait(1);
  startup(&DTcache→reader[j], DTcache→access_time);
  set_lock(self, DTcache→lock);
  zap_cache(DTcache);
  data→state = 10; wait(DTcache→access_time);
```

This code is used in section 356.

359. ⟨ Zap the instruction and data caches 359 ⟩ ≡

```
  if (¬Icache) {
    data→state = 11; goto switch1;
  }
  if (Icache→lock ∨ (j = get_reader(Icache)) < 0) wait(1);
  startup(&Icache→reader[j], Icache→access_time);
  set_lock(self, Icache→lock);
  zap_cache(Icache);
  data→state = 11; wait(Icache→access_time);
```

This code is used in section 356.

360. ⟨ Special cases for states in the first stage 266 ⟩ +≡

```
case 10: if (self→lockloc) *(self→lockloc) = Λ, self→lockloc = Λ;
  if (ITcache→lock ∨ (j = get_reader(ITcache)) < 0) wait(1);
  startup(&ITcache→reader[j], ITcache→access_time);
  set_lock(self, ITcache→lock);
  zap_cache(ITcache);
  data→state = 3; wait(ITcache→access_time);
case 11: if (self→lockloc) *(self→lockloc) = Λ, self→lockloc = Λ;
  if (wbuf_lock) wait(1);
  write_head = write_tail, write_ctl.state = 0;      /* zap the write buffer */
  if (¬Dcache) {
    data→state = 12; goto switch1;
  }
  if (Dcache→lock ∨ (j = get_reader(Dcache)) < 0) wait(1);
  startup(&Dcache→reader[j], Dcache→access_time);
  set_lock(self, Dcache→lock);
  zap_cache(Dcache);
  data→state = 12; wait(Dcache→access_time);
```

```
case 12: if (self→lockloc) *(self→lockloc) = Λ, self→lockloc = Λ;
  if (¬Scache) goto fin_ex;
  if (Scache→lock) wait(1);
  set_lock(self, Scache→lock);
  zap_cache(Scache);
  data→state = 3; wait(Scache→access_time);
```

361. ⟨ Clean the data caches 361 ⟩ ≡

```
  if (self→lockloc) *(self→lockloc) = Λ, self→lockloc = Λ;
  ⟨ Wait till write buffer is empty 362 ⟩;
  if (clean_co.next ∨ clean_lock) wait(1);
  set_lock(self, clean_lock);
  clean_ctl.i = sync; clean_ctl.state = 0; clean_ctl.x.o.h = 0;
  startup(&clean_co, 1);
  data→state = 13;
  data→interim = true;
  wait(1);
```

This code is used in section 356.

362. ⟨ Wait till write buffer is empty 362 ⟩ ≡

```
  if (write_head ≠ write_tail) {
    if (¬speed_lock) set_lock(self, speed_lock);
    wait(1);
  }
```

This code is used in sections 361 and 364.

363. The cleanup process might take a huge amount of time, so we must allow it to be interrupted. (Servicing the interruption might, of course, put more stuff into the cache.)

⟨ Special cases for states in the first stage 266 ⟩ +≡

```
case 13: if (¬clean_co.next) {
    data→interim = false; goto fin_ex;    /* it's done! */
  }
  if (trying_to_interrupt) goto fin_ex;    /* accept an interruption */
  wait(1);
```

---

access_time: **int**, §167.
clean_co: **coroutine**, §230.
clean_ctl: **control**, §230.
clean_lock: **lockvar**, §230.
control = **struct**, §44.
data: **register control** *, §124.
Dcache: **cache** *, §168.
DTcache: **cache** *, §168.
false = 0, §11.
fin_ex: label, §144.
get_reader: **static int** ( ), §183.
h: **tetra**, §17.
hot: **control** *, §60.
i: **internal_opcode**, §44.
Icache: **cache** *, §168.
interim: **bool**, §44.
ITcache: **cache** *, §168.
j: **register int**, §12.
ld = 56, §49.
ldunc = 59, §49.
lock: **lockvar**, §167.
lockloc: **coroutine** **, §23.
next: **coroutine** *, §23.
o: **octa**, §40.
owner: **coroutine** *, §44.
pst = 66, §49.
reader: **coroutine** *, §167.
reorder_bot: **control** *, §60.
reorder_top: **control** *, §60.
Scache: **cache** *, §168.
self: **register coroutine** *, §124.
set_lock = macro ( ), §37.
speed_lock: **lockvar**, §247.
startup: **static void** ( ), §31.
state: **int**, §44.
switch1: label, §130.
sync = 79, §49.
true = 1, §11.
trying_to_interrupt: **bool**, §315.
wait = macro ( ), §125.
wbuf_lock: **lockvar**, §247.
write_ctl: **control**, §248.
write_head: **write_node** *, §247.
write_tail: **write_node** *, §247.
x: **specnode**, §44.
zap_cache: **void** ( ), §181.

364. Now we consider SYNCD and SYNCID. When control comes to this part of the program, *data→y.o* is a virtual address and *data→z.o* is the corresponding physical address; $data\rightarrow xx + 1$ is the number of bytes we are supposed to be syncing; *data→b.o.l* is the number of bytes we can handle at once (either *Icache→bb* or *Dcache→bb* or 8192).

We need a more elaborate scheme to implement SYNCD and SYNCID than we have used for the "hint" instructions PRELD, PREGO, and PREST, because SYNCD and SYNCID are not merely hints. They cannot be converted into a sequence of cache-block-size commands at dispatch time, because we cannot be sure that the starting virtual address will be aligned with the beginning of a cache block. We need to realize that the bytes specified by SYNCD or SYNCID might cross a virtual page boundary—possibly with different protection bits on each page. We need to allow for interrupts. And we also need to keep the fetch buffer empty until a user's SYNCID has completely brought the memory up to date.

```
⟨ Special cases for states in later stages 272 ⟩ +≡
do_syncid: data→state = 30;
case 30: if (data ≠ old_hot) wait(1);
  if (¬Icache) {
    data→state = (data→loc.h & sign_bit ? 31 : 33); goto switch2;
  }
  ⟨ Clean the I-cache block for data→z.o, if any 365 ⟩;
  data→state = (data→loc.h & sign_bit ? 31 : 33); wait(Icache→access_time);
case 31: if (self→lockloc) *(self→lockloc) = Λ, self→lockloc = Λ;
  ⟨ Wait till write buffer is empty 362 ⟩;
  if (((data→b.o.l − 1) & ∼data→y.o.l) < data→xx) data→interim = true;
  if (¬Dcache) goto next_sync;
  ⟨ Clean the D-cache block for data→z.o, if any 366 ⟩;
  data→state = 32; wait(Dcache→access_time);
case 32: if (self→lockloc) *(self→lockloc) = Λ, self→lockloc = Λ;
  if (¬Scache) goto next_sync;
  ⟨ Clean the S-cache block for data→z.o, if any 367 ⟩;
  data→state = 35; wait(Scache→access_time);
do_syncd: data→state = 33;
case 33: if (data ≠ old_hot) wait(1);
  if (self→lockloc) *(self→lockloc) = Λ, self→lockloc = Λ;
  ⟨ Wait till write buffer is empty 362 ⟩;
  if (((data→b.o.l − 1) & ∼data→y.o.l) < data→xx) data→interim = true;
  if (¬Dcache)
    if (data→i ≡ syncd) goto fin_ex; else goto next_sync;
  ⟨ Use cleanup on the cache blocks for data→z.o, if any 368 ⟩;
  data→state = 34;
case 34: if (¬clean_co.next) goto next_sync;
  if (trying_to_interrupt ∧ data→interim ∧ data ≡ old_hot) {
    data→z.o = zero_octa;    /* anticipate RESUME_CONT */
    goto fin_ex;    /* accept an interruption */
  }
  wait(1);
next_sync: data→state = 35;
```

```
case 35: if (self→lockloc) *(self→lockloc) = Λ, self→lockloc = Λ;
  if (data→interim) ⟨Continue this command on the next cache block 369⟩;
  data→go.known = true;
  goto fin_ex;
```

365. ⟨Clean the I-cache block for *data→z.o*, if any 365⟩ ≡

```
  if (Icache→lock ∨ (j = get_reader(Icache)) < 0) wait(1);
  startup(&Icache→reader[j], Icache→access_time);
  set_lock(self, Icache→lock);
  p = cache_search(Icache, data→z.o);
  if (p) {
    demote_and_fix(Icache, p);
    clean_block(Icache, p);
  }
```

This code is used in section 364.

366. ⟨Clean the D-cache block for *data→z.o*, if any 366⟩ ≡

```
  if (Dcache→lock ∨ (j = get_reader(Dcache)) < 0) wait(1);
  startup(&Dcache→reader[j], Dcache→access_time);
  set_lock(self, Dcache→lock);
  p = cache_search(Dcache, data→z.o);
  if (p) {
    demote_and_fix(Dcache, p);
    clean_block(Dcache, p);
  }
```

This code is used in section 364.

367. ⟨Clean the S-cache block for *data→z.o*, if any 367⟩ ≡

```
  if (Scache→lock) wait(1);
  set_lock(self, Scache→lock);
  p = cache_search(Scache, data→z.o);
  if (p) {
    demote_and_fix(Scache, p);
    clean_block(Scache, p);
  }
```

This code is used in section 364.

---

access_time: **int**, §167.
b: **spec**, §44.
bb: **int**, §167.
cache_search: **static cacheblock** *( ), §193.
clean_block: **void** ( ), §179.
clean_co: **coroutine**, §230.
cleanup = 91, §129.
data: **register control** *, §124.
Dcache: **cache** *, §168.
demote_and_fix: **static cacheblock** *( ), §199.
fin_ex: label, §144.
get_reader: **static int** ( ), §183.
go: **specnode**, §44.
h: **tetra**, §17.
i: **internal_opcode**, §44.
Icache: **cache** *, §168.
interim: **bool**, §44.
j: **register int**, §12.
known: **bool**, §40.
l: **tetra**, §17.
loc: **octa**, §44.
lock: **lockvar**, §167.
lockloc: **coroutine** **, §23.
next: **coroutine** *, §23.
o: **octa**, §40.
old_hot: **control** *, §60.
p: **register cacheblock** *, §258.
reader: **coroutine** *, §167.
RESUME_CONT = 1, §320.
Scache: **cache** *, §168.
self: **register coroutine** *, §124.
set_lock = macro ( ), §37.
sign_bit = macro, §80.
startup: **static void** ( ), §31.
state: **int**, §44.
switch2: label, §135.
syncd = 64, §49.
true = 1, §11.
trying_to_interrupt: **bool**, §315.
wait = macro ( ), §125.
xx: **unsigned char**, §44.
y: **spec**, §44.
z: **spec**, §44.
zero_octa: **octa**, MMIX-ARITH §4.

368. ⟨ Use *cleanup* on the cache blocks for *data→z.o*, if any 368 ⟩ ≡

```
if (clean_co.next ∨ clean_lock) wait(1);
set_lock(self, clean_lock);
clean_ctl.i = syncd;
clean_ctl.state = 4;
clean_ctl.x.o.h = data→loc.h & sign_bit;
clean_ctl.z.o = data→z.o;
schedule(&clean_co, 1, 4);
```

This code is used in section 364.

369. We use the fact that cache block sizes are divisors of 8192.

⟨ Continue this command on the next cache block 369 ⟩ ≡

```
{
  data→interim = false;
  data→xx −= ((data→b.o.l − 1) & ∼data→y.o.l) + 1;
  data→y.o = incr(data→y.o, data→b.o.l);
  data→y.o.l &= −data→b.o.l;
  data→z.o.l = (data→z.o.l & −8192) + (data→y.o.l & 8191);
  if ((data→y.o.l & 8191) ≡ 0) goto square_one;
      /* maybe crossed a page boundary */
  if (data→i ≡ syncd) goto do_syncd; else goto do_syncid;
}
```

This code is used in section 364.

370. If the first page lacks proper protection, we still must try the second, in the rare case that a page boundary is spanned.

⟨ Special cases for states in later stages 272 ⟩ +≡

```
sync_check: if ((data→y.o.l ⊕ (data→y.o.l + data→xx)) ≥ 8192) {
    data→xx −= (8191 & ∼data→y.o.l) + 1;
    data→y.o = incr(data→y.o, 8192);
    data→y.o.l &= −8192;
    goto square_one;
  }
  goto fin_ex;
```

371. Input and output. We're done implementing the hardware, but there's still a small matter of software remaining, because we sometimes want to pretend that a real operating system is present without actually having one loaded. This simulator therefore implements a special feature: If `RESUME 1` is issued in location rT, the ten special I/O traps of MMIX-SIM are performed instantaneously behind the scenes.

Of course all claims of accurate simulation go out the door when this feature is used.

#define *max_sys_call* *Ftell*

⟨ Type definitions 11 ⟩ +≡
  typedef enum {
    Halt, *Fopen*, *Fclose*, *Fread*, *Fgets*, *Fgetws*, *Fwrite*, *Fputs*, *Fputws*, *Fseek*, *Ftell*
  } **sys_call**;

---

b: **spec**, §44.
clean_co: **coroutine**, §230.
clean_ctl: **control**, §230.
clean_lock: **lockvar**, §230.
cleanup = 91, §129.
data: **register control** *, §124.
do_syncd: label, §364.
do_syncid: label, §364.
false = 0, §11.
fin_ex: label, §144.
h: **tetra**, §17.
i: **internal_opcode**, §44.
incr: **octa** ( ), MMIX-ARITH §6.
interim: **bool**, §44.
l: **tetra**, §17.
loc: **octa**, §44.
next: **coroutine** *, §23.
o: **octa**, §40.
schedule: **static void** ( ), §28.
self: **register coroutine** *, §124.
set_lock = macro ( ), §37.
sign_bit = macro, §80.
square_one: label, §272.
state: **int**, §44.
syncd = 64, §49.
wait = macro ( ), §125.
x: **specnode**, §44.
xx: **unsigned char**, §44.
y: **spec**, §44.
z: **spec**, §44.

372. ⟨ Magically do an I/O operation, if *cool→loc* is rT 372 ⟩ ≡

```
if (cool→loc.l ≡ g[rT].o.l ∧ cool→loc.h ≡ g[rT].o.h) {
  register unsigned char yy, zz;
  octa ma, mb;
  if (g[rXX].o.l & #ffff0000) goto magic_done;
  yy = g[rXX].o.l ≫ 8, zz = g[rXX].o.l & #ff;
  if (yy > max_sys_call) goto magic_done;
  ⟨ Prepare memory arguments ma = M[a] and mb = M[b] if needed 380 ⟩;
  switch (yy) {
  case Halt: ⟨ Either halt or print warning 373 ⟩; break;
  case Fopen: g[rBB].o = mmix_fopen(zz, mb, ma); break;
  case Fclose: g[rBB].o = mmix_fclose(zz); break;
  case Fread: g[rBB].o = mmix_fread(zz, mb, ma); break;
  case Fgets: g[rBB].o = mmix_fgets(zz, mb, ma); break;
  case Fgetws: g[rBB].o = mmix_fgetws(zz, mb, ma); break;
  case Fwrite: g[rBB].o = mmix_fwrite(zz, mb, ma); break;
  case Fputs: g[rBB].o = mmix_fputs(zz, g[rBB].o); break;
  case Fputws: g[rBB].o = mmix_fputws(zz, g[rBB].o); break;
  case Fseek: g[rBB].o = mmix_fseek(zz, g[rBB].o); break;
  case Ftell: g[rBB].o = mmix_ftell(zz); break;
  }
magic_done: g[255].o = neg_one;      /* this will enable interrupts */
}
```

This code is used in section 322.

373. ⟨ Either halt or print warning 373 ⟩ ≡

```
if (¬zz) halted = true;
else if (zz ≡ 1) {
  octa trap_loc;
  trap_loc = incr(g[rWW].o, −4);
  if (¬(trap_loc.h ∨ trap_loc.l ≥ #f0))
    print_trip_warning(trap_loc.l ≫ 4, incr(g[rW].o, −4));
}
```

This code is used in section 372.

374. ⟨ Global variables 20 ⟩ +≡

```
char arg_count[] = {1, 3, 1, 3, 3, 3, 3, 2, 2, 2, 1};
```

375. The input/output operations invoked by TRAPs are done by subroutines in an auxiliary program module called MMIX-IO. Here we need only declare those subroutines, and write three primitive interfaces on which they depend.

376. ⟨ Global variables 20 ⟩ +≡

```
extern octa mmix_fopen ARGS((unsigned char, octa, octa));
extern octa mmix_fclose ARGS((unsigned char));
extern octa mmix_fread ARGS((unsigned char, octa, octa));
extern octa mmix_fgets ARGS((unsigned char, octa, octa));
extern octa mmix_fgetws ARGS((unsigned char, octa, octa));
extern octa mmix_fwrite ARGS((unsigned char, octa, octa));
extern octa mmix_fputs ARGS((unsigned char, octa));
```

```
extern octa mmix_fputws ARGS((unsigned char,octa));
extern octa mmix_fseek ARGS((unsigned char,octa));
extern octa mmix_ftell ARGS((unsigned char));
extern void print_trip_warning ARGS((int,octa));
```

377. ⟨Internal prototypes 13⟩ +≡

```
int mmgetchars ARGS((char *,int,octa,int));
void mmputchars ARGS((unsigned char *,int,octa));
char stdin_chr ARGS((void));
octa magic_read ARGS((octa));
void magic_write ARGS((octa,octa));
```

ARGS = macro, §6.
cool: **control** *, §60.
Fclose = 2, §371.
Fgets = 4, §371.
Fgetws = 5, §371.
Fopen = 1, §371.
Fputs = 7, §371.
Fputws = 8, §371.
Fread = 3, §371.
Fseek = 9, §371.
Ftell = 10, §371.
Fwrite = 6, §371.
g: **specnode** [], §86.
h: **tetra**, §17.
Halt = 0, §371.
halted: **bool**, §12.
incr: **octa** ( ), MMIX-ARITH §6.
l: **tetra**, §17.
loc: **octa**, §44.
max_sys_call = macro, §371.
mmix_fclose: **octa** ( ), MMIX-IO §11.
mmix_fgets: **octa** ( ), MMIX-IO §14.
mmix_fgetws: **octa** ( ), MMIX-IO §16.
mmix_fopen: **octa** ( ), MMIX-IO §8.
mmix_fputs: **octa** ( ), MMIX-IO §19.
mmix_fputws: **octa** ( ), MMIX-IO §20.
mmix_fread: **octa** ( ), MMIX-IO §12.
mmix_fseek: **octa** ( ), MMIX-IO §21.
mmix_ftell: **octa** ( ), MMIX-IO §22.
mmix_fwrite: **octa** ( ), MMIX-IO §18.
neg_one: **octa**, MMIX-ARITH §4.
o: **octa**, §40.
octa = **struct**, §17.
print_trip_warning: **void** ( ), MMIX-IO §23.
rBB = 7, §52.
rT = 13, §52.
rW = 24, §52.
rWW = 28, §52.
rXX = 29, §52.
true = 1, §11.

378. We need to cut through all the complications of buffers and caches in order to do magical I/O. The *magic_read* routine finds the current octabyte in a given physical address by looking at the write buffer, D-cache, S-cache, and memory until finding it.

```
⟨ Subroutines 14 ⟩ +≡
  octa magic_read(addr)
      octa addr;
  {
    register write_node *q;
    register cacheblock *p;
    for (q = write_tail; ; ) {
      if (q ≡ write_head) break;
      if (q ≡ wbuf_top) q = wbuf_bot; else q++;
      if ((q→addr.l & −8) ≡ (addr.l & −8) ∧ q→addr.h ≡ addr.h) return q→o;
    }
    if (Dcache) {
      p = cache_search(Dcache, addr);
      if (p) return p→data[(addr.l & (Dcache→bb − 1)) ≫ 3];
      if (((Dcache→outbuf.tag.l ⊕ addr.l) & −Dcache→bb) ≡ 0 ∧ Dcache→outbuf.tag.h ≡
            addr.h) return Dcache→outbuf.data[(addr.l & (Dcache→bb − 1)) ≫ 3];
      if (Scache) {
        p = cache_search(Scache, addr);
        if (p) return p→data[(addr.l & (Scache→bb − 1)) ≫ 3];
        if (((Scache→outbuf.tag.l ⊕ addr.l) & −Scache→bb) ≡ 0 ∧ Scache→outbuf.tag.h ≡
              addr.h) return Scache→outbuf.data[(addr.l & (Scache→bb − 1)) ≫ 3];
      }
    }
    return mem_read(addr);
  }
```

379. The *magic_write* routine changes the octabyte in a given physical address by changing it wherever it appears in a buffer or cache. Any "dirty" or "least recently used" status remains unchanged. (Yes, this *is* magic.)

```
⟨ Subroutines 14 ⟩ +≡
  void magic_write(addr, val)
      octa addr, val;
  {
    register write_node *q;
    register cacheblock *p;
    for (q = write_tail; ; ) {
      if (q ≡ write_head) break;
      if (q ≡ wbuf_top) q = wbuf_bot; else q++;
      if ((q→addr.l & −8) ≡ (addr.l & −8) ∧ q→addr.h ≡ addr.h) q→o = val;
    }
    if (Dcache) {
      p = cache_search(Dcache, addr);
      if (p) p→data[(addr.l & (Dcache→bb − 1)) ≫ 3] = val;
      if (((Dcache→inbuf.tag.l ⊕ addr.l) & −Dcache→bb) ≡ 0 ∧ Dcache→inbuf.tag.h ≡ addr.h)
        Dcache→inbuf.data[(addr.l & (Dcache→bb − 1)) ≫ 3] = val;
```

```
    if (((Dcache→outbuf.tag.l ⊕ addr.l) & −Dcache→bb) ≡ 0 ∧ Dcache→outbuf.tag.h ≡
          addr.h) Dcache→outbuf.data[(addr.l & (Dcache→bb − 1)) ≫ 3] = val;
    if (Scache) {
      p = cache_search(Scache, addr);
      if (p) p→data[(addr.l & (Scache→bb − 1)) ≫ 3] = val;
      if (((Scache→inbuf.tag.l⊕addr.l)&−Scache→bb) ≡ 0∧Scache→inbuf.tag.h ≡ addr.h)
        Scache→inbuf.data[(addr.l & (Scache→bb − 1)) ≫ 3] = val;
      if (((Scache→outbuf.tag.l ⊕ addr.l) & −Scache→bb) ≡ 0 ∧ Scache→outbuf.tag.h ≡
            addr.h) Scache→outbuf.data[(addr.l & (Scache→bb − 1)) ≫ 3] = val;
    }
  }
  mem_write(addr, val);
}
```

380. The conventions of our imaginary operating system require us to apply the trivial memory mapping in which segment i appears in a 2^{32}-byte page of physical addresses starting at $2^{32}i$.

⟨ Prepare memory arguments $ma = \mathrm{M}[a]$ and $mb = \mathrm{M}[b]$ if needed 380 ⟩ ≡

```
  if (arg_count[yy] ≡ 3) {
    octa arg_loc;

    arg_loc = g[rBB].o;
    if (arg_loc.h & #9fffffff) mb = zero_octa;
    else arg_loc.h ≫= 29, mb = magic_read(arg_loc);
    arg_loc = incr(g[rBB].o, 8);
    if (arg_loc.h & #9fffffff) ma = zero_octa;
    else arg_loc.h ≫= 29, ma = magic_read(arg_loc);
  }
```

This code is used in section 372.

addr: **octa**, §246.
arg_count: **char** [], §374.
bb: **int**, §167.
cache_search: **static cacheblock** ∗(), §193.
cacheblock = **struct**, §167.
data: **octa** ∗, §167.
Dcache: **cache** ∗, §168.
g: **specnode** [], §86.
h: **tetra**, §17.
inbuf: **cacheblock**, §167.
incr: **octa** ( ), MMIX-ARITH §6.
l: **tetra**, §17.
ma: **octa**, §372.
mb: **octa**, §372.
mem_read: **octa** ( ), §210.
mem_write: **void** ( ), §213.
o: **octa**, §246.
o: **octa**, §40.
octa = **struct**, §17.
outbuf: **cacheblock**, §167.
rBB = 7, §52.
Scache: **cache** ∗, §168.
tag: **octa**, §167.
wbuf_bot: **write_node** ∗, §247.
wbuf_top: **write_node** ∗, §247.
write_head: **write_node** ∗, §247.
write_node = **struct**, §246.
write_tail: **write_node** ∗, §247.
yy: **register unsigned char**, §372.
zero_octa: **octa**, MMIX-ARITH §4.

381. The subroutine *mmgetchars*(*buf*, *size*, *addr*, *stop*) reads characters starting at address *addr* in the simulated memory and stores them in *buf*, continuing until *size* characters have been read or some other stopping criterion has been met. If $stop < 0$ there is no other criterion; if $stop = 0$ a null character will also terminate the process; otherwise *addr* is even, and two consecutive null bytes starting at an even address will terminate the process. The number of bytes read and stored, exclusive of terminating nulls, is returned.

```
⟨Subroutines 14⟩ +≡
  int mmgetchars(buf, size, addr, stop)
      char *buf;
      int size;
      octa addr;
      int stop;
  {
    register char *p;
    register int m;
    octa a, x;
    if (((addr.h & #9fffffff) ∨ (incr(addr, size − 1).h & #9fffffff)) ∧ size) {
      fprintf(stderr, "Attempt␣to␣get␣characters␣from␣off␣the␣page!\n");
      return 0;
    }
    for (p = buf, m = 0, a = addr, a.h >>= 29; m < size; ) {
      x = magic_read(a);
      if ((a.l & #7) ∨ m > size − 8) ⟨Read and store one byte; return if done 382⟩
      else ⟨Read and store up to eight bytes; return if done 383⟩
    }
    return size;
  }
```

382. ⟨Read and store one byte; **return** if done 382⟩ ≡

```
  {
    if (a.l & #4) *p = (x.l >> (8 * ((~a.l) & #3))) & #ff;
    else *p = (x.h >> (8 * ((~a.l) & #3))) & #ff;
    if (¬*p ∧ stop ≥ 0) {
      if (stop ≡ 0) return m;
      if ((a.l & #1) ∧ *(p − 1) ≡ '\0') return m − 1;
    }
    p++, m++, a = incr(a, 1);
  }
```

This code is used in section 381.

383. ⟨Read and store up to eight bytes; **return** if done 383⟩ ≡

```
  {
    *p = x.h >> 24;
    if (¬*p ∧ (stop ≡ 0 ∨ (stop > 0 ∧ x.h < #10000))) return m;
    *(p + 1) = (x.h >> 16) & #ff;
    if (¬*(p + 1) ∧ stop ≡ 0) return m + 1;
    *(p + 2) = (x.h >> 8) & #ff;
    if (¬*(p + 2) ∧ (stop ≡ 0 ∨ (stop > 0 ∧ (x.h & #ffff) ≡ 0))) return m + 2;
```

```
    *(p + 3) = x.h & #ff;
    if (¬*(p + 3) ∧ stop ≡ 0) return m + 3;
    *(p + 4) = x.l ≫ 24;
    if (¬*(p + 4) ∧ (stop ≡ 0 ∨ (stop > 0 ∧ x.l < #10000))) return m + 4;
    *(p + 5) = (x.l ≫ 16) & #ff;
    if (¬*(p + 5) ∧ stop ≡ 0) return m + 5;
    *(p + 6) = (x.l ≫ 8) & #ff;
    if (¬*(p + 6) ∧ (stop ≡ 0 ∨ (stop > 0 ∧ (x.l & #ffff) ≡ 0))) return m + 6;
    *(p + 7) = x.l & #ff;
    if (¬*(p + 7) ∧ stop ≡ 0) return m + 7;
    p += 8, m += 8, a = incr(a, 8);
  }
```

This code is used in section 381.

384. The subroutine *mmputchars*(*buf*, *size*, *addr*) puts *size* characters into the simulated memory starting at address *addr*.

```
⟨ Subroutines 14 ⟩ +≡
  void mmputchars(buf, size, addr)
      unsigned char *buf;
      int size;
      octa addr;
  {
    register unsigned char *p;
    register int m;
    octa a, x;
    if (((addr.h & #9fffffff) ∨ (incr(addr, size − 1).h & #9fffffff)) ∧ size) {
      fprintf(stderr, "Attempt␣to␣put␣characters␣off␣the␣page!\n");
      return;
    }
    for (p = buf, m = 0, a = addr, a.h ≫= 29; m < size; ) {
      if ((a.l & #7) ∨ m > size − 8) ⟨ Load and write one byte 385 ⟩
      else ⟨ Load and write eight bytes 386 ⟩;
    }
  }
```

385. ⟨ Load and write one byte 385 ⟩ ≡

```
  {
    register int s = 8 * ((∼a.l) & #3);
    x = magic_read(a);
    if (a.l & #4) x.l ⊕= (((x.l ≫ s) ⊕ *p) & #ff) ≪ s;
    else x.h ⊕= (((x.h ≫ s) ⊕ *p) & #ff) ≪ s;
    magic_write(a, x);
    p++, m++, a = incr(a, 1);
  }
```

This code is used in section 384.

---

fprintf: **int** (), <stdio.h>.
h: **tetra**, §17.
incr: **octa** (), MMIX-ARITH §6.
l: **tetra**, §17.
magic_read: **octa** (), §378.
magic_write: **void** (), §379.
octa = **struct**, §17.
stderr: **FILE** *, <stdio.h>.

386. ⟨ Load and write eight bytes 386 ⟩ ≡

```
{
  x.h = (*p ≪ 24) + (*(p + 1) ≪ 16) + (*(p + 2) ≪ 8) + *(p + 3);
  x.l = (*(p + 4) ≪ 24) + (*(p + 5) ≪ 16) + (*(p + 6) ≪ 8) + *(p + 7);
  magic_write(a, x);
  p += 8, m += 8, a = incr(a, 8);
}
```

This code is used in section 384.

387. When standard input is being read by the simulated program at the same time as it is being used for interaction, we try to keep the two uses separate by maintaining a private buffer for the simulated program's `StdIn`. Online input is usually transmitted from the keyboard to a C program a line at a time; therefore an *fgets* operation works much better than *fread* when we prompt for new input. But there is a slight complication, because *fgets* might read a null character before coming to a newline character. We cannot deduce the number of characters read by *fgets* simply by looking at *strlen*(*stdin_buf*).

⟨ Subroutines 14 ⟩ +≡

```
char stdin_chr()
{
  register char *p;
  while (stdin_buf_start ≡ stdin_buf_end) {
    printf("StdIn>␣"); fflush(stdout);
    fgets(stdin_buf, 256, stdin);
    stdin_buf_start = stdin_buf;
    for (p = stdin_buf; p < stdin_buf + 254; p++)
      if (*p ≡ '\n') break;
    stdin_buf_end = p + 1;
  }
  return *stdin_buf_start++;
}
```

388. ⟨ Global variables 20 ⟩ +≡

```
char stdin_buf[256];      /* standard input to the simulated program */
char *stdin_buf_start;     /* current position in that buffer */
char *stdin_buf_end;      /* current end of that buffer */
```

389. Names of the sections.

⟨ Allocate a slot *p* in the S-cache 218 ⟩ Used in section 217.
⟨ Assign a functional unit if available, otherwise **goto** *stall* 82 ⟩ Used in section 75.
⟨ Begin an interruption and **break** 317 ⟩ Used in section 146.
⟨ Begin execution of a stage-two operation 351 ⟩ Used in section 135.
⟨ Begin execution of an operation 132 ⟩ Used in section 130.
⟨ Begin fetch with known physical address 296 ⟩ Used in section 288.
⟨ Begin fetch without I-cache lookup 295 ⟩ Used in section 291.
⟨ Cases 0 through 4, for the D-cache 233 ⟩ Used in section 232.
⟨ Cases 5 through 9, for the S-cache 234 ⟩ Used in section 232.
⟨ Cases for control of special coroutines 126, 215, 217, 222, 224, 232, 237, 257 ⟩ Used in section 125.
⟨ Cases for stage 1 execution 155, 313, 325, 327, 328, 329, 331, 356 ⟩ Used in section 132.
⟨ Cases to compute the results of register-to-register operation 137, 138, 139, 140, 141, 142, 143, 343, 344, 345, 346, 348, 350 ⟩ Used in section 132.
⟨ Cases to compute the virtual address of a memory operation 265 ⟩ Used in section 132.
⟨ Check for a hit in pending writes 278 ⟩ Used in section 273.
⟨ Check for external interrupt 314 ⟩ Used in section 64.
⟨ Check for *prest* with a fully spanned cache block 275 ⟩ Used in section 274.
⟨ Check for security violation, **break** if so 149 ⟩ Used in section 67.
⟨ Check for sufficient rename registers and memory slots, or **goto** *stall* 111 ⟩ Used in section 75.
⟨ Check the protection bits and get the physical address 269 ⟩ Used in sections 268, 270, and 272.
⟨ Clean the D-cache block for *data→z.o*, if any 366 ⟩ Used in section 364.
⟨ Clean the data caches 361 ⟩ Used in section 356.
⟨ Clean the I-cache block for *data→z.o*, if any 365 ⟩ Used in section 364.
⟨ Clean the S-cache block for *data→z.o*, if any 367 ⟩ Used in section 364.
⟨ Commit and/or deissue up to *commit_max* instructions 67 ⟩ Used in section 64.
⟨ Commit the hottest instruction, or **break** if it's not ready 146 ⟩ Used in section 67.
⟨ Commit to memory if possible, otherwise **break** 256 ⟩ Used in section 146.
⟨ Compute the new entry for *c→inbuf* and give the caller a sneak preview 245 ⟩ Used in section 237.
⟨ Continue this command on the next cache block 369 ⟩ Used in section 364.
⟨ Convert relative address to absolute address 84 ⟩ Used in section 75.
⟨ Copy data from *p* into *c→inbuf* 226 ⟩ Used in section 224.
⟨ Copy *Scache→inbuf* to slot *p* 220 ⟩ Used in section 217.
⟨ Copy the data from block *q* to *fetched* 294 ⟩ Used in sections 292 and 296.

---

a: **octa**, §384.
fflush: **int** ( ), `<stdio.h>`.
fgets: **char** ∗( ), `<stdio.h>`.
fread: **size_t** ( ), `<stdio.h>`.
h: **tetra**, §17.
incr: **octa** ( ), MMIX-ARITH §6.
l: **tetra**, §17.
m: **register int**, §384.
magic_write: **void** ( ), §379.
p: **register unsigned char** ∗, §384.
printf: **int** ( ), `<stdio.h>`.
stdin: **FILE** ∗, `<stdio.h>`.
stdout: **FILE** ∗, `<stdio.h>`.
strlen: **size_t** ( ), `<string.h>`.
x: **octa**, §384.

⟨ Declare **mmix_opcode** and **internal_opcode** 47, 49 ⟩ Used in section 44.
⟨ Deissue all but the hottest command 316 ⟩ Used in section 314.
⟨ Deissue the coolest instruction 145 ⟩ Used in section 67.
⟨ Determine the flags, f, and the internal opcode, i 80 ⟩ Used in section 75.
⟨ Dispatch an instruction to the *cool* block if possible, otherwise **goto** *stall* 101 ⟩ Used in section 75.
⟨ Dispatch one cycle's worth of instructions 74 ⟩ Used in section 64.
⟨ Do a simultaneous lookup in the D-cache 268 ⟩ Used in section 267.
⟨ Do a simultaneous lookup in the I-cache 292 ⟩ Used in section 291.
⟨ Do load/store stage 1 without D-cache lookup 270 ⟩ Used in section 267.
⟨ Do load/store stage 1 with known physical address 271 ⟩ Used in section 266.
⟨ Do load/store stage 2 without D-cache lookup 277 ⟩ Used in section 273.
⟨ Do stage 1 of `LDVTS` 353 ⟩ Used in section 352.
⟨ Do the final `SAVE` 340 ⟩ Used in section 339.
⟨ Either halt or print warning 373 ⟩ Used in section 372.
⟨ Execute all coroutines scheduled for the current time 125 ⟩ Used in section 64.
⟨ External prototypes 9, 38, 161, 175, 178, 180, 209, 212, 252 ⟩ Used in sections 3 and 5.
⟨ External routines 10, 39, 162, 176, 179, 181, 210, 213, 253 ⟩ Used in section 3.
⟨ External variables 4, 29, 59, 60, 66, 69, 77, 86, 87, 98, 115, 136, 150, 168, 207, 211, 214, 242, 247, 284, 349 ⟩ Used in sections 3 and 5.
⟨ Fill *Scache→inbuf* with clean memory data 219 ⟩ Used in section 217.
⟨ Finish a `CSWAP` 283 ⟩ Used in section 281.
⟨ Finish a store command 281 ⟩ Used in section 280.
⟨ Finish execution of an operation 144 ⟩ Used in section 130.
⟨ Forward the new data past the D-cache if it is write-through 263 ⟩ Used in section 257.
⟨ Generate an instruction to save $g[yy]$ 339 ⟩ Used in section 337.
⟨ Generate an instruction to unsave $g[yy]$ 333 ⟩ Used in section 332.
⟨ Get ready for the next step of `PREGO` 229 ⟩ Used in section 81.
⟨ Get ready for the next step of `PRELD` or `PREST` 228 ⟩ Used in section 81.
⟨ Get ready for the next step of `SAVE` 341 ⟩ Used in section 81.
⟨ Get ready for the next step of `UNSAVE` 335 ⟩ Used in section 81.
⟨ Global variables 20, 36, 41, 48, 50, 51, 53, 54, 65, 70, 78, 83, 88, 99, 107, 127, 148, 154, 194, 230, 235, 238, 248, 285, 303, 305, 315, 374, 376, 388 ⟩ Used in section 3.
⟨ Handle an internal `SAVE` when it's time to store 342 ⟩ Used in section 281.
⟨ Handle an internal `UNSAVE` when it's time to load 336 ⟩ Used in section 279.
⟨ Handle interrupt at end of execution stage 307 ⟩ Used in section 144.
⟨ Handle special cases for operations like *prego* and *ldvts* 289, 352 ⟩ Used in section 266.
⟨ Handle write-around when flushing to the S-cache 221 ⟩ Used in section 217.
⟨ Handle write-around when writing to the D-cache 259 ⟩ Used in section 257.
⟨ Header definitions 6, 7, 8, 52, 57, 129, 166 ⟩ Used in sections 3 and 5.
⟨ Ignore the item in *write_head* 264 ⟩ Used in section 257.
⟨ Initialize everything 22, 26, 61, 71, 79, 89, 116, 128, 153, 231, 236, 249, 286 ⟩ Used in section 10.
⟨ Insert an instruction to advance beta and L 112 ⟩ Used in section 110.

⟨ Insert an instruction to advance gamma 113 ⟩ Used in sections 110, 119, and 337.
⟨ Insert an instruction to decrease gamma 114 ⟩ Used in section 120.
⟨ Insert *data→b.o* into the proper field of *data→x.o*, checking for arithmetic exceptions if signed 282 ⟩ Used in section 281.
⟨ Insert dummy instruction for page table emulation 302 ⟩ Used in section 298.
⟨ Insert special operands when resuming an interrupted operation 324 ⟩ Used in section 103.
⟨ Install a new instruction into the *tail* position 304 ⟩ Used in section 301.
⟨ Install default fields in the *cool* block 100 ⟩ Used in section 75.
⟨ Install register X as the destination, or insert an internal command and **goto** *dispatch_done* if X is marginal 110 ⟩ Used in section 101.
⟨ Install the operand fields of the *cool* block 103 ⟩ Used in section 101.
⟨ Internal prototypes 13, 18, 24, 27, 30, 32, 34, 42, 45, 55, 62, 72, 90, 92, 94, 96, 156, 158, 169, 171, 173, 182, 184, 186, 188, 190, 192, 195, 198, 200, 202, 204, 240, 250, 254, 377 ⟩ Used in section 3.
⟨ Issue j pseudo-instructions to compute a page table entry 244 ⟩ Used in section 243.
⟨ Issue the *cool* instruction 81 ⟩ Used in section 75.
⟨ Load and write eight bytes 386 ⟩ Used in section 384.
⟨ Load and write one byte 385 ⟩ Used in section 384.
⟨ Local variables 12, 124, 258 ⟩ Used in section 10.
⟨ Look at the *head* instruction, and try to dispatch it if $j < dispatch\_max$ 75 ⟩ Used in section 74.
⟨ Look up the address in the DT-cache, and also in the D-cache if possible 267 ⟩ Used in section 266.
⟨ Look up the address in the IT-cache, and also in the I-cache if possible 291 ⟩ Used in section 288.
⟨ Magically do an I/O operation, if *cool→loc* is rT 372 ⟩ Used in section 322.
⟨ Make sure *cool_L* and *cool_G* are up to date 102 ⟩ Used in section 101.
⟨ Nullify the hottest instruction 147 ⟩ Used in section 146.
⟨ Other cases for the fetch coroutine 298, 301 ⟩ Used in section 288.
⟨ Pass *data* to the next stage of the pipeline 134 ⟩ Used in section 130.
⟨ Perform one cycle of the interrupt preparations 318 ⟩ Used in section 64.
⟨ Perform one machine cycle 64 ⟩ Used in section 10.
⟨ Predict a branch outcome 151 ⟩ Used in section 85.
⟨ Prepare for exceptional trip handler 308 ⟩ Used in section 307.
⟨ Prepare memory arguments $ma = M[a]$ and $mb = M[b]$ if needed 380 ⟩ Used in section 372.
⟨ Prepare to emulate the page translation 309 ⟩ Used in section 310.
⟨ Print all of c's cache blocks 177 ⟩ Used in section 176.
⟨ Read and store one byte; **return** if done 382 ⟩ Used in section 381.
⟨ Read and store up to eight bytes; **return** if done 383 ⟩ Used in section 381.
⟨ Read data into *c→inbuf* and wait for the bus 223 ⟩ Used in section 222.
⟨ Read from memory into *fetched* 297 ⟩ Used in section 296.
⟨ Record the result of branch prediction 152 ⟩ Used in section 75.
⟨ Recover from incorrect branch prediction 160 ⟩ Used in section 155.
⟨ Redirect the fetch if control changes at this inst 85 ⟩ Used in section 75.
⟨ Restart the fetch coroutine 287 ⟩ Used in sections 85, 160, 308, 309, and 316.
⟨ Resume an interrupted operation 323 ⟩ Used in section 322.

MMIX-SIM

1. Introduction. This program simulates a simplified version of the MMIX computer. Its main goal is to help people create and test MMIX programs for *The Art of Computer Programming* and related publications. It provides only a rudimentary terminal-oriented interface, but it has enough infrastructure to support a cool graphical user interface — which could be added by a motivated reader. (Hint, hint.)

MMIX is simplified in the following ways:

- There is no pipeline, and there are no caches. Thus, commands like SYNC and SYNCD and PREGO do nothing.
- Simulation applies only to user programs, not to an operating system kernel. Thus, all addresses must be nonnegative; "privileged" commands such as PUT rK,z or RESUME 1 or LDVTS x,y,z are not allowed; instructions should be executed only from addresses in segment 0 (addresses less than #2000000000000000). Certain special registers remain constant: rF = 0, rK = #ffffffffffffffff, rQ = 0; rT = #8000000500000000, rTT = #8000000600000000, rV = #369c200400000000.
- No trap interrupts are implemented, except for a few special cases of TRAP that provide rudimentary input-output.
- All instructions take a fixed amount of time, given by the rough estimates stated in the MMIX documentation. For example, MUL takes 10υ, LDB takes $\mu+\upsilon$; all times are expressed in terms of μ and υ, "mems" and "oops." The simulated clock increases by 2^{32} for each μ and 1 for each υ. But the interval counter rI decreases by 1 for each υ; and the usage count field of rU may increase by 1 (modulo 2^{47}) for each instruction.

2. To run this simulator, assuming UNIX conventions, you say '**mmix** ⟨options⟩ **progfile args...**', where **progfile** is an output of the MMIXAL assembler, **args...** is a sequence of optional command line arguments passed to the simulated program, and ⟨options⟩ is any subset of the following:

- **-t<n>** Trace each instruction the first n times it is executed. (The notation **<n>** in this option, and in several other options and interactive commands below, stands for a decimal integer.)
- **-e<x>** Trace each instruction that raises an arithmetic exception belonging to the given bit pattern. (The notation **<x>** in this option, and in several other commands below, stands for a hexadecimal integer.) The exception bits are DVWIOUZX as they appear in rA, namely #80 for D (integer divide check), #40 for V (integer overflow), ..., #01 for X (floating inexact). The option **-e** by itself is equivalent to **-eff**, tracing all eight exceptions.
- **-r** Trace details of the register stack. This option shows all the "hidden" loads and stores that occur when octabytes are written from the ring of local registers into memory, or read from memory into that ring. It also shows the full details of SAVE and UNSAVE operations.
- **-l<n>** List the source line corresponding to each traced instruction, filling gaps of length n or less. For example, if one instruction came from line 10 of the source

D.E. Knuth: MMIXware, LNCS 1750, pp. 332–421, 2014.
DOI: 10.1007/3-540-46611-8_8

file and the next instruction to be traced came from line 12, line 11 would be shown also, provided that $n \geq 1$. If `<n>` is omitted it is assumed to be 3.

- `-s` Show statistics of running time with each traced instruction.
- `-P` Show the program profile (that is, the frequency counts of each instruction that was executed) when the simulation ends.
- `-L<n>` List the source lines corresponding to each instruction that appears in the program profile, filling gaps of length n or less. This option implies `-P`. If `<n>` is omitted it is assumed to be 3.
- `-v` Be verbose: Turn on all options. (More precisely, the `-v` option is shorthand for `-t9999999999 -e -r -s -l10 -L10`.)
- `-q` Be quiet: Cancel all previously specified options.
- `-i` Go into interactive mode before starting the simulation.
- `-I` Go into interactive mode when the simulated program halts or pauses for a breakpoint.
- `-b<n>` Set the buffer size of source lines to $\max(72, n)$.
- `-c<n>` Set the capacity of the local register ring to $\max(256, n)$; this number must be a power of 2.
- `-f<filename>` Use the named file for standard input to the simulated program. This option should be used whenever the simulator is not being used interactively, because the simulator will not recognize end of file when standard input has been defined in any other way.
- `-D<filename>` Prepare the named file for use by other simulators, instead of actually doing a simulation.
- `-?` Print the "`Usage`" message, which summarizes the command line options.

The author recommends `-t2 -l -L` for initial offline debugging.

While the program is being simulated, an *interrupt* signal (usually control-C) will cause the simulator to break and go into interactive mode after tracing the current instruction, even if `-i` and `-I` were not specified on the command line.

---

running times, MMIX §50.

3. In interactive mode, the user is prompted 'mmix>' and a variety of commands can be typed online. Any command line option can be given in response to such a prompt (including the '-' that begins the option), and the following operations are also available:

• Simply typing ⟨return⟩ or n⟨return⟩ to the mmix> prompt causes one MMIX instruction to be executed and traced; then the user is prompted again.

• c continues simulation until the program halts or reaches a breakpoint. (Actually the command is 'c⟨return⟩', but we won't bother to mention the ⟨return⟩ in the following description.)

• q quits (terminates the simulation), after printing the profile (if it was requested) and the final statistics.

• s prints out the current statistics (the clock times and the current instruction location). We have already discussed the -s option on the command line, which causes these statistics to be printed automatically; but a lot of statistics can fill up a lot of file space, so users may prefer to see the statistics only on demand.

• l<n><t>, g<n><t>, $<n><t>, rA<t>, rB<t>, ..., rZZ<t>, and M<x><t> will show the current value of a local register, global register, dynamically numbered register, special register, or memory location. Here <t> specifies the type of value to be displayed; if <t> is '!', the value will be given in decimal notation; if <t> is '.' it will be given in floating point notation; if <t> is '#' it will be given in hexadecimal, and if <t> is '"' it will be given as a string of eight one-byte characters. Just typing <t> by itself will repeat the most recently shown value, perhaps in another format; for example, the command 'l10#' will show local register 10 in hexadecimal notation, then the command '!' will show it in decimal and '.' will show it as a floating point number. If <t> is empty, the previous type will be repeated; the default type is decimal. Register rA is equivalent to g22, according to the numbering used in GET and PUT commands.

The '<t>' in any of these commands can also have the form '=<value>', where the value is a decimal or floating point or hexadecimal or string constant. (The syntax rules for floating point constants appear in MMIX-ARITH. A string constant is treated as in the BYTE command of MMIXAL, but padded at the left with zeros if fewer than eight characters are specified.) This assigns a new value before displaying it. For example, 'l10=.1e3' sets local register 10 equal to 100; 'g250="ABCD",#a' sets global register 250 equal to #000000414243440a; 'M1000=-Inf' sets M_8[#1000] = #fff0000000000000, the representation of $-\infty$. Special registers other than rI cannot be set to values disallowed by PUT. Marginal registers cannot be set to nonzero values.

The command 'rI=250' sets the interval counter to 250; this will cause a break in simulation after 250υ have elapsed.

• +<n><t> shows the next n octabytes following the one most recently shown, in format <t>. For example, after 'l10#' a subsequent '+30' will show l11, l12, ..., l40 in hexadecimal notation. After 'g200=3' a subsequent '+30' will set g201, g202, ..., g230 equal to 3, but a subsequent '+30!' would merely display g201 through g230 in decimal notation. Memory addresses will advance by 8 instead of by 1. If <n> is empty, the default value $n = 1$ is used.

• @<x> sets the address of the next tetrabyte to be simulated, sort of like a GO command.

• t<x> says that the instruction in tetrabyte location x should always be traced, regardless of its frequency count.

• u<x> undoes the effect of t<x>.

• b[rwx]<x> sets breakpoints at tetrabyte x; here [rwx] stands for any subset of the letters r, w, and/or x, meaning to break when the tetrabyte is read, written, and/or executed. For example, 'bx1000' causes a break in the simulation just after the tetrabyte in #1000 is executed; 'b1000' undoes this breakpoint; 'brwx1000' causes a break just after any simulated instruction loads, stores, or appears in tetrabyte number #1000.

• T, D, P, S changes the "current segment" to either Text_Segment, Data_Segment, Pool_Segment, or Stack_Segment, respectively, namely to #0, #2000000000000000, #4000000000000000, or #6000000000000000. The current segment, initially #0, is added to all memory addresses in M, @, t, u, and b commands.

• B lists all current breakpoints and tracepoints.

• i<filename> reads a sequence of interactive commands from the specified file, one command per line, ignoring blank lines. This feature can be used to set many breakpoints or to display a number of key registers, etc. Included lines that begin with % or i are ignored; therefore an included file cannot include *another* file. Included lines that begin with a blank space are reproduced in the standard output, otherwise ignored.

• h (help) reminds the user of the available interactive commands.

4. Rudimentary I/O. Input and output are provided by the following ten primitive system calls:

• `Fopen`(*handle*, *name*, *mode*). Here *handle* is a one-byte integer, *name* is the address of the first byte of a string, and *mode* is one of the values `TextRead`, `TextWrite`, `BinaryRead`, `BinaryWrite`, `BinaryReadWrite`. An `Fopen` call associates *handle* with the external file called *name* and prepares to do input and/or output on that file. It returns 0 if the file was opened successfully; otherwise returns the value −1. If *mode* is `TextWrite`, `BinaryWrite`, or `BinaryReadWrite`, any previous contents of the named file are discarded. If *mode* is `TextRead` or `TextWrite`, the file consists of "lines" terminated by "newline" characters, and it is said to be a text file; otherwise the file consists of uninterpreted bytes, and it is said to be a binary file.

Text files and binary files are essentially equivalent in cases where this simulator is hosted by an operating system derived from UNIX; in such cases files can be written as text and read as binary or vice versa. But with other operating systems, text files and binary files often have quite different representations, and certain characters with byte codes less than `'␣'` are forbidden in text. Within any `MMIX` program, the newline character has byte code `#0a` = 10.

At the beginning of a program three handles have already been opened: The "standard input" file `StdIn` (handle 0) has mode `TextRead`, the "standard output" file `StdOut` (handle 1) has mode `TextWrite`, and the "standard error" file `StdErr` (handle 2) also has mode `TextWrite`. When this simulator is being run interactively, lines of standard input should be typed following a prompt that says '`StdIn>␣`', unless the `-f` option has been used. The standard output and standard error files of the simulated program are intermixed with the output of the simulator itself.

The input/output operations supported by this simulator can perhaps be understood most easily with reference to the standard library `stdio` that comes with the C language, because the conventions of C have been explained in hundreds of books. If we declare an array **FILE** $*file[256]$ and set $file[0] = stdin$, $file[1] = stdout$, and $file[2] = stderr$, then the simulated system call `Fopen`(*handle*, *name*, *mode*) is essentially equivalent to the C expression

$$(file[handle]?\ (file[handle] = freopen(name, mode\_string[mode], file[handle])):\ (file[handle] = fopen(name, mode\_string[mode])))?\ 0{:}\ -1,$$

if we predefine the values $mode\_string$[`TextRead`] = `"r"`, $mode\_string$[`TextWrite`] = `"w"`, $mode\_string$[`BinaryRead`] = `"rb"`, $mode\_string$[`BinaryWrite`] = `"wb"`, and $mode\_string$[`BinaryReadWrite`] = `"wb+"`.

• `Fclose`(*handle*). If the given file handle has been opened, it is closed—no longer associated with any file. Again the result is 0 if successful, or −1 if the file was already closed or unclosable. The C equivalent is

$$fclose(file[handle])\ ?\ -1 : 0$$

with the additional side effect of setting $file[handle] = \Lambda$.

• `Fread`(*handle*, *buffer*, *size*). The file handle should have been opened with mode `TextRead`, `BinaryRead`, or `BinaryReadWrite`. The next *size* characters are read into `MMIX`'s memory starting at address *buffer*. If an error occurs, the value $-1 - size$ is returned; otherwise, if the end of file does not intervene, 0 is returned; otherwise the negative value $n - size$ is returned, where n is the number of characters successfully read and stored. The statement

$$fread(buffer, 1, size, file[handle]) - size$$

has the equivalent effect in C, in the absence of file errors.

• `Fgets`(*handle*, *buffer*, *size*). The file handle should have been opened with mode `TextRead`, `BinaryRead`, or `BinaryReadWrite`. Characters are read into `MMIX`'s memory starting at address *buffer*, until either $size - 1$ characters have been read and stored or a newline character has been read and stored; the next byte in memory is then set to zero. If an error or end of file occurs before reading is complete, the memory contents are undefined and the value -1 is returned; otherwise the number of characters successfully read and stored is returned. The equivalent in C is

$$fgets(buffer, size, file[handle])\ ?\ strlen(buffer) : -1$$

if we assume that no null characters were read in; null characters may, however, precede a newline, and they are counted just like other characters.

• `Fgetws`(*handle*, *buffer*, *size*). This command is the same as `Fgets`, except that it applies to wyde characters instead of one-byte characters. Up to $size - 1$ wyde characters are read; a wyde newline is `#000a`. The C version, using conventions of the ISO multibyte string extension (MSE), is approximately

$$fgetws(buffer, size, file[handle])\ ?\ wcslen(buffer) : -1$$

where *buffer* now has type **wchar_t** $*$.

• `Fwrite`(*handle*, *buffer*, *size*). The file handle should have been opened with one of the modes `TextWrite`, `BinaryWrite`, or `BinaryReadWrite`. The next *size* characters are written from `MMIX`'s memory starting at address *buffer*. If no error occurs, 0 is returned; otherwise the negative value $n - size$ is returned, where n is the number of characters successfully written. The statement

$$fwrite(buffer, 1, size, file[handle]) - size$$

together with *fflush*(*file*[*handle*]) has the equivalent effect in C.

• `Fputs`(*handle*, *string*). The file handle should have been opened with one of the modes `TextWrite`, `BinaryWrite`, or `BinaryReadWrite`. One-byte characters are written from `MMIX`'s memory to the file, starting at address *string*, up to but not including the first byte equal to zero. The number of bytes written is returned, or -1 on error. The C version is

$$fputs(string, file[handle]) \geq 0\ ?\ strlen(string) : -1,$$

together with *fflush*(*file*[*handle*]).

• `Fputws`(*handle*, *string*). The file handle should have been opened with one of the modes `TextWrite`, `BinaryWrite`, or `BinaryReadWrite`. Wyde characters are written from `MMIX`'s memory to the file, starting at address *string*, up to but not including the first wyde equal to zero. The number of wydes written is returned, or -1 on error. The C+MSE version is

$$fputws(string, file[handle]) \ge 0 \; ? \; wcslen(string) : -1$$

together with *fflush*(*file*[*handle*]), where *string* now has type **wchar_t** ∗.

• `Fseek`(*handle*, *offset*). The file handle should have been opened with one of the modes `BinaryRead`, `BinaryWrite`, or `BinaryReadWrite`. This operation causes the next input or output operation to begin at *offset* bytes from the beginning of the file, if $offset \ge 0$, or at $-offset - 1$ bytes before the end of the file, if $offset < 0$. (For example, $offset = 0$ "rewinds" the file to its very beginning; $offset = -1$ moves forward all the way to the end.) The result is 0 if successful, or -1 if the stated positioning could not be done. The C version is

$$fseek(file[handle],\; offset < 0 \; ? \; offset + 1 : offset\;, \\ offset < 0 \; ? \; \texttt{SEEK\_END} : \texttt{SEEK\_SET}) ? \; -1 : 0.$$

If a file in mode `BinaryReadWrite` is used for both reading and writing, an `Fseek` command must be given when switching from input to output or from output to input.

• `Ftell`(*handle*). The file handle should have been opened with mode `BinaryRead`, `BinaryWrite`, or `BinaryReadWrite`. This operation returns the current file position, measured in bytes from the beginning, or -1 if an error has occurred. In this case the C function

$$ftell(file[handle])$$

has exactly the same meaning.

Although these ten operations are quite primitive, they provide the necessary functionality for extremely complex input/output behavior. For example, every function in the `stdio` library of C, with the exception of the two administrative operations *remove* and *rename*, can be implemented as a subroutine in terms of the six basic operations `Fopen`, `Fclose`, `Fread`, `Fwrite`, `Fseek`, and `Ftell`.

Notice that the `MMIX` function calls are much more consistent than those in the C library. The first argument is always a handle; the second, if present, is always an address; the third, if present, is always a size. *The result returned is always nonnegative if the operation was successful, negative if an anomaly arose.* These common features make the functions reasonably easy to remember.

5. The ten input/output operations of the previous section are invoked by `TRAP` commands with X = 0, Y = `Fopen` or `Fclose` or ... or `Ftell`, and Z = `Handle`. If there are two arguments, the second argument is placed in \$255. If there are three arguments, the address of the second is placed in \$255; the second argument is $M_8[\$255]$ and the third argument is $M_8[\$255 + 8]$. The returned value will be in \$255 when the system call is finished. (See the example below.)

6. The user program starts at symbolic location `Main`. At this time the global registers are initialized according to the `GREG` statements in the `MMIXAL` program, and \$255 is set to the numeric equivalent of `Main`. Local register \$0 is initially set to the number of *command line arguments*; and local register \$1 points to the first such argument, which is always a pointer to the program name. Each command line argument is a pointer to a string; the last such pointer is $M_8[\$0 \ll 3+\$1]$, and $M_8[\$0 \ll 3+\$1+8]$ is zero. (Register \$1 will point to an octabyte in `Pool_Segment`, and the command line strings will be in that segment too.) Location M[`Pool_Segment`] will be the address of the first unused octabyte of the pool segment.

Registers rA, rB, rD, rE, rF, rH, rI, rJ, rM, rP, rQ, and rR are initially zero, and rL = 2.

A subroutine library loaded with the user program might need to initialize itself. If an instruction has been loaded into tetrabyte M_4[#`f0`], the simulator actually begins execution at #`f0` instead of at `Main`; in this case \$255 holds the location of `Main`. (The routine at #`f0` can pass control to `Main` without increasing rL, if it starts with the slightly tricky sequence

```
PUT rW, $255;  PUT rB, $255;  SETML $255,#F700;  PUT rX,$255
```

and eventually says `RESUME`; this `RESUME` command will restore \$255 and rB. But the user program should *not* really count on the fact that rL is initially 2.)

7. The main program ends when `MMIX` executes the system call `TRAP 0`, which is often symbolically written '`TRAP 0,Halt,0`' to make its intention clear. The contents of \$255 at that time are considered to be the value "returned" by the main program, as in the *exit* statement of C; a nonzero value indicates an anomalous exit. All open files are closed when the program ends.

---

exit: **void** ( ), `<stdlib.h>`.

8. Here, for example, is a complete program that copies a text file to the standard output, given the name of the file to be copied. It includes all necessary error checking.

```
* SAMPLE PROGRAM: COPY A GIVEN FILE TO STANDARD OUTPUT
t        IS   $255
argc     IS   $0
argv     IS   $1
s        IS   $2
Buf_Size IS   1000
         LOC  Data_Segment
Buffer   LOC  @+Buf_Size
         GREG @
Arg0     OCTA 0,TextRead
Arg1     OCTA Buffer,Buf_Size
         LOC  #200                   main(argc,argv) {
Main     CMP  t,argc,2               if (argc==2) goto openit
         PBZ  t,OpenIt
         GETA t,1F                   fputs("Usage: ",stderr)
         TRAP 0,Fputs,StdErr
         LDOU t,argv,0               fputs(argv[0],stderr)
         TRAP 0,Fputs,StdErr
         GETA t,2F                   fputs(" filename\n",stderr)
Quit     TRAP 0,Fputs,StdErr
         NEG  t,0,1                  quit: exit(-1)
         TRAP 0,Halt,0
1H       BYTE "Usage: ",0
         LOC  (@+3)&-4               align to tetrabyte
2H       BYTE " filename",#a,0

OpenIt   LDOU s,argv,8               openit: s=argv[1]
         STOU s,Arg0
         LDA  t,Arg0                 fopen(argv[1],"r",file[3])
         TRAP 0,Fopen,3
         PBNN t,CopyIt               if (no error) goto copyit
         GETA t,1F                   fputs("Can't open file ",stderr)
         TRAP 0,Fputs,StdErr
         SET  t,s                    fputs(argv[1],stderr)
         TRAP 0,Fputs,StdErr
         GETA t,2F                   fputs("!\n",stderr)
         JMP  Quit                   goto quit
1H       BYTE "Can't open file ",0
         LOC  (@+3)&-4               align to tetrabyte
2H       BYTE "!",#a,0

CopyIt   LDA  t,Arg1                 copyit:
         TRAP 0,Fread,3              items=fread(buffer,1,buf_size,file[3])
```

```
        BN   t,EndIt            if (items < buf_size) goto endit
        LDA  t,Arg1             items=fwrite(buffer,1,buf_size,stdout)
        TRAP 0,Fwrite,StdOut
        PBNN t,CopyIt           if (items >= buf_size) goto copyit
Trouble GETA t,1F               trouble: fputs("Trouble w...!",stderr)
        JMP  Quit               goto quit
1H      BYTE "Trouble writing StdOut!",#a,0
EndIt   INCL t,Buf_Size
        BN   t,ReadErr          if (ferror(file[3])) goto readerr
        STO  t,Arg1+8
        LDA  t,Arg1             n=fwrite(buffer,1,items,stdout)
        TRAP 0,Fwrite,StdOut
        BN   t,Trouble          if (n < items) goto trouble
        TRAP 0,Halt,0           exit(0)
ReadErr GETA t,1F               readerr: fputs("Trouble r...!",stderr)
        JMP  Quit               goto quit }
1H      BYTE "Trouble reading!",#a,0
```

9. Basics. To get started, we define a type that provides semantic sugar.

```
⟨ Type declarations 9 ⟩ ≡
  typedef enum {
    false, true
  } bool;
```

See also sections 10, 16, 38, 39, 54, 55, 59, 64, and 135.

This code is used in section 141.

10. This program for the 64-bit MMIX architecture is based on 32-bit integer arithmetic, because nearly every computer available to the author at the time of writing (1999) was limited in that way. It uses subroutines from the MMIX-ARITH module, assuming only that type **tetra** represents unsigned 32-bit integers. The definition of **tetra** given here should be changed, if necessary, to agree with the definition in that module.

```
⟨ Type declarations 9 ⟩ +≡
  typedef unsigned int tetra;
    /* for systems conforming to the LP-64 data model */
  typedef struct {
    tetra h, l;
  } octa;    /* two tetrabytes make one octabyte */
  typedef unsigned char byte;    /* a monobyte */
```

11. We declare subroutines twice, once with a prototype and once with the old-style C conventions. The following hack makes this work with new compilers as well as the old standbys.

```
⟨ Preprocessor macros 11 ⟩ ≡
#ifdef __STDC__
#define ARGS(list) list
#else
#define ARGS(list) ()
#endif
```

See also sections 43 and 46.

This code is used in section 141.

12.

```
⟨ Subroutines 12 ⟩ ≡
  void print_hex ARGS((octa));
  void print_hex(o)
      octa o;
  {
    if (o.h) printf("%x%08x", o.h, o.l);
    else printf("%x", o.l);
  }
```

See also sections 13, 15, 17, 20, 26, 27, 42, 45, 47, 50, 82, 83, 91, 114, 117, 120, 137, 140, 143, 148, 154, 160, 162, 165, and 166.

This code is used in section 141.

__STDC__, Standard C. *printf*: **int** ( ), <stdio.h>.

13. Most of the subroutines in MMIX-ARITH return an octabyte as a function of two octabytes; for example, *oplus*(y, z) returns the sum of octabytes y and z. Division inputs the high half of a dividend in the global variable *aux* and returns the remainder in *aux*.

⟨ Subroutines 12 ⟩ +≡

```
extern octa zero_octa;  /* zero_octa.h = zero_octa.l = 0 */
extern octa neg_one;  /* neg_one.h = neg_one.l = −1 */
extern octa aux, val;  /* auxiliary data */
extern bool overflow;  /* flag set by signed multiplication and division */
extern int exceptions;  /* bits set by floating point operations */
extern int cur_round;  /* the current rounding mode */
extern char *next_char;  /* where a scanned constant ended */
extern octa oplus ARGS((octa y, octa z));  /* unsigned y + z */
extern octa ominus ARGS((octa y, octa z));  /* unsigned y − z */
extern octa incr ARGS((octa y, int delta));  /* unsigned y + δ (δ is signed) */
extern octa oand ARGS((octa y, octa z));  /* y ∧ z */
extern octa shift_left ARGS((octa y, int s));  /* y ≪ s, 0 ≤ s ≤ 64 */
extern octa shift_right ARGS((octa y, int s, int u));  /* y ≫ s, signed if ¬u */
extern octa omult ARGS((octa y, octa z));  /* unsigned (aux, x) = y × z */
extern octa signed_omult ARGS((octa y, octa z));  /* signed x = y × z */
extern octa odiv ARGS((octa x, octa y, octa z));
  /* unsigned (x, y)/z; aux = (x, y) mod z */
extern octa signed_odiv ARGS((octa y, octa z));  /* signed x = y/z */
extern int count_bits ARGS((tetra z));  /* x = ν(z) */
extern tetra byte_diff ARGS((tetra y, tetra z));  /* half of BDIF */
extern tetra wyde_diff ARGS((tetra y, tetra z));  /* half of WDIF */
extern octa bool_mult ARGS((octa y, octa z, bool xor));  /* MOR or MXOR */
extern octa load_sf ARGS((tetra z));  /* load short float */
extern tetra store_sf ARGS((octa x));  /* store short float */
extern octa fplus ARGS((octa y, octa z));  /* floating point x = y ⊕ z */
extern octa fmult ARGS((octa y, octa z));  /* floating point x = y ⊗ z */
extern octa fdivide ARGS((octa y, octa z));  /* floating point x = y ⊘ z */
extern octa froot ARGS((octa, int));  /* floating point x = √z */
extern octa fremstep ARGS((octa y, octa z, int delta));
  /* floating point x rem z = y rem z */
extern octa fintegerize ARGS((octa z, int mode));  /* floating point x = round(z) */
extern int fcomp ARGS((octa y, octa z));
  /* −1, 0, 1, or 2 if y < z, y = z, y > z, y ∥ z */
extern int fepscomp ARGS((octa y, octa z, octa eps, int sim));
  /* x = sim? [y ∼ z (ε)] : [y ≈ z (ε)] */
extern octa floatit ARGS((octa z, int mode, int unsgnd, int shrt));
  /* fix to float */
extern octa fixit ARGS((octa z, int mode));  /* float to fix */
extern void print_float ARGS((octa z));  /* print octabyte as floating decimal */
extern int scan_const ARGS((char *buf));
  /* val = floating or integer constant; returns the type */
```

14. Here's a quick check to see if arithmetic is in trouble.

```
#define panic(m)
        { fprintf(stderr, "Panic: %s!\n", m); exit(-2); }
```

⟨ Initialize everything 14 ⟩ ≡

```
  if (shift_left(neg_one, 1).h ≠ #fffffff)
    panic("Incorrect implementation of type tetra");
```

See also sections 18, 24, 32, 41, 77, and 147.

This code is used in section 141.

ARGS = macro ( ), §11.
aux: **octa**, MMIX-ARITH §4.
bool = **enum**, §9.
bool_mult: **octa** ( ), MMIX-ARITH §29.
byte_diff: **tetra** ( ), MMIX-ARITH §27.
count_bits: **int** ( ), MMIX-ARITH §26.
cur_round: **int**, MMIX-ARITH §30.
exceptions: **int**, MMIX-ARITH §32.
exit: **void** ( ), <stdlib.h>.
fcomp: **int** ( ), MMIX-ARITH §85.
fdivide: **octa** ( ), MMIX-ARITH §44.
fepscomp: **int** ( ), MMIX-ARITH §50.
fintegerize: **octa** ( ), MMIX-ARITH §86.
fixit: **octa** ( ), MMIX-ARITH §88.
floatit: **octa** ( ), MMIX-ARITH §89.
fmult: **octa** ( ), MMIX-ARITH §41.
fplus: **octa** ( ), MMIX-ARITH §46.
fprintf: **int** ( ), <stdio.h>.
fremstep: **octa** ( ), MMIX-ARITH §93.
froot: **octa** ( ), MMIX-ARITH §91.
h: **tetra**, §10.
incr: **octa** ( ), MMIX-ARITH §6.
l: **tetra**, §10.
load_sf: **octa** ( ), MMIX-ARITH §39.
neg_one: **octa**, MMIX-ARITH §4.
next_char: **char** *, MMIX-ARITH §69.
oand: **octa** ( ), MMIX-ARITH §25.
octa = **struct**, §10.
odiv: **octa** ( ), MMIX-ARITH §13.
ominus: **octa** ( ), MMIX-ARITH §5.
omult: **octa** ( ), MMIX-ARITH §8.
oplus: **octa** ( ), MMIX-ARITH §5.
overflow: **bool**, MMIX-ARITH §4.
print_float: **void** ( ), MMIX-ARITH §54.
scan_const: **int** ( ), MMIX-ARITH §68.
shift_left: **octa** ( ), MMIX-ARITH §7.
shift_right: **octa** ( ), MMIX-ARITH §7.
signed_odiv: **octa** ( ), MMIX-ARITH §24.
signed_omult: **octa** ( ), MMIX-ARITH §12.
stderr: **FILE** *, <stdio.h>.
store_sf: **tetra** ( ), MMIX-ARITH §40.
tetra = **unsigned int**, §10.
val: **octa**, MMIX-ARITH §69.
wyde_diff: **tetra** ( ), MMIX-ARITH §28.
zero_octa: **octa**, MMIX-ARITH §4.

15. Binary-to-decimal conversion is used when we want to see an octabyte as a signed integer. The identity $\lfloor (an+b)/10 \rfloor = \lfloor a/10 \rfloor n + \lfloor ((a \bmod 10)n + b)/10 \rfloor$ is helpful here.

```
#define sign_bit  ((unsigned) #80000000)

⟨ Subroutines 12 ⟩ +≡
  void print_int ARGS((octa));
  void print_int(o)
      octa o;
  {
    register tetra hi = o.h, lo = o.l, r, t;
    register int j;
    char dig[20];
    if (lo ≡ 0 ∧ hi ≡ 0) printf("0");
    else {
      if (hi & sign_bit) {
        printf("-");
        if (lo ≡ 0) hi = −hi;
        else lo = −lo, hi = ∼hi;
      }
      for (j = 0; hi; j++) {      /* 64-bit division by 10 */
        r = ((hi % 10) ≪ 16) + (lo ≫ 16);
        hi = hi/10;
        t = ((r % 10) ≪ 16) + (lo & #ffff);
        lo = ((r/10) ≪ 16) + (t/10);
        dig[j] = t % 10;
      }
      for ( ; lo; j++) {
        dig[j] = lo % 10;
        lo = lo/10;
      }
      for (j−−; j ≥ 0; j−−) printf("%c", dig[j] + '0');
    }
  }
```

16. Simulated memory. Chunks of simulated memory, 2048 bytes each, are kept in a tree structure organized as a *treap*, following ideas of Vuillemin, Aragon, and Seidel [*Communications of the ACM* **23** (1980), 229–239; *IEEE Symp. on Foundations of Computer Science* **30** (1989), 540–546]. Each node of the treap has two keys: One, called *loc*, is the base address of 512 simulated tetrabytes; it follows the conventions of an ordinary binary search tree, with all locations in the left subtree less than the *loc* of a node and all locations in the right subtree greater than that *loc*. The other, called *stamp*, can be thought of as the time the node was inserted into the tree; all subnodes of a given node have a larger *stamp*. By assigning time stamps at random, we maintain a tree structure that almost always is fairly well balanced.

Each simulated tetrabyte has an associated frequency count and source file reference.

```
⟨Type declarations 9⟩ +≡
  typedef struct {
    tetra tet;   /* the tetrabyte of simulated memory */
    tetra freq;   /* the number of times it was obeyed as an instruction */
    unsigned char bkpt;   /* breakpoint information for this tetrabyte */
    unsigned char file_no;   /* source file number, if known */
    unsigned short line_no;   /* source line number, if known */
  } mem_tetra;
  typedef struct mem_node_struct {
    octa loc;   /* location of the first of 512 simulated tetrabytes */
    tetra stamp;   /* time stamp for treap balancing */
    struct mem_node_struct *left, *right;   /* pointers to subtrees */
    mem_tetra dat[512];   /* the chunk of simulated tetrabytes */
  } mem_node;
```

17. The *stamp* value is actually only pseudorandom, based on the idea of Fibonacci hashing [see *Sorting and Searching*, Section 6.4]. This is good enough for our purposes, and it guarantees that no two stamps will be identical.

```
⟨Subroutines 12⟩ +≡
  mem_node *new_mem ARGS((void));
  mem_node *new_mem()
  {
    register mem_node *p;
    p = (mem_node *) calloc(1, sizeof(mem_node));
    if (¬p) panic("Can't allocate any more memory");
    p→stamp = priority;
    priority += #9e3779b9;   /* ⌊2^32(φ − 1)⌋ */
    return p;
  }
```

ARGS = macro ( ), §11.
calloc: **void** *( ), <stdlib.h>.
h: **tetra**, §10.
l: **tetra**, §10.
octa = **struct**, §10.
panic = macro ( ), §14.
printf: **int** ( ), <stdio.h>.
priority: **tetra**, §19.
tetra = **unsigned int**, §10.

18. Initially we start with a chunk for the pool segment, since the simulator will be putting command line information there before it runs the program.

```
⟨Initialize everything 14⟩ +≡
  mem_root = new_mem();
  mem_root→loc.h = #40000000;
  last_mem = mem_root;
```

19. ⟨Global variables 19⟩ ≡

```
  tetra priority = 314159265;   /* pseudorandom time stamp counter */
  mem_node *mem_root;   /* root of the treap */
  mem_node *last_mem;   /* the memory node most recently read or written */
  octa sclock;   /* simulated clock */
```

See also sections 25, 31, 40, 48, 52, 56, 61, 65, 76, 110, 113, 121, 129, 139, 144, and 151.

This code is used in section 141.

20. The *mem_find* routine finds a given tetrabyte in the simulated memory, inserting a new node into the treap if necessary.

```
⟨Subroutines 12⟩ +≡
  mem_tetra *mem_find ARGS((octa));
  mem_tetra *mem_find(addr)
      octa addr;
  {
    octa key;
    register int offset;
    register mem_node *p = last_mem;
    key.h = addr.h;
    key.l = addr.l & #ffff800;
    offset = addr.l & #7fc;
    if (p→loc.l ≠ key.l ∨ p→loc.h ≠ key.h)
      ⟨Search for key in the treap, setting last_mem and p to its location 21⟩;
    return &p→dat[offset ≫ 2];
  }
```

21. ⟨ Search for *key* in the treap, setting *last_mem* and *p* to its location 21 ⟩ ≡

```
{ register mem_node **q;
  for (p = mem_root; p; ) {
    if (key.l ≡ p→loc.l ∧ key.h ≡ p→loc.h) goto found;
    if ((key.l < p→loc.l ∧ key.h ≤ p→loc.h) ∨ key.h < p→loc.h) p = p→left;
    else p = p→right;
  }
  for (p = mem_root, q = &mem_root; p ∧ p→stamp < priority; p = *q) {
    if ((key.l < p→loc.l ∧ key.h ≤ p→loc.h) ∨ key.h < p→loc.h) q = &p→left;
    else q = &p→right;
  }
  *q = new_mem();
  (*q)→loc = key;
  ⟨ Fix up the subtrees of *q 22 ⟩;
  p = *q;
found: last_mem = p;
}
```

This code is used in section 20.

22. At this point we want to split the binary search tree *p* into two parts based on the given *key*, forming the left and right subtrees of the new node *q*. The effect will be as if *key* had been inserted before all of *p*'s nodes.

⟨ Fix up the subtrees of *q 22 ⟩ ≡

```
{
  register mem_node **l = &(*q)→left, **r = &(*q)→right;
  while (p) {
    if ((key.l < p→loc.l ∧ key.h ≤ p→loc.h) ∨ key.h < p→loc.h) *r = p, r = &p→left, p = *r;
    else *l = p, l = &p→right, p = *l;
  }
  *l = *r = Λ;
}
```

This code is used in section 21.

ARGS = macro ( ), §11.
dat: **mem_tetra** [], §16.
h: **tetra**, §10.
l: **tetra**, §10.
left: **mem_node** *, §16.
loc: **octa**, §16.
mem_node = **struct**, §16.
mem_tetra = **struct**, §16.
new_mem: **mem_node** *( ), §17.
octa = **struct**, §10.
right: **mem_node** *, §16.
stamp: **tetra**, §16.
tetra = **unsigned int**, §10.

23. Loading an object file. To get the user's program into memory, we read in an MMIX object, using modifications of the routines in the utility program MMOtype. Complete details of mmo format appear in the program for MMIXAL; a reader who hopes to understand this section ought to at least skim that documentation. Here we need to define only the basic constants used for interpretation.

```
#define mm #98 /* the escape code of mmo format */
#define lop_quote #0 /* the quotation lopcode */
#define lop_loc #1 /* the location lopcode */
#define lop_skip #2 /* the skip lopcode */
#define lop_fixo #3 /* the octabyte-fix lopcode */
#define lop_fixr #4 /* the relative-fix lopcode */
#define lop_fixrx #5 /* extended relative-fix lopcode */
#define lop_file #6 /* the file name lopcode */
#define lop_line #7 /* the file position lopcode */
#define lop_spec #8 /* the special hook lopcode */
#define lop_pre #9 /* the preamble lopcode */
#define lop_post #a /* the postamble lopcode */
#define lop_stab #b /* the symbol table lopcode */
#define lop_end #c /* the end-it-all lopcode */
```

24. We do not load the symbol table. (A more ambitious simulator could implement MMIXAL-style expressions for interactive debugging, but such enhancements are left to the interested reader.)

```
⟨Initialize everything 14⟩ +≡
  mmo_file = fopen(mmo_file_name, "rb");
  if (¬mmo_file) {
    register char *alt_name = (char *) calloc(strlen(mmo_file_name) + 5, sizeof(char));
    if (¬alt_name) panic("Can't␣allocate␣file␣name␣buffer");
    sprintf(alt_name, "%s.mmo", mmo_file_name);
    mmo_file = fopen(alt_name, "rb");
    if (¬mmo_file) {
      fprintf(stderr, "Can't␣open␣the␣object␣file␣%s␣or␣%s!\n", mmo_file_name,
          alt_name);
      exit(−3);
    }
    free(alt_name);
  }
  byte_count = 0;
```

25.
```
⟨Global variables 19⟩ +≡
  FILE *mmo_file; /* the input file */
  int postamble; /* have we encountered lop_post? */
  int byte_count; /* index of the next-to-be-read byte */
  byte buf[4]; /* the most recently read bytes */
  int yzbytes; /* the two least significant bytes */
  int delta; /* difference for relative fixup */
  tetra tet; /* buf bytes packed big-endianwise */
```

26. The tetrabytes of an mmo file are stored in friendly big-endian fashion, but this program is supposed to work also on computers that are little-endian. Therefore we read four successive bytes and pack them into a tetrabyte, instead of reading a single tetrabyte.

```
#define mmo_err
        {
          fprintf(stderr, "Bad␣object␣file!␣(Try␣running␣MMOtype.)\n");
          exit(−4);
        }
⟨ Subroutines 12 ⟩ +≡
  void read_tet ARGS((void));
  void read_tet()
  {
    if (fread(buf, 1, 4, mmo_file) ≠ 4) mmo_err;
    yzbytes = (buf[2] ≪ 8) + buf[3];
    tet = (((buf[0] ≪ 8) + buf[1]) ≪ 16) + yzbytes;
  }
```

27. ⟨ Subroutines 12 ⟩ +≡

```
  byte read_byte ARGS((void));
  byte read_byte()
  {
    register byte b;
    if (¬byte_count) read_tet();
    b = buf[byte_count];
    byte_count = (byte_count + 1) & 3;
    return b;
  }
```

28. ⟨ Load the preamble 28 ⟩ ≡

```
  read_tet();      /* read the first tetrabyte of input */
  if (buf[0] ≠ mm ∨ buf[1] ≠ lop_pre) mmo_err;
  if (ybyte ≠ 1) mmo_err;
  if (zbyte ≡ 0) obj_time = #ffffffff;
  else {
    j = zbyte − 1;
    read_tet(); obj_time = tet;     /* file creation time */
    for ( ; j > 0; j−−) read_tet();
  }
```

This code is used in section 32.

ARGS = macro ( ), §11.
byte = **unsigned char**, §10.
calloc: **void** ∗( ), <stdlib.h>.
exit: **void** ( ), <stdlib.h>.
FILE, <stdio.h>.
fopen: **FILE** ∗( ), <stdio.h>.
fprintf: **int** ( ), <stdio.h>.
fread: **size_t** ( ), <stdio.h>.
free: **void** ( ), <stdlib.h>.
j: **register int**, §62.
mmo_file_name = macro, §142.
obj_time: **tetra**, §31.
panic = macro ( ), §14.
sprintf: **int** ( ), <stdio.h>.
stderr: **FILE** ∗, <stdio.h>.
strlen: **size_t** ( ), <string.h>.
tetra = **unsigned int**, §10.
ybyte = macro, §33.
zbyte = macro, §33.

29. ⟨ Load the next item 29 ⟩ ≡

```
{
  read_tet();
loop: if (buf[0] ≡ mm)
      switch (buf[1]) {
      case lop_quote: if (yzbytes ≠ 1) mmo_err;
        read_tet(); break;
      ⟨ Cases for lopcodes in the main loop 33 ⟩
      case lop_post: postamble = 1;
        if (ybyte ∨ zbyte < 32) mmo_err;
        continue;
      default: mmo_err;
      }
    ⟨ Load tet as a normal item 30 ⟩;
}
```

This code is used in section 32.

30. In a normal situation, the newly read tetrabyte is simply supposed to be loaded into the current location. We load not only the current location but also the current file position, if *cur_line* is nonzero and *cur_loc* belongs to segment 0.

```
#define mmo_load(loc, val)  ll = mem_find(loc), ll→tet ⊕= val
```

⟨ Load *tet* as a normal item 30 ⟩ ≡

```
{
  mmo_load(cur_loc, tet);
  if (cur_line) {
    ll→file_no = cur_file;
    ll→line_no = cur_line;
    cur_line++;
  }
  cur_loc = incr(cur_loc, 4); cur_loc.l &= −4;
}
```

This code is used in section 29.

31. ⟨ Global variables 19 ⟩ +≡

```
octa cur_loc;    /* the current location */
int cur_file = −1;    /* the most recently selected file number */
int cur_line;    /* the current position in cur_file, if nonzero */
octa tmp;    /* an octabyte of temporary interest */
tetra obj_time;    /* when the object file was created */
```

32. ⟨ Initialize everything 14 ⟩ +≡

```
cur_loc.h = cur_loc.l = 0;
cur_file = −1;
cur_line = 0;
⟨ Load the preamble 28 ⟩;
do ⟨ Load the next item 29 ⟩ while (¬postamble);
⟨ Load the postamble 37 ⟩;
fclose(mmo_file);
cur_line = 0;
```

33. We have already implemented *lop_quote*, which falls through to the normal case after reading an extra tetrabyte. Now let's consider the other lopcodes in turn.

```
#define ybyte buf[2]   /* the next-to-least significant byte */
#define zbyte buf[3]   /* the least significant byte */

⟨ Cases for lopcodes in the main loop 33 ⟩ ≡
case lop_loc: if (zbyte ≡ 2) {
      j = ybyte; read_tet(); cur_loc.h = (j ≪ 24) + tet;
   } else if (zbyte ≡ 1) cur_loc.h = ybyte ≪ 24;
   else mmo_err;
   read_tet(); cur_loc.l = tet;
   continue;
case lop_skip: cur_loc = incr(cur_loc, yzbytes); continue;
```

See also sections 34, 35, and 36.

This code is used in section 29.

34. Fixups load information out of order, when future references have been resolved. The current file name and line number are not considered relevant.

```
⟨ Cases for lopcodes in the main loop 33 ⟩ +≡
case lop_fixo: if (zbyte ≡ 2) {
      j = ybyte; read_tet(); tmp.h = (j ≪ 24) + tet;
   } else if (zbyte ≡ 1) tmp.h = ybyte ≪ 24;
   else mmo_err;
   read_tet(); tmp.l = tet;
   mmo_load(tmp, cur_loc.h);
   mmo_load(incr(tmp, 4), cur_loc.l);
   continue;
case lop_fixr: delta = yzbytes;
   goto fixr;
case lop_fixrx: j = yzbytes; if (j ≠ 16 ∧ j ≠ 24) mmo_err;
   read_tet();
   delta = tet;
   if (delta & #fe000000) mmo_err;
fixr: tmp = incr(cur_loc, −(delta ≥ #1000000 ? (delta & #ffffff) − (1 ≪ j) : delta) ≪ 2);
   mmo_load(tmp, delta);
   continue;
```

---

buf: **byte** [], §25.
delta: **int**, §25.
fclose: **int** (), <stdio.h>.
file_no: **unsigned char**, §16.
h: **tetra**, §10.
incr: **octa** (), MMIX-ARITH §6.
j: **register int**, §62.
l: **tetra**, §10.
line_no: **unsigned short**, §16.
ll: **register mem_tetra** ∗, §62.
lop_fixo = #3, §23.
lop_fixr = #4, §23.
lop_fixrx = #5, §23.
lop_loc = #1, §23.
lop_post = #a, §23.
lop_quote = #0, §23.
lop_skip = #2, §23.
mem_find: **mem_tetra** ∗(), §20.
mm = #98, §23.
mmo_err = macro, §26.
mmo_file: **FILE** ∗, §25.
octa = **struct**, §10.
postamble: **int**, §25.
read_tet: **void** (), §26.
tet: **tetra**, §25.
tet: **tetra**, §16.
tetra = **unsigned int**, §10.
yzbytes: **int**, §25.

35. The space for file names isn't allocated until we are sure we need it.

```
⟨ Cases for lopcodes in the main loop 33 ⟩ +≡
case lop_file: if (file_info[ybyte].name) {
    if (zbyte) mmo_err;
    cur_file = ybyte;
  } else {
    if (¬zbyte) mmo_err;
    file_info[ybyte].name = (char *) calloc(4 * zbyte + 1, 1);
    if (¬file_info[ybyte].name) {
      fprintf(stderr, "No␣room␣to␣store␣the␣file␣name!\n"); exit(−5);
    }
    cur_file = ybyte;
    for (j = zbyte, p = file_info[ybyte].name; j > 0; j−−, p += 4) {
      read_tet();
      *p = buf[0]; *(p + 1) = buf[1]; *(p + 2) = buf[2]; *(p + 3) = buf[3];
    }
  }
  cur_line = 0; continue;
case lop_line: if (cur_file < 0) mmo_err;
  cur_line = yzbytes; continue;
```

36. Special bytes are ignored (at least for now).

```
⟨ Cases for lopcodes in the main loop 33 ⟩ +≡
case lop_spec: while (1) {
    read_tet();
    if (buf[0] ≡ mm) {
      if (buf[1] ≠ lop_quote ∨ yzbytes ≠ 1) goto loop;      /* end of special data */
      read_tet();
    }
  }
```

37. Since a chunk of memory holds 512 tetrabytes, the *ll* pointer in the following loop stays in the same chunk (namely, the first chunk of segment 3, also known as `Stack_Segment`).

```
⟨ Load the postamble 37 ⟩ ≡
  aux.h = #60000000; aux.l = #18;
  ll = mem_find(aux);
  (ll − 1)→tet = 2;      /* this will ultimately set rL = 2 */
  (ll − 5)→tet = argc;      /* and $0 = argc */
  (ll − 4)→tet = #40000000;
  (ll − 3)→tet = #8;      /* and $1 = Pool_Segment + 8 */
  G = zbyte; L = 0;
  for (j = G + G; j < 256 + 256; j++, ll++, aux.l += 4) read_tet(), ll→tet = tet;
  inst_ptr.h = (ll − 2)→tet, inst_ptr.l = (ll − 1)→tet;      /* Main */
  (ll + 2 * 12)→tet = G ≪ 24;
  g[255] = incr(aux, 12 * 8);      /* we will UNSAVE from here, to get going */
```

This code is used in section 32.

38. Loading and printing source lines. The loaded program generally contains cross references to the lines of symbolic source files, so that the context of each instruction can be understood. The following sections of this program make such information available when it is desired.

Source file data is kept in a **file_node** structure:

```
⟨ Type declarations 9 ⟩ +≡
  typedef struct {
    char *name;      /* name of source file */
    int line_count;     /* number of lines in the file */
    long *map;     /* pointer to map of file positions */
  } file_node;
```

39. In partial preparation for the day when source files are in Unicode, we define a type **Char** for the source characters.

```
⟨ Type declarations 9 ⟩ +≡
  typedef char Char;     /* bytes that will become wydes some day */
```

40.

```
⟨ Global variables 19 ⟩ +≡
  file_node file_info[256];     /* data about each source file */
  int buf_size;     /* size of buffer for source lines */
  Char *buffer;
```

41. As in MMIXAL, we prefer source lines of length 72 characters or less, but the user is allowed to increase the limit. (Longer lines will silently be truncated to the buffer size when the simulator lists them.)

```
⟨ Initialize everything 14 ⟩ +≡
  if (buf_size < 72) buf_size = 72;
  buffer = (Char *) calloc(buf_size + 1, sizeof(Char));
  if (¬buffer) panic("Can't␣allocate␣source␣line␣buffer");
```

argc: **int**, §141.
aux: **octa**, MMIX-ARITH §4.
buf: **byte** [], §25.
calloc: **void** *(), <stdlib.h>.
cur_file: **int**, §31.
cur_line: **int**, §31.
exit: **void** (), <stdlib.h>.
fprintf: **int** (), <stdio.h>.
g: **octa** [], §76.
G: **register int**, §75.
h: **tetra**, §10.
incr: **octa** (), MMIX-ARITH §6.
inst_ptr: **octa**, §61.
j: **register int**, §62.
l: **tetra**, §10.
L: **register int**, §75.
ll: **register mem_tetra** *, §62.
loop: label, §29.
lop_file = #6, §23.
lop_line = #7, §23.
lop_quote = #0, §23.
lop_spec = #8, §23.
mem_find: **mem_tetra** *(), §20.
mm = #98, §23.
mmo_err = macro, §26.
p: **register char** *, §62.
panic = macro (), §14.
read_tet: **void** (), §26.
rL = 20, §55.
stderr: **FILE** *, <stdio.h>.
tet: **tetra**, §16.
tet: **tetra**, §25.
ybyte = macro, §33.
yzbytes: **int**, §25.
zbyte = macro, §33.

42. The first time we are called upon to list a line from a given source file, we make a map of starting locations for each line. Source files should contain at most 65535 lines. We assume that they contain no null characters.

```
⟨ Subroutines 12 ⟩ +≡
  void make_map ARGS((void));
  void make_map()
  {
    long map[65536];
    register int k, l;
    register long *p;
    ⟨ Check if the source file has been modified 44 ⟩;
    for (l = 1; l < 65536 ∧ ¬feof(src_file); l++) {
      map[l] = ftell(src_file);
    loop: if (¬fgets(buffer, buf_size, src_file)) break;
      if (buffer[strlen(buffer) − 1] ≠ '\n') goto loop;
    }
    file_info[cur_file].line_count = l;
    file_info[cur_file].map = p = (long *) calloc(l, sizeof(long));
    if (¬p) panic("No␣room␣for␣a␣source-line␣map");
    for (k = 1; k < l; k++) p[k] = map[k];
  }
```

43. We want to warn the user if the source file has changed since the object file was written. The standard C library doesn't provide the information we need; so we use the UNIX system function *stat*, in hopes that other operating systems provide a similar way to do the job.

```
⟨ Preprocessor macros 11 ⟩ +≡
#include <sys/types.h>
#include <sys/stat.h>
```

44. ⟨ Check if the source file has been modified 44 ⟩ ≡

```
  {
    struct stat stat_buf;
    if (stat(file_info[cur_file].name, &stat_buf) ≥ 0)
      if ((tetra) stat_buf.st_mtime > obj_time) fprintf(stderr,
           "Warning:␣File␣%s␣was␣modified;␣it␣may␣not␣match␣the␣program!\n",
           file_info[cur_file].name);
  }
```

This code is used in section 42.

45. Source lines are listed by the *print_line* routine, preceded by 12 characters containing the line number. If a file error occurs, nothing is printed—not even an error message; the absence of listed data is itself a message.

```
⟨ Subroutines 12 ⟩ +≡
  void print_line ARGS((int));
  void print_line(k)
      int k;
  {
```

```
  char buf[11];
  if (k ≥ file_info[cur_file].line_count) return;
  if (fseek(src_file, file_info[cur_file].map[k], SEEK_SET) ≠ 0) return;
  if (¬fgets(buffer, buf_size, src_file)) return;
  sprintf(buf, "%d:␣␣␣␣", k);
  printf("line␣%.6s␣%s", buf, buffer);
  if (buffer[strlen(buffer) − 1] ≠ '\n') printf("\n");
  line_shown = true;
}
```

46. ⟨ Preprocessor macros 11 ⟩ +≡

```
#ifndef SEEK_SET
#define SEEK_SET 0    /* code for setting the file pointer to a given offset */
#endif
```

47. The *show_line* routine is called when we want to output line *cur_line* of source file number *cur_file*, assuming that *cur_line* ≠ 0. Its job is primarily to maintain continuity, by opening or reopening the *src_file* if the source file changes, and by connecting the previously output lines to the new one. Sometimes no output is necessary, because the desired line has already been printed.

⟨ Subroutines 12 ⟩ +≡

```
void show_line ARGS((void));
void show_line()
{
  register int k;
  if (shown_file ≠ cur_file) ⟨ Prepare to list lines from a new source file 49 ⟩
  else if (shown_line ≡ cur_line) return;   /* already shown */
  if (cur_line > shown_line + gap + 1 ∨ cur_line < shown_line) {
    if (shown_line > 0)
      if (cur_line < shown_line) printf("--------\n");
          /* indicate upward move */
      else printf("␣␣␣␣␣...\n");   /* indicate the gap */
    print_line(cur_line);
  } else for (k = shown_line + 1; k ≤ cur_line; k++) print_line(k);
  shown_line = cur_line;
}
```

ARGS = macro ( ), §11.
buf_size: **int**, §40.
buffer: **Char** ∗, §40.
calloc: **void** ∗( ), <stdlib.h>.
cur_file: **int**, §31.
cur_line: **int**, §31.
feof: **int** ( ), <stdio.h>.
fgets: **char** ∗( ), <stdio.h>.
file_info: **file_node** [ ], §40.
fprintf: **int** ( ), <stdio.h>.
fseek: **int** ( ), <stdio.h>.
ftell: **long** ( ), <stdio.h>.
gap: **int**, §48.
line_count: **int**, §38.
line_shown: **bool**, §48.
map: **long** ∗, §38.
name: **char** ∗, §38.
obj_time: **tetra**, §31.
panic = macro ( ), §14.
printf: **int** ( ), <stdio.h>.
SEEK_SET = macro, <stdio.h>.
shown_file: **int**, §48.
shown_line: **int**, §48.
sprintf: **int** ( ), <stdio.h>.
src_file: **FILE** ∗, §48.
st_mtime: **time_t**, <sys/stat.h>.
stat: **int** ( ), <sys/stat.h>.
stderr: **FILE** ∗, <stdio.h>.
strlen: **size_t** ( ), <string.h>.
tetra = **unsigned int**, §10.
true = 1, §9.

48. ⟨ Global variables 19 ⟩ +≡

```
FILE *src_file;    /* the currently open source file */
int shown_file = −1;    /* index of the most recently listed file */
int shown_line;    /* the line most recently listed in shown_file */
int gap;    /* minimum gap between consecutively listed source lines */
bool line_shown;    /* did we list anything recently? */
bool showing_source;    /* are we listing source lines? */
int profile_gap;    /* the gap when printing final frequencies */
bool profile_showing_source;    /* showing_source within final frequencies */
```

49. ⟨ Prepare to list lines from a new source file 49 ⟩ ≡

```
{
  if (¬src_file) src_file = fopen(file_info[cur_file].name, "r");
  else freopen(file_info[cur_file].name, "r", src_file);
  if (¬src_file) {
    fprintf(stderr, "Warning:␣I␣can't␣open␣file␣%s;␣source␣listing␣omitted.\n",
        file_info[cur_file].name);
    showing_source = false;
    return;
  }
  printf("\"%s\"\n", file_info[cur_file].name);
  shown_file = cur_file;
  shown_line = 0;
  if (¬file_info[cur_file].map) make_map();
}
```

This code is used in section 47.

50. Here is a simple application of *show_line*. It is a recursive routine that prints the frequency counts of all instructions that occur in a given subtree of the simulated memory and that were executed at least once. The subtree is traversed in symmetric order; therefore the frequencies appear in increasing order of the instruction locations.

⟨ Subroutines 12 ⟩ +≡

```
void print_freqs ARGS((mem_node *));
void print_freqs(p)
    mem_node *p;
{
  register int j;
  octa cur_loc;
  if (p→left) print_freqs(p→left);
  for (j = 0; j < 512; j++)
    if (p→dat[j].freq) ⟨ Print frequency data for location p→loc + 4 * j 51 ⟩;
  if (p→right) print_freqs(p→right);
}
```

51. An ellipsis (. . .) is printed between frequency data for nonconsecutive instructions, unless source line information intervenes.

```
⟨ Print frequency data for location p→loc + 4 ∗ j 51 ⟩ ≡
  {
    cur_loc = incr(p→loc, 4 ∗ j);
    if (showing_source ∧ p→dat[j].line_no) {
      cur_file = p→dat[j].file_no, cur_line = p→dat[j].line_no;
      line_shown = false;
      show_line();
      if (line_shown) goto loc_implied;
    }
    if (cur_loc.l ≠ implied_loc.l ∨ cur_loc.h ≠ implied_loc.h)
      if (profile_started) printf("␣␣␣␣␣␣␣␣␣0.␣␣␣␣␣␣␣␣...\n");
  loc_implied: printf("%10d.␣%08x%08x:␣%08x␣(%s)\n", p→dat[j].freq, cur_loc.h, cur_loc.l,
        p→dat[j].tet, info[p→dat[j].tet ≫ 24].name);
    implied_loc = incr(cur_loc, 4); profile_started = true;
  }
```

This code is used in section 50.

52. ⟨ Global variables 19 ⟩ +≡

```
  octa implied_loc;      /∗ location following the last shown frequency data ∗/
  bool profile_started;  /∗ have we printed at least one frequency count? ∗/
```

53. ⟨ Print all the frequency counts 53 ⟩ ≡

```
  {
    printf("\nProgram␣profile:\n");
    shown_file = cur_file = −1; shown_line = cur_line = 0;
    gap = profile_gap;
    showing_source = profile_showing_source;
    implied_loc = neg_one;
    print_freqs(mem_root);
  }
```

This code is used in section 141.

ARGS = macro ( ), §11.
bool = **enum**, §9.
cur_file: **int**, §31.
cur_line: **int**, §31.
dat: **mem_tetra** [ ], §16.
false = 0, §9.
FILE, `<stdio.h>`.
file_info: **file_node** [ ], §40.
file_no: **unsigned char**, §16.
fopen: **FILE** ∗( ), `<stdio.h>`.
fprintf: **int** ( ), `<stdio.h>`.
freopen: **FILE** ∗( ), `<stdio.h>`.
freq: **tetra**, §16.
h: **tetra**, §10.
incr: **octa** ( ), MMIX-ARITH §6.
info: **op_info** [ ], §65.
l: **tetra**, §10.
left: **mem_node** ∗, §16.
line_no: **unsigned short**, §16.
loc: **octa**, §16.
make_map: **void** ( ), §42.
map: **long** ∗, §38.
mem_node = **struct**, §16.
mem_root: **mem_node** ∗, §19.
name: **char** ∗, §38.
neg_one: **octa**, MMIX-ARITH §4.
octa = **struct**, §10.
printf: **int** ( ), `<stdio.h>`.
right: **mem_node** ∗, §16.
show_line: **void** ( ), §47.
stderr: **FILE** ∗, `<stdio.h>`.
tet: **tetra**, §16.
true = 1, §9.

54. Lists. This simulator needs to deal with 256 different opcodes, so we might as well enumerate them now.

⟨ Type declarations 9 ⟩ +≡

```
typedef enum {
  TRAP, FCMP, FUN, FEQL, FADD, FIX, FSUB, FIXU,
  FLOT, FLOTI, FLOTU, FLOTUI, SFLOT, SFLOTI, SFLOTU, SFLOTUI,
  FMUL, FCMPE, FUNE, FEQLE, FDIV, FSQRT, FREM, FINT,
  MUL, MULI, MULU, MULUI, DIV, DIVI, DIVU, DIVUI,
  ADD, ADDI, ADDU, ADDUI, SUB, SUBI, SUBU, SUBUI,
  IIADDU, IIADDUI, IVADDU, IVADDUI, VIIIADDU, VIIIADDUI, XVIADDU, XVIADDUI,
  CMP, CMPI, CMPU, CMPUI, NEG, NEGI, NEGU, NEGUI,
  SL, SLI, SLU, SLUI, SR, SRI, SRU, SRUI,
  BN, BNB, BZ, BZB, BP, BPB, BOD, BODB,
  BNN, BNNB, BNZ, BNZB, BNP, BNPB, BEV, BEVB,
  PBN, PBNB, PBZ, PBZB, PBP, PBPB, PBOD, PBODB,
  PBNN, PBNNB, PBNZ, PBNZB, PBNP, PBNPB, PBEV, PBEVB,
  CSN, CSNI, CSZ, CSZI, CSP, CSPI, CSOD, CSODI,
  CSNN, CSNNI, CSNZ, CSNZI, CSNP, CSNPI, CSEV, CSEVI,
  ZSN, ZSNI, ZSZ, ZSZI, ZSP, ZSPI, ZSOD, ZSODI,
  ZSNN, ZSNNI, ZSNZ, ZSNZI, ZSNP, ZSNPI, ZSEV, ZSEVI,
  LDB, LDBI, LDBU, LDBUI, LDW, LDWI, LDWU, LDWUI,
  LDT, LDTI, LDTU, LDTUI, LDO, LDOI, LDOU, LDOUI,
  LDSF, LDSFI, LDHT, LDHTI, CSWAP, CSWAPI, LDUNC, LDUNCI,
  LDVTS, LDVTSI, PRELD, PRELDI, PREGO, PREGOI, GO, GOI,
  STB, STBI, STBU, STBUI, STW, STWI, STWU, STWUI,
  STT, STTI, STTU, STTUI, STO, STOI, STOU, STOUI,
  STSF, STSFI, STHT, STHTI, STCO, STCOI, STUNC, STUNCI,
  SYNCD, SYNCDI, PREST, PRESTI, SYNCID, SYNCIDI, PUSHGO, PUSHGOI,
  OR, ORI, ORN, ORNI, NOR, NORI, XOR, XORI,
  AND, ANDI, ANDN, ANDNI, NAND, NANDI, NXOR, NXORI,
  BDIF, BDIFI, WDIF, WDIFI, TDIF, TDIFI, ODIF, ODIFI,
  MUX, MUXI, SADD, SADDI, MOR, MORI, MXOR, MXORI,
  SETH, SETMH, SETML, SETL, INCH, INCMH, INCML, INCL,
  ORH, ORMH, ORML, ORL, ANDNH, ANDNMH, ANDNML, ANDNL,
  JMP, JMPB, PUSHJ, PUSHJB, GETA, GETAB, PUT, PUTI,
  POP, RESUME, SAVE, UNSAVE, SYNC, SWYM, GET, TRIP
} mmix_opcode;
```

55. We also need to enumerate the special names for special registers.

⟨ Type declarations 9 ⟩ +≡

```
typedef enum {
  rB, rD, rE, rH, rJ, rM, rR, rBB, rC, rN, rO, rS, rI, rT, rTT, rK, rQ, rU, rV, rG, rL,
      rA, rF, rP, rW, rX, rY, rZ, rWW, rXX, rYY, rZZ
} special_reg;
```

56. ⟨ Global variables 19 ⟩ +≡

```
char *special_name[32] = {"rB", "rD", "rE", "rH", "rJ", "rM", "rR", "rBB", "rC", "rN",
    "rO", "rS", "rI", "rT", "rTT", "rK", "rQ", "rU", "rV", "rG", "rL", "rA", "rF", "rP",
    "rW", "rX", "rY", "rZ", "rWW", "rXX", "rYY", "rZZ"};
```

57. Here are the bit codes for arithmetic exceptions. These codes, except `H_BIT`, are defined also in MMIX-ARITH.

```
#define X_BIT (1 << 8)  /* floating inexact */
#define Z_BIT (1 << 9)  /* floating division by zero */
#define U_BIT (1 << 10) /* floating underflow */
#define O_BIT (1 << 11) /* floating overflow */
#define I_BIT (1 << 12) /* floating invalid operation */
#define W_BIT (1 << 13) /* float-to-fix overflow */
#define V_BIT (1 << 14) /* integer overflow */
#define D_BIT (1 << 15) /* integer divide check */
#define H_BIT (1 << 16) /* trip */
```

58. The *bkpt* field associated with each tetrabyte of memory has bits associated with forced tracing and/or breaking for reading, writing, and/or execution.

```
#define trace_bit (1 << 3)
#define read_bit (1 << 2)
#define write_bit (1 << 1)
#define exec_bit (1 << 0)
```

59. To complete our lists of lists, we enumerate the rudimentary operating system calls that are built in to `MMIXAL`.

```
#define max_sys_call Ftell

⟨Type declarations 9⟩ +≡
  typedef enum {
    Halt, Fopen, Fclose, Fread, Fgets, Fgetws, Fwrite, Fputs, Fputws, Fseek, Ftell
  } sys_call;
```

bkpt: **unsigned char**, §16.

60. The main loop. Now let's plunge in to the guts of the simulator, the master switch that controls most of the action.

```
⟨ Perform one instruction 60 ⟩ ≡
  {
    if (resuming) loc = incr(inst_ptr, −4), inst = g[rX].l;
    else ⟨ Fetch the next instruction 63 ⟩;
    op = inst ≫ 24; xx = (inst ≫ 16) & #ff; yy = (inst ≫ 8) & #ff; zz = inst & #ff;
    f = info[op].flags; yz = inst & #ffff;
    x = y = z = a = b = zero_octa; exc = 0; old_L = L;
    if (f & rel_addr_bit) ⟨ Convert relative address to absolute address 70 ⟩;
    ⟨ Install operand fields 71 ⟩;
    if (f & X_is_dest_bit)
      ⟨ Install register X as the destination, adjusting the register stack if necessary 80 ⟩;
    w = oplus(y, z);
    if (loc.h ≥ #20000000) goto privileged_inst;
    switch (op) {
    ⟨ Cases for individual MMIX instructions 84 ⟩;
    }
    ⟨ Check for trip interrupt 122 ⟩;
    ⟨ Update the clocks 127 ⟩;
    ⟨ Trace the current instruction, if requested 128 ⟩;
    if (resuming ∧ op ≠ RESUME) resuming = false;
  }
```

This code is used in section 141.

61. Operands x and a are usually destinations (results), computed from the source operands y, z, and/or b.

```
⟨ Global variables 19 ⟩ +≡
  octa w, x, y, z, a, b, ma, mb;    /* operands */
  octa *x_ptr;    /* destination */
  octa loc;    /* location of the current instruction */
  octa inst_ptr;    /* location of the next instruction */
  tetra inst;    /* the current instruction */
  int old_L;    /* value of L before the current instruction */
  int exc;    /* exceptions raised by the current instruction */
  int tracing_exceptions;    /* exception bits that cause tracing */
  int rop;    /* ropcode of a resumed instruction */
  int round_mode;    /* the style of floating point rounding just used */
  bool resuming;    /* are we resuming an interrupted instruction? */
  bool halted;    /* did the program come to a halt? */
  bool breakpoint;    /* should we pause after the current instruction? */
  bool tracing;    /* should we trace the current instruction? */
  bool stack_tracing;    /* should we trace details of the register stack? */
  bool interacting;    /* are we in interactive mode? */
  bool interact_after_break;    /* should we go into interactive mode? */
  bool tripping;    /* are we about to go to a trip handler? */
  bool good;    /* did the last branch instruction guess correctly? */
  tetra trace_threshold;    /* each instruction should be traced this many times */
```

62. ⟨ Local registers 62 ⟩ ≡

```
register mmix_opcode op;    /* operation code of the current instruction */
register int xx, yy, zz, yz;    /* operand fields of the current instruction */
register tetra f;  /* properties of the current op */
register int i, j, k;   /* miscellaneous indices */
register mem_tetra *ll;    /* current place in the simulated memory */
register char *p;    /* current place in a string */
```

See also section 75.

This code is used in section 141.

63. ⟨ Fetch the next instruction 63 ⟩ ≡

```
{
  loc = inst_ptr;
  ll = mem_find(loc);
  inst = ll→tet;
  cur_file = ll→file_no;
  cur_line = ll→line_no;
  ll→freq++;
  if (ll→bkpt & exec_bit) breakpoint = true;
  tracing = breakpoint ∨ (ll→bkpt & trace_bit) ∨ (ll→freq ≤ trace_threshold);
  inst_ptr = incr(inst_ptr, 4);
}
```

This code is used in section 60.

64. Much of the simulation is table-driven, based on a static data structure called the **op_info** for each operation code.

⟨ Type declarations 9 ⟩ +≡

```
typedef struct {
  char *name;    /* symbolic name of an opcode */
  unsigned char flags;    /* its instruction format */
  unsigned char third_operand;    /* its special register input */
  unsigned char mems;    /* how many μ it costs */
  unsigned char oops;    /* how many υ it costs */
  char *trace_format;    /* how it appears when traced */
} op_info;
```

---

bkpt: **unsigned char**, §16.
bool = **enum**, §9.
cur_file: **int**, §31.
cur_line: **int**, §31.
exec_bit = macro, §58.
false = 0, §9.
file_no: **unsigned char**, §16.
freq: **tetra**, §16.
g: **octa** [], §76.
h: **tetra**, §10.
incr: **octa** ( ), MMIX-ARITH §6.
info: **op_info** [], §65.
l: **tetra**, §10.
L: **register int**, §75.
line_no: **unsigned short**, §16.
mem_find: **mem_tetra** *( ), §20.
mem_tetra = **struct**, §16.
mmix_opcode = **enum**, §54.
octa = **struct**, §10.
oplus: **octa** ( ), MMIX-ARITH §5.
privileged_inst: label, §107.
rel_addr_bit = #40, §65.
RESUME = #f9, §54.
rX = 25, §55.
tet: **tetra**, §16.
tetra = **unsigned int**, §10.
trace_bit = macro, §58.
true = 1, §9.
X_is_dest_bit = #20, §65.
zero_octa: **octa**, MMIX-ARITH §4.

65. For example, the *flags* field of *info*[*op*] tells us how to obtain the operands from the X, Y, and Z fields of the current instruction. Each entry records special properties of an operation code, in binary notation: #1 means Z is an immediate value, #2 means rZ is a source operand, #4 means Y is an immediate value, #8 means rY is a source operand, #10 means rX is a source operand, #20 means rX is a destination, #40 means YZ is part of a relative address, #80 means a push or pop or unsave instruction.

The *trace_format* field will be explained later.

```
#define Z_is_immed_bit #1
#define Z_is_source_bit #2
#define Y_is_immed_bit #4
#define Y_is_source_bit #8
#define X_is_source_bit #10
#define X_is_dest_bit #20
#define rel_addr_bit #40
#define push_pop_bit #80
```

⟨ Global variables 19 ⟩ +≡

```
  op_info info[256] = {⟨ Info for arithmetic commands 66 ⟩, ⟨ Info for branch
      commands 67 ⟩, ⟨ Info for load/store commands 68 ⟩, ⟨ Info for logical and control
      commands 69 ⟩};
```

66. ⟨ Info for arithmetic commands 66 ⟩ ≡

```
  {"TRAP", #0a, 255, 0, 5, "%r"},
      {"FCMP", #2a, 0, 0, 1, "%l␣=␣%.y␣cmp␣%.z␣=␣%x"},
      {"FUN", #2a, 0, 0, 1, "%l␣=␣[%.y(||)%.z]␣=␣%x"},
      {"FEQL", #2a, 0, 0, 1, "%l␣=␣[%.y(==)%.z]␣=␣%x"},
      {"FADD", #2a, 0, 0, 4, "%l␣=␣%.y␣%(+%)␣%.z␣=␣%.x"},
      {"FIX", #26, 0, 0, 4, "%l␣=␣%(fix%)␣%.z␣=␣%x"},
      {"FSUB", #2a, 0, 0, 4, "%l␣=␣%.y␣%(-%)␣%.z␣=␣%.x"},
      {"FIXU", #26, 0, 0, 4, "%l␣=␣%(fix%)␣%.z␣=␣%#x"},
      {"FLOT", #26, 0, 0, 4, "%l␣=␣%(flot%)␣%z␣=␣%.x"},
      {"FLOTI", #25, 0, 0, 4, "%l␣=␣%(flot%)␣%z␣=␣%.x"},
      {"FLOTU", #26, 0, 0, 4, "%l␣=␣%(flot%)␣%#z␣=␣%.x"},
      {"FLOTUI", #25, 0, 0, 4, "%l␣=␣%(flot%)␣%z␣=␣%.x"},
      {"SFLOT", #26, 0, 0, 4, "%l␣=␣%(sflot%)␣%z␣=␣%.x"},
      {"SFLOTI", #25, 0, 0, 4, "%l␣=␣%(sflot%)␣%z␣=␣%.x"},
      {"SFLOTU", #26, 0, 0, 4, "%l␣=␣%(sflot%)␣%#z␣=␣%.x"},
      {"SFLOTUI", #25, 0, 0, 4, "%l␣=␣%(sflot%)␣%z␣=␣%.x"},
      {"FMUL", #2a, 0, 0, 4, "%l␣=␣%.y␣%(*%)␣%.z␣=␣%.x"},
      {"FCMPE", #2a, rE, 0, 4, "%l␣=␣%.y␣cmp␣%.z␣(%.b))␣=␣%x"},
      {"FUNE", #2a, rE, 0, 1, "%l␣=␣[%.y(||)%.z␣(%.b)]␣=␣%x"},
      {"FEQLE", #2a, rE, 0, 4, "%l␣=␣[%.y(==)%.z␣(%.b)]␣=␣%x"},
      {"FDIV", #2a, 0, 0, 40, "%l␣=␣%.y␣%(/%)␣%.z␣=␣%.x"},
      {"FSQRT", #26, 0, 0, 40, "%l␣=␣%(sqrt%)␣%.z␣=␣%.x"},
      {"FREM", #2a, 0, 0, 4, "%l␣=␣%.y␣%(rem%)␣%.z␣=␣%.x"},
      {"FINT", #26, 0, 0, 4, "%l␣=␣%(int%)␣%.z␣=␣%.x"},
      {"MUL", #2a, 0, 0, 10, "%l␣=␣%y␣*␣%z␣=␣%x"},
      {"MULI", #29, 0, 0, 10, "%l␣=␣%y␣*␣%z␣=␣%x"},
      {"MULU", #2a, 0, 0, 10, "%l␣=␣%#y␣*␣%#z␣=␣%#x,␣rH=%#a"},
```

```
{"MULUI",#29,0,0,10,"%l␣=␣%#y␣*␣%z␣=␣%#x,␣rH=%#a"},
{"DIV",#2a,0,0,60,"%l␣=␣%y␣/␣%z␣=␣%x,␣rR=%a"},
{"DIVI",#29,0,0,60,"%l␣=␣%y␣/␣%z␣=␣%x,␣rR=%a"},
{"DIVU",#2a,rD,0,60,"%l␣=␣%#b%0y␣/␣%#z␣=␣%#x,␣rR=%#a"},
{"DIVUI",#29,rD,0,60,"%l␣=␣%#b%0y␣/␣%z␣=␣%#x,␣rR=%#a"},
{"ADD",#2a,0,0,1,"%l␣=␣%y␣+␣%z␣=␣%x"},
{"ADDI",#29,0,0,1,"%l␣=␣%y␣+␣%z␣=␣%x"},
{"ADDU",#2a,0,0,1,"%l␣=␣%#y␣+␣%#z␣=␣%#x"},
{"ADDUI",#29,0,0,1,"%l␣=␣%#y␣+␣%z␣=␣%#x"},
{"SUB",#2a,0,0,1,"%l␣=␣%y␣-␣%z␣=␣%x"},
{"SUBI",#29,0,0,1,"%l␣=␣%y␣-␣%z␣=␣%x"},
{"SUBU",#2a,0,0,1,"%l␣=␣%#y␣-␣%#z␣=␣%#x"},
{"SUBUI",#29,0,0,1,"%l␣=␣%#y␣-␣%z␣=␣%#x"},
{"2ADDU",#2a,0,0,1,"%l␣=␣%#y␣<<1+␣%#z␣=␣%#x"},
{"2ADDUI",#29,0,0,1,"%l␣=␣%#y␣<<1+␣%z␣=␣%#x"},
{"4ADDU",#2a,0,0,1,"%l␣=␣%#y␣<<2+␣%#z␣=␣%#x"},
{"4ADDUI",#29,0,0,1,"%l␣=␣%#y␣<<2+␣%z␣=␣%#x"},
{"8ADDU",#2a,0,0,1,"%l␣=␣%#y␣<<3+␣%#z␣=␣%#x"},
{"8ADDUI",#29,0,0,1,"%l␣=␣%#y␣<<3+␣%z␣=␣%#x"},
{"16ADDU",#2a,0,0,1,"%l␣=␣%#y␣<<4+␣%#z␣=␣%#x"},
{"16ADDUI",#29,0,0,1,"%l␣=␣%#y␣<<4+␣%z␣=␣%#x"},
{"CMP",#2a,0,0,1,"%l␣=␣%y␣cmp␣%z␣=␣%x"},
{"CMPI",#29,0,0,1,"%l␣=␣%y␣cmp␣%z␣=␣%x"},
{"CMPU",#2a,0,0,1,"%l␣=␣%#y␣cmp␣%#z␣=␣%x"},
{"CMPUI",#29,0,0,1,"%l␣=␣%#y␣cmp␣%z␣=␣%x"},
{"NEG",#26,0,0,1,"%l␣=␣%y␣-␣%z␣=␣%x"},
{"NEGI",#25,0,0,1,"%l␣=␣%y␣-␣%z␣=␣%x"},
{"NEGU",#26,0,0,1,"%l␣=␣%y␣-␣%#z␣=␣%#x"},
{"NEGUI",#25,0,0,1,"%l␣=␣%y␣-␣%z␣=␣%#x"},
{"SL",#2a,0,0,1,"%l␣=␣%y␣<<␣%#z␣=␣%x"},
{"SLI",#29,0,0,1,"%l␣=␣%y␣<<␣%z␣=␣%x"},
{"SLU",#2a,0,0,1,"%l␣=␣%#y␣<<␣%#z␣=␣%#x"},
{"SLUI",#29,0,0,1,"%l␣=␣%#y␣<<␣%z␣=␣%#x"},
{"SR",#2a,0,0,1,"%l␣=␣%y␣>>␣%#z␣=␣%x"},
{"SRI",#29,0,0,1,"%l␣=␣%y␣>>␣%z␣=␣%x"},
{"SRU",#2a,0,0,1,"%l␣=␣%#y␣>>␣%#z␣=␣%#x"},
{"SRUI",#29,0,0,1,"%l␣=␣%#y␣>>␣%z␣=␣%#x"}
```

This code is used in section 65.

flags: **unsigned char**, §64.
op: **register mmix_opcode**, §62.
op_info = **struct**, §64.
rD = 1, §55.
rE = 2, §55.
trace_format: **char** *, §64.

67. ⟨ Info for branch commands 67 ⟩ ≡

```
{"BN", #50, 0, 0, 1, "%b<0?␣%t%g"},
    {"BNB", #50, 0, 0, 1, "%b<0?␣%t%g"},
    {"BZ", #50, 0, 0, 1, "%b==0?␣%t%g"},
    {"BZB", #50, 0, 0, 1, "%b==0?␣%t%g"},
    {"BP", #50, 0, 0, 1, "%b>0?␣%t%g"},
    {"BPB", #50, 0, 0, 1, "%b>0?␣%t%g"},
    {"BOD", #50, 0, 0, 1, "%b␣odd?␣%t%g"},
    {"BODB", #50, 0, 0, 1, "%b␣odd?␣%t%g"},
    {"BNN", #50, 0, 0, 1, "%b>=0?␣%t%g"},
    {"BNNB", #50, 0, 0, 1, "%b>=0?␣%t%g"},
    {"BNZ", #50, 0, 0, 1, "%b!=0?␣%t%g"},
    {"BNZB", #50, 0, 0, 1, "%b!=0?␣%t%g"},
    {"BNP", #50, 0, 0, 1, "%b<=0?␣%t%g"},
    {"BNPB", #50, 0, 0, 1, "%b<=0?␣%t%g"},
    {"BEV", #50, 0, 0, 1, "%b␣even?␣%t%g"},
    {"BEVB", #50, 0, 0, 1, "%b␣even?␣%t%g"},
    {"PBN", #50, 0, 0, 1, "%b<0?␣%t%g"},
    {"PBNB", #50, 0, 0, 1, "%b<0?␣%t%g"},
    {"PBZ", #50, 0, 0, 1, "%b==0?␣%t%g"},
    {"PBZB", #50, 0, 0, 1, "%b==0?␣%t%g"},
    {"PBP", #50, 0, 0, 1, "%b>0?␣%t%g"},
    {"PBPB", #50, 0, 0, 1, "%b>0?␣%t%g"},
    {"PBOD", #50, 0, 0, 1, "%b␣odd?␣%t%g"},
    {"PBODB", #50, 0, 0, 1, "%b␣odd?␣%t%g"},
    {"PBNN", #50, 0, 0, 1, "%b>=0?␣%t%g"},
    {"PBNNB", #50, 0, 0, 1, "%b>=0?␣%t%g"},
    {"PBNZ", #50, 0, 0, 1, "%b!=0?␣%t%g"},
    {"PBNZB", #50, 0, 0, 1, "%b!=0?␣%t%g"},
    {"PBNP", #50, 0, 0, 1, "%b<=0?␣%t%g"},
    {"PBNPB", #50, 0, 0, 1, "%b<=0?␣%t%g"},
    {"PBEV", #50, 0, 0, 1, "%b␣even?␣%t%g"},
    {"PBEVB", #50, 0, 0, 1, "%b␣even?␣%t%g"},
    {"CSN", #3a, 0, 0, 1, "%l␣=␣%y<0?␣%z:␣%b␣=␣%x"},
    {"CSNI", #39, 0, 0, 1, "%l␣=␣%y<0?␣%z:␣%b␣=␣%x"},
    {"CSZ", #3a, 0, 0, 1, "%l␣=␣%y==0?␣%z:␣%b␣=␣%x"},
    {"CSZI", #39, 0, 0, 1, "%l␣=␣%y==0?␣%z:␣%b␣=␣%x"},
    {"CSP", #3a, 0, 0, 1, "%l␣=␣%y>0?␣%z:␣%b␣=␣%x"},
    {"CSPI", #39, 0, 0, 1, "%l␣=␣%y>0?␣%z:␣%b␣=␣%x"},
    {"CSOD", #3a, 0, 0, 1, "%l␣=␣%y␣odd?␣%z:␣%b␣=␣%x"},
    {"CSODI", #39, 0, 0, 1, "%l␣=␣%y␣odd?␣%z:␣%b␣=␣%x"},
    {"CSNN", #3a, 0, 0, 1, "%l␣=␣%y>=0?␣%z:␣%b␣=␣%x"},
    {"CSNNI", #39, 0, 0, 1, "%l␣=␣%y>=0?␣%z:␣%b␣=␣%x"},
    {"CSNZ", #3a, 0, 0, 1, "%l␣=␣%y!=0?␣%z:␣%b␣=␣%x"},
    {"CSNZI", #39, 0, 0, 1, "%l␣=␣%y!=0?␣%z:␣%b␣=␣%x"},
    {"CSNP", #3a, 0, 0, 1, "%l␣=␣%y<=0?␣%z:␣%b␣=␣%x"},
    {"CSNPI", #39, 0, 0, 1, "%l␣=␣%y<=0?␣%z:␣%b␣=␣%x"},
    {"CSEV", #3a, 0, 0, 1, "%l␣=␣%y␣even?␣%z:␣%b␣=␣%x"},
    {"CSEVI", #39, 0, 0, 1, "%l␣=␣%y␣even?␣%z:␣%b␣=␣%x"},
```

```
{"ZSN", #2a, 0, 0, 1, "%l␣=␣%y<0?␣%z:␣0␣=␣%x"},
{"ZSNI", #29, 0, 0, 1, "%l␣=␣%y<0?␣%z:␣0␣=␣%x"},
{"ZSZ", #2a, 0, 0, 1, "%l␣=␣%y==0?␣%z:␣0␣=␣%x"},
{"ZSZI", #29, 0, 0, 1, "%l␣=␣%y==0?␣%z:␣0␣=␣%x"},
{"ZSP", #2a, 0, 0, 1, "%l␣=␣%y>0?␣%z:␣0␣=␣%x"},
{"ZSPI", #29, 0, 0, 1, "%l␣=␣%y>0?␣%z:␣0␣=␣%x"},
{"ZSOD", #2a, 0, 0, 1, "%l␣=␣%y␣odd?␣%z:␣0␣=␣%x"},
{"ZSODI", #29, 0, 0, 1, "%l␣=␣%y␣odd?␣%z:␣0␣=␣%x"},
{"ZSNN", #2a, 0, 0, 1, "%l␣=␣%y>=0?␣%z:␣0␣=␣%x"},
{"ZSNNI", #29, 0, 0, 1, "%l␣=␣%y>=0?␣%z:␣0␣=␣%x"},
{"ZSNZ", #2a, 0, 0, 1, "%l␣=␣%y!=0?␣%z:␣0␣=␣%x"},
{"ZSNZI", #29, 0, 0, 1, "%l␣=␣%y!=0?␣%z:␣0␣=␣%x"},
{"ZSNP", #2a, 0, 0, 1, "%l␣=␣%y<=0?␣%z:␣0␣=␣%x"},
{"ZSNPI", #29, 0, 0, 1, "%l␣=␣%y<=0?␣%z:␣0␣=␣%x"},
{"ZSEV", #2a, 0, 0, 1, "%l␣=␣%y␣even?␣%z:␣0␣=␣%x"},
{"ZSEVI", #29, 0, 0, 1, "%l␣=␣%y␣even?␣%z:␣0␣=␣%x"}
```

This code is used in section 65.

68. ⟨ Info for load/store commands 68 ⟩ ≡

```
{"LDB",#2a,0,1,1,"%l␣=␣M1[%#y+%#z]␣=␣%x"},
    {"LDBI",#29,0,1,1,"%l␣=␣M1[%#y%?+]␣=␣%x"},
    {"LDBU",#2a,0,1,1,"%l␣=␣M1[%#y+%#z]␣=␣%#x"},
    {"LDBUI",#29,0,1,1,"%l␣=␣M1[%#y%?+]␣=␣%#x"},
    {"LDW",#2a,0,1,1,"%l␣=␣M2[%#y+%#z]␣=␣%x"},
    {"LDWI",#29,0,1,1,"%l␣=␣M2[%#y%?+]␣=␣%x"},
    {"LDWU",#2a,0,1,1,"%l␣=␣M2[%#y+%#z]␣=␣%#x"},
    {"LDWUI",#29,0,1,1,"%l␣=␣M2[%#y%?+]␣=␣%#x"},
    {"LDT",#2a,0,1,1,"%l␣=␣M4[%#y+%#z]␣=␣%x"},
    {"LDTI",#29,0,1,1,"%l␣=␣M4[%#y%?+]␣=␣%x"},
    {"LDTU",#2a,0,1,1,"%l␣=␣M4[%#y+%#z]␣=␣%#x"},
    {"LDTUI",#29,0,1,1,"%l␣=␣M4[%#y%?+]␣=␣%#x"},
    {"LDO",#2a,0,1,1,"%l␣=␣M8[%#y+%#z]␣=␣%x"},
    {"LDOI",#29,0,1,1,"%l␣=␣M8[%#y%?+]␣=␣%x"},
    {"LDOU",#2a,0,1,1,"%l␣=␣M8[%#y+%#z]␣=␣%#x"},
    {"LDOUI",#29,0,1,1,"%l␣=␣M8[%#y%?+]␣=␣%#x"},
    {"LDSF",#2a,0,1,1,"%l␣=␣(M4[%#y+%#z])␣=␣%.x"},
    {"LDSFI",#29,0,1,1,"%l␣=␣(M4[%#y%?+])␣=␣%.x"},
    {"LDHT",#2a,0,1,1,"%l␣=␣M4[%#y+%#z]<<32␣=␣%#x"},
    {"LDHTI",#29,0,1,1,"%l␣=␣M4[%#y%?+]<<32␣=␣%#x"},
    {"CSWAP",#3a,0,2,2,"%l␣=␣[M8[%#y+%#z]==%a]␣=␣%x,␣%r"},
    {"CSWAPI",#39,0,2,2,"%l␣=␣[M8[%#y%?+]==%a]␣=␣%x,␣%r"},
    {"LDUNC",#2a,0,1,1,"%l␣=␣M8[%#y+%#z]␣=␣%#x"},
    {"LDUNCI",#29,0,1,1,"%l␣=␣M8[%#y%?+]␣=␣%#x"},
    {"LDVTS",#2a,0,0,1,""},
    {"LDVTSI",#29,0,0,1,""},
    {"PRELD",#0a,0,0,1,"[%#y+%#z␣..␣%#x]"},
    {"PRELDI",#09,0,0,1,"[%#y%?+␣..␣%#x]"},
    {"PREGO",#0a,0,0,1,"[%#y+%#z␣..␣%#x]"},
    {"PREGOI",#09,0,0,1,"[%#y%?+␣..␣%#x]"},
    {"GO",#2a,0,0,3,"%l␣=␣%#x,␣->␣%#y+%#z"},
    {"GOI",#29,0,0,3,"%l␣=␣%#x,␣->␣%#y%?+"},
    {"STB",#1a,0,1,1,"M1[%#y+%#z]␣=␣%b,␣M8[%#w]=%#a"},
    {"STBI",#19,0,1,1,"M1[%#y%?+]␣=␣%b,␣M8[%#w]=%#a"},
    {"STBU",#1a,0,1,1,"M1[%#y+%#z]␣=␣%#b,␣M8[%#w]=%#a"},
    {"STBUI",#19,0,1,1,"M1[%#y%?+]␣=␣%#b,␣M8[%#w]=%#a"},
    {"STW",#1a,0,1,1,"M2[%#y+%#z]␣=␣%b,␣M8[%#w]=%#a"},
    {"STWI",#19,0,1,1,"M2[%#y%?+]␣=␣%b,␣M8[%#w]=%#a"},
    {"STWU",#1a,0,1,1,"M2[%#y+%#z]␣=␣%#b,␣M8[%#w]=%#a"},
    {"STWUI",#19,0,1,1,"M2[%#y%?+]␣=␣%#b,␣M8[%#w]=%#a"},
    {"STT",#1a,0,1,1,"M4[%#y+%#z]␣=␣%b,␣M8[%#w]=%#a"},
    {"STTI",#19,0,1,1,"M4[%#y%?+]␣=␣%b,␣M8[%#w]=%#a"},
    {"STTU",#1a,0,1,1,"M4[%#y+%#z]␣=␣%#b,␣M8[%#w]=%#a"},
    {"STTUI",#19,0,1,1,"M4[%#y%?+]␣=␣%#b,␣M8[%#w]=%#a"},
    {"STO",#1a,0,1,1,"M8[%#y+%#z]␣=␣%b"},
    {"STOI",#19,0,1,1,"M8[%#y%?+]␣=␣%b"},
    {"STOU",#1a,0,1,1,"M8[%#y+%#z]␣=␣%#b"},
    {"STOUI",#19,0,1,1,"M8[%#y%?+]␣=␣%#b"},
```

```
{"STSF", #1a, 0, 1, 1, "%(M4[%#y+%#z]%)␣=␣%.b,␣M8[%#w]=%#a"},
{"STSFI", #19, 0, 1, 1, "%(M4[%#y%?+]%)␣=␣%.b,␣M8[%#w]=%#a"},
{"STHT", #1a, 0, 1, 1, "M4[%#y+%#z]␣=␣%#b>>32,␣M8[%#w]=%#a"},
{"STHTI", #19, 0, 1, 1, "M4[%#y%?+]␣=␣%#b>>32,␣M8[%#w]=%#a"},
{"STCO", #0a, 0, 1, 1, "M8[%#y+%#z]␣=␣%b"},
{"STCOI", #09, 0, 1, 1, "M8[%#y%?+]␣=␣%b"},
{"STUNC", #1a, 0, 1, 1, "M8[%#y+%#z]␣=␣%#b"},
{"STUNCI", #19, 0, 1, 1, "M8[%#y%?+]␣=␣%#b"},
{"SYNCD", #0a, 0, 0, 1, "[%#y+%#z␣..␣%#x]"},
{"SYNCDI", #09, 0, 0, 1, "[%#y%?+␣..␣%#x]"},
{"PREST", #0a, 0, 0, 1, "[%#y+%#z␣..␣%#x]"},
{"PRESTI", #09, 0, 0, 1, "[%#y%?+␣..␣%#x]"},
{"SYNCID", #0a, 0, 0, 1, "[%#y+%#z␣..␣%#x]"},
{"SYNCIDI", #09, 0, 0, 1, "[%#y%?+␣..␣%#x]"},
{"PUSHGO", #aa, 0, 0, 3, "%lrO=%#b,␣rL=%a,␣rJ=%#x,␣->␣%#y+%#z"},
{"PUSHGOI", #a9, 0, 0, 3, "%lrO=%#b,␣rL=%a,␣rJ=%#x,␣->␣%#y%?+"}
```

This code is used in section 65.

69. ⟨ Info for logical and control commands 69 ⟩ ≡

```
{"OR", #2a, 0, 0, 1, "%l␣=␣%#y␣|␣%#z␣=␣%#x"},
    {"ORI", #29, 0, 0, 1, "%l␣=␣%#y␣|␣%z␣=␣%#x"},
    {"ORN", #2a, 0, 0, 1, "%l␣=␣%#y␣|~␣%#z␣=␣%#x"},
    {"ORNI", #29, 0, 0, 1, "%l␣=␣%#y␣|~␣%z␣=␣%#x"},
    {"NOR", #2a, 0, 0, 1, "%l␣=␣%#y␣~|␣%#z␣=␣%#x"},
    {"NORI", #29, 0, 0, 1, "%l␣=␣%#y␣~|␣%z␣=␣%#x"},
    {"XOR", #2a, 0, 0, 1, "%l␣=␣%#y␣^␣%#z␣=␣%#x"},
    {"XORI", #29, 0, 0, 1, "%l␣=␣%#y␣^␣%z␣=␣%#x"},
    {"AND", #2a, 0, 0, 1, "%l␣=␣%#y␣&␣%#z␣=␣%#x"},
    {"ANDI", #29, 0, 0, 1, "%l␣=␣%#y␣&␣%z␣=␣%#x"},
    {"ANDN", #2a, 0, 0, 1, "%l␣=␣%#y␣\\␣%#z␣=␣%#x"},
    {"ANDNI", #29, 0, 0, 1, "%l␣=␣%#y␣\\␣%z␣=␣%#x"},
    {"NAND", #2a, 0, 0, 1, "%l␣=␣%#y␣~&␣%#z␣=␣%#x"},
    {"NANDI", #29, 0, 0, 1, "%l␣=␣%#y␣~&␣%z␣=␣%#x"},
    {"NXOR", #2a, 0, 0, 1, "%l␣=␣%#y␣~^␣%#z␣=␣%#x"},
    {"NXORI", #29, 0, 0, 1, "%l␣=␣%#y␣~^␣%z␣=␣%#x"},
    {"BDIF", #2a, 0, 0, 1, "%l␣=␣%#y␣bdif␣%#z␣=␣%#x"},
    {"BDIFI", #29, 0, 0, 1, "%l␣=␣%#y␣bdif␣%z␣=␣%#x"},
    {"WDIF", #2a, 0, 0, 1, "%l␣=␣%#y␣wdif␣%#z␣=␣%#x"},
    {"WDIFI", #29, 0, 0, 1, "%l␣=␣%#y␣wdif␣%z␣=␣%#x"},
    {"TDIF", #2a, 0, 0, 1, "%l␣=␣%#y␣tdif␣%#z␣=␣%#x"},
    {"TDIFI", #29, 0, 0, 1, "%l␣=␣%#y␣tdif␣%z␣=␣%#x"},
    {"ODIF", #2a, 0, 0, 1, "%l␣=␣%#y␣odif␣%#z␣=␣%#x"},
    {"ODIFI", #29, 0, 0, 1, "%l␣=␣%#y␣odif␣%z␣=␣%#x"},
    {"MUX", #2a, rM, 0, 1, "%l␣=␣%#b?␣%#y:␣%#z␣=␣%#x"},
    {"MUXI", #29, rM, 0, 1, "%l␣=␣%#b?␣%#y:␣%z␣=␣%#x"},
    {"SADD", #2a, 0, 0, 1, "%l␣=␣nu(%#y\\%#z)␣=␣%x"},
    {"SADDI", #29, 0, 0, 1, "%l␣=␣nu(%#y%?\\)␣=␣%x"},
    {"MOR", #2a, 0, 0, 1, "%l␣=␣%#y␣mor␣%#z␣=␣%#x"},
    {"MORI", #29, 0, 0, 1, "%l␣=␣%#y␣mor␣%z␣=␣%#x"},
    {"MXOR", #2a, 0, 0, 1, "%l␣=␣%#y␣mxor␣%#z␣=␣%#x"},
    {"MXORI", #29, 0, 0, 1, "%l␣=␣%#y␣mxor␣%z␣=␣%#x"},
    {"SETH", #20, 0, 0, 1, "%l␣=␣%#z"},
    {"SETMH", #20, 0, 0, 1, "%l␣=␣%#z"},
    {"SETML", #20, 0, 0, 1, "%l␣=␣%#z"},
    {"SETL", #20, 0, 0, 1, "%l␣=␣%#z"},
    {"INCH", #30, 0, 0, 1, "%l␣=␣%#y␣+␣%#z␣=␣%#x"},
    {"INCMH", #30, 0, 0, 1, "%l␣=␣%#y␣+␣%#z␣=␣%#x"},
    {"INCML", #30, 0, 0, 1, "%l␣=␣%#y␣+␣%#z␣=␣%#x"},
    {"INCL", #30, 0, 0, 1, "%l␣=␣%#y␣+␣%#z␣=␣%#x"},
    {"ORH", #30, 0, 0, 1, "%l␣=␣%#y␣|␣%#z␣=␣%#x"},
    {"ORMH", #30, 0, 0, 1, "%l␣=␣%#y␣|␣%#z␣=␣%#x"},
    {"ORML", #30, 0, 0, 1, "%l␣=␣%#y␣|␣%#z␣=␣%#x"},
    {"ORL", #30, 0, 0, 1, "%l␣=␣%#y␣|␣%#z␣=␣%#x"},
    {"ANDNH", #30, 0, 0, 1, "%l␣=␣%#y␣\\␣%#z␣=␣%#x"},
    {"ANDNMH", #30, 0, 0, 1, "%l␣=␣%#y␣\\␣%#z␣=␣%#x"},
    {"ANDNML", #30, 0, 0, 1, "%l␣=␣%#y␣\\␣%#z␣=␣%#x"},
    {"ANDNL", #30, 0, 0, 1, "%l␣=␣%#y␣\\␣%#z␣=␣%#x"},
```

```
{"JMP", #40, 0, 0, 1, "->␣%#z"},
{"JMPB", #40, 0, 0, 1, "->␣%#z"},
{"PUSHJ", #e0, 0, 0, 1, "%lrO=%#b,␣rL=%a,␣rJ=%#x,␣->␣%#z"},
{"PUSHJB", #e0, 0, 0, 1, "%lrO=%#b,␣rL=%a,␣rJ=%#x,␣->␣%#z"},
{"GETA", #60, 0, 0, 1, "%l␣=␣%#z"},
{"GETAB", #60, 0, 0, 1, "%l␣=␣%#z"},
{"PUT", #02, 0, 0, 1, "%s␣=␣%r"},
{"PUTI", #01, 0, 0, 1, "%s␣=␣%r"},
{"POP", #80, rJ, 0, 3, "%lrL=%a,␣rO=%#b,␣->␣%#y%?+"},
{"RESUME", #00, 0, 0, 5, "{%#b}␣->␣%#z"},
{"SAVE", #20, 0, 20, 1, "%l␣=␣%#x"},
{"UNSAVE", #82, 0, 20, 1, "%#z:␣rG=%x,␣...,␣rL=%a"},
{"SYNC", #01, 0, 0, 1, ""},
{"SWYM", #00, 0, 0, 1, ""},
{"GET", #20, 0, 0, 1, "%l␣=␣%s␣=␣%#x"},
{"TRIP", #0a, 255, 0, 5, "rW=%#w,␣rX=%#x,␣rY=%#y,␣rZ=%#z,␣rB=%#b,␣g[255]=%#a"}
```

This code is used in section 65.

70. ⟨Convert relative address to absolute address 70⟩ ≡

```
{
  if ((op & #fe) ≡ JMP) yz = inst & #ffffff;
  if (op & 1) yz −= (op ≡ JMPB ? #1000000 : #10000);
  y = inst_ptr; z = incr(loc, yz ≪ 2);
}
```

This code is used in section 60.

71. ⟨Install operand fields 71⟩ ≡

```
if (resuming ∧ rop ≠ RESUME_AGAIN)
  ⟨Install special operands when resuming an interrupted operation 126⟩
else {
  if (f & #10) ⟨Set b from register X 74⟩;
  if (info[op].third_operand) ⟨Set b from special register 79⟩;
  if (f & #1) z.l = zz;
  else if (f & #2) ⟨Set z from register Z 72⟩
  else if ((op & #f0) ≡ SETH) ⟨Set z as an immediate wyde 78⟩;
  if (f & #4) y.l = yy;
  else if (f & #8) ⟨Set y from register Y 73⟩;
}
```

This code is used in section 60.

---

b: **octa**, §61.
f: **register tetra**, §62.
incr: **octa** (), MMIX-ARITH §6.
info: **op_info** [], §65.
inst: **tetra**, §61.
inst_ptr: **octa**, §61.
JMP = #f0, §54.
JMPB = #f1, §54.
l: **tetra**, §10.
loc: **octa**, §61.
op: **register mmix_opcode**, §62.
RESUME_AGAIN = 0, §125.
resuming: **bool**, §61.
rJ = 4, §55.
rM = 5, §55.
rop: **int**, §61.
SETH = #e0, §54.
third_operand: **unsigned char**, §64.
y: **octa**, §61.
yy: **register int**, §62.
yz: **register int**, §62.
z: **octa**, §61.
zz: **register int**, §62.

72. There are 256 global registers, $g[0]$ through $g[255]$; the first 32 of them are used for the special registers rA, rB, etc. There are *lring_mask* + 1 local registers, usually 256 but the user can increase this to a larger power of 2 if desired.

The current values of rL, rG, rO, and rS are kept in separate variables called L, G, O, and S for convenience. (In fact, O and S actually hold the values rO/8 and rS/8, modulo *lring_size*.)

```
⟨ Set z from register Z 72 ⟩ ≡
  {
    if (zz ≥ G) z = g[zz];
    else if (zz < L) z = l[(O + zz) & lring_mask];
  }
```

This code is used in section 71.

73.
```
⟨ Set y from register Y 73 ⟩ ≡
  {
    if (yy ≥ G) y = g[yy];
    else if (yy < L) y = l[(O + yy) & lring_mask];
  }
```

This code is used in section 71.

74.
```
⟨ Set b from register X 74 ⟩ ≡
  {
    if (xx ≥ G) b = g[xx];
    else if (xx < L) b = l[(O + xx) & lring_mask];
  }
```

This code is used in section 71.

75.
```
⟨ Local registers 62 ⟩ +≡
  register int G, L, O;    /* accessible copies of key registers */
```

76.
```
⟨ Global variables 19 ⟩ +≡
  octa g[256];    /* global registers */
  octa *l;    /* local registers */
  int lring_size;    /* the number of local registers (a power of 2) */
  int lring_mask;    /* one less than lring_size */
  int S;    /* congruent to rS ≫ 3 modulo lring_size */
```

77. Several of the global registers have constant values, because of the way MMIX has been simplified in this simulator.

Special register rN has a constant value identifying the time of compilation. (The macro `ABSTIME` is defined externally in the file `abstime.h`, which should have just been created by ABSTIME; ABSTIME is a trivial program that computes the value of the standard library function *time*(Λ). We assume that this number, which is the number of seconds in the "UNIX epoch," is less than 2^{32}. Beware: Our assumption will fail in February of 2106.)

```
#define VERSION 1    /* version of the MMIX architecture that we support */
#define SUBVERSION 0    /* secondary byte of version number */
#define SUBSUBVERSION 1    /* further qualification to version number */
```

⟨ Initialize everything 14 ⟩ +≡
```
g[rK] = neg_one;
g[rN].h = (VERSION ≪ 24) + (SUBVERSION ≪ 16) + (SUBSUBVERSION ≪ 8);
g[rN].l = ABSTIME;      /* see comment and warning above */
g[rT].h = #80000005;
g[rTT].h = #80000006;
g[rV].h = #369c2004;
if (lring_size < 256) lring_size = 256;
lring_mask = lring_size − 1;
if (lring_size & lring_mask)
   panic("The␣number␣of␣local␣registers␣must␣be␣a␣power␣of␣2");
l = (octa *) calloc(lring_size, sizeof(octa));
if (¬l) panic("No␣room␣for␣the␣local␣registers");
cur_round = ROUND_NEAR;
```

78. In operations like INCH, we want z to be the yz field, shifted left 48 bits. We also want y to be register X, which has previously been placed in b; then INCH can be simulated as if it were ADDU.

⟨ Set z as an immediate wyde 78 ⟩ ≡
```
{
   switch (op & 3) {
   case 0: z.h = yz ≪ 16; break;
   case 1: z.h = yz; break;
   case 2: z.l = yz ≪ 16; break;
   case 3: z.l = yz; break;
   }
   y = b;
}
```
This code is used in section 71.

79. ⟨ Set b from special register 79 ⟩ ≡
```
b = g[info[op].third_operand];
```
This code is used in section 71.

ABSTIME = macro, abstime.h.
b: **octa**, §61.
calloc: **void** *( ), <stdlib.h>.
cur_round: **int**, MMIX-ARITH §30.
h: **tetra**, §10.
info: **op_info** [ ], §65.
l: **tetra**, §10.
neg_one: **octa**, MMIX-ARITH §4.
octa = **struct**, §10.
op: **register mmix_opcode**, §62.
panic = macro ( ), §14.
rA = 21, §55.
rB = 0, §55.
rK = 15, §55.
rN = 9, §55.
ROUND_NEAR = 4, §100.
rT = 13, §55.
rTT = 14, §55.
rV = 18, §55.
third_operand: **unsigned char**, §64.
time: **time_t** ( ), <time.h>.
xx: **register int**, §62.
y: **octa**, §61.
yy: **register int**, §62.
yz: **register int**, §62.
z: **octa**, §61.
zz: **register int**, §62.

80. ⟨ Install register X as the destination, adjusting the register stack if necessary 80 ⟩ ≡

```
if (xx ≥ G) {
  sprintf(lhs, "$%d=g[%d]", xx, xx);
  x_ptr = &g[xx];
} else {
  while (xx ≥ L) ⟨ Increase rL 81 ⟩;
  sprintf(lhs, "$%d=l[%d]", xx, (O + xx) & lring_mask);
  x_ptr = &l[(O + xx) & lring_mask];
}
```

This code is used in section 60.

81. ⟨ Increase rL 81 ⟩ ≡

```
{
  l[(O + L) & lring_mask] = zero_octa;
  L = g[rL].l = L + 1;
  if (((S − O − L) & lring_mask) ≡ 0) stack_store();
}
```

This code is used in section 80.

82. The *stack_store* routine advances the "gamma" pointer in the ring of local registers, by storing the oldest local register into memory location rS and advancing rS.

```
#define test_store_bkpt(ll) if ((ll)→bkpt & write_bit) breakpoint = tracing = true
⟨ Subroutines 12 ⟩ +≡
  void stack_store ARGS((void));
  void stack_store()
  {
    register mem_tetra *ll = mem_find(g[rS]);
    register int k = S & lring_mask;

    ll→tet = l[k].h; test_store_bkpt(ll);
    (ll + 1)→tet = l[k].l; test_store_bkpt(ll + 1);
    if (stack_tracing) {
      tracing = true;
      if (cur_line) show_line();
      printf("␣␣␣␣␣␣␣␣␣␣␣␣␣M8[#%08x%08x]=l[%d]=#%08x%08x,␣rS+=8\n", g[rS].h,
          g[rS].l, k, l[k].h, l[k].l);
    }
    g[rS] = incr(g[rS], 8), S++;
  }
```

83. The *stack_load* routine is essentially the inverse of *stack_store*.

```
#define test_load_bkpt(ll) if ((ll)→bkpt & read_bit) breakpoint = tracing = true
⟨ Subroutines 12 ⟩ +≡
  void stack_load ARGS((void));
  void stack_load()
  {
    register mem_tetra *ll;
    register int k;
```

```
    S--, g[rS] = incr(g[rS], -8);
    ll = mem_find(g[rS]);
    k = S & lring_mask;
    l[k].h = ll->tet; test_load_bkpt(ll);
    l[k].l = (ll + 1)->tet; test_load_bkpt(ll + 1);
    if (stack_tracing) {
      tracing = true;
      if (cur_line) show_line();
      printf("␣␣␣␣␣␣␣␣␣␣␣␣␣rS-=8,␣l[%d]=M8[#%08x%08x]=#%08x%08x\n", k, g[rS].h,
          g[rS].l, l[k].h, l[k].l);
    }
  }
```

ARGS = macro ( ), §11.
bkpt: **unsigned char**, §16.
breakpoint: **bool**, §61.
cur_line: **int**, §31.
g: **octa** [ ], §76.
G: **register int**, §75.
h: **tetra**, §10.
incr: **octa** ( ), MMIX-ARITH §6.
l: **octa** ∗, §76.
L: **register int**, §75.
l: **tetra**, §10.
lhs: **char** [ ], §139.
lring_mask: **int**, §76.
mem_find: **mem_tetra** ∗( ), §20.
mem_tetra = **struct**, §16.
O: **register int**, §75.
printf: **int** ( ), <stdio.h>.
read_bit = macro, §58.
rL = 20, §55.
rS = 11, §55.
S: **int**, §76.
show_line: **void** ( ), §47.
sprintf: **int** ( ), <stdio.h>.
stack_tracing: **bool**, §61.
tet: **tetra**, §16.
tracing: **bool**, §61.
true = 1, §9.
write_bit = macro, §58.
x_ptr: **octa** ∗, §61.
xx: **register int**, §62.
zero_octa: **octa**, MMIX-ARITH §4.

84. Simulating the instructions. The master switch branches in 256 directions, one for each `MMIX` instruction.

Let's start with `ADD`, since it is somehow the most typical case—not too easy, and not too hard. The task is to compute $x = y + z$, and to signal overflow if the sum is out of range. Overflow occurs if and only if y and z have the same sign but the sum has a different sign.

Overflow is one of the eight arithmetic exceptions. We record such exceptions in a variable called *exc*, which is set to zero at the beginning of each cycle and used to update rA at the end.

The main control routine has put the input operands into octabytes y and z. It has also made *x_ptr* point to the octabyte where the result should be placed.

```
⟨ Cases for individual MMIX instructions 84 ⟩ ≡
case ADD: case ADDI: x = w;     /* w = oplus(y, z) */
  if (((y.h ⊕ z.h) & sign_bit) ≡ 0 ∧ ((y.h ⊕ x.h) & sign_bit) ≠ 0) exc |= V_BIT;
store_x: *x_ptr = x; break;
```

See also sections 85, 86, 87, 88, 89, 90, 92, 93, 94, 95, 96, 97, 101, 102, 104, 106, 107, 108, and 124.

This code is used in section 60.

85. Other cases of signed and unsigned addition and subtraction are, of course, similar. Overflow occurs in the calculation $x = y - z$ if and only if it occurs in the calculation $y = x + z$.

```
⟨ Cases for individual MMIX instructions 84 ⟩ +≡
case SUB: case SUBI: case NEG: case NEGI: x = ominus(y, z);
  if (((x.h ⊕ z.h) & sign_bit) ≡ 0 ∧ ((x.h ⊕ y.h) & sign_bit) ≠ 0) exc |= V_BIT;
  goto store_x;
case ADDU: case ADDUI: case INCH: case INCMH: case INCML: case INCL: x = w;
  goto store_x;
case SUBU: case SUBUI: case NEGU: case NEGUI: x = ominus(y, z); goto store_x;
case IIADDU: case IIADDUI: case IVADDU: case IVADDUI: case VIIIADDU:
  case VIIIADDUI: case XVIADDU: case XVIADDUI:
  x = oplus(shift_left(y, ((op & #f) ≫ 1) − 3), z); goto store_x;
case SETH: case SETMH: case SETML: case SETL: case GETA: case GETAB: x = z;
  goto store_x;
```

86. Let's get the simple bitwise operations out of the way too.

```
⟨ Cases for individual MMIX instructions 84 ⟩ +≡
case OR: case ORI: case ORH: case ORMH: case ORML: case ORL: x.h = y.h | z.h;
  x.l = y.l | z.l; goto store_x;
case ORN: case ORNI: x.h = y.h | ∼z.h; x.l = y.l | ∼z.l; goto store_x;
case NOR: case NORI: x.h = ∼(y.h | z.h); x.l = ∼(y.l | z.l); goto store_x;
case XOR: case XORI: x.h = y.h ⊕ z.h; x.l = y.l ⊕ z.l; goto store_x;
case AND: case ANDI: x.h = y.h & z.h; x.l = y.l & z.l; goto store_x;
case ANDN: case ANDNI: case ANDNH: case ANDNMH: case ANDNML: case ANDNL:
  x.h = y.h & ∼z.h; x.l = y.l & ∼z.l; goto store_x;
case NAND: case NANDI: x.h = ∼(y.h & z.h); x.l = ∼(y.l & z.l); goto store_x;
case NXOR: case NXORI: x.h = ∼(y.h ⊕ z.h); x.l = ∼(y.l ⊕ z.l); goto store_x;
```

87. The less simple bit manipulations are almost equally simple, given the subroutines of MMIX-ARITH. The MUX operation has three inputs; in such cases the inputs appear in y, z, and b.

```
#define shift_amt (z.h ∨ z.l ≥ 64 ? 64 : z.l)
⟨ Cases for individual MMIX instructions 84 ⟩ +≡
case SL: case SLI: x = shift_left(y, shift_amt);
  a = shift_right(x, shift_amt, 0);
  if (a.h ≠ y.h ∨ a.l ≠ y.l) exc |= V_BIT;
  goto store_x;
case SLU: case SLUI: x = shift_left(y, shift_amt); goto store_x;
case SR: case SRI: case SRU: case SRUI: x = shift_right(y, shift_amt, op & #2);
  goto store_x;
case MUX: case MUXI: x.h = (y.h & b.h) | (z.h & ∼b.h); x.l = (y.l & b.l) | (z.l & ∼b.l);
  goto store_x;
case SADD: case SADDI: x.l = count_bits(y.h & ∼z.h) + count_bits(y.l & ∼z.l); goto store_x;
case MOR: case MORI: x = bool_mult(y, z, false); goto store_x;
case MXOR: case MXORI: x = bool_mult(y, z, true); goto store_x;
case BDIF: case BDIFI: x.h = byte_diff(y.h, z.h); x.l = byte_diff(y.l, z.l); goto store_x;
case WDIF: case WDIFI: x.h = wyde_diff(y.h, z.h); x.l = wyde_diff(y.l, z.l); goto store_x;
case TDIF: case TDIFI: if (y.h > z.h) x.h = y.h − z.h;
tdif_l: if (y.l > z.l) x.l = y.l − z.l; goto store_x;
case ODIF: case ODIFI: if (y.h > z.h) x = ominus(y, z);
  else if (y.h ≡ z.h) goto tdif_l;
  goto store_x;
```

88. When an operation has two outputs, the primary output is placed in x and the auxiliary output is placed in a.

```
⟨ Cases for individual MMIX instructions 84 ⟩ +≡
case MUL: case MULI: x = signed_omult(y, z);
test_overflow: if (overflow) exc |= V_BIT;
  goto store_x;
case MULU: case MULUI: x = omult(y, z); a = g[rH] = aux; goto store_x;
case DIV: case DIVI: if (¬z.l ∧ ¬z.h) aux = y, exc |= D_BIT, overflow = false;
  else x = signed_odiv(y, z);
  a = g[rR] = aux; goto test_overflow;
case DIVU: case DIVUI: x = odiv(b, y, z); a = g[rR] = aux; goto store_x;
```

89. The floating point routines of MMIX-ARITH record exceptional events in a variable called *exceptions*. Here we simply merge those bits into the *exc* variable. The U_BIT is not exactly the same as "underflow," but the true definition of underflow will be applied when *exc* is combined with rA.

```
⟨ Cases for individual MMIX instructions 84 ⟩ +≡
case FADD: x = fplus(y, z);
fin_float: round_mode = cur_round;
store_fx: exc |= exceptions; goto store_x;
case FSUB: a = z; if (fcomp(a, zero_octa) ≠ 2) a.h ⊕= sign_bit;
  x = fplus(y, a); goto fin_float;
case FMUL: x = fmult(y, z); goto fin_float;
```

```
case FDIV: x = fdivide(y, z); goto fin_float;
case FREM: x = fremstep(y, z, 2500); goto fin_float;
case FSQRT: x = froot(z, y.l);
fin_unifloat: if (y.h ∨ y.l > 4) goto illegal_inst;
  round_mode = (y.l ? y.l : cur_round); goto store_fx;
case FINT: x = fintegerize(z, y.l); goto fin_unifloat;
case FIX: x = fixit(z, y.l); goto fin_unifloat;
case FIXU: x = fixit(z, y.l); exceptions &= ~W_BIT; goto fin_unifloat;
case FLOT: case FLOTI: case FLOTU: case FLOTUI: case SFLOT: case SFLOTI:
  case SFLOTU: case SFLOTUI: x = floatit(z, y.l, op & #2, op & #4); goto fin_unifloat;
```


a: **octa**, §61.
aux: **octa**, MMIX-ARITH §4.
b: **octa**, §61.
BDIF = #d0, §54.
BDIFI = #d1, §54.
bool_mult: **octa** ( ), MMIX-ARITH §29.
byte_diff: **tetra** ( ), MMIX-ARITH §27.
count_bits: **int** ( ), MMIX-ARITH §26.
cur_round: **int**, MMIX-ARITH §30.
D_BIT = macro, §57.
DIV = #1c, §54.
DIVI = #1d, §54.
DIVU = #1e, §54.
DIVUI = #1f, §54.
exc: **int**, §61.
exceptions: **int**, MMIX-ARITH §32.
FADD = #04, §54.
false = 0, §9.
fcomp: **int** ( ), MMIX-ARITH §85.
FDIV = #14, §54.
fdivide: **octa** ( ), MMIX-ARITH §44.
FINT = #17, §54.
fintegerize: **octa** ( ), MMIX-ARITH §86.
FIX = #05, §54.
fixit: **octa** ( ), MMIX-ARITH §88.
FIXU = #07, §54.
floatit: **octa** ( ), MMIX-ARITH §89.
FLOT = #08, §54.
FLOTI = #09, §54.
FLOTU = #0a, §54.
FLOTUI = #0b, §54.
FMUL = #10, §54.
fmult: **octa** ( ), MMIX-ARITH §41.
fplus: **octa** ( ), MMIX-ARITH §46.
FREM = #16, §54.
fremstep: **octa** ( ), MMIX-ARITH §93.
froot: **octa** ( ), MMIX-ARITH §91.
FSQRT = #15, §54.
FSUB = #06, §54.
g: **octa** [ ], §76.
h: **tetra**, §10.
illegal_inst: label, §107.
l: **tetra**, §10.
MOR = #dc, §54.
MORI = #dd, §54.
MUL = #18, §54.
MULI = #19, §54.
MULU = #1a, §54.
MULUI = #1b, §54.
MUX = #d8, §54.
MUXI = #d9, §54.
MXOR = #de, §54.
MXORI = #df, §54.
ODIF = #d6, §54.
ODIFI = #d7, §54.
odiv: **octa** ( ), MMIX-ARITH §13.
ominus: **octa** ( ), MMIX-ARITH §5.
omult: **octa** ( ), MMIX-ARITH §8.
op: **register mmix_opcode**, §62.
overflow: **bool**, MMIX-ARITH §4.
rH = 3, §55.
round_mode: **int**, §61.
rR = 6, §55.
SADD = #da, §54.
SADDI = #db, §54.
SFLOT = #0c, §54.
SFLOTI = #0d, §54.
SFLOTU = #0e, §54.
SFLOTUI = #0f, §54.
shift_left: **octa** ( ), MMIX-ARITH §7.
shift_right: **octa** ( ), MMIX-ARITH §7.
sign_bit = macro, §15.
signed_odiv: **octa** ( ), MMIX-ARITH §24.
signed_omult: **octa** ( ), MMIX-ARITH §12.
SL = #38, §54.
SLI = #39, §54.
SLU = #3a, §54.
SLUI = #3b, §54.
SR = #3c, §54.
SRI = #3d, §54.
SRU = #3e, §54.
SRUI = #3f, §54.
store_x: label, §84.
TDIF = #d4, §54.
TDIFI = #d5, §54.
true = 1, §9.
U_BIT = macro, §57.
V_BIT = macro, §57.
W_BIT = macro, §57.
WDIF = #d2, §54.
WDIFI = #d3, §54.
wyde_diff: **tetra** ( ), MMIX-ARITH §28.
x: **octa**, §61.
y: **octa**, §61.
z: **octa**, §61.
zero_octa: **octa**, MMIX-ARITH §4.

90. We have now done all of the arithmetic operations except for the cases that compare two registers and yield a value of −1 or 0 or 1.

```
#define cmp_zero store_x   /* x is 0 by default */

⟨ Cases for individual MMIX instructions 84 ⟩ +≡
case CMP: case CMPI: if ((y.h & sign_bit) > (z.h & sign_bit)) goto cmp_neg;
  if ((y.h & sign_bit) < (z.h & sign_bit)) goto cmp_pos;
case CMPU: case CMPUI: if (y.h < z.h) goto cmp_neg;
  if (y.h > z.h) goto cmp_pos;
  if (y.l < z.l) goto cmp_neg;
  if (y.l ≡ z.l) goto cmp_zero;
cmp_pos: x.l = 1; goto store_x;
cmp_neg: x = neg_one; goto store_x;
case FCMPE: k = fepscomp(y, z, b, true);
  if (k) goto cmp_zero_or_invalid;
case FCMP: k = fcomp(y, z);
  if (k < 0) goto cmp_neg;
cmp_fin: if (k ≡ 1) goto cmp_pos;
cmp_zero_or_invalid: if (k ≡ 2) exc |= I_BIT;
  goto cmp_zero;
case FUN: if (fcomp(y, z) ≡ 2) goto cmp_pos; else goto cmp_zero;
case FEQL: if (fcomp(y, z) ≡ 0) goto cmp_pos; else goto cmp_zero;
case FEQLE: k = fepscomp(y, z, b, false);
  goto cmp_fin;
case FUNE: if (fepscomp(y, z, b, true) ≡ 2) goto cmp_pos; else goto cmp_zero;
```

91. We have now done all the register-register operations except for the conditional commands. Conditional commands and branch commands all make use of a simple subroutine that determines whether a given octabyte satisfies the condition of a given opcode.

```
⟨ Subroutines 12 ⟩ +≡
  int register_truth ARGS((octa, mmix_opcode));
  int register_truth(o, op)
      octa o;
      mmix_opcode op;
  { register int b;
    switch ((op ≫ 1) & #3) {
    case 0: b = o.h ≫ 31; break;   /* negative? */
    case 1: b = (o.h ≡ 0 ∧ o.l ≡ 0); break;   /* zero? */
    case 2: b = (o.h < sign_bit ∧ (o.h ∨ o.l)); break;   /* positive? */
    case 3: b = o.l & #1; break;   /* odd? */
    }
    if (op & #8) return b ⊕ 1;
    else return b;
  }
```

92. The b operand will be zero on the ZS operations; it will be the contents of register X on the CS operations.

```
⟨ Cases for individual MMIX instructions 84 ⟩ +≡
case CSN: case CSNI: case CSZ: case CSZI:
  case CSP: case CSPI: case CSOD: case CSODI:
  case CSNN: case CSNNI: case CSNZ: case CSNZI:
  case CSNP: case CSNPI: case CSEV: case CSEVI:
  case ZSN: case ZSNI: case ZSZ: case ZSZI:
  case ZSP: case ZSPI: case ZSOD: case ZSODI:
  case ZSNN: case ZSNNI: case ZSNZ: case ZSNZI:
  case ZSNP: case ZSNPI: case ZSEV: case ZSEVI:
  x = register_truth(y, op) ? z : b; goto store_x;
```

ARGS = macro ( ), §11.
b: **octa**, §61.
CMP = #30, §54.
CMPI = #31, §54.
CMPU = #32, §54.
CMPUI = #33, §54.
CSEV = #6e, §54.
CSEVI = #6f, §54.
CSN = #60, §54.
CSNI = #61, §54.
CSNN = #68, §54.
CSNNI = #69, §54.
CSNP = #6c, §54.
CSNPI = #6d, §54.
CSNZ = #6a, §54.
CSNZI = #6b, §54.
CSOD = #66, §54.
CSODI = #67, §54.
CSP = #64, §54.
CSPI = #65, §54.
CSZ = #62, §54.
CSZI = #63, §54.
exc: **int**, §61.
false = 0, §9.
FCMP = #01, §54.
FCMPE = #11, §54.
fcomp: **int** ( ), MMIX-ARITH §85.
fepscomp: **int** ( ), MMIX-ARITH §50.
FEQL = #03, §54.
FEQLE = #13, §54.
FUN = #02, §54.
FUNE = #12, §54.
h: **tetra**, §10.
I_BIT = macro, §57.
k: **register int**, §62.
l: **tetra**, §10.
mmix_opcode = **enum**, §54.
neg_one: **octa**, MMIX-ARITH §4.
octa = **struct**, §10.
op: **register mmix_opcode**, §62.
sign_bit = macro, §15.
store_x: label, §84.
true = 1, §9.
x: **octa**, §61.
y: **octa**, §61.
z: **octa**, §61.
ZSEV = #7e, §54.
ZSEVI = #7f, §54.
ZSN = #70, §54.
ZSNI = #71, §54.
ZSNN = #78, §54.
ZSNNI = #79, §54.
ZSNP = #7c, §54.
ZSNPI = #7d, §54.
ZSNZ = #7a, §54.
ZSNZI = #7b, §54.
ZSOD = #76, §54.
ZSODI = #77, §54.
ZSP = #74, §54.
ZSPI = #75, §54.
ZSZ = #72, §54.
ZSZI = #73, §54.

93. Didn't that feel good, when 32 opcodes reduced to a single case? We get to do it one more time. Happiness!

```
⟨ Cases for individual MMIX instructions 84 ⟩ +≡
case BN: case BNB: case BZ: case BZB:
  case BP: case BPB: case BOD: case BODB:
  case BNN: case BNNB: case BNZ: case BNZB:
  case BNP: case BNPB: case BEV: case BEVB:
  case PBN: case PBNB: case PBZ: case PBZB:
  case PBP: case PBPB: case PBOD: case PBODB:
  case PBNN: case PBNNB: case PBNZ: case PBNZB:
  case PBNP: case PBNPB: case PBEV: case PBEVB:
  x.l = register_truth(b, op);
  if (x.l) {
    inst_ptr = z;
    good = (op ≥ PBN);
  } else good = (op < PBN);
  if (good) good_guesses++;
  else {
    bad_guesses++, sclock.l += 2;      /* penalty is 2υ for bad guess */
    if (g[rI].l ≤ 2 ∧ g[rI].l ∧ g[rI].h ≡ 0) tracing = breakpoint = true;
    g[rI] = incr(g[rI], −2);
  }
  break;
```

94. Memory operations are next on our agenda. The memory address, $y + z$, has already been placed in w.

```
⟨ Cases for individual MMIX instructions 84 ⟩ +≡
case LDB: case LDBI: case LDBU: case LDBUI:
  i = 56; j = (w.l & #3) ≪ 3;
  goto fin_ld;
case LDW: case LDWI: case LDWU: case LDWUI:
  i = 48; j = (w.l & #2) ≪ 3;
  goto fin_ld;
case LDT: case LDTI: case LDTU: case LDTUI:
  i = 32; j = 0; goto fin_ld;
case LDHT: case LDHTI: i = j = 0;
fin_ld: ll = mem_find(w); test_load_bkpt(ll);
  x.h = ll→tet;
  x = shift_right(shift_left(x, j), i, op & #2);
check_ld: if (w.h & sign_bit) goto privileged_inst;
  goto store_x;
case LDO: case LDOI: case LDOU: case LDOUI: case LDUNC: case LDUNCI: w.l &= −8;
  ll = mem_find(w);
  test_load_bkpt(ll); test_load_bkpt(ll + 1);
  x.h = ll→tet; x.l = (ll + 1)→tet;
  goto check_ld;
case LDSF: case LDSFI: ll = mem_find(w); test_load_bkpt(ll);
  x = load_sf(ll→tet); goto check_ld;
```

95. ⟨ Cases for individual MMIX instructions 84 ⟩ +≡

```
case STB: case STBI: case STBU: case STBUI:
  i = 56; j = (w.l & #3) ≪ 3;
  goto fin_pst;
case STW: case STWI: case STWU: case STWUI:
  i = 48; j = (w.l & #2) ≪ 3;
  goto fin_pst;
case STT: case STTI: case STTU: case STTUI:
  i = 32; j = 0;
fin_pst: ll = mem_find(w);
  if ((op & #2) ≡ 0) {
    a = shift_right(shift_left(b, i), i, 0);
    if (a.h ≠ b.h ∨ a.l ≠ b.l) exc |= V_BIT;
  }
  ll→tet ⊕= (ll→tet ⊕ (b.l ≪ (i − 32 − j))) & ((((tetra) −1) ≪ (i − 32)) ≫ j);
  goto fin_st;
case STSF: case STSFI: ll = mem_find(w);
  ll→tet = store_sf(b); exc = exceptions;
  goto fin_st;
case STHT: case STHTI: ll = mem_find(w); ll→tet = b.h;
fin_st: test_store_bkpt(ll);
  w.l &= −8; ll = mem_find(w);
  a.h = ll→tet; a.l = (ll + 1)→tet;      /* for trace output */
  goto check_st;
case STCO: case STCOI: b.l = xx;
case STO: case STOI: case STOU: case STOUI: case STUNC: case STUNCI: w.l &= −8;
  ll = mem_find(w);
  test_store_bkpt(ll); test_store_bkpt(ll + 1);
  ll→tet = b.h; (ll + 1)→tet = b.l;
check_st: if (w.h & sign_bit) goto privileged_inst;
  break;
```

96. The CSWAP operation has elements of both loading and storing. We shuffle some of the operands around so that they will appear correctly in the trace output.

⟨ Cases for individual MMIX instructions 84 ⟩ +≡

```
case CSWAP: case CSWAPI: w.l &= −8; ll = mem_find(w);
  test_load_bkpt(ll); test_load_bkpt(ll + 1);
  a = g[rP];
  if (ll→tet ≡ a.h ∧ (ll + 1)→tet ≡ a.l) {
    x.h = 0, x.l = 1;
    test_store_bkpt(ll); test_store_bkpt(ll + 1);
    ll→tet = b.h, (ll + 1)→tet = b.l;
    strcpy(rhs, "M8[%#w]=%#b");
  } else {
    b.h = ll→tet, b.l = (ll + 1)→tet;
    g[rP] = b;
    strcpy(rhs, "rP=%#b");
  }
  goto check_ld;
```

97. The GET command is permissive, but PUT is restrictive.

```
⟨ Cases for individual MMIX instructions 84 ⟩ +≡
case GET: if (yy ≠ 0 ∨ zz ≥ 32) goto illegal_inst;
  x = g[zz];
  goto store_x;
case PUT: case PUTI: if (yy ≠ 0 ∨ xx ≥ 32) goto illegal_inst;
  strcpy(rhs, "%z␣=␣%#z");
  if (xx ≥ 8) {
    if (xx ≤ 11 ∧ xx ≠ 8) goto illegal_inst;      /* can't change rN, rO, rS */
    if (xx ≤ 18) goto privileged_inst;
    if (xx ≡ rA) ⟨ Get ready to update rA 100 ⟩
    else if (xx ≡ rL) ⟨ Set L = z = min(z, L) 98 ⟩
    else if (xx ≡ rG) ⟨ Get ready to update rG 99 ⟩;
  }
  g[xx] = z; zz = xx; break;
```

98. ⟨ Set $L = z = \min(z, L)$ 98 ⟩ ≡

```
{
  x = z; strcpy(rhs, z.h ? "min(rL,%#x)␣=␣%z" : "min(rL,%x)␣=␣%z");
  if (z.l > L ∨ z.h) z.h = 0, z.l = L;
  else old_L = L = z.l;
}
```

This code is used in section 97.

---

a: **octa**, §61.
b: **octa**, §61.
check_ld: label, §94.
CSWAP = #94, §54.
CSWAPI = #95, §54.
exc: **int**, §61.
exceptions: **int**, MMIX-ARITH §32.
g: **octa** [], §76.
GET = #fe, §54.
h: **tetra**, §10.
i: **register int**, §62.
illegal_inst: label, §107.
j: **register int**, §62.
l: **tetra**, §10.
L: **register int**, §75.
ll: **register mem_tetra** *, §62.
mem_find: **mem_tetra** *(), §20.
old_L: **int**, §61.
op: **register mmix_opcode**, §62.
privileged_inst: label, §107.
PUT = #f6, §54.
PUTI = #f7, §54.
rA = 21, §55.
rG = 19, §55.
rhs = macro, §139.
rL = 20, §55.
rP = 23, §55.
shift_left: **octa** (), MMIX-ARITH §7.
shift_right: **octa** (), MMIX-ARITH §7.
sign_bit = macro, §15.
STB = #a0, §54.
STBI = #a1, §54.
STBU = #a2, §54.
STBUI = #a3, §54.
STCO = #b4, §54.
STCOI = #b5, §54.
STHT = #b2, §54.
STHTI = #b3, §54.
STO = #ac, §54.
STOI = #ad, §54.
store_sf: **tetra** (), MMIX-ARITH §40.
store_x: label, §84.
STOU = #ae, §54.
STOUI = #af, §54.
strcpy: **char** *(), <string.h>.
STSF = #b0, §54.
STSFI = #b1, §54.
STT = #a8, §54.
STTI = #a9, §54.
STTU = #aa, §54.
STTUI = #ab, §54.
STUNC = #b6, §54.
STUNCI = #b7, §54.
STW = #a4, §54.
STWI = #a5, §54.
STWU = #a6, §54.
STWUI = #a7, §54.
test_load_bkpt = macro (), §83.
test_store_bkpt = macro (), §82.
tet: **tetra**, §16.
tetra = **unsigned int**, §10.
V_BIT = macro, §57.
w: **octa**, §61.
x: **octa**, §61.
xx: **register int**, §62.
yy: **register int**, §62.
z: **octa**, §61.
zz: **register int**, §62.

99. ⟨ Get ready to update rG 99 ⟩ ≡

```
{
  if (z.h ≠ 0 ∨ z.l > 255 ∨ z.l < L ∨ z.l < 32) goto illegal_inst;
  for (j = z.l; j < G; j++) g[j] = zero_octa;
  G = z.l;
}
```

This code is used in section 97.

100.

```
#define ROUND_OFF 1
#define ROUND_UP 2
#define ROUND_DOWN 3
#define ROUND_NEAR 4
```

⟨ Get ready to update rA 100 ⟩ ≡

```
{
  if (z.h ≠ 0 ∨ z.l ≥ #40000) goto illegal_inst;
  cur_round = (z.l ≥ #10000 ? z.l ≫ 16 : ROUND_NEAR);
}
```

This code is used in section 97.

101. Pushing and popping are rather delicate, because we want to trace them coherently.

⟨ Cases for individual MMIX instructions 84 ⟩ +≡

```
case PUSHGO: case PUSHGOI: inst_ptr = w; goto push;
case PUSHJ: case PUSHJB: inst_ptr = z;
push: if (xx ≥ G) {
    xx = L++;
    if (((S − O − L) & lring_mask) ≡ 0) stack_store( );
  }
  x.l = xx; l[(O + xx) & lring_mask] = x;      /* the "hole" records the amount pushed */
  sprintf(lhs, "l[%d]=%d,␣", (O + xx) & lring_mask, xx);
  x = g[rJ] = incr(loc, 4);
  L −= xx + 1; O += xx + 1;
  b = g[rO] = incr(g[rO], (xx + 1) ≪ 3);
sync_L: a.l = g[rL].l = L; break;
case POP: if (xx ≠ 0 ∧ xx ≤ L) y = l[(O + xx − 1) & lring_mask];
  if (g[rS].l ≡ g[rO].l) stack_load( );
  k = l[(O − 1) & lring_mask].l & #ff;
  while ((tetra)(O − S) ≤ (tetra) k) stack_load( );
  L = k + (xx ≤ L ? xx : L + 1);
  if (L > G) L = G;
  if (L > k) {
    l[(O − 1) & lring_mask] = y;
    if (y.h) sprintf(lhs, "l[%d]=#%x%08x,␣", (O − 1) & lring_mask, y.h, y.l);
    else sprintf(lhs, "l[%d]=#%x,␣", (O − 1) & lring_mask, y.l);
  } else lhs[0] = '\0';
  y = g[rJ]; z.l = yz ≪ 2; inst_ptr = oplus(y, z);
  O −= k + 1; b = g[rO] = incr(g[rO], −((k + 1) ≪ 3));
  goto sync_L;
```

102. To complete our simulation of MMIX's register stack, we need to implement SAVE and UNSAVE.

```
⟨ Cases for individual MMIX instructions 84 ⟩ +≡
case SAVE: if (xx < G ∨ yy ≠ 0 ∨ zz ≠ 0) goto illegal_inst;
  l[(O + L) & lring_mask].l = L, L++;
  if (((S − O − L) & lring_mask) ≡ 0) stack_store();
  O += L; g[rO] = incr(g[rO], L ≪ 3);
  L = g[rL].l = 0;
  while (g[rO].l ≠ g[rS].l) stack_store();
  for (k = G; ; ) {
    ⟨ Store g[k] in the register stack 103 ⟩;
    if (k ≡ 255) k = rB;
    else if (k ≡ rR) k = rP;
    else if (k ≡ rZ + 1) break;
    else k++;
  }
  O = S, g[rO] = g[rS];
  x = incr(g[rO], −8); goto store_x;
```

---

a: **octa**, §61.
b: **octa**, §61.
cur_round: **int**, MMIX-ARITH §30.
g: **octa** [], §76.
G: **register int**, §75.
h: **tetra**, §10.
illegal_inst: label, §107.
incr: **octa** ( ), MMIX-ARITH §6.
inst_ptr: **octa**, §61.
j: **register int**, §62.
k: **register int**, §62.
L: **register int**, §75.
l: **tetra**, §10.
l: **octa** ∗, §76.
lhs: **char** [], §139.
loc: **octa**, §61.
lring_mask: **int**, §76.
O: **register int**, §75.
oplus: **octa** ( ), MMIX-ARITH §5.
POP = #f8, §54.
PUSHGO = #be, §54.
PUSHGOI = #bf, §54.
PUSHJ = #f2, §54.
PUSHJB = #f3, §54.
rB = 0, §55.
rJ = 4, §55.
rL = 20, §55.
rO = 10, §55.
rP = 23, §55.
rR = 6, §55.
rS = 11, §55.
rZ = 27, §55.
S: **int**, §76.
SAVE = #fa, §54.
sprintf: **int** ( ), <stdio.h>.
stack_load: **void** ( ), §83.
stack_store: **void** ( ), §82.
store_x: label, §84.
tetra = **unsigned int**, §10.
w: **octa**, §61.
x: **octa**, §61.
xx: **register int**, §62.
y: **octa**, §61.
yy: **register int**, §62.
yz: **register int**, §62.
z: **octa**, §61.
zero_octa: **octa**, MMIX-ARITH §4.
zz: **register int**, §62.

103. This part of the program naturally has a lot in common with the *stack_store* subroutine. (There's a little white lie in the section name; if k is $rZ+1$, we store rG and rA, not $g[k]$.)

⟨Store $g[k]$ in the register stack 103⟩ ≡

```
ll = mem_find(g[rS]);
if (k ≡ rZ + 1) x.h = G ≪ 24, x.l = g[rA].l;
else x = g[k];
ll→tet = x.h; test_store_bkpt(ll);
(ll + 1)→tet = x.l; test_store_bkpt(ll + 1);
if (stack_tracing) {
  tracing = true;
  if (cur_line) show_line();
  if (k ≥ 32) printf("␣␣␣␣␣␣␣␣␣␣␣␣␣M8[#%08x%08x]=g[%d]=#%08x%08x,␣rS+=8\n",
      g[rS].h, g[rS].l, k, x.h, x.l);
  else printf("␣␣␣␣␣␣␣␣␣␣␣␣␣M8[#%08x%08x]=%s=#%08x%08x,␣rS+=8\n", g[rS].h,
      g[rS].l, k ≡ rZ + 1 ? "(rG,rA)" : special_name[k], x.h, x.l);
}
S++, g[rS] = incr(g[rS], 8);
```

This code is used in section 102.

104. ⟨Cases for individual MMIX instructions 84⟩ +≡

```
case UNSAVE: if (xx ≠ 0 ∨ yy ≠ 0) goto illegal_inst;
  z.l &= −8; g[rS] = incr(z, 8);
  for (k = rZ + 1; ; ) {
    ⟨Load g[k] from the register stack 105⟩;
    if (k ≡ rP) k = rR;
    else if (k ≡ rB) k = 255;
    else if (k ≡ G) break;
    else k−−;
  }
  S = g[rS].l ≫ 3;
  stack_load();
  k = l[S & lring_mask].l & #ff;
  for (j = 0; j < k; j++) stack_load();
  O = S; g[rO] = g[rS]; L = k > G ? G : k;
  g[rL].l = L; a = g[rL]; g[rG].l = G; break;
```

105. ⟨Load $g[k]$ from the register stack 105⟩ ≡

```
g[rS] = incr(g[rS], −8);
ll = mem_find(g[rS]);
test_load_bkpt(ll); test_load_bkpt(ll + 1);
if (k ≡ rZ + 1) {
  x.l = G = g[rG].l = ll→tet ≫ 24, a.l = g[rA].l = (ll + 1)→tet & #3ffff;
  if (G < 32) x.l = G = g[rG].l = 32;
} else g[k].h = ll→tet, g[k].l = (ll + 1)→tet;
if (stack_tracing) {
  tracing = true;
  if (cur_line) show_line();
  if (k ≥ 32) printf("␣␣␣␣␣␣␣␣␣␣␣␣␣rS−=8,␣g[%d]=M8[#%08x%08x]=#%08x%08x\n", k,
      g[rS].h, g[rS].l, ll→tet, (ll + 1)→tet);
```

```
    else if (k ≡ rZ + 1) printf("␣␣␣␣␣␣␣␣␣␣␣␣␣(rG,rA)=M8[#%08x%08x]=#%08x%08x\n",
            g[rS].h, g[rS].l, ll→tet, (ll + 1)→tet);
    else printf("␣␣␣␣␣␣␣␣␣␣␣␣␣rS-=8,␣%s=M8[#%08x%08x]=#%08x%08x\n",
            special_name[k], g[rS].h, g[rS].l, ll→tet, (ll + 1)→tet);
  }
```

This code is used in section 104.

106. The cache maintenance instructions don't affect this simulation, because there are no caches. But if the user has invoked them, we do provide a bit of information when tracing, indicating the scope of the instruction.

```
⟨ Cases for individual MMIX instructions 84 ⟩ +≡
case SYNCID: case SYNCIDI: case PREST: case PRESTI: case SYNCD: case SYNCDI:
  case PREGO: case PREGOI: case PRELD: case PRELDI: x = incr(w, xx); break;
```

107. Several loose ends remain to be nailed down.

```
⟨ Cases for individual MMIX instructions 84 ⟩ +≡
case GO: case GOI: x = inst_ptr; inst_ptr = w; goto store_x;
case JMP: case JMPB: inst_ptr = z;
case SWYM: break;
case SYNC: if (xx ≠ 0 ∨ yy ≠ 0 ∨ zz > 7) goto illegal_inst;
  if (zz ≤ 3) break;
case LDVTS: case LDVTSI: privileged_inst: strcpy(lhs, "!privileged");
  goto break_inst;
illegal_inst: strcpy(lhs, "!illegal");
break_inst: breakpoint = tracing = true;
  if (¬interacting ∧ ¬interact_after_break) halted = true;
  break;
```

108. Trips and traps. We have now implemented 253 of the 256 instructions: all but `TRIP`, `TRAP`, and `RESUME`.

The `TRIP` instruction simply turns `H_BIT` on in the *exc* variable; this will trigger an interruption to location 0.

The `TRAP` instruction is not simulated, except for the system calls mentioned in the introduction.

```
⟨ Cases for individual MMIX instructions 84 ⟩ +≡
case TRIP: exc |= H_BIT; break;
case TRAP: if (xx ≠ 0 ∨ yy > max_sys_call) goto privileged_inst;
  strcpy(rhs, trap_format[yy]);
  g[rWW] = inst_ptr;
  g[rXX].h = sign_bit, g[rXX].l = inst;
  g[rYY] = y, g[rZZ] = z;
  z.h = 0, z.l = zz;
  a = incr(b, 8);
  ⟨ Prepare memory arguments ma = M[a] and mb = M[b] if needed 111 ⟩;
  switch (yy) {
  case Halt: ⟨ Either halt or print warning 109 ⟩; g[rBB] = g[255]; break;
  case Fopen: g[rBB] = mmix_fopen((unsigned char) zz, mb, ma); break;
  case Fclose: g[rBB] = mmix_fclose((unsigned char) zz); break;
  case Fread: g[rBB] = mmix_fread((unsigned char) zz, mb, ma); break;
  case Fgets: g[rBB] = mmix_fgets((unsigned char) zz, mb, ma); break;
  case Fgetws: g[rBB] = mmix_fgetws((unsigned char) zz, mb, ma); break;
  case Fwrite: g[rBB] = mmix_fwrite((unsigned char) zz, mb, ma); break;
  case Fputs: g[rBB] = mmix_fputs((unsigned char) zz, b); break;
  case Fputws: g[rBB] = mmix_fputws((unsigned char) zz, b); break;
  case Fseek: g[rBB] = mmix_fseek((unsigned char) zz, b); break;
  case Ftell: g[rBB] = mmix_ftell((unsigned char) zz); break;
  }
  x = g[255] = g[rBB]; break;
```

109. ⟨ Either halt or print warning 109 ⟩ ≡

```
  if (¬zz) halted = breakpoint = true;
  else if (zz ≡ 1) {
    if (loc.h ∨ loc.l ≥ #90) goto privileged_inst;
    print_trip_warning(loc.l ≫ 4, incr(g[rW], −4));
  } else goto privileged_inst;
```

This code is used in section 108.

110. ⟨ Global variables 19 ⟩ +≡

```
  char arg_count[] = {1, 3, 1, 3, 3, 3, 3, 2, 2, 2, 1};
  char *trap_format[] = {"Halt(%z)",
      "$255␣=␣Fopen(%!z,M8[%#b]=%#q,M8[%#a]=%p)␣=␣%x",
      "$255␣=␣Fclose(%!z)␣=␣%x", "$255␣=␣Fread(%!z,M8[%#b]=%#q,M8[%#a]=%p)␣=␣%x",
      "$255␣=␣Fgets(%!z,M8[%#b]=%#q,M8[%#a]=%p)␣=␣%x",
      "$255␣=␣Fgetws(%!z,M8[%#b]=%#q,M8[%#a]=%p)␣=␣%x",
      "$255␣=␣Fwrite(%!z,M8[%#b]=%#q,M8[%#a]=%p)␣=␣%x",
      "$255␣=␣Fputs(%!z,%#b)␣=␣%x", "$255␣=␣Fputws(%!z,%#b)␣=␣%x",
      "$255␣=␣Fseek(%!z,%b)␣=␣%x", "$255␣=␣Ftell(%!z)␣=␣%x"};
```

111. ⟨Prepare memory arguments $ma = M[a]$ and $mb = M[b]$ if needed 111⟩ ≡

```
if (arg_count[yy] ≡ 3) {
  ll = mem_find(b); test_load_bkpt(ll); test_load_bkpt(ll + 1);
  mb.h = ll→tet, mb.l = (ll + 1)→tet;
  ll = mem_find(a); test_load_bkpt(ll); test_load_bkpt(ll + 1);
  ma.h = ll→tet, ma.l = (ll + 1)→tet;
}
```

This code is used in section 108.

112. The input/output operations invoked by TRAPs are done by subroutines in an auxiliary program module called MMIX-IO. Here we need only declare those subroutines, and write three primitive interfaces on which they depend.

113. ⟨Global variables 19⟩ +≡

```
extern void mmix_io_init ARGS((void));
extern octa mmix_fopen ARGS((unsigned char, octa, octa));
extern octa mmix_fclose ARGS((unsigned char));
extern octa mmix_fread ARGS((unsigned char, octa, octa));
extern octa mmix_fgets ARGS((unsigned char, octa, octa));
extern octa mmix_fgetws ARGS((unsigned char, octa, octa));
extern octa mmix_fwrite ARGS((unsigned char, octa, octa));
extern octa mmix_fputs ARGS((unsigned char, octa));
extern octa mmix_fputws ARGS((unsigned char, octa));
extern octa mmix_fseek ARGS((unsigned char, octa));
extern octa mmix_ftell ARGS((unsigned char));
extern void print_trip_warning ARGS((int, octa));
extern void mmix_fake_stdin ARGS((FILE *));
```

---

a: **octa**, §61.
ARGS = macro ( ), §11.
b: **octa**, §61.
breakpoint: **bool**, §61.
exc: **int**, §61.
Fclose = 2, §59.
Fgets = 4, §59.
Fgetws = 5, §59.
FILE, <stdio.h>.
Fopen = 1, §59.
Fputs = 7, §59.
Fputws = 8, §59.
Fread = 3, §59.
Fseek = 9, §59.
Ftell = 10, §59.
Fwrite = 6, §59.
g: **octa** [], §76.
h: **tetra**, §10.
H_BIT = macro, §57.
Halt = 0, §59.
halted: **bool**, §61.
incr: **octa** ( ), MMIX-ARITH §6.
inst: **tetra**, §61.
inst_ptr: **octa**, §61.
l: **tetra**, §10.
ll: **register mem_tetra** *, §62.
loc: **octa**, §61.
ma: **octa**, §61.
max_sys_call = macro, §59.
mb: **octa**, §61.
mem_find: **mem_tetra** *( ), §20.
mmix_fake_stdin: **void** ( ), MMIX-IO §10.
mmix_fclose: **octa** ( ), MMIX-IO §11.
mmix_fgets: **octa** ( ), MMIX-IO §14.
mmix_fgetws: **octa** ( ), MMIX-IO §16.
mmix_fopen: **octa** ( ), MMIX-IO §8.
mmix_fputs: **octa** ( ), MMIX-IO §19.
mmix_fputws: **octa** ( ), MMIX-IO §20.
mmix_fread: **octa** ( ), MMIX-IO §12.
mmix_fseek: **octa** ( ), MMIX-IO §21.
mmix_ftell: **octa** ( ), MMIX-IO §22.
mmix_fwrite: **octa** ( ), MMIX-IO §18.
mmix_io_init: **void** ( ), MMIX-IO §7.
octa = **struct**, §10.
print_trip_warning: **void** ( ), MMIX-IO §23.
privileged_inst: label, §107.
rBB = 7, §55.
rhs = macro, §139.
rW = 24, §55.
rWW = 28, §55.
rXX = 29, §55.
rYY = 30, §55.
rZZ = 31, §55.
sign_bit = macro, §15.
strcpy: **char** *( ), <string.h>.
test_load_bkpt = macro ( ), §83.
tet: **tetra**, §16.
TRAP = #00, §54.
TRIP = #ff, §54.
true = 1, §9.
x: **octa**, §61.
xx: **register int**, §62.
y: **octa**, §61.
yy: **register int**, §62.
z: **octa**, §61.
zz: **register int**, §62.

114. The subroutine *mmgetchars*(*buf*, *size*, *addr*, *stop*) reads characters starting at address *addr* in the simulated memory and stores them in *buf*, continuing until *size* characters have been read or some other stopping criterion has been met. If $stop < 0$ there is no other criterion; if $stop = 0$ a null character will also terminate the process; otherwise *addr* is even, and two consecutive null bytes starting at an even address will terminate the process. The number of bytes read and stored, exclusive of terminating nulls, is returned.

```
⟨ Subroutines 12 ⟩ +≡
  int mmgetchars ARGS((char *, int, octa, int));
  int mmgetchars(buf, size, addr, stop)
      char *buf;
      int size;
      octa addr;
      int stop;
  {
    register char *p;
    register int m;
    register mem_tetra *ll;
    register tetra x;
    octa a;
    for (p = buf, m = 0, a = addr; m < size; ) {
      ll = mem_find(a); test_load_bkpt(ll);
      x = ll→tet;
      if ((a.l & #3) ∨ m > size − 4) ⟨ Read and store one byte; return if done 115 ⟩
      else ⟨ Read and store up to four bytes; return if done 116 ⟩
    }
    return size;
  }
```

115. ⟨ Read and store one byte; **return** if done 115 ⟩ ≡

```
  {
    *p = (x ≫ (8 * ((∼a.l) & #3))) & #ff;
    if (¬*p ∧ stop ≥ 0) {
      if (stop ≡ 0) return m;
      if ((a.l & #1) ∧ *(p − 1) ≡ '\0') return m − 1;
    }
    p++, m++, a = incr(a, 1);
  }
```

This code is used in section 114.

116. ⟨ Read and store up to four bytes; **return** if done 116 ⟩ ≡

```
  {
    *p = x ≫ 24;
    if (¬*p ∧ (stop ≡ 0 ∨ (stop > 0 ∧ x < #10000))) return m;
    *(p + 1) = (x ≫ 16) & #ff;
    if (¬*(p + 1) ∧ stop ≡ 0) return m + 1;
    *(p + 2) = (x ≫ 8) & #ff;
    if (¬*(p + 2) ∧ (stop ≡ 0 ∨ (stop > 0 ∧ (x & #ffff) ≡ 0))) return m + 2;
    *(p + 3) = x & #ff;
```

```
    if (¬*(p + 3) ∧ stop ≡ 0) return m + 3;
    p += 4, m += 4, a = incr(a, 4);
  }
```

This code is used in section 114.

117. The subroutine *mmputchars*(*buf*, *size*, *addr*) puts *size* characters into the simulated memory starting at address *addr*.

```
⟨ Subroutines 12 ⟩ +≡
  void mmputchars ARGS((unsigned char *, int, octa));
  void mmputchars(buf, size, addr)
      unsigned char *buf;
      int size;
      octa addr;
  {
    register unsigned char *p;
    register int m;
    register mem_tetra *ll;
    octa a;
    for (p = buf, m = 0, a = addr; m < size; ) {
      ll = mem_find(a); test_store_bkpt(ll);
      if ((a.l & #3) ∨ m > size − 4) ⟨ Load and write one byte 118 ⟩
      else ⟨ Load and write four bytes 119 ⟩;
    }
  }
```

118. ⟨ Load and write one byte 118 ⟩ ≡

```
  {
    register int s = 8 * ((~a.l) & #3);
    ll→tet ⊕= (((ll→tet ≫ s) ⊕ *p) & #ff) ≪ s;
    p++, m++, a = incr(a, 1);
  }
```

This code is used in section 117.

119. ⟨ Load and write four bytes 119 ⟩ ≡

```
  {
    ll→tet = (*p ≪ 24) + (*(p + 1) ≪ 16) + (*(p + 2) ≪ 8) + *(p + 3);
    p += 4, m += 4, a = incr(a, 4);
  }
```

This code is used in section 117.

ARGS = macro ( ), §11.
incr: **octa** ( ), MMIX-ARITH §6.
l: **tetra**, §10.
mem_find: **mem_tetra** *( ), §20.
mem_tetra = **struct**, §16.
octa = **struct**, §10.
test_load_bkpt = macro ( ), §83.
test_store_bkpt = macro ( ), §82.
tet: **tetra**, §16.
tetra = **unsigned int**, §10.

120. When standard input is being read by the simulated program at the same time as it is being used for interaction, we try to keep the two uses separate by maintaining a private buffer for the simulated program's `StdIn`. Online input is usually transmitted from the keyboard to a C program a line at a time; therefore an *fgets* operation works much better than *fread* when we prompt for new input. But there is a slight complication, because *fgets* might read a null character before coming to a newline character. We cannot deduce the number of characters read by *fgets* simply by looking at *strlen*(*stdin_buf*).

```
⟨Subroutines 12⟩ +≡
  char stdin_chr ARGS((void));
  char stdin_chr()
  {
    register char *p;
    while (stdin_buf_start ≡ stdin_buf_end) {
      if (interacting) {
        printf("StdIn>␣"); fflush(stdout);
      }
      if (¬fgets(stdin_buf, 256, stdin))
        panic("End␣of␣file␣on␣standard␣input;␣use␣the␣-f␣option,␣not␣<");
      stdin_buf_start = stdin_buf;
      for (p = stdin_buf; p < stdin_buf + 254; p++)
        if (*p ≡ '\n') break;
      stdin_buf_end = p + 1;
    }
    return *stdin_buf_start++;
  }
```

121. ⟨Global variables 19⟩ +≡

```
  char stdin_buf[256];      /* standard input to the simulated program */
  char *stdin_buf_start;    /* current position in that buffer */
  char *stdin_buf_end;      /* current end of that buffer */
```

122. Just after executing each instruction, we do the following. Underflow that is exact and not enabled is ignored. (This applies also to underflow that was triggered by `RESUME_SET`.)

```
⟨Check for trip interrupt 122⟩ ≡
  if ((exc & (U_BIT + X_BIT)) ≡ U_BIT ∧ ¬(g[rA].l & U_BIT)) exc &= ~U_BIT;
  if (exc) {
    if (exc & tracing_exceptions) tracing = true;
    j = exc & (g[rA].l | H_BIT);    /* find all exceptions that have been enabled */
    if (j) ⟨Initiate a trip interrupt 123⟩;
    g[rA].l |= exc ≫ 8;
  }
```

This code is used in section 60.

123. ⟨Initiate a trip interrupt 123⟩ ≡

```
  {
    tripping = true;
    for (k = 0; ¬(j & H_BIT); j ≪= 1, k++) ;
```

```
    exc &= ~(H_BIT >> k);    /* trips taken are not logged as events */
    g[rW] = inst_ptr;
    inst_ptr.h = 0, inst_ptr.l = k << 4;
    g[rX].h = sign_bit, g[rX].l = inst;
    if ((op & #e0) ≡ STB) g[rY] = w, g[rZ] = b;
    else g[rY] = y, g[rZ] = z;
    g[rB] = g[255];
    g[255] = g[rJ];
    if (op ≡ TRIP) w = g[rW], x = g[rX], a = g[255];
  }
```

This code is used in section 122.

124. We are finally ready for the last case.

⟨ Cases for individual MMIX instructions 84 ⟩ +≡

```
case RESUME: if (xx ∨ yy ∨ zz) goto illegal_inst;
  inst_ptr = z = g[rW];
  b = g[rX];
  if (¬(b.h & sign_bit)) ⟨ Prepare to perform a ropcode 125 ⟩;
  break;
```

---

a: **octa**, §117.
ARGS = macro ( ), §11.
b: **octa**, §61.
exc: **int**, §61.
fflush: **int** ( ), <stdio.h>.
fgets: **char** ∗( ), <stdio.h>.
fread: **size_t** ( ), <stdio.h>.
g: **octa** [], §76.
h: **tetra**, §10.
H_BIT = macro, §57.
illegal_inst: label, §107.
inst: **tetra**, §61.
inst_ptr: **octa**, §61.
interacting: **bool**, §61.
j: **register int**, §62.
k: **register int**, §62.
l: **tetra**, §10.
op: **register mmix_opcode**, §62.
panic = macro ( ), §14.
printf: **int** ( ), <stdio.h>.
rA = 21, §55.
rB = 0, §55.
RESUME = #f9, §54.
RESUME_SET = 2, §125.
rJ = 4, §55.
rW = 24, §55.
rX = 25, §55.
rY = 26, §55.
rZ = 27, §55.
sign_bit = macro, §15.
STB = #a0, §54.
stdin: **FILE** ∗, <stdio.h>.
stdout: **FILE** ∗, <stdio.h>.
strlen: **size_t** ( ), <string.h>.
tracing: **bool**, §61.
tracing_exceptions: **int**, §61.
TRIP = #ff, §54.
tripping: **bool**, §61.
true = 1, §9.
U_BIT = macro, §57.
w: **octa**, §61.
x: **register tetra**, §114.
X_BIT = macro, §57.
xx: **register int**, §62.
y: **octa**, §61.
yy: **register int**, §62.
z: **octa**, §61.
zz: **register int**, §62.

125. Here we check to see if the ropcode restrictions hold. If so, the ropcode will actually be obeyed on the next fetch phase.

```
#define RESUME_AGAIN 0   /* repeat the command in rX as if in location rW − 4 */
#define RESUME_CONT 1   /* same, but substitute rY and rZ for operands */
#define RESUME_SET 2   /* set register $X to rZ */
```

⟨ Prepare to perform a ropcode 125 ⟩ ≡

```
{
  rop = b.h ≫ 24;   /* the ropcode is the leading byte of rX */
  switch (rop) {
  case RESUME_CONT: if ((1 ≪ (b.l ≫ 28)) & #8f30) goto illegal_inst;
  case RESUME_SET: k = (b.l ≫ 16) & #ff;
    if (k ≥ L ∧ k < G) goto illegal_inst;
  case RESUME_AGAIN: if ((b.l ≫ 24) ≡ RESUME) goto illegal_inst;
    break;
  default: goto illegal_inst;
  }
  resuming = true;
}
```

This code is used in section 124.

126. ⟨ Install special operands when resuming an interrupted operation 126 ⟩ ≡

```
if (rop ≡ RESUME_SET) {
  op = ORI;
  y = g[rZ];
  z = zero_octa;
  exc = g[rX].h & #ff00;
  f = X_is_dest_bit;
} else {   /* RESUME_CONT */
  y = g[rY];
  z = g[rZ];
}
```

This code is used in section 71.

127. We don't want to count the UNSAVE that bootstraps the whole process.

⟨ Update the clocks 127 ⟩ ≡

```
if (sclock.l ∨ sclock.h ∨ ¬resuming) {
  sclock.h += info[op].mems;   /* clock goes up by 2^32 for each μ */
  sclock = incr(sclock, info[op].oops);   /* clock goes up by 1 for each υ */
  if ((¬(loc.h & sign_bit) ∨ (g[rU].h & #8000)) ∧
      ((op & (g[rU].h ≫ 16)) ≡ (g[rU].h ≫ 24))) {
    g[rU].l++;
    if (g[rU].l ≡ 0) { g[rU].h++; if (g[rU].h & #7fff ≡ 0) g[rU].h −= #8000; }
  }   /* usage counter counts matched instructions simulated */
  if (g[rI].l ≤ info[op].oops ∧ g[rI].l ∧ g[rI].h ≡ 0) tracing = breakpoint = true;
  g[rI] = incr(g[rI], −info[op].oops);   /* interval υ timer counts down */
}
```

This code is used in section 60.

128. Tracing. After an instruction has been executed, we often want to display its effect. This part of the program prints out a symbolic interpretation of what has just happened.

```
⟨ Trace the current instruction, if requested 128 ⟩ ≡
  if (tracing) {
    if (showing_source ∧ cur_line) show_line();
    ⟨ Print the frequency count, the location, and the instruction 130 ⟩;
    ⟨ Print a stream-of-consciousness description of the instruction 131 ⟩;
    if (showing_stats ∨ breakpoint) show_stats(breakpoint);
    just_traced = true;
  } else if (just_traced) {
    printf("␣..............................................\n");
    just_traced = false;
    shown_line = −gap − 1;    /* gap will not be filled */
  }
```

This code is used in section 60.

129. ⟨ Global variables 19 ⟩ +≡

```
  bool showing_stats;   /* should traced instructions also show the statistics? */
  bool just_traced;   /* was the previous instruction traced? */
```

b: **octa**, §61.
bool = **enum**, §9.
breakpoint: **bool**, §61.
cur_line: **int**, §31.
exc: **int**, §61.
f: **register tetra**, §62.
false = 0, §9.
G: **register int**, §75.
g: **octa** [], §76.
gap: **int**, §48.
h: **tetra**, §10.
illegal_inst: label, §107.
incr: **octa** (), MMIX-ARITH §6.
info: **op_info** [], §65.
k: **register int**, §62.
L: **register int**, §75.
l: **tetra**, §10.
loc: **octa**, §61.
mems: **unsigned char**, §64.
oops: **unsigned char**, §64.
op: **register mmix_opcode**, §62.
ORI = #c1, §54.
printf: **int** (), <stdio.h>.
RESUME = #f9, §54.
resuming: **bool**, §61.
rI = 12, §55.
rop: **int**, §61.
rU = 17, §55.
rX = 25, §55.
rY = 26, §55.
rZ = 27, §55.
sclock: **octa**, §19.
show_line: **void** (), §47.
show_stats: **void** (), §140.
showing_source: **bool**, §48.
shown_line: **int**, §48.
sign_bit = macro, §15.
tracing: **bool**, §61.
true = 1, §9.
X_is_dest_bit = #20, §65.
y: **octa**, §61.
z: **octa**, §61.
zero_octa: **octa**, MMIX-ARITH §4.

130. ⟨ Print the frequency count, the location, and the instruction 130 ⟩ ≡

```
if (resuming ∧ op ≠ RESUME) {
  switch (rop) {
  case RESUME_AGAIN:
    printf("␣␣␣␣␣␣␣␣␣␣␣(%08x%08x:␣%08x␣(%s))␣", loc.h, loc.l, inst, info[op].name);
    break;
  case RESUME_CONT: printf("␣␣␣␣␣␣␣␣␣␣␣(%08x%08x:␣%04xrYrZ␣(%s))␣", loc.h, loc.l,
        inst ≫ 16, info[op].name); break;
  case RESUME_SET: printf("␣␣␣␣␣␣␣␣␣␣␣(%08x%08x:␣..%02x..rZ␣(SET))␣", loc.h,
        loc.l, (inst ≫ 16) & #ff); break;
  }
} else {
  ll = mem_find(loc);
  printf("%10d.␣%08x%08x:␣%08x␣(%s)␣", ll→freq, loc.h, loc.l, inst, info[op].name);
}
```

This code is used in section 128.

131. This part of the simulator was inspired by ideas of E. H. Satterthwaite, *Software—Practice and Experience* **2** (1972), 197–217. Online debugging tools have improved significantly since Satterthwaite published his work, but good offline tools are still valuable; alas, today's algebraic programming languages do not provide tracing facilities that come anywhere close to the level of quality that Satterthwaite was able to demonstrate for ALGOL in 1970.

⟨ Print a stream-of-consciousness description of the instruction 131 ⟩ ≡

```
if (lhs[0] ≡ '!') printf("%s␣instruction!\n", lhs + 1);     /* privileged or illegal */
else {
  ⟨ Print changes to rL 132 ⟩;
  if (z.l ≡ 0 ∧ (op ≡ ADDUI ∨ op ≡ ORI)) p = "%l␣=␣%y␣=␣%#x";     /* LDA, SET */
  else p = info[op].trace_format;
  for ( ; *p; p++) ⟨ Interpret character *p in the trace format 133 ⟩;
  if (exc) printf(",␣rA=#%05x", g[rA].l);
  if (tripping) tripping = false, printf(",␣->␣#%02x", inst_ptr.l);
  printf("\n");
}
```

This code is used in section 128.

132. Push, pop, and UNSAVE instructions display changes to rL and rO explicitly; otherwise the change is implicit, if $L \neq old\_L$.

⟨ Print changes to rL 132 ⟩ ≡

```
if (L ≠ old_L ∧ ¬(f & push_pop_bit)) printf("rL=%d,␣", L);
```

This code is used in section 131.

133. Each MMIX instruction has a *trace format* string, which defines its symbolic representation. For example, the string for ADD is `"%l␣=␣%y␣+␣%z␣=␣%x"`; if the instruction is, say, `ADD $1,$2,$3` with $\$2 = 5$ and $\$3 = 8$, and if the stack offset is 100, the trace output will be `"$1=l[101]␣=␣5␣+␣8␣=␣13"`.

Percent signs (`%`) induce special format conventions, as follows:

• `%a`, `%b`, `%p`, `%q`, `%w`, `%x`, `%y`, and `%z` stand for the numeric contents of octabytes a, b, ma, mb, w, x, y, and z, respectively; a "style" character may follow the percent sign in this case, as explained below.

• `%(` and `%)` are brackets that indicate the mode of floating point rounding. If *round_mode* = ROUND_NEAR, ROUND_OFF, ROUND_UP, ROUND_DOWN, the corresponding brackets are `(` and `)`, `[` and `]`, `^` and `^`, `_` and `_`. Such brackets are placed around a floating point operator; for example, floating point addition is denoted by '`[+]`' when the current rounding mode is rounding-off.

• `%l` stands for the string *lhs*, which usually represents the "left hand side" of the instruction just performed, formatted as a register number and its equivalent in the ring of local registers (e.g., '`$1=l[101]`') or as a register number and its equivalent in the array of global registers (e.g., '`$255=g[255]`'). The POP instruction uses *lhs* to indicate how the "hole" in the register stack was plugged.

• `%r` means to switch to string *rhs* and continue formatting from there. This mechanism allows us to use variable formats for opcodes like TRAP that have several variants.

• `%t` means to print either '`Yes, ->loc`' (where `loc` is the location of the next instruction) or '`No`', depending on the value of x.

• `%g` means to print '` (bad guess)`' if *good* is *false*.

• `%s` stands for the name of special register $g[zz]$.

• `%?` stands for omission of the following operator if $z = 0$. For example, the memory address of LDBI is described by '`%#y%?+`'; this means to treat the address as simply '`%#y`' if $z = 0$, otherwise as '`%#y+%z`'. This case is used only when z is a relatively small number ($z.h = 0$).

⟨ Interpret character $*p$ in the trace format 133 ⟩ ≡

```
{
  if (*p ≠ '%') fputc(*p, stdout);
  else {
    style = decimal;
  char_switch:
    switch (*++p) {
    ⟨ Cases for formatting characters 134 ⟩;
    default: printf("BUG!!");      /* can't happen */
    }
  }
}
```

This code is used in section 131.

134. Octabytes are printed as decimal numbers unless a "style" character intervenes between the percent sign and the name of the octabyte: '#' denotes hexadecimal notation, prefixed by #; '0' denotes hexadecimal notation with no prefixed # and with leading zeros not suppressed; '.' denotes floating decimal notation; and '!' means to use the names StdIn, StdOut, or StdErr if the value is 0, 1, or 2.

```
⟨ Cases for formatting characters 134 ⟩ ≡
case '#': style = hex; goto char_switch;
case '0': style = zhex; goto char_switch;
case '.': style = floating; goto char_switch;
case '!': style = handle; goto char_switch;
```

See also sections 136 and 138.

This code is used in section 133.

135.
```
⟨ Type declarations 9 ⟩ +≡
  typedef enum {
    decimal, hex, zhex, floating, handle
  } fmt_style;
```

136.
```
⟨ Cases for formatting characters 134 ⟩ +≡
case 'a': trace_print(a); break;
case 'b': trace_print(b); break;
case 'p': trace_print(ma); break;
case 'q': trace_print(mb); break;
case 'w': trace_print(w); break;
case 'x': trace_print(x); break;
case 'y': trace_print(y); break;
case 'z': trace_print(z); break;
```

---

a: **octa**, §61.
b: **octa**, §61.
false = 0, §9.
fputc: **int** ( ), <stdio.h>.
g: **octa** [ ], §76.
good: **bool**, §61.
h: **tetra**, §10.
lhs: **char** [ ], §139.
ma: **octa**, §61.
mb: **octa**, §61.
p: **register char** *, §62.
printf: **int** ( ), <stdio.h>.
rhs = macro, §139.
ROUND_DOWN = 3, §100.
round_mode: **int**, §61.
ROUND_NEAR = 4, §100.
ROUND_OFF = 1, §100.
ROUND_UP = 2, §100.
stdout: **FILE** *, <stdio.h>.
style: **fmt_style**, §137.
trace_print: **void** ( ), §137.
w: **octa**, §61.
x: **octa**, §61.
y: **octa**, §61.
z: **octa**, §61.
zz: **register int**, §62.

137. ⟨ Subroutines 12 ⟩ +≡

```
fmt_style style;
char *stream_name[] = {"StdIn", "StdOut", "StdErr"};
void trace_print ARGS((octa));
void trace_print(o)
    octa o;
{
  switch (style) {
  case decimal: print_int(o); return;
  case hex: fputc('#', stdout); print_hex(o); return;
  case zhex: printf("%08x%08x", o.h, o.l); return;
  case floating: print_float(o); return;
  case handle: if (o.h ≡ 0 ∧ o.l < 3) printf(stream_name[o.l]);
    else print_int(o); return;
  }
}
```

138. ⟨ Cases for formatting characters 134 ⟩ +≡

```
case '(': fputc(left_paren[round_mode], stdout); break;
case ')': fputc(right_paren[round_mode], stdout); break;
case 't': if (x.l) printf("␣Yes,␣->␣#"), print_hex(inst_ptr);
  else printf("␣No"); break;
case 'g': if (¬good) printf("␣(bad␣guess)"); break;
case 's': printf(special_name[zz]); break;
case '?': p++; if (z.l) printf("%c%d", *p, z.l); break;
case 'l': printf(lhs); break;
case 'r': p = switchable_string; break;
```

139. **#define** *rhs* &*switchable_string*[1]

⟨ Global variables 19 ⟩ +≡

```
char left_paren[] = {0, '[', '^', '_', '('};      /* denotes the rounding mode */
char right_paren[] = {0, ']', '^', '_', ')'};      /* denotes the rounding mode */
char switchable_string[48];      /* holds rhs; position 0 is ignored */
  /* switchable_string must be able to hold any trap_format */
char lhs[32];
int good_guesses, bad_guesses;      /* branch prediction statistics */
```

140. ⟨Subroutines 12⟩ +≡

```
void show_stats ARGS((bool));
void show_stats(verbose)
    bool verbose;
{
  octa o;
  printf("␣␣%d␣instruction%s,␣%d␣mem%s,␣%d␣oop%s;␣%d␣good␣guess%s,␣%d␣bad\n",
      g[rU].l, g[rU].l ≡ 1 ? "" : "s",
      sclock.h, sclock.h ≡ 1 ? "" : "s",
      sclock.l, sclock.l ≡ 1 ? "" : "s",
      good_guesses, good_guesses ≡ 1 ? "" : "es", bad_guesses);
  if (¬verbose) return;
  o = halted ? incr(inst_ptr, −4) : inst_ptr;
  printf("␣␣(%s␣at␣location␣#%08x%08x)\n", halted ? "halted" : "now", o.h, o.l);
}
```

ARGS = macro ( ), §11.
bool = **enum**, §9.
decimal = 0, §135.
floating = 3, §135.
fmt_style = **enum**, §135.
fputc: **int** ( ), <stdio.h>.
g: **octa** [ ], §76.
good: **bool**, §61.
h: **tetra**, §10.
halted: **bool**, §61.
handle = 4, §135.
hex = 1, §135.
incr: **octa** ( ), MMIX-ARITH §6.
inst_ptr: **octa**, §61.
l: **tetra**, §10.
octa = **struct**, §10.
p: **register char** ∗, §62.
print_float: **void** ( ), MMIX-ARITH §54.
print_hex: **void** ( ), §12.
print_int: **void** ( ), §15.
printf: **int** ( ), <stdio.h>.
round_mode: **int**, §61.
rU = 17, §55.
sclock: **octa**, §19.
special_name: **char** ∗[ ], §56.
stdout: **FILE** ∗, <stdio.h>.
trap_format: **char** ∗[ ], §110.
x: **octa**, §61.
z: **octa**, §61.
zhex = 2, §135.
zz: **register int**, §62.

141. Running the program. Now we are ready to fit the pieces together into a working simulator.

```
#include <stdio.h>
#include <stdlib.h>
#include <ctype.h>
#include <string.h>
#include <signal.h>
#include "abstime.h"
  ⟨ Preprocessor macros 11 ⟩
  ⟨ Type declarations 9 ⟩
  ⟨ Global variables 19 ⟩
  ⟨ Subroutines 12 ⟩

  int main(argc, argv)
       int argc;
       char *argv[];
  {
    ⟨ Local registers 62 ⟩;
    mmix_io_init();
    ⟨ Process the command line 142 ⟩;
    ⟨ Initialize everything 14 ⟩;
    ⟨ Load the command line arguments 163 ⟩;
    ⟨ Get ready to UNSAVE the initial context 164 ⟩;
    while (1) {
      if (interrupt ∧ ¬breakpoint) breakpoint = interacting = true, interrupt = false;
      else {
        breakpoint = false;
        if (interacting) ⟨ Interact with the user 149 ⟩;
      }
      if (halted) break;
      do ⟨ Perform one instruction 60 ⟩ while ((¬interrupt ∧ ¬breakpoint) ∨ resuming);
      if (interact_after_break) interacting = true, interact_after_break = false;
    }
  end_simulation: if (profiling) ⟨ Print all the frequency counts 53 ⟩;
    if (interacting ∨ profiling ∨ showing_stats) show_stats(true);
    return g[255].l;      /* provide rudimentary feedback for non-interactive runs */
  }
```

142. Here we process the command line options; when we finish, **cur_arg* should be the name of the object file to be loaded and simulated.

We assume that *argv*[0] is never null. (The author believes strongly that the wizards who decided to allow *argc* = 0 were mistaken when they defined the C89 standard; hence he has taken no pains to avoid system crashes when people try to invoke any of his programs with a null environment. Null invocations are contrary to the intent of C's designers.)

```
#define mmo_file_name  *cur_arg

⟨ Process the command line 142 ⟩ ≡
  myself = argv[0];
```

```
for (cur_arg = argv + 1; *cur_arg ∧ (*cur_arg)[0] ≡ '-'; cur_arg++)
  scan_option(*cur_arg + 1, true);
if (¬*cur_arg) scan_option("?", true);     /* exit with usage note */
argc −= cur_arg − argv;   /* this is the argc of the user program */
```

This code is used in section 141.

breakpoint: **bool**, §61.
cur_arg: **char** **, §144.
false = 0, §9.
g: **octa** [], §76.
halted: **bool**, §61.
interact_after_break: **bool**, §61.
interacting: **bool**, §61.
interrupt: **bool**, §144.
l: **tetra**, §10.
mmix_io_init: **void** (), MMIX-IO §7.
myself: **char** *, §144.
profiling: **bool**, §144.
resuming: **bool**, §61.
scan_option: **void** (), §143.
show_stats: **void** (), §140.
showing_stats: **bool**, §129.
true = 1, §9.

143. Careful readers of the following subroutine will notice a little white bug: A tracing specification like `t1000000000` or even `t0000000000` or even `t!!!!!!!!!!` is silently converted to `t4294967295`.

The `-b` and `-c` options are effective only on the command line, but they are harmless while interacting.

```
⟨ Subroutines 12 ⟩ +≡
  void scan_option ARGS((char *, bool));
  void scan_option(arg, usage)
      char *arg;     /* command line argument (without the '-') */
      bool usage;     /* should we exit with usage note if unrecognized? */
  {
    register int k;
    switch (*arg) {
    case 't': if (strlen(arg) > 10) trace_threshold = #ffffffff;
      else if (sscanf(arg + 1, "%d", &trace_threshold) ≠ 1) trace_threshold = 0;
      return;
    case 'e': if (¬*(arg + 1)) tracing_exceptions = #ff;
      else if (sscanf(arg + 1, "%x", &tracing_exceptions) ≠ 1) tracing_exceptions = 0;
      return;
    case 'r': stack_tracing = true; return;
    case 's': showing_stats = true; return;
    case 'l': if (¬*(arg + 1)) gap = 3;
      else if (sscanf(arg + 1, "%d", &gap) ≠ 1) gap = 0;
      showing_source = true; return;
    case 'L': if (¬*(arg + 1)) profile_gap = 3;
      else if (sscanf(arg + 1, "%d", &profile_gap) ≠ 1) profile_gap = 0;
      profile_showing_source = true;
    case 'P': profiling = true; return;
    case 'v': trace_threshold = #ffffffff; tracing_exceptions = #ff;
      stack_tracing = true; showing_stats = true;
      gap = 10, showing_source = true;
      profile_gap = 10, profile_showing_source = true, profiling = true;
      return;
    case 'q': trace_threshold = tracing_exceptions = 0;
      stack_tracing = showing_stats = showing_source = false;
      profiling = profile_showing_source = false;
      return;
    case 'i': interacting = true; return;
    case 'I': interact_after_break = true; return;
    case 'b': if (sscanf(arg + 1, "%d", &buf_size) ≠ 1) buf_size = 0; return;
    case 'c': if (sscanf(arg + 1, "%d", &lring_size) ≠ 1) lring_size = 0; return;
    case 'f': ⟨ Open a file for simulated standard input 145 ⟩; return;
    case 'D': ⟨ Open a file for dumping binary output 146 ⟩; return;
    default: if (usage) {
        fprintf(stderr, "Usage:␣%s␣<options>␣progfile␣command␣line-args...\n",
            myself);
        for (k = 0; usage_help[k][0]; k++) fprintf(stderr, usage_help[k]);
        exit(−1);
```

```
      } else for (k = 0; usage_help[k][1] ≠ 'b'; k++) printf(usage_help[k]);
      return;
    }
  }
```

ARGS = macro ( ), §11.
bool = **enum**, §9.
buf_size: **int**, §40.
exit: **void** ( ), <stdlib.h>.
false = 0, §9.
fprintf: **int** ( ), <stdio.h>.
gap: **int**, §48.
interact_after_break: **bool**, §61.
interacting: **bool**, §61.
lring_size: **int**, §76.
myself: **char** *, §144.
printf: **int** ( ), <stdio.h>.
profile_gap: **int**, §48.
profile_showing_source: **bool**, §48.
profiling: **bool**, §144.
showing_source: **bool**, §48.
showing_stats: **bool**, §129.
sscanf: **int** ( ), <stdio.h>.
stack_tracing: **bool**, §61.
stderr: **FILE** *, <stdio.h>.
strlen: **size_t** ( ), <string.h>.
trace_threshold: **tetra**, §61.
tracing_exceptions: **int**, §61.
true = 1, §9.
usage_help: **char** *[ ], §144.

144. ⟨ Global variables 19 ⟩ +≡

```
char *myself;   /* argv[0], the name of this simulator */
char **cur_arg;   /* pointer to current place in the argument vector */
bool interrupt;   /* has the user interrupted the simulation recently? */
bool profiling;   /* should we print the profile at the end? */
FILE *fake_stdin;   /* file substituted for the simulated StdIn */
FILE *dump_file;   /* file used for binary dumps */
char *usage_help[] = {
"␣with␣these␣options:␣(<n>=decimal␣number,␣<x>=hex␣number)\n",
    "-t<n>␣trace␣each␣instruction␣the␣first␣n␣times\n",
    "-e<x>␣trace␣each␣instruction␣with␣an␣exception␣matching␣x\n",
    "-r␣␣␣␣trace␣hidden␣details␣of␣the␣register␣stack\n",
    "-l<n>␣list␣source␣lines␣when␣tracing,␣filling␣gaps␣<=␣n\n",
    "-s␣␣␣␣show␣statistics␣after␣each␣traced␣instruction\n",
    "-P␣␣␣␣print␣a␣profile␣when␣simulation␣ends\n",
    "-L<n>␣list␣source␣lines␣with␣the␣profile\n",
    "-v␣␣␣␣be␣verbose:␣show␣almost␣everything\n",
    "-q␣␣␣␣be␣quiet:␣show␣only␣the␣simulated␣standard␣output\n",
    "-i␣␣␣␣run␣interactively␣(prompt␣for␣online␣commands)\n",
    "-I␣␣␣␣interact,␣but␣only␣after␣the␣program␣halts\n",
    "-b<n>␣change␣the␣buffer␣size␣for␣source␣lines\n",
    "-c<n>␣change␣the␣cyclic␣local␣register␣ring␣size\n",
    "-f<filename>␣use␣given␣file␣to␣simulate␣standard␣input\n",
    "-D<filename>␣dump␣a␣file␣for␣use␣by␣other␣simulators\n",
    ""};
char *interactive_help[] = {
"The␣interactive␣commands␣are:\n",
    "<return>␣␣trace␣one␣instruction\n",
    "n␣␣␣␣␣␣␣␣␣trace␣one␣instruction\n",
    "c␣␣␣␣␣␣␣␣␣continue␣until␣halt␣or␣breakpoint\n",
    "q␣␣␣␣␣␣␣␣␣quit␣the␣simulation\n",
    "s␣␣␣␣␣␣␣␣␣show␣current␣statistics\n",
    "l<n><t>␣␣␣set␣and/or␣show␣local␣register␣in␣format␣t\n",
    "g<n><t>␣␣␣set␣and/or␣show␣global␣register␣in␣format␣t\n",
    "rA<t>␣␣␣␣␣set␣and/or␣show␣register␣rA␣in␣format␣t\n",
    "$<n><t>␣␣␣set␣and/or␣show␣dynamic␣register␣in␣format␣t\n",
    "M<x><t>␣␣␣set␣and/or␣show␣memory␣octabyte␣in␣format␣t\n",
    "+<n><t>␣␣␣set␣and/or␣show␣n␣additional␣octabytes␣in␣format␣t\n",
    "␣<t>␣is␣!␣(decimal)␣or␣.␣(floating)␣or␣#␣(hex)␣or␣\"␣(string)\n",
    "␣␣␣␣␣or␣<empty>␣(previous␣<t>)␣or␣=<value>␣(change␣value)\n",
    "@<x>␣␣␣␣␣␣go␣to␣location␣x\n",
    "b[rwx]<x>␣set␣or␣reset␣breakpoint␣at␣location␣x\n",
    "t<x>␣␣␣␣␣␣trace␣location␣x\n",
    "u<x>␣␣␣␣␣␣untrace␣location␣x\n",
    "T␣␣␣␣␣␣␣␣␣set␣current␣segment␣to␣Text_Segment\n",
    "D␣␣␣␣␣␣␣␣␣set␣current␣segment␣to␣Data_Segment\n",
    "P␣␣␣␣␣␣␣␣␣set␣current␣segment␣to␣Pool_Segment\n",
    "S␣␣␣␣␣␣␣␣␣set␣current␣segment␣to␣Stack_Segment\n",
    "B␣␣␣␣␣␣␣␣␣show␣all␣current␣breakpoints␣and␣tracepoints\n",
```

```
"i<file>␣␣␣insert␣commands␣from␣file\n",
"-<option>␣change␣a␣tracing/listing/profile␣option\n",
"-?␣␣␣␣␣␣␣␣show␣the␣tracing/listing/profile␣options␣␣\n",
""};
```

145. ⟨ Open a file for simulated standard input 145 ⟩ ≡

```
if (fake_stdin) fclose(fake_stdin);
fake_stdin = fopen(arg + 1, "r");
if (¬fake_stdin) fprintf(stderr, "Sorry,␣I␣can't␣open␣file␣%s!\n", arg + 1);
else mmix_fake_stdin(fake_stdin);
```

This code is used in section 143.

146. ⟨ Open a file for dumping binary output 146 ⟩ ≡

```
dump_file = fopen(arg + 1, "wb");
if (¬dump_file) fprintf(stderr, "Sorry,␣I␣can't␣open␣file␣%s!\n", arg + 1);
```

This code is used in section 143.

147. ⟨ Initialize everything 14 ⟩ +≡

```
signal(SIGINT, catchint);    /* now catchint will catch the first interrupt */
```

148. ⟨ Subroutines 12 ⟩ +≡

```
void catchint ARGS((int));
void catchint(n)
    int n;
{
  interrupt = true;
  signal(SIGINT, catchint);    /* now catchint will catch the next interrupt */
}
```

---

arg: **char** ∗, §143.
ARGS = macro ( ), §11.
argv: **char** ∗[ ], §141.
bool = **enum**, §9.
fclose: **int** ( ), <stdio.h>.
FILE, <stdio.h>.
fopen: **FILE** ∗( ), <stdio.h>.
fprintf: **int** ( ), <stdio.h>.
mmix_fake_stdin: **void** ( ), MMIX-IO §10.
SIGINT = macro, <signal.h>.
signal: **void** (∗( ))( ), <signal.h>.
stderr: **FILE** ∗, <stdio.h>.
true = 1, §9.

149. ⟨ Interact with the user 149 ⟩ ≡

```
{ register int repeating;
interact: ⟨ Put a new command in command_buf 150 ⟩;
  p = command_buf;
  repeating = 0;
  switch (*p) {
  case '\n': case 'n': breakpoint = tracing = true;     /* trace one inst and break */
  case 'c': goto resume_simulation;     /* continue until breakpoint */
  case 'q': goto end_simulation;
  case 's': show_stats(true); goto interact;
  case '-': k = strlen(p); if (p[k − 1] ≡ '\n') p[k − 1] = '\0';
    scan_option(p + 1, false); goto interact;
  ⟨ Cases that change cur_disp_mode 152 ⟩;
  ⟨ Cases that define cur_disp_type 153 ⟩;
  ⟨ Cases that set and clear tracing and breakpoints 161 ⟩;
  default: what_say: k = strlen(command_buf);
    if (k < 10 ∧ command_buf[k − 1] ≡ '\n') command_buf[k − 1] = '\0';
    else strcpy(command_buf + 9, "...");
    printf("Eh? Sorry, I don't understand `%s'. (Type h for help)\n",
        command_buf);
    goto interact;
  case 'h': for (k = 0; interactive_help[k][0]; k++) printf(interactive_help[k]);
    goto interact;
  }
check_syntax: if (*p ≠ '\n') {
    if (¬*p)
    incomplete_str: printf("Syntax error: Incomplete command!\n");
    else {
      p[strlen(p) − 1] = '\0';
      printf("Syntax error; I'm ignoring `%s'!\n", p);
    }
  }
  while (repeating) ⟨ Display and/or set the value of the current octabyte 156 ⟩;
  goto interact;
resume_simulation: ;
}
```

This code is used in section 141.

150. ⟨ Put a new command in *command_buf* 150 ⟩ ≡

```
{ register bool ready = false;
incl_read: while (incl_file ∧ ¬ready)
    if (¬fgets(command_buf, command_buf_size, incl_file)) {
      fclose(incl_file);
      incl_file = Λ;
    } else if (command_buf[0] ≠ '\n' ∧ command_buf[0] ≠ 'i' ∧ command_buf[0] ≠ '%')
      if (command_buf[0] ≡ ' ') printf("%s", command_buf);
      else ready = true;
  while (¬ready) {
    printf("mmix> "); fflush(stdout);
```

```
      if (¬fgets(command_buf, command_buf_size, stdin)) command_buf[0] = 'q';
      if (command_buf[0] ≠ 'i') ready = true;
      else {
        command_buf[strlen(command_buf) − 1] = '\0';
        incl_file = fopen(command_buf + 1, "r");
        if (incl_file) goto incl_read;
        if (isspace(command_buf[1])) incl_file = fopen(command_buf + 2, "r");
        if (incl_file) goto incl_read;
        printf("Can't␣open␣file␣`%s'!\n", command_buf + 1);
      }
    }
  }
```

This code is used in section 149.

151.

```
#define command_buf_size 1024
        /* make it plenty long, for floating point tests */

⟨ Global variables 19 ⟩ +≡
  char command_buf[command_buf_size];
  FILE *incl_file;     /* file of commands included by `i' */
  char cur_disp_mode = 'l';    /* 'l' or 'g' or '$' or 'M' */
  char cur_disp_type = '!';    /* '!' or '.' or '#' or '"' */
  bool cur_disp_set;     /* was the last <t> of the form =<val>? */
  octa cur_disp_addr;     /* the h half is relevant only in mode 'M' */
  octa cur_seg;     /* current segment offset */
  char spec_reg_code[] = {rA, rB, rC, rD, rE, rF, rG, rH, rI, rJ, rK, rL, rM, rN, rO, rP,
      rQ, rR, rS, rT, rU, rV, rW, rX, rY, rZ};
  char spec_regg_code[] = {0, rBB, 0, 0, 0, 0, 0, 0, 0, 0, 0, 0, 0, 0, 0, 0, 0, 0, 0, rTT, 0, 0, rWW,
      rXX, rYY, rZZ};
```


bool = **enum**, §9.
breakpoint: **bool**, §61.
end_simulation: label, §141.
false = 0, §9.
fclose: **int** (), <stdio.h>.
fflush: **int** (), <stdio.h>.
fgets: **char** *(), <stdio.h>.
FILE, <stdio.h>.
fopen: **FILE** *(), <stdio.h>.
h: **tetra**, §10.
interactive_help: **char** *[], §144.
isspace: **int** (), <ctype.h>.
k: **register int**, §62.
octa = **struct**, §10.
p: **register char** *, §62.
printf: **int** (), <stdio.h>.
rA = 21, §55.
rB = 0, §55.
rBB = 7, §55.
rC = 8, §55.
rD = 1, §55.
rE = 2, §55.
rF = 22, §55.
rG = 19, §55.
rH = 3, §55.
rI = 12, §55.
rJ = 4, §55.
rK = 15, §55.
rL = 20, §55.
rM = 5, §55.
rN = 9, §55.
rO = 10, §55.
rP = 23, §55.
rQ = 16, §55.
rR = 6, §55.
rS = 11, §55.
rT = 13, §55.
rTT = 14, §55.
rU = 17, §55.
rV = 18, §55.
rW = 24, §55.
rWW = 28, §55.
rX = 25, §55.
rXX = 29, §55.
rY = 26, §55.
rYY = 30, §55.
rZ = 27, §55.
rZZ = 31, §55.
scan_option: **void** (), §143.
show_stats: **void** (), §140.
stdin: **FILE** *, <stdio.h>.
stdout: **FILE** *, <stdio.h>.
strcpy: **char** *(), <string.h>.
strlen: **size_t** (), <string.h>.
tracing: **bool**, §61.
true = 1, §9.

152. ⟨ Cases that change *cur_disp_mode* 152 ⟩ ≡

```
case 'l': case 'g': case '$': cur_disp_mode = *p++;
  for (cur_disp_addr.l = 0; isdigit(*p); p++)
    cur_disp_addr.l = 10 * cur_disp_addr.l + *p - '0';
  goto new_mode;
case 'r': p++; cur_disp_mode = 'g';
  if (*p < 'A' ∨ *p > 'Z') goto what_say;
  if (*(p + 1) ≠ *p) cur_disp_addr.l = spec_reg_code[*p - 'A'], p++;
  else if (spec_regg_code[*p - 'A']) cur_disp_addr.l = spec_regg_code[*p - 'A'], p += 2;
  else goto what_say;
  goto new_mode;
case 'M': cur_disp_mode = *p;
  cur_disp_addr = scan_hex(p + 1, cur_seg); cur_disp_addr.l &= -8; p = next_char;
new_mode: cur_disp_set = false;      /* the '=' is remembered only by '+' */
  repeating = 1;
  goto scan_type;
case '+': if (¬isdigit(*(p + 1))) repeating = 1;
  for (p++; isdigit(*p); p++) repeating = 10 * repeating + *p - '0';
  if (repeating) {
    if (cur_disp_mode ≡ 'M') cur_disp_addr = incr(cur_disp_addr, 8);
    else cur_disp_addr.l++;
  }
  goto scan_type;
```

This code is used in section 149.

153. ⟨ Cases that define *cur_disp_type* 153 ⟩ ≡

```
case '!': case '.': case '#': case '"': cur_disp_set = false;
  repeating = 1;
set_type: cur_disp_type = *p++; break;
scan_type: if (*p ≡ '!' ∨ *p ≡ '.' ∨ *p ≡ '#' ∨ *p ≡ '"') goto set_type;
  if (*p ≠ '=') break;
  goto scan_eql;
case '=': repeating = 1;
scan_eql: cur_disp_set = true;
  val = zero_octa;
  if (*++p ≡ '#') cur_disp_type = *p, val = scan_hex(p + 1, zero_octa);
  else if (*p ≡ '"' ∨ *p ≡ '\'') goto scan_string;
  else cur_disp_type = (scan_const(p) > 0 ? '.' : '!');
  p = next_char;
  if (*p ≠ ',') break;
  val.h = 0; val.l &= #ff;
scan_string: cur_disp_type = '"';
  ⟨ Scan a string constant 155 ⟩; break;
```

This code is used in section 149.

154. ⟨ Subroutines 12 ⟩ +≡

```
  octa scan_hex ARGS((char *, octa));
  octa scan_hex(s, offset)
      char *s;
      octa offset;
```

```
{
  register char *p;
  octa o;

  o = zero_octa;
  for (p = s; isxdigit(*p); p++) {
    o = incr(shift_left(o,4), *p - '0');
    if (*p ≥ 'a') o = incr(o, '0' - 'a' + 10);
    else if (*p ≥ 'A') o = incr(o, '0' - 'A' + 10);
  }
  next_char = p;
  return oplus(o, offset);
}
```

155. ⟨Scan a string constant 155⟩ ≡

```
while (*p ≡ ',') {
  if (*++p ≡ '#') {
    aux = scan_hex(p + 1, zero_octa), p = next_char;
    val = incr(shift_left(val,8), aux.l & #ff);
  } else if (isdigit(*p)) {
    for (k = *p++ - '0'; isdigit(*p); p++) k = (10 * k + *p - '0') & #ff;
    val = incr(shift_left(val,8), k);
  }
  else if (*p ≡ '\n') goto incomplete_str;
}
if (*p ≡ '\'' ∧ *(p + 2) ≡ *p) *p = *(p + 2) = '"';
if (*p ≡ '"') {
  for (p++; *p ∧ *p ≠ '\n' ∧ *p ≠ '"'; p++) val = incr(shift_left(val,8), *p);
  if (*p ∧ *p++ ≡ '"')
    if (*p ≡ ',') goto scan_string;
}
```

This code is used in section 153.

ARGS = macro ( ), §11.
aux: **octa**, MMIX-ARITH §4.
cur_disp_addr: **octa**, §151.
cur_disp_mode: **char**, §151.
cur_disp_set: **bool**, §151.
cur_disp_type: **char**, §151.
cur_seg: **octa**, §151.
false = 0, §9.
h: **tetra**, §10.
incomplete_str: label, §149.
incr: **octa** ( ), MMIX-ARITH §6.
isdigit: **int** ( ), <ctype.h>.
isxdigit: **int** ( ), <ctype.h>.
k: **register int**, §62.
l: **tetra**, §10.
next_char: **char** *, MMIX-ARITH §69.
octa = **struct**, §10.
oplus: **octa** ( ), MMIX-ARITH §5.
p: **register char** *, §62.
repeating: **register int**, §149.
scan_const: **int** ( ), MMIX-ARITH §68.
shift_left: **octa** ( ), MMIX-ARITH §7.
spec_reg_code: **char** [ ], §151.
spec_regg_code: **char** [ ], §151.
true = 1, §9.
val: **octa**, MMIX-ARITH §69.
what_say: label, §149.
zero_octa: **octa**, MMIX-ARITH §4.

156. ⟨ Display and/or set the value of the current octabyte 156 ⟩ ≡

```
{
  if (cur_disp_set) ⟨ Set the current octabyte to val 157 ⟩;
  ⟨ Display the current octabyte 159 ⟩;
  fputc('\n', stdout);
  repeating --;
  if (¬repeating) break;
  if (cur_disp_mode ≡ 'M') cur_disp_addr = incr(cur_disp_addr, 8);
  else cur_disp_addr.l++;
}
```

This code is used in section 149.

157. ⟨ Set the current octabyte to *val* 157 ⟩ ≡

```
switch (cur_disp_mode) {
case 'l': l[cur_disp_addr.l & lring_mask] = val; break;
case '$': k = cur_disp_addr.l & #ff;
  if (k < L) l[(O + k) & lring_mask] = val; else if (k ≥ G) g[k] = val;
  break;
case 'g': k = cur_disp_addr.l & #ff;
  if (k < 32) ⟨ Set g[k] = val only if permissible 158 ⟩;
  g[k] = val; break;
case 'M': if (¬(cur_disp_addr.h & sign_bit)) {
    ll = mem_find(cur_disp_addr);
    ll→tet = val.h; (ll + 1)→tet = val.l;
  } break;
}
```

This code is used in section 156.

158. Here we essentially simulate a PUT command, but we simply **break** if the PUT is illegal or privileged.

⟨ Set $g[k] = val$ only if permissible 158 ⟩ ≡

```
if (k ≥ 9 ∧ k ≠ rI) {
  if (k ≤ 19) break;
  if (k ≡ rA) {
    if (val.h ≠ 0 ∨ val.l ≥ #40000) break;
    cur_round = (val.l ≥ #10000 ? val.l ≫ 16 : ROUND_NEAR);
  } else if (k ≡ rG) {
    if (val.h ≠ 0 ∨ val.l > 255 ∨ val.l < L ∨ val.l < 32) break;
    for (j = val.l; j < G; j++) g[j] = zero_octa;
    G = val.l;
  } else if (k ≡ rL) {
    if (val.h ≡ 0 ∧ val.l < L) L = val.l;
    else break;
  }
}
```

This code is used in section 157.

159. ⟨Display the current octabyte 159⟩ ≡

```
switch (cur_disp_mode) {
case 'l': k = cur_disp_addr.l & lring_mask;
  printf("l[%d]=", k); aux = l[k]; break;
case '$': k = cur_disp_addr.l & #ff;
  if (k < L)
    printf("$%d=l[%d]=", k, (O + k) & lring_mask), aux = l[(O + k) & lring_mask];
  else if (k >= G) printf("$%d=g[%d]=", k, k), aux = g[k];
  else printf("$%d=", k), aux = zero_octa;
  break;
case 'g': k = cur_disp_addr.l & #ff;
  printf("g[%d]=", k); aux = g[k]; break;
case 'M': if (cur_disp_addr.h & sign_bit) aux = zero_octa;
  else {
    ll = mem_find(cur_disp_addr);
    aux.h = ll->tet; aux.l = (ll + 1)->tet;
  }
  printf("M8[#"); print_hex(cur_disp_addr); printf("]="); break;
}
switch (cur_disp_type) {
case '!': print_int(aux); break;
case '.': print_float(aux); break;
case '#': fputc('#', stdout); print_hex(aux); break;
case '"': print_string(aux); break;
}
```

This code is used in section 156.

---

aux: **octa**, MMIX-ARITH §4.
cur_disp_addr: **octa**, §151.
cur_disp_mode: **char**, §151.
cur_disp_set: **bool**, §151.
cur_disp_type: **char**, §151.
cur_round: **int**, MMIX-ARITH §30.
fputc: **int** ( ), <stdio.h>.
g: **octa** [ ], §76.
G: **register int**, §75.
h: **tetra**, §10.
incr: **octa** ( ), MMIX-ARITH §6.
j: **register int**, §62.
k: **register int**, §62.
l: **tetra**, §10.
l: **octa** ∗, §76.
L: **register int**, §75.
ll: **register mem_tetra** ∗, §62.
lring_mask: **int**, §76.
mem_find: **mem_tetra** ∗( ), §20.
O: **register int**, §75.
print_float: **void** ( ), MMIX-ARITH §54.
print_hex: **void** ( ), §12.
print_int: **void** ( ), §15.
print_string: **void** ( ), §160.
printf: **int** ( ), <stdio.h>.
rA = 21, §55.
repeating: **register int**, §149.
rG = 19, §55.
rI = 12, §55.
rL = 20, §55.
ROUND_NEAR = 4, §100.
sign_bit = macro, §15.
stdout: **FILE** ∗, <stdio.h>.
tet: **tetra**, §16.
val: **octa**, MMIX-ARITH §69.
zero_octa: **octa**, MMIX-ARITH §4.

160. ⟨ Subroutines 12 ⟩ +≡

```
void print_string ARGS((octa));
void print_string(o)
    octa o;
{
  register int k, state, b;
  for (k = state = 0; k < 8; k++) {
    b = ((k < 4 ? o.h >> (8 * (3 - k)) : o.l >> (8 * (7 - k)))) & #ff;
    if (b ≡ 0) {
      if (state) printf("%s,0", state > 1 ? "\"" : ""), state = 1;
    } else if (b ≥ '␣' ∧ b ≤ '~')
      printf("%s%c", state > 1 ? "" : state ≡ 1 ? ",\"" : "\"", b), state = 2;
    else printf("%s#%x", state > 1 ? "\"," : state ≡ 1 ? "," : "", b), state = 1;
  }
  if (state ≡ 0) printf("0");
  else if (state > 1) printf("\"");
}
```

161. ⟨ Cases that set and clear tracing and breakpoints 161 ⟩ ≡

```
case '@': inst_ptr = scan_hex(p + 1, cur_seg); p = next_char;
  halted = false; break;
case 't': case 'u': k = *p;
  val = scan_hex(p + 1, cur_seg); p = next_char;
  if (val.h < #20000000) {
    ll = mem_find(val);
    if (k ≡ 't') ll→bkpt |= trace_bit;
    else ll→bkpt &= ~trace_bit;
  }
  break;
case 'b': for (k = 0, p++; ¬isxdigit(*p); p++)
    if (*p ≡ 'r') k |= read_bit;
    else if (*p ≡ 'w') k |= write_bit;
    else if (*p ≡ 'x') k |= exec_bit;
  val = scan_hex(p, cur_seg); p = next_char;
  if (¬(val.h & sign_bit)) {
    ll = mem_find(val);
    ll→bkpt = (ll→bkpt & −8) | k;
  }
  break;
case 'T': cur_seg.h = 0; goto passit;
case 'D': cur_seg.h = #20000000; goto passit;
case 'P': cur_seg.h = #40000000; goto passit;
case 'S': cur_seg.h = #60000000; goto passit;
case 'B': show_breaks(mem_root);
passit: p++; break;
```

This code is used in section 149.

162. ⟨Subroutines 12⟩ +≡

```
void show_breaks ARGS((mem_node *));
void show_breaks(p)
    mem_node *p;
{
  register int j;
  octa cur_loc;
  if (p->left) show_breaks(p->left);
  for (j = 0; j < 512; j++)
    if (p->dat[j].bkpt) {
      cur_loc = incr(p->loc, 4 * j);
      printf("  %08x%08x %c%c%c%c\n", cur_loc.h, cur_loc.l,
          p->dat[j].bkpt & trace_bit ? 't' : '-', p->dat[j].bkpt & read_bit ? 'r' : '-',
          p->dat[j].bkpt & write_bit ? 'w' : '-', p->dat[j].bkpt & exec_bit ? 'x' : '-');
    }
  if (p->right) show_breaks(p->right);
}
```

163. We put pointers to the command line strings in octabytes M_8[Pool_Segment + $8*(k+1)$] for $0 \le k < argc$; the strings themselves are octabyte-aligned, starting at M_8[Pool_Segment + $8*(argc+2)$]. The location of the first free octabyte in the pool segment is placed in M_8[Pool_Segment].

⟨Load the command line arguments 163⟩ ≡

```
x.h = #40000000, x.l = #8;
loc = incr(x, 8 * (argc + 1));
for (k = 0; k < argc; k++, cur_arg++) {
  ll = mem_find(x);
  ll->tet = loc.h, (ll + 1)->tet = loc.l;
  ll = mem_find(loc);
  mmputchars((unsigned char *) *cur_arg, strlen(*cur_arg), loc);
  x.l += 8, loc.l += 8 + (strlen(*cur_arg) & -8);
}
x.l = 0; ll = mem_find(x); ll->tet = loc.h, (ll + 1)->tet = loc.l;
```

This code is used in section 141.

---

argc: **int**, §141.
ARGS = macro ( ), §11.
bkpt: **unsigned char**, §16.
cur_arg: **char** ∗∗, §144.
cur_seg: **octa**, §151.
dat: **mem_tetra** [], §16.
exec_bit = macro, §58.
false = 0, §9.
h: **tetra**, §10.
halted: **bool**, §61.
incr: **octa** ( ), MMIX-ARITH §6.
inst_ptr: **octa**, §61.
isxdigit: **int** ( ), <ctype.h>.
k: **register int**, §62.
l: **tetra**, §10.
left: **mem_node** ∗, §16.
ll: **register mem_tetra** ∗, §62.
loc: **octa**, §16.
loc: **octa**, §61.
mem_find: **mem_tetra** ∗( ), §20.
mem_node = **struct**, §16.
mem_root: **mem_node** ∗, §19.
mmputchars: **void** ( ), §117.
next_char: **char** ∗, MMIX-ARITH §69.
octa = **struct**, §10.
p: **register char** ∗, §62.
printf: **int** ( ), <stdio.h>.
read_bit = macro, §58.
right: **mem_node** ∗, §16.
scan_hex: **octa** ( ), §154.
sign_bit = macro, §15.
strlen: **size_t** ( ), <string.h>.
tet: **tetra**, §16.
trace_bit = macro, §58.
val: **octa**, MMIX-ARITH §69.
write_bit = macro, §58.
x: **octa**, §61.

164. ⟨ Get ready to UNSAVE the initial context 164 ⟩ ≡

```
x.h = 0, x.l = #f0;
ll = mem_find(x);
if (ll→tet) inst_ptr = x;
resuming = true;
rop = RESUME_AGAIN;
g[rX].l = ((tetra) UNSAVE ≪ 24) + 255;
if (dump_file) {
  x.l = 1;
  dump(mem_root);
  dump_tet(0), dump_tet(0);
  exit(0);
}
```

This code is used in section 141.

165. The special option '-D<filename>' can be used to prepare binary files needed by the MMIX-in-MMIX simulator of Section 1.4.3′. (See *The Art of Computer Programming*, Volume 1, Fascicle 1.) This option puts big-endian octabytes into a given file; a location l is followed by one or more nonzero octabytes $M_8[l]$, $M_8[l+8]$, $M_8[l+16]$, ..., followed by zero. The simulated simulator knows how to load programs in such a format (see exercise 1.4.3′–20), and so does the meta-simulator MMMIX.

⟨ Subroutines 12 ⟩ +≡

```
void dump ARGS((mem_node *));
void dump_tet ARGS((tetra));
void dump(p)
    mem_node *p;
{
  register int j;
  octa cur_loc;

  if (p→left) dump(p→left);
  for (j = 0; j < 512; j += 2)
    if (p→dat[j].tet ∨ p→dat[j + 1].tet) {
      cur_loc = incr(p→loc, 4 * j);
      if (cur_loc.l ≠ x.l ∨ cur_loc.h ≠ x.h) {
        if (x.l ≠ 1) dump_tet(0), dump_tet(0);
        dump_tet(cur_loc.h); dump_tet(cur_loc.l); x = cur_loc;
      }
      dump_tet(p→dat[j].tet);
      dump_tet(p→dat[j + 1].tet);
      x = incr(x, 8);
    }
  if (p→right) dump(p→right);
}
```

166. ⟨ Subroutines 12 ⟩ +≡

```
void dump_tet(t)
    tetra t;
{
  fputc(t >> 24, dump_file);
  fputc((t >> 16) & #ff, dump_file);
  fputc((t >> 8) & #ff, dump_file);
  fputc(t & #ff, dump_file);
}
```

ARGS = macro ( ), §11.
dat: **mem_tetra** [ ], §16.
dump_file: **FILE** ∗, §144.
exit: **void** ( ), <stdlib.h>.
fputc: **int** ( ), <stdio.h>.
g: **octa** [ ], §76.
h: **tetra**, §10.
incr: **octa** ( ), MMIX-ARITH §6.
inst_ptr: **octa**, §61.
l: **tetra**, §10.
left: **mem_node** ∗, §16.
ll: **register mem_tetra** ∗, §62.
loc: **octa**, §16.
mem_find: **mem_tetra** ∗( ), §20.
mem_node = **struct**, §16.
mem_root: **mem_node** ∗, §19.
octa = **struct**, §10.
RESUME_AGAIN = 0, §125.
resuming: **bool**, §61.
right: **mem_node** ∗, §16.
rop: **int**, §61.
rX = 25, §55.
tet: **tetra**, §16.
tetra = **unsigned int**, §10.
true = 1, §9.
UNSAVE = #fb, §54.
x: **octa**, §61.

167. Names of the sections.

⟨ Cases for formatting characters 134, 136, 138 ⟩ Used in section 133.
⟨ Cases for individual MMIX instructions 84, 85, 86, 87, 88, 89, 90, 92, 93, 94, 95, 96, 97, 101, 102, 104, 106, 107, 108, 124 ⟩ Used in section 60.
⟨ Cases for lopcodes in the main loop 33, 34, 35, 36 ⟩ Used in section 29.
⟨ Cases that change *cur_disp_mode* 152 ⟩ Used in section 149.
⟨ Cases that define *cur_disp_type* 153 ⟩ Used in section 149.
⟨ Cases that set and clear tracing and breakpoints 161 ⟩ Used in section 149.
⟨ Check for trip interrupt 122 ⟩ Used in section 60.
⟨ Check if the source file has been modified 44 ⟩ Used in section 42.
⟨ Convert relative address to absolute address 70 ⟩ Used in section 60.
⟨ Display and/or set the value of the current octabyte 156 ⟩ Used in section 149.
⟨ Display the current octabyte 159 ⟩ Used in section 156.
⟨ Either halt or print warning 109 ⟩ Used in section 108.
⟨ Fetch the next instruction 63 ⟩ Used in section 60.
⟨ Fix up the subtrees of $*q$ 22 ⟩ Used in section 21.
⟨ Get ready to UNSAVE the initial context 164 ⟩ Used in section 141.
⟨ Get ready to update rA 100 ⟩ Used in section 97.
⟨ Get ready to update rG 99 ⟩ Used in section 97.
⟨ Global variables 19, 25, 31, 40, 48, 52, 56, 61, 65, 76, 110, 113, 121, 129, 139, 144, 151 ⟩ Used in section 141.
⟨ Increase rL 81 ⟩ Used in section 80.
⟨ Info for arithmetic commands 66 ⟩ Used in section 65.
⟨ Info for branch commands 67 ⟩ Used in section 65.
⟨ Info for load/store commands 68 ⟩ Used in section 65.
⟨ Info for logical and control commands 69 ⟩ Used in section 65.
⟨ Initialize everything 14, 18, 24, 32, 41, 77, 147 ⟩ Used in section 141.
⟨ Initiate a trip interrupt 123 ⟩ Used in section 122.
⟨ Install operand fields 71 ⟩ Used in section 60.
⟨ Install register X as the destination, adjusting the register stack if necessary 80 ⟩ Used in section 60.
⟨ Install special operands when resuming an interrupted operation 126 ⟩ Used in section 71.
⟨ Interact with the user 149 ⟩ Used in section 141.
⟨ Interpret character $*p$ in the trace format 133 ⟩ Used in section 131.
⟨ Load and write four bytes 119 ⟩ Used in section 117.
⟨ Load and write one byte 118 ⟩ Used in section 117.
⟨ Load $g[k]$ from the register stack 105 ⟩ Used in section 104.
⟨ Load *tet* as a normal item 30 ⟩ Used in section 29.
⟨ Load the command line arguments 163 ⟩ Used in section 141.
⟨ Load the next item 29 ⟩ Used in section 32.
⟨ Load the postamble 37 ⟩ Used in section 32.
⟨ Load the preamble 28 ⟩ Used in section 32.
⟨ Local registers 62, 75 ⟩ Used in section 141.
⟨ Open a file for dumping binary output 146 ⟩ Used in section 143.

⟨ Open a file for simulated standard input 145 ⟩ Used in section 143.
⟨ Perform one instruction 60 ⟩ Used in section 141.
⟨ Prepare memory arguments $ma = \mathrm{M}[a]$ and $mb = \mathrm{M}[b]$ if needed 111 ⟩ Used in section 108.
⟨ Prepare to list lines from a new source file 49 ⟩ Used in section 47.
⟨ Prepare to perform a ropcode 125 ⟩ Used in section 124.
⟨ Preprocessor macros 11, 43, 46 ⟩ Used in section 141.
⟨ Print a stream-of-consciousness description of the instruction 131 ⟩ Used in section 128.
⟨ Print all the frequency counts 53 ⟩ Used in section 141.
⟨ Print changes to rL 132 ⟩ Used in section 131.
⟨ Print frequency data for location $p\text{-}loc + 4 * j$ 51 ⟩ Used in section 50.
⟨ Print the frequency count, the location, and the instruction 130 ⟩ Used in section 128.
⟨ Process the command line 142 ⟩ Used in section 141.
⟨ Put a new command in *command_buf* 150 ⟩ Used in section 149.
⟨ Read and store one byte; **return** if done 115 ⟩ Used in section 114.
⟨ Read and store up to four bytes; **return** if done 116 ⟩ Used in section 114.
⟨ Scan a string constant 155 ⟩ Used in section 153.
⟨ Search for *key* in the treap, setting *last_mem* and *p* to its location 21 ⟩ Used in section 20.
⟨ Set b from register X 74 ⟩ Used in section 71.
⟨ Set b from special register 79 ⟩ Used in section 71.
⟨ Set $g[k] = val$ only if permissible 158 ⟩ Used in section 157.
⟨ Set $L = z = \min(z, L)$ 98 ⟩ Used in section 97.
⟨ Set the current octabyte to *val* 157 ⟩ Used in section 156.
⟨ Set y from register Y 73 ⟩ Used in section 71.
⟨ Set z as an immediate wyde 78 ⟩ Used in section 71.
⟨ Set z from register Z 72 ⟩ Used in section 71.
⟨ Store $g[k]$ in the register stack 103 ⟩ Used in section 102.
⟨ Subroutines 12, 13, 15, 17, 20, 26, 27, 42, 45, 47, 50, 82, 83, 91, 114, 117, 120, 137, 140, 143, 148, 154, 160, 162, 165, 166 ⟩ Used in section 141.
⟨ Trace the current instruction, if requested 128 ⟩ Used in section 60.
⟨ Type declarations 9, 10, 16, 38, 39, 54, 55, 59, 64, 135 ⟩ Used in section 141.
⟨ Update the clocks 127 ⟩ Used in section 60.

MMIXAL

1. Definition of MMIXAL. This program takes input written in `MMIXAL`, the `MMIX` assembly language, and translates it into binary files that can be loaded and executed on `MMIX` simulators. `MMIXAL` is much simpler than the "industrial strength" assembly languages that computer manufacturers usually provide, because it is primarily intended for the simple demonstration programs in *The Art of Computer Programming*. Yet it tries to have enough features to serve also as the back end of compilers for C and other high-level languages.

Instructions for using the program appear at the end of this document (see page 487). First we will discuss the input and output languages in detail; then we'll consider the translation process, step by step; then we'll put everything together.

2. A program in `MMIXAL` consists of a series of *lines*, each of which usually contains a single instruction. However, lines with no instructions are possible, and so are lines with two or more instructions.

Each instruction has three parts called its label field, opcode field, and operand field; these fields are separated from each other by one or more spaces. The label field, which is often empty, consists of all characters up to the first blank space. The opcode field, which is never empty, runs from the first nonblank after the label to the next blank space. The operand field, which again might be empty, runs from the next nonblank character (if any) to the first blank or semicolon that isn't part of a string or character constant. If the operand field is followed by a semicolon, possibly with intervening blanks, a new instruction begins immediately after the semicolon; otherwise the rest of the line is ignored. The end of a line is treated as a blank space for the purposes of these rules, with the additional proviso that string or character constants are not allowed to extend from one line to another.

The label field must begin with a letter or a digit; otherwise the entire line is treated as a comment. Popular ways to introduce comments, either at the beginning of a line or after the operand field, are to precede them by the character `%` as in TeX, or by `//` as in C++; `MMIXAL` is not very particular. However, Lisp-style comments introduced by single semicolons will fail if they follow an instruction, because they will be assumed to introduce another instruction.

3. `MMIXAL` has no built-in macro capability, nor does it know how to include header files and such things. But users can run their files through a standard C preprocessor to obtain `MMIXAL` programs in which macros and such things have been expanded. (Caution: The preprocessor also removes C-style comments, unless it is told not to do so.) Literate programming tools could also be used for preprocessing.

If a line begins with the special form '`#` ⟨ integer ⟩ ⟨ string ⟩', this program interprets it as a *line directive* emitted by a preprocessor. For example,

```
# 13 "foo.mms"
```

means that the following line was line 13 in the user's source file `foo.mms`. Line directives allow us to correlate errors with the user's original file; we also pass them to the output, for use by simulators and debuggers.

D.E. Knuth: MMIXware, LNCS 1750, pp. 422–493, 2014.
DOI: 10.1007/3-540-46611-8_9

4. MMIXAL deals primarily with *symbols* and *constants*, which it interprets and combines to form machine language instructions and data. Constants are simplest, so we will discuss them first.

A *decimal constant* is a sequence of digits, representing a number in radix 10. A *hexadecimal constant* is a sequence of hexadecimal digits, preceded by #, representing a number in radix 16:

⟨ digit ⟩ ⟶ 0 | 1 | 2 | 3 | 4 | 5 | 6 | 7 | 8 | 9
⟨ hex digit ⟩ ⟶ ⟨ digit ⟩ | A | B | C | D | E | F | a | b | c | d | e | f
⟨ decimal constant ⟩ ⟶ ⟨ digit ⟩ | ⟨ decimal constant ⟩⟨ digit ⟩
⟨ hex constant ⟩ ⟶ #⟨ hex digit ⟩ | ⟨ hex constant ⟩⟨ hex digit ⟩

Constants whose value is 2^{64} or more are reduced modulo 2^{64}.

5. A *character constant* is a single character enclosed in single quote marks; it denotes the ASCII or Unicode number corresponding to that character. For example, 'a' represents the constant #61, also known as 97. The quoted character can be anything except the character that the C library calls \n or *newline*; that character should be represented as #a.

⟨ character constant ⟩ ⟶ '⟨ single byte character except newline ⟩'
⟨ constant ⟩ ⟶ ⟨ decimal constant ⟩ | ⟨ hex constant ⟩ | ⟨ character constant ⟩

Notice that ''' represents a single quote, the code #27; and '\' represents a backslash, the code #5c. MMIXAL characters are never "quoted" by backslashes as in the C language.

In the present implementation a character constant will always be at most 255, since wyde character input is not supported. But if the input were in Unicode one could write, say, 'א' or 'Ж' for #05d0 or #0416. The present program does not support Unicode directly because basic software for inputting and outputting 16-bit characters was still in a primitive state at the time of writing. But the data structures below are designed so that a change to Unicode will not be difficult when the time is ripe.

6. A *string constant* like "Hello" is an abbreviation for a sequence of one or more character constants separated by commas: 'H','e','l','l','o'. Any character except newline or the double quote mark " can appear between the double quotes of a string constant. Similarly, "高德纳" is an abbrevation for '高','德','纳' (namely #9ad8,#5fb7,#7eb3) when Unicode is supported.

7. A *symbol* in `MMIXAL` is any sequence of letters and digits, beginning with a letter. A colon '`:`' or underscore symbol '`_`' is regarded as a letter, for purposes of this definition. All extended-ASCII characters like '`é`', whose 8-bit code exceeds 126, are also treated as letters.

⟨ letter ⟩ ⟶ `A` | `B` | ⋯ | `Z` | `a` | `b` | ⋯ | `z` | `:` | `_` | ⟨ character with code value > 126 ⟩
⟨ symbol ⟩ ⟶ ⟨ letter ⟩ | ⟨ symbol ⟩⟨ letter ⟩ | ⟨ symbol ⟩⟨ digit ⟩

In future implementations, when `MMIXAL` is used with Unicode, all wyde characters whose 16-bit code exceeds 126 will be regarded as letters; thus `MMIXAL` symbols will be able to involve Greek letters or Chinese characters or thousands of other glyphs.

8. A symbol is said to be *fully qualified* if it begins with a colon. Every symbol that is not fully qualified is an abbreviation for the fully qualified symbol obtained by placing the *current prefix* in front of it; the current prefix is always fully qualified. At the beginning of an `MMIXAL` program the current prefix is simply the single character '`:`', but the user can change it with the `PREFIX` command. For example,

```
ADD     x,y,z              % means ADD :x,:y,:z
PREFIX  Foo:               % current prefix is :Foo:
ADD     x,y,z              % means ADD :Foo:x,:Foo:y,:Foo:z
PREFIX  Bar:               % current prefix is :Foo:Bar:
ADD     :x,y,:z            % means ADD :x,:Foo:Bar:y,:z
PREFIX  :                  % current prefix reverts to :
ADD     x,Foo:Bar:y,Foo:z  % means ADD :x,:Foo:Bar:y,:Foo:z
```

This mechanism allows large programs to avoid conflicts between symbol names, when parts of the program are independent and/or written by different users. The current prefix conventionally ends with a colon, but this convention need not be obeyed.

9. A *local symbol* is a decimal digit followed by one of the letters `B`, `F`, or `H`, meaning "backward," "forward," or "here":

⟨ local operand ⟩ ⟶ ⟨ digit ⟩ `B` | ⟨ digit ⟩ `F`
⟨ local label ⟩ ⟶ ⟨ digit ⟩ `H`

The `B` and `F` forms are permitted only in the operand field of `MMIXAL` instructions; the `H` form is permitted only in the label field. A local operand such as `2B` stands for the last local label `2H` in instructions before the current one, or 0 if `2H` has not yet appeared as a label. A local operand such as `2F` stands for the first `2H` in instructions after the current one. Thus, in a sequence such as

```
2H JMP 2F
2H JMP 2B
```

the first instruction jumps to the second and the second jumps to the first.

Local symbols are useful for references to nearby points of a program, in cases where no meaningful name is appropriate. They can also be useful in special situations where a redefinable symbol is needed; for example, an instruction like

```
9H IS 9B+1
```

will maintain a running counter.

10. Each symbol receives a value called its *equivalent* when it appears in the label field of an instruction; it is said to be *defined* after its equivalent has been established. A few symbols, like `rA` and `ROUND_OFF` and `Fopen`, are predefined because they refer to fixed constants associated with the `MMIX` hardware or its rudimentary operating system; otherwise every symbol should be defined exactly once. The two appearances of '`2H`' in the example above do not violate this rule, because the second '`2H`' is not the same symbol as the first.

A predefined symbol can be redefined (given a new equivalent). After it has been redefined it acts like an ordinary symbol and cannot be redefined again. A complete list of the predefined symbols appears in the program listing below.

Equivalents are either *pure* or *register numbers.* A pure equivalent is an unsigned octabyte, but a register number equivalent is a one-byte value, between 0 and 255. A dollar sign is used to change a pure number into a register number; for example, '`$20`' means register number 20.

11. Constants and symbols are combined into *expressions* in a simple way:

⟨ primary expression ⟩ ⟶ ⟨ constant ⟩ | ⟨ symbol ⟩ | ⟨ local operand ⟩ | `@` |
    `(`⟨ expression ⟩`)` | ⟨ unary operator ⟩⟨ primary expression ⟩
⟨ term ⟩ ⟶ ⟨ primary expression ⟩ | ⟨ term ⟩⟨ strong operator ⟩⟨ primary expression ⟩
⟨ expression ⟩ ⟶ ⟨ term ⟩ | ⟨ expression ⟩⟨ weak operator ⟩⟨ term ⟩
⟨ unary operator ⟩ ⟶ `+` | `-` | `~` | `$` | `&`
⟨ strong operator ⟩ ⟶ `*` | `/` | `//` | `%` | `<<` | `>>` | `&`
⟨ weak operator ⟩ ⟶ `+` | `-` | `|` | `^`

Each expression has a value that is either pure or a register number. The character `@` stands for the current location, which is always pure. The unary operators `+`, `-`, `~`, `$`, and `&` mean, respectively, "do nothing," "subtract from zero," "complement the bits," "change from pure value to register number," and "take the serial number." Only the first of these, `+`, can be applied to a register number. The last unary operator, `&`, applies only to symbols, and it is of interest primarily to system programmers; it converts a symbol to the unique positive integer that is used to identify it in the binary file output by `MMIXAL`.

Binary operators come in two flavors, strong and weak. The strong ones are essentially concerned with multiplication or division: `x*y`, `x/y`, `x//y`, `x%y`, `x<<y`, `x>>y`, and `x&y` stand respectively for $(x\times y) \bmod 2^{64}$ (multiplication), $\lfloor x/y \rfloor$ (division), $\lfloor 2^{64}x/y \rfloor$ (fractional division), $x \bmod y$ (remainder), $(x \times 2^y) \bmod 2^{64}$ (left shift), $\lfloor x/2^y \rfloor$ (right shift), and $x \mathbin{\&} y$ (bitwise and) on unsigned octabytes. Division is legal only if $y > 0$; fractional division is legal only if $x < y$. None of the strong binary operations can be applied to register numbers.

The weak binary operations `x+y`, `x-y`, `x|y`, and `x^y` stand respectively for $(x + y) \bmod 2^{64}$ (addition), $(x - y) \bmod 2^{64}$ (subtraction), $x \mid y$ (bitwise or), and $x \oplus y$ (bitwise exclusive-or) on unsigned octabytes. These operations can be applied to register numbers only in four contexts: ⟨ register ⟩ + ⟨ pure ⟩, ⟨ pure ⟩ + ⟨ register ⟩, ⟨ register ⟩ − ⟨ pure ⟩ and ⟨ register ⟩ − ⟨ register ⟩. For example, if `x` denotes `$1` and `y` denotes `$10`, then `x+3` and `3+x` denote `$4`, and `y-x` denotes the pure value `9`.

Register numbers within expressions are allowed to be arbitrary octabytes, but a register number assigned as the equivalent of a symbol should not exceed 255.

(Incidentally, one might ask why the designer of `MMIXAL` did not simply adopt the existing rules of C for expressions. The primary reason is that the designers of C chose to give `<<`, `>>`, and `&` a lower precedence than `+`; but in `MMIXAL` we want to be able to write things like `o<<24+x<<16+y<<8+z` or `@+yz<<2` or `@+(#100-@)&#ff`. Since the conventions of C were inappropriate, it was better to make a clean break, not pretending to have a close relationship with that language. The new rules are quite easily memorized, because `MMIXAL` has just two levels of precedence, and the strong binary operations are all essentially multiplicative by nature while the weak binary operations are essentially additive.)

12. A symbol is called a *future reference* until it has been defined. `MMIXAL` restricts the use of future references, so that programs can be assembled quickly in one pass over the input; therefore all expressions can be evaluated when the `MMIXAL` processor first sees them.

The restrictions are easily stated: Future references cannot be used in expressions together with unary or binary operators (except the unary `+`, which does nothing); moreover, future references can appear as operands only in instructions that have relative addresses (namely branches, probable branches, `JMP`, `PUSHJ`, `GETA`) or in octabyte constants (the pseudo-operation `OCTA`). Thus, for example, one can say `JMP 1F` or `JMP 1B-4`, but not `JMP 1F-4`.

13. We noted earlier that each `MMIXAL` instruction contains a label field, an opcode field, and an operand field. The label field is either empty or a symbol or local label; when it is nonempty, the symbol or local label receives an equivalent. The operand field is either empty or a sequence of expressions separated by commas; when it is empty, it is equivalent to the simple operand field '`0`'.

⟨ instruction ⟩ ⟶ ⟨ label ⟩⟨ opcode ⟩⟨ operand list ⟩
⟨ label ⟩ ⟶ ⟨ empty ⟩ | ⟨ symbol ⟩ | ⟨ local label ⟩
⟨ operand list ⟩ ⟶ ⟨ empty ⟩ | ⟨ expression list ⟩
⟨ expression list ⟩ ⟶ ⟨ expression ⟩ | ⟨ expression list ⟩`,`⟨ expression ⟩

The opcode field contains either a symbolic `MMIX` operation name (like `ADD`), or an *alias operation*, or a *pseudo-operation*. Alias operations are alternate names for `MMIX` operations whose standard names are inappropriate in certain contexts. Pseudo-operations do not correspond directly to `MMIX` commands, but they govern the assembly process in important ways.

There are two alias operations:

• `SET $X,$Y` is equivalent to `OR $X,$Y,0`; it sets register X to register Y. Similarly, `SET $X,Y` (when `Y` is not a register) is equivalent to `SETL $X,Y`.
• `LDA $X,$Y,$Z` is equivalent to `ADDU $X,$Y,$Z`; it loads the address of memory location \$Y+\$Z into register X. Similarly, `LDA $X,$Y,Z` is equivalent to `ADDU $X,$Y,Z`.

The symbolic operation names for genuine `MMIX` operations should not include the suffix `I` for an immediate operation or the suffix `B` for a backward jump; `MMIXAL` determines such things automatically. Thus, one never writes `ADDI` or `JMPB` in the source input to `MMIXAL`, although such opcodes might appear when a simulator or debugger or disassembler is presenting a numeric instruction in symbolic form.

⟨ opcode ⟩ ⟶ ⟨ symbolic `MMIX` operation ⟩ | ⟨ alias operation ⟩
| ⟨ pseudo-operation ⟩
⟨ symbolic `MMIX` operation ⟩ ⟶ `TRAP` | `FCMP` | ··· | `TRIP`
⟨ alias operation ⟩ ⟶ `SET` | `LDA`
⟨ pseudo-operation ⟩ ⟶ `IS` | `LOC` | `PREFIX` | `GREG` | `LOCAL` | `BSPEC` | `ESPEC`
| `BYTE` | `WYDE` | `TETRA` | `OCTA`

14. `MMIX` operations like `ADD` require exactly three expressions as operands. The first two must be register numbers. The third must be either a register number or a pure number between 0 and 255; in the latter case, `ADD` becomes `ADDI` in the assembled output. Thus, for example, the command "set register 1 to the sum of register 2 and register 3" could be expressed as

```
ADD $1,$2,$3
```

or as, say,

```
ADD x,y,y+1
```

if the equivalent of `x` is `$1` and the equivalent of `y` is `$2`. The command "subtract 5 from register 1" could be expressed as

```
SUB $1,$1,5
```

or as

```
SUB x,x,5
```

but not as '`SUBI $1,$1,5`' or '`SUBI x,x,5`'.

`MMIX` operations like `FLOT` require either three operands (register, pure, register/pure) or only two (register, register/pure). In the first case the middle operand is the rounding mode, which is best expressed in terms of the predefined symbolic values `ROUND_CURRENT`, `ROUND_OFF`, `ROUND_UP`, `ROUND_DOWN`, `ROUND_NEAR`, for $(0,1,2,3,4)$ respectively. In the second case the middle operand is understood to be zero (namely, `ROUND_CURRENT`).

`MMIX` operations like `SETL` or `INCH`, which involve a wyde intermediate constant, require exactly two operands, (register, pure). The value of the second operand should fit in two bytes.

`MMIX` operations like `BNZ`, which mention a register and a relative address, also require two operands. The first operand should be a register number. The second operand should yield a result r in the range $-2^{16} \le r < 2^{16}$ when the current location is subtracted from it and the result is divided by 4. The second operand might also be undefined; in that case, the eventual value must satisfy the restriction stated for defined values. The opcodes `GETA` and `PUSHJ` are similar, except that the first operand to `PUSHJ` might also be pure (see below). The `JMP` operation is also similar, but it has only one operand, and it allows the larger address range $-2^{24} \le r < 2^{24}$.

`MMIX` operations that refer to memory, like `LDO` and `STHT` and `GO`, are treated like `ADD` if they have three operands, except that the first operand should be pure (not a register number) in the case of `PRELD`, `PREGO`, `PREST`, `STCO`, `SYNCD`, and `SYNCID`. These opcodes also accept a special two-operand form, in which the second operand stands for a *base address* and an immediate offset (see below).

The first operand of `PUSHJ` and `PUSHGO` can be either a pure number or a register number. In the first case ('`PUSHJ 2,Sub`' or '`PUSHGO 2,Sub`') the programmer might be thinking "let's push down two registers"; in the second case ('`PUSHJ $2,Sub`' or '`PUSHGO $2,Sub`') the programmer might be thinking "let's make register 2 the hole position for this subroutine call." Both cases result in the same assembled output.

The remaining MMIX opcodes are idiosyncratic:

```
NEG r,p,z;
PUT s,z;
GET r,s;
POP p,yz;
RESUME xyz;
SAVE r,0;
UNSAVE r;
SYNC xyz;
TRAP x,y,z  or  TRAP x,yz  or  TRAP xyz;
```

SWYM and TRIP are like TRAP. Here s is an integer between 0 and 31, preferably given by one of the predefined symbols rA, rB, ... for special register codes; r is a register number; p is a pure byte; x, y, and z are either register numbers or pure bytes; yz and xyz are pure values that fit respectively in two and three bytes.

All of these rules can be summarized by saying that MMIXAL treats each MMIX opcode in the most natural way. When there are three operands, they affect fields X, Y, and Z of the assembled MMIX instruction; when there are two operands, they affect fields X and YZ; when there is just one operand, it affects field XYZ.

15. In all cases when the opcode corresponds to an MMIX operation, the MMIXAL instruction tells the assembler to carry out four steps: (1) Align the current location so that it is a multiple of 4, by adding 1, 2, or 3 if necessary; (2) Define the equivalent of the label field to be the current location, if the label is nonempty; (3) Evaluate the operands and assemble the specified MMIX instruction into the current location; (4) Increase the current location by 4.

16. Now let's consider the pseudo-operations, starting with the simplest cases.

• ⟨label⟩ `IS` ⟨expression⟩ defines the value of the label to be the value of the expression, which must not be a future reference. The expression may be either pure or a register number.

• ⟨label⟩ `LOC` ⟨expression⟩ first defines the label to be the value of the current location, if the label is nonempty. Then the current location is changed to the value of the expression, which must be pure.

For example, '`LOC #1000`' will start assembling subsequent instructions or data in location whose hexadecimal value is #`1000`. '`X LOC @+500`' defines `X` to be the address of the first of 500 bytes in memory; assembly will continue at location `X` + 500. The operation of aligning the current location to a multiple of 256, if it is not already aligned in that way, can be expressed as '`LOC @+(256-@)&255`'.

A less trivial example arises if we want to emit instructions and data into two separate areas of memory, but we want to intermix them in the `MMIXAL` source file. We could start by defining `8H` and `9H` to be the starting addresses of the instruction and data segments, respectively. Then, a sequence of instructions could be enclosed in '`LOC 8B`; ...; `8H IS @`'; a sequence of data could be enclosed in '`LOC 9B`; ...; `9H IS @`'. Any number of such sequences could then be combined. Instead of the two pseudo-instructions '`8H IS @; LOC 9B`' one could in fact write simply '`8H LOC 9B`' when switching from instructions to data.

• `PREFIX` ⟨symbol⟩ redefines the current prefix to be the given symbol (fully qualified). The label field should be blank.

17. The next pseudo-operations assemble bytes, wydes, tetrabytes, or octabytes of data.

• ⟨label⟩ `BYTE` ⟨expression list⟩ defines the label to be the current location, if the label field is nonempty; then it assembles one byte for each expression in the expression list, and advances the current location by the number of bytes. The expressions should all be pure numbers that fit in one byte.

String constants are often used in such expression lists. For example, if the current location is #`1000`, the instruction `BYTE "Hello",0` assembles six bytes containing the constants `'H'`, `'e'`, `'l'`, `'l'`, `'o'`, and `0` into locations #`1000`, ..., #`1005`, and advances the current location to #`1006`.

• ⟨label⟩ `WYDE` ⟨expression list⟩ is similar, but it first makes the current location even, by adding 1 to it if necessary. Then it defines the label (if a nonempty label is present), and assembles each expression as a two-byte value. The current location is advanced by twice the number of expressions in the list. The expressions should all be pure numbers that fit in two bytes.

• ⟨label⟩ `TETRA` ⟨expression list⟩ is similar, but it aligns the current location to a multiple of 4 before defining the label; then it assembles each expression as a four-byte value. The current location is advanced by $4n$ if there are n expressions in the list. Each expression should be a pure number that fits in four bytes.

• ⟨label⟩ `OCTA` ⟨expression list⟩ is similar, but it first aligns the current location to a multiple of 8; it assembles each expression as an eight-byte value. The current location is advanced by $8n$ if there are n expressions in the list. Any or all of the expressions may be future references, but they should all be defined as pure numbers eventually.

18. Global registers are important for accessing memory in `MMIX` programs. They could be allocated by hand, and defined with `IS` instructions, but `MMIXAL` provides a mechanism that is usually much more convenient:

• $\langle$label$\rangle$ `GREG` $\langle$expression$\rangle$ allocates a new global register, and assigns its number as the equivalent of the label. At the beginning of assembly, the current global threshold G is \$255. Each distinct `GREG` instruction decreases G by 1; the final value of G will be the initial value of rG when the assembled program is loaded.

The value of the expression will be loaded into the global register at the beginning of the program. *If this value is nonzero, it should remain constant throughout the program execution*; such global registers are considered to be *base addresses.* Two or more base addresses with the same constant value are assigned to the same global register number.

Base addresses can simplify memory accesses in an important way. Suppose, for example, five octabyte values appear in a data segment, and their addresses are called `AA`, `BB`, `CC`, `DD`, and `EE`:

```
AA LOC @+8;BB LOC @+8;CC LOC @+8;DD LOC @+8;EE LOC @+8
```

Then if you say `Base GREG AA`, you will be able to write simply '`LDO $1,AA`' to bring `AA` into register `$1`, and '`LDO $2,CC`' to bring `CC` into register `$2`.

Here's how it works: Whenever a memory operation such as `LDO` or `STB` or `GO` has only two operands, the second operand should be a pure number whose value can be expressed as $b+\delta$, where $0 \le \delta < 256$ and b is the value of a base address in one of the preceding `GREG` commands. The `MMIXAL` processor will find the closest base address and manufacture an appropriate command. For example, the instruction '`LDO $2,CC`' in the example of the preceding paragraph would be converted automatically to '`LDO $2,Base,16`'.

If no base address is close enough, an error message will be generated, unless this program is run with the `-x` option on the command line. The `-x` option inserts additional instructions if necessary, using global register 255, so that any address is accessible. For example, if there is no base address that allows `LDO $2,FF` to be implemented in a single instruction, but if `FF` equals `Base+1000`, then the `-x` option would assemble two instructions,

```
SETL $255,1000; LDO $2,Base,$255
```

in place of `LDO $2,FF`. Caution: The `-x` feature makes the number of actual `MMIX` instructions hard to predict, so extreme care must be used if your style of coding includes relative branch instructions in dangerous forms like '`BNZ x,@+8`'.

This base address convention can be used also with the alias operation `LDA`. For example, '`LDA $3,CC`' loads the address of `CC` into register 3, by assembling the instruction '`ADDU $3,Base,16`'.

MMIXAL also allows a two-operand form for memory operations such as

```
LDO $1,$2
```

to be an abbreviation for 'LDO $1,$2,0'.

When MMIXAL programs use subroutines with a memory stack in addition to the built-in register stack, they usually begin with the instructions 'sp GREG 0;fp GREG 0'; these instructions allocate a *stack pointer* sp=$254 and a *frame pointer* fp=$253. However, subroutine libraries are free to implement any conventions for global registers and stacks that they like.

19. Short programs rarely run out of global registers, but long programs need a mechanism to check that GREG hasn't been used too often. The following pseudo-instruction provides the necessary safety valve:

• LOCAL ⟨expression⟩ ensures that the expression will be a local register in the program being assembled. The expression should be a register number, and the label field should be blank. At the close of assembly, MMIXAL will report an error if the final value of G does not exceed all register numbers that are declared local in this way.

A LOCAL instruction need not be given unless the register number is 32 or more. (MMIX always considers $0 through $31 to be local, so MMIXAL implicitly acts as if the instruction 'LOCAL $31' were present.)

20. Finally, there are two pseudo-instructions to pass information and hints to the loading routine and/or to debuggers that will be using the assembled program.

• BSPEC ⟨expression⟩ begins "special mode"; the ⟨expression⟩ should have a value that fits in two bytes, and the label field should be blank.

• ESPEC ends "special mode"; the operand field is ignored, and the label field should be blank.

All material assembled between BSPEC and ESPEC is passed directly to the output, but not loaded as part of the assembled program. Ordinary MMIX instructions cannot appear in special mode; only the pseudo-operations IS, PREFIX, BYTE, WYDE, TETRA, OCTA, GREG, and LOCAL are allowed. The operand of BSPEC should have a value that fits in two bytes; this value identifies the kind of data that follows. (For example, BSPEC 0 might introduce information about subroutine calling conventions at the current location, and BSPEC 1 might introduce line numbers from a high-level-language program that was compiled into the code at the current place. System routines often need to pass such information through an assembler to the operating system, hence MMIXAL provides a general-purpose conduit.)

21. A program should begin at the special symbolic location `Main` (more precisely, at the address corresponding to the fully qualified symbol `:Main`). This symbol always has serial number 1, and it must always be defined.

Locations should not receive assembled data more than once. (More precisely, the loader will load the bitwise xor of all the data assembled for each byte position; but the general rule "do not load two things into the same byte" is safest.) All locations that do not receive assembled data are initially zero, except that the loading routine will put register stack data into segment 3, and the operating system may put command line data and debugger data into segment 2. (The rudimentary `MMIX` operating system starts a program with the number of command line arguments in \$0, and a pointer to the beginning of an array of argument pointers in \$1.) Segments 2 and 3 should not get assembled data, unless the user is a true hacker who is willing to take the risk that such data might crash the system.

22. Binary MMO output. When the `MMIXAL` processor assembles a file called `foo.mms`, it produces a binary output file called `foo.mmo`. (The suffix `mms` stands for "`MMIX` symbolic," and `mmo` stands for "`MMIX` object.") Such `mmo` files have a simple structure consisting of a sequence of tetrabytes. Some of the tetrabytes are instructions to a loading routine; others are data to be loaded.

Loader instructions are distinguished from tetrabytes of data by their first (most significant) byte, which has the special escape-code value #98, called *mm* in the program below. This code value corresponds to `MMIX`'s opcode `LDVTS`, which is unlikely to occur in tetras of data. The second byte X of a loader instruction is the loader opcode, called the *lopcode*. The third and fourth bytes, Y and Z, are operands. Sometimes they are combined into a single 16-bit operand called YZ.

#define *mm* #98

23. A small, contrived example will help explain the basic ideas of mmo format. Consider the following input file, called `test.mms`:

```
% A peculiar example of MMIXAL
     LOC   Data_Segment       % location #2000000000000000
     OCTA  1F                 % a future reference
a    GREG  @                  % $254 is base address for ABCD
ABCD BYTE  "ab"               % two bytes of data
     LOC   #123456789         % switch to the instruction segment
Main JMP   1F                 % another future reference
     LOC   @+#4000            % skip past 16384 bytes
2H   LDB   $3,ABCD+1          % use the base address
     BZ    $3,1F; TRAP        % and refer to the future again
# 3 "foo.mms"                 % this comment is a line directive
     LOC   2B-4*10            % move 10 tetras before previous location
1H   JMP   2B                 % resolve previous references to 1F
     BSPEC 5                  % begin special data of type 5
     TETRA &a<<8              % four bytes of special data
     WYDE  a-$0               % two more bytes of special data
     ESPEC                    % end a special data packet
     LOC   ABCD+2             % resume the data segment
     BYTE  "cd",#98           % assemble three more bytes of data
```

It defines a silly program that essentially puts `'b'` into register 3; the program halts when it gets to an all-zero `TRAP` instruction following the `BZ`. But the assembled output of this file illustrates most of the features of `MMIX` objects, and in fact `test.mms` was the first test file tried by the author when the `MMIXAL` processor was originally written.

The binary output file `test.mmo` assembled from `test.mms` consists of the following tetrabytes, shown in hexadecimal notation with brief comments. Fuller explanations appear with the descriptions of individual lopcodes below.

`98090101`	*lop_pre* 1,1 (preamble, version 1, 1 tetra)
`36f4a363`	(the file creation time)
`98012001`	*lop_loc* #20,1 (data segment, 1 tetra)
`00000000`	(low tetrabyte of address in data segment)
`00000000`	(high tetrabyte of `OCTA 1F`)
`00000000`	(low tetrabyte, will be fixed up later)
`61620000`	(`"ab"`, padded with trailing zeros)
`98010002`	*lop_loc* 0,2 (instruction segment, 2 tetras)
`00000001`	(high tetrabyte of address in instruction segment)
`2345678c`	(low tetrabyte of address, after alignment)
`98060002`	*lop_file* 0,2 (file name 0, 2 tetras)
`74657374`	(`"test"`)
`2e6d6d73`	(`".mms"`)
`98070007`	*lop_line* 7 (line 7 of the current file)
`f0000000`	(`JMP 1F`, will be fixed up later)
`98024000`	*lop_skip* #4000 (advance 16384 bytes)

98070009	*lop_line* 9 (line 9 of the current file)
8103fe01	(`LDB $3,a,1`, uses base address `a`)
42030000	(`BZ $3,1F`, will be fixed later)
9807000a	*lop_line* 10 (stay on line 10)
00000000	(`TRAP`)
98010002	*lop_loc* 0, 2 (instruction segment, 2 tetras)
00000001	(high tetrabyte of address in instruction segment)
2345a768	(low tetrabyte of address `1H`)
98050010	*lop_fixrx* 16 (fix 16-bit relative address)
0100fff5	(fixup for location `@-4*-11`)
98040ff7	*lop_fixr* #`ff7` (fix `@-4*#ff7`)
98032001	*lop_fixo* #20, 1 (data segment, 1 tetra)
00000000	(low tetrabyte of data segment address to fix)
98060102	*lop_file* 1, 2 (file name 1, 2 tetras)
666f6f2e	(`"foo."`)
6d6d7300	(`"mms",0`)
98070004	*lop_line* 4 (line 4 of the current file)
f000000a	(`JMP 2B`)
98080005	*lop_spec* 5 (begin special data of type 5)
00000200	(`TETRA &a<<8`)
00fe0000	(`WYDE a-$0`)
98012001	*lop_loc* #20,1 (data segment, 1 tetra)
0000000a	(low tetrabyte of address in data segment)
00006364	(`"cd"` with leading zeros, because of alignment)
98000001	*lop_quote* (don't treat next tetrabyte as a lopcode)
98000000	(`BYTE #98`, padded with trailing zeros)
980a00fe	*lop_post* $254 (begin postamble, G is 254)
20000000	(high tetrabyte of the initial contents of $254)
00000008	(low tetrabyte of base address $254)
00000001	(high tetrabyte of the initial contents of $255)
2345678c	(low tetrabyte of $255, is address of `Main`)
980b0000	*lop_stab* (begin symbol table)
203a5040	(compressed form for symbol table as a ternary trie)
50404020	
41204220	
43094408	
83404020	(`ABCD` = #2000000000000008, serial 3)
4d206120	
69056e01	
2345678c	
81400f61	(`Main` = #000000012345678c, serial 1)
fe820000	(`a` = $254, serial 2)
980c000a	*lop_end* (end symbol table, 10 tetras)

---

lop_end = #`c`, §24.
lop_file = #`6`, §24.
lop_fixo = #`3`, §24.
lop_fixr = #`4`, §24.
lop_fixrx = #`5`, §24.
lop_line = #`7`, §24.
lop_loc = #`1`, §24.
lop_post = #`a`, §24.
lop_pre = #`9`, §24.
lop_quote = #`0`, §24.
lop_skip = #`2`, §24.
lop_spec = #`8`, §24.
lop_stab = #`b`, §24.

24. When a tetrabyte of the `mmo` file does not begin with the escape code, it is loaded into the current location λ, and λ is increased to the next higher multiple of 4. (If λ is not a multiple of 4, the tetrabyte actually goes into location $\lambda \wedge (-4) = 4\lfloor \lambda/4 \rfloor$, according to `MMIX`'s usual conventions.) The current line number is also increased by 1, if it is nonzero.

When a tetrabyte does begin with the escape code, its next byte is the lopcode defining a loader instruction. There are thirteen lopcodes:

• *lop_quote*: X = #`00`, YZ = 1. Treat the next tetra as an ordinary tetrabyte, even if it begins with the escape code.

• *lop_loc*: X = #`01`, Y = high byte, Z = tetra count (Z = 1 or 2). Set the current location to the 64-bit address defined by the next Z tetras, plus 2^{56}Y. Usually Y = 0 (for the instruction segment) or Y = #`20` (for the data segment). If Z = 2, the high tetra appears first.

• *lop_skip*: X = #`02`, YZ = delta. Increase the current location by YZ.

• *lop_fixo*: X = #`03`, Y = high byte, Z = tetra count (Z = 1 or 2). Load the value of the current location λ into octabyte P, where P is the 64-bit address defined by the next Z tetras plus 2^{56}Y as in *lop_loc*. (The octabyte at P was previously assembled as zero because of a future reference.)

• *lop_fixr*: X = #`04`, YZ = delta. Load YZ into the YZ field of the tetrabyte in location P, where P is $\lambda - 4$YZ, namely the address that precedes the current location by YZ tetrabytes. (This tetrabyte was previously loaded with an `MMIX` instruction that takes a relative address: a branch, probable branch, `JMP`, `PUSHJ`, or `GETA`. Its YZ field was previously assembled as zero because of a future reference.)

• *lop_fixrx*: X = #`05`, Y = 0, Z = 16 or 24. Proceed as in *lop_fixr*, but load δ into tetrabyte P = $\lambda - 4\delta$ instead of loading YZ into P = $\lambda -$ 4YZ. Here δ is the value of the tetrabyte following the *lop_fixrx* instruction; its leading byte will be either 0 or 1. If the leading byte is 1, δ should be treated as the *negative* number ($\delta \wedge$#**`ffffff`**) $- 2^{\mathrm{Z}}$ when calculating the address P. (The latter case arises only rarely, but it is needed when fixing up a relative "future" reference that ultimately leads to a "backward" instruction. The value of δ that is xored into location P in such cases will change `BZ` to `BZB`, or `JMP` to `JMPB`, etc.; we have Z = 24 when fixing a `JMP`, Z = 16 otherwise.)

• *lop_file*: X = #`06`, Y = file number, Z = tetra count. Set the current file number to Y and the current line number to zero. If this file number has occurred previously, Z should be zero; otherwise Z should be positive, and the next Z tetrabytes are the characters of the file name in big-endian order. Trailing zeros follow the file name if its length is not a multiple of 4.

• *lop_line*: X = #`07`, YZ = line number. Set the current line number to YZ. If the line number is nonzero, the current file and current line should correspond to the source location that generated the next data to be loaded, for use in diagnostic messages. (The `MMIXAL` processor gives precise line numbers to the sources of tetrabytes in segment 0, which tend to be instructions, but not to the sources of tetrabytes assembled in other segments.)

• *lop_spec*: X = #`08`, YZ = type. Begin special data of type YZ. The subsequent tetrabytes, continuing until the next loader operation other than *lop_quote*, comprise the special data. A *lop_quote* instruction allows tetrabytes of special data to begin with the escape code.

• *lop_pre*: X = #09, Y = 1, Z = tetra count. A *lop_pre* instruction, which defines the "preamble," must be the first tetrabyte of every `mmo` file. The Y field specifies the version number of `mmo` format, currently 1; other version numbers may be defined later, but version 1 should always be supported as described in the present document. The Z tetrabytes following a *lop_pre* command provide additional information that might be of interest to system routines. If $Z > 0$, the first tetra of additional information records the time that this `mmo` file was created, measured in seconds since 00:00:00 Greenwich Mean Time on 1 Jan 1970.

• *lop_post*: X = #0a, Y = 0, Z = G (must be 32 or more). This instruction begins the *postamble*, which follows all instructions and data to be loaded. It causes the loaded program to begin with rG equal to the stated value of G, and with \$G, G+1, ..., \$255 initially set to the values of the next $(256-G)*2$ tetrabytes. These tetrabytes specify $256-G$ octabytes in big-endian fashion (high half first).

• *lop_stab*: X = #0b, YZ = 0. This instruction must appear immediately after the $(256-G)*2$ tetrabytes following *lop_post*. It is followed by the symbol table, which lists the equivalents of all user-defined symbols in a compact form that will be described later.

• *lop_end*: X = #0c, YZ = tetra count. This instruction must be the very last tetrabyte of each `mmo` file. Furthermore, exactly YZ tetrabytes must appear between it and the *lop_stab* command. (Therefore a program can easily find the symbol table without reading forward through the entire `mmo` file.)

A separate routine called `MMOtype` is available to translate binary `mmo` files into human-readable form.

```
#define lop_quote #0   /* the quotation lopcode */
#define lop_loc #1   /* the location lopcode */
#define lop_skip #2   /* the skip lopcode */
#define lop_fixo #3   /* the octabyte-fix lopcode */
#define lop_fixr #4   /* the relative-fix lopcode */
#define lop_fixrx #5   /* extended relative-fix lopcode */
#define lop_file #6   /* the file name lopcode */
#define lop_line #7   /* the file position lopcode */
#define lop_spec #8   /* the special hook lopcode */
#define lop_pre #9   /* the preamble lopcode */
#define lop_post #a   /* the postamble lopcode */
#define lop_stab #b   /* the symbol table lopcode */
#define lop_end #c   /* the end-it-all lopcode */
```

25. Many readers will have noticed that `MMIXAL` has no facilities for relocatable output, nor does `mmo` format support such features. The author's first drafts of `MMIXAL` and `mmo` did allow relocatable objects, with external linkages, but the rules were substantially more complicated and therefore inconsistent with the goals of *The Art of Computer Programming*. The present design might actually prove to be superior to the current practice, now that computer memory is significantly cheaper than it used to be, because one-pass assembly and loading are extremely fast when relocatability and external linkages are disallowed. Different program modules can be assembled together about as fast as they could be linked together under a relocatable scheme, and they can communicate with each other in much more flexible ways. Debugging tools are enhanced when open-source libraries are combined with user programs, and such libraries will certainly improve in quality when their source form is accessible to a larger community of users.

26. Basic data types. This program for the 64-bit `MMIX` architecture is based on 32-bit integer arithmetic, because nearly every computer available to the author at the time of writing was limited in that way. Details of the basic arithmetic appear in a separate program module called MMIX-ARITH, because the same routines are needed also for the simulators. The definition of type **tetra** should be changed, if necessary, to conform with the definitions found in MMIX-ARITH.

```
⟨ Type definitions 26 ⟩ ≡
  typedef unsigned int tetra;    /* assumes that an int is exactly 32 bits wide */
  typedef struct {
    tetra h, l;
  } octa;    /* two tetrabytes make one octabyte */
  typedef enum {
    false, true
  } bool;
```

See also sections 30, 54, 58, 62, 68, and 82.

This code is used in section 136.

27.
```
⟨ Global variables 27 ⟩ ≡
  extern octa zero_octa;    /* zero_octa.h = zero_octa.l = 0 */
  extern octa neg_one;    /* neg_one.h = neg_one.l = −1 */
  extern octa aux;    /* auxiliary output of a subroutine */
  extern bool overflow;    /* set by certain subroutines for signed arithmetic */
```

See also sections 33, 36, 37, 43, 46, 51, 56, 60, 63, 67, 69, 77, 83, 90, 105, 120, 133, 139, and 143.

This code is used in section 136.

28. Most of the subroutines in MMIX-ARITH return an octabyte as a function of two octabytes; for example, *oplus* (y, z) returns the sum of octabytes y and z. Division inputs the high half of a dividend in the global variable *aux* and returns the remainder in *aux*.

```
⟨ Subroutines 28 ⟩ ≡
  extern octa oplus ARGS((octa y, octa z));    /* unsigned y + z */
  extern octa ominus ARGS((octa y, octa z));    /* unsigned y − z */
  extern octa incr ARGS((octa y, int delta));    /* unsigned y + δ (δ is signed) */
  extern octa oand ARGS((octa y, octa z));    /* y ∧ z */
  extern octa shift_left ARGS((octa y, int s));    /* y ≪ s, 0 ≤ s ≤ 64 */
  extern octa shift_right ARGS((octa y, int s, int u));    /* y ≫ s, signed if ¬u */
  extern octa omult ARGS((octa y, octa z));    /* unsigned (aux, x) = y × z */
  extern octa odiv ARGS((octa x, octa y, octa z));
    /* unsigned (x, y)/z; aux = (x, y) mod z */
```

See also sections 41, 42, 44, 45, 47, 48, 49, 50, 52, 55, 57, 59, 73, and 74.

This code is used in section 136.

`ARGS` = macro ( ), §31.
aux: **octa**, MMIX-ARITH §4.
incr: **octa** ( ), MMIX-ARITH §6.
neg_one: **octa**, MMIX-ARITH §4.
oand: **octa** ( ), MMIX-ARITH §25.
odiv: **octa** ( ), MMIX-ARITH §13.
ominus: **octa** ( ), MMIX-ARITH §5.
omult: **octa** ( ), MMIX-ARITH §8.
oplus: **octa** ( ), MMIX-ARITH §5.
overflow: **bool**, MMIX-ARITH §4.
shift_left: **octa** ( ), MMIX-ARITH §7.
shift_right: **octa** ( ), MMIX-ARITH §7.
zero_octa: **octa**, MMIX-ARITH §4.

29. Here's a rudimentary check to see if arithmetic is in trouble.

⟨ Initialize everything 29 ⟩ ≡
```
acc = shift_left(neg_one, 1);
if (acc.h ≠ #ffffffff) panic("Type␣tetra␣is␣not␣implemented␣correctly");
```
See also sections 32, 61, 71, 84, 91, and 140.

This code is used in section 136.

30. Future versions of this program will work with symbols formed from Unicode characters, but the present code limits itself to an 8-bit subset. The type **Char** is defined here in order to ease the later transition: At present, **Char** is the same as **char**, but **Char** can be changed to a 16-bit type in the Unicode version.

Other changes will also be necessary when the transition to Unicode is made; for example, some calls of *fprintf* will become calls of *fwprintf*, and some occurrences of `%s` will become `%ls` in print formats. The switchable type name **Char** provides at least a first step towards a brighter future with Unicode.

⟨ Type definitions 26 ⟩ +≡
```
typedef char Char;    /* bytes that will become wydes some day */
```

31. While we're talking about classic systems versus future systems, we might as well define the `ARGS` macro, which makes function prototypes available on ANSI C systems without making them uncompilable on older systems. Each subroutine below is declared first with a prototype, then with an old-style definition.

⟨ Preprocessor definitions 31 ⟩ ≡
```
#ifdef __STDC__
#define ARGS(list) list
#else
#define ARGS(list) ()
#endif
```
See also section 39.

This code is used in section 136.

32. Basic input and output. Input goes into a buffer that is normally limited to 72 characters. This limit can be raised, by using the `-b` option when invoking the assembler; but short buffers will keep listings from becoming unwieldy, because a symbolic listing adds 19 characters per line.

```
⟨ Initialize everything 29 ⟩ +≡
  if (buf_size < 72) buf_size = 72;
  buffer = (Char *) calloc(buf_size + 1, sizeof(Char));
  lab_field = (Char *) calloc(buf_size + 1, sizeof(Char));
  op_field = (Char *) calloc(buf_size, sizeof(Char));
  operand_list = (Char *) calloc(buf_size, sizeof(Char));
  err_buf = (Char *) calloc(buf_size + 60, sizeof(Char));
  if (¬buffer ∨ ¬lab_field ∨ ¬op_field ∨ ¬operand_list ∨ ¬err_buf)
    panic("No␣room␣for␣the␣buffers");
```

33.
```
⟨ Global variables 27 ⟩ +≡
  Char *buffer;   /* raw input of the current line */
  Char *buf_ptr;   /* current position within buffer */
  Char *lab_field;   /* copy of the label field of the current instruction */
  Char *op_field;   /* copy of the opcode field of the current instruction */
  Char *operand_list;   /* copy of the operand field of the current instruction */
  Char *err_buf;   /* place where dynamic error messages are sprinted */
```

34.
```
⟨ Get the next line of input text, or break if the input has ended 34 ⟩ ≡
  if (¬fgets(buffer, buf_size + 1, src_file)) break;
  line_no++;
  line_listed = false;
  j = strlen(buffer);
  if (buffer[j − 1] ≡ '\n') buffer[j − 1] = '\0';   /* remove the newline */
  else if ((j = fgetc(src_file)) ≠ EOF) ⟨ Flush the excess part of an overlong line 35 ⟩;
  if (buffer[0] ≡ '#') ⟨ Check for a line directive 38 ⟩;
  buf_ptr = buffer;
```

This code is used in section 136.

__STDC__, Standard C.
acc: **octa**, §83.
buf_size: **int**, §139.
calloc: **void** *(), <stdlib.h>.
EOF = (−1), <stdio.h>.
false = 0, §26.
fgetc: **int** (), <stdio.h>.
fgets: **char** *(), <stdio.h>.
fprintf: **int** (), <stdio.h>.
fwprintf: **int** (), multibyte string function.
h: **tetra**, §26.
j: **register int**, §136.
line_listed: **bool**, §36.
line_no: **int**, §36.
neg_one: **octa**, MMIX-ARITH §4.
panic = macro (), §45.
shift_left: **octa** (), MMIX-ARITH §7.
src_file: **FILE** *, §139.
strlen: **size_t** (), <string.h>.

35. ⟨ Flush the excess part of an overlong line 35 ⟩ ≡

```
{
  while (j ≠ '\n' ∧ j ≠ EOF) j = fgetc(src_file);
  if (¬long_warning_given) {
    long_warning_given = true;
    err("*trailing␣characters␣of␣long␣input␣line␣have␣been␣dropped");
    fprintf(stderr,
        "(say␣`-b␣<number>'␣to␣increase␣the␣length␣of␣my␣input␣buffer)\n");
  } else err("*trailing␣characters␣dropped");
}
```

This code is used in section 34.

36. ⟨ Global variables 27 ⟩ +≡

```
int cur_file;    /* index of the current file in filename */
int line_no;    /* current position in the file */
bool line_listed;    /* have we listed the buffer contents? */
bool long_warning_given;    /* have we given the hint about -b? */
```

37. We keep track of source file name and line number at all times, for error reporting and for synchronization data in the object file. Up to 256 different source file names can be remembered.

⟨ Global variables 27 ⟩ +≡

```
Char *filename[257];    /* source file names, including those in line directives */
int filename_count;    /* how many filename entries have we filled? */
```

38. If the current line is a line directive, it will also be treated as a comment by the assembler.

⟨ Check for a line directive 38 ⟩ ≡

```
{
  for (p = buffer + 1; isspace(*p); p++) ;
  for (j = 0; isdigit(*p); p++) j = 10 * j + *p − '0';
  for ( ; isspace(*p); p++) ;
  if (*p ≡ '\"') {
    if (¬filename[filename_count]) {
      filename[filename_count] = (Char *) calloc(FILENAME_MAX + 1, sizeof(Char));
      if (¬filename[filename_count])
        panic("Capacity␣exceeded:␣Out␣of␣filename␣memory");
    }
    for (p++, k = 0; *p ∧ *p ≠ '\"' ∧ k < FILENAME_MAX; p++, k++)
      filename[filename_count][k] = *p;
    if (k ≡ FILENAME_MAX) panic("Capacity␣exceeded:␣File␣name␣too␣long");
    if (*p ≡ '\"' ∧ *(p − 1) ≠ '\"') {    /* yes, it's a line directive */
      filename[filename_count][k] = '\0';
      for (k = 0; strcmp(filename[k], filename[filename_count]) ≠ 0; k++) ;
      if (k ≡ filename_count) {
        if (filename_count ≡ 256)
          panic("Capacity␣exceeded:␣More␣than␣256␣file␣names");
        filename_count++;
      }
```

```
      cur_file = k;
      line_no = j - 1;
    }
  }
}
```

This code is used in section 34.

39. Archaic versions of the C library do not define FILENAME_MAX.

```
⟨ Preprocessor definitions 31 ⟩ +≡
#ifndef FILENAME_MAX
#define FILENAME_MAX 256
#endif
```

40. ⟨ Local variables 40 ⟩ ≡

```
  register Char *p, *q;     /* the place where we're currently scanning */
```

See also section 65.

This code is used in section 136.

41. The next several subroutines are useful for preparing a listing of the assembled results. In such a listing, which the user can request with a command line option, we fill the leftmost 19 columns with a representation of the output that has been assembled from the input in the buffer. Sometimes the assembled output requires more than one line, because we have room to output only a tetrabyte per line.

The *flush_listing_line* subroutine is called when we have finished generating one line's worth of assembled material. Its parameter is a string to be printed between the assembled material and the buffer contents, if the input line hasn't yet been echoed. The length of this string should be 19 minus the number of characters already printed on the current line of the listing.

```
⟨ Subroutines 28 ⟩ +≡
  void flush_listing_line ARGS((char *));
  void flush_listing_line(s)
      char *s;
  {
    if (line_listed) fprintf(listing_file, "\n");
    else {
      fprintf(listing_file, "%s%s\n", s, buffer);
      line_listed = true;
    }
  }
```

ARGS = macro ( ), §31.
bool = **enum**, §26.
buffer: **Char** *, §33.
calloc: **void** *( ), `<stdlib.h>`.
Char = **char**, §30.
EOF = (−1), `<stdio.h>`.
err = macro ( ), §45.
fgetc: **int** ( ), `<stdio.h>`.
FILENAME_MAX = macro, `<stdio.h>`.
fprintf: **int** ( ), `<stdio.h>`.
isdigit: **int** ( ), `<ctype.h>`.
isspace: **int** ( ), `<ctype.h>`.
j: **register int**, §136.
k: **register int**, §136.
listing_file: **FILE** *, §139.
panic = macro ( ), §45.
src_file: **FILE** *, §139.
stderr: **FILE** *, `<stdio.h>`.
strcmp: **int** ( ), `<string.h>`.
true = 1, §26.

42. Only the three least significant hex digits of a location are shown on the listing, unless the other digits have changed. The following subroutine prints an extra line when a change needs to be shown.

```
⟨ Subroutines 28 ⟩ +≡
  void update_listing_loc ARGS((int));
  void update_listing_loc(k)
      int k;      /* the location to display, mod 4 */
  {
    if (cur_loc.h ≠ listing_loc.h ∨ ((cur_loc.l ⊕ listing_loc.l) & #fffff000)) {
      fprintf(listing_file, "%08x%08x:", cur_loc.h, (cur_loc.l & −4) | k);
      flush_listing_line("␣␣");
    }
    listing_loc.h = cur_loc.h; listing_loc.l = (cur_loc.l & −4) | k;
  }
```

43.
```
⟨ Global variables 27 ⟩ +≡
  octa cur_loc;     /* current location of assembled output */
  octa listing_loc;     /* current location on the listing */
  unsigned char hold_buf[4];     /* assembled bytes */
  unsigned char held_bits;     /* which bytes of hold_buf are active? */
  unsigned char listing_bits;     /* which of them haven't been listed yet? */
  bool spec_mode;     /* are we between BSPEC and ESPEC? */
  tetra spec_mode_loc;     /* number of bytes in the current special output */
```

44. When bytes are assembled, they are placed into the *hold_buf*. More precisely, a byte assembled for a location that is j plus a multiple of 4 is placed into *hold_buf*[j]; two auxiliary variables, *held_bits* and *listing_bits*, are then increased by $1 \ll j$. Furthermore, *listing_bits* is increased by $\#10 \ll j$ if that byte is a future reference to be resolved later.

The bytes are held until we need to output them. The *listing_clear* routine lists any that have been held but not yet shown. It should be called only when *listing_bits* $\neq 0$.

```
⟨ Subroutines 28 ⟩ +≡
  void listing_clear ARGS((void));
  void listing_clear()
  {
    register int j, k;
    for (k = 0; k < 4; k++)
      if (listing_bits & (1 ≪ k)) break;
    if (spec_mode) fprintf(listing_file, "␣␣␣␣␣␣␣␣␣");
    else {
      update_listing_loc(k);
      fprintf(listing_file, "␣...%03x:␣", (listing_loc.l & #ffc) | k);
    }
    for (j = 0; j < 4; j++)
      if (listing_bits & (#10 ≪ j)) fprintf(listing_file, "xx");
      else if (listing_bits & (1 ≪ j)) fprintf(listing_file, "%02x", hold_buf[j]);
      else fprintf(listing_file, "␣␣");
    flush_listing_line("␣␣");
```

```
  listing_bits = 0;
}
```

ARGS = macro ( ), §31.
bool = **enum**, §26.
BSPEC = #104, §62.
ESPEC = #105, §62.
flush_listing_line: **void** ( ), §41.
fprintf: **int** ( ), <stdio.h>.
h: **tetra**, §26.
l: **tetra**, §26.
listing_file: **FILE** *, §139.
octa = **struct**, §26.
tetra = **unsigned int**, §26.

45. Error messages are written to *stderr*. If the message begins with '*' it is merely a warning; if it begins with '!' it is fatal; otherwise the error is probably serious enough to make manual correction necessary, yet it is not tragic. Errors and warnings appear also on the optional listing file.

```
#define err(m)
        { report_error(m); if (m[0] ≠ '*') goto bypass; }
#define derr(m, p)
        { sprintf(err_buf, m, p);
          report_error(err_buf); if (err_buf[0] ≠ '*') goto bypass; }
#define dderr(m, p, q)
        { sprintf(err_buf, m, p, q);
          report_error(err_buf); if (err_buf[0] ≠ '*') goto bypass; }
#define panic(m)
        { sprintf(err_buf, "!%s", m); report_error(err_buf); }
#define dpanic(m, p)
        { err_buf[0] = '!'; sprintf(err_buf + 1, m, p); report_error(err_buf); }
```

⟨ Subroutines 28 ⟩ +≡

```
  void report_error ARGS((char *));
  void report_error(message)
      char *message;
  {
    if (¬filename[cur_file]) filename[cur_file] = "(nofile)";
    if (message[0] ≡ '*') fprintf(stderr, "\"%s\",␣line␣%d␣warning:␣%s\n",
          filename[cur_file], line_no, message + 1);
    else if (message[0] ≡ '!') fprintf(stderr, "\"%s\",␣line␣%d␣fatal␣error:␣%s\n",
          filename[cur_file], line_no, message + 1);
    else {
      fprintf(stderr, "\"%s\",␣line␣%d:␣%s!\n", filename[cur_file], line_no, message);
      err_count++;
    }
    if (listing_file) {
      if (¬line_listed) flush_listing_line("******************␣");
      if (message[0] ≡ '*')
        fprintf(listing_file, "************␣warning:␣%s\n", message + 1);
      else if (message[0] ≡ '!')
        fprintf(listing_file, "********␣fatal␣error:␣%s!\n", message + 1);
      else fprintf(listing_file, "**********␣error:␣%s!\n", message);
    }
    if (message[0] ≡ '!') exit(−2);
  }
```

46. ⟨ Global variables 27 ⟩ +≡

```
  int err_count;     /* this many errors were found */
```

47. Output to the binary *obj_file* occurs four bytes at a time. The bytes are assembled in small buffers, not output as single tetrabytes, because we want the output to be big-endian even when the assembler is running on a little-endian machine.

```
#define mmo_write(buf)
        if (fwrite(buf, 1, 4, obj_file) ≠ 4) dpanic("Can't␣write␣on␣%s", obj_file_name)
```

```
⟨ Subroutines 28 ⟩ +≡
  void mmo_clear ARGS((void));
  void mmo_out ARGS((void));
  unsigned char lop_quote_command[4] = {mm, lop_quote, 0, 1};
  void mmo_clear()      /* clears hold_buf, when held_bits ≠ 0 */
  {
    if (hold_buf[0] ≡ mm) mmo_write(lop_quote_command);
    mmo_write(hold_buf);
    if (listing_file ∧ listing_bits) listing_clear();
    held_bits = 0;
    hold_buf[0] = hold_buf[1] = hold_buf[2] = hold_buf[3] = 0;
    mmo_cur_loc = incr(mmo_cur_loc, 4); mmo_cur_loc.l &= −4;
    if (mmo_line_no) mmo_line_no++;
  }
  unsigned char mmo_buf[4];
  int mmo_ptr;
  void mmo_out()      /* output the contents of mmo_buf */
  {
    if (held_bits) mmo_clear();
    mmo_write(mmo_buf);
  }
```

ARGS = macro ( ), §31.
bypass: label, §102.
cur_file: **int**, §36.
err_buf: **Char** ∗, §33.
exit: **void** ( ), `<stdlib.h>`.
filename: **Char** ∗[ ], §37.
flush_listing_line: **void** ( ), §41.
fprintf: **int** ( ), `<stdio.h>`.
fwrite: **size_t** ( ), `<stdio.h>`.
held_bits: **unsigned char**, §43.
hold_buf: **unsigned char** [ ], §43.
incr: **octa** ( ), MMIX-ARITH §6.
l: **tetra**, §26.
line_listed: **bool**, §36.
line_no: **int**, §36.
listing_bits: **unsigned char**, §43.
listing_clear: **void** ( ), §44.
listing_file: **FILE** ∗, §139.
lop_quote = #0, §24.
mm = #98, §22.
mmo_cur_loc: **octa**, §51.
mmo_line_no: **int**, §51.
obj_file: **FILE** ∗, §139.
obj_file_name: **char** [ ], §139.
sprintf: **int** ( ), `<stdio.h>`.
stderr: **FILE** ∗, `<stdio.h>`.

48. ⟨ Subroutines 28 ⟩ +≡

```
void mmo_tetra ARGS((tetra));
void mmo_byte ARGS((unsigned char));
void mmo_lop ARGS((char, unsigned char, unsigned char));
void mmo_lopp ARGS((char, unsigned short));

void mmo_tetra(t)    /* output a tetrabyte */
    tetra t;
{
  mmo_buf[0] = t >> 24; mmo_buf[1] = (t >> 16) & #ff;
  mmo_buf[2] = (t >> 8) & #ff; mmo_buf[3] = t & #ff;
  mmo_out();
}
void mmo_byte(b)
    unsigned char b;
{
  mmo_buf[(mmo_ptr++) & 3] = b;
  if (¬(mmo_ptr & 3)) mmo_out();
}
void mmo_lop(x, y, z)    /* output a loader operation */
    char x;
    unsigned char y, z;
{
  mmo_buf[0] = mm; mmo_buf[1] = x; mmo_buf[2] = y; mmo_buf[3] = z;
  mmo_out();
}
void mmo_lopp(x, yz)    /* output a loader operation with two-byte operand */
    char x;
    unsigned short yz;
{
  mmo_buf[0] = mm; mmo_buf[1] = x; mmo_buf[2] = yz >> 8; mmo_buf[3] = yz & #ff;
  mmo_out();
}
```

49. The *mmo_loc* subroutine makes the current location in the object file equal to *cur_loc*.

⟨ Subroutines 28 ⟩ +≡

```
void mmo_loc ARGS((void));
void mmo_loc()
{
  octa o;
  if (held_bits) mmo_clear();
  o = ominus(cur_loc, mmo_cur_loc);
  if (o.h ≡ 0 ∧ o.l < #10000) {
    if (o.l) mmo_lopp(lop_skip, o.l);
  } else {
    if (cur_loc.h & #ffffff) {
      mmo_lop(lop_loc, 0, 2);
      mmo_tetra(cur_loc.h);
```

```
    } else mmo_lop(lop_loc, cur_loc.h >> 24, 1);
    mmo_tetra(cur_loc.l);
  }
  mmo_cur_loc = cur_loc;
}
```

50. Similarly, the *mmo_sync* subroutine makes sure that the current file and line number in the output file agree with *cur_file* and *line_no*.

```
⟨Subroutines 28⟩ +≡
  void mmo_sync ARGS((void));
  void mmo_sync()
  {
    register int j;
    register unsigned char *p;
    if (cur_file ≠ mmo_cur_file) {
      if (filename_passed[cur_file]) mmo_lop(lop_file, cur_file, 0);
      else {
        mmo_lop(lop_file, cur_file, (strlen(filename[cur_file]) + 3) >> 2);
        for (j = 0, p = filename[cur_file]; *p; p++, j = (j + 1) & 3) {
          mmo_buf[j] = *p;
          if (j ≡ 3) mmo_out();
        }
        if (j) {
          for ( ; j < 4; j++) mmo_buf[j] = 0;
          mmo_out();
        }
        filename_passed[cur_file] = 1;
      }
      mmo_cur_file = cur_file;
      mmo_line_no = 0;
    }
    if (line_no ≠ mmo_line_no) {
      if (line_no ≥ #10000)
        panic("I can't deal with line numbers exceeding 65535");
      mmo_lopp(lop_line, line_no);
      mmo_line_no = line_no;
    }
  }
```

ARGS = macro ( ), §31.
cur_file: **int**, §36.
cur_loc: **octa**, §43.
filename: **Char** *[ ], §37.
filename_passed: **char** [ ], §51.
h: **tetra**, §26.
held_bits: **unsigned char**, §43.
l: **tetra**, §26.
line_no: **int**, §36.
lop_file = #6, §24.
lop_line = #7, §24.
lop_loc = #1, §24.
lop_skip = #2, §24.
mm = #98, §22.
mmo_buf: **unsigned char** [ ], §47.
mmo_clear: **void** ( ), §47.
mmo_cur_file: **int**, §51.
mmo_cur_loc: **octa**, §51.
mmo_line_no: **int**, §51.
mmo_out: **void** ( ), §47.
mmo_ptr: **int**, §47.
octa = **struct**, §26.
ominus: **octa** ( ), MMIX-ARITH §5.
panic = macro ( ), §45.
strlen: **size_t** ( ), <string.h>.
tetra = **unsigned int**, §26.

51. ⟨ Global variables 27 ⟩ +≡

```
octa mmo_cur_loc;	/* current location in the object file */
int mmo_line_no;	/* current line number in the mmo output so far */
int mmo_cur_file;	/* index of the current file in the mmo output so far */
char filename_passed[256];	/* has a filename been recorded in the output? */
```

52. Here is a basic subroutine that assembles k bytes starting at *cur_loc*. The value of k should be 1, 2, or 4, and *cur_loc* should be a multiple of k. The *x_bits* parameter tells which bytes, if any, are part of a future reference.

⟨ Subroutines 28 ⟩ +≡

```
void assemble ARGS((char, tetra, unsigned char));
void assemble(k, dat, x_bits)
    char k;
    tetra dat;
    unsigned char x_bits;
{
  register int j, jj, l;
  if (spec_mode) l = spec_mode_loc;
  else {
    l = cur_loc.l;
    ⟨ Make sure cur_loc and mmo_cur_loc refer to the same tetrabyte 53 ⟩;
    if (¬held_bits ∧ ¬(cur_loc.h & #e0000000)) mmo_sync();
  }
  for (j = 0; j < k; j++) {
    jj = (l + j) & 3;
    hold_buf[jj] = (dat ≫ (8 * (k − 1 − j))) & #ff;
    held_bits |= 1 ≪ jj;
    listing_bits |= 1 ≪ jj;
  }
  listing_bits |= x_bits;
  if (((l + k) & 3) ≡ 0) {
    if (listing_file) listing_clear();
    mmo_clear();
  }
  if (spec_mode) spec_mode_loc += k;
  else cur_loc = incr(cur_loc, k);
}
```

53. ⟨ Make sure *cur_loc* and *mmo_cur_loc* refer to the same tetrabyte 53 ⟩ ≡

```
if (cur_loc.h ≠ mmo_cur_loc.h ∨ ((cur_loc.l ⊕ mmo_cur_loc.l) & #fffffffc)) mmo_loc();
```

This code is used in section 52.

54. The symbol table. Symbols are stored and retrieved by means of a *ternary search trie*, following ideas of Bentley and Sedgewick. (See *ACM–SIAM Symp. on Discrete Algorithms* **8** (1997), 360–369; R. Sedgewick, *Algorithms in C* (Reading, Mass.: Addison–Wesley, 1998), §15.4.) Each trie node stores a character, and there are branches to subtries for the cases where a given character is less than, equal to, or greater than the character in the trie. There also is a pointer to a symbol table entry if a symbol ends at the current node.

```
⟨Type definitions 26⟩ +≡
  typedef struct ternary_trie_struct {
    unsigned short ch;    /* the (possibly wyde) character stored here */
    struct ternary_trie_struct *left, *mid, *right;
      /* downward in the ternary trie */
    struct sym_tab_struct *sym;    /* equivalents of symbols */
  } trie_node;
```

55. We allocate trie nodes in chunks of 1000 at a time.

```
⟨Subroutines 28⟩ +≡
  trie_node *new_trie_node ARGS((void));
  trie_node *new_trie_node()
  {
    register trie_node *t = next_trie_node;
    if (t ≡ last_trie_node) {
      t = (trie_node *) calloc(1000, sizeof(trie_node));
      if (¬t) panic("Capacity␣exceeded:␣Out␣of␣trie␣memory");
      last_trie_node = t + 1000;
    }
    next_trie_node = t + 1;
    return t;
  }
```

56.
```
⟨Global variables 27⟩ +≡
  trie_node *trie_root;    /* root of the trie */
  trie_node *op_root;    /* root of subtrie for opcodes */
  trie_node *next_trie_node, *last_trie_node;    /* allocation control */
  trie_node *cur_prefix;    /* root of subtrie for unqualified symbols */
```

ARGS = macro ( ), §31.
calloc: **void** *( ), <stdlib.h>.
cur_loc: **octa**, §43.
h: **tetra**, §26.
held_bits: **unsigned char**, §43.
hold_buf: **unsigned char** [ ], §43.
incr: **octa** ( ), MMIX-ARITH §6.
l: **tetra**, §26.
listing_bits: **unsigned char**, §43.
listing_clear: **void** ( ), §44.
listing_file: **FILE** *, §139.
mmo_clear: **void** ( ), §47.
mmo_loc: **void** ( ), §49.
mmo_sync: **void** ( ), §50.
octa = **struct**, §26.
panic = macro ( ), §45.
spec_mode: **bool**, §43.
spec_mode_loc: **tetra**, §43.
sym_tab_struct: **struct**, §58.
tetra = **unsigned int**, §26.

57. The *trie_search* subroutine starts at a given node of the trie and finds a given string in its middle subtrie, inserting new nodes if necessary. The string ends with the first nonletter or nondigit; the location of the terminating character is stored in global variable *terminator*.

```
#define isletter(c) (isalpha(c) ∨ c ≡ '_' ∨ c ≡ ':' ∨ (unsigned int)(c) > 126)
⟨ Subroutines 28 ⟩ +≡
  trie_node *trie_search ARGS((trie_node *, Char *));
  Char *terminator;    /* where the search ended */
  trie_node *trie_search(t, s)
      trie_node *t;
      Char *s;
  {
    register trie_node *tt = t;
    register unsigned char *p = (unsigned char *) s;
    while (1) {
      if (¬isletter(*p) ∧ ¬isdigit(*p)) {
        terminator = (Char *) p; return tt;
      }
      if (tt→mid) {
        tt = tt→mid;
        while (*p ≠ tt→ch) {
          if (*p < tt→ch) {
            if (tt→left) tt = tt→left;
            else {
              tt→left = new_trie_node(); tt = tt→left; goto store_new_char;
            }
          } else {
            if (tt→right) tt = tt→right;
            else {
              tt→right = new_trie_node(); tt = tt→right; goto store_new_char;
            }
          }
        }
        p++;
      } else {
        tt→mid = new_trie_node(); tt = tt→mid;
      store_new_char: tt→ch = *p++;
      }
    }
  }
```

58. Symbol table nodes hold the serial numbers and equivalents of defined symbols. They also hold "fixup information" for undefined symbols; this will allow the loader to correct any previously assembled instructions that refer to such symbols when they are eventually defined.

In the symbol table node for a defined symbol, the *link* field has one of the special codes `DEFINED` or `REGISTER` or `PREDEFINED`, and the *equiv* field holds the defined value. The *serial* number is a unique identifier for all user-defined symbols.

In the symbol table node for an undefined symbol, the *equiv* field is ignored. The *link* field points to the first node of fixup information; that node is, in turn, a symbol table node that might link to other fixups. The *serial* number in a fixup node is either 0 or 1 or 2, meaning respectively "fixup the octabyte pointed to by *equiv*" or "fixup the relative address in the YZ field of the instruction pointed to by *equiv*" or "fixup the relative address in the XYZ field of the instruction pointed to by *equiv*."

```
#define DEFINED (sym_node *) 1    /* code value for octabyte equivalents */
#define REGISTER (sym_node *) 2    /* code value for register-number equivalents */
#define PREDEFINED (sym_node *) 3    /* code value for not-yet-used equivalents */
#define fix_o 0    /* serial code for octabyte fixup */
#define fix_yz 1    /* serial code for relative fixup */
#define fix_xyz 2    /* serial code for JMP fixup */
```

⟨ Type definitions 26 ⟩ +≡

```
typedef struct sym_tab_struct {
  int serial;    /* serial number of symbol; type number for fixups */
  struct sym_tab_struct *link;    /* DEFINED status or link to fixup */
  octa equiv;    /* the equivalent value */
} sym_node;
```

ARGS = macro ( ), §31.
ch: **unsigned short**, §54.
Char = **char**, §30.
isalpha: **int** ( ), <ctype.h>.
isdigit: **int** ( ), <ctype.h>.
left: **trie_node** *, §54.
mid: **trie_node** *, §54.
new_trie_node: **trie_node** *( ), §55.
octa = **struct**, §26.
right: **trie_node** *, §54.
trie_node = **struct**, §54.

59. The allocation of new symbol table nodes proceeds in chunks, like the allocation of trie nodes. But in this case we also have the possibility of reusing old fixup nodes that are no longer needed.

```
#define recycle_fixup(pp) pp->link = sym_avail, sym_avail = pp
⟨ Subroutines 28 ⟩ +≡
  sym_node *new_sym_node ARGS((bool));
  sym_node *new_sym_node(serialize)
      bool serialize;   /* should the new node receive a unique serial number? */
  {
    register sym_node *p = sym_avail;
    if (p) {
      sym_avail = p->link; p->link = Λ; p->serial = 0; p->equiv = zero_octa;
    } else {
      p = next_sym_node;
      if (p ≡ last_sym_node) {
        p = (sym_node *) calloc(1000, sizeof(sym_node));
        if (¬p) panic("Capacity␣exceeded:␣Out␣of␣symbol␣memory");
        last_sym_node = p + 1000;
      }
      next_sym_node = p + 1;
    }
    if (serialize) p->serial = ++serial_number;
    return p;
  }
```

60. ⟨ Global variables 27 ⟩ +≡

```
  int serial_number;
  sym_node *sym_root;   /* root of the sym */
  sym_node *next_sym_node, *last_sym_node;   /* allocation control */
  sym_node *sym_avail;   /* stack of recycled symbol table nodes */
```

61. We initialize the trie by inserting all the predefined symbols. Opcodes are given the prefix ^, to distinguish them from ordinary symbols; this character nicely divides uppercase letters from lowercase letters.

```
⟨ Initialize everything 29 ⟩ +≡
  trie_root = new_trie_node();
  cur_prefix = trie_root;
  op_root = new_trie_node();
  trie_root->mid = op_root;
  trie_root->ch = ':';
  op_root->ch = '^';
  ⟨ Put the MMIX opcodes and MMIXAL pseudo-ops into the trie 64 ⟩;
  ⟨ Put the special register names into the trie 66 ⟩;
  ⟨ Put other predefined symbols into the trie 70 ⟩;
```

62. Most of the assembly work can be table driven, based on bits that are stored as the "equivalents" of opcode symbols like ^ADD.

```
#define rel_addr_bit #1   /* is YZ or XYZ relative? */
#define immed_bit #2   /* should opcode be immediate if Z or YZ not register? */
#define zar_bit #4   /* should register status of Z be ignored? */
#define zr_bit #8   /* must Z be a register? */
#define yar_bit #10   /* should register status of Y be ignored? */
#define yr_bit #20   /* must Y be a register? */
#define xar_bit #40   /* should register status of X be ignored? */
#define xr_bit #80   /* must X be a register? */
#define yzar_bit #100   /* should register status of YZ be ignored? */
#define yzr_bit #200   /* must YZ be a register? */
#define xyzar_bit #400   /* should register status of XYZ be ignored? */
#define xyzr_bit #800   /* must XYZ be a register? */
#define one_arg_bit #1000   /* is it OK to have zero or one operand? */
#define two_arg_bit #2000   /* is it OK to have exactly two operands? */
#define three_arg_bit #4000   /* is it OK to have exactly three operands? */
#define many_arg_bit #8000   /* is it OK to have more than three operands? */
#define align_bits #30000   /* how much alignment: byte, wyde, tetra, or octa? */
#define no_label_bit #40000   /* should the label be blank? */
#define mem_bit #80000   /* must YZ be a memory reference? */
#define spec_bit #100000   /* is this opcode allowed in SPEC mode? */

⟨ Type definitions 26 ⟩ +≡
  typedef struct {
    Char *name;   /* symbolic opcode */
    short code;   /* numeric opcode */
    int bits;   /* treatment of operands */
  } op_spec;

  typedef enum {
    SET = #100, IS, LOC, PREFIX, BSPEC, ESPEC, GREG, LOCAL,
    BYTE, WYDE, TETRA, OCTA
  } pseudo_op;
```

ARGS = macro ( ), §31.
bool = **enum**, §26.
calloc: **void** *( ), <stdlib.h>.
ch: **unsigned short**, §54.
Char = **char**, §30.
cur_prefix: **trie_node** *, §56.
equiv: **octa**, §58.
link: **sym_node** *, §58.
mid: **trie_node** *, §54.
new_trie_node: **trie_node** *( ), §55.
op_root: **trie_node** *, §56.
panic = macro ( ), §45.
serial: **int**, §58.
sym_node = **struct**, §58.
trie_root: **trie_node** *, §56.
zero_octa: **octa**, MMIX-ARITH §4.

63. ⟨ Global variables 27 ⟩ +≡

```
op_spec op_init_table[] = {
{"TRAP", #00, #27554}, {"FCMP", #01, #240a8},
{"FUN", #02, #240a8}, {"FEQL", #03, #240a8},
{"FADD", #04, #240a8}, {"FIX", #05, #26288},
{"FSUB", #06, #240a8}, {"FIXU", #07, #26288},
{"FLOT", #08, #26282}, {"FLOTU", #0a, #26282},
{"SFLOT", #0c, #26282}, {"SFLOTU", #0e, #26282},
{"FMUL", #10, #240a8}, {"FCMPE", #11, #240a8},
{"FUNE", #12, #240a8}, {"FEQLE", #13, #240a8},
{"FDIV", #14, #240a8}, {"FSQRT", #15, #26288},
{"FREM", #16, #240a8}, {"FINT", #17, #26288},
{"MUL", #18, #240a2}, {"MULU", #1a, #240a2},
{"DIV", #1c, #240a2}, {"DIVU", #1e, #240a2},
{"ADD", #20, #240a2}, {"ADDU", #22, #240a2},
{"SUB", #24, #240a2}, {"SUBU", #26, #240a2},
{"2ADDU", #28, #240a2}, {"4ADDU", #2a, #240a2},
{"8ADDU", #2c, #240a2}, {"16ADDU", #2e, #240a2},
{"CMP", #30, #240a2}, {"CMPU", #32, #240a2},
{"NEG", #34, #26082}, {"NEGU", #36, #26082},
{"SL", #38, #240a2}, {"SLU", #3a, #240a2},
{"SR", #3c, #240a2}, {"SRU", #3e, #240a2},
{"BN", #40, #22081}, {"BZ", #42, #22081},
{"BP", #44, #22081}, {"BOD", #46, #22081},
{"BNN", #48, #22081}, {"BNZ", #4a, #22081},
{"BNP", #4c, #22081}, {"BEV", #4e, #22081},
{"PBN", #50, #22081}, {"PBZ", #52, #22081},
{"PBP", #54, #22081}, {"PBOD", #56, #22081},
{"PBNN", #58, #22081}, {"PBNZ", #5a, #22081},
{"PBNP", #5c, #22081}, {"PBEV", #5e, #22081},
{"CSN", #60, #240a2}, {"CSZ", #62, #240a2},
{"CSP", #64, #240a2}, {"CSOD", #66, #240a2},
{"CSNN", #68, #240a2}, {"CSNZ", #6a, #240a2},
{"CSNP", #6c, #240a2}, {"CSEV", #6e, #240a2},
{"ZSN", #70, #240a2}, {"ZSZ", #72, #240a2},
{"ZSP", #74, #240a2}, {"ZSOD", #76, #240a2},
{"ZSNN", #78, #240a2}, {"ZSNZ", #7a, #240a2},
{"ZSNP", #7c, #240a2}, {"ZSEV", #7e, #240a2},
{"LDB", #80, #a60a2}, {"LDBU", #82, #a60a2},
{"LDW", #84, #a60a2}, {"LDWU", #86, #a60a2},
{"LDT", #88, #a60a2}, {"LDTU", #8a, #a60a2},
{"LDO", #8c, #a60a2}, {"LDOU", #8e, #a60a2},
{"LDSF", #90, #a60a2}, {"LDHT", #92, #a60a2},
{"CSWAP", #94, #a60a2}, {"LDUNC", #96, #a60a2},
{"LDVTS", #98, #a60a2}, {"PRELD", #9a, #a6022},
{"PREGO", #9c, #a6022}, {"GO", #9e, #a60a2},
{"STB", #a0, #a60a2}, {"STBU", #a2, #a60a2},
{"STW", #a4, #a60a2}, {"STWU", #a6, #a60a2},
{"STT", #a8, #a60a2}, {"STTU", #aa, #a60a2},
```

```
{"STO",#ac,#a60a2},{"STOU",#ae,#a60a2},
{"STSF",#b0,#a60a2},{"STHT",#b2,#a60a2},
{"STCO",#b4,#a6022},{"STUNC",#b6,#a60a2},
{"SYNCD",#b8,#a6022},{"PREST",#ba,#a6022},
{"SYNCID",#bc,#a6022},{"PUSHGO",#be,#a6062},
{"OR",#c0,#240a2},{"ORN",#c2,#240a2},
{"NOR",#c4,#240a2},{"XOR",#c6,#240a2},
{"AND",#c8,#240a2},{"ANDN",#ca,#240a2},
{"NAND",#cc,#240a2},{"NXOR",#ce,#240a2},
{"BDIF",#d0,#240a2},{"WDIF",#d2,#240a2},
{"TDIF",#d4,#240a2},{"ODIF",#d6,#240a2},
{"MUX",#d8,#240a2},{"SADD",#da,#240a2},
{"MOR",#dc,#240a2},{"MXOR",#de,#240a2},
{"SETH",#e0,#22080},{"SETMH",#e1,#22080},
{"SETML",#e2,#22080},{"SETL",#e3,#22080},
{"INCH",#e4,#22080},{"INCMH",#e5,#22080},
{"INCML",#e6,#22080},{"INCL",#e7,#22080},
{"ORH",#e8,#22080},{"ORMH",#e9,#22080},
{"ORML",#ea,#22080},{"ORL",#eb,#22080},
{"ANDNH",#ec,#22080},{"ANDNMH",#ed,#22080},
{"ANDNML",#ee,#22080},{"ANDNL",#ef,#22080},
{"JMP",#f0,#21001},{"PUSHJ",#f2,#22041},
{"GETA",#f4,#22081},{"PUT",#f6,#22002},
{"POP",#f8,#23000},{"RESUME",#f9,#21000},
{"SAVE",#fa,#22080},{"UNSAVE",#fb,#23a00},
{"SYNC",#fc,#21000},{"SWYM",#fd,#27554},
{"GET",#fe,#22080},{"TRIP",#ff,#27554},
{"SET",SET,#22180},{"LDA",#22,#a60a2},
{"IS",IS,#101400},{"LOC",LOC,#1400},
{"PREFIX",PREFIX,#141000},
{"BYTE",BYTE,#10f000},{"WYDE",WYDE,#11f000},
{"TETRA",TETRA,#12f000},{"OCTA",OCTA,#13f000},
{"BSPEC",BSPEC,#41400},{"ESPEC",ESPEC,#141000},
{"GREG",GREG,#101000},{"LOCAL",LOCAL,#141800}};
int op_init_size;    /* the number of items in op_init_table */
```

BSPEC = #104, §62.
BYTE = #108, §62.
ESPEC = #105, §62.
GREG = #106, §62.
IS = #101, §62.
LOC = #102, §62.
LOCAL = #107, §62.
OCTA = #10b, §62.
op_spec = struct, §62.
PREFIX = #103, §62.
SET = #100, §62.
TETRA = #10a, §62.
WYDE = #109, §62.

64. ⟨ Put the MMIX opcodes and MMIXAL pseudo-ops into the trie 64 ⟩ ≡

```
op_init_size = (sizeof op_init_table)/sizeof(op_spec);
for (j = 0; j < op_init_size; j++) {
  tt = trie_search(op_root, op_init_table[j].name);
  pp = tt->sym = new_sym_node(false);
  pp->link = PREDEFINED;
  pp->equiv.h = op_init_table[j].code, pp->equiv.l = op_init_table[j].bits;
}
```

This code is used in section 61.

65. ⟨ Local variables 40 ⟩ +≡

```
register trie_node *tt;
register sym_node *pp, *qq;
```

66. ⟨ Put the special register names into the trie 66 ⟩ ≡

```
for (j = 0; j < 32; j++) {
  tt = trie_search(trie_root, special_name[j]);
  pp = tt->sym = new_sym_node(false);
  pp->link = PREDEFINED;
  pp->equiv.l = j;
}
```

This code is used in section 61.

67. ⟨ Global variables 27 ⟩ +≡

```
Char *special_name[32] = {"rB", "rD", "rE", "rH", "rJ", "rM", "rR", "rBB", "rC", "rN",
    "rO", "rS", "rI", "rT", "rTT", "rK", "rQ", "rU", "rV", "rG", "rL", "rA", "rF", "rP",
    "rW", "rX", "rY", "rZ", "rWW", "rXX", "rYY", "rZZ"};
```

68. ⟨ Type definitions 26 ⟩ +≡

```
typedef struct {
  Char *name;
  tetra h, l;
} predef_spec;
```

69. ⟨ Global variables 27 ⟩ +≡

```
predef_spec predefs[] = {{"ROUND_CURRENT", 0, 0}, {"ROUND_OFF", 0, 1}, {"ROUND_UP", 0,
    2}, {"ROUND_DOWN", 0, 3}, {"ROUND_NEAR", 0, 4},
  {"Inf", #7ff00000, 0},
  {"Data_Segment", #20000000, 0}, {"Pool_Segment", #40000000, 0}, {"Stack_Segment",
    #60000000, 0},
  {"D_BIT", 0, #80}, {"V_BIT", 0, #40}, {"W_BIT", 0, #20}, {"I_BIT", 0, #10}, {"O_BIT", 0,
    #08}, {"U_BIT", 0, #04}, {"Z_BIT", 0, #02}, {"X_BIT", 0, #01},
  {"D_Handler", 0, #10}, {"V_Handler", 0, #20}, {"W_Handler", 0, #30}, {"I_Handler", 0,
    #40}, {"O_Handler", 0, #50}, {"U_Handler", 0, #60}, {"Z_Handler", 0, #70},
    {"X_Handler", 0, #80},
  {"StdIn", 0, 0}, {"StdOut", 0, 1}, {"StdErr", 0, 2},
  {"TextRead", 0, 0}, {"TextWrite", 0, 1}, {"BinaryRead", 0, 2}, {"BinaryWrite", 0, 3},
    {"BinaryReadWrite", 0, 4},
  {"Halt", 0, 0}, {"Fopen", 0, 1}, {"Fclose", 0, 2}, {"Fread", 0, 3}, {"Fgets", 0, 4},
    {"Fgetws", 0, 5}, {"Fwrite", 0, 6}, {"Fputs", 0, 7}, {"Fputws", 0, 8}, {"Fseek", 0, 9},
    {"Ftell", 0, 10}};
int predef_size;
```

70. ⟨ Put other predefined symbols into the trie 70 ⟩ ≡

```
predef_size = (sizeof predefs)/sizeof(predef_spec);
for (j = 0; j < predef_size; j++) {
   tt = trie_search(trie_root, predefs[j].name);
   pp = tt→sym = new_sym_node(false);
   pp→link = PREDEFINED;
   pp→equiv.h = predefs[j].h, pp→equiv.l = predefs[j].l;
}
```

This code is used in section 61.

71. We place Main into the trie at the beginning of assembly, so that it will show up as an undefined symbol if the user specifies no starting point.

⟨ Initialize everything 29 ⟩ +≡

```
trie_search(trie_root, "Main")→sym = new_sym_node(true);
```

---

bits: **int**, §62.
Char = **char**, §30.
code: **short**, §62.
equiv: **octa**, §58.
false = 0, §26.
h: **tetra**, §26.
j: **register int**, §136.
l: **tetra**, §26.
link: **sym_node** ∗, §58.
name: **Char** ∗, §62.
new_sym_node: **sym_node** ∗( ), §59.
op_init_size: **int**, §63.
op_init_table: **op_spec** [ ], §63.
op_root: **trie_node** ∗, §56.
op_spec = **struct**, §62.
PREDEFINED = macro, §58.
sym: **sym_node** ∗, §54.
sym_node = **struct**, §58.
tetra = **unsigned int**, §26.
trie_node = **struct**, §54.
trie_root: **trie_node** ∗, §56.
trie_search: **trie_node** ∗( ), §57.
true = 1, §26.

72. At the end of assembly we traverse the entire symbol table, visiting each symbol in lexicographic order and transmitting the trie structure to the output file. We detect any undefined future references at this time.

The order of traversal has a simple recursive pattern: To traverse the subtrie rooted at t, we

traverse *t*→*left*, if the left subtrie is nonempty;
visit *t*→*sym*, if this symbol table entry is present;
traverse *t*→*mid*, if the middle subtrie is nonempty;
traverse *t*→*right*, if the right subtrie is nonempty.

This pattern leads to a compact representation in the `mmo` file, usually requiring fewer than two bytes per trie node plus the bytes needed to encode the equivalents and serial numbers. Each node of the trie is encoded as a "master byte" followed by the encodings of the left subtrie, character, equivalent, middle subtrie, and right subtrie. The master byte is the sum of

#`80`, if the character occupies two bytes instead of one;
#`40`, if the left subtrie is nonempty;
#`20`, if the middle subtrie is nonempty;
#`10`, if the right subtrie is nonempty;
#`01` to #`08`, if the symbol's equivalent is one to eight bytes long;
#`09` to #`0e`, if the symbol's equivalent is 2^{61} plus one to six bytes;
#`0f`, if the symbol's equivalent is \$0 plus one byte;

the character is omitted if the middle subtrie and the equivalent are both empty. The "equivalent" of an undefined symbol is zero, but stated as two bytes long. Symbol equivalents are followed by the serial number, represented as a sequence of one or more bytes in radix 128; the final byte of the serial number is tagged by adding 128. (Thus, serial number $2^{14}-1$ is encoded as #`7fff`; serial number 2^{14} is #`010080`.)

73. First we prune the trie by removing all predefined symbols that the user did not redefine.

⟨ Subroutines 28 ⟩ +≡

```
trie_node *prune ARGS((trie_node *));
trie_node *prune(t)
    trie_node *t;
{
  register int useful = 0;
  if (t→sym) {
    if (t→sym→serial) useful = 1;
    else t→sym = Λ;
  }
  if (t→left) {
    t→left = prune(t→left);
    if (t→left) useful = 1;
  }
```

```
  if (t→mid) {
    t→mid = prune(t→mid);
    if (t→mid) useful = 1;
  }
  if (t→right) {
    t→right = prune(t→right);
    if (t→right) useful = 1;
  }
  if (useful) return t;
  else return Λ;
}
```

74. Then we output the trie by following the recursive traversal pattern.

```
⟨ Subroutines 28 ⟩ +≡
  void out_stab ARGS((trie_node *));
  void out_stab(t)
      trie_node *t;
  {
    register int m = 0, j;
    register sym_node *pp;
    if (t→ch > #ff) m += #80;
    if (t→left) m += #40;
    if (t→mid) m += #20;
    if (t→right) m += #10;
    if (t→sym) {
      if (t→sym→link ≡ REGISTER) m += #f;
      else if (t→sym→link ≡ DEFINED) ⟨ Encode the length of t→sym→equiv 76 ⟩
      else if (t→sym→link ∨ t→sym→serial ≡ 1) ⟨ Report an undefined symbol 79 ⟩;
    }
    mmo_byte(m);
    if (t→left) out_stab(t→left);
    if (m & #2f) ⟨ Visit t and traverse t→mid 75 ⟩;
    if (t→right) out_stab(t→right);
  }
```

ARGS = macro ( ), §31.
ch: **unsigned short**, §54.
DEFINED = macro, §58.
equiv: **octa**, §58.
left: **trie_node** *, §54.
link: **sym_node** *, §58.
mid: **trie_node** *, §54.
mmo_byte: **void** ( ), §48.
REGISTER = macro, §58.
right: **trie_node** *, §54.
serial: **int**, §58.
sym: **sym_node** *, §54.
sym_node = **struct**, §58.
trie_node = **struct**, §54.

75. A global variable called *sym_buf* holds all characters on middle branches to the current trie node; *sym_ptr* is the first currently unused character in *sym_buf*.

```
⟨ Visit t and traverse t→mid 75 ⟩ ≡
  {
    if (m & #80) mmo_byte(t→ch ≫ 8);
    mmo_byte(t→ch & #ff);
    *sym_ptr++ = (m & #80 ? '?' : t→ch);      /* Unicode? not yet */
    m &= #f; if (m ∧ t→sym→link) {
      if (listing_file) ⟨ Print symbol sym_buf and its equivalent 78 ⟩;
      if (m ≡ 15) m = 1;
      else if (m > 8) m −= 8;
      for ( ; m > 0; m−−)
        if (m > 4) mmo_byte((t→sym→equiv.h ≫ (8 * (m − 5))) & #ff);
        else mmo_byte((t→sym→equiv.l ≫ (8 * (m − 1))) & #ff);
      for (m = 0; m < 4; m++)
        if (t→sym→serial < (1 ≪ (7 * (m + 1)))) break;
      for ( ; m ≥ 0; m−−) mmo_byte(((t→sym→serial ≫ (7 * m)) & #7f) + (m ? 0 : #80));
    }
    if (t→mid) out_stab(t→mid);
    sym_ptr−−;
  }
```

This code is used in section 74.

76.

```
⟨ Encode the length of t→sym→equiv 76 ⟩ ≡
  { register tetra x;
    if ((t→sym→equiv.h & #ffff0000) ≡ #20000000)
      m += 8, x = t→sym→equiv.h − #20000000;      /* data segment */
    else x = t→sym→equiv.h;
    if (x) m += 4; else x = t→sym→equiv.l;
    for (j = 1; j < 4; j++)
      if (x < (1 ≪ (8 * j))) break;
    m += j;
  }
```

This code is used in section 74.

77. We make room for symbols up to 999 bytes long. Strictly speaking, the program should check if this limit is exceeded; but really!

```
⟨ Global variables 27 ⟩ +≡
  Char sym_buf[1000];
  Char *sym_ptr;
```

78. The initial ':' of each fully qualified symbol is omitted here, since most users of MMIXAL will probably not need the PREFIX feature. One consequence of this omission is that the one-character symbol ':' itself, which is allowed by the rules of MMIXAL, is printed as the null string.

```
⟨ Print symbol sym_buf and its equivalent 78 ⟩ ≡
  {
    *sym_ptr = '\0';
    fprintf(listing_file, "␣%s␣=␣", sym_buf + 1);
    pp = t→sym;
    if (pp→link ≡ DEFINED) fprintf(listing_file, "#%08x%08x", pp→equiv.h, pp→equiv.l);
    else if (pp→link ≡ REGISTER) fprintf(listing_file, "$%03d", pp→equiv.l);
    else fprintf(listing_file, "?");
    fprintf(listing_file, "␣(%d)\n", pp→serial);
  }
```

This code is used in section 75.

79. ⟨ Report an undefined symbol 79 ⟩ ≡

```
  {
    *sym_ptr = (m & #80 ? '?' : t→ch);      /* Unicode? not yet */
    *(sym_ptr + 1) = '\0';
    fprintf(stderr, "undefined␣symbol:␣%s\n", sym_buf + 1);
    err_count++;
    m += 2;
  }
```

This code is used in section 74.

80. ⟨ Check and output the trie 80 ⟩ ≡

```
  op_root→mid = Λ;      /* annihilate all the opcodes */
  prune(trie_root);
  sym_ptr = sym_buf;
  if (listing_file) fprintf(listing_file, "\nSymbol␣table:\n");
  mmo_lop(lop_stab, 0, 0);
  out_stab(trie_root);
  while (mmo_ptr & 3) mmo_byte(0);
  mmo_lopp(lop_end, mmo_ptr ≫ 2);
```

This code is used in section 142.

---

ch: **unsigned short**, §54.
Char = **char**, §30.
DEFINED = macro, §58.
equiv: **octa**, §58.
err_count: **int**, §46.
fprintf: **int** ( ), <stdio.h>.
h: **tetra**, §26.
j: **register int**, §74.
l: **tetra**, §26.
link: **sym_node** *, §58.
listing_file: **FILE** *, §139.
lop_end = #c, §24.
lop_stab = #b, §24.
m: **register int**, §74.
mid: **trie_node** *, §54.
mmo_byte: **void** ( ), §48.
mmo_lop: **void** ( ), §48.
mmo_lopp: **void** ( ), §48.
mmo_ptr: **int**, §47.
op_root: **trie_node** *, §56.
out_stab: **void**, §74.
pp: **register sym_node** *, §74.
prune: **trie_node** *( ), §73.
REGISTER = macro, §58.
serial: **int**, §58.
stderr: **FILE** *, <stdio.h>.
sym: **sym_node** *, §54.
t: **trie_node** *, §74.
tetra = **unsigned int**, §26.
trie_root: **trie_node** *, §56.

81. Expressions. The most intricate part of the assembly process is the task of scanning and evaluating expressions in the operand field. Fortunately, MMIXAL's expressions have a simple structure that can be handled easily with a stack-based approach.

Two stacks hold pending data as the operand field is scanned and evaluated. The *op_stack* contains operators that have not yet been performed; the *val_stack* contains values that have not yet been used. After an entire operand list has been scanned, the *op_stack* will be empty and the *val_stack* will hold the operand values needed to assemble the current instruction.

82. Entries on *op_stack* have one of the constant values defined here, and they have one of the precedence levels defined here.

Entries on *val_stack* have *equiv*, *link*, and *status* fields; the *link* points to a trie node if the expression is a symbol that has not yet been subjected to any operations.

```
⟨ Type definitions 26 ⟩ +≡
  typedef enum {
    negate, serialize, complement, registerize, inner_lp,
        plus, minus, times, over, frac, mod, shl, shr, and, or, xor,
        outer_lp, outer_rp, inner_rp
  } stack_op;
  typedef enum {
    zero, weak, strong, unary
  } prec;
  typedef enum {
    pure, reg_val, undefined
  } stat;
  typedef struct {
    octa equiv;   /* current value */
    trie_node *link;   /* trie reference for symbol */
    stat status;   /* pure, reg_val, or undefined */
  } val_node;
```

```
83. #define top_op op_stack[op_ptr − 1]   /* top entry on the operator stack */
#define top_val val_stack[val_ptr − 1]   /* top entry on the value stack */
#define next_val val_stack[val_ptr − 2]   /* next-to-top entry of the value stack */

⟨ Global variables 27 ⟩ +≡
  stack_op *op_stack;   /* stack for pending operators */
  int op_ptr;   /* number of items on op_stack */
  val_node *val_stack;   /* stack for pending operands */
  int val_ptr;   /* number of items on val_stack */
  prec precedence[] = {unary, unary, unary, unary, zero,
      weak, weak, strong, strong, strong, strong, strong, strong, strong, weak, weak,
      zero, zero, zero};   /* precedences of the respective stack_op values */
  stack_op rt_op;   /* newly scanned operator */
  octa acc;   /* temporary accumulator */
```

84. ⟨ Initialize everything 29 ⟩ +≡

```
op_stack = (stack_op *) calloc(buf_size, sizeof(stack_op));
val_stack = (val_node *) calloc(buf_size, sizeof(val_node));
if (¬op_stack ∨ ¬val_stack) panic("No␣room␣for␣the␣stacks");
```

85. The operand field of an instruction will have been copied into a separate **Char** array called *operand_list* when we reach this part of the program.

⟨ Scan the operand field 85 ⟩ ≡

```
p = operand_list;
val_ptr = 0;     /* val_stack is empty */
op_stack[0] = outer_lp, op_ptr = 1;
  /* op_stack contains an "outer left parenthesis" */
while (1) {
  ⟨ Scan opening tokens until putting something on val_stack 86 ⟩;
scan_close: ⟨ Scan a binary operator or closing token, rt_op 97 ⟩;
  while (precedence[top_op] ≥ precedence[rt_op])
    ⟨ Perform the top operation on op_stack 98 ⟩;
hold_op: op_stack[op_ptr++] = rt_op;
}
operands_done:
```

This code is used in section 102.

---

buf_size: **int**, §139.
calloc: **void** ∗( ), <stdlib.h>.
octa = **struct**, §26.
operand_list: **Char** ∗, §33.
p: **register Char** ∗, §40.
panic = macro ( ), §45.
trie_node = **struct**, §54.

86. A comment that follows an empty operand list needs to be detected here.

```
⟨ Scan opening tokens until putting something on val_stack 86 ⟩ ≡
scan_open: if (isletter(*p)) ⟨ Scan a symbol 87 ⟩
  else if (isdigit(*p)) {
    if (*(p + 1) ≡ 'F') ⟨ Scan a forward local 88 ⟩
    else if (*(p + 1) ≡ 'B') ⟨ Scan a backward local 89 ⟩
    else ⟨ Scan a decimal constant 94 ⟩;
  } else switch (*p++) {
    case '#': ⟨ Scan a hexadecimal constant 95 ⟩; break;
    case '\'': ⟨ Scan a character constant 92 ⟩; break;
    case '\"': ⟨ Scan a string constant 93 ⟩; break;
    case '@': ⟨ Scan the current location 96 ⟩; break;
    case '-': op_stack[op_ptr++] = negate;
    case '+': goto scan_open;
    case '&': op_stack[op_ptr++] = serialize; goto scan_open;
    case '~': op_stack[op_ptr++] = complement; goto scan_open;
    case '$': op_stack[op_ptr++] = registerize; goto scan_open;
    case '(': op_stack[op_ptr++] = inner_lp; goto scan_open;
    default:
      if (p ≡ operand_list + 1) {    /* treat operand list as empty */
        operand_list[0] = '0', operand_list[1] = '\0', p = operand_list;
        goto scan_open;
      }
      if (*(p - 1)) derr("syntax␣error␣at␣character␣`%c'", *(p - 1));
      derr("syntax␣error␣after␣character␣`%c'", *(p - 2));
  }
```

This code is used in section 85.

87. ⟨ Scan a symbol 87 ⟩ ≡

```
  {
    if (*p ≡ ':') tt = trie_search(trie_root, p + 1);
    else tt = trie_search(cur_prefix, p);
    p = terminator;
  symbol_found: val_ptr++;
    pp = tt→sym;
    if (¬pp) pp = tt→sym = new_sym_node(true);
    top_val.link = tt, top_val.equiv = pp→equiv;
    if (pp→link ≡ PREDEFINED) pp→link = DEFINED;
    top_val.status = (pp→link ≡ DEFINED ? pure : pp→link ≡ REGISTER ? reg_val : undefined);
  }
```

This code is used in section 86.

88. ⟨ Scan a forward local 88 ⟩ ≡
```
{
  tt = &forward_local_host[*p - '0']; p += 2; goto symbol_found;
}
```
This code is used in section 86.

89. ⟨ Scan a backward local 89 ⟩ ≡
```
{
  tt = &backward_local_host[*p - '0']; p += 2; goto symbol_found;
}
```
This code is used in section 86.

90. Statically allocated variables *forward_local_host*[*j*] and *backward_local_host*[*j*] masquerade as nodes of the trie.

⟨ Global variables 27 ⟩ +≡
```
trie_node forward_local_host[10], backward_local_host[10];
sym_node forward_local[10], backward_local[10];
```

91. Initially 0H, 1H, ..., 9H are defined to be zero.

⟨ Initialize everything 29 ⟩ +≡
```
for (j = 0; j < 10; j++) {
  forward_local_host[j].sym = &forward_local[j];
  backward_local_host[j].sym = &backward_local[j];
  backward_local[j].link = DEFINED;
}
```

complement = 2, §82.
cur_prefix: **trie_node** ∗, §56.
DEFINED = macro, §58.
derr = macro ( ), §45.
equiv: **octa**, §82.
equiv: **octa**, §58.
inner_lp = 4, §82.
isdigit: **int** ( ), <ctype.h>.
isletter = macro ( ), §57.
j: **register int**, §136.
link: **trie_node** ∗, §82.
link: **sym_node** ∗, §58.
negate = 0, §82.
new_sym_node: **sym_node** ∗( ), §59.
op_ptr: **int**, §83.
op_stack: **stack_op** ∗, §83.
operand_list: **Char** ∗, §33.
p: **register Char** ∗, §40.
pp: **register sym_node** ∗, §65.
PREDEFINED = macro, §58.
pure = 0, §82.
reg_val = 1, §82.
REGISTER = macro, §58.
registerize = 3, §82.
serialize = 1, §82.
status: **stat**, §82.
sym: **sym_node** ∗, §54.
sym_node = **struct**, §58.
terminator: **Char** ∗, §57.
top_val = macro, §83.
trie_node = **struct**, §54.
trie_root: **trie_node** ∗, §56.
trie_search: **trie_node** ∗( ), §57.
true = 1, §26.
tt: **register trie_node** ∗, §65.
undefined = 2, §82.
val_ptr: **int**, §83.
val_stack: **val_node** ∗, §83.

92. We have already checked to make sure that the character constant is legal.

```
⟨Scan a character constant 92⟩ ≡
  acc.h = 0, acc.l = (unsigned char) *p;
  p += 2;
  goto constant_found;
```

This code is used in section 86.

93.

```
⟨Scan a string constant 93⟩ ≡
  acc.h = 0, acc.l = (unsigned char) *p;
  if (*p ≡ '\"') {
    p++;
    acc.l = 0;
    err("*null␣string␣is␣treated␣as␣zero");
  } else if (*(p + 1) ≡ '\"') p += 2;
  else *p = '\"', *−−p = ',';
  goto constant_found;
```

This code is used in section 86.

94.

```
⟨Scan a decimal constant 94⟩ ≡
  acc.h = 0, acc.l = *p − '0';
  for (p++; isdigit(*p); p++) {
    acc = oplus(acc, shift_left(acc, 2));
    acc = incr(shift_left(acc, 1), *p − '0');
  }
constant_found: val_ptr++;
  top_val.link = Λ;
  top_val.equiv = acc;
  top_val.status = pure;
```

This code is used in section 86.

95.

```
⟨Scan a hexadecimal constant 95⟩ ≡
  if (¬isxdigit(*p)) err("illegal␣hexadecimal␣constant");
  acc.h = acc.l = 0;
  for ( ; isxdigit(*p); p++) {
    acc = incr(shift_left(acc, 4), *p − '0');
    if (*p ≥ 'a') acc = incr(acc, '0' − 'a' + 10);
    else if (*p ≥ 'A') acc = incr(acc, '0' − 'A' + 10);
  }
  goto constant_found;
```

This code is used in section 86.

96.

```
⟨Scan the current location 96⟩ ≡
  acc = cur_loc;
  goto constant_found;
```

This code is used in section 86.

97.

```
⟨Scan a binary operator or closing token, rt_op 97⟩ ≡
  switch (*p++) {
  case '+': rt_op = plus; break;
  case '-': rt_op = minus; break;
```

```
case '*': rt_op = times; break;
case '/': if (*p ≠ '/') rt_op = over;
  else p++, rt_op = frac; break;
case '%': rt_op = mod; break;
case '<': rt_op = shl; goto sh_check;
case '>': rt_op = shr;
sh_check: p++; if (*(p − 1) ≡ *(p − 2)) break;
  derr("syntax␣error␣at␣'%c'", *(p − 2));
case '&': rt_op = and; break;
case '|': rt_op = or; break;
case '^': rt_op = xor; break;
case ')': rt_op = inner_rp; break;
case '\0': case ',': rt_op = outer_rp; break;
default: derr("syntax␣error␣at␣'%c'", *(p − 1));
}
```

This code is used in section 85.

98. ⟨ Perform the top operation on *op_stack* 98 ⟩ ≡

```
switch (op_stack[−− op_ptr]) {
case inner_lp: if (rt_op ≡ inner_rp) goto scan_close;
  err("*missing␣right␣parenthesis"); break;
case outer_lp: if (rt_op ≡ outer_rp) {
    if (top_val.status ≡ reg_val ∧ (top_val.equiv.l > #ff ∨ top_val.equiv.h)) {
      err("*register␣number␣too␣large,␣will␣be␣reduced␣mod␣256");
      top_val.equiv.h = 0, top_val.equiv.l &= #ff;
    }
    if (¬*(p − 1)) goto operands_done;
    else rt_op = outer_lp; goto hold_op;    /* comma */
  } else {
    op_ptr++; err("*missing␣left␣parenthesis");
    goto scan_close;
  }
⟨ Cases for unary operators 100 ⟩
⟨ Cases for binary operators 99 ⟩
}
```

This code is used in section 85.

acc: **octa**, §83.
and = 13, §82.
cur_loc: **octa**, §43.
derr = macro ( ), §45.
equiv: **octa**, §82.
err = macro ( ), §45.
frac = 9, §82.
h: **tetra**, §26.
hold_op: label, §85.
incr: **octa** ( ), MMIX-ARITH §6.
inner_lp = 4, §82.
inner_rp = 18, §82.
isdigit: **int** ( ), <ctype.h>.
isxdigit: **int** ( ), <ctype.h>.
l: **tetra**, §26.
link: **trie_node** *, §82.
minus = 6, §82.
mod = 10, §82.
op_ptr: **int**, §83.
op_stack: **stack_op** *, §83.
operands_done: label, §85.
oplus: **octa** ( ), MMIX-ARITH §5.
or = 14, §82.
outer_lp = 16, §82.
outer_rp = 17, §82.
over = 8, §82.
p: **register Char** *, §40.
plus = 5, §82.
pure = 0, §82.
reg_val = 1, §82.
rt_op: **stack_op**, §83.
scan_close: label, §85.
shift_left: **octa** ( ), MMIX-ARITH §7.
shl = 11, §82.
shr = 12, §82.
status: **stat**, §82.
times = 7, §82.
top_val = macro, §83.
val_ptr: **int**, §83.
xor = 15, §82.

99. Now we come to the part where equivalents are changed by unary or binary operators found in the expression being scanned.

The most typical operator, and in some ways the fussiest one to deal with, is binary addition. Once we've written the code for this case, the other cases almost take care of themselves.

```
⟨ Cases for binary operators 99 ⟩ ≡
case plus: if (top_val.status ≡ undefined) err("cannot␣add␣an␣undefined␣quantity");
  if (next_val.status ≡ undefined) err("cannot␣add␣to␣an␣undefined␣quantity");
  if (top_val.status ≡ reg_val ∧ next_val.status ≡ reg_val)
    err("cannot␣add␣two␣register␣numbers");
  next_val.equiv = oplus(next_val.equiv, top_val.equiv);
fin_bin: next_val.status = (top_val.status ≡ next_val.status ? pure : reg_val); val_ptr−−;
delink: top_val.link = Λ; break;
```

See also section 101.

This code is used in section 98.

100.

```
#define unary_check(verb)
    if (top_val.status ≠ pure) derr("can␣%s␣pure␣values␣only", verb)

⟨ Cases for unary operators 100 ⟩ ≡
case negate: unary_check("negate");
  top_val.equiv = ominus(zero_octa, top_val.equiv); goto delink;
case complement: unary_check("complement");
  top_val.equiv.h = ∼top_val.equiv.h, top_val.equiv.l = ∼top_val.equiv.l;
  goto delink;
case registerize: unary_check("registerize");
  top_val.status = reg_val; goto delink;
case serialize: if (¬top_val.link) err("can␣take␣serial␣number␣of␣symbol␣only");
  top_val.equiv.h = 0, top_val.equiv.l = top_val.link→sym→serial;
  top_val.status = pure; goto delink;
```

This code is used in section 98.

101.

```
#define binary_check(verb) if (top_val.status ≠ pure ∨ next_val.status ≠ pure)
        derr("can␣%s␣pure␣values␣only", verb)

⟨ Cases for binary operators 99 ⟩ +≡
case minus: if (top_val.status ≡ undefined)
    err("cannot␣subtract␣an␣undefined␣quantity");
  if (next_val.status ≡ undefined)
    err("cannot␣subtract␣from␣an␣undefined␣quantity");
  if (top_val.status ≡ reg_val ∧ next_val.status ≠ reg_val)
    err("cannot␣subtract␣register␣number␣from␣pure␣value");
  next_val.equiv = ominus(next_val.equiv, top_val.equiv); goto fin_bin;
case times: binary_check("multiply");
  next_val.equiv = omult(next_val.equiv, top_val.equiv); goto fin_bin;
case over: case mod: binary_check("divide");
  if (top_val.equiv.l ≡ 0 ∧ top_val.equiv.h ≡ 0) err("*division␣by␣zero");
  next_val.equiv = odiv(zero_octa, next_val.equiv, top_val.equiv);
  if (op_stack[op_ptr] ≡ mod) next_val.equiv = aux;
  goto fin_bin;
```

```
case frac: binary_check("compute␣a␣ratio␣of");
  if (next_val.equiv.h ≥ top_val.equiv.h ∧ (next_val.equiv.l ≥
       top_val.equiv.l ∨ next_val.equiv.h > top_val.equiv.h)) err("*illegal␣fraction");
  next_val.equiv = odiv(next_val.equiv, zero_octa, top_val.equiv); goto fin_bin;
case shl: case shr: binary_check("compute␣a␣bitwise␣shift␣of");
  if (top_val.equiv.h ∨ top_val.equiv.l > 63) next_val.equiv = zero_octa;
  else if (op_stack[op_ptr] ≡ shl)
    next_val.equiv = shift_left(next_val.equiv, top_val.equiv.l);
  else next_val.equiv = shift_right(next_val.equiv, top_val.equiv.l, 1);
  goto fin_bin;
case and: binary_check("compute␣bitwise␣and␣of");
  next_val.equiv.h &= top_val.equiv.h, next_val.equiv.l &= top_val.equiv.l;
  goto fin_bin;
case or: binary_check("compute␣bitwise␣or␣of");
  next_val.equiv.h |= top_val.equiv.h, next_val.equiv.l |= top_val.equiv.l;
  goto fin_bin;
case xor: binary_check("compute␣bitwise␣xor␣of");
  next_val.equiv.h ⊕= top_val.equiv.h, next_val.equiv.l ⊕= top_val.equiv.l;
  goto fin_bin;
```


and = 13, §82.
aux: **octa**, MMIX-ARITH §4.
complement = 2, §82.
derr = macro ( ), §45.
equiv: **octa**, §82.
err = macro ( ), §45.
frac = 9, §82.
h: **tetra**, §26.
l: **tetra**, §26.
link: **trie_node** ∗, §82.
minus = 6, §82.
mod = 10, §82.
negate = 0, §82.
next_val = macro, §83.
odiv: **octa** ( ), MMIX-ARITH §13.
ominus: **octa** ( ), MMIX-ARITH §5.
omult: **octa** ( ), MMIX-ARITH §8.
op_ptr: **int**, §83.
op_stack: **stack_op** ∗, §83.
oplus: **octa** ( ), MMIX-ARITH §5.
or = 14, §82.
over = 8, §82.
plus = 5, §82.
pure = 0, §82.
reg_val = 1, §82.
registerize = 3, §82.
serial: **int**, §58.
serialize = 1, §82.
shift_left: **octa** ( ), MMIX-ARITH §7.
shift_right: **octa** ( ), MMIX-ARITH §7.
shl = 11, §82.
shr = 12, §82.
status: **stat**, §82.
sym: **sym_node** ∗, §54.
times = 7, §82.
top_val = macro, §83.
undefined = 2, §82.
val_ptr: **int**, §83.
xor = 15, §82.
zero_octa: **octa**, MMIX-ARITH §4.

102. Assembling an instruction. Now let's move up from the expression level to the instruction level. We get to this part of the program at the beginning of a line, or after a semicolon at the end of an instruction earlier on the current line. Our current position in the buffer is the value of *buf_ptr*.

```
⟨Process the next MMIXAL instruction or comment 102⟩ ≡
  p = buf_ptr; buf_ptr = "";
  ⟨Scan the label field; goto bypass if there is none 103⟩;
  ⟨Scan the opcode field; goto bypass if there is none 104⟩;
  ⟨Copy the operand field 106⟩;
  buf_ptr = p;
  if (spec_mode ∧ ¬(op_bits & spec_bit))
    derr("cannot␣use␣`%s'␣in␣special␣mode", op_field);
  if ((op_bits & no_label_bit) ∧ lab_field[0]) {
    derr("*label␣field␣of␣`%s'␣instruction␣is␣ignored", op_field);
    lab_field[0] = '\0';
  }
  if (op_bits & align_bits) ⟨Align the location pointer 107⟩;
  ⟨Scan the operand field 85⟩;
  if (opcode ≡ GREG) ⟨Allocate a global register 108⟩;
  if (lab_field[0]) ⟨Define the label 109⟩;
  ⟨Do the operation 116⟩;
bypass:
```

This code is used in section 136.

```
103. ⟨Scan the label field; goto bypass if there is none 103⟩ ≡
  if (¬*p) goto bypass;
  q = lab_field;
  if (¬isspace(*p)) {
    if (¬isdigit(*p) ∧ ¬isletter(*p)) goto bypass;     /* comment */
    for (*q++ = *p++; isdigit(*p) ∨ isletter(*p); p++, q++) *q = *p;
    if (*p ∧ ¬isspace(*p)) derr("label␣syntax␣error␣at␣`%c'", *p);
  }
  *q = '\0';
  if (isdigit(lab_field[0]) ∧ (lab_field[1] ≠ 'H' ∨ lab_field[2]))
    derr("improper␣local␣label␣`%s'", lab_field);
  for (p++; isspace(*p); p++) ;
```

This code is used in section 102.

104. We copy the opcode field to a special buffer because we might want to refer to the symbolic opcode in error messages.

```
⟨Scan the opcode field; goto bypass if there is none 104⟩ ≡
  q = op_field; while (isletter(*p) ∨ isdigit(*p)) *q++ = *p++; *q = '\0';
  if (¬isspace(*p) ∧ *p ∧ op_field[0]) derr("opcode␣syntax␣error␣at␣`%c'", *p);
  pp = trie_search(op_root, op_field)→sym;
  if (¬pp) {
    if (op_field[0]) derr("unknown␣operation␣code␣`%s'", op_field);
    if (lab_field[0]) derr("*no␣opcode;␣label␣`%s'␣will␣be␣ignored", lab_field);
    goto bypass;
  }
```

```
  opcode = pp→equiv.h, op_bits = pp→equiv.l;
  while (isspace(*p)) p++;
```

This code is used in section 102.

105. ⟨ Global variables 27 ⟩ +≡

```
  tetra opcode;     /* numeric code for MMIX operation or MMIXAL pseudo-op */
  tetra op_bits;    /* flags describing an operator's special characteristics */
```

106. We copy the operand field to a special buffer so that we can change string constants while scanning them later.

⟨ Copy the operand field 106 ⟩ ≡

```
  q = operand_list;
  while (*p) {
    if (*p ≡ ';') break;
    if (*p ≡ '\'') {
      *q++ = *p++;
      if (¬*p) err("incomplete␣character␣constant");
      *q++ = *p++;
      if (*p ≠ '\'') err("illegal␣character␣constant");
    } else if (*p ≡ '\"') {
      for (*q++ = *p++; *p ∧ *p ≠ '\"'; p++, q++) *q = *p;
      if (¬*p) err("incomplete␣string␣constant");
    }
    *q++ = *p++;
    if (isspace(*p)) break;
  }
  while (isspace(*p)) p++;
  if (*p ≡ ';') p++;
  else p = "";      /* if not followed by semicolon, rest of the line is a comment */
  if (q ≡ operand_list) *q++ = '0';     /* change empty operand field to '0' */
  *q = '\0';
```

This code is used in section 102.

---

align_bits = #30000, §62.
buf_ptr: **Char** *, §33.
derr = macro ( ), §45.
equiv: **octa**, §58.
err = macro ( ), §45.
GREG = #106, §62.
h: **tetra**, §26.
isdigit: **int** ( ), <ctype.h>.
isletter = macro ( ), §57.
isspace: **int** ( ), <ctype.h>.
l: **tetra**, §26.
lab_field: **Char** *, §33.
no_label_bit = #40000, §62.
op_field: **Char** *, §33.
op_root: **trie_node** *, §56.
operand_list: **Char** *, §33.
p: **register Char** *, §40.
pp: **register sym_node** *, §65.
q: **register Char** *, §40.
spec_bit = #100000, §62.
spec_mode: **bool**, §43.
sym: **sym_node** *, §54.
tetra = **unsigned int**, §26.
trie_search: **trie_node** *( ), §57.

107. It is important to do the alignment in this step before defining the label or evaluating the operand field.

```
⟨ Align the location pointer 107 ⟩ ≡
  {
    j = (op_bits & align_bits) ≫ 16;
    acc.h = −1, acc.l = −(1 ≪ j);
    cur_loc = oand(incr(cur_loc, (1 ≪ j) − 1), acc);
  }
```

This code is used in section 102.

108. ⟨ Allocate a global register 108 ⟩ ≡

```
  {
    if (val_stack[0].equiv.l ∨ val_stack[0].equiv.h) {
      for (j = greg; j < 255; j++)
        if (greg_val[j].l ≡ val_stack[0].equiv.l ∧ greg_val[j].h ≡ val_stack[0].equiv.h) {
          cur_greg = j;
          goto got_greg;
        }
    }
    if (greg ≡ 32) err("too␣many␣global␣registers");
    greg−−;
    greg_val[greg] = val_stack[0].equiv; cur_greg = greg;
  got_greg: ;
  }
```

This code is used in section 102.

109. If the label is, say 2H, we will already have used the old value of 2B when evaluating the operands. Furthermore, an operand of 2F will have been treated as undefined, which it still is.

Symbols can be defined more than once, but only if each definition gives them the same equivalent value.

A warning message is given when a predefined symbol is being redefined, if its predefined value has already been used.

```
⟨ Define the label 109 ⟩ ≡
  {
    sym_node *new_link = DEFINED;
    acc = cur_loc;
    if (opcode ≡ IS) {
      if (val_stack[0].status ≡ undefined) err("the␣operand␣is␣undefined");
      cur_loc = val_stack[0].equiv;
      if (val_stack[0].status ≡ reg_val) new_link = REGISTER;
    } else if (opcode ≡ GREG) cur_loc.h = 0, cur_loc.l = cur_greg, new_link = REGISTER;
    ⟨ Find the symbol table node, pp 111 ⟩;
    if (pp→link ≡ DEFINED ∨ pp→link ≡ REGISTER) {
      if (pp→equiv.l ≠ cur_loc.l ∨ pp→equiv.h ≠ cur_loc.h ∨ pp→link ≠ new_link) {
        if (pp→serial) derr("symbol␣'%s'␣is␣already␣defined", lab_field);
        pp→serial = ++serial_number;
        derr("*redefinition␣of␣predefined␣symbol␣'%s'", lab_field);
```

```
      }
    } else if (pp→link ≡ PREDEFINED) pp→serial = ++serial_number;
    else if (pp→link) {
      if (new_link ≡ REGISTER) err("future␣reference␣cannot␣be␣to␣a␣register");
      do ⟨Fix prior references to this label 112⟩ while (pp→link);
    }
    if (isdigit(lab_field[0])) pp = &backward_local[lab_field[0] − '0'];
    pp→equiv = cur_loc; pp→link = new_link;
    ⟨Fix references that might be in the val_stack 110⟩;
    if (listing_file ∧ (opcode ≡ IS ∨ opcode ≡ LOC))
      ⟨Make special listing to show the label equivalent 115⟩;
    cur_loc = acc;
  }
```

This code is used in section 102.

110. ⟨Fix references that might be in the *val_stack* 110⟩ ≡

```
  if (¬isdigit(lab_field[0]))
    for (j = 0; j < val_ptr; j++)
      if (val_stack[j].status ≡ undefined ∧ val_stack[j].link→sym ≡ pp) {
        val_stack[j].status = (new_link ≡ REGISTER ? reg_val : pure);
        val_stack[j].equiv = cur_loc;
      }
```

This code is used in section 109.

111. ⟨Find the symbol table node, *pp* 111⟩ ≡

```
  if (isdigit(lab_field[0])) pp = &forward_local[lab_field[0] − '0'];
  else {
    if (lab_field[0] ≡ ':') tt = trie_search(trie_root, lab_field + 1);
    else tt = trie_search(cur_prefix, lab_field);
    pp = tt→sym;
    if (¬pp) pp = tt→sym = new_sym_node(true);
  }
```

This code is used in section 109.

---

acc: **octa**, §83.
align_bits = #30000, §62.
backward_local: **sym_node** [], §90.
cur_greg: **int**, §143.
cur_loc: **octa**, §43.
cur_prefix: **trie_node** ∗, §56.
DEFINED = macro, §58.
derr = macro (), §45.
equiv: **octa**, §82.
equiv: **octa**, §58.
err = macro (), §45.
forward_local: **sym_node** [], §90.
GREG = #106, §62.
greg: **int**, §143.
greg_val: **octa** [], §133.
h: **tetra**, §26.
incr: **octa** (), MMIX-ARITH §6.
IS = #101, §62.
isdigit: **int** (), <ctype.h>.
j: **register int**, §136.
l: **tetra**, §26.
lab_field: **Char** ∗, §33.
link: **sym_node** ∗, §58.
link: **trie_node** ∗, §82.
listing_file: **FILE** ∗, §139.
LOC = #102, §62.
new_sym_node: **sym_node** ∗(), §59.
oand: **octa** (), MMIX-ARITH §25.
op_bits: **tetra**, §105.
opcode: **tetra**, §105.
pp: **register sym_node** ∗, §65.
PREDEFINED = macro, §58.
pure = 0, §82.
reg_val = 1, §82.
REGISTER = macro, §58.
serial: **int**, §58.
serial_number: **int**, §60.
status: **stat**, §82.
sym: **sym_node** ∗, §54.
sym_node = **struct**, §58.
trie_root: **trie_node** ∗, §56.
trie_search: **trie_node** ∗(), §57.
true = 1, §26.
tt: **register trie_node** ∗, §65.
undefined = 2, §82.
val_ptr: **int**, §83.
val_stack: **val_node** ∗, §83.

112. ⟨ Fix prior references to this label 112 ⟩ ≡

```
{
  qq = pp→link;
  pp→link = qq→link;
  mmo_loc();
  if (qq→serial ≡ fix_o) ⟨ Fix a future reference from an octabyte 113 ⟩
  else ⟨ Fix a future reference from a relative address 114 ⟩;
  recycle_fixup(qq);
}
```

This code is used in section 109.

113. ⟨ Fix a future reference from an octabyte 113 ⟩ ≡

```
{
  if (qq→equiv.h & #ffffff) {
    mmo_lop(lop_fixo, 0, 2);
    mmo_tetra(qq→equiv.h);
  } else mmo_lop(lop_fixo, qq→equiv.h ≫ 24, 1);
  mmo_tetra(qq→equiv.l);
}
```

This code is used in section 112.

114. ⟨ Fix a future reference from a relative address 114 ⟩ ≡

```
{
  octa o;
  o = ominus(cur_loc, qq→equiv);
  if (o.l & 3)
    dderr("*relative␣address␣in␣location␣#%08x%08x␣not␣divisible␣by␣4",
        qq→equiv.h, qq→equiv.l);
  o = shift_right(o, 2, 0);  k = 0;
  if (o.h ≡ 0)
    if (o.l < #10000) mmo_lopp(lop_fixr, o.l);
    else if (qq→serial ≡ fix_xyz ∧ o.l < #1000000) {
      mmo_lop(lop_fixrx, 0, 24);  mmo_tetra(o.l);
    } else k = 1;
  else if (o.h ≡ #ffffffff)
    if (qq→serial ≡ fix_xyz ∧ o.l ≥ #ff000000) {
      mmo_lop(lop_fixrx, 0, 24);  mmo_tetra(o.l & #1ffffff);
    } else if (qq→serial ≡ fix_yz ∧ o.l ≥ #ffff0000) {
      mmo_lop(lop_fixrx, 0, 16);  mmo_tetra(o.l & #100ffff);
    } else k = 1;
  else k = 1;
  if (k) dderr("relative␣address␣in␣location␣#%08x%08x␣is␣too␣far␣away",
        qq→equiv.h, qq→equiv.l);
}
```

This code is used in section 112.

```
115. ⟨Make special listing to show the label equivalent 115⟩ ≡
  if (new_link ≡ DEFINED) {
    fprintf(listing_file, "(%08x%08x)", cur_loc.h, cur_loc.l);
    flush_listing_line("␣");
  } else {
    fprintf(listing_file, "($%03d)", cur_loc.l & #ff);
    flush_listing_line("␣␣␣␣␣␣␣␣␣␣␣␣␣");
  }
```

This code is used in section 109.

```
116. ⟨Do the operation 116⟩ ≡
  future_bits = 0;
  if (op_bits & many_arg_bit) ⟨Do a many-operand operation 117⟩
  else switch (val_ptr) {
    case 1: if (¬(op_bits & one_arg_bit))
          derr("opcode␣`%s'␣needs␣more␣than␣one␣operand", op_field);
      ⟨Do a one-operand operation 129⟩;
    case 2: if (¬(op_bits & two_arg_bit))
          if (op_bits & one_arg_bit)
            derr("opcode␣`%s'␣must␣not␣have␣two␣operands", op_field)
          else derr("opcode␣`%s'␣must␣have␣more␣than␣two␣operands", op_field);
      if ((op_bits & (three_arg_bit + mem_bit)) ≡ three_arg_bit) goto make_two_three;
      ⟨Do a two-operand operation 124⟩;
    make_two_three: val_stack[2] = val_stack[1], val_ptr = 3;
      val_stack[1].equiv = zero_octa, val_stack[1].link = Λ, val_stack[1].status = pure;
        /* insert 0 as the second operand */
    case 3: if (¬(op_bits & three_arg_bit))
          derr("opcode␣`%s'␣must␣not␣have␣three␣operands", op_field);
      ⟨Do a three-operand operation 119⟩;
    default: derr("too␣many␣operands␣for␣opcode␣`%s'", op_field);
  }
```

This code is used in section 102.

---

cur_loc: **octa**, §43.
dderr = macro ( ), §45.
DEFINED = macro, §58.
derr = macro ( ), §45.
equiv: **octa**, §58.
equiv: **octa**, §82.
fix_o = 0, §58.
fix_xyz = 2, §58.
fix_yz = 1, §58.
flush_listing_line: **void** ( ), §41.
fprintf: **int** ( ), <stdio.h>.
future_bits: **int**, §120.
h: **tetra**, §26.
k: **register int**, §136.
l: **tetra**, §26.
link: **sym_node** *, §58.
link: **trie_node** *, §82.
listing_file: **FILE** *, §139.
lop_fixo = #3, §24.
lop_fixr = #4, §24.
lop_fixrx = #5, §24.
many_arg_bit = #8000, §62.
mem_bit = #80000, §62.
mmo_loc: **void** ( ), §49.
mmo_lop: **void** ( ), §48.
mmo_lopp: **void** ( ), §48.
mmo_tetra: **void** ( ), §48.
new_link: **sym_node** *, §109.
octa = **struct**, §26.
ominus: **octa** ( ), MMIX-ARITH §5.
one_arg_bit = #1000, §62.
op_bits: **tetra**, §105.
op_field: **Char** *, §33.
pp: **register sym_node** *, §65.
pure = 0, §82.
qq: **register sym_node** *, §65.
recycle_fixup = macro ( ), §59.
serial: **int**, §58.
shift_right: **octa** ( ), MMIX-ARITH §7.
status: **stat**, §82.
three_arg_bit = #4000, §62.
two_arg_bit = #2000, §62.
val_ptr: **int**, §83.
val_stack: **val_node** *, §83.
zero_octa: **octa**, MMIX-ARITH §4.

117. The many-operand operators are BYTE, WYDE, TETRA, and OCTA.

```
⟨ Do a many-operand operation 117 ⟩ ≡
  for (j = 0; j < val_ptr; j++) {
    ⟨ Deal with cases where val_stack[j] is impure 118 ⟩;
    k = 1 ≪ (opcode − BYTE);
    if ((val_stack[j].equiv.h ∧ opcode < OCTA) ∨
          (val_stack[j].equiv.l > #ffff ∧ opcode < TETRA) ∨
          (val_stack[j].equiv.l > #ff ∧ opcode < WYDE))
      if (k ≡ 1) err("*constant␣doesn't␣fit␣in␣one␣byte")
      else derr("*constant␣doesn't␣fit␣in␣%d␣bytes", k);
    if (k < 8) assemble(k, val_stack[j].equiv.l, 0);
    else if (val_stack[j].status ≡ undefined) assemble(4, 0, #f0), assemble(4, 0, #f0);
    else assemble(4, val_stack[j].equiv.h, 0), assemble(4, val_stack[j].equiv.l, 0);
  }
```

This code is used in section 116.

118.

```
⟨ Deal with cases where val_stack[j] is impure 118 ⟩ ≡
  if (val_stack[j].status ≡ reg_val) err("*register␣number␣used␣as␣a␣constant")
  else if (val_stack[j].status ≡ undefined) {
    if (opcode ≠ OCTA) err("undefined␣constant");
    pp = val_stack[j].link→sym;
    qq = new_sym_node(false);
    qq→link = pp→link;
    pp→link = qq;
    qq→serial = fix_o;
    qq→equiv = cur_loc;
  }
```

This code is used in section 117.

119.

```
⟨ Do a three-operand operation 119 ⟩ ≡
  ⟨ Do the Z field 121 ⟩;
  ⟨ Do the Y field 122 ⟩;
assemble_X: ⟨ Do the X field 123 ⟩;
assemble_inst: assemble(4, (opcode ≪ 24) + xyz, future_bits);
  break;
```

This code is used in section 116.

120. Individual fields of an instruction are placed into global variables z, y, x, yz, and/or xyz.

```
⟨ Global variables 27 ⟩ +≡
  tetra z, y, x, yz, xyz;     /* pieces for assembly */
  int future_bits;     /* places where there are future references */
```

121.

```
⟨ Do the Z field 121 ⟩ ≡
  if (val_stack[2].status ≡ undefined) err("Z␣field␣is␣undefined");
  if (val_stack[2].status ≡ reg_val) {
    if (¬(op_bits & (immed_bit + zr_bit + zar_bit)))
      derr("*Z␣field␣of␣`%s'␣should␣not␣be␣a␣register␣number", op_field);
  } else if (op_bits & immed_bit) opcode++;     /* immediate */
```

```
  else if (op_bits & zr_bit)
    derr("*Z␣field␣of␣‘%s’␣should␣be␣a␣register␣number", op_field);
  if (val_stack[2].equiv.h ∨ val_stack[2].equiv.l > #ff)
    err("*Z␣field␣doesn’t␣fit␣in␣one␣byte");
  z = val_stack[2].equiv.l & #ff;
```

This code is used in section 119.

122. ⟨Do the Y field 122⟩ ≡

```
  if (val_stack[1].status ≡ undefined) err("Y␣field␣is␣undefined");
  if (val_stack[1].status ≡ reg_val) {
    if (¬(op_bits & (yr_bit + yar_bit)))
      derr("*Y␣field␣of␣‘%s’␣should␣not␣be␣a␣register␣number", op_field);
  } else if (op_bits & yr_bit)
    derr("*Y␣field␣of␣‘%s’␣should␣be␣a␣register␣number", op_field);
  if (val_stack[1].equiv.h ∨ val_stack[1].equiv.l > #ff)
    err("*Y␣field␣doesn’t␣fit␣in␣one␣byte");
  y = val_stack[1].equiv.l & #ff; yz = (y ≪ 8) + z;
```

This code is used in section 119.

123. ⟨Do the X field 123⟩ ≡

```
  if (val_stack[0].status ≡ undefined) err("X␣field␣is␣undefined");
  if (val_stack[0].status ≡ reg_val) {
    if (¬(op_bits & (xr_bit + xar_bit)))
      derr("*X␣field␣of␣‘%s’␣should␣not␣be␣a␣register␣number", op_field);
  } else if (op_bits & xr_bit)
    derr("*X␣field␣of␣‘%s’␣should␣be␣a␣register␣number", op_field);
  if (val_stack[0].equiv.h ∨ val_stack[0].equiv.l > #ff)
    err("*X␣field␣doesn’t␣fit␣in␣one␣byte");
  x = val_stack[0].equiv.l & #ff; xyz = (x ≪ 16) + yz;
```

This code is used in section 119.

---

assemble: **void** (), §52.
BYTE = #108, §62.
cur_loc: **octa**, §43.
derr = macro (), §45.
equiv: **octa**, §82.
equiv: **octa**, §58.
err = macro (), §45.
false = 0, §26.
fix_o = 0, §58.
h: **tetra**, §26.
immed_bit = #2, §62.
j: **register int**, §136.
k: **register int**, §136.
l: **tetra**, §26.
link: **trie_node** ∗, §82.
link: **sym_node** ∗, §58.
new_sym_node: **sym_node** ∗(), §59.
OCTA = #10b, §62.
op_bits: **tetra**, §105.
op_field: **Char** ∗, §33.
opcode: **tetra**, §105.
pp: **register sym_node** ∗, §65.
qq: **register sym_node** ∗, §65.
reg_val = 1, §82.
serial: **int**, §58.
status: **stat**, §82.
sym: **sym_node** ∗, §54.
TETRA = #10a, §62.
tetra = **unsigned int**, §26.
undefined = 2, §82.
val_ptr: **int**, §83.
val_stack: **val_node** ∗, §83.
WYDE = #109, §62.
xar_bit = #40, §62.
xr_bit = #80, §62.
yar_bit = #10, §62.
yr_bit = #20, §62.
zar_bit = #4, §62.
zr_bit = #8, §62.

124. ⟨ Do a two-operand operation 124 ⟩ ≡

```
if (val_stack[1].status ≡ undefined) {
  if (op_bits & rel_addr_bit)
    ⟨ Assemble YZ as a future reference and goto assemble_X 125 ⟩
  else err("YZ␣field␣is␣undefined");
} else if (val_stack[1].status ≡ reg_val) {
  if (¬(op_bits & (immed_bit + yzr_bit + yzar_bit)))
    derr("*YZ␣field␣of␣`%s'␣should␣not␣be␣a␣register␣number", op_field);
  if (opcode ≡ SET) val_stack[1].equiv.l <<= 8, opcode = #c1;    /* change to OR */
  else if (op_bits & mem_bit) val_stack[1].equiv.l <<= 8, opcode++;
      /* silently append ,0 */
} else {    /* val_stack[1].status ≡ pure */
  if (op_bits & mem_bit)
    ⟨ Assemble YZ as a memory address and goto assemble_X 127 ⟩;
  if (opcode ≡ SET) opcode = #e3;    /* change to SETL */
  else if (op_bits & immed_bit) opcode++;    /* immediate */
  else if (op_bits & yzr_bit) {
    derr("*YZ␣field␣of␣`%s'␣should␣be␣a␣register␣number", op_field);
  }
  if (op_bits & rel_addr_bit)
    ⟨ Assemble YZ as a relative address and goto assemble_X 126 ⟩;
}
if (val_stack[1].equiv.h ∨ val_stack[1].equiv.l > #ffff)
  err("*YZ␣field␣doesn't␣fit␣in␣two␣bytes");
yz = val_stack[1].equiv.l & #ffff;
goto assemble_X;
```

This code is used in section 116.

125. ⟨ Assemble YZ as a future reference and **goto** *assemble_X* 125 ⟩ ≡

```
{
  pp = val_stack[1].link→sym;
  qq = new_sym_node(false);
  qq→link = pp→link;
  pp→link = qq;
  qq→serial = fix_yz;
  qq→equiv = cur_loc;
  yz = 0;
  future_bits = #c0;
  goto assemble_X;
}
```

This code is used in section 124.

126. ⟨ Assemble YZ as a relative address and **goto** *assemble_X* 126 ⟩ ≡

```
{
  octa source, dest;

  if (val_stack[1].equiv.l & 3) err("*relative␣address␣is␣not␣divisible␣by␣4");
  source = shift_right(cur_loc, 2, 0);
  dest = shift_right(val_stack[1].equiv, 2, 0);
  acc = ominus(dest, source);
```

```
    if (¬(acc.h & #80000000)) {
      if (acc.l > #ffff ∨ acc.h)
        err("relative␣address␣is␣more␣than␣#ffff␣tetrabytes␣forward");
    } else {
      acc = incr(acc, #10000);
      opcode++;
      if (acc.l > #ffff ∨ acc.h)
        err("relative␣address␣is␣more␣than␣#10000␣tetrabytes␣backward");
    }
    yz = acc.l;
    goto assemble_X;
  }
```

This code is used in section 124.

127. ⟨ Assemble YZ as a memory address and **goto** *assemble_X* 127 ⟩ ≡

```
  {
    octa o;
    o = val_stack[1].equiv, k = 0;
    for (j = greg; j < 255; j++)
      if (greg_val[j].h ∨ greg_val[j].l) {
        acc = ominus(val_stack[1].equiv, greg_val[j]);
        if (acc.h ≤ o.h ∧ (acc.l ≤ o.l ∨ acc.h < o.h)) o = acc, k = j;
      }
    if (o.l ≤ #ff ∧ ¬o.h ∧ k) yz = (k ≪ 8) + o.l, opcode++;
    else if (¬expanding) err("no␣base␣address␣is␣close␣enough␣to␣the␣address␣A")
    else ⟨ Assemble instructions to put supplementary data in $255 128 ⟩;
    goto assemble_X;
  }
```

This code is used in section 124.

---

acc: **octa**, §83.
assemble_X: label, §119.
cur_loc: **octa**, §43.
derr = macro ( ), §45.
equiv: **octa**, §82.
equiv: **octa**, §58.
err = macro ( ), §45.
expanding: **int**, §139.
false = 0, §26.
fix_yz = 1, §58.
future_bits: **int**, §120.
greg: **int**, §143.
greg_val: **octa** [], §133.
h: **tetra**, §26.
immed_bit = #2, §62.
incr: **octa** ( ), MMIX-ARITH §6.
j: **register int**, §136.
k: **register int**, §136.
l: **tetra**, §26.
link: **trie_node** ∗, §82.
link: **sym_node** ∗, §58.
mem_bit = #80000, §62.
new_sym_node: **sym_node** ∗( ), §59.
octa = **struct**, §26.
ominus: **octa** ( ), MMIX-ARITH §5.
op_bits: **tetra**, §105.
op_field: **Char** ∗, §33.
opcode: **tetra**, §105.
pp: **register sym_node** ∗, §65.
pure = 0, §82.
qq: **register sym_node** ∗, §65.
reg_val = 1, §82.
rel_addr_bit = #1, §62.
serial: **int**, §58.
SET = #100, §62.
shift_right: **octa** ( ), MMIX-ARITH §7.
status: **stat**, §82.
sym: **sym_node** ∗, §54.
undefined = 2, §82.
val_stack: **val_node** ∗, §83.
yz: **tetra**, §120.
yzar_bit = #100, §62.
yzr_bit = #200, §62.

128. **#define** SETH #e0
#define SETL #e3
#define ORH #e8
#define ORL #eb

⟨ Assemble instructions to put supplementary data in $255 128 ⟩ ≡

```
{
  for (j = SETH; j ≤ ORL; j++) {
    switch (j & 3) {
    case 0: yz = o.h ≫ 16; break;      /* SETH */
    case 1: yz = o.h & #ffff; break;     /* SETMH or ORMH */
    case 2: yz = o.l ≫ 16; break;      /* SETML or ORML */
    case 3: yz = o.l & #ffff; break;     /* SETL or ORL */
    }
    if (yz ∨ j ≡ SETL) {
      assemble(4, (j ≪ 24) + (255 ≪ 16) + yz, 0);
      j |= ORH;
    }
  }
  if (k) yz = (k ≪ 8) + 255;      /* Y = $k, Z = $255 */
  else yz = 255 ≪ 8, opcode++;      /* Y = $255, Z = 0 */
}
```

This code is used in section 127.

129. ⟨ Do a one-operand operation 129 ⟩ ≡

```
if (val_stack[0].status ≡ undefined) {
  if (op_bits & rel_addr_bit)
    ⟨ Assemble XYZ as a future reference and goto assemble_inst 130 ⟩
  else if (opcode ≠ PREFIX) err("the␣operand␣is␣undefined");
} else if (val_stack[0].status ≡ reg_val) {
  if (¬(op_bits & (xyzr_bit + xyzar_bit)))
    derr("*operand␣of␣`%s'␣should␣not␣be␣a␣register␣number", op_field);
} else {     /* val_stack[0].status ≡ pure */
  if (op_bits & xyzr_bit)
    derr("*operand␣of␣`%s'␣should␣be␣a␣register␣number", op_field);
  if (op_bits & rel_addr_bit)
    ⟨ Assemble XYZ as a relative address and goto assemble_inst 131 ⟩;
}
if (opcode > #ff) ⟨ Do a pseudo-operation and goto bypass 132 ⟩;
if (val_stack[0].equiv.h ∨ val_stack[0].equiv.l > #ffffff)
  err("*XYZ␣field␣doesn't␣fit␣in␣three␣bytes");
xyz = val_stack[0].equiv.l & #ffffff;
goto assemble_inst;
```

This code is used in section 116.

130. ⟨ Assemble XYZ as a future reference and **goto** *assemble_inst* 130 ⟩ ≡

```
{
  pp = val_stack[0].link→sym;
  qq = new_sym_node(false);
  qq→link = pp→link;
```

```
    pp→link = qq;
    qq→serial = fix_xyz;
    qq→equiv = cur_loc;
    xyz = 0;
    future_bits = #e0;
    goto assemble_inst;
  }
```

This code is used in section 129.

131. ⟨ Assemble XYZ as a relative address and **goto** *assemble_inst* 131 ⟩ ≡

```
  {
    octa source, dest;
    if (val_stack[0].equiv.l & 3) err("*relative␣address␣is␣not␣divisible␣by␣4");
    source = shift_right(cur_loc, 2, 0);
    dest = shift_right(val_stack[0].equiv, 2, 0);
    acc = ominus(dest, source);
    if (¬(acc.h & #80000000)) {
      if (acc.l > #ffffff ∨ acc.h)
        err("relative␣address␣is␣more␣than␣#ffffff␣tetrabytes␣forward");
    } else {
      acc = incr(acc, #1000000);
      opcode++;
      if (acc.l > #ffffff ∨ acc.h)
        err("relative␣address␣is␣more␣than␣#1000000␣tetrabytes␣backward");
    }
    xyz = acc.l;
    goto assemble_inst;
  }
```

This code is used in section 129.

---

acc: **octa**, §83.
assemble: **void** ( ), §52.
assemble_inst: label, §119.
bypass: label, §102.
cur_loc: **octa**, §43.
derr = macro ( ), §45.
equiv: **octa**, §82.
equiv: **octa**, §58.
err = macro ( ), §45.
false = 0, §26.
fix_xyz = 2, §58.
future_bits: **int**, §120.
h: **tetra**, §26.
incr: **octa** ( ), MMIX-ARITH §6.
j: **register int**, §136.
k: **register int**, §136.
l: **tetra**, §26.
link: **trie_node** ∗, §82.
link: **sym_node** ∗, §58.
new_sym_node: **sym_node** ∗( ), §59.
o: **octa**, §127.
octa = **struct**, §26.
ominus: **octa** ( ), MMIX-ARITH §5.
op_bits: **tetra**, §105.
op_field: **Char** ∗, §33.
opcode: **tetra**, §105.
pp: **register sym_node** ∗, §65.
PREFIX = #103, §62.
pure = 0, §82.
qq: **register sym_node** ∗, §65.
reg_val = 1, §82.
rel_addr_bit = #1, §62.
serial: **int**, §58.
shift_right: **octa** ( ), MMIX-ARITH §7.
status: **stat**, §82.
sym: **sym_node** ∗, §54.
undefined = 2, §82.
val_stack: **val_node** ∗, §83.
xyz: **tetra**, §120.
xyzar_bit = #400, §62.
xyzr_bit = #800, §62.
yz: **tetra**, §120.

132. ⟨ Do a pseudo-operation and **goto** *bypass* 132 ⟩ ≡

```
switch (opcode) {
case LOC: cur_loc = val_stack[0].equiv;
case IS: goto bypass;
case PREFIX: if (¬val_stack[0].link) err("not␣a␣valid␣prefix");
  cur_prefix = val_stack[0].link; goto bypass;
case GREG: if (listing_file) ⟨ Make listing for GREG 134 ⟩;
  goto bypass;
case LOCAL: if (val_stack[0].equiv.l > lreg) lreg = val_stack[0].equiv.l;
  if (listing_file) {
    fprintf(listing_file, "($%03d)", val_stack[0].equiv.l);
    flush_listing_line("␣␣␣␣␣␣␣␣␣␣␣␣␣");
  }
  goto bypass;
case BSPEC: if (val_stack[0].equiv.l > #ffff ∨ val_stack[0].equiv.h)
    err("*operand␣of␣'BSPEC'␣doesn't␣fit␣in␣two␣bytes");
  mmo_loc(); mmo_sync();
  mmo_lopp(lop_spec, val_stack[0].equiv.l);
  spec_mode = true; spec_mode_loc = 0; goto bypass;
case ESPEC: spec_mode = false; goto bypass;
}
```

This code is used in section 129.

133. ⟨ Global variables 27 ⟩ +≡

```
octa greg_val[256];    /* initial values of global registers */
```

134. ⟨ Make listing for GREG 134 ⟩ ≡

```
if (val_stack[0].equiv.l ∨ val_stack[0].equiv.h) {
  fprintf(listing_file, "($%03d=#%08x", cur_greg, val_stack[0].equiv.h);
  flush_listing_line("␣␣␣␣");
  fprintf(listing_file, "␣␣␣␣␣␣␣␣␣%08x)", val_stack[0].equiv.l);
  flush_listing_line("␣");
} else {
  fprintf(listing_file, "($%03d)", cur_greg);
  flush_listing_line("␣␣␣␣␣␣␣␣␣␣␣␣␣");
}
```

This code is used in section 132.

135. Running the program. On a UNIX-like system, the command

```
mmixal [options] sourcefilename
```

will assemble the `MMIXAL` program in file `sourcefilename`, writing any error messages on the standard error file. (Nothing is written to the standard output.) The options, which may appear in any order, are:

- `-o objectfilename` Send the output to a binary file called `objectfilename`. If no `-o` specification is given, the object file name is obtained from the input file name by changing the final letter from '`s`' to '`o`', or by appending '`.mmo`' if `sourcefilename` doesn't end with `s`.
- `-l listingname` Output a listing of the assembled input and output to a text file called `listingname`.
- `-x` Expand memory-oriented commands that cannot be assembled as single instructions, by assembling auxiliary instructions that make temporary use of global register $255.
- `-b bufsize` Allow up to `bufsize` characters per line of input.

BSPEC = #104, §62.
bypass: label, §102.
cur_greg: **int**, §143.
cur_loc: **octa**, §43.
cur_prefix: **trie_node** *, §56.
equiv: **octa**, §82.
err = macro ( ), §45.
ESPEC = #105, §62.
false = 0, §26.
flush_listing_line: **void** ( ), §41.
fprintf: **int** ( ), `<stdio.h>`.
GREG = #106, §62.
h: **tetra**, §26.
IS = #101, §62.
l: **tetra**, §26.
link: **trie_node** *, §82.
listing_file: **FILE** *, §139.
LOC = #102, §62.
LOCAL = #107, §62.
lop_spec = #8, §24.
lreg: **int**, §143.
mmo_loc: **void** ( ), §49.
mmo_lopp: **void** ( ), §48.
mmo_sync: **void** ( ), §50.
octa = **struct**, §26.
opcode: **tetra**, §105.
PREFIX = #103, §62.
spec_mode: **bool**, §43.
spec_mode_loc: **tetra**, §43.
true = 1, §26.
val_stack: **val_node** *, §83.

136. Here, finally, is the overall structure of this program.

```
#include <stdio.h>
#include <stdlib.h>
#include <ctype.h>
#include <string.h>
#include <time.h>
  ⟨ Preprocessor definitions 31 ⟩
  ⟨ Type definitions 26 ⟩
  ⟨ Global variables 27 ⟩
  ⟨ Subroutines 28 ⟩
  int main(argc, argv)
      int argc; char *argv[];
  {
    register int j, k;     /* all-purpose integers */
    ⟨ Local variables 40 ⟩;
    ⟨ Process the command line 137 ⟩;
    ⟨ Initialize everything 29 ⟩;
    while (1) {
      ⟨ Get the next line of input text, or break if the input has ended 34 ⟩;
      while (1) {
        ⟨ Process the next MMIXAL instruction or comment 102 ⟩;
        if (¬*buf_ptr) break;
      }
      if (listing_file) {
        if (listing_bits) listing_clear();
        else if (¬line_listed) flush_listing_line("␣␣␣␣␣␣␣␣␣␣␣␣␣␣␣␣␣␣␣");
      }
    }
    ⟨ Finish the assembly 142 ⟩;
  }
```

137. The space after "-b" is optional, because MMIX-SIM does not use a space in this context.

```
⟨ Process the command line 137 ⟩ ≡
  for (j = 1; j < argc − 1 ∧ argv[j][0] ≡ '-'; j++)
    if (¬argv[j][2]) {
      if (argv[j][1] ≡ 'x') expanding = 1;
      else if (argv[j][1] ≡ 'o') j++, strcpy(obj_file_name, argv[j]);
      else if (argv[j][1] ≡ 'l') j++, strcpy(listing_name, argv[j]);
      else if (argv[j][1] ≡ 'b' ∧ sscanf(argv[j + 1], "%d", &buf_size) ≡ 1) j++;
      else break;
    } else if (argv[j][1] ≠ 'b' ∨ sscanf(argv[j] + 2, "%d", &buf_size) ≠ 1) break;
  if (j ≠ argc − 1) {
    fprintf(stderr, "Usage:␣%s␣%s␣sourcefilename\n", argv[0],
        "[-x]␣[-l␣listingname]␣[-b␣buffersize]␣[-o␣objectfilename]");
    exit(−1);
  }
```

```
src_file_name = argv[j];
```

This code is used in section 136.

138. ⟨ Open the files 138 ⟩ ≡

```
src_file = fopen(src_file_name, "r");
if (¬src_file) dpanic("Can't␣open␣the␣source␣file␣%s", src_file_name);
if (¬obj_file_name[0]) {
  j = strlen(src_file_name);
  if (src_file_name[j − 1] ≡ 's') {
    strcpy(obj_file_name, src_file_name); obj_file_name[j − 1] = 'o';
  }
  else sprintf(obj_file_name, "%s.mmo", src_file_name);
}
obj_file = fopen(obj_file_name, "wb");
if (¬obj_file) dpanic("Can't␣open␣the␣object␣file␣%s", obj_file_name);
if (listing_name[0]) {
  listing_file = fopen(listing_name, "w");
  if (¬listing_file) dpanic("Can't␣open␣the␣listing␣file␣%s", listing_name);
}
```

This code is used in section 140.

139. ⟨ Global variables 27 ⟩ +≡

```
char *src_file_name;    /* name of the MMIXAL input file */
char obj_file_name[FILENAME_MAX + 1];    /* name of the binary output file */
char listing_name[FILENAME_MAX + 1];    /* name of the optional listing file */
FILE *src_file, *obj_file, *listing_file;
int expanding;    /* are we expanding instructions when base address fail? */
int buf_size;    /* maximum number of characters per line of input */
```

140. ⟨ Initialize everything 29 ⟩ +≡

```
⟨ Open the files 138 ⟩;
filename[0] = src_file_name;
filename_count = 1;
⟨ Output the preamble 141 ⟩;
```

141. ⟨ Output the preamble 141 ⟩ ≡

```
mmo_lop(lop_pre, 1, 1);
mmo_tetra(time(Λ));
mmo_cur_file = −1;
```

This code is used in section 140.

---

buf_ptr: **Char** *, §33.
dpanic = macro ( ), §45.
exit: **void** ( ), <stdlib.h>.
FILE, <stdio.h>.
filename: **Char** *[ ], §37.
filename_count: **int**, §37.
FILENAME_MAX = macro, <stdio.h>.
flush_listing_line: **void** ( ), §41.
fopen: **FILE** *( ), <stdio.h>.
fprintf: **int** ( ), <stdio.h>.
line_listed: **bool**, §36.
listing_bits: **unsigned char**, §43.
listing_clear: **void** ( ), §44.
lop_pre = #9, §24.
mmo_cur_file: **int**, §51.
mmo_lop: **void** ( ), §48.
mmo_tetra: **void** ( ), §48.
sprintf: **int** ( ), <stdio.h>.
sscanf: **int** ( ), <stdio.h>.
stderr: **FILE** *, <stdio.h>.
strcpy: **char** *( ), <string.h>.
strlen: **size_t** ( ), <string.h>.
time: **time_t** ( ), <time.h>.

142. ⟨ Finish the assembly 142 ⟩ ≡

```
if (lreg ≥ greg)
   dpanic("Danger:␣Must␣reduce␣the␣number␣of␣GREGs␣by␣%d", lreg − greg + 1);
⟨ Output the postamble 144 ⟩;
⟨ Check and output the trie 80 ⟩;
⟨ Report any undefined local symbols 145 ⟩;
if (err_count) {
   if (err_count > 1) fprintf(stderr, "(%d␣errors␣were␣found.)\n", err_count);
   else fprintf(stderr, "(One␣error␣was␣found.)\n");
}
exit(err_count);
```

This code is used in section 136.

143. ⟨ Global variables 27 ⟩ +≡

```
int greg = 255;     /* global register allocator */
int cur_greg;     /* global register just allocated */
int lreg = 32;     /* local register allocator */
```

144. ⟨ Output the postamble 144 ⟩ ≡

```
mmo_lop(lop_post, 0, greg);
greg_val[255] = trie_search(trie_root, "Main")→sym→equiv;
for (j = greg; j < 256; j++) {
   mmo_tetra(greg_val[j].h);
   mmo_tetra(greg_val[j].l);
}
```

This code is used in section 142.

145. ⟨ Report any undefined local symbols 145 ⟩ ≡

```
for (j = 0; j < 10; j++)
   if (forward_local[j].link)
      err_count++, fprintf(stderr, "undefined␣local␣symbol␣%dF\n", j);
```

This code is used in section 142.

---

dpanic = macro ( ), §45.
equiv: **octa**, §58.
err_count: **int**, §46.
exit: **void** ( ), `<stdlib.h>`.
forward_local: **sym_node** [ ], §90.
fprintf: **int** ( ), `<stdio.h>`.
greg_val: **octa** [ ], §133.
h: **tetra**, §26.
j: **register int**, §136.
l: **tetra**, §26.
link: **sym_node** ∗, §58.
lop_post = #**a**, §24.
mmo_lop: **void** ( ), §48.
mmo_tetra: **void** ( ), §48.
stderr: **FILE** ∗, `<stdio.h>`.
sym: **sym_node** ∗, §54.
trie_root: **trie_node** ∗, §56.
trie_search: **trie_node** ∗( ), §57.

146. Names of the sections.

⟨ Open the files 138 ⟩ Used in section 140.
⟨ Output the postamble 144 ⟩ Used in section 142.
⟨ Output the preamble 141 ⟩ Used in section 140.
⟨ Perform the top operation on *op_stack* 98 ⟩ Used in section 85.
⟨ Preprocessor definitions 31, 39 ⟩ Used in section 136.
⟨ Print symbol *sym_buf* and its equivalent 78 ⟩ Used in section 75.
⟨ Process the command line 137 ⟩ Used in section 136.
⟨ Process the next `MMIXAL` instruction or comment 102 ⟩ Used in section 136.
⟨ Put other predefined symbols into the trie 70 ⟩ Used in section 61.
⟨ Put the `MMIX` opcodes and `MMIXAL` pseudo-ops into the trie 64 ⟩ Used in section 61.
⟨ Put the special register names into the trie 66 ⟩ Used in section 61.
⟨ Report an undefined symbol 79 ⟩ Used in section 74.
⟨ Report any undefined local symbols 145 ⟩ Used in section 142.
⟨ Scan a backward local 89 ⟩ Used in section 86.
⟨ Scan a binary operator or closing token, *rt_op* 97 ⟩ Used in section 85.
⟨ Scan a character constant 92 ⟩ Used in section 86.
⟨ Scan a decimal constant 94 ⟩ Used in section 86.
⟨ Scan a forward local 88 ⟩ Used in section 86.
⟨ Scan a hexadecimal constant 95 ⟩ Used in section 86.
⟨ Scan a string constant 93 ⟩ Used in section 86.
⟨ Scan a symbol 87 ⟩ Used in section 86.
⟨ Scan opening tokens until putting something on *val_stack* 86 ⟩ Used in section 85.
⟨ Scan the current location 96 ⟩ Used in section 86.
⟨ Scan the label field; **goto** *bypass* if there is none 103 ⟩ Used in section 102.
⟨ Scan the opcode field; **goto** *bypass* if there is none 104 ⟩ Used in section 102.
⟨ Scan the operand field 85 ⟩ Used in section 102.
⟨ Subroutines 28, 41, 42, 44, 45, 47, 48, 49, 50, 52, 55, 57, 59, 73, 74 ⟩ Used in section 136.
⟨ Type definitions 26, 30, 54, 58, 62, 68, 82 ⟩ Used in section 136.
⟨ Visit t and traverse $t\to mid$ 75 ⟩ Used in section 74.

MMMIX

1. Introduction. This CWEB program simulates how the MMIX computer might be implemented with a high-performance pipeline in many different configurations. All of the complexities of MMIX's architecture are treated, except for multiprocessing and low-level details of memory mapped input/output.

The present program module, which contains the main routine for the MMIX meta-simulator, is primarily devoted to administrative tasks. Other modules do the actual work after this module has told them what to do.

2. A user typically invokes the meta-simulator with a UNIX-like command line of the general form '`mmmix configfile progfile`', where the `configfile` describes the characteristics of an MMIX implementation and the `progfile` contains a program to be downloaded and run. Rules for configuration files appear in the module called `mmix-config`. The program file is either an "MMIX binary file" dumped by MMIX-SIM, or an ASCII text file that describes hexadecimal data in a rudimentary format. It is assumed to be binary if its name ends with the extension '`.mmb`'.

```
#include <stdio.h>
#include <stdlib.h>
#include <string.h>
#include "mmix-pipe.h"
  char *config_file_name, *prog_file_name;
  ⟨ Global variables 5 ⟩
  ⟨ Subroutines 10 ⟩
  int main(argc, argv)
      int argc;
      char *argv[];
  {
    ⟨ Parse the command line 3 ⟩;
    MMIX_config(config_file_name);
    MMIX_init();
    mmix_io_init();
    ⟨ Input the program 4 ⟩;
    ⟨ Run the simulation interactively 13 ⟩;
    printf("Simulation␣ended␣at␣time␣%d.\n", ticks.l);
    print_stats();
    return 0;
  }
```

3. The command line might also contain options, some day. For now I'm forgetting them and simplifying everything until I gain further experience.

```
⟨ Parse the command line 3 ⟩ ≡
  if (argc ≠ 3) {
    fprintf(stderr, "Usage:␣%s␣configfile␣progfile\n", argv[0]);
    exit(−3);
  }
  config_file_name = argv[1];
```

D.E. Knuth: MMIXware, LNCS 1750, pp. 494–509, 2014.
DOI: 10.1007/3-540-46611-8_10

prog_file_name = *argv*[2];

This code is used in section 2.

4. ⟨Input the program 4⟩ ≡

if (*strlen*(*prog_file_name*) > 4 ∧ *strcmp*(*prog_file_name* + *strlen*(*prog_file_name*) − 4, ".mmb") ≡ 0) ⟨Input an MMIX binary file 9⟩

else ⟨Input a rudimentary hexadecimal file 6⟩;

fclose(*prog_file*);

This code is used in section 2.

exit: **void** (), <stdlib.h>.
fclose: **int** (), <stdio.h>.
fprintf: **int** (), <stdio.h>.
l: **tetra**, MMIX-PIPE §17.
MMIX_config: **void** (), MMIX-CONFIG §38.
MMIX_init: **void** (), MMIX-PIPE §10.
mmix_io_init: **void** (), MMIX-IO §7.
print_stats: **void** (), MMIX-PIPE §162.
printf: **int** (), <stdio.h>.
prog_file: **FILE** *, §5.
stderr: **FILE** *, <stdio.h>.
strcmp: **int** (), <string.h>.
strlen: **size_t** (), <string.h>.
ticks: **Extern octa**, MMIX-PIPE §87.

5. Hexadecimal input to memory. A rudimentary hexadecimal input format is implemented here so that the simulator can be run with essentially arbitrary data in the simulated memory. The rules of this format are extremely simple: Each line of the file either begins with (i) 12 hexadecimal digits followed by a colon; or (ii) a space followed by 16 hexadecimal digits. In case (i), the 12 hex digits specify a 48-bit physical address, called the current location. In case (ii), the 16 hex digits specify an octabyte to be stored in the current location; the current location is then increased by 8. The current location should be a multiple of 8, but its three least significant bits are actually ignored. Arbitrary comments can follow the specification of a new current location or a new octabyte, as long as each line is less than 99 characters long. For example, the file

```
0123456789ab:  SILLY EXAMPLE
 0123456789abcdef first octabyte
 fedbca9876543210 second
```

places the octabyte #`0123456789abcdef` into memory location #`0123456789a8` and #`fedcba9876543210` into location #`0123456789b0`.

```
#define BUF_SIZE 100
⟨ Global variables 5 ⟩ ≡
  octa cur_loc;
  octa cur_dat;
  bool new_chunk;
  char buffer[BUF_SIZE];
  FILE *prog_file;
```

See also sections 16 and 25.

This code is used in section 2.

6. ⟨ Input a rudimentary hexadecimal file 6 ⟩ ≡

```
{
  prog_file = fopen(prog_file_name, "r");
  if (¬prog_file) {
    fprintf(stderr, "Panic:␣Can't␣open␣MMIX␣hexadecimal␣file␣%s!\n",
        prog_file_name);
    exit(−3);
  }
  new_chunk = true;
  while (1) {
    if (¬fgets(buffer, BUF_SIZE, prog_file)) break;
    if (buffer[strlen(buffer) − 1] ≠ '\n') {
      fprintf(stderr, "Panic:␣Hexadecimal␣file␣line␣too␣long:␣'%s...'!\n", buffer);
      exit(−3);
    }
```

```
      if (buffer[12] ≡ ':') ⟨Change the current location 7⟩
      else if (buffer[0] ≡ '␣') ⟨Read an octabyte and advance cur_loc 8⟩
      else {
        fprintf(stderr, "Panic:␣Improper␣hexadecimal␣file␣line:␣`%s'!\n", buffer);
        exit(−3);
      }
    }
  }
```

This code is used in section 4.

7. ⟨Change the current location 7⟩ ≡

```
  {
    if (sscanf(buffer, "%4x%8x", &cur_loc.h, &cur_loc.l) ≠ 2) {
      fprintf(stderr, "Panic:␣Improper␣hexadecimal␣file␣location:␣`%s'!\n", buffer);
      exit(−3);
    }
    new_chunk = true;
  }
```

This code is used in section 6.

8. ⟨Read an octabyte and advance *cur_loc* 8⟩ ≡

```
  {
    if (sscanf(buffer + 1, "%8x%8x", &cur_dat.h, &cur_dat.l) ≠ 2) {
      fprintf(stderr, "Panic:␣Improper␣hexadecimal␣file␣data:␣`%s'!\n", buffer);
      exit(−3);
    }
    if (new_chunk) mem_write(cur_loc, cur_dat);
    else mem_hash[last_h].chunk[(cur_loc.l & #ffff) ≫ 3] = cur_dat;
    cur_loc.l += 8;
    if ((cur_loc.l & #fff8) ≠ 0) new_chunk = false;
    else {
      new_chunk = true;
      if ((cur_loc.l & #ffff0000) ≡ 0) cur_loc.h++;
    }
  }
```

This code is used in section 6.

---

bool = **enum**, MMIX-PIPE §11.
chunk: **octa** ∗, MMIX-PIPE §206.
exit: **void** ( ), <stdlib.h>.
false = 0, MMIX-PIPE §11.
fgets: **char** ∗( ), <stdio.h>.
FILE, <stdio.h>.
fopen: **FILE** ∗( ), <stdio.h>.
fprintf: **int** ( ), <stdio.h>.
h: **tetra**, MMIX-PIPE §17.
l: **tetra**, MMIX-PIPE §17.
last_h: **int**, MMIX-PIPE §211.
mem_hash: **chunknode** ∗, MMIX-PIPE §207.
mem_write: **void** ( ), MMIX-PIPE §213.
octa = **struct**, MMIX-PIPE §17.
prog_file_name, §2.
sscanf: **int** ( ), <stdio.h>.
stderr: **FILE** ∗, <stdio.h>.
strlen: **size_t** ( ), <string.h>.
true = 1, MMIX-PIPE §11.

9. Binary input to memory. When the program file was dumped by MMIX-SIM, it has the simple format discussed in exercise 1.4.3′–20 of the MMIX fascicle [*The Art of Computer Programming*, Volume 1, Fascicle 1]. We assume that such a program has text, data, pool, and stack segments, as in the conventions of that book. We load it into four 2^{32}-byte pages of physical memory, one for each segment; page zero of segment i is mapped to physical location $2^{32}i$. Page tables are kept in physical locations starting at $2^{32}\times 4$; static traps begin at $2^{32}\times 5$ and dynamic traps at $2^{32}\times 6$. (These conventions agree with the special register settings rT = #8000000500000000, rTT = #8000000600000000, rV = #369c200400000000 assumed by the stripped-down simulator.)

```
⟨ Input an MMIX binary file 9 ⟩ ≡
  {
    prog_file = fopen(prog_file_name, "rb");
    if (¬prog_file) {
      fprintf(stderr, "Panic:␣Can't␣open␣MMIX␣binary␣file␣%s!\n", prog_file_name);
      exit(−3);
    }
    while (1) {
      if (¬undump_octa()) break;
      new_chunk = true;
      cur_loc = cur_dat;
      if (cur_loc.h & #9fffffff) bad_address = true;
      else bad_address = false, cur_loc.h ≫= 29;
          /* apply trivial mapping function for each segment */
      ⟨ Input consecutive octabytes beginning at cur_loc 11 ⟩;
    }
    ⟨ Set up the canned environment 12 ⟩;
  }
```

This code is used in section 4.

10. The *undump_octa* routine reads eight bytes from the binary file *prog_file* into the global octabyte *cur_dat*, taking care as usual to be big-endian regardless of the host computer's bias.

```
⟨ Subroutines 10 ⟩ ≡
  static bool undump_octa ARGS((void));
  static bool undump_octa()
  {
    register int t0, t1, t2, t3;
    t0 = fgetc(prog_file); if (t0 ≡ EOF) return false;
    t1 = fgetc(prog_file); if (t1 ≡ EOF) goto oops;
    t2 = fgetc(prog_file); if (t2 ≡ EOF) goto oops;
    t3 = fgetc(prog_file); if (t3 ≡ EOF) goto oops;
    cur_dat.h = (t0 ≪ 24) + (t1 ≪ 16) + (t2 ≪ 8) + t3;
    t0 = fgetc(prog_file); if (t0 ≡ EOF) goto oops;
    t1 = fgetc(prog_file); if (t1 ≡ EOF) goto oops;
    t2 = fgetc(prog_file); if (t2 ≡ EOF) goto oops;
    t3 = fgetc(prog_file); if (t3 ≡ EOF) goto oops;
    cur_dat.l = (t0 ≪ 24) + (t1 ≪ 16) + (t2 ≪ 8) + t3;
```

```
    return true;
  oops: fprintf(stderr, "Premature␣end␣of␣file␣on␣%s!\n", prog_file_name);
    return false;
  }
```

See also sections 17 and 20.

This code is used in section 2.

11. ⟨Input consecutive octabytes beginning at *cur_loc* 11⟩ ≡

```
  while (1) {
    if (¬undump_octa()) {
      fprintf(stderr, "Unexpected␣end␣of␣file␣on␣%s!\n", prog_file_name);
      break;
    }
    if (¬(cur_dat.h ∨ cur_dat.l)) break;
    if (bad_address) {
      fprintf(stderr, "Panic:␣Unsupported␣virtual␣address␣%08x%08x!\n", cur_loc.h,
          cur_loc.l);
      exit(−5);
    }
    if (new_chunk) mem_write(cur_loc, cur_dat);
    else mem_hash[last_h].chunk[(cur_loc.l & #ffff) ≫ 3] = cur_dat;
    cur_loc.l += 8;
    if ((cur_loc.l & #fff8) ≠ 0) new_chunk = false;
    else {
      new_chunk = true;
      if ((cur_loc.l & #ffff0000) ≡ 0) {
        bad_address = true;
        cur_loc.h = (cur_loc.h ≪ 29) + 1;
      }
    }
  }
```

This code is used in section 9.

ARGS = macro ( ), MMIX-PIPE §6.
bad_address: **bool**, §25.
bool = **enum**, MMIX-PIPE §11.
chunk: **octa** ∗, MMIX-PIPE §206.
cur_dat: **octa**, §5.
cur_loc: **octa**, §5.
EOF = (−1), <stdio.h>.
exit: **void** ( ), <stdlib.h>.
false = 0, MMIX-PIPE §11.
fgetc: **int** ( ), <stdio.h>.
fopen: **FILE** ∗( ), <stdio.h>.
fprintf: **int** ( ), <stdio.h>.
h: **tetra**, MMIX-PIPE §17.
l: **tetra**, MMIX-PIPE §17.
last_h: **int**, MMIX-PIPE §211.
mem_hash: **chunknode** ∗, MMIX-PIPE §207.
mem_write: **void** ( ), MMIX-PIPE §213.
new_chunk: **bool**, §5.
prog_file: **FILE** ∗, §5.
prog_file_name, §2.
stderr: **FILE** ∗, <stdio.h>.
true = 1, MMIX-PIPE §11.

12. The primitive operating system assumed in simple programs of *The Art of Computer Programming* will set up text segment, data segment, pool segment, and stack segment as in MMIX-SIM. The runtime stack will be initialized if we `UNSAVE` from the last location loaded in the `.mmb` file.

```
#define rQ 16

⟨Set up the canned environment 12⟩ ≡
  if (cur_loc.h ≠ 3) {
    fprintf(stderr, "Panic:␣MMIX␣binary␣file␣didn't␣set␣up␣the␣stack!\n");
    exit(−6);
  }
  inst_ptr.o = mem_read(incr(cur_loc, −8 ∗ 14));   /∗ Main ∗/
  inst_ptr.p = Λ;
  cur_loc.h = #60000000;
  g[255].o = incr(cur_loc, −8);   /∗ place to UNSAVE ∗/
  cur_dat.l = #90;
  if (mem_read(cur_dat).h) inst_ptr.o = cur_dat;   /∗ start at #90 if nonzero ∗/
  head→inst = (UNSAVE ≪ 24) + 255, tail−−;   /∗ prefetch a fabricated command ∗/
  head→loc = incr(inst_ptr.o, −4);   /∗ in case the UNSAVE is interrupted ∗/
  g[rT].o.h = #80000005, g[rTT].o.h = #80000006;
  cur_dat.h = (RESUME ≪ 24) + 1, cur_dat.l = 0, cur_loc.h = 5, cur_loc.l = 0;
  mem_write(cur_loc, cur_dat);   /∗ the primitive trap handler ∗/
  cur_dat.l = cur_dat.h, cur_dat.h = (NEGI ≪ 24) + (255 ≪ 16) + 1;
  cur_loc.h = 6, cur_loc.l = 8;
  mem_write(cur_loc, cur_dat);   /∗ the primitive dynamic trap handler ∗/
  cur_dat.h = (GET ≪ 24) + rQ, cur_dat.l = (PUTI ≪ 24) + (rQ ≪ 16), cur_loc.l = 0;
  mem_write(cur_loc, cur_dat);   /∗ more of the primitive dynamic trap handler ∗/
  cur_dat.h = 0, cur_dat.l = 7;   /∗ generate a PTE with rwx permission ∗/
  cur_loc.h = 4;   /∗ beginning of skeleton page table ∗/
  mem_write(cur_loc, cur_dat);   /∗ PTE for the text segment ∗/
  ITcache→set[0][0].tag = zero_octa;
  ITcache→set[0][0].data[0] = cur_dat;   /∗ prime the IT cache ∗/
  cur_dat.l = 6;   /∗ PTE with read and write permission only ∗/
  cur_dat.h = 1, cur_loc.l = 3 ≪ 13;
  mem_write(cur_loc, cur_dat);   /∗ PTE for the data segment ∗/
  cur_dat.h = 2, cur_loc.l = 6 ≪ 13;
  mem_write(cur_loc, cur_dat);   /∗ PTE for the pool segment ∗/
  cur_dat.h = 3, cur_loc.l = 9 ≪ 13;
  mem_write(cur_loc, cur_dat);   /∗ PTE for the stack segment ∗/
  g[rK].o = neg_one;   /∗ enable all interrupts ∗/
  g[rV].o.h = #369c2004;
  page_bad = false, page_r = 4 ≪ (32 − 13), page_s = 32, page_mask.l = #ffffffff;
  page_b[1] = 3, page_b[2] = 6, page_b[3] = 9, page_b[4] = 12;
```

This code is used in section 9.

cur_dat: **octa**, §5.
cur_loc: **octa**, §5.
data: **octa** *, MMIX-PIPE §167.
exit: **void** (), `<stdlib.h>`.
false = 0, MMIX-PIPE §11.
fprintf: **int** (), `<stdio.h>`.
g: **int**, MMIX-PIPE §167.
GET = #fe, MMIX-PIPE §47.
h: **tetra**, MMIX-PIPE §17.
head: **fetch** *, MMIX-PIPE §69.
incr: **octa** (), MMIX-ARITH §6.
inst: **tetra**, MMIX-PIPE §68.
inst_ptr: **spec**, MMIX-PIPE §284.
ITcache: **cache** *, MMIX-PIPE §168.
l: **tetra**, MMIX-PIPE §17.
loc: **octa**, MMIX-PIPE §44.
mem_read: **octa** (), MMIX-PIPE §210.
mem_write: **void** (), MMIX-PIPE §213.
neg_one: **octa**, MMIX-ARITH §4.
NEGI = #35, MMIX-PIPE §47.
o: **octa**, MMIX-PIPE §40.
p: **specnode** *, MMIX-PIPE §40.
page_b: **int** [], MMIX-PIPE §238.
page_bad: **bool**, MMIX-PIPE §238.
page_mask: **octa**, MMIX-PIPE §238.
page_r: **int**, MMIX-PIPE §238.
page_s: **int**, MMIX-PIPE §238.
PUTI = #f7, MMIX-PIPE §47.
RESUME = #f9, MMIX-PIPE §47.
$rK = 15$, MMIX-PIPE §52.
$rT = 13$, MMIX-PIPE §52.
$rTT = 14$, MMIX-PIPE §52.
$rV = 18$, MMIX-PIPE §52.
set: **cacheset** *, MMIX-PIPE §167.
stderr: **FILE** *, `<stdio.h>`.
tag: **octa**, MMIX-PIPE §167.
tail: **fetch** *, MMIX-PIPE §69.
UNSAVE = #fb, MMIX-PIPE §47.
zero_octa: **octa**, MMIX-ARITH §4.

13. Interaction. When prompted for instructions, this simulator understands the following terse commands:

- ⟨ positive integer ⟩: Run for this many clock cycles.
- `@`⟨ hexadecimal integer ⟩: Set the instruction pointer to this virtual address; successive instructions will be fetched from here.
- `k`: Toggle the sign bit of the instruction pointer.
- `b`⟨ hexadecimal integer ⟩: Set the breakpoint to this virtual address; simulation will pause when an instruction from the breakpoint address enters the fetch buffer.
- `v`⟨ hexadecimal integer ⟩: Set the desired level of diagnostic output; each bit in the hexadecimal integer enables certain printouts when the simulator is running. Bit #`1` shows instructions when issued, deissued, or committed; #`2` shows the pipeline and locks after each cycle; #`4` shows each coroutine activation; #`8` each coroutine scheduling; #`10` reports when reading from an uninitialized chunk of memory; #`20` asks for online input when reading from addresses $\geq 2^{48}$; #`40` reports all I/O to memory address $\geq 2^{48}$; #`80` shows details of branch prediction; #`100` displays full cache contents including blocks with invalid tags.
- `-`⟨ integer ⟩: Deissue this many instructions.
- `l`⟨ integer ⟩ or `g`⟨ integer ⟩: Show current "hot" contents of a local or global register.
- `m`⟨ hexadecimal integer ⟩: Show current contents of a physical memory address. (This value may not be up to date; newer values might appear in the write buffer and/or in the caches.)
- `f`⟨ hexadecimal integer ⟩: Insert a tetrabyte into the fetch buffer. (Use with care!)
- `i`⟨ integer ⟩: Set the interval counter rI to the given value; this will trigger an interrupt after the specified number of cycles.
- `IT`, `DT`, `I`, `D`, or `S`: Show current contents of a cache.
- `D*` or `S*`: Show dirty blocks of a cache.
- `p`: Show current contents of the pipeline.
- `s`: Show current statistics on branch prediction and speed of instruction issue.
- `h`: Help (show the possibilities for interaction).
- `q`: Quit.

```
⟨ Run the simulation interactively 13 ⟩ ≡
  while (1) {
    printf("mmmix>␣"); fflush(stdout);
    fgets(buffer, BUF_SIZE, stdin);
    switch (buffer[0]) {
    default: what_say:
      printf("Eh?␣Sorry,␣I␣don't␣understand.␣(Type␣h␣for␣help)\n");
      continue;
    case 'q': case 'x': goto done;
      ⟨ Cases for interaction 14 ⟩
    }
  }
```

done:

This code is used in section 2.

14. ⟨ Cases for interaction 14 ⟩ ≡

```
case 'h': case '?': printf("The␣interactive␣commands␣are␣as␣follows:\n");
  printf("␣<n>␣to␣run␣for␣n␣cycles\n");
  printf("␣@<x>␣to␣take␣next␣instruction␣from␣location␣x\n");
  printf("␣k␣␣␣␣to␣change␣the␣sign␣bit␣of␣the␣instruction␣location\n");
  printf("␣b<x>␣to␣pause␣when␣location␣x␣is␣fetched\n");
  printf("␣v<x>␣to␣print␣specified␣diagnostics␣when␣running;\n");
  printf("␣␣␣␣x=1[insts␣enter/leave␣pipe]+2[whole␣pipeline␣each␣cycle]+\n");
  printf("␣␣␣␣␣␣4[coroutine␣activations]+8[coroutine␣scheduling]+\n");
  printf("␣␣␣␣␣␣10[uninitialized␣read]+20[online␣I/O␣read]+\n");
  printf("␣␣␣␣␣␣40[I/O␣read/write]+80[branch␣prediction␣details]+\n");
  printf("␣␣␣␣␣␣100[invalid␣cache␣blocks␣displayed␣too]\n");
  printf("␣-<n>␣to␣deissue␣n␣instructions\n");
  printf("␣l<n>␣to␣print␣current␣value␣of␣local␣register␣n\n");
  printf("␣g<n>␣to␣print␣current␣value␣of␣global␣register␣n\n");
  printf("␣m<x>␣to␣print␣current␣value␣of␣memory␣address␣x\n");
  printf("␣f<x>␣to␣insert␣instruction␣x␣into␣the␣fetch␣buffer\n");
  printf("␣i<n>␣to␣initiate␣a␣timer␣interrupt␣after␣n␣cycles\n");
  printf("␣IT,␣DT,␣I,␣D,␣or␣S␣to␣print␣current␣cache␣contents\n");
  printf("␣D*␣or␣S*␣to␣print␣dirty␣blocks␣of␣a␣cache\n");
  printf("␣p␣to␣print␣current␣pipeline␣contents\n");
  printf("␣s␣to␣print␣current␣stats\n");
  printf("␣h␣to␣print␣this␣message\n");
  printf("␣q␣to␣exit\n");
  printf("(Here␣<n>␣is␣a␣decimal␣integer,␣<x>␣is␣hexadecimal.)\n");
  continue;
```

See also sections 15, 18, 19, 21, 22, 23, and 24.

This code is used in section 13.

BUF_SIZE = 100, §5.
buffer: **char** [ ], §5.
fflush: **int** ( ), <stdio.h>.
fgets: **char** *( ), <stdio.h>.
printf: **int** ( ), <stdio.h>.
stdin: **FILE** *, <stdio.h>.
stdout: **FILE** *, <stdio.h>.

15. ⟨ Cases for interaction 14 ⟩ +≡

```
case '0': case '1': case '2': case '3': case '4': case '5': case '6': case '7':
  case '8': case '9':
  if (sscanf(buffer, "%d", &n) ≠ 1) goto what_say;
  printf("Running␣%d␣at␣time␣%d", n, ticks.l);
  if (bp.h ≡ (tetra) −1 ∧ bp.l ≡ (tetra) −1) printf("\n");
  else printf("␣with␣breakpoint␣%08x%08x\n", bp.h, bp.l);
  MMIX_run(n, bp); continue;
case '@': inst_ptr.o = read_hex(buffer + 1); goto new_inst_ptr;
case 'k': inst_ptr.o.h ⊕= #80000000;    /* shortcut to kernel mode */
  if (¬ticks.l ∧ head) head→loc.h ⊕= #80000000;    /* fix the UNSAVE loc */
new_inst_ptr: if (inst_ptr.o.h & #80000000) g[rK].o.h &= −2;
      /* disable interrupts on P_BIT */
  inst_ptr.p = Λ; continue;
case 'b': bp = read_hex(buffer + 1); continue;
case 'v': verbose = read_hex(buffer + 1).l; continue;
```

16. ⟨ Global variables 5 ⟩ +≡

```
  int n, m;    /* temporary integer */
  octa bp = {−1, −1};    /* breakpoint */
  octa tmp;    /* an octabyte of temporary interest */
  static unsigned char d[BUF_SIZE];
```

17. Here's a simple program to read an octabyte in hexadecimal notation from a buffer. It changes the buffer by storing a null character after the input.

⟨ Subroutines 10 ⟩ +≡

```
  octa read_hex ARGS((char *));
  octa read_hex(p)
      char *p;
  {
    register int j, k;
    octa val;

    val.h = val.l = 0;
    for (j = 0; ; j++) {
      if (p[j] ≥ '0' ∧ p[j] ≤ '9') d[j] = p[j] − '0';
      else if (p[j] ≥ 'a' ∧ p[j] ≤ 'f') d[j] = p[j] − 'a' + 10;
      else if (p[j] ≥ 'A' ∧ p[j] ≤ 'F') d[j] = p[j] − 'A' + 10;
      else break;
    }
    p[j] = '\0';
    for (j−−, k = 0; k ≤ j; k++) {
      if (k ≥ 8) val.h += d[j − k] ≪ (4 * k − 32);
      else val.l += d[j − k] ≪ (4 * k);
    }
    return val;
  }
```

18. ⟨ Cases for interaction 14 ⟩ +≡

```
case '-': if (sscanf(buffer + 1, "%d", &n) ≠ 1 ∨ n < 0) goto what_say;
  if (cool ≤ hot) m = hot − cool; else m = (hot − reorder_bot) + 1 + (reorder_top − cool);
```

```
  if (n > m) deissues = m; else deissues = n;
  continue;
case 'l': if (sscanf(buffer + 1, "%d", &n) ≠ 1 ∨ n < 0) goto what_say;
  if (n ≥ lring_size) goto what_say;
  printf("␣␣l[%d]=%08x%08x\n", n, l[n].o.h, l[n].o.l); continue;
case 'm': tmp = mem_read(read_hex(buffer + 1));
  printf("␣␣m[%s]=%08x%08x\n", buffer + 1, tmp.h, tmp.l); continue;
```

19. The register stack pointers, rO and rS, are not kept up to date in the g array. Therefore we have to deduce their values by examining the pipeline.

```
⟨ Cases for interaction 14 ⟩ +≡
case 'g': if (sscanf(buffer + 1, "%d", &n) ≠ 1 ∨ n < 0) goto what_say;
  if (n ≥ 256) goto what_say;
  if (n ≡ rO ∨ n ≡ rS) {
    if (hot ≡ cool)     /* pipeline empty */
      g[rO].o = sl3(cool_O), g[rS].o = sl3(cool_S);
    else g[rO].o = sl3(hot→cur_O), g[rS].o = sl3(hot→cur_S);
  }
  printf("␣␣g[%d]=%08x%08x\n", n, g[n].o.h, g[n].o.l);
  continue;
```

20. ⟨ Subroutines 10 ⟩ +≡

```
  static octa sl3 ARGS((octa));
  static octa sl3(y)     /* shift left by 3 bits */
      octa y;
  {
    register tetra yhl = y.h ≪ 3, ylh = y.l ≫ 29;
    y.h = yhl + ylh; y.l ≪= 3;
    return y;
  }
```

ARGS = macro ( ), MMIX-PIPE §6.
BUF_SIZE = 100, §5.
buffer: **char** [ ], §5.
cool: **control** ∗, MMIX-PIPE §60.
cool_O: **octa**, MMIX-PIPE §98.
cool_S: **octa**, MMIX-PIPE §98.
cur_O: **octa**, MMIX-PIPE §44.
cur_S: **octa**, MMIX-PIPE §44.
deissues: **int**, MMIX-PIPE §60.
g: **int**, MMIX-PIPE §167.
h: **tetra**, MMIX-PIPE §17.
head: **fetch** ∗, MMIX-PIPE §69.
hot: **control** ∗, MMIX-PIPE §60.
inst_ptr: **spec**, MMIX-PIPE §284.
l: **tetra**, MMIX-PIPE §17.
loc: **octa**, MMIX-PIPE §44.
lring_size: **int**, MMIX-PIPE §86.
mem_read: **octa** ( ), MMIX-PIPE §210.
MMIX_run: **void** ( ), MMIX-PIPE §10.
o: **octa**, MMIX-PIPE §40.
octa = **struct**, MMIX-PIPE §17.
p: **specnode** ∗, MMIX-PIPE §40.
P_BIT = 1 ≪ 0, MMIX-PIPE §54.
printf: **int** ( ), <stdio.h>.
reorder_bot: **control** ∗, MMIX-PIPE §60.
reorder_top: **control** ∗, MMIX-PIPE §60.
rK = 15, MMIX-PIPE §52.
rO = 10, MMIX-PIPE §52.
rS = 11, MMIX-PIPE §52.
sscanf: **int** ( ), <stdio.h>.
tetra = **unsigned int**, MMIX-PIPE §17.
ticks: **Extern octa**, MMIX-PIPE §87.
verbose: **int**, MMIX-PIPE §4.
what_say: label, §13.

21. ⟨ Cases for interaction 14 ⟩ +≡

```
case 'I': print_cache(buffer[1] ≡ 'T' ? ITcache : Icache, false); continue;
case 'D': print_cache(buffer[1] ≡ 'T' ? DTcache : Dcache,
  buffer[1] ≡ '*'); continue;
case 'S': print_cache(Scache, buffer[1] ≡ '*'); continue;
case 'p': print_pipe(); print_locks(); continue;
case 's': print_stats(); continue;
case 'i': if (sscanf(buffer + 1, "%d", &n) ≡ 1) g[rI].o = incr(zero_octa, n);
  continue;
```

22. ⟨ Cases for interaction 14 ⟩ +≡

```
case 'f': tmp = read_hex(buffer + 1);
  {
    register fetch *new_tail;
    if (tail ≡ fetch_bot) new_tail = fetch_top;
    else new_tail = tail − 1;
    if (new_tail ≡ head) printf("Sorry,␣the␣fetch␣buffer␣is␣full!\n");
    else {
      tail→loc = inst_ptr.o;
      tail→inst = tmp.l;
      tail→interrupt = 0;
      tail→noted = false;
      tail = new_tail;
    }
    continue;
  }
```

23. A hidden case here, for me when debugging. It essentially disables the translation caches, by mapping everything to zero.

⟨ Cases for interaction 14 ⟩ +≡

```
case 'd': if (ticks.l)
    printf("Sorry:␣I␣disable␣ITcache␣and␣DTcache␣only␣at␣the␣beginning!\n");
  else {
    ITcache→set[0][0].tag = zero_octa;
    ITcache→set[0][0].data[0] = seven_octa;
    DTcache→set[0][0].tag = zero_octa;
    DTcache→set[0][0].data[0] = seven_octa;
    g[rK].o = neg_one;
    page_bad = false;
    page_mask = neg_one;
    inst_ptr.p = (specnode *) 1;
  } continue;
```

24. And another case, for me when kludging. At the moment, it simply lists the functional unit names.

But I might decide to put other stuff here when giving a demo.

```
⟨ Cases for interaction 14 ⟩ +≡
case '!': {
    register int j;
    for (j = 0; j < funit_count; j++) printf("unit %s %d\n", funit[j].name, funit[j].k);
  }
  continue;
```

25. ⟨ Global variables 5 ⟩ +≡

```
  bool bad_address;
  extern bool page_bad;
  extern octa page_mask;
  extern int page_r, page_s, page_b[5];
  extern octa zero_octa;
  extern octa neg_one;
  octa seven_octa = {0, 7};
  extern octa incr ARGS((octa y, int delta));     /* unsigned y + δ (δ is signed) */
  extern void mmix_io_init ARGS((void));
  extern void MMIX_config ARGS((char *));
```

ARGS = macro ( ), MMIX-PIPE §6.
bool = **enum**, MMIX-PIPE §11.
buffer: **char** [ ], §5.
data: **octa** *, MMIX-PIPE §167.
Dcache: **cache** *, MMIX-PIPE §168.
DTcache: **cache** *, MMIX-PIPE §168.
false = 0, MMIX-PIPE §11.
fetch = **struct**, MMIX-PIPE §68.
fetch_bot: **fetch** *, MMIX-PIPE §69.
fetch_top: **fetch** *, MMIX-PIPE §69.
funit: **func** *, MMIX-PIPE §77.
funit_count: **int**, MMIX-PIPE §77.
g: **int**, MMIX-PIPE §167.
head: **fetch** *, MMIX-PIPE §69.
Icache: **cache** *, MMIX-PIPE §168.
incr: **octa** ( ), MMIX-ARITH §6.
inst: **tetra**, MMIX-PIPE §68.
inst_ptr: **spec**, MMIX-PIPE §284.
interrupt: **unsigned int**, MMIX-PIPE §68.
ITcache: **cache** *, MMIX-PIPE §168.
k: **register int**, §17.
l: **tetra**, MMIX-PIPE §17.
loc: **octa**, MMIX-PIPE §44.
MMIX_config: **void** ( ), MMIX-CONFIG §38.
mmix_io_init: **void** ( ), MMIX-IO §7.
n: **int**, §16.
name: **char** *, MMIX-PIPE §167.
neg_one: **octa**, MMIX-ARITH §4.
noted: **bool**, MMIX-PIPE §68.
o: **octa**, MMIX-PIPE §40.
octa = **struct**, MMIX-PIPE §17.
p: **specnode** *, MMIX-PIPE §40.
page_b: **int** [ ], MMIX-PIPE §238.
page_bad: **bool**, MMIX-PIPE §238.
page_mask: **octa**, MMIX-PIPE §238.
page_r: **int**, MMIX-PIPE §238.
page_s: **int**, MMIX-PIPE §238.
print_cache: **void** ( ), MMIX-PIPE §176.
print_locks: **void** ( ), MMIX-PIPE §39.
print_pipe: **void** ( ), MMIX-PIPE §253.
print_stats: **void** ( ), MMIX-PIPE §162.
printf: **int** ( ), <stdio.h>.
read_hex: **octa** ( ), §17.
rI = 12, MMIX-PIPE §52.
rK = 15, MMIX-PIPE §52.
Scache: **cache** *, MMIX-PIPE §168.
set: **cacheset** *, MMIX-PIPE §167.
specnode = **struct**, MMIX-PIPE §40.
sscanf: **int** ( ), <stdio.h>.
tag: **octa**, MMIX-PIPE §167.
tail: **fetch** *, MMIX-PIPE §69.
ticks: **Extern octa**, MMIX-PIPE §87.
tmp: **octa**, §16.
zero_octa: **octa**, MMIX-ARITH §4.

26. Names of the sections.

⟨ Cases for interaction 14, 15, 18, 19, 21, 22, 23, 24 ⟩ Used in section 13.
⟨ Change the current location 7 ⟩ Used in section 6.
⟨ Global variables 5, 16, 25 ⟩ Used in section 2.
⟨ Input a rudimentary hexadecimal file 6 ⟩ Used in section 4.
⟨ Input an `MMIX` binary file 9 ⟩ Used in section 4.
⟨ Input consecutive octabytes beginning at *cur_loc* 11 ⟩ Used in section 9.
⟨ Input the program 4 ⟩ Used in section 2.
⟨ Parse the command line 3 ⟩ Used in section 2.
⟨ Read an octabyte and advance *cur_loc* 8 ⟩ Used in section 6.
⟨ Run the simulation interactively 13 ⟩ Used in section 2.
⟨ Set up the canned environment 12 ⟩ Used in section 9.
⟨ Subroutines 10, 17, 20 ⟩ Used in section 2.

MMOTYPE

1. Introduction. This program reads a binary mmo file output by the MMIXAL processor and lists it in human-readable form. It lists only the symbol table, if invoked with the -s option. It lists also the tetrabytes of input, if invoked with the -v option.

```
#include <stdio.h>
#include <stdlib.h>
#include <time.h>
#include <string.h>
  ⟨ Prototype preparations 5 ⟩
  ⟨ Type definitions 7 ⟩
  ⟨ Global variables 4 ⟩
  ⟨ Subroutines 8 ⟩
  int main(argc, argv)
      int argc; char *argv[];
  {
    register int j, delta, postamble = 0;
    register char *p;
    ⟨ Process the command line 2 ⟩;
    ⟨ Initialize everything 3 ⟩;
    ⟨ List the preamble 23 ⟩;
    do ⟨ List the next item 13 ⟩ while (¬postamble);
    ⟨ List the postamble 24 ⟩;
    ⟨ List the symbol table 25 ⟩;
    return 0;
  }
```

2. ⟨ Process the command line 2 ⟩ ≡

```
  listing = 1, verbose = 0;
  for (j = 1; j < argc − 1 ∧ argv[j][0] ≡ '-' ∧ argv[j][2] ≡ '\0'; j++) {
    if (argv[j][1] ≡ 's') listing = 0;
    else if (argv[j][1] ≡ 'v') verbose = 1;
    else break;
  }
  if (j ≠ argc − 1) {
    fprintf(stderr, "Usage:␣%s␣[-s]␣[-v]␣mmofile\n", argv[0]);
    exit(−1);
  }
```

This code is used in section 1.

3. ⟨ Initialize everything 3 ⟩ ≡

```
  mmo_file = fopen(argv[argc − 1], "rb");
  if (¬mmo_file) {
    fprintf(stderr, "Can't␣open␣file␣%s!\n", argv[argc − 1]);
    exit(−2);
  }
```

See also sections 12 and 17.

This code is used in section 1.

D.E. Knuth: MMIXware, LNCS 1750, pp. 510–523, 2014.
DOI: 10.1007/3-540-46611-8_11

4. ⟨ Global variables 4 ⟩ ≡

```
int listing;    /* are we listing everything? */
int verbose;    /* are we also showing the tetras of input as they are read? */
FILE *mmo_file;    /* the input file */
```

See also sections 11, 16, and 29.

This code is used in section 1.

5. ⟨ Prototype preparations 5 ⟩ ≡

```
#ifdef __STDC__
#define ARGS(list) list
#else
#define ARGS(list) ()
#endif
```

This code is used in section 1.

6. A complete definition of mmo format appears in the MMIXAL document. Here we need to define only the basic constants used for interpretation.

```
#define mm #98    /* the escape code of mmo format */
#define lop_quote #0    /* the quotation lopcode */
#define lop_loc #1    /* the location lopcode */
#define lop_skip #2    /* the skip lopcode */
#define lop_fixo #3    /* the octabyte-fix lopcode */
#define lop_fixr #4    /* the relative-fix lopcode */
#define lop_fixrx #5    /* extended relative-fix lopcode */
#define lop_file #6    /* the file name lopcode */
#define lop_line #7    /* the file position lopcode */
#define lop_spec #8    /* the special hook lopcode */
#define lop_pre #9    /* the preamble lopcode */
#define lop_post #a    /* the postamble lopcode */
#define lop_stab #b    /* the symbol table lopcode */
#define lop_end #c    /* the end-it-all lopcode */
```

__STDC__, Standard C.
exit: **void** ( ), <stdlib.h>.
FILE, <stdio.h>.
fopen: **FILE** *( ), <stdio.h>.
fprintf: **int** ( ), <stdio.h>.
stderr: **FILE** *, <stdio.h>.

7. Low-level arithmetic. This program is intended to work correctly whenever an **int** has at least 32 bits.

```
⟨ Type definitions 7 ⟩ ≡
  typedef unsigned char byte;    /* a monobyte */
  typedef unsigned int tetra;    /* a tetrabyte */
  typedef struct { tetra h, l;
  } octa;    /* an octabyte */
```

This code is used in section 1.

8. The *incr* subroutine adds a signed integer to an (unsigned) octabyte.

```
⟨ Subroutines 8 ⟩ ≡
  octa incr ARGS((octa, int));
  octa incr(o, delta)
      octa o;
      int delta;
  {
    register tetra t;
    octa x;
    if (delta ≥ 0) {
      t = #ffffffff − delta;
      if (o.l ≤ t) x.l = o.l + delta, x.h = o.h;
      else x.l = o.l − t − 1, x.h = o.h + 1;
    }
    else {
      t = −delta;
      if (o.l ≥ t) x.l = o.l − t, x.h = o.h;
      else x.l = o.l + (#ffffffff + delta) + 1, x.h = o.h − 1;
    }
    return x;
  }
```

See also sections 9, 10, and 26.

This code is used in section 1.

9. Low-level input. The tetrabytes of an mmo file are stored in friendly big-endian fashion, but this program is supposed to work also on computers that are little-endian. Therefore we read four successive bytes and pack them into a tetrabyte, instead of reading a single tetrabyte.

```
⟨ Subroutines 8 ⟩ +≡
  void read_tet ARGS((void));
  void read_tet()
  {
    if (fread(buf, 1, 4, mmo_file) ≠ 4) {
      fprintf(stderr, "Unexpected␣end␣of␣file␣after␣%d␣tetras!\n", count);
      exit(−3);
    }
    yz = (buf[2] ≪ 8) + buf[3];
    tet = (((buf[0] ≪ 8) + buf[1]) ≪ 16) + yz;
    if (verbose) printf("␣␣%08x\n", tet);
    count++;
  }
```

10. ⟨ Subroutines 8 ⟩ +≡

```
  byte read_byte ARGS((void));
  byte read_byte()
  {
    register byte b;
    if (¬byte_count) read_tet();
    b = buf[byte_count];
    byte_count = (byte_count + 1) & 3;
    return b;
  }
```

11. ⟨ Global variables 4 ⟩ +≡

```
  int count;    /* the number of tetrabytes we've read */
  int byte_count;    /* index of the next-to-be-read byte */
  byte buf[4];    /* the most recently read bytes */
  int yz;    /* the two least significant bytes */
  tetra tet;    /* buf bytes packed big-endianwise */
```

12. ⟨ Initialize everything 3 ⟩ +≡

```
  count = byte_count = 0;
```

ARGS = macro ( ), §5.
exit: **void** ( ), <stdlib.h>.
fprintf: **int** ( ), <stdio.h>.
fread: **size_t** ( ), <stdio.h>.
mmo_file: **FILE** ∗, §4.
printf: **int** ( ), <stdio.h>.
stderr: **FILE** ∗, <stdio.h>.
verbose: **int**, §4.

13. The main loop. Now for the bread-and-butter part of this program.

```
⟨ List the next item 13 ⟩ ≡
  {
    read_tet();
  loop: if (buf[0] ≡ mm)
        switch (buf[1]) {
        case lop_quote: if (yz ≠ 1) err("YZ␣field␣of␣lop_quote␣should␣be␣1");
          read_tet(); break;
        ⟨ Cases for lopcodes in the main loop 18 ⟩
        default: err("Unknown␣lopcode");
        }
    if (listing) ⟨ List tet as a normal item 15 ⟩;
  }
```

This code is used in section 1.

14. We want to catch all cases where the rules of mmo format are not obeyed. The *err* macro ameliorates this somewhat tedious chore.

```
#define err(m)
        { fprintf(stderr, "Error␣in␣tetra␣%d:␣%s!\n", count, m); continue; }
```

15. In a normal situation, the newly read tetrabyte is simply supposed to be loaded into the current location. We list not only the current location but also the current file position, if *cur_line* is nonzero and *cur_loc* belongs to segment 0.

```
⟨ List tet as a normal item 15 ⟩ ≡
  {
    printf("%08x%08x:␣%08x", cur_loc.h, cur_loc.l, tet);
    if (¬cur_line) printf("\n");
    else {
      if (cur_loc.h & #e0000000) printf("\n");
      else {
        if (cur_file ≡ listed_file) printf("␣(line␣%d)\n", cur_line);
        else {
          printf("␣(\"%s\",␣line␣%d)\n", file_name[cur_file], cur_line);
          listed_file = cur_file;
        }
      }
      cur_line++;
    }
    cur_loc = incr(cur_loc, 4); cur_loc.l &= −4;
  }
```

This code is used in section 13.

16. ⟨ Global variables 4 ⟩ +≡

```
  octa cur_loc;      /* the current location */
  int listed_file;      /* the most recently listed file number */
  int cur_file;     /* the most recently selected file number */
  int cur_line;      /* the current position in cur_file */
  char *file_name[256];      /* file names seen */
  octa tmp;     /* an octabyte of temporary interest */
```

17. ⟨ Initialize everything 3 ⟩ +≡
cur_loc.h = *cur_loc.l* = 0;
listed_file = *cur_file* = −1;
cur_line = 0;

---

buf: **byte** [ ], §11.
count: **int**, §11.
fprintf: **int** ( ), <stdio.h>.
h: **tetra**, §7.
incr: **octa** ( ), §8.
l: **tetra**, §7.
listing: **int**, §4.
lop_quote = #0, §6.
mm = #98, §6.
octa = **struct**, §7.
printf: **int** ( ), <stdio.h>.
read_tet: **void** ( ), §9.
stderr: **FILE** *, <stdio.h>.
tet: **tetra**, §11.
yz: **int**, §11.

18. The simple lopcodes. We have already implemented *lop_quote*, which falls through to the normal case after reading an extra tetrabyte. Now let's consider the other lopcodes in turn.

```
#define y buf[2]    /* the next-to-least significant byte */
#define z buf[3]    /* the least significant byte */
```

⟨ Cases for lopcodes in the main loop 18 ⟩ ≡

```
case lop_loc: if (z ≡ 2) {
    j = y; read_tet(); cur_loc.h = (j ≪ 24) + tet;
  } else if (z ≡ 1) cur_loc.h = y ≪ 24;
  else err("Z␣field␣of␣lop_loc␣should␣be␣1␣or␣2");
  read_tet(); cur_loc.l = tet;
  continue;
case lop_skip: cur_loc = incr(cur_loc, yz); continue;
```

See also sections 19, 20, 21, and 22.

This code is used in section 13.

19. Fixups load information out of order, when future references have been resolved. The current file name and line number are not considered relevant.

⟨ Cases for lopcodes in the main loop 18 ⟩ +≡

```
case lop_fixo: if (z ≡ 2) {
    j = y; read_tet(); tmp.h = (j ≪ 24) + tet;
  } else if (z ≡ 1) tmp.h = y ≪ 24;
  else err("Z␣field␣of␣lop_fixo␣should␣be␣1␣or␣2");
  read_tet(); tmp.l = tet;
  if (listing) printf("%08x%08x:␣%08x%08x\n", tmp.h, tmp.l, cur_loc.h, cur_loc.l);
  continue;
case lop_fixr: delta = yz;
  goto fixr;
case lop_fixrx: j = yz; if (j ≠ 16 ∧ j ≠ 24)
    err("YZ␣field␣of␣lop_fixrx␣should␣be␣16␣or␣24");
  read_tet();
  delta = tet;
  if (delta & #fe000000) err("increment␣of␣lop_fixrx␣is␣too␣large");
fixr: tmp = incr(cur_loc, −(delta ≥ #1000000 ? (delta & #ffffff) − (1 ≪ j) : delta) ≪ 2);
  if (listing) printf("%08x%08x:␣%08x\n", tmp.h, tmp.l, delta);
  continue;
```

20. The space for file names isn't allocated until we are sure we need it.

⟨ Cases for lopcodes in the main loop 18 ⟩ +≡

```
case lop_file: if (file_name[y]) {
    for (j = z; j > 0; j−−) read_tet();
    cur_file = y;
    if (z) err("Two␣file␣names␣with␣the␣same␣number");
  } else {
    if (¬z) err("No␣name␣given␣for␣newly␣selected␣file");
    file_name[y] = (char *) calloc(4 * z + 1, 1);
```

```
    if (¬file_name[y]) {
      fprintf(stderr, "No␣room␣to␣store␣the␣file␣name!\n"); exit(−4);
    }
    cur_file = y;
    for (j = z, p = file_name[y]; j > 0; j−−, p += 4) {
      read_tet();
      *p = buf[0]; *(p + 1) = buf[1]; *(p + 2) = buf[2]; *(p + 3) = buf[3];
    }
  }
  cur_line = 0; continue;
case lop_line: if (cur_file < 0) err("No␣file␣was␣selected␣for␣lop_line");
  cur_line = yz; continue;
```

21. Special bytes in the file might be in synch with the current location and/or the current file position, so we list those parameters too.

```
⟨ Cases for lopcodes in the main loop 18 ⟩ +≡
case lop_spec: if (listing) {
    printf("Special␣data␣%d␣at␣loc␣%08x%08x", yz, cur_loc.h, cur_loc.l);
    if (¬cur_line) printf("\n");
    else if (cur_file ≡ listed_file) printf("␣(line␣%d)\n", cur_line);
    else {
      printf("␣(\"%s\",␣line␣%d)\n", file_name[cur_file], cur_line);
      listed_file = cur_file;
    }
  }
  while (1) {
    read_tet();
    if (buf[0] ≡ mm) {
      if (buf[1] ≠ lop_quote ∨ yz ≠ 1) goto loop;      /* end of special data */
      read_tet();
    }
    if (listing) printf("␣␣␣␣␣␣␣␣␣␣␣␣␣␣␣␣␣␣␣␣%08x\n", tet);
  }
```

buf: **byte** [], §11.
calloc: **void** *(), <stdlib.h>.
cur_file: **int**, §16.
cur_line: **int**, §16.
cur_loc: **octa**, §16.
delta: **int**, §8.
err = macro (), §14.
exit: **void** (), <stdlib.h>.
file_name: **char** *[], §16.
fprintf: **int** (), <stdio.h>.
h: **tetra**, §7.
incr: **octa** (), §8.
j: **register int**, §1.
l: **tetra**, §7.
listed_file: **int**, §16.
listing: **int**, §4.
loop: label, §13.
lop_file = #6, §6.
lop_fixo = #3, §6.
lop_fixr = #4, §6.
lop_fixrx = #5, §6.
lop_line = #7, §6.
lop_loc = #1, §6.
lop_quote = #0, §6.
lop_skip = #2, §6.
lop_spec = #8, §6.
mm = #98, §6.
p: **register char** *, §1.
printf: **int** (), <stdio.h>.
read_tet: **void** (), §9.
stderr: **FILE** *, <stdio.h>.
tet: **tetra**, §11.
tmp: **octa**, §16.
yz: **int**, §11.

22. The other cases shouldn't appear in the main loop.

```
⟨ Cases for lopcodes in the main loop 18 ⟩ +≡
case lop_pre: err("Can't␣have␣another␣preamble");
case lop_post: postamble = 1;
  if (y) err("Y␣field␣of␣lop_post␣should␣be␣zero");
  if (z < 32) err("Z␣field␣of␣lop_post␣must␣be␣32␣or␣more");
  continue;
case lop_stab: err("Symbol␣table␣must␣follow␣postamble");
case lop_end: err("Symbol␣table␣can't␣end␣before␣it␣begins");
```

23. The preamble and postamble. Now here's what we do before and after the main loop.

```
⟨ List the preamble 23 ⟩ ≡
  read_tet();    /* read the first tetrabyte of input */
  if (buf[0] ≠ mm ∨ buf[1] ≠ lop_pre) {
    fprintf(stderr, "Input␣is␣not␣an␣MMO␣file␣(first␣two␣bytes␣are␣wrong)!\n");
    exit(−5);
  }
  if (y ≠ 1) fprintf(stderr,
        "Warning:␣I'm␣reading␣this␣file␣as␣version␣1,␣not␣version␣%d!\n", y);
  if (z > 0) {
    j = z;
    read_tet();
    if (listing) printf("File␣was␣created␣%s", asctime(localtime((time_t *) &tet)));
    for (j−−; j > 0; j−−) {
      read_tet();
      if (listing) printf("Preamble␣data␣%08x\n", tet);
    }
  }
```

This code is used in section 1.

24. ⟨ List the postamble 24 ⟩ ≡

```
  for (j = z; j < 256; j++) {
    read_tet(); tmp.h = tet; read_tet();
    if (listing) {
      if (tmp.h ∨ tet) printf("g%03d:␣%08x%08x\n", j, tmp.h, tet);
      else printf("g%03d:␣0\n", j);
    }
  }
```

This code is used in section 1.

---

asctime: **char** ∗( ), <time.h>.
buf: **byte** [], §11.
err = macro ( ), §14.
exit: **void** ( ), <stdlib.h>.
fprintf: **int** ( ), <stdio.h>.
h: **tetra**, §7.
j: **register int**, §1.
listing: **int**, §4.
localtime: **struct tm** ∗( ), <time.h>.
lop_end = #c, §6.
lop_post = #a, §6.
lop_pre = #9, §6.
lop_stab = #b, §6.
mm = #98, §6.
postamble: **register int**, §1.
printf: **int** ( ), <stdio.h>.
read_tet: **void** ( ), §9.
stderr: **FILE** ∗, <stdio.h>.
tet: **tetra**, §11.
tmp: **octa**, §16.
y = macro, §18.
z = macro, §18.

25. The symbol table. Finally we come to the symbol table, which is the most interesting part of this program because it recursively traces an implicit ternary trie structure.

```
⟨ List the symbol table 25 ⟩ ≡
  read_tet();
  if (buf[0] ≠ mm ∨ buf[1] ≠ lop_stab) {
    fprintf(stderr, "Symbol␣table␣does␣not␣follow␣the␣postamble!\n");
    exit(−6);
  }
  if (yz) fprintf(stderr, "YZ␣field␣of␣lop_stab␣should␣be␣zero!\n");
  printf("Symbol␣table␣(beginning␣at␣tetra␣%d):\n", count);
  stab_start = count;
  sym_ptr = sym_buf;
  print_stab();
  ⟨ Check the lop_end 30 ⟩;
```

This code is used in section 1.

26. The main work is done by a recursive subroutine called *print_stab*, which manipulates a global array *sym_buf* containing the current symbol prefix; the global variable *sym_ptr* points to the first unfilled character of that array.

```
⟨ Subroutines 8 ⟩ +≡
  void print_stab ARGS((void));
  void print_stab()
  {
    register int m = read_byte();    /* the master control byte */
    register int c;    /* the character at the current trie node */
    register int j, k;
    if (m & #40) print_stab();    /* traverse the left subtrie, if it is nonempty */
    if (m & #2f) {
      ⟨ Read the character c 27 ⟩;
      *sym_ptr++ = c;
      if (sym_ptr ≡ &sym_buf[sym_length_max]) {
        fprintf(stderr, "Oops,␣the␣symbol␣is␣too␣long!\n"); exit(−7);
      }
      if (m & #f) ⟨ Print the current symbol with its equivalent and serial number 28 ⟩;
      if (m & #20) print_stab();    /* traverse the middle subtrie */
      sym_ptr−−;
    }
    if (m & #10) print_stab();    /* traverse the right subtrie, if it is nonempty */
  }
```

27. The present implementation doesn't support Unicode; characters with more than 8-bit codes are printed as '?'. However, the changes for 16-bit codes would be quite easy if proper fonts for Unicode output were available. In that case, *sym_buf* would be an array of wyde characters.

```
⟨ Read the character c 27 ⟩ ≡
  if (m & #80) j = read_byte();      /* 16-bit character */
  else j = 0;
  c = read_byte();
  if (j) c = '?';      /* oops, we can't print (j ≪ 8) + c easily at this time */
```

This code is used in section 26.

28. ⟨ Print the current symbol with its equivalent and serial number 28 ⟩ ≡

```
{
  *sym_ptr = '\0';
  j = m & #f;
  if (j ≡ 15) sprintf(equiv_buf, "$%03d", read_byte());
  else if (j ≤ 8) {
    strcpy(equiv_buf, "#");
    for ( ; j > 0; j−−) sprintf(equiv_buf + strlen(equiv_buf), "%02x", read_byte());
    if (strcmp(equiv_buf, "#0000") ≡ 0) strcpy(equiv_buf, "?");      /* undefined */
  } else {
    strncpy(equiv_buf, "#20000000000000", 33 − 2 * j);
    equiv_buf[33 − 2 * j] = '\0';
    for ( ; j > 8; j−−) sprintf(equiv_buf + strlen(equiv_buf), "%02x", read_byte());
  }
  for (j = k = read_byte(); ; k = read_byte(), j = (j ≪ 7) + k)
    if (k ≥ 128) break;      /* the serial number is now j − 128 */
  printf("␣␣␣␣%s␣=␣%s␣(%d)\n", sym_buf + 1, equiv_buf, j − 128);
}
```

This code is used in section 26.

29. **#define** *sym_length_max* 1000

```
⟨ Global variables 4 ⟩ +≡
  int stab_start;      /* where the symbol table began */
  char sym_buf[sym_length_max];
    /* the characters on middle transitions to current node */
  char *sym_ptr;      /* the character in sym_buf following the current prefix */
  char equiv_buf[20];      /* equivalent of the current symbol */
```

ARGS = macro ( ), §5.
buf: **byte** [ ], §11.
count: **int**, §11.
exit: **void** ( ), <stdlib.h>.
fprintf: **int** ( ), <stdio.h>.
lop_end = #c, §6.
lop_stab = #b, §6.
mm = #98, §6.
printf: **int** ( ), <stdio.h>.
read_byte: **byte** ( ), §10.
read_tet: **void** ( ), §9.
sprintf: **int** ( ), <stdio.h>.
stderr: **FILE** *, <stdio.h>.
strcmp: **int** ( ), <string.h>.
strcpy: **char** *( ), <string.h>.
strlen: **size_t** ( ), <string.h>.
strncpy: **char** *( ), <string.h>.
yz: **int**, §11.

30. ⟨ Check the *lop_end* 30 ⟩ ≡

```
while (byte_count)
  if (read_byte()) fprintf(stderr, "Nonzero␣byte␣follows␣the␣symbol␣table!\n");
read_tet();
if (buf[0] ≠ mm ∨ buf[1] ≠ lop_end)
  fprintf(stderr, "The␣symbol␣table␣isn't␣followed␣by␣lop_end!\n");
else if (count ≠ stab_start + yz + 1)
  fprintf(stderr, "YZ␣field␣at␣lop_end␣should␣have␣been␣%d!\n", count − yz − 1);
else {
  if (verbose) printf("Symbol␣table␣ends␣at␣tetra␣%d.\n", count);
  if (fread(buf, 1, 1, mmo_file))
    fprintf(stderr, "Extra␣bytes␣follow␣the␣lop_end!\n");
}
```

This code is used in section 25.

31. Names of the sections.

⟨ Cases for lopcodes in the main loop 18, 19, 20, 21, 22 ⟩ Used in section 13.
⟨ Check the *lop_end* 30 ⟩ Used in section 25.
⟨ Global variables 4, 11, 16, 29 ⟩ Used in section 1.
⟨ Initialize everything 3, 12, 17 ⟩ Used in section 1.
⟨ List *tet* as a normal item 15 ⟩ Used in section 13.
⟨ List the next item 13 ⟩ Used in section 1.
⟨ List the postamble 24 ⟩ Used in section 1.
⟨ List the preamble 23 ⟩ Used in section 1.
⟨ List the symbol table 25 ⟩ Used in section 1.
⟨ Print the current symbol with its equivalent and serial number 28 ⟩ Used in section 26.
⟨ Process the command line 2 ⟩ Used in section 1.
⟨ Prototype preparations 5 ⟩ Used in section 1.
⟨ Read the character *c* 27 ⟩ Used in section 26.
⟨ Subroutines 8, 9, 10, 26 ⟩ Used in section 1.
⟨ Type definitions 7 ⟩ Used in section 1.

---

buf: **byte** [ ], §11.
byte_count: **int**, §11.
count: **int**, §11.
fprintf: **int** ( ), <stdio.h>.
fread: **size_t** ( ), <stdio.h>.
lop_end = #c, §6.
mm = #98, §6.
mmo_file: **FILE** *, §4.
printf: **int** ( ), <stdio.h>.
read_byte: **byte** ( ), §10.
read_tet: **void** ( ), §9.
stab_start: **int**, §29.
stderr: **FILE** *, <stdio.h>.
verbose: **int**, §4.
yz: **int**, §11.

MASTER INDEX

The following list, a compilation of the indexes produced from all the MMIXware programs and documentation, shows the section numbers where each identifier makes an appearance. Underlined numbers indicate a place of definition. Single-letter identifiers are indexed only when they are defined.

Further characteristics of the program segments, such as 'system dependencies', can also be found here, together with significant error messages and other indexable things like the names of people whose work is cited.

Digits follow letters in the lexicographic order of this index. For example, '*t1*' follows '*tt*'; and '16ADDU' precedes '2ADDU'.